Reinforcement Learning
Theory and Applications

Edited by
Cornelius Weber
Mark Elshaw
Norbert Michael Mayer

Reinforcement Learning, Theory and Applications
Edited by Cornelius Weber, Mark Elshaw and Norbert Michael Mayer

Republished by InTech
Janeza Trdine 9, 51000 Rijeka, Croatia

Technical Editor Teodora Smiljanic

Cover Designer Dino Smrekar

Additional hard copies can be obtained from orders@intechopen.com

Reinforcement Learning, Theory and Applications, Edited by Cornelius Weber, Mark Elshaw and Norbert Michael Mayer
p. cm.
ISBN 978-3-902613-14-1

For EU product safety concerns:
IN TECH d.o.o., Prolaz Marije Krucifikse Kozulić 3, 51000 Rijeka, Croatia,
info@intechopen.com or visit our website at intechopen.com.

Preface

Brains rule the world, and brain-like computation is increasingly used in computers and electronic devices. Brain-like computation is about processing and interpreting data or directly putting forward and performing actions. Learning is a very important aspect. This book is on reinforcement learning which involves performing actions to achieve a goal. Two other learning paradigms exist. Supervised learning has initially been successful in prediction and classification tasks, but is not brain-like. Unsupervised learning is about understanding the world by passively mapping or clustering given data according to some order principles, and is associated with the cortex in the brain. In reinforcement learning an agent learns by trial and error to perform an action to receive a reward, thereby yielding a powerful method to develop goal-directed action strategies. It is predominately associated with the basal ganglia in the brain.

The first 11 chapters of this book, Theory, describe and extend the scope of reinforcement learning. The remaining 11 chapters, Applications, show that there is already wide usage in numerous fields. Reinforcement learning can tackle control tasks that are too complex for traditional, hand-designed, non-learning controllers. As learning computers can deal with technical complexities, the tasks of human operators remain to specify goals on increasingly higher levels.

This book shows that reinforcement learning is a very dynamic area in terms of theory and applications and it shall stimulate and encourage new research in this field. We would like to thank all contributors to this book for their research and effort.

Summary of Theory:

Chapters 1 and 2 create a link to supervised and unsupervised learning, respectively, by regarding reinforcement learning as a prediction problem, and chapter 3 looks at fuzzy-control with a reinforcement-based genetic algorithm. Reinforcement algorithms are modified in chapter 4 for future parallel and quantum computing, and in chapter 5 for a more general class of state-action spaces, described by grammars. Then follow biological views; in chapter 6 how reinforcement learning occurs on a single neuron level by considering the interaction between a spatio-temporal learning rule and Hebbian learning, and in a global brain view of chapter 7, unsupervised learning is depicted as a means of data pre-processing and arrangement for reinforcement algorithms. A table presents a ready-to-implement description of standard reinforcement learning algorithms. The following chapters consider multi agent systems where a single agent has only partial view of the entire system. Multiple agents can work cooperatively on a common goal, as considered in chapter 8, or rewards can be individual but interdependent, such as in game play, as considered in chapters 9, 10 and 11.

Summary of Applications:
Chapter 12 continues with game applications where a robot cup middle size league robot learns a strategic soccer move. A dialogue manager for man-machine dialogues in chapter 13 interacts with humans by communication and database queries, dependent on interaction strategies that govern the Markov decision processes. Chapters 14, 15, 16 and 17 tackle control problems that may be typical for classical methods of control like PID controllers and hand-set rules. However, traditional methods fail if the systems are too complex, time-varying, if knowledge of the state is imprecise, or if there are multiple objectives. These chapters report examples of computer applications that are tackled only with reinforcement learning such as water allocation improvement, building environmental control, chemical processing and industrial process control. The reinforcement-controlled systems may continue learning during operation. The next three chapters involve path optimization. In chapter 18, internet routers explore different links to find more optimal routes to a destination address. Chapter 19 deals with optimizing a travel sequence w.r.t. both time and distance. Chapter 20 proposes an untypical application of path optimization: a path from a given pattern to a target pattern provides a distance measure. An unclassified medical image can thereby be classified dependent on whether a path from it is shorter to an image of healthy or unhealthy tissue, specifically considering lung nodules classification using 3D geometric measures extracted from the lung lesions Computerized Tomography (CT) images. Chapter 21 presents a physicians' decision support system for diagnosis and treatment, involving a knowledgebase server. In chapter 22 a reinforcement learning sub-module improves the efficiency for the exchange of messages in a decision support system in air traffic management.

January 2008

Cornelius Weber
Mark Elshaw
Norbert Michael Mayer

Contents

1

Neural Forecasting Systems

Takashi Kuremoto, Masanao Obayashi and Kunikazu Kobayashi
Yamaguchi University
Japan

1. Introduction

Artificial neural network models (NN) have been widely adopted on the field of time series forecasting in the last two decades. As a kind of soft-computing method, neural forecasting systems can be built more easily because of their learning algorithms than traditional linear or nonlinear models which need to be constructed by advanced mathematic techniques and long process to find optimized parameters of models. The good ability of function approximation and strong performance of sample learning of NN have been known by using error back propagation learning algorithm (BP) with a feed forward multi-layer NN called multi-layer perceptron (MLP) (Rumelhart et. al, 1986), and after this mile stone of neural computing, there have been more than 5,000 publications on NN for forecasting (Crone & Nikolopoulos, 2007).

To simulate complex phenomenon, chaos models have been researched since the middle of last century (Lorenz, 1963; May, 1976). For NN models, the radial basis function network (RBFN) was employed on chaotic time series prediction in the early time (Casdagli, 1989). To design the structure of hidden-layer of RBFN, a cross-validated subspace method is proposed, and the system was applied to predict noisy chaotic time series (Leung & Wang, 2001). A two-layered feed-forward NN, which has its all hidden units with hyperbolic tangent activation function and the final output unit with linear function, gave a high accuracy of prediction for the Lorenz system, Henon and Logistic map (Oliveira et. al, 2000).

To real data of time series, NN and advanced NN models (Zhang, 2003) are reported to provide more accurate forecasting results comparing with traditional statistical model (i.e. the autoregressive integrated moving average (ARIMA)(Box & Jankins, 1976)), and the performances of different NNs for financial time series are confirmed by Kodogiannis & Lolis (Kodogiannis & Lolis, 2002). Furthermore, using benchmark data, several time series forecasting competitions have been held in the past decades, many kinds of NN methods showed their powerful ability of prediction versus other new techniques, e.g. vector quantization, fuzzy logic, Bayesian methods, Kalman filter or other filtering techniques, support vector machine, etc (Lendasse et. al, 2007; Crone & Nikolopoulos, 2007).

Meanwhile, reinforcement learning (RL), a kind of goal-directed learning, has been generally applied in control theory, autonomous system, and other fields of intelligent computation (Sutton & Barto, 1998). When the environment of an agent belongs to Markov decision process (MDP) or the Partially Observable Markov Decision Processes (POMDP), behaviours of exploring let the agent obtain reward or punishment from the environment, and the policy of action then is modified to adapt to acquire more reward. When prediction

error for a time series is considered as reward or punishment from the environment, one can use RL to train predictors constructed by neural networks.
In this chapter, two kinds of neural forecasting systems using RL are introduced in detail: a self-organizing fuzzy neural network (SOFNN) (Kuremoto et al., 2003) and a multi-layer perceptron (MLP) predictor (Kuremoto et al., 2005). The results of experiments using Lorenz chaos showed the efficiency of the method comparing with the results by a conventional learning method (BP).

2. Architecture of neural forecasting system

The flow chart of neural forecasting processing is generally used by which in Fig. 1. The *t*th step time series data $y(t)$ can be embedded into a new *n*-dimensional space $\mathbf{x}(t)$ according to Takens Theorem (Takens, 1981). Eq. (1) shows the detail of reconstructed vector space which serves input layer of NN, here τ is an arbitrary delay. An example of 3-dimensional reconstruction is shown in Fig. 2. The output layer of neural forecasting systems is usually with one neuron whose output $\hat{y}(t+1)$ equals prediction result.

$$\begin{aligned}\mathbf{x}(t) &= (x_1(t), x_2(t), \cdots, x_n(t)) \\ &= (y(t), y(t-\tau), \cdots, y(t-(n-1)\tau)\end{aligned} \tag{1}$$

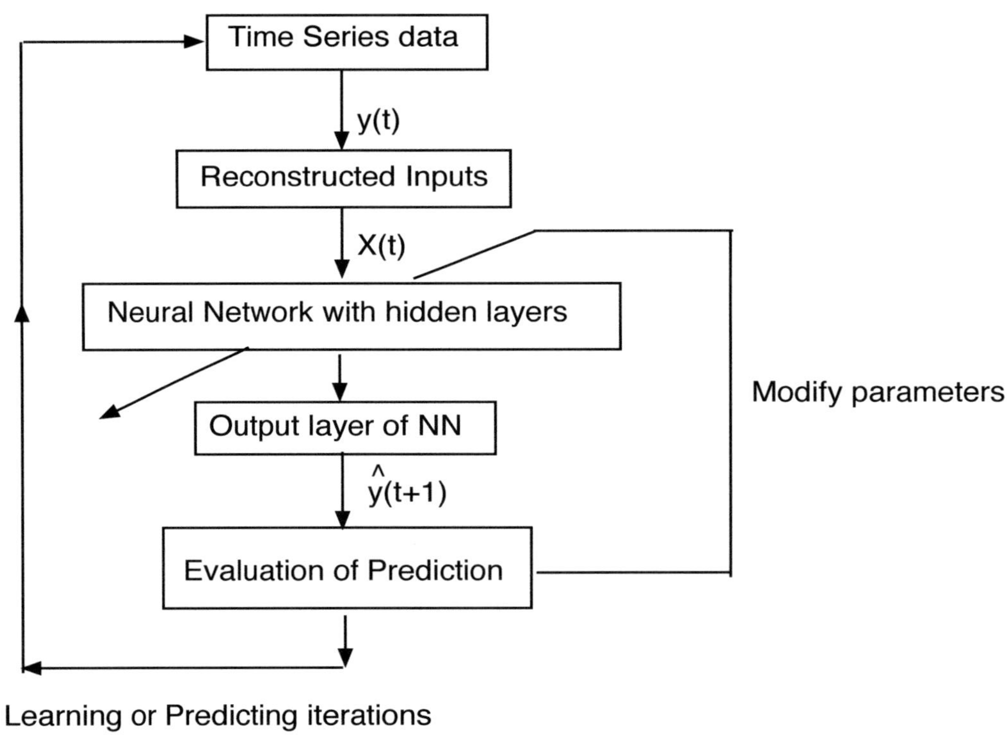

Fig. 1. Flow chart of neural forecasting methods.

There are various architectures of NN models, including MLP, RBFN, recurrent neural network (RNN), autoregressive recurrent neural network (ARNN), neuro-fuzzy hybrid network, ARIMA-NN hybrid model, SOFNN, and so on. The training rules of NNs are also very different not only well-known methods, i.e., BP, orthogonal least squares (OLS), fuzzy inference, but also evolutional computation, i.e., genetic algorithm (GA), particle swarm optimization (PSO), genetic programming (GP), RL, and so on.

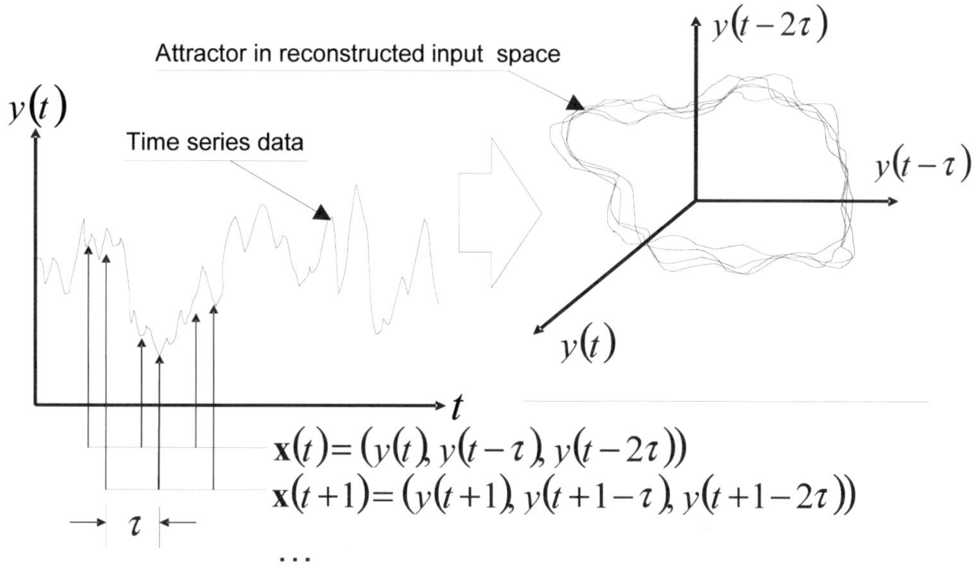

Fig. 2. Embedding a time series into a 3-dimensional space.

2.1 MLP with BP

MLP, a feed-forward multi-layer network, is one of the most famous classical neural forecasting systems whose structure is shown in Fig. 3. BP is commonly used as its learning rule, and the system performs fine efficiency in the function approximation and nonlinear prediction.

For the hidden layer, let the number of neurons is *K*, the output of neuron k is H_k, then the output of MLP is obtained by Eq. (2) and Eq. (3).

$$\hat{y}(t+1) = f(\sum_{k=1}^{K} w_{yk} H_k) \tag{2}$$

$$H_k = f(\sum_{i=1}^{n} w_{ki} x_i(t)) \tag{3}$$

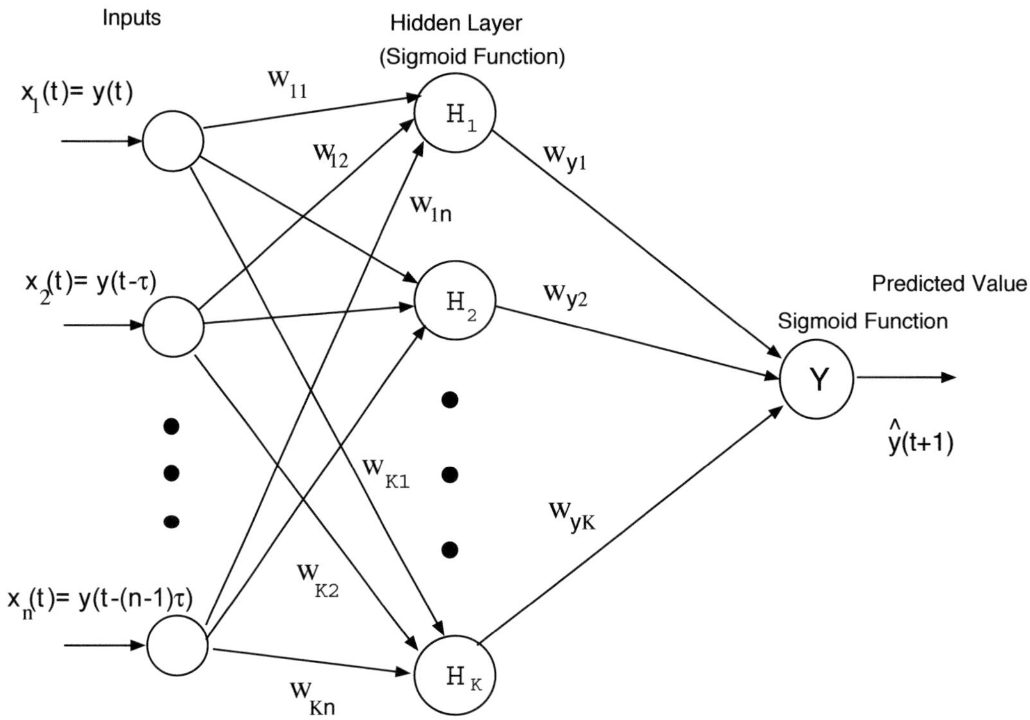

Fig. 3. A MLP with n input neurons, one hidden layer, and one neuron in output layer using BP training algorithm.

Here w_{yk}, w_{ki} represent the connection of kth hidden neuron with output neuron and input neurons, respectively. Activation function $f(u)$ is a sigmoid function (or hyperblolic tangent function) given by Eq. (4).

$$f(u) = \frac{1}{1 + \exp(-\beta u)} \tag{4}$$

Gradient parameter β is usually set to 1.0, and to correspond to $f(u)$, the scale of time series data should be adjusted to (0.0, 1.0).
BP is a supervised learning algorithm, using sample data trains NN providing more correct output data by modifying all of connections between layers. Conventionally, the error function is given by the mean square error as Eq. (5).

$$E(W) = \frac{1}{S}\sum_{t=0}^{S-1}(y(t+1) - \hat{y}(t+1))^2 \tag{5}$$

Here S is the size of train data set, $y(t+1)$ is the actual data in time series. The error is minimized by adjusting the weights according to Eq. (6), Eq. (7) and Eq. (2), Eq. (3).

$$W(w_{yk}, w_{ik})^{new} = \alpha W(w_{yk}, w_{ik})^{old} - \eta \Delta W(w_{yk}, w_{ik}) \tag{6}$$

$$\Delta W(w_{yk}, w_{ik}) = (\partial E / \partial w_{yk}, \partial E / \partial w_{ik}) \tag{7}$$

Here α is a discount parameter (0.0< $\alpha \leq 1.0$), η is the learning rate (0.0 < $\eta \leq 1.0$). The training iteration keeps to be executed until the error function converges enough.

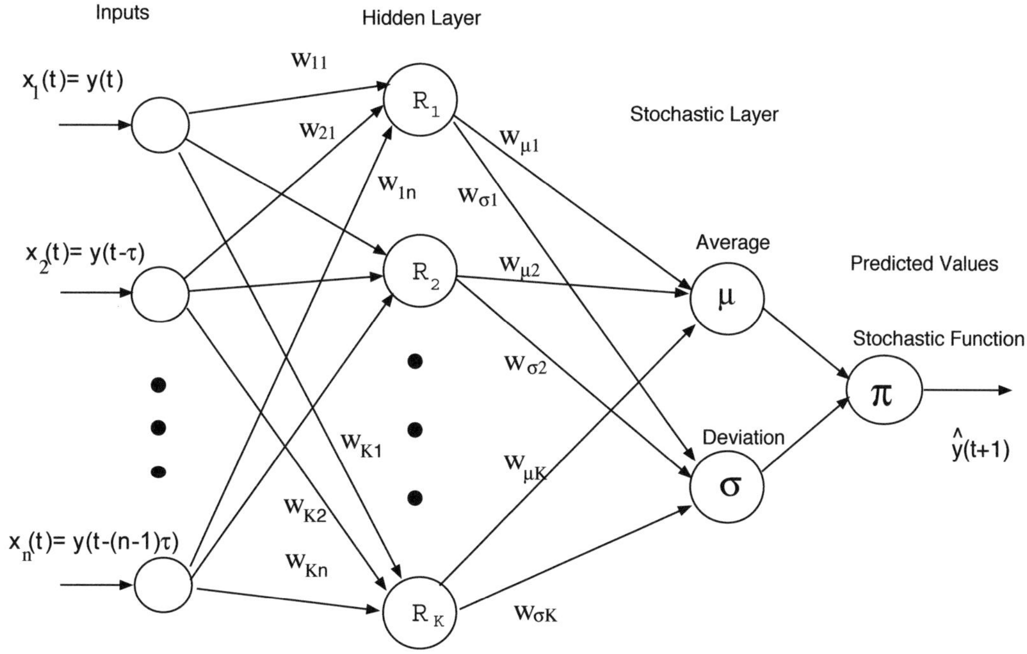

Fig. 4. A MLP with *n* input neurons, two hidden layers, and one neuron in output layer using RL training algorithm.

2.2 MLP with RL

One important feature of RL is its statistical action policy, which brings out exploration of adaptive solutions. Fig. 4 shows a MLP which output layer is designed by a neuron with Gaussian function. A hidden layer consists of variables of the distribution function is added. The activation function of units in each hidden layer is still sigmoid function (or hyperbolic tangent function) (Eq. (8)-(10)).

$$\mu = \frac{1}{1 + \exp(-\beta_1 \sum R_k w_{\mu k})} \tag{8}$$

$$\sigma = \frac{1}{1 + \exp(-\beta_2 \sum R_k w_{\sigma k})} \tag{9}$$

$$R_k = \frac{1}{1 + \exp(-\beta_3 \sum x_i(t) w_{ki})} \tag{10}$$

And the prediction value is given according to Eq. (11).

$$\pi(\hat{y}(t+1),\mathbf{w},\mathbf{x}(t)) = \frac{1}{\sqrt{2\pi\sigma}}\exp\left\{-\frac{(\hat{y}(t+1)-\mu)^2}{2\sigma^2}\right\} \tag{11}$$

Here $\beta_1, \beta_2, \beta_3$ are gradient constants, $\mathbf{w}$ ($w_{\mu k}$, $w_{\sigma k}$, w_{ki}) represents the connection of kth hidden neuron with neuron μ,σ in statistical hidden layer and input neurons, respectively. The modification of $\mathbf{w}$ is calculated by RL algirthm which will be described in section 3.

2.3 SOFNN with RL

A neuro-fuzzy hybrid forecasting system, SOFNN, using RL training algorithm is shown in Fig. 5. A hidden layer consists of fuzzy membership functions $B_{ij}(x_i(t))$ is designed to categorize input data of each dimension in $\mathbf{x}(x_1(t), x_2(t),..., x_n(t))$, t = 1, 2, ..., S (Eq. (12)). The fuzzy reference λ_k, which calculates the fitness for an input set $\mathbf{x}(t)$, is executed by fuzzy rules layer (Eq. 13).

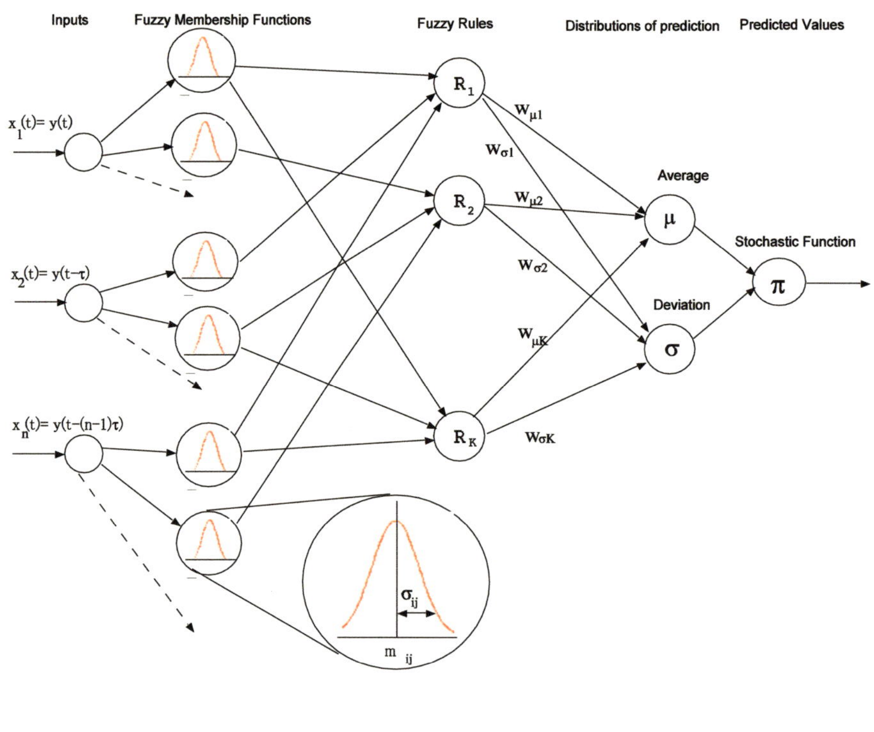

Fig. 5. A SOFNN with n input neurons, three hidden layers, and one neuron in output layer using RL training algorithm.

$$B_{ij}\left(x_i(t)\right) = \exp\left\{-\frac{\left(x_i(t) - m_{ij}\right)^2}{2\sigma_{ij}^{\ 2}}\right\} \tag{12}$$

$$\lambda_k(X(t)) = \prod_{i=1}^{n} B_{ic}(x_i(t)) \tag{13}$$

Where $i = 1, 2, ..., n$, j means the number of membership function which is 1 initially, m_{ij}, σ_{ij} are the mean and standard deviation of jth membership function for input $x_i(t)$, c means each of membership function which connects with kth rule, respectively. $c \in j$, ($j = 1, 2, ..., l$), and l is the maximum number of membership functions. If an adaptive threshold of $B_{ij}\left(x_i(t)\right)$ is considered, then the multiplication or combination of membership functions and rules can be realized automatically, the network owns self-organizing function to deal with different features of inputs.
The output of neurons μ, σ in stochastic layer is given by Eq. (14), Eq. (15) respectively.

$$\mu = \frac{\sum_k \lambda_k \ w_{\mu k}}{\sum_k \lambda_k} \tag{14}$$

$$\sigma = \frac{\sum_k \lambda_k \ w_{\sigma k}}{\sum_k \lambda_k} \tag{15}$$

Where $w_{\mu k}$, $w_{\sigma k}$ are the connections between μ, σ and rules, and μ, σ are the mean and standard deviation of stochastic function $\pi\left(\hat{y}(t+1), \mathbf{w}, \mathbf{x}(t)\right)$ whose description is given by Eq. (11). The output of system can be obtained by generating a random data according this probability function.

3. SGA of RL

3.1 Algorithm of SGA

A RL algorithm, Stochastic Gradient Ascent (SGA), is proposed by Kimura and Kobayashi (Kimura & Kobayashi, 1996, 1998) to deal with POMDP and continuous action space. Experimental results reported that SGA learning algorithm was successful for cart-pole control and maze problem. In the case of time series forecasting, the output of predictor can be considered as an action of agent, and the prediction error can be used as reward or punishment from the environment, so SGA can be used to train a neural forecasting system by renewing internal variable vector of NN (Kuremoto et. al, 2003, 2005).
The SGA algorithm is given below.

Step 1. Observe an input $\mathbf{x}(t)$ from training data of time series.

Step 2. Predict a future data $\hat{y}(t+1)$ according to a probability $\pi(\hat{y}(t+1), \mathbf{w}, \mathbf{x}(t))$.
Step 3. Receive the immediate reward r_t by calculating the prediction error.

$$r_t = \begin{cases} r & if\ |\hat{y}(t+1) - y(t+1)| \le \varepsilon \\ -r & if\ |\hat{y}(t+1) - y(t+1)| > \varepsilon \end{cases} \quad (16)$$

Here r , ε are evaluation constants greater than or equal to zero.
Step 4. Calculate characteristic eligibility $e_i(t)$ and eligibility trace $\overline{D}_i(t)$.

$$e_i(t) = \frac{\partial}{\partial w_i} \ln\{\pi(\hat{y}(t+1), \mathbf{w}, \mathbf{x}(t))\} \quad (17)$$

$$\overline{D}_i(t) = e_i(t) + \gamma \overline{D}_i(t-1) \quad (18)$$

Here $\gamma(0 \le \gamma < 1)$ is a discount factor, w_i denotes ith internal variable vector.
Step 5. Calculate $\Delta w_i(t)$ by Eq. (19).

$$\Delta w_i(t) = (r_t - b)\overline{D}_i(t) \quad (19)$$

Here b denotes the reinforcement baseline.
Step 6. Improve policy by renewing its internal variable $\mathbf{w}$ by Eq. (20).

$$\mathbf{w} \leftarrow \mathbf{w} + \alpha_s \Delta\mathbf{w}(t) \quad (20)$$

Here $\Delta\mathbf{w}(t) = (\Delta w_1(t), \Delta w_2(t), \cdots, \Delta w_i(t), \cdots)$ denotes synaptic weights, and other internal variables of forecasting system, α_s is a positive learning rate.
Step 7. For next time step t+1, return to step 1.
Characteristic eligibility $e_i(t)$, shown in Eq. (17), means that the change of the policy function is concerning with the change of system internal variable vector (Williams, 1992). In fact, the algorithm combines reward/punishment to modify the stochastic policy with its internal variable renewing by step 4 and step 5. The finish condition of training iteration is also decided by the enough convergence of prediction error of sample data.

3.2 SGA for MLP

For the MLP forecasting system described in section 2.2 (Fig. 4), the characteristic eligibility $e_i(t)$ of Eq. (21)-(23) can be derived from Eq. (8)-(11) with the internal viable $w_{\mu k}$, $w_{\sigma k}$, w_{ki} respectively.

$$e_{w_{\mu k}} = \frac{\partial}{\partial w_{\mu k}} \ln(\pi) = \frac{\partial\{\ln(\pi)\}}{\partial \mu} \frac{\partial \mu}{\partial w_{\mu k}} \\ = \frac{\beta_1 R_k \mu(1-\mu)(\hat{y}(t+1)-\mu)}{\sigma^2} \tag{21}$$

$$e_{w_{\sigma k}} = \frac{\partial}{\partial w_{\sigma k}} \ln(\pi) = \frac{\partial\{\ln(\pi)\}}{\partial \sigma} \frac{\partial \sigma}{\partial w_{\sigma k}} \\ = \beta_2 R_k (1-\sigma) \frac{1}{\sigma} \left(\frac{(\hat{y}(t+1)-\mu)^2}{\sigma^2} - 1 \right) \tag{22}$$

$$e_{w_{ki}} = \frac{\partial}{\partial w_{ki}} \ln(\pi) = \frac{\partial\{\ln(\pi)\}}{\partial \mu} \frac{\partial \mu}{\partial R_k} \frac{\partial R_k}{\partial w_{ki}} + \frac{\partial\{\ln(\pi)\}}{\partial \sigma} \frac{\partial \sigma}{\partial R_k} \frac{\partial R_k}{\partial w_{ki}} \\ = \beta_3 x_i(t)(1-R_k)(w_{\mu k} e_{w_{\mu k}} + w_{\sigma k} e_{w_{\sigma k}}) \tag{23}$$

The initial values of $w_{\mu k}$, $w_{\sigma k}$, w_{ki} are random numbers in (0, 1) at the first iteration of training. Gradient constants $\beta_1, \beta_2, \beta_3$ and reward parameters r, ε denoted by Eq. (16) have empirical values.

3.3 SGA for SOFNN

For the SOFNN forecasting system described in section 2.3 (Fig. 5), the characteristic eligibility $e_i(t)$ of Eq. (24)-(27) can be derived from Eq. (11)-(15) with the internal viable $w_{\mu k}$, $w_{\sigma k}$, m_{ij}, σ_{ij} respectively.

$$e_{w_{\mu k}} = \frac{\partial}{\partial w_{\mu k}} \ln(\pi) = \frac{\partial\{\ln(\pi)\}}{\partial \mu} \frac{\partial \mu}{\partial w_{\mu k}} \\ = \frac{\hat{y}(t+1)-\mu}{\sigma^2} \frac{\lambda_k}{\sum_k \lambda_k} \tag{24}$$

$$e_{w_{\sigma k}} = \frac{\partial}{\partial w_{\sigma k}} \ln(\pi) = \frac{\partial\{\ln(\pi)\}}{\partial \sigma} \frac{\partial \sigma}{\partial w_{\sigma k}} \\ = \frac{1}{\sigma} \left(\frac{(\hat{y}(t+1)-\mu)^2}{\sigma^2} - 1 \right) \frac{\lambda_k}{\sum_k \lambda_k} \tag{25}$$

$$
\begin{aligned}
e_{m_{ij}} &= \frac{\partial}{\partial m_{ij}} \ln(\pi) \\
&= \sum_{k} \left\{ \left(\frac{\partial\{\ln(\pi)\}}{\partial \mu} \frac{\partial \mu}{\partial \lambda_k} + \frac{\partial\{\ln(\pi)\}}{\partial \sigma} \frac{\partial \sigma}{\partial \lambda_k} \right) \frac{\partial \lambda_k}{\partial B_{ij}} \right\} \frac{\partial B_{ij}}{\partial m_{ij}} \\
&= \sum_{k} \left\{ \left(\begin{array}{l} \dfrac{\hat{y}(t+1)-\mu}{\sigma^2} \dfrac{w_{\mu k}-\mu}{\sum_k \lambda_k} + \\ \dfrac{1}{\sigma}\left(\dfrac{(\hat{y}(t+1)-\mu)^2}{\sigma^2} - 1\right) \dfrac{w_{\sigma k}-\sigma}{\sum_k \lambda_k} \end{array} \right) \frac{\lambda_k}{B_{ij}} \right\} \frac{x_i - m_{ij}}{\sigma_{ij}^2} B_{ik}
\end{aligned}
\tag{26}
$$

$$
\begin{aligned}
e_{\sigma_{ij}} &= \frac{\partial}{\partial \sigma_{ij}} \ln(\pi) \\
&= \sum_{k} \left\{ \left(\frac{\partial\{\ln(\pi)\}}{\partial \mu} \frac{\partial \mu}{\partial \lambda_k} + \frac{\partial\{\ln(\pi)\}}{\partial \sigma} \frac{\partial \sigma}{\partial \lambda_k} \right) \frac{\partial \lambda_k}{\partial B_{ij}} \right\} \frac{\partial B_{ij}}{\partial \sigma_{ij}} \\
&= \sum_{k} \left\{ \left(\begin{array}{l} \dfrac{\hat{y}(t+1)-\mu}{\sigma^2} \dfrac{w_{\mu k}-\mu}{\sum_k \lambda_k} \\ + \dfrac{1}{\sigma}\left(\dfrac{(\hat{y}(t+1)-\mu)^2}{\sigma^2} - 1\right) \dfrac{w_{\sigma k}-\sigma}{\sum_k \lambda_k} \end{array} \right) \frac{\lambda_k}{B_{ij}} \right\} \frac{(x_i - m_{ij})^2}{\sigma_{ij}^3} B_{ik}
\end{aligned}
\tag{27}
$$

Here membership function B_{ik} is described by Eq. (12), fuzzy inference λ_k is described by Eq. (13). The initial values of $w_{\mu k}, w_{\sigma k}, m_{ij}, \sigma_{ij}$ are random numbers included in (0, 1) at the first iteration of training. Reward *r*, threshold of evaluation error ε denoted by Eq. (16) have empirical values.

4. Experiments

A chaotic time series generated by Lorenz equations was used as benchmark for forecasting experiments which were MLP using BP, MLP using SGA, SOFNN using SGA. Prediction precision was evaluated by the mean square error (MSE) between forecasted values and time series data.

4.1 Lorenz chaos

A butterfly-like attractor generated by the three ordinary differential equations (Eq. (28)) is very famous on the early stage of chaos phenomenon study (Lorenz, 1969).

$$\begin{cases} \dot{o}(t) = \delta p(t) - \delta o(t) \\ \dot{p}(t) = -o(t)q(t) + \phi o(t) - p(t) \\ \dot{q}(t) = o(t)p(t) - \varphi q(t) \end{cases} \tag{28}$$

Here δ, ϕ, φ are constants. The chaotic time series was obtained from dimension $o(t)$ of Eq. (29) in forecasting experiments, where $\Delta t = 0.005$, $\delta = 16.0$, $\phi = 45.92$, $\varphi = 4.0$.

$$\begin{cases} o(t+1) = o(t) + \Delta t \sigma (p(t) - o(t)) \\ p(t+1) = p(t) - \Delta t (o(t)q(t) - \phi o(t) + p(t)) \\ q(t+1) = q(t) + \Delta t (o(t)p(t) - \varphi q(t)) \end{cases} \tag{29}$$

The size of sample data for training is 1,000, and the continued 500 data were served as unknown data for evaluating the accuracy of short-term (i.e. one-step ahead) prediction.

4.2 Experiment of MLP using BP

It is very important and difficult to construct a good architecture of MLP for nonlinear prediction. An experimental study (Oliveira et. al, 2000) showed the different prediction results for Lorenz time series by the architecture of $n : 2n : n : 1$, where n denotes the embedding dimension and the cases of n = 2, 3, 4 were investigated for different term predictions (long-term prediction).

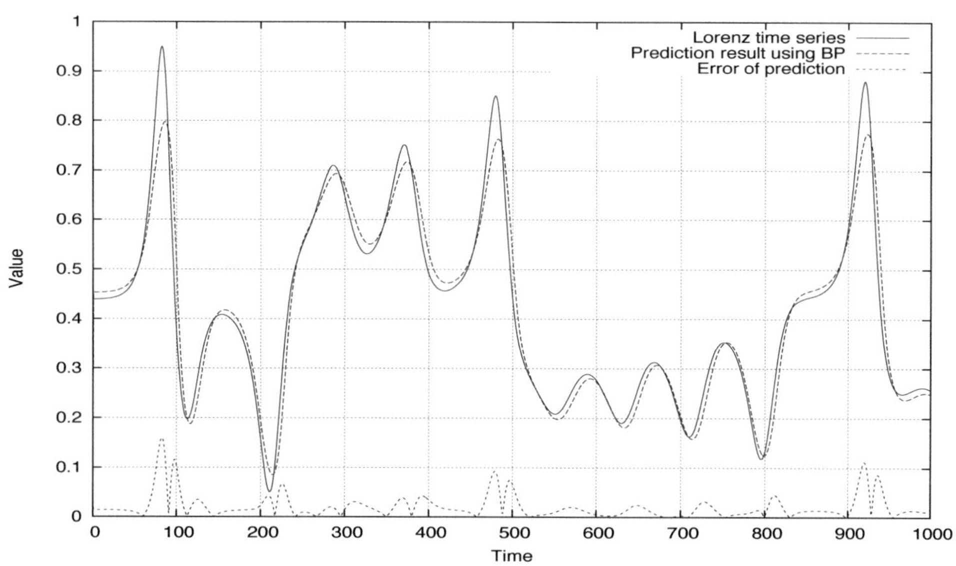

Fig. 6. Prediction results after 2,000 iterations of training by MLP using BP.

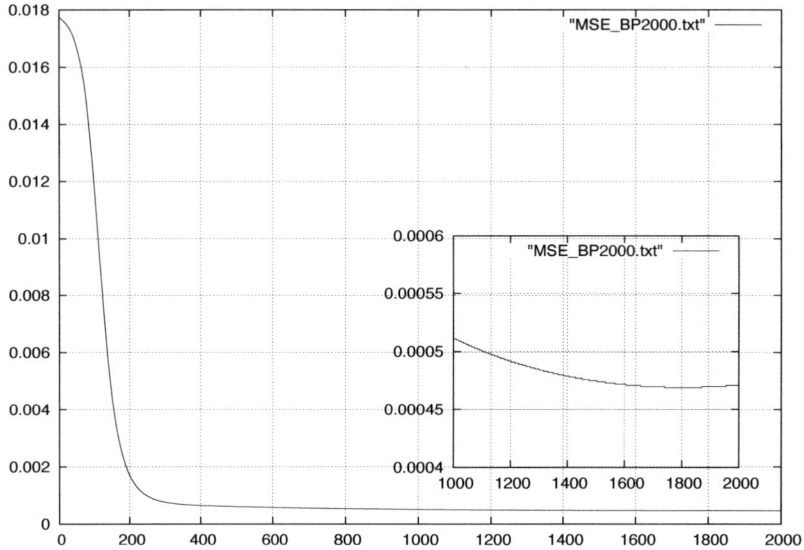

Fig. 7. Prediction error (MSE) in training iteration of MLP using BP.

For short-term prediction here, a three-layer MLP using BP and *3* : *6* : *1* structure shown in Fig. 3 was used in experiment, and time delay τ =1 was used in embedding input space. Gradient constant of sigmoid function β = 1.0, discount constant α = 1.0, learning rate η = 0.01,

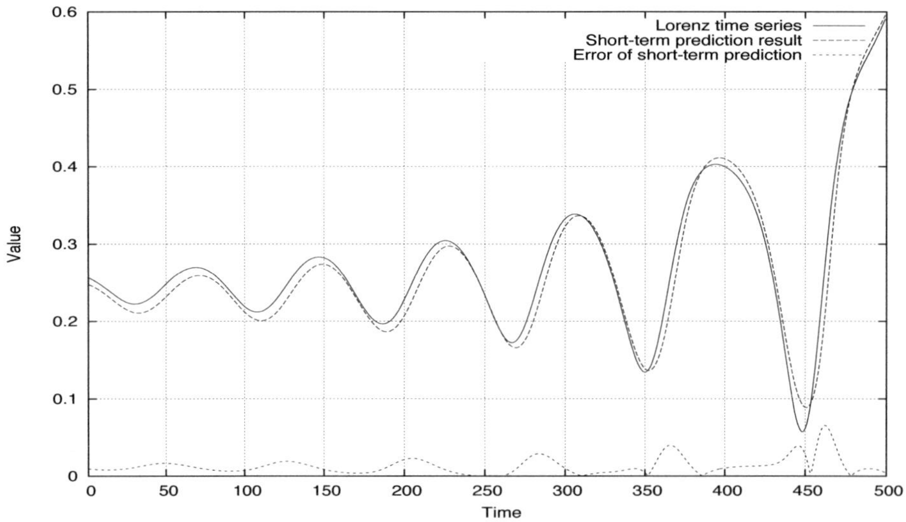

Fig. 8. One-step ahead forecasting results by MLP using BP.

and the finish condition of training was set to $E(W) < 5.0\times10^{-4}$. The prediction results after training 2,000 times are shown in Fig. 6, and the change of prediction error according to the iteration of training is shown in Fig. 7. The one-step ahead prediction results are shown in Fig. 8. The 500 steps MSE of one-step ahead forecasting by MLP using BP was 0.0129.

4.3 Experiment of MLP using SGA

A four-layer MLP forecasting system with SGA and *3 : 60 : 2 : 1* structure shown in Fig. 4 was used in experiment, and time delay τ =1 was used in embedding input space. Gradient

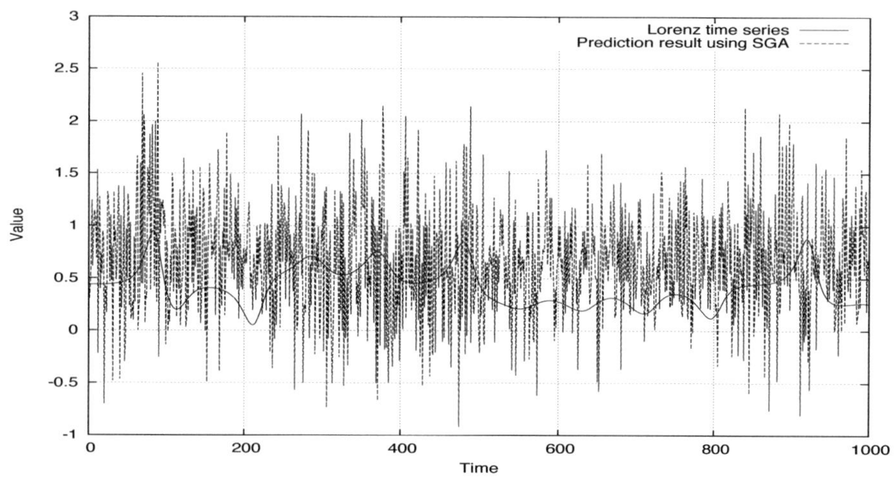

Fig.9. Prediction results before iteration by MLP using SGA.

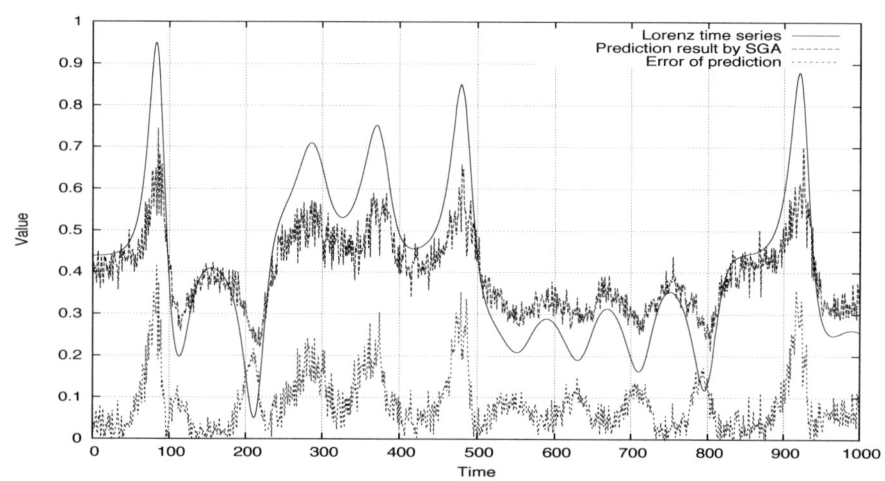

Fig. 10. Prediction results after 5,000 iterations of training by MLP using SGA.

constants of sigmoid functions $\beta_1 = 8.0, \beta_2 = 18.0, \beta_3 = 10.0$, discount constant $\gamma = 0.9$, learning rate $\alpha_{wij} = \alpha_{w\sigma k} = 2.0\times10^{-6}, \alpha_{w\mu k} = 2.0\times10^{-5}$, the reward was set by Eq. (30), and the finish condition of training was set to 30,000 iterations where the convergence $E(W)$ could be observed. The prediction results after 0, 5,000, 30,000 iterations of training are shown in Fig. 9, Fig. 10 and Fig. 11 respectively. The change of prediction error during training is shown in Fig. 12. The one-step ahead prediction results are shown in Fig. 13. The 500 steps MSE of one-step ahead forecasting by MLP using SGA was 0.0112, forecasting accuracy was 13.2% upped than MLP using BP.

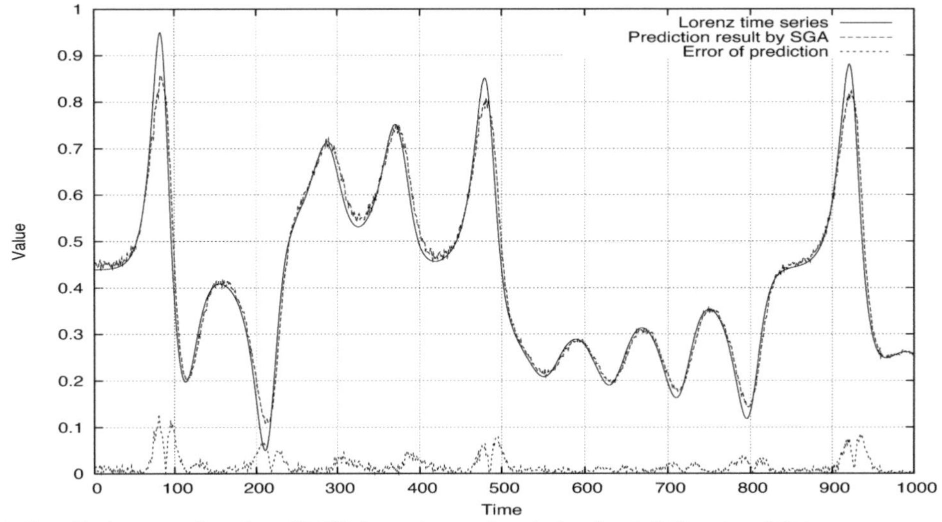

Fig. 11. Prediction results after 30,000 iterations of training by MLP using SGA.

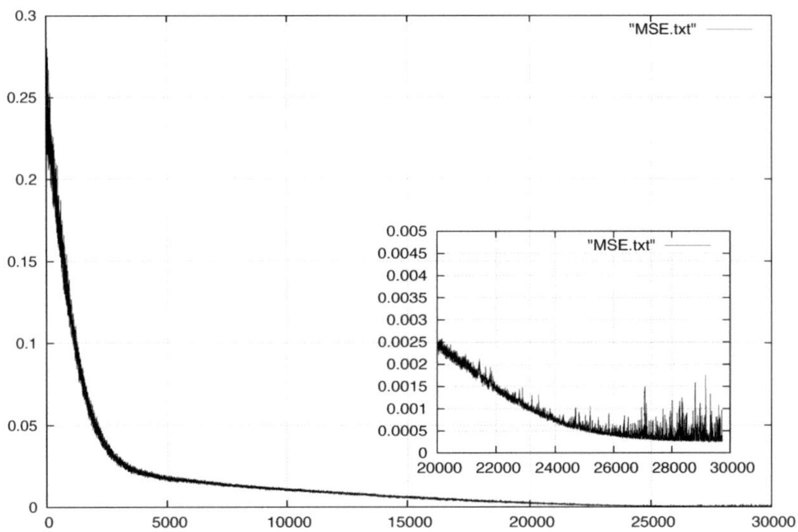

Fig. 12. Prediction error (MSE) in training iteration of MLP using SGA.

$$r_t = \begin{cases} 4.0E-4 & if \ \left|\hat{y}(t+1) - y(t+1)\right| \le 0.1 \\ -4.0E-4 & if \ \left|\hat{y}(t+1) - y(t+1)\right| > 0.1 \end{cases} \tag{30}$$

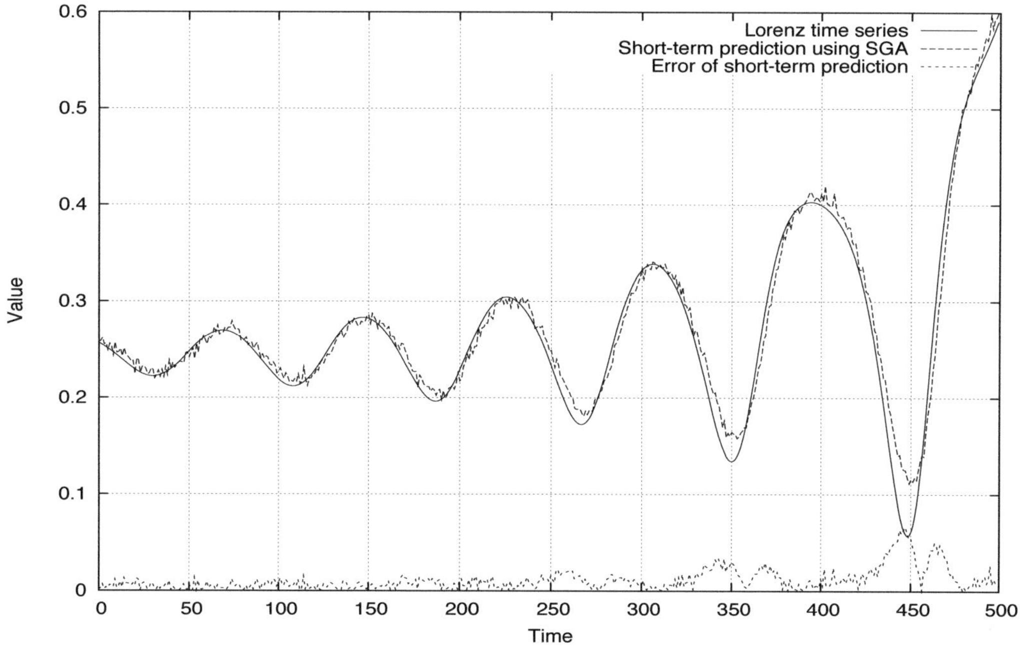

Fig. 13. One-step ahead forecasting results by MLP using SGA.

4.4 Experiment of SOFNN using SGA

A five-layer SOFNN forecasting system with SGA and structure shown in Fig. 5 was used in experiment, time delay τ =2 was used in 3, 4, or 5-dimensional embedding input spaces. Initial value of weight $w_{\mu k}$ had random values in (0.0, 1.0), $w_{\sigma k} = 0.5, m_{ij} = 0.0, \sigma_{ij} = 15.0$ and discount γ = 0.9, learning rate $\alpha_{mij} = \alpha_{w\sigma ij} = \alpha_{w\sigma k} = 3.0\times10^{-6}, \alpha_{w\mu k} = 2.0\times10^{-3}$, the reward *r* was set by Eq. (31), and the finish condition of training was also set to 30,000 iterations where the convergence *E*(*W*) could be observed. The prediction results after training are shown in Fig. 14, where the number of input neurons was 4 and data scale of results was modified into (0.0, 1.0). The change of prediction error during the training is shown in Fig. 15. The one-step ahead prediction results are shown in Fig. 16. The 500 steps MSE of one-step ahead forecasting by SOFNN using SGA was 0.00048, forecasting accuracy was 95.7% and 96.3% upped than the case by MLP using BP and by MLP using SGA respectively.

$$r_t = \begin{cases} 1.5 & if \ \left|\hat{y}(t+1) - y(t+1)\right| \le 1.5 \\ -1.5 & if \ \left|\hat{y}(t+1) - y(t+1)\right| > 1.5 \end{cases} \tag{31}$$

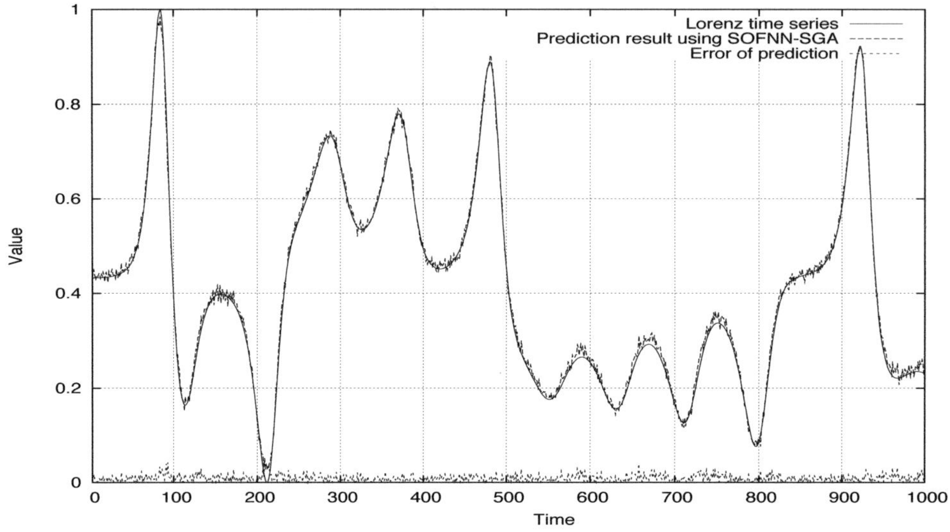

Fig. 14. Prediction results after 30,000 iterations of training by SOFNN using SGA.

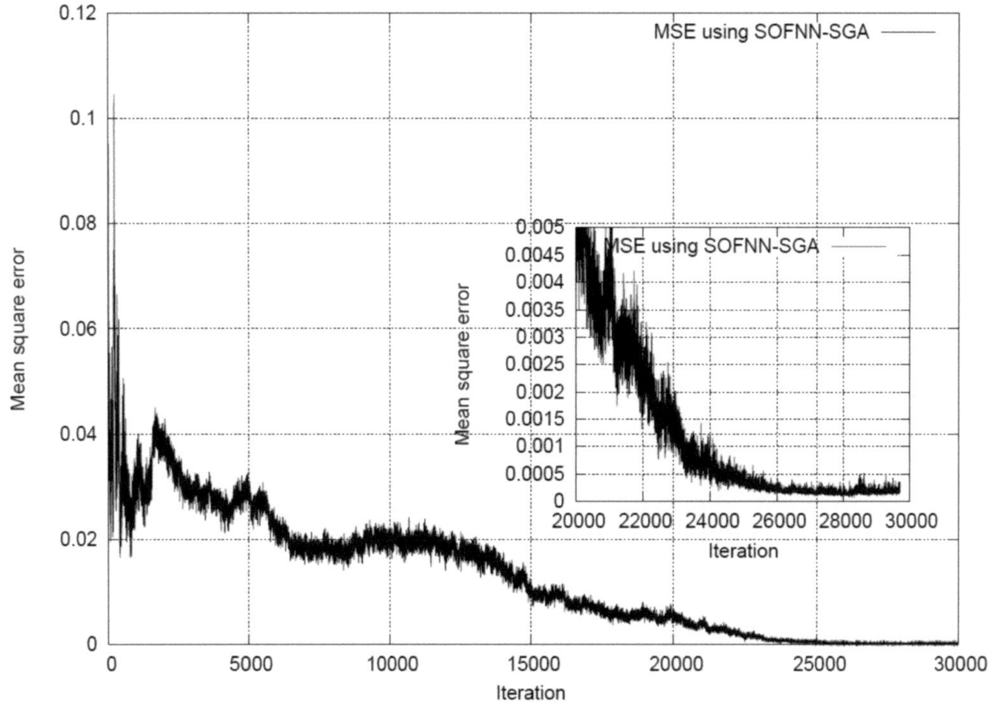

Fig. 15. Prediction error (MSE) in training iteration of SOFNN using SGA.

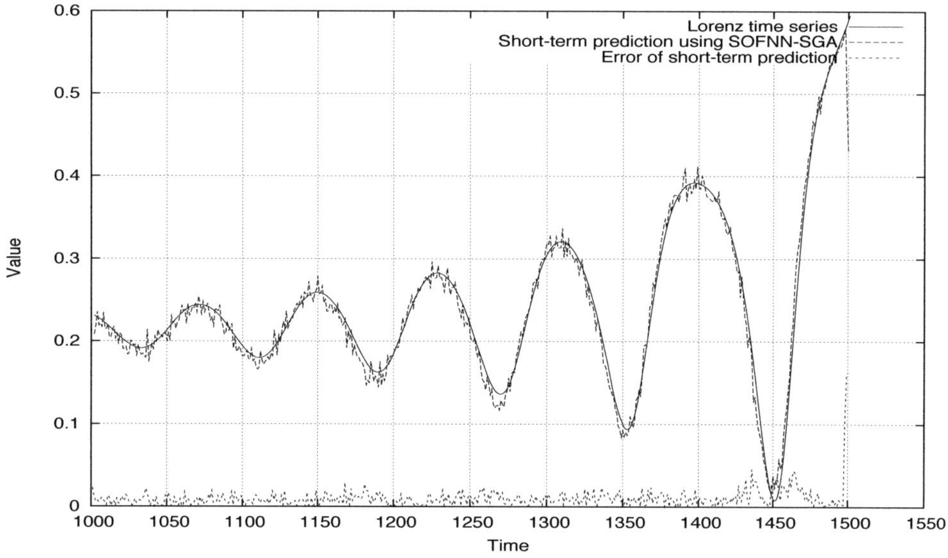

Fig. 16. One-step ahead forecasting results by SOFNN using SGA.

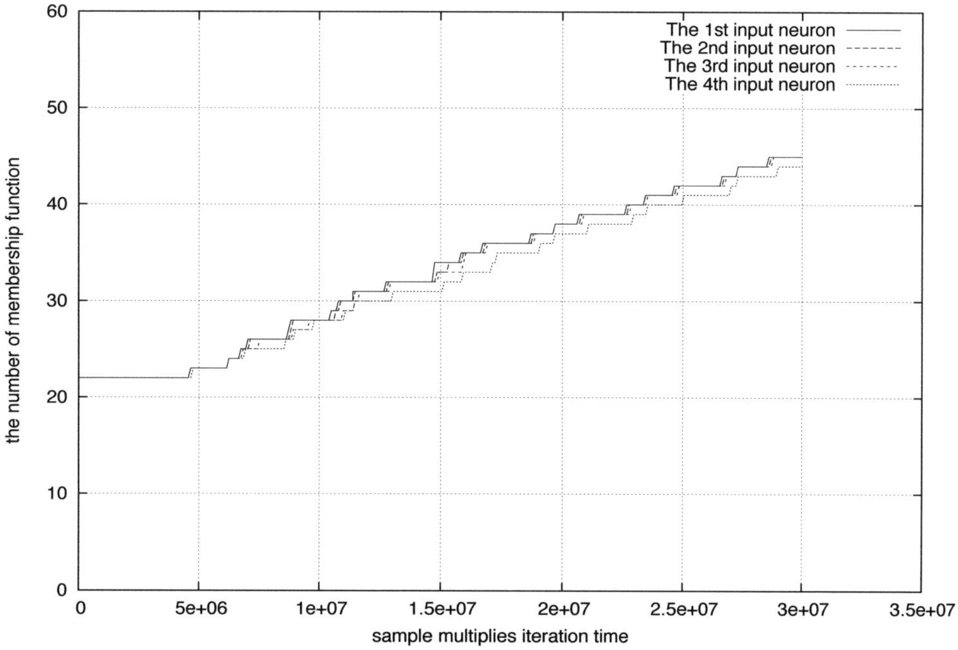

Fig. 17. The number of membership function neurons of SOFNN using SGA increased in training experiment.

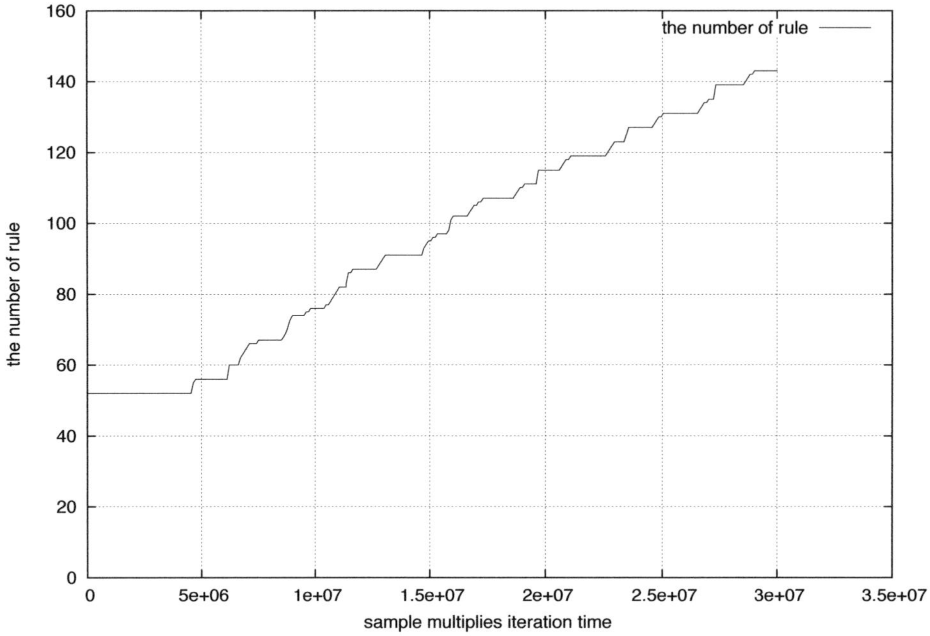

Fig. 18. The number of rules of SOFNN using SGA increased in training experiment.

One advanced feature of SOFNN is its data-driven structure building. The number of membership function neurons and rules increased with samples (1,000 steps in training of experiment) and iterations (30,000 times in training of experiment), which can be confirmed by Fig. 17 and Fig. 18. The number of membership function neurons for the 4 input neurons was 44, 44, 44, 45 respectively, and the number of rules was 143 when the training finished.

5. Conclusion

Though RL has been developed as one of the most important methods of machine learning, it is still seldom adopted in forecasting theory and prediction systems. Two kinds of neural forecasting systems using SGA learning were described in this chapter, and the experiments of training and short-term forecasting showed their successful performances comparing with the conventional NN prediction method. Though the iterations of MLP with SGA and SOFNN with SGA in training experiments took more than that of MLP with BP, both of their computation time were not more than a few minutes by a computer with 3.0GHz CPU. A problem of these RL forecasting systems is that the value of reward in SGA algorithm influences learning convergence seriously, the optimum reward should be searched experimentally for different time series. Another problem of SOFNN with SGA is how to tune up initial value of deviation parameter in membership function and the threshold those were also modified by observing prediction error in training experiments. In fact, when SOFNN with SGA was applied on an neural forecasting competition "NN3" where 11 time series sets were used as benchmark, it did not work sufficiently in the long-term prediction comparing with the results of other methods (Kuremoto et. al, 2007; Crone & Nikolopoulos,

2007). All these problems remain to be resolved, and it is expected that RL forecasting systems will be developed remarkably in the future.

Acknowledgements

We would like to thank Mr. Yamamoto A. and Mr. Teramori N. for their early work in experiments, and a part of this study was supported by MEXT-KAKENHI (15700161) and JSPS-KAKENHI (18500230).

6.References

Box, G. E. P. & Jenkins, G. (1970). *Time series analysis: Forecasting and control*. Holden-Day, ISBN-10 0816211043, San Francisco

Casdagli, M. (1989). Nonlinear prediction of chaotic time series. *Physica D: Nonlinear Phenomena*. Vol. 35, pp. 335-356

Crone, S. & Nikolopoulos, K. (2007). Results of the NN3 neural network forecasting competition. *The 27th International Symposium on Forecasting*. Program, pp. 129

Engle, R. F. (1982). Autoregressive conditional heteroscedasticity with estimates of the variance of U. K. inflation. *Econometrica*. Vol. 50, pp. 987-1008

Kimura, H., Yamamura, M. & Kobayashi S. (1996). Reinforcement learning in partially observable Markov decision process: A stochastic gradient ascent (in Japanese). *Journal of Japanese Society for Artificial Intelligent*, pp. 761-768

Kimura, H. & Kobayashi S. (1998). Reinforcement learning for continuous action using stochastic gradient ascent. *Intelligent Autonomous Systems*, pp. 288-295

Kodogiannis, V. & Lolis, A. (2002). Forecasting financial time series using neural network and fuzzy system-based techniques. *Neural computing & applications*. Vol. 11, pp. 90-102

Kuremoto, T., Obayashi, M., Yamamoto, A. & Kobayashi, K. (2003). Predicting chaotic time series by reinforcement learning. *Proceedings of the 2nd International Conference on Computational Intelligence, Robotics and Autonomous Systems* (CIRAS '03), Singapore

Kuremoto, T., Obayashi, & Kobayashi, K. (2005). Nonlinear prediction by reinforcement learning. In: *Lecture Notes in Computer Science*, Vol. 3644, pp.1085-1094, Springer, ISBN 0302-9743 (Print) 1611-3349 (Online), Berlin

Kuremoto, T., Obayashi, & Kobayashi, K. (2007). Forecasting time series by SOFNN with reinforcement learning. *The 27th International Symposium on Forecasting*. Program, pp. 99

Lendasse, A., Oja, E., Simula, O. & Verleysen, M. (2007). Time series prediction competition: The CATS benchmark. *Neurocomputing*. Vol. 70, pp. 2325-2329

Leung, H., Lo, T., & Wang S. (2001). Prediction of noisy chaotic time series using an optimal radial basis function. *IEEE Transaction on Neural Networks*. Vol. 12, pp.1163-1172

Lorenz, E. N. (1963). Deterministic nonperiodic flow. *Journal of the atmosphere Sciences*. Vol. 20, pp. 130-141

May, R. M. (1976). Simple mathematical models with very complicated dynamics. *Nature*, Vol. 261, pp. 459-467

Oliveira, K. A., Vannucci, A. & Silva, E. C. (2000). Using artificial neural networks to forecast chaotic time series. *Physica A*. Vol. 284, pp. 393-404

Rumelhart, D. E., Hinton, G. E. & R. J. Williams, R. J. (1986). Learning representation by back-propagating errors. *Nature*. Vol. 232, No. 9, pp. 533-536

Sutton, R. S. & Barto, A. G. (1998). *Reinforcement learning: an introduction*. The MIT Press, ISBN 0-262-19398-1, Cambridge

Takens., F. (1981). Detecting strange attractor in turbulence. *Lecture Notes in Mathematics*, Vol. 898, pp. 366-381, Springer-Verlag, Berlin

Williams., R. J. (1992). Simple statistical gradient following algorithms for connectionist reinforecement learning. *Machine Learning*, Vol. 8, pp. 229-256

Zhang, G. P. (2003). Time series forecasting using a hybrid ARIMA and neural network model. *Neurocomputing*, Vol. 50, pp. 159-175

2

Reinforcement Learning in System Identification

Mariela Cerrada and Jose Aguilar
Universidad de los Andes
Mérida-Venezuela

1. Introduction

The Reinforcement Learning (RL) problem has been widely researched an applied in several areas (Sutton & Barto, 1998; Sutton, 1988; Singh & Sutton, 1996; Schapire & Warmuth, 1996; Tesauro, 1995; Si & Wang, 2001; Van Buijtenen et al., 1998). In dynamical environments, a learning agent gets rewards or penalties, according to its performance for learning good actions.

In identification problems, information from the environment is needed in order to propose an approximate system model, thus, RL can be used for taking the on-line information taking. Off-line learning algorithms have reported suitable results in system identification (Ljung, 1997); however these results are bounded on the available data, their quality and quantity. In this way, the development of on-line learning algorithms for system identification is an important contribution.

In this work, it is presented an on-line learning algorithm based on RL using the Temporal Difference (TD) method, for identification purposes. Here, the basic propositions of RL with TD are used and, as a consequence, the linear TD(λ) algorithm proposed in (Sutton & Barto, 1998) is modified and adapted for systems identification and the reinforcement signal is generically defined according to the temporal difference and the identification error. Thus, the main contribution of this paper is the proposition of a generic on-line identification algorithm based on RL.

The proposed algorithm is applied in the parameters adjustment of a Dynamical Adaptive Fuzzy Model (DAFM) (Cerrada et al., 2002; Cerrada et al., 2005). In this case, the prediction function is a non-linear function of the fuzzy model parameters and a non-linear TD(λ) algorithm is obtained for the on-line adjustment of the DAFM parameters.

In the next section the basic aspects about the RL problem and the DAFM are revised. Third section is devoted to the proposed on-line learning algorithm for identification purposes. The algorithm performance for time-varying non-linear systems identification is showed with an illustrative example in section fourth. Finally, conclusions are presented.

2. Theoretical background

2.1 Reinforcement learning and temporal differences

RL deals with the problem of learning based on trial and error in order to achieve the overall objective (Sutton & Barto, 1998). RL are related to problems where the learning agent does not know what it must do. Thus, the agent must discover an action policy for maximize the *expected gain* defined by the rewards that the agents gets. At time *t*, *(t=0, 1, 2, ...)*, the agent receives the *state* S_t and based on this information it choises an *action* a_t. As a consequence, the agent receives a *reinforcement signal or reward* r_{t+1}. In case of the infinite time domain, a *discount* weights the received reward and the *discounted expected gain* is defined as:

$$R_t = \sum_{k=0}^{\infty} \mu^k r_{t+k+1} \tag{1}$$

where μ, $0 < \mu \leq 1$, is the *discount rate,* and it determines the current value of the futures rewards.

On the other hand, TD method permits to solve the prediction problem taking into account the difference (error) between two prediction values at successive instants *t* and *t+1*, given by a function *P*. According to the TD method, the adjustment law for the parameter vector θ of the prediction function $P(\theta)$ in given by the following equation (Sutton, 1988) :

$$\theta_{t+1} = \theta_t + \eta \left[P(x_{t+1}, \theta_t) - P(x_t, \theta_t) \right] \frac{\partial P(x_t, \theta_t)}{\partial \theta} \tag{2}$$

where x_t is a vector of available data at time *t* and η, $0 < \eta \leq 1$, is the learning rate. The term between parentheses is the *temporal difference* and the equation (2) is the *TD algorithm* that can be used on-line in a incremental way.

RL problem can be viewed as a prediction problem where the objective is the estimation of the discounted gain defined by equation (1), by using the *TD* algorithm.

Let $\hat{R}_t$ be the prediction of R_t. Then, from equation (1):

$$R_t = r_{t+1} + \mu R_{t+1} \tag{3}$$

The real value of R_{t+1} is not available, then, by replacing it by its estimated value in (3), the prediction error is defined by the following equation:

$$\Delta = R_t - \hat{R}_t = r_{t+1} + \mu \hat{R}_{t+1} - \hat{R}_t \tag{4}$$

which describe a temporal difference. The reinforcement value r_{t+1} is defined in order to obtain at time *t+1* a better prediction of R_t, given by $\hat{R}_t$, based on available information. In this manner, a good estimation in the RL problem means the optimization of R_t .

Thus, denoting $\hat{R}$ as *P* and by replacing the temporal difference in (2) by that one defined in (4), the parameters adjustment law is:

$$\theta_{t+1} = \theta_t + \eta \left[r_{t+1} + \mu \, P(x_{t+1}, \theta_t) - P(x_t, \theta_t) \right] \frac{\partial P(x_t, \theta_t)}{\partial \theta} \tag{5}$$

The learning agent using the equation (5) for the parameters adjustment is called *Adaptive-Heuristic-Critic* (Sutton & Barto, 1998). In on-line applications, the time *t* is the same iteration time in the learning process by using equation (5).

2.2 Dynamical adaptive fuzzy models

Without loss of generality, a fuzzy logic model MISO (Multiple Inputs-Single Output), is a linguistic model defined by the following M fuzzy rules:

$$\theta_{t+1} = \theta_t + \eta \left[r_{t+1} + \mu\, P(x_{t+1}, \theta_t) - P(x_t, \theta_t) \right] \frac{\partial P(x_t, \theta_t)}{\partial \theta} \tag{6}$$

where x_i is a vector of linguistic input on the domain of discourse U_i ; y is the linguistic output variable on the domain of discourse V; F_i^l and G^l are fuzzy sets on U_i and V, respectively, $(i=1,\dots,n)$ and $(l=1,\dots,M)$, each one defined by their membership functions.
The DAFM is obtained from the previous rule base (6), by supposing input values defined by fuzzy singleton, gaussian membership functions of the fuzzy sets defined for the fuzzy output variables and the defuzzification method given by center-average method. Then, the inference mechanism provides the following model (Cerrada et al., 2005):

$$y(X) = \frac{\sum_{l=1}^{M} \gamma^l \left(\prod_{i=1}^{n} \exp\left[-\frac{(x_i - \alpha_i^l)^2}{\beta_i^l} \right] \right)}{\sum_{l=1}^{M} \left(\prod_{i=1}^{n} \exp\left[-\frac{(x_i - \alpha_i^l)^2}{\beta_i^l} \right] \right)} \tag{7}$$

where $\underline{X}=(x_1\ x_2\ \dots\ x_n)^T$ is a vector of linguistic input variables x_i at time t; $\alpha(v_i^l,t_j)$, $\beta(w_i^l,t_j)$ and $\gamma(u^l,t_j)$ are time-depending functions; v_i^l and w_i^l are parameters associated to the variable x_i in the rule l; u^l is a parameter associated to the center of the output fuzzy set in the rule l.
Definition. Let $x_i(t_j)$ be the value of the input variable x_i to the DAFM at time t_j to obtain the output $y(t_j)$. The generic structure of the functions $\alpha_i^l(v_i^l,t_j)$, $\beta_i^l(w_i^l,t_j)$ and $\gamma^l(u^l,t_j)$ in equation (7), are defined by the following equations (Cerrada et al., 2005):

$$\alpha_i^l = f(v_i^l, \bar{x}_i(t_j)) = v_i^l \frac{\sum_{k=j-\delta_1}^{j} x_i(t_k)}{\delta_1 + 1} \qquad \delta_1 \in N \tag{8}$$

$$\beta_i^l = f(w_i^l, \sigma_i^2(t_j)) = w_i^l \left| \frac{\sum_{k=j-\delta_1}^{j} (x_i(t_k) - \bar{x}_i(t_k))^2}{\delta_1 + 1} + \varepsilon \right|, \quad \varepsilon \in \Re, \delta_1 \in N, \bar{x}_i(t_o) = x_i(0) \tag{9}$$

$$\gamma^l = f(u^l, \overline{y}(t_j)) = u^l\, \overline{y}(t_j) \tag{10}$$

where:

$$\overline{y}(t_j) = \frac{\sum_{k=j-\delta_2}^{j-1} y(t_k)}{\delta_2}, \quad \delta_2 \in N; \quad y(t_o) = y(0) \tag{11}$$

or

$$\overline{y}(t_j)=\frac{\sum_{k=1}^{j-1} y(t_k)}{j-1},\quad y(t_o)=y(0) \tag{12}$$

The parameters v_i^l, w_i^l and u^l can be on-line or off-line adjusted by using the following iterative generic algorithm:

$$\theta(k+1)=\theta(k)+\eta\Delta_\theta \tag{13}$$

where $\theta(t)$ denotes the vector of parameters at time t, Δ_θ is the parameter increment at time t and η, $0<\eta<1$, is the learning rate. Tuning algorithm by using off-line gradient-based learning is presented in (Cerrada et al., 2002; Cerrada et al., 2005).
In this work, the initial values of parameters are randomly selected on certain interval, the number of rules M is fixed and it is not adjusted during the learning process. The input variables x_i are also known, then, the number of adjustable parameters is fixed.
Clearly, by taking the functions $\alpha_i^l(v_i^l,t_j)$, $\beta_i^l(w_i^l,t_j)$ and $\gamma^l(u^l,t_j)$ as parameters in equation (7), a classical Adaptive Fuzzy Model (AFM) is obtained (Wang, 1994). The mentioned parameters are also adjusted by using the learning algorithm (13). Comparisons between the performances of the AFM and DAMF in system identification are provided in (Cerrada et al., 2005).

3. RL-based on-line identification algorithm

In this work, the fuzzy identification problem is solved by using the weighted identification error as a prediction function in the RL problem, and by suitably defining the reinforcement value according to the identification error. Thus, the minimization of the prediction error (4) drives to the minimization of the identification error.
The *critic* (learning agent) is used in order to predict the performance on the identification as an approximator of the system's behavior. The prediction function is defined as a function of the *identification error* $e(t,\theta_t)=y(t)-y_e(t,\theta_t)$, where $y(t)$ denotes the real value of the system output at time t and $y_e(t,\theta_t)$ denotes the estimated value given by the identification model by using the available values of θ at time t.
Let P_t be the proposed non-linear prediction function, defined as a cumulative addition on an interval of time, given by the following equation :

$$P(x_t,\theta_t)=\frac{1}{2}\sum_{k=t-K}^{t}(\mu\lambda)^{t-k}\, e^2(x_k,\theta_t) \tag{14}$$

where $e(x_k,\theta_t)=y(k)-y_e(x_k,\theta_t)$ defines the identification error at time k and the value of θ at time t, and K defines the size of the time interval. Then:

$$\frac{\partial P(x_t,\theta_t)}{\partial\theta}=\sum_{k=t-K}^{t}(\mu\lambda)^{t-k} e(x_k,\theta_t)\Psi(k,\theta_t) \tag{15}$$

where:

$$\Psi(k,\theta_t)=\frac{\partial e(x_k,\theta_t)}{\partial\theta}=-\frac{\partial y_e(k,\theta_t)}{\partial\theta} \tag{16}$$

By replacing (15) into (5), the following learning algorithm for the parameters adjustment is obtained:

$$\theta_{t+1}=\theta_t+\eta\left[r_{t+1}+\mu P(x_{t+1},\theta_t)-P(x_t,\theta_t)\right]\sum_{k=t-K}^{t}(\mu\lambda)^{t-k}e(x_k,\theta_t)\Psi(k,\theta_t) \tag{17}$$

where expression in equation (15) can be viewed as the *eligibility trace* (Sutton & Barto, 1998), which stores the temporal record of the identification errors weighted by the parameter λ. From (14), the function $P(x_{t+1},\theta_t)$ is obtained in the following manner:

$$\begin{aligned}P(x_{t+1},\theta_t)&=\frac{1}{2}\sum_{k=t-K}^{t+1}(\mu\lambda)^{t+1-k}e^2(x_k,\theta_t)\\&=\frac{1}{2}\left[e^2(x_{t+1},\theta_t)+\sum_{k=t-K}^{t}(\mu\lambda)^{t+1-k}e^2(x_k,\theta_t)\right]\\&=\frac{1}{2}e^2(x_{t+1},\theta_t)+\mu\lambda\left[\frac{1}{2}\sum_{k=t-K}^{t}(\mu\lambda)^{t-k}e^2(x_k,\theta_t)\right]\\&=\frac{1}{2}e^2(x_{t+1},\theta_t)+\mu\lambda P(x_t,\theta_t)\end{aligned} \tag{18}$$

By replacing (18) into (17), the learning algorithm is given.
In the prediction problem, a good estimation of R_t is expected; that implies $P(x_t,\theta_t)$ goes to $r_{t+1}+\mu P(x_{t+1},\theta_t)$. This condition is obtained from equation (4). Given that the prediction function is the weighted sum of the square identification error $e^2(t)$, then it is expected that:

$$0\le r_{t+1}+\mu P(x_{t+1},\theta_t)<P(x_t,\theta_t) \tag{19}$$

On the other hand, a suitable adjustment of identification model means that the following condition is accomplished:

$$0\le P(x_{t+1},\theta_t)<P(x_t,\theta_t) \tag{20}$$

The reinforcement r_{t+1} is defined in order to accomplish the expected condition (19) and taking into account the condition (20). Then, by using equations (14) and (18), the reinforcement signal is defined as:

$$r_{t+1}=-\frac{1}{2}\mu e^2(x_{t+1},\theta_t)\qquad\text{if}\quad P(x_{t+1},\theta_t)>P(x_t,\theta_t) \tag{21}$$

$$r_{t+1}=0\qquad\text{if}\quad P(x_{t+1},\theta_t)\le P(x_t,\theta_t) \tag{22}$$

In this way, the identification error into the prediction function $P(x_{t+1},\theta_t)$, according to the equation (18), is rejected by using the reinforcement in equation (22). The learning rate η in (17) is defined by the following equation:

$$\eta(k) = \frac{\eta(k-1)}{\rho + \eta(k-1)}; \quad 0 < \rho < 1 \tag{23}$$

Thus, an accurate adjustment of parameters is expected. Usually, $\eta(0)$ is around 1, and ρ is around 0. Parameters μ and λ can depend on the system dynamic: small values in case of slow dynamical systems, and values around 1 in case of fast dynamical systems.
In this work, the proposed RL-based algorithm is applied to fuzzy identification and the identification model is provided by the DAFM in (7). Then, the prediction function P is a non-linear function of the fuzzy model parameters and a non-linear approach of $TD(\lambda)$ is obtained.

3.1 Descent-gradient-based analysis

The proposed identification learning algorithm can be studied like a descent-gradient method with respect to the parametric predictive function P. In the descent-gradient method for optimization, the objective is to find the minimal value of the error measure on the parameters space, denoted by $J(\theta)$, by using the following algorithm for the parameters adjustment:

$$\theta_{t+1} = \theta_t + \Delta\theta_t = \theta_t + 2\alpha\left[E\{z \mid x_t\} - P(x_t,\theta)\right]\nabla_\theta P(x_t,\theta) \tag{24}$$

In this case, a error measure is defined as:

$$J(\theta,x) = \left(E\{z \mid x\} - P(x,\theta)\right)^2 \tag{25}$$

where $E\{z \mid x\}$ is the expected value of the real value z, from the knowledge of the available data x.
In this work, the learning algorithm (17) is like a learning algorithm (24), based on the descent-gradient method, where $r_{t+1}+\mu P(x_{t+1}, \theta_t)$ is the expected value $E\{z \mid x\}$ in (25). By appropriate selecting r_{t+1} according to (21) and (22), the expected value in the learning problem is defined in two ways:

$$E\{z \mid x\} = \mu P(x_{t+1}, \theta_t) \quad \text{if} \quad P(x_{t+1},\theta_t) \le P(x_t,\theta_t) \tag{26}$$

or

$$E\{z \mid x\} = \mu^2 \lambda P(x_t, \theta_t) \quad \text{if} \quad P(x_{t+1},\theta_t) > P(x_t,\theta_t) \tag{27}$$

Then, the parameters adjustment is made on each iteration in order to attain the expected value of the prediction function P according to the predicted value of $P(x_{t+1}, \theta_t)$ and the real value $P(x_t,\theta_t)$. In both of cases, the expected value is minor than the obtained real value $P(x_t,\theta_t)$ and the selected value of r_{t+1} defines the magnitude of the defined error measure.

4. Illustrative example

This section shows an illustrative example applied to fuzzy identification of time-varying non-linear systems by using the proposed on-line RL-based identification algorithm and the DAFM described in section 2.2. Comparisons by using off-line gradient-based tuning

algorithm are presented in order to highlight the algorithm performance. For off-line adjustment purposes, the input-output training data is obtained from Pseudo-Random Binary Signal (PRBS) input signal. The performance of the fuzzy identification is evaluated according to the identification relative error $(e_r=(y(t)-y_e(t))/y(t))$ normalized on $[0,1]$.
The system is described by the following difference equation:

$$y(k+1)=g[y(k),y(k-1)]+u(k) \tag{28}$$

where

$$g[y(k),y(k-1)]=\frac{y(k)y(k-1)[y(k)+a(k)]}{1+y^2(k)+y^2(k-1)} \tag{29}$$
$$a(k)=2.5+2.5\ sen(2\pi k/250)$$

In this case, the unknown function $g=[.]$ is estimated by using the DAFM and, additionally, a sudden change on $a(k)$ is proposed by setting $a(k)=0,\ k>400$. After an extensive training phase, the fuzzy model with $M=8$, $\delta_1=4$ and $\delta_2=1$ (in equations (8),(9),(11)), has been chosen. In this case, the fuzzy identification performance is adequate and the Root Mean Square Error (RMSE) is 0.1285 in validation phase. Figure 1 shows the performance of the DAFM using the off-line gradient-based tuning algorithm with initial conditions on the interval $[0,1]$ and using the following input signal:

$$u(k)=\begin{cases} sen(2\pi k/25) & 1<k<100 \quad y \quad k>500 \\ 3+(0.5sen(2\pi k/250)+0.5sen(2\pi k/25)) & 100<k<500 \end{cases} \tag{30}$$

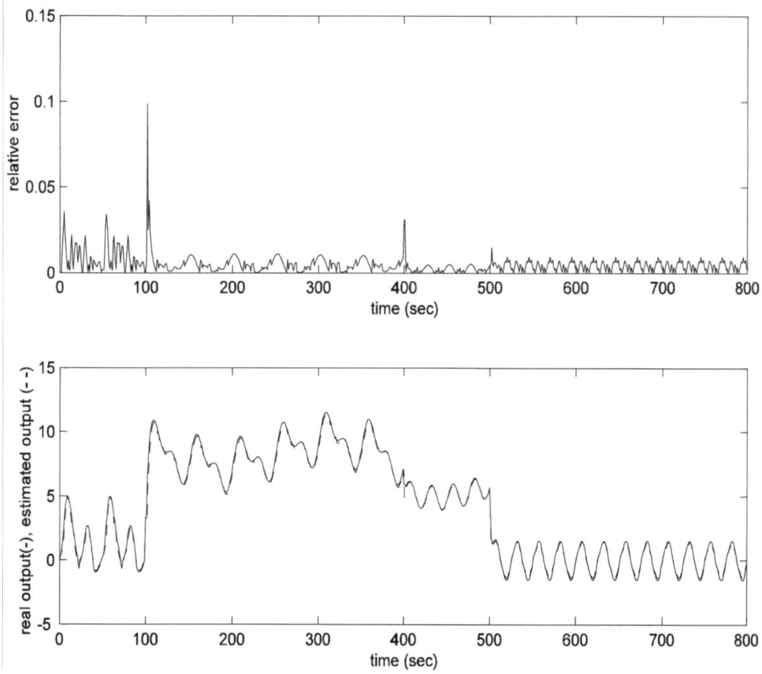

Fig. 1. Fuzzy identification using off-line tuning algorithm and DAFM

In the following, fuzzy identification performance by using the DAFM with the proposed RL-based tuning algorithm is presented. Equation (17) is used for the parameters adjustment with the prediction function defined in (14) and the reinforcement defined in (21)-(22). Here, $\lambda=\mu=0.9$, $K=5$ and the learning rate is set up by the equation (23) with $\rho=0.01$. Note that the iteration index t is the same time k in system (28). After experimental proofs, the performance approaching the accuracy obtained from off-line adjustment is obtained with $M=6$ and initial conditions on $[0.5,1.5]$. Here, the RMSE= 0.0838 is achieved. Figure 2 shows the tuning algorithm performance and table 1 shows the comparative values related to the RMSE.

M	**RMSE off-line**	**RMSE On-line**
6	0.1110	0.0838
8	0.1285	0.1084
10	0.1327	0.1044
15	0.1069	0.0860
20	0.1398	0.1056

Table 1. Comparison between the on-line proposed algorithm and off-line tuning

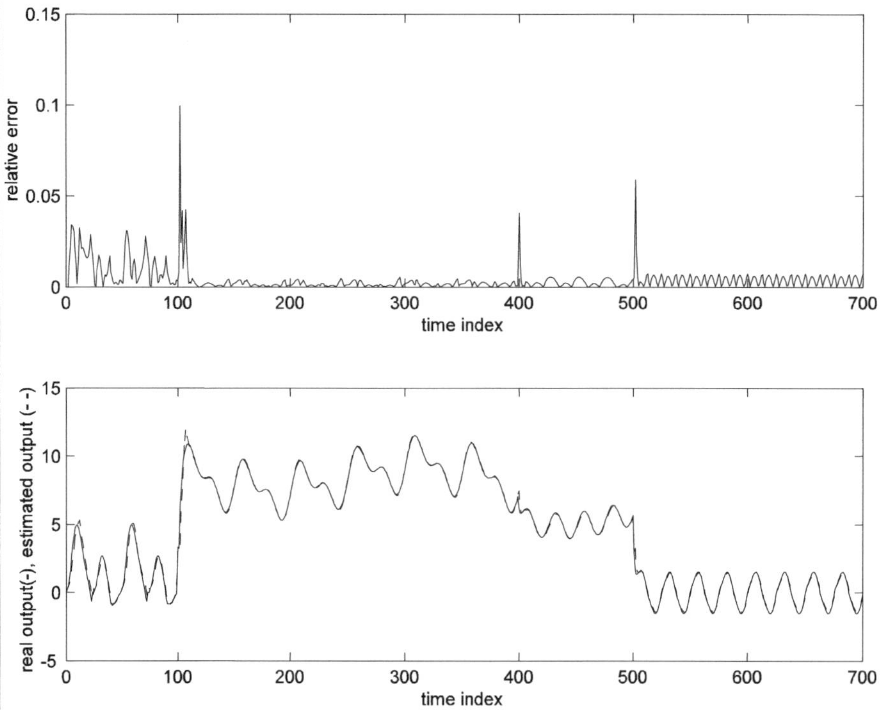

Fig. 2. Fuzzy identification using RL-based tuning algorithm and DAFM

4.1 Initial condition dependence

In order to show the algorithm sensibility according to the initial conditions of the fuzzy model parameters, the following figures show the tuning algorithm performance. In this case, the system is described by the equation (31):

$$y(k+1)=\frac{y(k)y(k-1)y(k-2)u(k-1)(y(k-2)-1)+u(k)}{a(k)+y(k-2)^2+y(k-1)^2} \qquad (31)$$
$$a(k)=1+0.1\,sen(2\pi k/100)$$

where:

$$u(k)=\begin{cases} sen(2\pi k/250) & 1<k<500 \text{ and } 801<k<1000 \\ 1.5+(0.8sen(2\pi k/250)+0.2sen(2\pi k/25)) & 501<k<800 \end{cases} \qquad (32)$$

Figure 3 shows the tuning process by using a model with *M=20* and initial conditions on the interval *[0.5,1.5]*. In this case, even when the initial error is large, the tuning algorithm performance also shows an adequate performance and the tuning process has an suitable evolution (here, a sudden change on *a(k)* is not considered). Figure 4 shows the tuning process by using a model with initial conditions on the interval *[0,1]* an also a suitable performance of the proposed identification algorithm is shown.

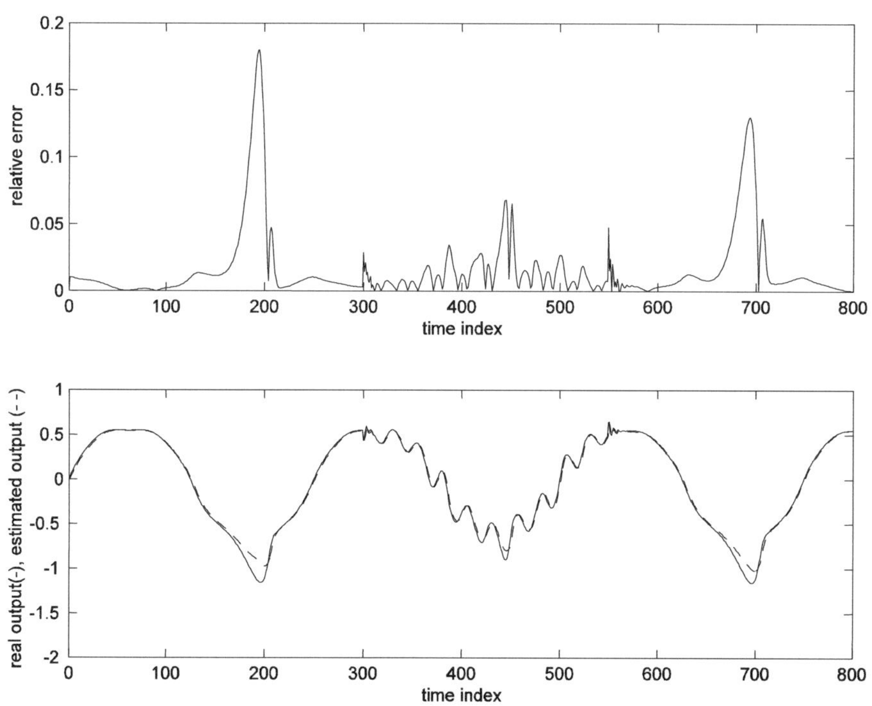

Fig. 3. Fuzzy identification using RL-based tuning algorithm and DAFM with initial conditions on *[0.5,1.5]*.

The previous tests show the performance and the sensibility of the proposed on-line algorithm is adequate in terms of (a) The initial conditions of the DAFM parameters, (b) Changes on the internal dynamic (the term $a(k)$ in the example) and (c) Changes on the inputs signal (the proposed input $u(k)$).
These ones are very important aspects to be evaluated in order to consider an on-line identification algorithm. In the example, even though the initial error depends on the initial conditions of the DAFM parameters, a good evolution of the learning algorithm is accomplished. Table 1 also shows the number of rules M do not strongly determines the global performance of the proposed on-line algorithm although a similar RMSE could be obtained with a low number of rules and off-line tuning. However, this one could be not reached whether good quality and quantity of historical data is not available in off-line approaches.

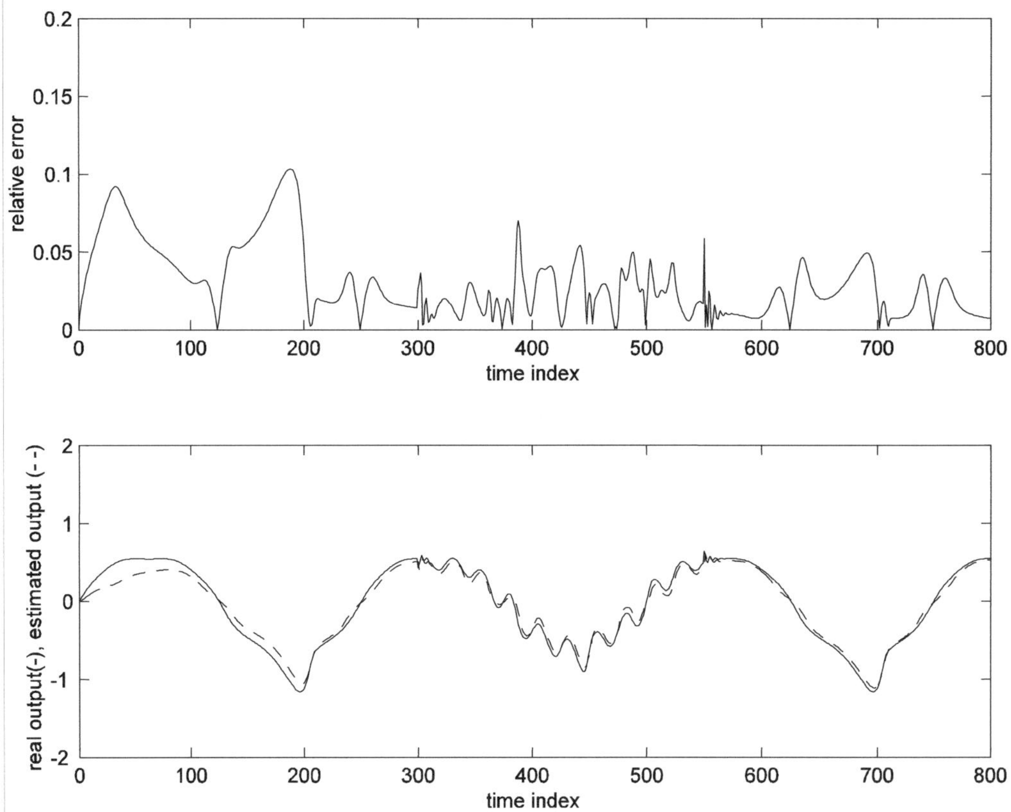

Fig. 4. Fuzzy identification using RL-based tuning algorithm and DAFM with initial conditions on *[0,1]*.

5. Acknowledgment

This work has been partially presented in the International Symposium on Neural Networks ISNN 2006.

6. Conclusion

This work proposes an on-line tuning algorithm based on reinforcement learning for the identification problem. Both the prediction function and the reinforcement signal have been defined by taking into account the identification error, according to the classical recursive identification algorithms. The presence of the reinforcement signal in the proposed tuning algorithm permits to reject the identification error into the prediction function, then, the parameters adjustment not only depends on the gradient direction.

The proposed algorithm has been applied in fuzzy identification, then, the prediction function is a non-linear function of the fuzzy model parameters. In this case, the proposed identification model is a Dynamical Adaptive Fuzzy Model (DAFM) that has reported a good performance in identification problems.

In order to show the algorithm performance, an illustrative example related to time-varying non-linear system identification using a DAFM has been developed. The obtained results have been compared by using the off-line gradient-based learning algorithm. The performance obtained by using the DAFM with the proposed on-line algorithm is adequate in terms of the main aspects to be taken into account in on-line identification: the initial conditions of the model parameters, the changes on the internal dynamic and the changes on the input signal.

Even when similar results could be obtained by using the DAFM with off-line tuning, in this case good quality and quantity of available historical data is needed to reach a suitable validation phase in off-line tuning. This one highlights the use of the on-line learning algorithms and the proposed RL-based on-line tuning algorithm could be an important contribution for the system identification in dynamical environments with perturbations, for example, in process control area.

7. References

Cerrada, M.; Aguilar, J.; Colina, E. & Titli, A. (2002). An approach for dynamical adaptive fuzzy modeling, *Proceedings of IEEE-FUZZ 2002 International Conference on Fuzzy Systems*, pp. 156-161, Hawai-USA, May 2002, Canada

Cerrada, M.; Aguilar, J.; Colina, E. & Titli, A. (2005). Dynamical membership functions: an approach for adaptive fuzzy modelling. *Fuzzy Sets and Systems*, Vol. 152, No. 3, (June 2005) (513-533)

Ljung, L. (1997). *System Identification. Theory for the User*, Prentice Hall, New York

Schapire, R.E. & Warmuth, M.K. (1996). On the worst-case analysis of temporal differences learning algorithms. *Machine Learning*, Vol. 22, (95-121)

Si, J. & Wang, Y-T. (2001). On line learning control by association and reinforcement. *IEEE Transactions on Neural Networks*, Vol. 12, No. 2, (264-276)

Singh, S.P. & Sutton, R.S. (1996). Reinforcement learning with replacing eligibility traces. *Machine Learning*, Vol. 22, (123-158)

Sutton, R.S. & Barto, A.G. (1998). *Reinforcement Learning. An Introduction,* The MIT Press, Cambridge

Sutton, R.S. (1988). Learning to predict by the methods of temporal differences. *Machine Learning,* Vol. 3, (9-44)

Tesauro, G. (1995). Temporal difference learning and TD-Gammon. *Communications of the Association for Computing Machinery*, Vol. 38, No. 3, (58-68)

Van Buijtenen, W.M.; Schram, G.; Babuska, R. & Verbruggen, H.B. (1995). Adaptive fuzzy control of satellite attitude by reinforcement learning. *IEEE Transactions on Fuzzy Systems*, Vol. 6, No. 2, (185-194)

Wang, L.X. (1994). *Adaptive Fuzzy Systems and Control,* Prentice Hall, New Jersey

3

Reinforcement Evolutionary Learning for Neuro-Fuzzy Controller Design

Cheng-Jian Lin+
National University of Kaohsiung, Kaohsiung, Taiwan

1. Introduction

In recent years, the concept of the fuzzy logic or artificial neural networks for control problems has grown into a popular research area [1]-[3]. The reason is that classical control theory usually requires a mathematical model for designing controllers. The inaccuracy of mathematical modeling of plants usually degrades the performance of the controllers, especially for nonlinear and complex control problems [4], [25]. Fuzzy logic has the ability to express the ambiguity of human thinking and translate expert knowledge into computable numerical data.

A fuzzy system consists of a set of fuzzy IF-THEN rules that describe the input-output mapping relationship of the networks. Obviously, it is difficult for human experts to examine all the input-output data from a complex system to find proper rules for a fuzzy system. To cope with this difficulty, several approaches that are used to generate the fuzzy IF-THEN rules from numerical data have been proposed [5]-[8]. These methods were developed for supervised learning; i.e., the correct "target" output values are given for each input pattern to guide the learning of the network. However, most of the supervised learning algorithms for neuro-fuzzy networks require precise training data to tune the networks for various applications. For some real world applications, precise training data are usually difficult and expensive, if not impossible, to obtain. For this reason, there has been a growing interest in reinforcement learning algorithms for use in fuzzy [9]-[10] or neural controller [11]-[12] design.

In the design of a fuzzy controller, adjusting the required parameters is important. To do this, back-propagation (BP) training was widely used in [11]-[12], [18]. It is a powerful training technique that can be applied to networks with a forward structure. Since the steepest descent technique is used in BP training to minimize the error function, the algorithms may reach the local minima very fast and never find the global solution.

The development of genetic algorithms (GAs) has provided another approach for adjusting parameters in the design of controllers. GA is a parallel and global technique [9], [19]. Because it simultaneously evaluates many points in a search space, it is more likely to converge toward the global solution. Some researchers have developed methods to design and implement fuzzy controllers by using GAs. Karr [2] used a GA to generate membership

+ Corresponding author. Email:chlin@nuk.edu.tw

functions for a fuzzy system. In Karr's work, a user needs to declare an exhaustive rule set and then use a GA to design only the membership functions. In [20], a fuzzy controller design method that used a GA to find the membership functions and the rule sets simultaneously was proposed. Lin [27] proposed a hybrid learning method which combines the GA and the least-squares estimate (LSE) method to construct a neuron-fuzzy controller. In [20] and [27], the input space was partitioned into a grid. The number of fuzzy rules (i.e., the length of each chromosome in the GA) increased exponentially as the dimension of the input space increased. To overcome this problem, Juang [26] adopted a flexible partition approach in the precondition part. The method has the admirable property of small network size and high learning accuracy.

Recently, some researchers [9], [19], [28]-[29] applied GA methods to implement reinforcement learning in the design of fuzzy controllers. Lin and Jou [9] proposed GA-based fuzzy reinforcement learning to control magnetic bearing systems. In [19], Juang and his colleagues proposed genetic reinforcement learning in designing fuzzy controllers. The GA adopted in [19] was based upon traditional symbiotic evolution which, when applied to fuzzy controller design, complements the local mapping property of a fuzzy rule. In [28], Er and Deng proposed dynamic Q-Learning for on-line tuning the fuzzy inference systems. Kaya and Alhajj [29] proposed a novel multiagent reinforcement learning approach based on fuzzy OLAP association rules mining. However, these approaches encountered one or more of the following major problems: 1) the initial values of the populations were generated randomly; 2) the mutational value was generated by the constant range while the mutation point is also generated randomly; 3) the population sizes always depend on the problem which is to be solved.

In this chapter, we propose a reinforcement sequential-search-based genetic algorithm (R-SSGA) method for solving above-mentioned problems. Unlike the traditional reinforcement learning, we formulate a number of time steps before failure occurs as the fitness function. The new sequential-search-based genetic algorithm (SSGA) is also proposed to perform parameter learning. Moreover, the SSGA method is different from traditional GA, which the better chromosomes will be initially generated while the better mutation points will be determined for performing efficient mutation. Compared with traditional genetic algorithm, the SSGA method generates initialize population efficiently and decides efficient mutation points to perform mutation. The advantages of the proposed R-SSGA method are summarized as follows: (1) The R-SSGA method can reduce the population sizes to a minimum size (4); (2) The chromosome which has the best performance will be chosen to perform the mutation operator in each generation. (3) The R-SSGA method converges more quickly than existing traditional genetic methods.

This chapter is organized as follows. Section 2 introduces the sequential-search-based genetic algorithm. A reinforcement sequential-search-based genetic algorithm is presented in Section 3. In Section 4, the proposed R-SSGA method is evaluated using two different control problems, and its performances are benchmarked against other structures. Finally, conclusions on the proposed algorithm are summarized in the last section.

2. The sequential-search-based genetic algorithm

A new genetic learning algorithm, called sequential-search-based genetic algorithm (SSGA), is proposed to adjust the parameters for the desired outputs. The proposed SSGA method is different from a traditional genetic algorithm [9], [19]. The SSGA method generates initial population efficiently and decides efficient mutation points to perform mutation. Like traditional genetic algorithm [9], [19], the proposed SSGA method consists of two major operators: reproduction, crossover. Before the details of these two operators are explained, coding, initialization and efficient mutation are discussed as follows:

Coding step: The first step in the SSGA method is to code a neuro-fuzzy controller into a chromosome. We adopt a Takagi-Sugeno-Kang (TSK) type neuro-fuzzy controller [13] to be the structure of the proposed SSGA method. A TSK-type neuro-fuzzy controller employs different implication and aggregation methods than the standard Mamdani controller [1]. Instead of using fuzzy sets the conclusion part of a rule, is a linear combination of the crisp inputs.

$$\text{IF } x_1 \text{ is } A_{1j}(m_{1j}, \sigma_{1j}) \text{and } x_2 \text{ is } A_{2j}(m_{2j}, \sigma_{2j}) \ldots \text{and } x_n \text{ is } A_{nj}(m_{nj}, \sigma_{nj})$$

$$THEN\ y'=w_0+w_1x_1+\ldots+w_ix_i \tag{1}$$

where m_{ij} and σ_{ij} represent a Gaussian membership function with mean and deviation with ith dimension and jth rule node. A fuzzy rule in Fig. 1 is represented the form in Eq. (1).

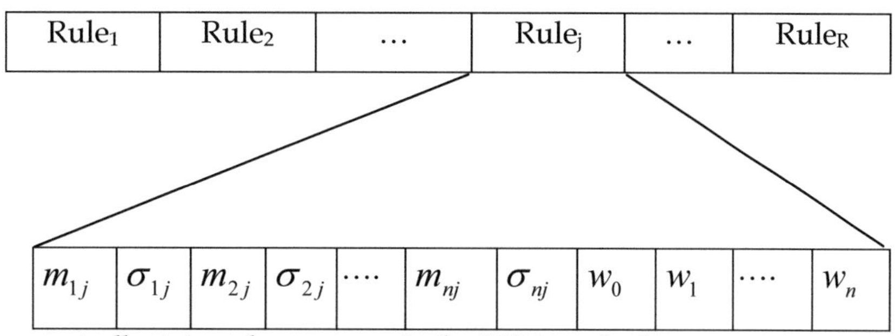

Fig. 1. Coding a fuzzy controller into a chromosome in the SSGA method.

Initialization step: Before the SSGA method is designed, individuals forming an initial population should be generated. Unlike traditional genetic algorithm, an initial population is generated randomly within a fixed range. In the SSGA method, the initial population is generated efficiently to ensure that chromosomes with good genes can be generated. The detailed steps of the initialization method are described as follows:

- **Step 0:** The first chromosome that represents a TSK-type fuzzy controller will be generated initially. The following formulations show how to generate the chromosomes:

$$Deviation\text{: } Chr_j[p]=random[\sigma_{\min}, \sigma_{\max}] \tag{2}$$

where p=2, 4, 6, …, 2*n

$$Mean\text{: } Chr_j[p]= random[m_{\min}, m_{\max}] \tag{3}$$

where p=1, 3, 5, …, 2*n-1

$$Weight\text{: } Chr_j[p]= random\ [w_{\min}, w_{\max}] \tag{4}$$

where p=2*n +1,..., 2*n +(1+n)

where Chr_j means chromosome in *i*th rule and *p* represent the *p*th gene in a Chr_j; $[\sigma_{\min}, \sigma_{\max}]$, $[m_{\min}, m_{\max}]$, and $[w_{\min}, w_{\max}]$ represent the predefined ranges of deviation, mean, and weight. The ranges are determined by practical experimentation or trial-and-error tests.

- **Step 1:** To generate the other chromosomes, we use the SSGA method to generate the new chromosomes. The search algorithm of the SSGA method is similar to the local search procedure in [14]. In the SSGA method, every gene in the previous chromosomes is selected using a sequential search and the gene's value is updated to evaluate the performance based on the fitness value. The details of the SSGA method are as follows:
  (a) Sequentially search for a gene in the previous chromosome.
  (b) Update the chosen gene in (a) according to the following formula:

$$Chr_j[p]=\begin{cases}\mathrm{Chr_j}[p]+\Delta(fitness\_value, \sigma_{\max}-\mathrm{Chr_j}[p]), if \alpha>0.5 \\ \mathrm{Chr_j}[p]-\Delta(fitness\_value, \mathrm{Chr_j}[p]-\sigma_{\min}), if \alpha<0.5\end{cases} \tag{5}$$

where p=2, 4, 6, …, 2*n

$$Chr_j[p]=\begin{cases}\mathrm{Chr_j}[p]+\Delta(fitness\_value, m_{\max}-\mathrm{Chr_j}[p]), if \alpha>0.5 \\ \mathrm{Chr_j}[p]-\Delta(fitness\_value, \mathrm{Chr_j}[p]-m_{\min}), if \alpha<0.5\end{cases} \tag{6}$$

where p=1, 3, 5, …, 2*n-1

$$\mathrm{Chr_j}[\mathrm{p}]=\begin{cases}\mathrm{Chr_j}[p]+\Delta(fitness\_value, w_{\max}-\mathrm{Chr_j}[p]), if \alpha>0.5 \\ \mathrm{Chr_j}[p]-\Delta(fitness\_value, \mathrm{Chr_j}[p]-w_{\min}), if \alpha<0.5\end{cases} \tag{7}$$

where p=2*n +1,..., 2*n +(1+n)

$$\text{where } \Delta(fitness\_value, v) = v * \lambda * (1/fitness\_value)^{\lambda} \tag{8}$$

  where $\alpha, \lambda \in [0,1]$ are the random values; $fitness\_value$ is the fitness computed using Eq (11); *p* represents the *p*th gene in a chromosome; *j* represents the *j*th rule, respectively. The function $\Delta(fitness\_value, v)$ returns a value, such that $\Delta(fitness\_value, v)$ comes close to 0 as $fitness\_value$ increases. This property causes the mutation operator to search the space uniformly during the initial stage (when $fitness\_value$ is small) and locally during the later stages, thus increasing the probability of generating children closer to its successor than a random choice and reducing the number of generations.
  (c) If the new gene that is generated from (b) can improve the fitness value, then replace the old gene with the new gene in the chromosome. If not, recover the old gene in the chromosome. After this, go to (a) until every gene is selected. The pseudo code for the SSGA method is listed in Figure 2. The $Chr_{k,j}$ represents the *k*th chromosome and

*j*th rule in a fuzzy controller. And *Nf* denote the size of the population, $fitness(Chr_{k,j\_new})$ is a fitness function by Eq.(11) using the *k*th new chromosome.

```
Procedure Sequential-Search-Based Genetic Algorithm
Begin
      Let p=0,i=0;
   Repeat
      k=k+1;
      Repeat
        j=j+1;
        Repeat
              p=p+1;
              Perform Chr_{k,j_new}=inttialize(Chr_{k,j_old}[p]);by(5)to(8);
          Evaluate fitness(Chr_{k,j_new}) and fitness(Chr_{k,j_old}) by(11);
              If fitness(Chr_{k,j_new}) >fitness(Chr_{k,j_old}) Then
            Chr_{k,j_old} = Chr_{k,j_new;}; else Chr_{k,j_new} = Chr_{k,j_old};
        Until p=2*n+(1+n);
      Until j=R;
   Until k=Nf;
End
```

Fig. 2. The pseudo code for the SSGA method.

- **Step 2**: If no genes are selected to improve the fitness value in step 1, than the new chromosome will be generated according to step 0. After the new chromosome is generated, the initialization method returns to step 1 until the total number of chromosomes is generated.

The firing strength of a fuzzy rule is calculated by performing the "AND" operation on the truth values of each variable to its corresponding fuzzy sets,

$$u_j = \prod_{i=1}^{n} \exp\left(-\frac{\left[u_i^{(1)} - m_{ij}\right]^2}{\sigma_{ij}^2}\right) \tag{9}$$

where m_{ij} and σ_{ij} are, respectively, the center and the width of the Gaussian membership function of the *j*th term of the *i*th input variable x_i. The output of a fuzzy system is computed by

$$u_{out} = \frac{\sum_j u_j \sum_{i=0}^{n} w_{ij} x_i}{\sum_j u_j} \tag{10}$$

where the weight w_j is the output action strength associated with the jth rule and u_{out} is the output of the network.

Efficient mutation step: Although reproduction and crossover will produce many new strings, they do not introduce any new information to the population at the site of an individual. Mutation is an operator that randomly alters the allele of a gene. We use an efficient mutation operation, which is unlike the traditional mutation, to mutate the chromosomes. In the SSGA method, we perform efficient mutation using the best fitness value chromosome of every generation. And we use the SSGA method to decide on the mutation points. When the mutation points are selected, we use Eqs. (5) to (7) to update the genes. The efficient mutation of an individual is shown in Fig. 3.

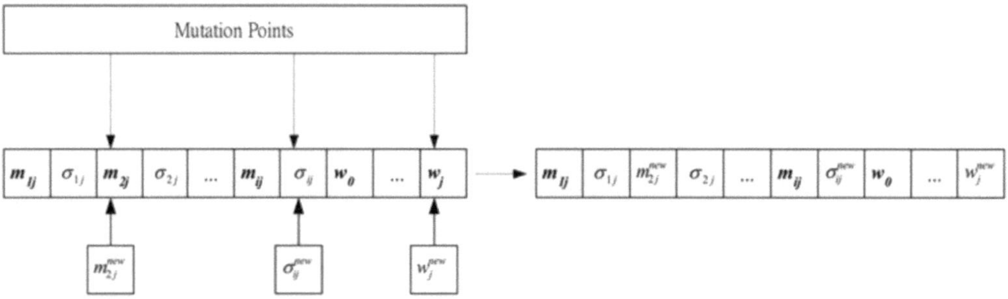

Fig. 3. Efficient mutation operation using 3 mutation points with jth rule.

Reproduction step: Reproduction is a process in which individual strings are copied according to their fitness value. In this study, we use the roulette-wheel selection method [15] – a simulated roulette is spun – for this reproduction process. The best performing individuals in the top half of the population [19] advances to the next generation. The other half is generated to perform crossover and mutation operations on individuals in the top half of the parent generation.

Crossover step: Reproduction directs the search toward the best existing individuals but does not create any new individuals. In nature, an offspring has two parents and inherits genes from both. The main operator working on the parents is the crossover operator, the operation of which occurred for a selected pair with a crossover rate that was set to 0.5 in this study. The first step is to select the individuals from the population for the crossover. Tournament selection [15] is used to select the top-half of the best performing individuals [19]. The individuals are crossed and separated using a two-point crossover that is the new individuals are created by exchanging the site's values between the selected sites of parents' individual. After this operation, the individuals with poor performances are replaced by the newly produced offspring.

The aforementioned steps are done repeatedly and stopped when the predetermined condition is achieved.

3. Reinforcement sequential-search-based genetic algorithm (R-SSGA)

Unlike the supervised learning problem, in which the correct "target" output values are given for each input pattern to perform neuron-fuzzy controller learning, the reinforcement learning problem has only very simple "evaluative" or "critical" information, rather than "instructive" information, available for learning. In the extreme case, there is only a single bit of information to indicate whether the output is right or wrong. Figure 4 shows how the R-SSGA method and its training environment interact in a reinforcement learning problem. The environment supplies a time-varying input vector to the R-SSGA method, receives its time-varying output/action vectors and then provides a reinforcement signal. Therefore, the reinforcement signal indicates whether a success or a failure occurs.

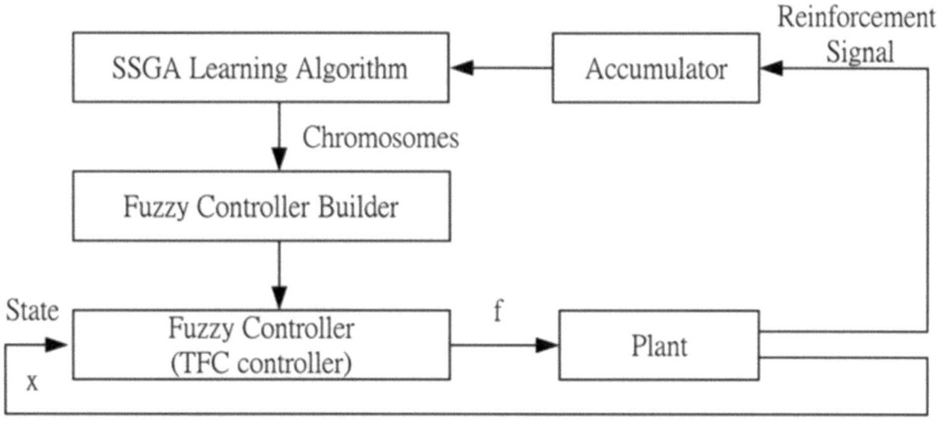

Fig. 4. The proposed R-SSGA method.

As show in Fig. 4, the R-SSGA method consists of a TSK-type fuzzy controller which acts as the control network to determine a proper action according to the current input vector (environment state). The structure of the R-SSGA method is different from Barto and his colleagues' actor-critic architecture [16]-[17]. Two neuron-like adaptive elements are integrated in this system [16]-[17]. They are the associative search element (ASE) used as a controller, and the adaptive critic element (ACE) used as a predictor. Temporal difference techniques and single-parameter stochastic exploration are used in [16]. The input to the R-SSGA method is the state of the plant, and the output is a control action of the state, denoted by f. The only available feedback is a reinforcement signal that notifies the R-SSGA method only when a failure occurs. An accumulator plays a role which is a relative performance measure shown in Fig. 4. It accumulates the number of time steps before a failure occurs [30]. Thus, the feedback takes the form of an accumulator that determines how long the experiment is still a "success"; this is used as a relative measure of the fitness of the proposed R-SSGA method. That is, the accumulator will indicate the "fitness" of the current R-SSGA method. The key to this learning algorithm is formulating a number of time steps before failure occurs and using this formulation as the fitness function of the R-SSGA method. The advantage of the proposed method need not use the critical network as either a multi-step or single-step predictor.

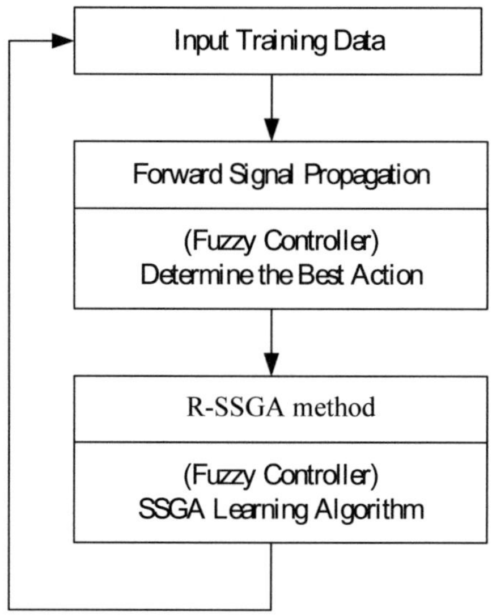

Fig. 5. Flowchart of the R-SSGA method

Figure 5 shows the flowchart of the R-SSGA method. The R-SSGA method runs in a feedforward fashion to control the environment (plant) until a failure occurs. Our relative measure of fitness function takes the form of an accumulator that determines how long the experiment is a "success". In this way, according to a defined fitness function, a fitness value is assigned to each string in the population where high fitness values means good fit. Thus, we use a number of time steps before failure occurs to define the fitness function. The fitness function is defined by:

$$\text{Fitness\_Value (i)} = \text{TIME-STEP(i)} \tag{11}$$

where *TIME-STEP(i)* represents how long the experiment is still a "success" about the *i*th population. Eq.(11) reflects the fact that long-time steps before failure occurs (to keep the desired control goal longer) mean higher fitness of the R-SSGA method.

4. Illustrative examples

To verify the performance of the proposed R-SSGA method, two control examples—the cart-pole balancing system and a water bath temperature control system—are presented in this section. For the two computer simulations, the initial parameters are given in Table 1 before training.

In this example, we shall apply the R-SSGA method to the classic control problem of the cart-pole balancing. This problem is often used as an example of inherently unstable and dynamic systems to demonstrate both modern and classic control techniques [22]-[23] or reinforcement learning schemes [18]-[19], and is now used as a control benchmark. As shown in Fig. 6, the cart-pole balancing problem is the problem of learning how to balance an upright pole. The bottom of the pole is hinged to the left or right of a cart that travels along a finite-length track. Both the cart and the pole can move only in the vertical plane; that is, each has only one degree of freedom.

Table 1: The initial parameters before training

Parameters	*Value*
Population Size	*4*
Crossover Rate	*0.5*
Coding Type	*Real Number*
$[\sigma_{\min}, \sigma_{\max}]$	*[0,1]*
$[m_{\min}, m_{\max}]$	*[0,1]*
$[w_{\min}, w_{\max}]$	*[-20,20]*

Example 1. Cart-Pole Balancing System

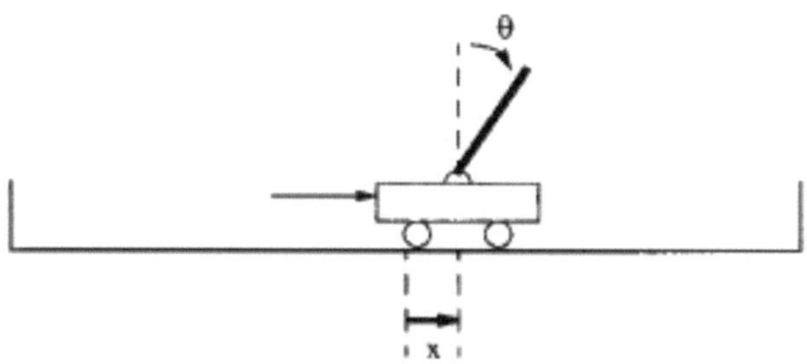

Fig. 6. The cart-pole balancing system.

There are four state variables in the system: θ, the angle of the pole in an upright position (in degrees); $\dot{\theta}$, the angular velocity of the pole (in degrees/seconds); x, the horizontal position of the cart's center (in meters); and $\dot{x}$, the velocity of the cart (in meters/seconds). The only control action is *f*, which is the amount of force (in *Newtons*) applied to the cart to move it left or right. The system fails when the pole falls past a certain angle ($\pm 12^{o}$ is used here) or when the cart runs into the boundary of the track (the distance is 2.4*m* from the center to each boundary of the track). The goal of this control problem is to determine a sequence of forces that, when applied to the cart, balance the pole so that it is upright. The motion equations that we used were:

$$\theta(t+1) = \theta(t) + \Delta\dot{\theta}(t) \tag{12}$$

$$\begin{aligned}\dot{\theta}(t+1) = \dot{\theta}(t) + \Delta \frac{(m+m_p)g\sin\theta(t)}{(4/3)(m+m_p)l - m_p l\cos^2\theta(t)} \\ - \frac{\cos\theta(t)\left[f(t) + m_p l\dot{\theta}(t)^2\sin\theta(t) - \mu_c \operatorname{sgn}(\dot{x}(t))\right]}{(4/3)(m+m_p)l - m_p l\cos^2\theta(t)} \\ - \frac{\dfrac{\mu_p(m+m_p)\dot{\theta}(t)}{m_p l}}{(4/3)(m+m_p)l - m_p l\cos^2\theta(t)}\end{aligned} \tag{13}$$

$$x(t+1) = x(t) + \Delta\dot{x}(t) \tag{14}$$

$$\begin{aligned}x(t+1) = \dot{x}(t) + \Delta \frac{f(t) + m_p l\left[\dot{\theta}(t)^2\sin\theta(t) - \ddot{\theta}(t)\cos\theta(t)\right]}{(m+m_p)} \\ - \frac{\mu_c \operatorname{sgn}(\dot{x}(t))}{(m+m_p)}\end{aligned} \tag{15}$$

where

l = *0.5* m, the length of the pole;

m = 1.1 kg, combined mass of the pole and the cart;

m_p = 0.1 kg, mass of the pole;

g = 9.8 m/s, acceleration due to the gravity; (16)

μ_c = 0.0005, coefficient of friction of the cart on the track,

μ_p = 0.000002, coefficient of friction of the pole on the cart,

Δ = 0.02(s), sampling interval.

The constraints on the variables were $-12^\circ \le \theta \le 12^\circ$, -2.4$m \le x \le$ 2.4m, and -10$N \le f \le$ 10N. A control strategy was deemed successful if it balanced a pole for 100,000 time steps.

The four input variables $(\theta, \dot{\theta}, x, \dot{x})$ and the output f_t are normalized between 0 and 1 over the following ranges, $\theta \in$[-12,12], $\dot{\theta} \in$ [-60,60], $x \in$ [-2.4,2.4], $\dot{x} \in$ [-3,3], $f_t \in$ [-10,10]. The fitness function in this example is defined in Eq.(11) to train the R-SSGA method where Eq.(11) is used to calculate how long it takes the cart-pole balancing system to fail and receives a penalty signal of -1 when the pole falls past a certain angle ($|\theta| > 12°C$) and when the cart runs into the boundaries of the tracks falls($|x| > 2.4m$). In this experiment, the initial values were set to (0, 0, 0, 0). And we set four rules constitute a TSK-Type fuzzy controller.

A total of five runs were performs. Each run started at same initial state. The simulation result in Fig.7 (a) shows that the R-SSGA method learned on average to balance the pole at the *16*th generation. In this figure, each run indicates that the largest fitness value in the current generation was selected before the cart-pole balancing system failed. When the proposed R-SSGA learning method is stopped, we choose the best string in the population in the final generation and tested it on the cart-pole balancing system. The final fuzzy rules generated by the R-SSGA method are described as follows:

Rule 1: IF x_1 is $A_{11}(0.38,0.35)$ and x_2 is $A_{21}(5.67,0.32)$ and x_3 is $A_{31}(0.19,1.91)$
and x_4 is $A_{41}(0.40,0.825)$
THEN $y'=-2.94+0.42x_1-0.20x_2-0.70x_3+0.40x_4$

Rule 2: IF x_1 is $A_{12}(0.52,1.70)$ and x_2 is $A_{22}(7.43,0.39)$ and x_3 is $A_{32}(0.37,14.9)$
and x_4 is $A_{42}(1.28,0.44)$
THEN $y'=12.21+12.16x_1-0.25x_2+0.32x_3+4.66x_4$

Rule 3: IF x_1 is $A_{13}(0.52,6.66)$ and x_2 is $A_{23}(12.1,0.39)$ and x_3 is $A_{33}(0.37,9.64)$
and x_4 is $A_{43}(1.28,0.44)$
THEN $y'=11.93+9.63x_1-0.25x_2+0.32x_3+9.64x_4$

Rule 4: IF x_1 is $A_{14}(0.52,17)$ and x_2 is $A_{24}(9.29,0.39)$ and x_3 is $A_{34}(0.37,3.98)$
and x_4 is $A_{44}(1.28,0.44)$
THEN $y'=11.93-3.98x_1-0.25x_2+0.32x_3+10.29x_4$

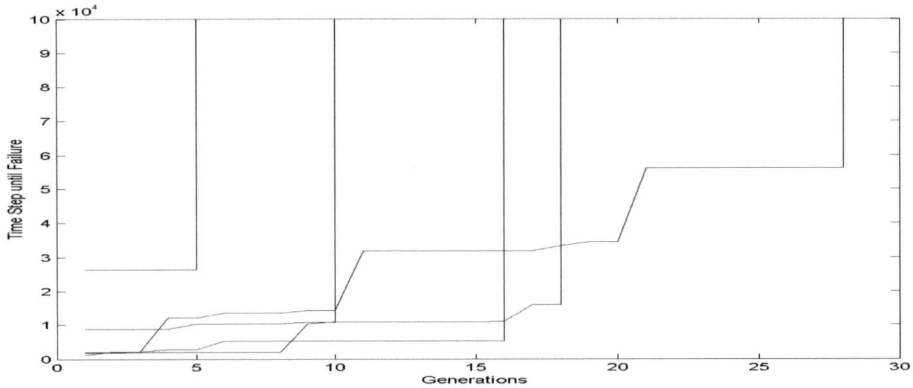

(a)

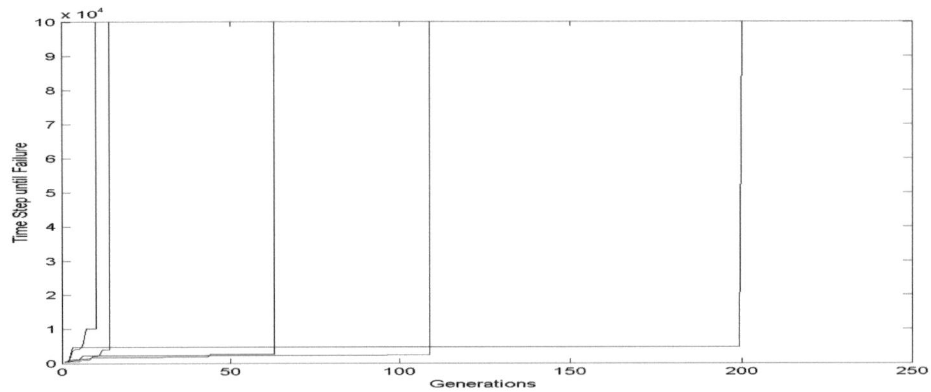

(b)

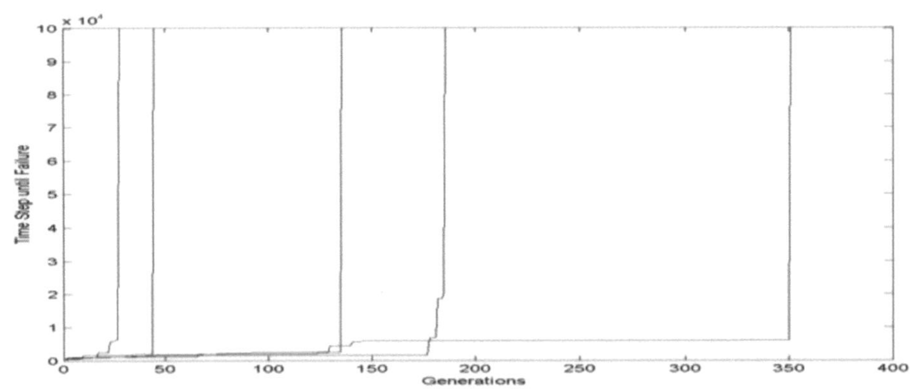

(c)

Fig. 7. The performance of (a) the R-SSGA method, (b) the SEFC method [19], and (c) the TGFC method [9] on the cart-pole balancing system.

Figure 8(a) show the angular deviation of the pole when the cart-pole balancing system was controlled by the well-trained R-SSGA method starting at the initial state: $r(0)=0, \dot{r}(0)=0, \theta(0)=0, \dot{\theta}(0)=0$. The average angular deviation was 0.006^0.

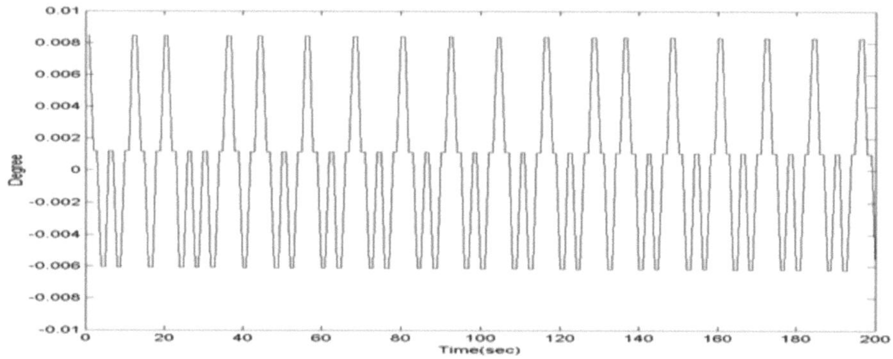

(a)

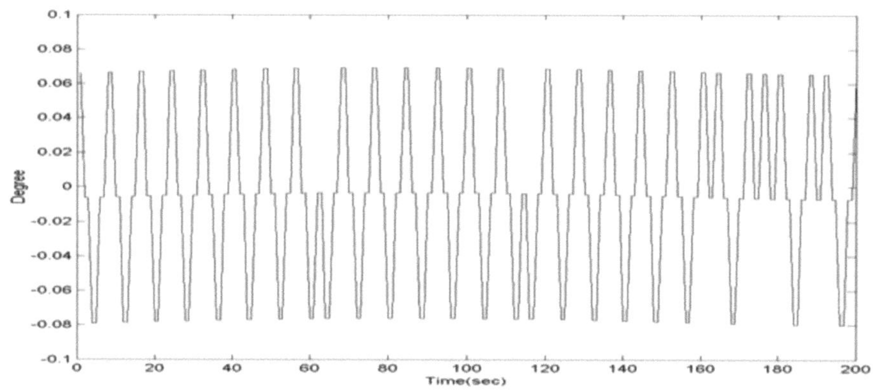

(b)

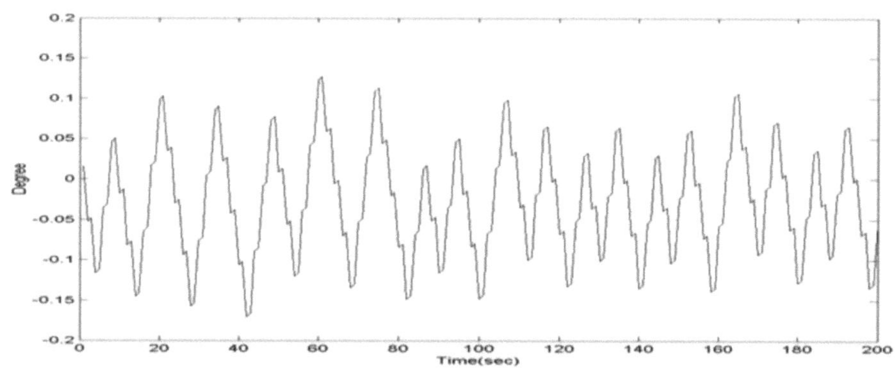

(c)

Fig. 8. Angular deviation of the pole by a trained (a) the R-SSGA method, (b) the SEFC method [19], and (c) the TGFC method [9].

In the experiment, we compare the performance of our system with the symbiotic evolution fuzzy controller (SEFC) [19] and the traditional genetic fuzzy controller (TGFC) [9]. In the SEFC and TGFC, the population sizes were also set to 50, and the crossover and mutation probabilities were set to 0.5 and 0.3, respectively. Figures 7 (b) and (c) show that the SEFC method and the TGFC method learned on average to balance the pole at the 80th and 149th generation. In this example, we compare the CPU times of the R-SSGA method with the SEFC and the TGFC methods. Table 2 shows the CPU times of the three methods. As shown in Table 2, our method obtains shorter CPU times than the SEFC and the TGFC methods. Figures 8(b) and 8(c) show the angular deviation of the pole when the cart-pole balancing system was controlled by the [19] and [9] models. The average angular deviation of the [19] and [9] models were 0.06^0 and 0.1^0. We also try to control the cart-pole balancing system at a different initial state: $r(0) = 0.6, \dot{r}(0) = 0.3, \theta(0) = 3, \dot{\theta}(0) = 1$. Figure 9 (a)-(c) shows the angular deviation of the pole when the cart-pole balancing system was controlled by the R-SSGA, the SEFC [19], and the TGFC [9] models at the initial state: $r(0) = 0.6, \dot{r}(0) = 0.3, \theta(0) = 3, \dot{\theta}(0) = 1$.

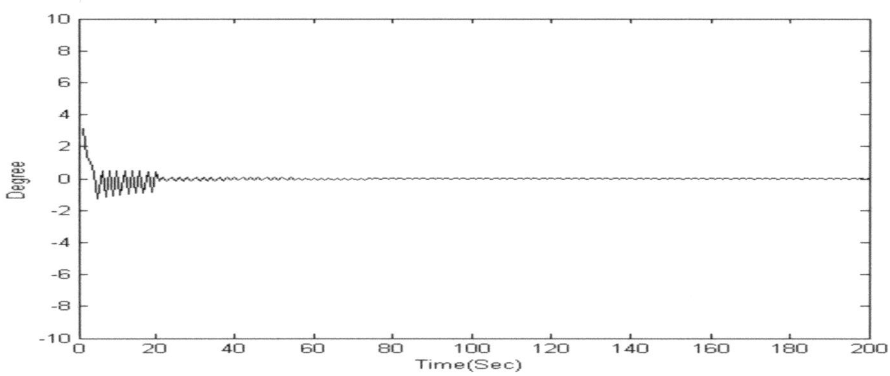

(a)

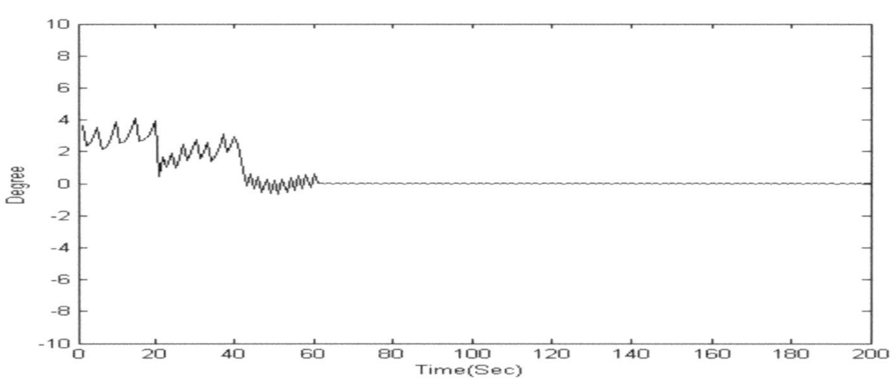

(b)

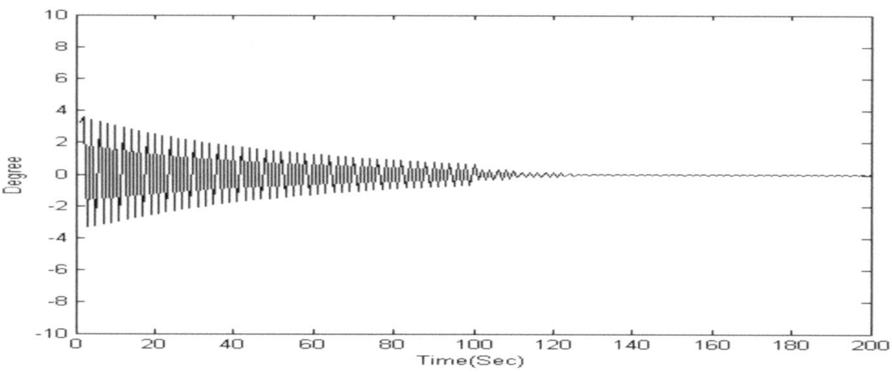

(c)

Fig. 9. Angular deviation of the pole by a trained (a) the R-SSGA method, (b) the SEFC method [19], and (c) the TGFC method [9] at the initial state: $r(0) = 0.6, \dot{r}(0) = 0.3, \theta(0) = 3, \dot{\theta}(0) = 1$.

Table 3 shows the number of pole-balance trials (which reflects the number of training episodes required) measured. The GENITOR [24] and SANE (Symbiotic Adaptive Neuro-Evolution) [21] were applied to the same control problem, and the simulation results are listed in Table 3. In GENITOR, the normal evolution algorithm was used to evolve the weights in a fully connected two-layer neural network, with additional connections from each input unit to the output layer. The network has five input units, five hidden units and one output unit. In SANE, the traditional symbiotic evolution algorithm was used to evolve a two-layer neural network with five input units, eight hidden units, and two output units. An individual in SANE represents a hidden unit with five specified connections to the input and output units. In Table 3 we can see that the proposed method is feasible and effective. And the proposed R-SSGA method only took 4 rules and the population size was 4.

Method	**Mean (Sec)**	**Best (Sec)**	**Worst (Sec)**
R-SSGA	**20**	**3**	**60**
SEFC [19]	36	4	236
TGFC [9]	165	8	412

Table 2. Performance comparison of the R-SSGA, the SEFC, and the TGFC methods.

Method	Mean	Best	Worst
GENITOR [24]	2578	415	12964
SANE [21]	1691	46	4461
TGFC [9]	80	26	200
SEFC [19]	149	10	350
R-SSGA	**17**	**5**	**29**

Table 3. Performance comparison of various existing models in Example 1.

In this example, to verify the performance of our proposed method, we use five different initial states for the R-SSGA, the SEFC, and the TGFC methods. The five different initial states are shown as follows:

S1: $r(0) = 0.8, \dot{r}(0) = 0.2, \theta(0) = 8, \dot{\theta}(0) = 3$

S2: $r(0) = 0.3, \dot{r}(0) = 0.1, \theta(0) = 2, \dot{\theta}(0) = 0$

S3: $r(0) = 0.5, \dot{r}(0) = 0.1, \theta(0) = 4, \dot{\theta}(0) = 2$

S4: $r(0) = 0.7, \dot{r}(0) = 0.4, \theta(0) = 6, \dot{\theta}(0) = 3$

S5: $r(0) = 0.2, \dot{r}(0) = 0.1, \theta(0) = 2, \dot{\theta}(0) = 1$

Figure 10 (a)-(c) show that the R-SSGA, the SEFC, and the TGFC methods learned on average to balance the pole at the 78th, 105th, and 166th generation. Figure 11(a)-(c) show the angular deviation of the pole when the cart-pole balancing system was controlled by the R-SSGA method, the SEFC method [19], and the TGFC method [9] that starting at the initial state: $r(0) = 0, \dot{r}(0) = 0, \theta(0) = 0, \dot{\theta}(0) = 0$. The average angular deviations were 0.01^0, 0.04^0, and 0.08^0. Table 4 shows the number of pole-balance trials measured of the R-SSGA, the SEFC [19], and the TGFC [9] methods. In Table 4, we see that the proposed method obtains a better performance than some existing methods [9], [19].

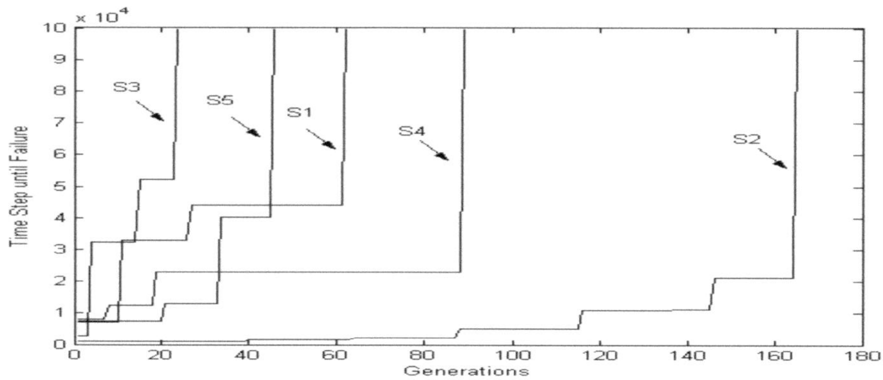

(a)

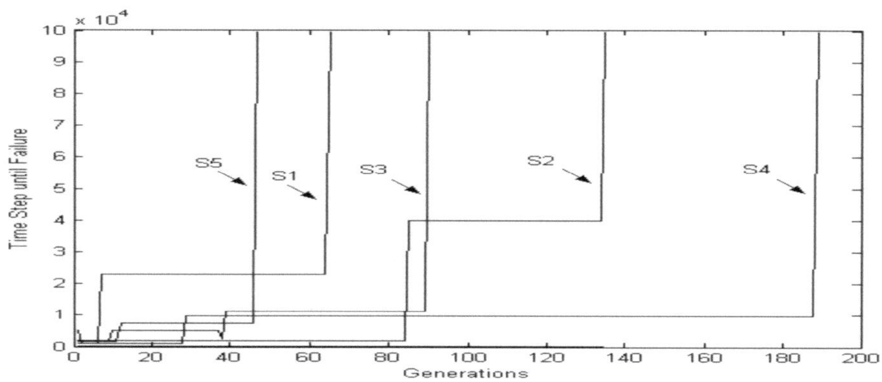

(b)

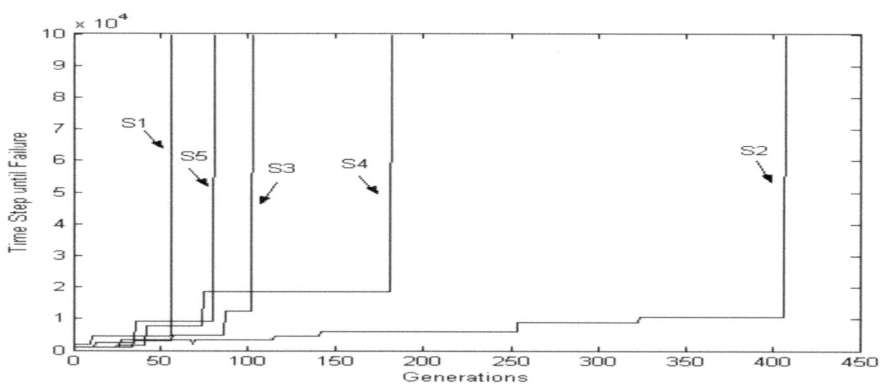

(c)

Fig. 10. The performance of (a) the R-SSGA method, (b) the SEFC method [19], and (c) the TGFC method [9] on the cart-pole balancing system starting at five different initial states.

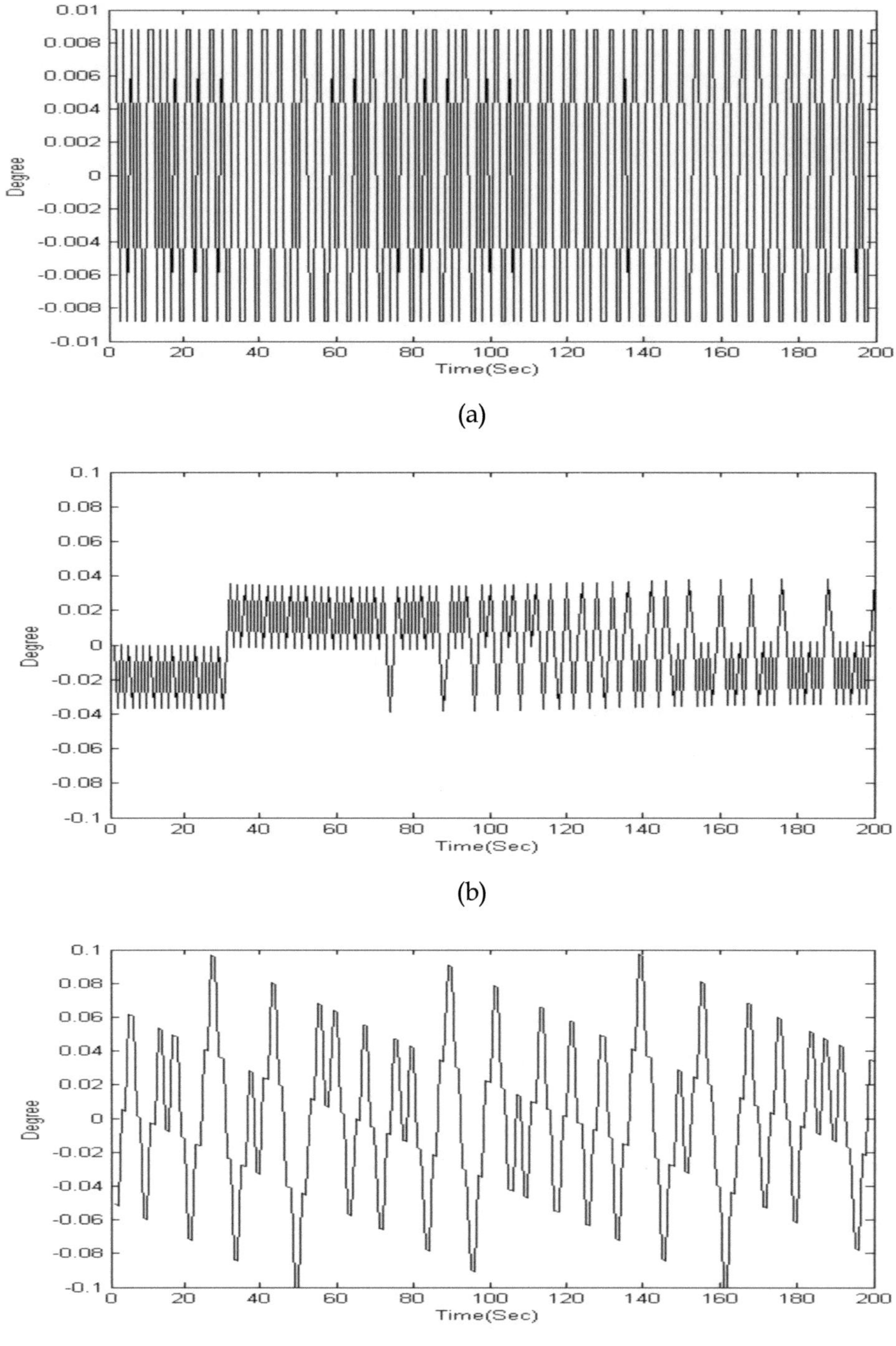

Fig. 11. Angular deviation of the pole by a trained (a) the R-SSGA method, (b) the SEFC method [19], and (c) the TGFC method [9].

Table 4: Performance comparison of existing models in Example 1.

Method	Mean	Best	Worst
TGFC [9]	166	57	407
SEFC [19]	105	47	189
R-SSGA	**78**	**24**	**165**

Example 2. Water Bath Temperature Control System

The goal of this simulation was to control the temperature of a water bath system given by

$$\frac{dy(t)}{dt} = \frac{u(t)}{C} + \frac{Y_0 - y(t)}{RC} \tag{17}$$

where $y(t)$ is the system output temperature in $^{\circ}C$; $u(t)$ is the heat flowing into the system; Y_0 is the room temperature; C is the equivalent system thermal capacity; and R is the equivalent thermal resistance between the system borders and the surroundings.

Assuming that R and C are essentially constant, we rewrite the system in Eq.(17) into discrete-time form with some reasonable approximation. The system

$$y(t+1) = e^{-\alpha Ts} y(k) + \frac{\frac{\beta}{\alpha}(1-e^{-\alpha Ts})}{1+e^{0.5y(k)-40}} u(k) + [1-e^{-\alpha Ts}] y_0 \tag{18}$$

is obtained, where α and β are constant values describing R and C. The system parameters used in this example were α=$1.0015e^{-4}$, β=$8.67973e^{-3}$, and Y_0=25.0($^{\circ}C$), which were obtained from a real water bath plant in [3]. The input $u(k)$ was limited to 0, and the voltage was 5V. The sampling period was Ts=30. The system configuration is shown in Fig. 12, where y_{ref} was the desired temperature of the controlled plant.

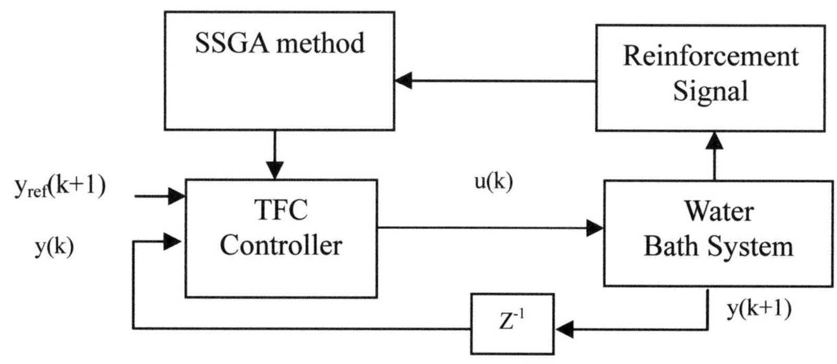

Fig. 12. Flow diagram of using the R-SSGA method for solving the temperature control problem.

In this example, y_{ref} and $y(k)$ and the output $u(k)$ were normalized between 0 and 1 over the following ranges: y_{ref} :[25,85], $y(k)$:[25,85], and $u(k)$:[0,5]. The values of floating-point numbers were initially assigned using the R-SSGA method initially. The fitness function was set for each reassigned regulation temperature T=35, 55, and 75, starting from the current temperature and again after 10 time steps. The control temperature error should be within $\pm 1.5\,^{\circ}C$; otherwise failure occurs. In the R-SSGA method, we set five rules constitute a TSK-Type fuzzy controller using the proposed R-SSGA method. A total of five runs were performed. Each run started at same initial state.
The simulation result in Fig. 13(a) shows that the R-SSGA method learned on average to success at the 25th generation. In this figure, each run indicates that the largest fitness value in the current generation was selected before the water bath temperature system failed. When the R-SSGA learning is stopped, we chose the best string in the population in the final generation and tested it with two different examples in the water bath temperature control system. The final fuzzy rules of a TSK-Type fuzzy controller by the R-SSGA method are described as follows:

Rule 1: IF x_1 is A_{11}(1.23, 0.75) and x_2 is A_{21}(0.13, 0.81)

THEN y'=7.09 +8.50 x_1+1.51 x_2

Rule 2: IF x_1 is A_{12}(0.18, 0.352) and x_2 is A_{22}(1.09, 0.45)

THEN y'=-19.41-14.051 x_1 -16.81 x_2

Rule 3: IF x_1 is A_{13}(0.19, 0.36) and x_2 is A_{23}(1.10, 0.46)

THEN y'=-19.42 -14.05 x_1 -16.80 x_2

Rule 4: IF x_1 is A_{14}(0.0001 1.27) and x_2 is A_{24}(1.09, 0.45)

THEN y'=5.40+ 8.47 x_1 -16.81 x_2

Rule 5: IF x_1 is A_{15}(5.0, 0.66) and x_2 is A_{25}(0.14, 0.08)

THEN y'=-4.85-5.88 x_1 +9.45 x_2

where $A_{ij}(m_{ij}, \sigma_{ij})$ represents a Gaussian membership function with mean m_{ij} and deviation σ_{ij} in ith input dimension and jth rule. In this example, as with example 1, we also compare the performance of our system with the SEFC method [19] and the TGFC method [9]. Figures 13 (b) and 10(c) show the performance of [19] and [9] methods. In this figure we can see that the SEFC and TGFC methods learned on average to balance the pole at the *49*th and *96*th generation but in our model just take 25 generations.

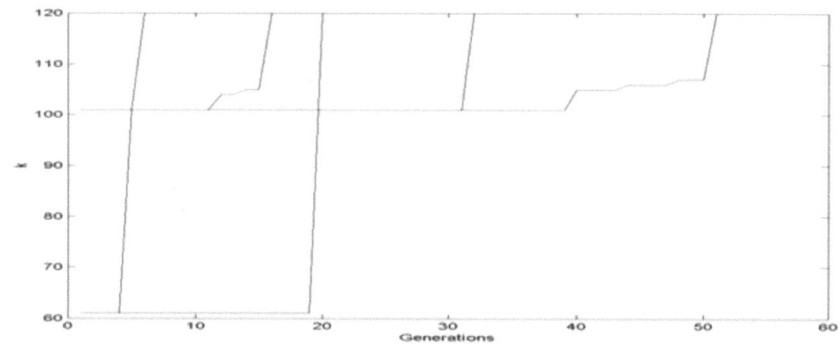

(a)

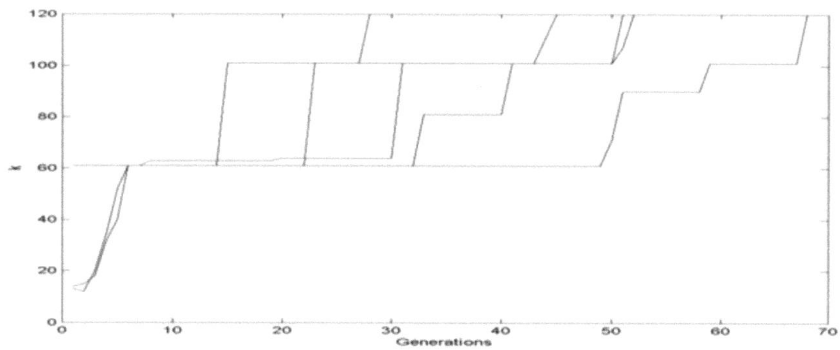

(b)

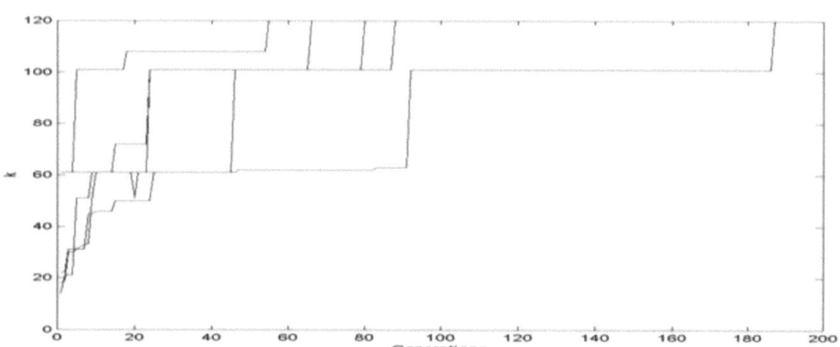

(c)

Fig. 13. The performance of the water bath system for (a) the R-SSGA method, (b) the SEFC method [19] and, (c) the TGFC method [9].

For testing the controller system, we compare the three methods (the R-SSGA, SEFC, and TGFC methods). The three methods are applied to the water bath temperature control

system. The comparison performance measures included a set points regulation and a change of parameters.
The first task was to control the simulated system to follow three set points

$$y_{ref}(k) = \begin{cases} 35°c, & for \quad k \le 40 \\ 55°c, & for \quad 40 < k \le 80 \\ 75°c, & for \quad 80 < k \le 120. \end{cases} \tag{19}$$

The regulation performance of the R-SSGA method is shown in Fig. 14(a). The error curves of the three methods are shown in Fig. 14(b). In this figure, the R-SSGA method obtains smaller errors than others.

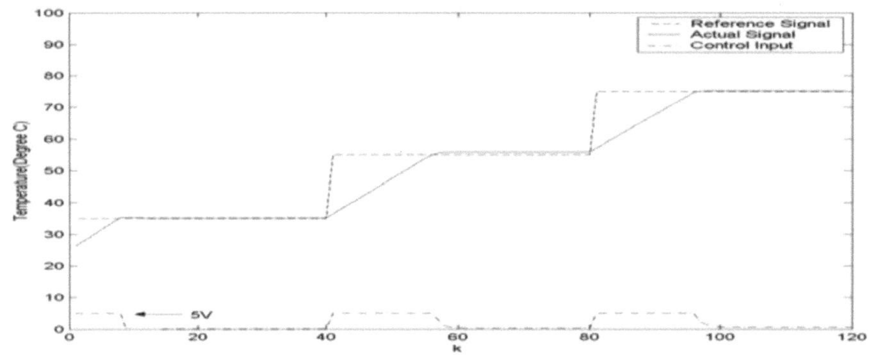

(a)

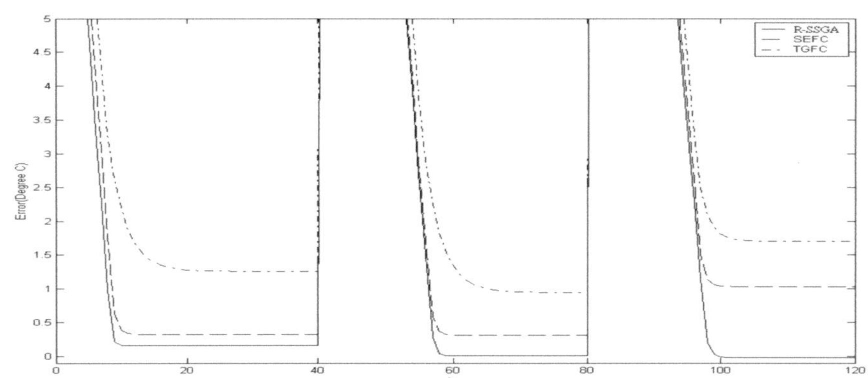

(b)

Fig. 14. (a) Final regulation performance of the R-SSGA method for water bath system. (b) The error curves of the R-SSGA method, the SEFC method and the TGFC method.

In the second set of simulations, the tracking capability of the R-SSGA method with respect to ramp-reference signals is studied. We define

$$y_{ref}(k) = \begin{cases} 34°C & for \quad k \le 30 \\ (34 + 0.5 * (k - 30))°C & for \quad 30 < k \le 50 \\ (44 + 0.8 * (k - 50))°C & for \quad 50 < k \le 70 \\ (60 + 0.5 * (k - 70))°C & for \quad 70 < k \le 90 \\ 70°C & for \quad 90 < k \le 120 \end{cases} \tag{20}$$

The tracking performance of the R-SSGA method is shown in Fig. 15(a). The corresponding errors of the three methods are shown in Fig. 15(b). The results show the good control and disturbance rejection capabilities of the trained R-SSGA method in the water bath system.

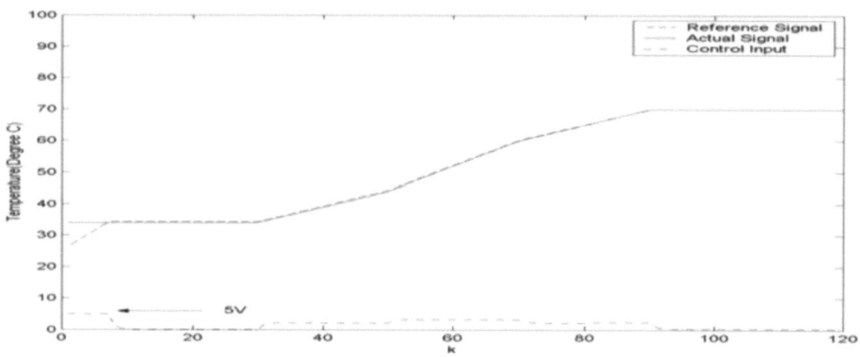

(a)

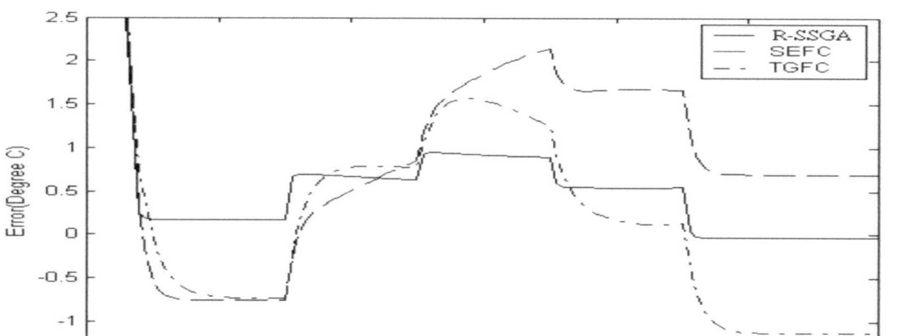

(b)

Fig. 15. (a) The tracking of the R-SSGA method when a change occurs in the water bath system. (b) The error curves of the R-SSGA method, the SEFC method [19], and the TGFC method [9].

To test their regulation performance, a performance index, sum of absolute error (SAE), is defined by

$$SAE = \sum_{k} \left| y_{ref}(k) - y(k) \right| \tag{21}$$

where $y_{ref}(k)$ and $y(k)$ are the reference output and the actual output of the simulated system, respectively. Table 5 shows the comparison the SAE among the R-SSGA method, the SEFC method, and the TGFC method. As show in Table 5, the proposed R-SSGA method has better performance than that of the others. And the proposed method only takes 5 rules and the populations' size is minimized to 4.

$SAE=\sum_{k=1}^{120} \lvert y_{ref}(k)-y(k) \rvert$	**R-SSGA**	SEFC [19]	TGFC [9]
Regulation Performance	**360.04**	370.12	400.12
Tracking Performance	**54.187**	90.81	104.221

Table 5: Performance comparison of various existing models in Example 2.

5. Conclusions

A novel reinforcement sequential-search-based genetic algorithm (R-SSGA) is proposed. The better chromosomes will be initially generated while the better mutation points will be determined for performing efficient mutation. We formulate a number of time steps before failure occurs as the fitness function. The proposed R-SSGA method makes the design of TSK-Type fuzzy controllers more practical for real-world applications, since it greatly lessens the quality and quantity requirements of the teaching signals. Two typical examples were presented to show the fundamental applications of the proposed R-SSGA method. Simulation results have shown that 1) the R-SSGA method converges quickly; 2) the R-SSGA method requires a small number of population sizes (only 4); 3) the R-SSGA method obtains a smaller average angular deviation than other methods.

6. Acknowledgement

This research is supported by the National Science Council of R.O.C. under grant NSC 95-2221-E-324- 028-MY2.

7. References

C. T. Lin and C. S. G. Lee, *Neural Fuzzy Systems: A neural-fuzzy synergism to intelligent systems.* Englewood Cliffs, NJ: Prentice-Hall, May 1996. (with disk).

C. L. Karr and E. J. Gentry, "Fuzzy control of ph using genetic algorithms," *IEEE Trans. on Fuzzy Syst.*, vol. 1, pp. 46–53, Feb. 1993.

J. Tanomaru and S. Omatu, "Process control by on-line trained neural controllers," *IEEE Trans. on Ind. Electron.*, Vol. 39, pp. 511-521, 1992.

K.J. °Astrom and B. Wittenmark, *Adaptive Control*. Reading, MA: Addison-Wesley, 1989.

C. J. Lin and C. H. Chen, "Nonlinear system control using compensatory neuro-fuzzy networks," *IEICE Trans. Fundamentals*, vol. E86-A, no. 9, pp. 2309-2316, Sept. 2003.

C. F. Juang and C. T. Lin, "An online self-constructing neural fuzzy inference network and its applications," *IEEE Trans. Fuzzy Syst.*, vol. 6, no. 1, pp.12-32, Feb. 1998.

C. W. Anderson, "Learning and problem solving with multilayer connectionist systems," Ph.D. dissertation, Univ. Massachusetts, Amherst, 1986.

A. G. Barto and M. I. Jordan, "Gradient following without backpropagation in layered networks," in *Proc. IEEE 1st Annual Conf. Neural Networks*, vol. 2, San Diego, CA, pp. 629–636, 1987.

C. T. Lin and C. P. Jo, "GA-based fuzzy reinforcement learning for control of a magnetic bearing system," *IEEE Trans. Syst., Man, Cybern., Part B*, vol. 30, no. 2, pp. 276-289, Apr. 2000.

X. W. Yan, Z.D. Deng and Z.Q. Sun, "Competitive Takagi-Sugeno fuzzy reinforcement learning," in *Proc. IEEE Int. Conf. Control Applications.*, pp. 878-883, Sept. 2001.

G.rigore O., "Reinforcement learning neural network used in control of nonlinear systems, " in *Proc. IEEE Int. Conf. Industrial Technology.*, vol. 1, pp. 19-22, Jan. 2000.

X. Xu and H. G. He, "Residual-gradient-based neural reinforcement learning for the optimal control of an acrobat," in *Proc. IEEE Int. Conf. Intelligent Control.*, pp. 27-30, Oct. 2002.

T. Takagi, M. Sugeno, "Fuzzy identification of systems and its applications to modeling and control", *IEEE Trans. Syst., Man, Cybern.*, vol. 1, no. 1, pp. 116-32, 1985.

J.-S. R. Jang, C. T. Sun, and E. Mizutani, *Neuro-Fuzzy and Soft Computing*, Ch. 17, Prentice-Hall, 1997.

O. Cordon, F. Herrera, F. Hoffmann, and L. Magdalena, *Genetic fuzzy systems evolutionary tuning and learning of fuzzy knowledge bases.* Advances in Fuzzy Systems-Applications and Theory, vol.19, NJ: World Scientific Publishing, 2001.

A. G. Barto and R. S. Sutton, "Landmark learning: An illustration of associative search, " *Biol. Cybern.* Vol. 42, pp. 1-8, 1981.

A. G. Barto, R. S. Sutton, and C. W. Anderson, "Neuron like adaptive elements that can solve difficult learning control problem," *IEEE Trans. Syst., Man, Cybern.*, vol. SMC-13, no 5, pp. 834-847, 1983.

C. T. Lin and C. S. G. Lee, "Reinforcement structure/parameter learning for neural-network-based fuzzy logic control systems," *IEEE Trans. Fuzzy Syst.*, vol. 2, pp. 46–63, Feb. 1994.

C. F. Juang, J. Y. Lin and C. T. Lin, "Genetic reinforcement learning through symbiotic evolution for fuzzy controller design," *IEEE Trans. Syst., Man, Cybern., Part B*, vol. 30, no. 2, pp. 290-302, Apr. 2000.

A. Homaifar and E. McCormick, "Simultaneous design of membership functions and rule sets for fuzzy controllers using genetic algorithms," *IEEE Trans. Fuzzy Syst.*, vol. 3, no. 9, pp. 129-139, May 1995.

D. E. Moriarty and R. Miikkulainen, "Efficient reinforcement learning through symbiotic evolution," *Mach. Learn.*, vol. 22, pp. 11–32, 1996.

R. H. Cannon, Jr., *Dynamics of Physical Systems.* New York: Mc- Graw-Hill, 1967.

K. C. Cheok and N. K. Loh, "A ball-balancing demonstration of optimal and disturbance-accommodating control," *IEEE Contr. Syst. Mag.*, pp. 54–57, 1987.

D. Whitley, S. Dominic, R. Das, and C. W. Anderson, "Genetic reinforcement learning for neuro control problems," *Mach. Learn.*, vol. 13, pp. 259–284, 1993.

J. Hauser, S. Sastry, and P. Kokotovic, "Nonolinear control via approximate input-output linearization: the ball and beam example," *IEEE Trans. Automatic Control*, vol. 37, pp. 392-398, Mar. 1992.

C. F. Juang, "A TSK-type recurrent fuzzy network for dynamic systems processing by neural network and genetic algorithms," *IEEE Trans. on Fuzzy Systems*, Vol. 10, No. 2, pp. 155-170, April, 2002.

C. J. Lin, "A GA-based neural fuzzy system for temperature control," *Fuzzy Sets and Systems*, Vol. 143, pp. 311-333, 2004.

M. J. Er and C. Deng, "Online tuning of fuzzy inference systems using dynamic Q-Learning," *IEEE Trans. Syst., Man, Cybern., Part B*, vol. 34, no. 3, pp. 1478-1489, June 2004.

M. Kaya, R. Alhajj, "Fuzzy OLAP association rules mining-based modular reinforcement learning approach for multiagent systems," *IEEE Trans. on Syst., Man, Cybern., Part B*, vol. 35, no. 2, pp. 326-338, Apr. 2005.

C. J. Lin, "A GA-based neural network with supervised and reinforcement learning," *Journal of The Chinese Institute of Electrical Engineering*, Vol. 9, No. 1, pp.11-24.

4

Superposition-Inspired Reinforcement Learning and Quantum Reinforcement Learning

Chun-Lin Chen and Dao-Yi Dong
Nanjing University & Institute of Systems Science, CAS
China

1. Introduction

Reinforcement Learning (RL) remains an active research area for a long time (Kaelbling et al., 1996; Sutton & Barto, 1998) and is still one of the most rapidly developing machine learning methods in recent years (Barto & Mahadevan, 2003). Related algorithms and techniques have been used in different applications such as motion control, operations research, robotics and sequential decision process (He & Jagannathan, 2005; Kondo & Ito, 2004; Morimoto & Doya, 2001; Chen et al., 2006b). However how to speed up learning has always been one of the key problems for the theoretical research and applications of RL methods (Sutton & Barto, 1998).

Recently there comes up a new approach for solving this problem owning to the rapid development of quantum information and quantum computation (Preskill, 1998; Nielsen & Chuang, 2000). Some results have shown that quantum computation can efficiently speed up the solutions of some classical problems, and even can solve some difficult problems that classical algorithms can not solve. Two important quantum algorithms, Shor's factoring algorithm (Shor, 1994; Ekert & Jozsa, 1996) and Grover's searching algorithm (Grover, 1996; Grover, 1997), have been proposed in 1994 and 1996 respectively. Shor's factoring algorithm can give an exponential speedup for factoring large integers into prime numbers and its experimental demonstration has been realized using nuclear magnetic resonance (Vandersypen et al., 2001). Grover's searching algorithm can achieve a square speedup over classical algorithms in unsorted database searching and its experimental implementations have also been demonstrated using nuclear magnetic resonance (Chuang et al., 1998; Jones, 1998a; Jones et al., 1998b) and quantum optics (Kwiat et al., 2000; Scully & Zubairy, 2001).

Taking advantage of quantum computation, the algorithm integration inspired by quantum characteristics will not only improve the performance of existing algorithms on traditional computers, but also promote the development of related research areas such as quantum computer and machine learning. According to our recent research results (Dong et al., 2005a; Dong et al., 2006a; Dong et al., 2006b; Chen et al., 2006a; Chen et al., 2006c; Chen & Dong, 2007; Dong et al., 2007a; Dong et al., 2007b), in this chapter the RL methods based on quantum theory are introduced following the developing roadmap from Superposition-Inspired Reinforcement Learning (SIRL) to Quantum Reinforcement Learning (QRL).

As for SIRL methods we concern mainly about the exploration policy. Inspired by the superposition principle of quantum state, in a RL system, a probabilistic exploration policy is proposed to mimic the state collapse phenomenon according to quantum measurement postulate, which leads to a good balance between exploration and exploitation. In this way, the simulated experiments show that SIRL may accelerate the learning process and allow avoiding the locally optimal policies.

When SIRL is extended to quantum mechanical systems, QRL theory is proposed naturally (Dong et al., 2005a, Dong et al., 2007b). In a QRL system, the state value can be represented with quantum state and be obtained by randomly observing the quantum state, which will lead to state collapse according to quantum measurement postulate. The occurrence probability of eigenvalue is determined by probability amplitude, which is updated according to rewards. So this approach represents the whole state-action space with the superposition of quantum state, which leads to real parallel computing and a good tradeoff between exploration and exploitation using probability as well.

Besides the introduction of SIRL and QRL methods, in this chapter, the relationship between different theories and algorithms are briefly analyzed, and their applications are also introduced respectively. The organization of this chapter is as follows. Section 2 gives a brief introduction to the fundamentals of quantum computation, which include the superposition principle, parallel computation and quantum gates. In Section 3, the SIRL method is presented in a probabilistic version through mimicking the quantum behaviors. Section 4 gives the introduction of QRL method based on quantum superposition and quantum parallelism. Related issues and future work are discussed as a conclusion in Section 5.

2. Fundamentals of quantum computation

2.1 State superposition and quantum parallel computation

In quantum computation, information unit (also called as qubit) is represented with quantum state and a qubit is an arbitrary superposition state of two-state quantum system (Dirac's representation) (Preskill, 1998):

$$|\psi\rangle = \alpha|0\rangle + \beta|1\rangle \tag{1}$$

where α and β are complex coefficients and satisfy $|\alpha|^2 + |\beta|^2 = 1$. $|0\rangle$ and $|1\rangle$ are two orthogonal states (also called basis vectors of quantum state $|\psi\rangle$), and they correspond to logic states 0 and 1. $|\alpha|^2$ represents the occurrence probability of $|0\rangle$ when the qubit is measured, and $|\beta|^2$ is the probability of obtaining result $|1\rangle$. The physical carrier of a qubit is any two-state quantum system such as two-level atom, spin-1/2 particle and polarized photon. The value of classical bit is either Boolean value 0 or value 1, but a qubit can be prepared in the coherent superposition state of 0 and 1, i.e. a qubit can simultaneously store 0 and 1, which is the main difference between classical computation and quantum computation.

According to quantum computation theory, the quantum computing process can be looked upon as a unitary transformation U from input qubits to output qubits. If one applies a transformation U to a superposition state, the transformation will act on all basis vectors of this superposition state and the output will be a new superposition state by superposing the results of all basis vectors. So when one processes function $f(x)$ by the method, the transformation U can simultaneously work out many different results for a certain input x. This is analogous with parallel process of classical computer and is called quantum parallelism. The powerful ability of quantum algorithm is just derived from the parallelism of quantum computation.

Suppose the input qubit $|z\rangle$ lies in the superposition state:

$$|z\rangle = \frac{1}{\sqrt{2}}(|0\rangle + |1\rangle) \tag{2}$$

The transformation U_z describing computing process is defined as the following:

$$U_z : |z, y\rangle \rightarrow |z, y \oplus f(z)\rangle \tag{3}$$

where $|z, y\rangle$ represents the input joint state and $|z, y \oplus f(z)\rangle$ is the output joint state. Let $y = 0$ and we can easily obtain (Nielsen & Chuang, 2000):

$$U_z |z\rangle = \frac{1}{\sqrt{2}}(|0, f(0)\rangle + |1, f(1)\rangle) \tag{4}$$

The result contains information about both $f(0)$ and $f(1)$, and we seem to evaluate $f(z)$ for two values of z simultaneously.

Now consider an n-qubit cluster and it lies in the following superposition state:

$$|\psi\rangle = \sum_{x=00\cdots0}^{\overbrace{11\cdots1}^{n}} C_x |x\rangle \qquad (\text{where } \sum_{x=00\cdots0}^{\overbrace{11\cdots1}^{n}} |C_x|^2 = 1) \tag{5}$$

where C_x is complex coefficients and $|C_x|^2$ represents occurrence probability of $|x\rangle$ when state $|\psi\rangle$ is measured. $|x\rangle$ can take on 2^n values, so the superposition state can be looked upon as the superposition state of all integers from 0 to $2^n - 1$. Since U is a unitary transformation, computing function $f(x)$ can give (Preskill, 1998):

$$U \sum_{x=00\cdots0}^{\overbrace{11\cdots1}^{n}} C_x |x,0\rangle = \sum_{x=00\cdots0}^{\overbrace{11\cdots1}^{n}} C_x U |x,0\rangle = \sum_{x=00\cdots0}^{\overbrace{11\cdots1}^{n}} C_x |x, f(x)\rangle \tag{6}$$

Based on the above analysis, it is easy to find that an n-qubit cluster can simultaneously process 2^n states. However, this is different from the classical parallel computation, where multiple circuits built to compute $f(x)$ are executed simultaneously, since quantum parallel computation doesn't necessarily make a tradeoff between computation time and needed physical space. In fact, quantum parallelism employs a single circuit to evaluate the function for multiple values of x simultaneously by exploiting the quantum state superposition principle and provides an exponential-scale computation space in the n-qubit linear physical space. Therefore quantum computation can effectively increase the computing speed of some important classical functions. So it is possible to obtain significant result through fusing quantum computation into reinforcement learning theory.

2.2 Quantum gates

Analogous to classical computer, quantum computer accomplishes some quantum computation tasks through quantum gates. A quantum gate or quantum logic gate is a basic quantum circuit operating on a small number of qubits. They can be represented by unitary matrices. Here we will introduce several simple quantum gates including quantum NOT gate, Hadamard gate, phase gate and quantum CNOT gate. The detailed description of quantum gates can refer to (Nielsen & Chuang, 2000).

A quantum NOT gate maps $|0\rangle \to |1\rangle$ and $|1\rangle \to |0\rangle$ respectively and that can be described by the following matrix:

$$U_{NOT} = \begin{bmatrix} 0 & 1 \\ 1 & 0 \end{bmatrix} \tag{7}$$

When a quantum NOT gate is applied on a single qubit with state $|\psi\rangle = \alpha |0\rangle + \beta |1\rangle$, then the output will become $|\psi\rangle = \alpha |1\rangle + \beta |0\rangle$. The symbol for the NOT gate is drawn in Fig.1 (a).

The Hadamard gate is one of the most useful quantum gates and can be represented as:

$$H = \frac{1}{\sqrt{2}} \begin{bmatrix} 1 & 1 \\ 1 & -1 \end{bmatrix} \tag{8}$$

Through the Hadamard gate, a qubit in the state $|0\rangle$ is transformed into a superposition state in the two states, i.e.

$$H|0\rangle \equiv \frac{1}{\sqrt{2}} \begin{bmatrix} 1 & 1 \\ 1 & -1 \end{bmatrix} \begin{pmatrix} 1 \\ 0 \end{pmatrix} = \frac{1}{\sqrt{2}} \begin{pmatrix} 1 \\ 1 \end{pmatrix} = \frac{1}{\sqrt{2}} |0\rangle + \frac{1}{\sqrt{2}} |1\rangle \tag{9}$$

Another important gate is phase gate which can be expressed as

$$U_p = \begin{bmatrix} 1 & 0 \\ 0 & i \end{bmatrix} \tag{10}$$

U_p generates a relative phase π between the two basis states of the input state, i.e.

$$U_p |\psi\rangle = \alpha |0\rangle + i\beta |1\rangle \tag{11}$$

The CNOT gate acts on two qubits simultaneously and can be represented by the following matrix:

$$U_{CNOT} = \begin{bmatrix} 1 & 0 & 0 & 0 \\ 0 & 1 & 0 & 0 \\ 0 & 0 & 0 & 1 \\ 0 & 0 & 1 & 0 \end{bmatrix} \tag{12}$$

The symbol for the CNOT gate is shown as in Fig.1 (b). If the first control qubit is equal to $|1\rangle$, then CNOT gate flips the target (second) qubit. Otherwise the target remains unaffected. This can be described as follows:

$$\begin{cases} U_{CNOT}|00\rangle = |00\rangle \\ U_{CNOT}|01\rangle = |01\rangle \\ U_{CNOT}|10\rangle = |11\rangle \\ U_{CNOT}|11\rangle = |10\rangle \end{cases} \tag{13}$$

Just like AND and NOT form a universal set for classical boolen circuits, the CNOT gate combined with one qubit rotation gate can implement any kind of quantum calculation.

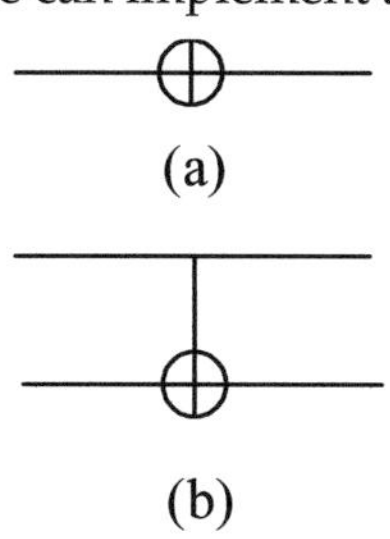

Fig. 1. Symbols for NOT and CNOT gate

3. Superposition-inspired reinforcement learning

Similar the standard RL, SIRL is also a RL method that is designed for the traditional computer, instead of a quantum algorithm. However, it borrows the ideas from quantum characteristics and provides an alternative exploration strategy, i.e., action selection method. In this section, the SIRL will be presented after a brief introduction of the standard RL theory and the existing exploration strategies.

3.1 Reinforcement learning and exploration strategy

Standard framework of RL is based on discrete-time, finite Markov decision processes (MDPs) (Sutton & Barto, 1998). RL algorithms assume that state S and action $A_{(s_n)}$ can be divided into discrete values. At a certain step, the agent observes the state of the environment (inside and outside of the agent) s_t, and then choose an action a_t. After executing the action, the agent receives a reward r_{t+1}, which reflects how good that action is (in a short-term sense).

The goal of reinforcement learning is to learn a mapping from states to actions, that is to say, the agent is to learn a policy $\pi : S \times \cup_{i\in S} A_{(i)} \to [0,1]$, so that expected sum of discounted reward of each state will be maximized:

$$\begin{aligned} V_{(s)}^{\pi} &= E\{r_{t+1} + \gamma r_{t+2} + \gamma^2 r_{t+3} + \cdots \mid s_t = s, \pi\} \\ &= E[r_{t+1} + \gamma V_{(s_{t+1})}^{\pi} \mid s_t = s, \pi] \\ &= \sum_{a\in A_s} \pi(s,a)[r_s^a + \gamma \sum_{s'} p_{ss'}^a V_{(s')}^{\pi}] \end{aligned} \tag{14}$$

where $\gamma \in [0,1)$ is discounted factor, $\pi(s,a)$ is the probability of selecting action a according to state s under policy π, $p_{ss'}^a = \Pr\{s_{t+1} = s' \mid s_t = s, a_t = a\}$ is probability for state transition and $r_s^a = E\{r_{t+1} \mid s_t = s, a_t = a\}$ is expected one-step reward. Then we have the optimal state-value function

$$V_{(s)}^{*} = \max_{a\in A_s}[r_s^a + \gamma \sum_{s'} p_{ss'}^a V_{(s')}^{*}] \tag{15}$$

$$\pi^* = \arg\max_{\pi} V_{(s)}^{\pi}, \quad \forall s \in S \tag{16}$$

In dynamic programming, (15) is also called Bellman equation of V^*.

As for state-action pairs, there are similar value functions and Bellman equations, where $Q^{\pi}(s,a)$ stands for the value of taking action a in state s under policy π:

$$\begin{aligned} Q_{(s,a)}^{\pi} &= E\{r_{t+1} + \gamma r_{t+2} + \gamma^2 r_{t+3} + \ldots \mid s_t = s, a_t = a, \pi\} \\ &= r_s^a + \gamma \sum_{s'} p_{ss'}^a V^{\pi}(s') \\ &= r_s^a + \gamma \sum_{s'} p_{ss'}^a \sum_{a'} \pi(s',a') Q_{(s',a')}^{\pi} \end{aligned} \tag{17}$$

$$Q_{(s,a)}^{*} = \max_{\pi} Q_{(s,a)} = r_s^a + \gamma \sum_{s'} p_{ss'}^a \max_{a'} Q_{(s',a')}^{*} \tag{18}$$

Let α be the learning rate, the one-step update rule of Q-learning (a widely used reinforcement learning algorithm) (Watkins & Dayan, 1992) is:

$$Q(s_t,a_t) \leftarrow (1-\alpha)Q(s_t,a_t) + \alpha(r_{t+1} + \gamma \max_{a'} Q(s_{t+1},a')) \tag{19}$$

Besides Q-learning, there are also many other RL algorithms such as temporal difference (TD), SARSA and multi-step version of these algorithms. For more detail, please refer to (Sutton & Barto, 1998).

To approach the optimal policy effectively and efficiently, the RL algorithms always need a certain exploration strategy. One widely used exploration strategy is ε-greedy ($\varepsilon \in [0,1)$), where the optimal action is selected with probability $1-\varepsilon$ and a random action is selected with probability ε. Sutton and Barto (Sutton & Barto, 1998) have compared the performance of RL for different ε, which shows that a nonzero ε is usually better than $\varepsilon = 0$ (i.e., blind greedy strategy). Moreover, the exploration probability ε can be reduced over time, which moves the agent from exploration to exploitation. The ε-greedy method is simple and effective, but it has one drawback that when it explores it chooses equally among all actions. This means that it makes no difference to choose the worst action or the next-to-best action. Another problem is that it is difficult to choose a proper parameter ε which can offer the optimal balancing between exploration and exploitation.

Another kind of action selection methods are randomized strategies, such as Boltzmann exploration (i.e., Softmax method) (Sutton & Barto, 1998) and Simulated Annealing (SA) method (Guo et al., 2004). It uses a positive parameter τ called the temperature and chooses action with the probability proportional to $\exp(Q_{(s,a)}/\tau)$. Compared with ε-greedy method, the greedy action is still given the highest selection probability, but all the others are ranked and weighted according to their value estimates. It can also move from exploration to exploitation by adjusting the "temperature" parameter τ. It is natural to sample actions according to this distribution, but it is very difficult to set and adjust a good parameter τ and may converge unnecessarily slowly unless the parameter τ is manually tuned with great care. It also has another potential shortcoming that it may works badly when the values of the actions are close and the best action can not be separated from the others. A third problem is that when the parameter τ is reduced over time to acquire more exploitation, there is no effective mechanism to guarantee re-exploration when necessary.

Therefore, the existing exploration strategies usually suffer from the difficulties to hold the good balancing between exploration and exploitation and to provide an easy method of parameter setting. Hence new ideas are necessary to explore more effective exploration strategies to achieve better performance. Inspired by the main characteristics of quantum computation, we present the SIRL algorithm with a probabilistic exploration policy.

3.2 Superposition-inspired RL

The exploration strategy for SIRL is inspired by the state superposition principle of a quantum system and collapse postulate, where a combined action form is adopted to provide a probabilistic mechanism for each state in the SIRL system. At state s, the action to be selected is represented as:

$$a_s = f(s) = \frac{c_1}{a_1} + \frac{c_2}{a_2} + \ldots + \frac{c_m}{a_m} = \sum_{i=1}^{m} \frac{c_i}{a_i} \tag{20}$$

Where $\sum_{i=1}^{m} c_i = 1$, $0 \le c_i \le 1$, $i = 1,2,...m$. a_s is the action to be selected at state s and the action selection set is $\{a_1, a_2, ..., a_m\}$. Equation (20) is not for numerical computation and it just means that at the state s, the agent will choose the action a_i with the occurrence probability c_i, which leads to a natural exploration strategy for SIRL.

After the execution of action a_i from state s, the corresponding probability c_i is updated according to the immediate reward r and the estimated value of the next state $V(s')$.

$$c_i \leftarrow c_i + k(r + V(s')) \tag{21}$$

where k is the updating step and the probability distribution $(c_1, c_2, ..., c_m)$ is normalized after each updating process. The procedural algorithm of standard SIRL is shown as in Fig. 2.

Procedural SIRL:

Initialize $V(s)$ arbitrarily, π to the policy to be evaluated

$$\pi : a_s = f(s) = \frac{c_1}{a_1} + \frac{c_2}{a_2} + ... + \frac{c_m}{a_m} = \sum_{i=1}^{m} \frac{c_i}{a_i}$$

Repeat (for each episode):
  Initialize s
  Repeat (for each step of episode):
    $a \leftarrow$ action given by π for s
    Take action a: observe reward, r, and next state, s'
      $V(s) \leftarrow V(s) + \alpha[r + \gamma V(s') - V(s)]$
      $c_i \leftarrow c_i + k(r + V(s'))$
      $s \leftarrow s'$
  until s is terminal
until the learning process ends

Fig. 2. A standard SIRL algorithm

In the SIRL algorithm, the exploration policy is accomplished through a probability distribution over the action set. When the agent is going to choose an action at a certain state, the action a_i will be selected with probability c_i, which is also updated along with the value funcion updating. Comparing the SIRL algorithm with basic RL algorithms, the main difference is that with the probabilistic exploration policy, the SIRL algorithm makes better tradeoff between exporation and exploitation without bothering to tune it by the designers.

3.3 Simulated experiments

The performance of the SIRL algorithm is tested with two examples, which are a puzzle problem and a mobile robot navigation problem.

1. The puzzle problem

First, let's consider a puzzle problem as shown in Fig. 3, which is in a $13\times13(0\sim12)$ gridworld environment. From any state the agent can perform one of four primary actions: up, down, left and right, and actions that would lead into a blocked cell are not executed. The task is to find an optimal policy which will let the agent move from *S*(11,1) to *G*(1,11) with minimized cost (number of moving steps).

The experiment setting is as follows. Once the agent finds the goal state it receives a reward of 100 and then ends this episode. All steps are punished by a reward of -1. The discount factor γ is set to 0.99 for all the algorithms that we have carried out in this example. In this experiment, we compare the proposed method with TD algorithm. For the action selection policy of TD algorithm, we use ε-greedy policy (ε = 0.01). As for SIRL method, the action selecting policy uses the values of c_i to denote the probability of an action, which is defined as $a_s = f(s) = \frac{c_1}{a_1} + \frac{c_2}{a_2} + \ldots + \frac{c_m}{a_m} = \sum_{i=1}^{m} \frac{c_i}{a_i}$. For the four cell-to-cell actions c_i is initialized uniformly.

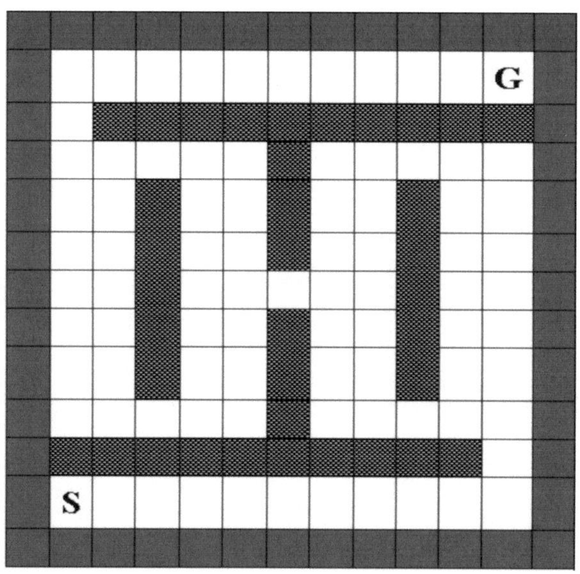

Fig. 3. A puzzle problem. The task is to move from start (S) to goal (G) with minimum number of steps

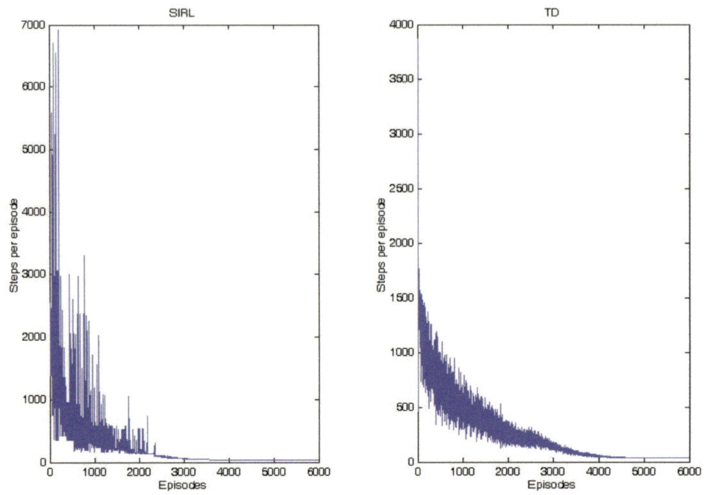

Fig. 4. Performance of SIRL (the left figure) compared with TD algorithm (the right figure)

The experimental results of the SIRL method compared with TD method are plotted in Fig. 4. It is obvious that at the beginning phase SIRL with this superposition-inspired exploration strategy learns extraordinarily fast, and then steadily converges to the optimal policy that costs 40 steps to the goal *G*. The results show that the SIRL method makes a good tradeoff between exploration and exploitation.

2. Mobile robot navigation

A simulation environment has also been set up with a larger grid-map of 400×600. And the configuration of main parameters is as follows: learning rate $\alpha = 0.5$, discount factor $\gamma = 0.9$. Fig. 5. shows the result in complex indoor environment, which verifies the effectiveness of robot learning using SIRL for navigation in large unknown environments.

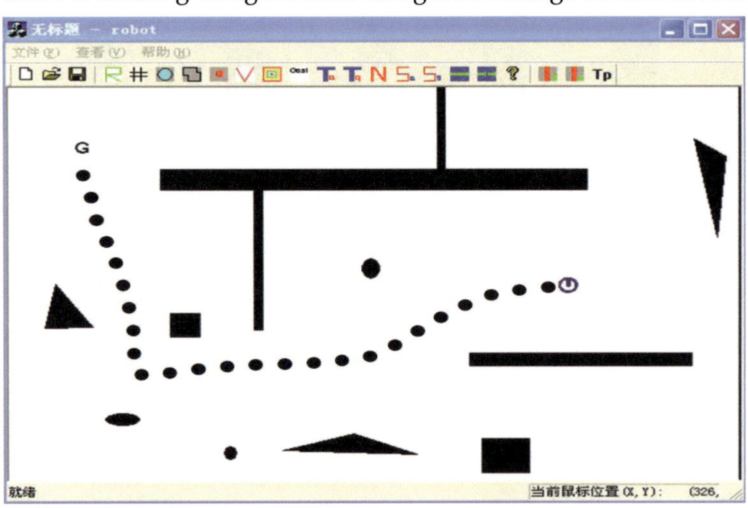

Fig. 5. Simulation result of robot navigation in indoor environment

4. Quantum reinforcement learning

When the SIRL is applied to a real quantum system, for example, to run the algorithm on a quantum computer, the representation and the computation mode will be dramatically different, which will lead to quantum reinforcement learning (QRL). Then we can take the most advantages of this quantum algorithm, such as the speeding up due to quantum parallel computation.

4.1 Representation

One of the most fundamental principles of quantum mechanics is the state superposition principle. As we represent a QRL system with quantum concepts, similarly, we have the following definitions and propositions for QRL.

Definition 1: (Eigenvalue of states or actions) States S or actions a in a RL system are denoted as corresponding orthogonal quantum states $|\mathrm{s}_\mathrm{n}\rangle$ (or $|\mathrm{a}_\mathrm{n}\rangle$) and are called the eigenvalue of states or actions in QRL.

Then we get the set of eigenvalues of states: $\mathrm{S} = \{|\mathrm{s}_\mathrm{n}\rangle\}$ and that of actions for state i: $\mathrm{A}_{(\mathrm{i})} = \{|\mathrm{a}_\mathrm{n}\rangle\}$.

Corollary 1: Every possible state $|\mathrm{s}\rangle$ or action $|\mathrm{a}\rangle$ can be expanded in terms of an orthogonal complete set of functions, respectively. We have

$$|s\rangle = \sum_n \beta_n |s_n\rangle \tag{22}$$

$$|a\rangle = \sum_n \beta_n |a_n\rangle \tag{23}$$

where β_n is probability amplitude, which can be a complex number, $|s_n\rangle$ and $|a_n\rangle$ are eigenvalues of states and actions, respectively. And the β_n in equation (22) is not necessarily the same as the ones in equation (23), which just mean this corollary holds for both of $|s\rangle$ and $|a\rangle$. $|\beta_n|^2$ means the probability of corresponding eigenvalues and satisfies

$$\sum_n |\beta_n|^2 = 1 \tag{24}$$

Proof: (sketch)

(1) State space $\{|s\rangle\}$ in QRL system is a N-dimension Hilbert space,

(2) States $\{|s_n\rangle\}$ in traditional RL system are the eigenvalue of states $|s\rangle$ in QRL system, (Definition 1)

Then $\{|s_n\rangle\}$ are N linear independent vectors for this N-dimension Hilbert space, according to the definition of Hilbert space, any possible state $|s\rangle$ can be expanded in terms of the complete set of $|s_n\rangle$. And it is the same for action space $\{|a\rangle\}$.

So the states and actions in QRL are different from those in traditional RL.

1. The sum of several states (or actions) does not have a definite meaning in traditional RL, but the sum of states (or actions) in QRL is still a possible state (or action) of the same quantum system, and it will simultaneously take on the superposition state of some eigenvalues.
2. The measurement value of $|s\rangle$ relates to its probability density. When $|s\rangle$ takes on an eigenstate $|s_i\rangle$, its value is exclusive. Otherwise, its value has the probability of $|\beta_i|^2$ to be one of the eigenstate $|s_i\rangle$.

Like what has been described in Section 2, quantum computation is built upon the concept of qubit. Now we consider the systems of multiple qubits and propose a formal representation of them for QRL system.

Let N_s and N_a be the numbers of states and actions respectively, then choose numbers m and n, which are characterized by the following inequalities:

$$N_s \leq 2^m \leq 2N_s,\ N_a \leq 2^n \leq 2N_a \tag{25}$$

And use m and n qubits to represent eigenstate set $S=\{s\}$ and eigenaction set $A=\{a\}$ respectively:

$$s: \begin{bmatrix} a_1 \big| a_2 \big| \cdots \big| a_m \\ b_1 \big| b_2 \big| \cdots \big| b_m \end{bmatrix}, \text{ where } |a_i|^2+|b_i|^2=1,\ i=1,2,...m$$

$$a: \begin{bmatrix} \alpha_1 \big| \alpha_2 \big| \cdots \big| \alpha_n \\ \beta_1 \big| \beta_2 \big| \cdots \big| \beta_n \end{bmatrix}, \text{ where } |\alpha_i|^2+|\beta_i|^2=1,\ i=1,2,...n$$

Thus the states and actions of a QRL system may lie in superposition states:

$$|s^{(m)}\rangle = \sum_{s=00\cdots0}^{\overbrace{11...1}^{m}} C_s |s\rangle \tag{26}$$

$$|a^{(n)}\rangle = \sum_{a=00\cdots0}^{\overbrace{11...1}^{n}} C_a |a\rangle \tag{27}$$

where C_s and C_a can be complex numbers and satisfy

$$\sum_{s=00\cdots0}^{\overbrace{11...1}^{m}} |C_s|^2 = 1 \tag{28}$$

$$\sum_{a=00\cdots0}^{\overbrace{11...1}^{n}} |C_a|^2 = 1 \tag{29}$$

4.2 Action selection policy

In QRL, the agent is also to learn a policy $\pi : S \times \cup_{i\in S} A_{(i)} \rightarrow [0,1]$, which will maximize the expected sum of discounted reward of each state. That is to say, the mapping from states to actions is $f(s) = \pi : S \rightarrow A$, and we have

$$f(s) = |a_s^{(n)}\rangle = \sum_{a=00\cdots0}^{\overbrace{11...1}^{n}} C_a |a\rangle \tag{30}$$

where C_a is probability amplitude of action $|a\rangle$ and satisfies (29).

Definition 2: (Collapse) When a quantum state $|\psi\rangle = \sum_n \beta_n |\psi_n\rangle$ is measured, it will be changed and collapse randomly into one $|\psi_n\rangle$ of its eigenstates with corresponding probability $|\langle\psi_n|\psi\rangle|^2$:

$$|\langle\psi_n|\psi\rangle|^2 = |(|\psi_n\rangle)^* |\psi\rangle|^2 = |\beta_n|^2 \tag{31}$$

Then when an action $|a_s^{(n)}\rangle$ is measured, we will get $|a\rangle$ with the occurrence probability of $|C_a|^2$. In QRL algorithm, we will amplify the probability of "good" action according to corresponding rewards. It is obvious that the *collapse* action selection method is not a real action selection method theoretically. It is just a fundamental phenomenon when a quantum state is measured, which results in a good balancing between exploration and exploitation and a natural "action selection" without setting parameters.

4.3 Value function updating and reinforcement strategy

In Corollary 1 we pointed out that every possible state of QRL $|s\rangle$ can be expanded in terms of an orthogonal complete set of eigenstate $|s_n\rangle$: $|s\rangle = \sum_n \beta_n |s_n\rangle$. If we use an *m*-qubit register, it will be $|s^{(m)}\rangle = \sum_{s=00\cdots0}^{\overbrace{11...1}^{m}} C_s |s\rangle$.

According to quantum parallel computation theory, a certain unitary transformation U from input qubit to output qubit can be implemented. Suppose we have such a "quantum black box" which can simultaneously process these 2^m states with the value updating rule

$$V(s) \leftarrow V(s) + \alpha(r + V(s') - V(s)) \tag{32}$$

where α is learning rate, and r is the immediate reward. It is like parallel value updating of traditional RL over all states, however, it provides an exponential-scale computation space in the *m*-qubit linear physical space and can speed up the solutions of related functions.

The reinforcement strategy is accomplished by changing the probability amplitudes of the actions according to the updated value function. As we know that action selection is executed by measuring action $|a_s^{(n)}\rangle$ related to certain state $|s^{(m)}\rangle$, which will collapse to $|a\rangle$ with the occurrence probability of $|C_a|^2$. So it is no doubt that probability amplitude updating is the key of recording the "trial-and-error" experience and learning to be more intelligent. When an action $|a\rangle$ is executed, it should be able to memorize whether it is "good" or "bad" by changing its probability amplitude C_a. For more details, please refer to (Chen et al., 2006a; Dong et al., 2006b; Dong et al., 2007b).

As action $|a_s^{(n)}\rangle$ is the superposition of *n* possible eigenactions, to find out $|a\rangle$ and to change its probability amplitudes are usually interactional for a quantum system. So we simply update the probability amplitude of $|a_s^{(n)}\rangle$ without searching $|a\rangle$, which is inspired by Grover's searching algorithm (Grover, 1996).

The updating of probability amplitude is based on Grover iteration. First, prepare the equally weighted superposition of all eigenactions

$$|a_0^{(n)}\rangle = \frac{1}{\sqrt{2^n}}\left(\sum_{a=00\cdots0}^{\overbrace{11...1}^{n}} |a\rangle\right) \tag{33}$$

This process can be done easily by applying the Hadamard transformation to each qubit of an initial state $|a = 0\rangle$. We know that $|a\rangle$ is an eigenaction and can get

$$\langle a | a_0^{(n)} \rangle = \frac{1}{\sqrt{2^n}} \tag{34}$$

Now assume the eigenaction to be reinforced is $|a_j\rangle$, and we can construct Grover iteration through combining two reflections U_{a_j} and $U_{a_0^{(n)}}$ (Preskill, 1998; Nielsen & Chuang, 2000)

$$U_{a_j} = I - 2|a_j\rangle\langle a_j| \tag{35}$$

$$U_{a_0^{(n)}} = 2|a_0^{(n)}\rangle\langle a_0^{(n)}| - I \tag{36}$$

where I is unitary matrix. U_{a_j} flips the sign of the action $|a_j\rangle$, but acts trivially on any action orthogonal to $|a_j\rangle$. This transformation has a simple geometrical interpretation. Acting on any vector in the 2^n-dimensional Hilbert space, U_{a_j} reflects the vector about the hyperplane orthogonal to $|a_j\rangle$. On the other hand, $U_{a_0^{(n)}}$ preserves $|a_0^{(n)}\rangle$, but flips the sign of any vector orthogonal to $|a_0^{(n)}\rangle$. Grover iteration is the unitary transformation

$$U_{Grov} = U_{a_0^{(n)}} U_{a_j} \tag{37}$$

By repeatedly applying the transformation U_{Grov} on $|a_0^{(n)}\rangle$, we can enhance the probability amplitude of the basis action $|a_j\rangle$ while suppressing the amplitude of all other actions. This can also be looked upon as a kind of rotation in two-dimensional space. Applying Grover iteration U_{Grov} for K times on $|a_0^{(n)}\rangle$ can be represented as

$$U_{Grov}^{K} |a_0^{(n)}\rangle = \sin((2K+1)\theta)|a_j\rangle + \cos((2K+1)\theta)|\phi\rangle \tag{38}$$

where $|\phi\rangle = \sqrt{\frac{1}{2^n - 1}} \sum_{a \neq a_j} |a\rangle$, θ satisfying $\sin\theta = 1/\sqrt{2^n}$. Through repeating Grover iteration, we can reinforce the probability amplitude of corresponding action according to the reward value.

Thus when an action $|a_0^{(n)}\rangle$ is executed, the probability amplitude of $|a_j\rangle$ is updated by carrying out $[k(r + V(s'))]$ (an integer) times of Grover iteration. k is a parameter and the probability amplitudes will be normalized with $\sum_a |C_a|^2 = 1$ after each updating.

4.4 Quantum reinforcement learning algorithm

The procedural form of a standard QRL algorithm is described as Fig. 6 (Dong et al., 2007b). QRL is inspired by the superposition principle of quantum state and quantum parallel computation. The state value can be represented with quantum state and be obtained by randomly observing the simulated quantum state, which will lead to state collapse according to quantum measurement postulate. And the occurrence probability of eigenvalue is determined by probability amplitude, which is updated according to rewards. So this approach represents the whole state-action space with the superposition of quantum state and makes a good tradeoff between exploration and exploitation using probability. The merit of QRL is twofold. First, as for simulation algorithm on traditional computer it is an effective algorithm with novel representation and computation methods. Second, the representation and computation mode are consistent with quantum parallel computation system and can speed up learning in exponential scale with quantum computer or quantum logic gates.

In this QRL algorithm we use temporal difference (TD) prediction for the state value updating, and TD algorithm has been proved to converge for absorbing Markov chain when the stepsize is nonnegative and digressive (Sutton & Barto, 1998; Watkins & Dayan, 1992). Since QRL is a stochastic iterative algorithm and Bertsekas and Tsitsiklis have verified the convergence of stochastic iterative algorithms (Bertsekas & Tsitsiklis, 1996), we give the convergence result about the QRL algorithm as Theorem 1. The proof and related discussions can be found in (Dong et al., 2006a; Chen et al., 2006c; Dong et al., 2007b):

Theorem 1: For any Markov chain, quantum reinforcement learning algorithm converges at the optimal state value function $V(s)^*$ with probability 1 under proper exploration policy when the following conditions hold (where α_k is stepsize and nonnegative):

$$\lim_{T\to\infty}\sum_{k=1}^{T}\alpha_k=\infty, \qquad \lim_{T\to\infty}\sum_{k=1}^{T}\alpha_k^2<\infty \tag{39}$$

From the procedure of QRL in Fig. 6, we can see that the learning process of QRL is carried out through parallel computation, which also provides a mechanism of parallel updating. Sutton and Barto (Sutton & Barto, 1998) have pointed out that for the basic RL algorithms the parallel updating does not affect such performances of RL as learning speed and convergence in general. But we find that the parallel updating will speed up the learning process for the RL algorithms with a hierarchical setting (Sutton et al., 1999; Barto & Mahadevan, 2003; Chen et al., 2005), because the parallel updating rules give more chance to the updating of the upper level learning process and this experience for the agent can work as the "sub-goals" intrinsically that will speed up the lower learning process.

Procedure QRL:

Initialize $|s^{(m)}\rangle = \sum_{s=00\cdots0}^{11\cdots1} C_s |s\rangle$, $f(s) = |a_s^{(n)}\rangle = \sum_{a=00\cdots0}^{11\cdots1} C_a |a\rangle$ and $V(s)$ arbitrarily

Repeat (for each episode)

For all states $|s^{(m)}\rangle = \sum_{s=00\cdots0}^{11\cdots1} C_s |s\rangle$:

1. Observe $f(s) = |a_s^{(n)}\rangle$ and get $|a\rangle$;
2. Take action $|a\rangle$, observe next state $|s'\rangle$, reward r, then
   (a) Update state value: $V(s) \leftarrow V(s) + \alpha(r + \gamma V(s') - V(s))$
   (b) Update probability amplitudes:
   repeat for $[k(r + V(s'))]$ times
   $$\mathrm{U}_{Grov} |a_s^{(n)}\rangle = U_{a_0^{(n)}} U_a |a_s^{(n)}\rangle$$

Until for all states $|\Delta V(s)| \leq \varepsilon$.

Fig. 6. The algorithm of a standard QRL (Dong et al., 2007b)

4.5 Physical implementation

Now let's simply consider the physical realization of QRL and detailed discussion can be found in (Dong et al., 2006b). In QRL algorithm, the three main operations occur in preparing the equally weighted superposition state for calculating the times of Grover iteration, initializing the quantum system for representing states or actions, and carrying out a certain times of Grover iteration for updating probability amplitude according to reward value. In fact, we can initialize the quantum system by equally weighted superposition for representing states or actions. So the main operations required are preparing the equally weighted superposition state and carrying out Grover iteration. These can be implemented using the Hadamard transform and the conditional phase shift operation, both of which are relatively easy in quantum computation.

Consider a quantum system described by *n* qubits, it has 2^{n} possible states. To prepare an equally weighted superposition state, initially let each qubit lie in the state $|0\rangle$, then we can perform the transformation H on each qubit independently in sequence and thus change the state of the system. The state transition matrix representing this operation will be of dimension $2^{\mathrm{n}} \times 2^{\mathrm{n}}$ and it can be implemented by *n* shunt-wound Hadamard gates. This process can be represented into:

$$H^{\otimes n} | \overbrace{00\cdots0}^{n} \rangle = \frac{1}{\sqrt{2^n}} \sum_{a=00\cdots0}^{\overbrace{11...1}^{n}} | a \rangle \qquad (40)$$

The other operation is the conditional phase shift operation which is an important element to carry out the Grover iteration. According to quantum information theory, this transformation may be efficiently implemented using phase gates on a quantum computer. The conditional phase shift operation does not change the probability of each state since the square of the absolute value of the amplitude in each state stays the same.

4.6 Simulated experiments

The presented QRL algorithm is also tested using two examples: Prisoner's Diploma and the control of a five-qubit system.

1. Prisoner's Diploma

The first example is derived from typical Prisoners' Dilemma. In the Prisoners' Dilemma, each of the two prisoners, prisoner I and prisoner II, must independently make the action selection to agree to give evidence against the other guy or to refuse to do so. The situation is as described in Table 1 with the entries giving the length of the prison sentence (years in prison) for each prisoner, in every possible situation. In this case, each of the prisoners is assumed to minimize his sentence. As we know, this play may lead to Nash equilibrium by giving the action selection *(agree to give evidence, agree to give evidence)* with the outcome of (3, 3) years in prison.

prisoner II / **Prisoner I**	**Agree to give evidence**	**Refuse to give evidence**
Agree	(3, 3)	(0, 5)
Refuse	(5, 0)	(1, 1)

Table 1. The Prisoners' Dilemma

Now, we assume that this Prisoners game can be played repeatedly. Each of them can choose to agree or refuse to give evidence against the other guy and the probabilities of the action selection *(agree to give evidence, agree to give evidence)* are initially equal. To find a better outcome, the two prisoners try to improve their action selection using learning. By applying the QRL method proposed in this chapter, we get the results as shown in Fig. 6 and Fig. 7 (Chen et al., 2006a; Chen et al., 2006c). From the results, it is obvious that the two prisoners get smarter when they try to cooperate indeliberately and both of them select the action of *"Refuse to give evidence"* after about 40 episodes of play. Then they steadily get the outcome of (1, 1) instead of (3, 3) (Nash equilibrium).

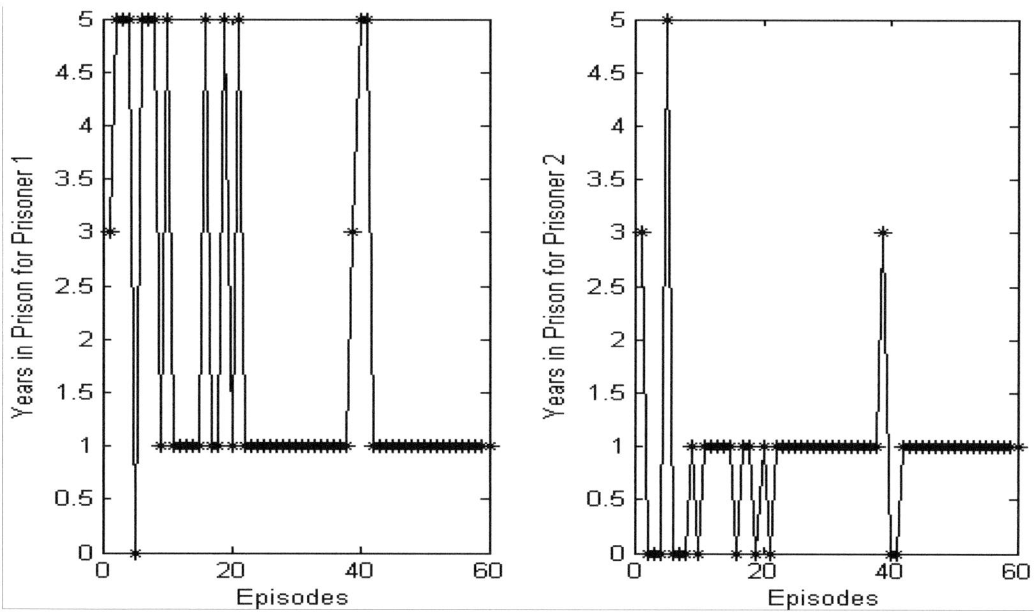

Fig. 6. The outcome (years in prison) of the Prisoners problem for each prisoner

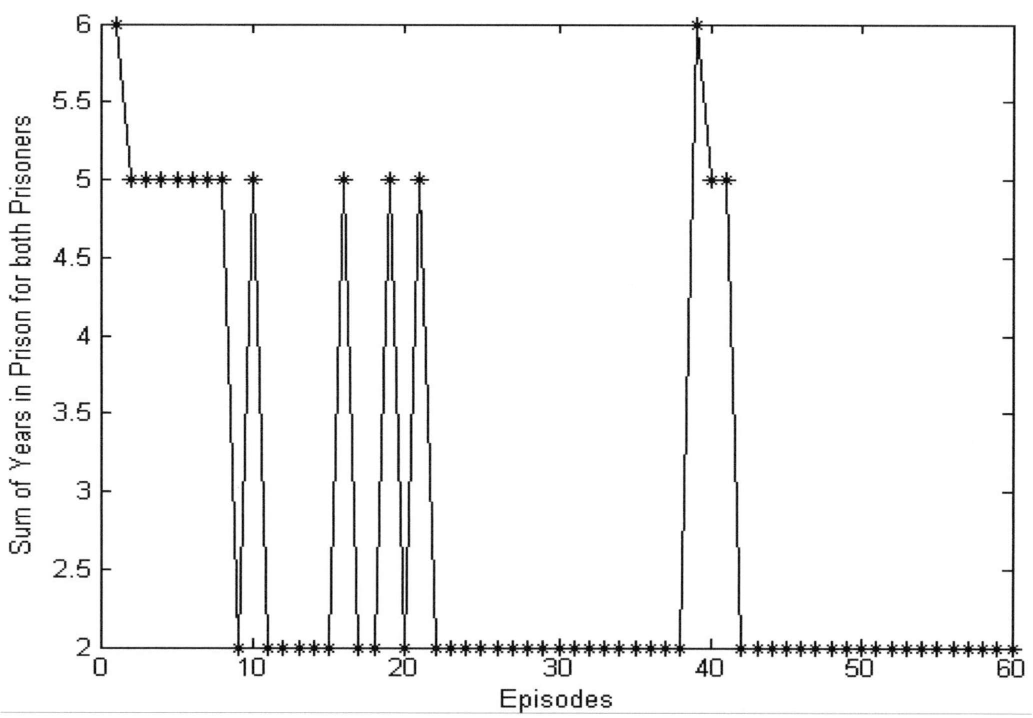

Fig. 7. The whole outcome of the Prisoners problem (Sum of years in prison for both prisoners)

2. Control of a five-qubit system

The second axample is about the control of a five-qubit system (Dong et al., 2006c). With the development of quantum information technology, quantum control theory has drawn the attention of many scientists (Chen et al., 2005). The objective of quantum control is to determine how to drive quantum systems from an initial given quantum state to a pre-determined target quantum state with some given time. According to quantum mechanics, the state $|\psi(\mathrm{t})\rangle$ of arbitary time *t* can be reached through an evolution on the initial state $|\psi(0)\rangle$. It can be expressed as

$$|\psi(\mathrm{t})\rangle = \hat{\mathrm{U}}\,|\psi(0)\rangle \tag{41}$$

where $\hat{\mathrm{U}}$ is a unitary operator and satisfies:

$$\hat{\mathrm{U}}\hat{\mathrm{U}}^{+} = \hat{\mathrm{U}}^{+}\hat{\mathrm{U}} = \mathrm{I} \tag{42}$$

where $\hat{\mathrm{U}}^{+}$ is the Hermitian conjugate operator of $\hat{\mathrm{U}}$. So the control problem of quantum state can be converted into finding appropriate unitary operator $\hat{\mathrm{U}}$.

In this example, we consider the five-qubit system, it has 32 eigenstates. In practical quantum information technology, some state transitions can easily be completed through appropriate unitary transformations but the other ones are not easy to be accomplished. Assume we know its state transitions satisfy the following equations through some experiments:

$|00001\rangle = \hat{\mathrm{U}}_{00}\,|00000\rangle$; $|00010\rangle = \hat{\mathrm{U}}_{01}\,|00001\rangle$; $|00011\rangle = \hat{\mathrm{U}}_{02}\,|00010\rangle$;

$|00100\rangle = \hat{\mathrm{U}}_{03}\,|00011\rangle$; $|00101\rangle = \hat{\mathrm{U}}_{04}\,|00100\rangle$; $|00111\rangle = \hat{\mathrm{U}}_{11}\,|00001\rangle$;

$|01000\rangle = \hat{\mathrm{U}}_{12}\,|00010\rangle$; $|01010\rangle = \hat{\mathrm{U}}_{14}\,|00100\rangle$; $|01011\rangle = \hat{\mathrm{U}}_{15}\,|00101\rangle$;

$|01000\rangle = \hat{\mathrm{U}}_{21}\,|00111\rangle$; $|01011\rangle = \hat{\mathrm{U}}_{24}\,|01010\rangle$; $|01101\rangle = \hat{\mathrm{U}}_{31}\,|00111\rangle$;

$|10000\rangle = \hat{\mathrm{U}}_{34}\,|01010\rangle$; $|10001\rangle = \hat{\mathrm{U}}_{35}\,|01011\rangle$; $|01101\rangle = \hat{\mathrm{U}}_{40}\,|01100\rangle$;

$|10001\rangle = \hat{\mathrm{U}}_{44}\,|10000\rangle$; $|10010\rangle = \hat{\mathrm{U}}_{50}\,|01100\rangle$; $|10110\rangle = \hat{\mathrm{U}}_{54}\,|10000\rangle$;

$|10111\rangle = \hat{\mathrm{U}}_{55}\,|10001\rangle$; $|10101\rangle = \hat{\mathrm{U}}_{62}\,|10100\rangle$; $|10110\rangle = \hat{\mathrm{U}}_{63}\,|10101\rangle$;

$|10111\rangle = \hat{\mathrm{U}}_{64}\,|10110\rangle$; $|11000\rangle = \hat{\mathrm{U}}_{70}\,|10010\rangle$; $|11100\rangle = \hat{\mathrm{U}}_{74}\,|10110\rangle$;

$|11101\rangle = \hat{\mathrm{U}}_{75}\,|10111\rangle$; $|11001\rangle = \hat{\mathrm{U}}_{80}\,|11001\rangle$; $|11101\rangle = \hat{\mathrm{U}}_{84}\,|11100\rangle$;

$|11111\rangle = \hat{\mathrm{U}}_{91}\,|11001\rangle$

In the above equations, $\hat{\mathrm{U}}$ is reversible operator. For example, we can easily get

$$|00000\rangle = \hat{U}_{00}^{-1}\,|00001\rangle \tag{43}$$

Assume the other transitions are impossible except the above transitions and corresponding inverse transitions. If the initial state and the target state are $|11100\rangle$ and $|11111\rangle$ respectively, the following task is to find optimal control sequence through QRL.

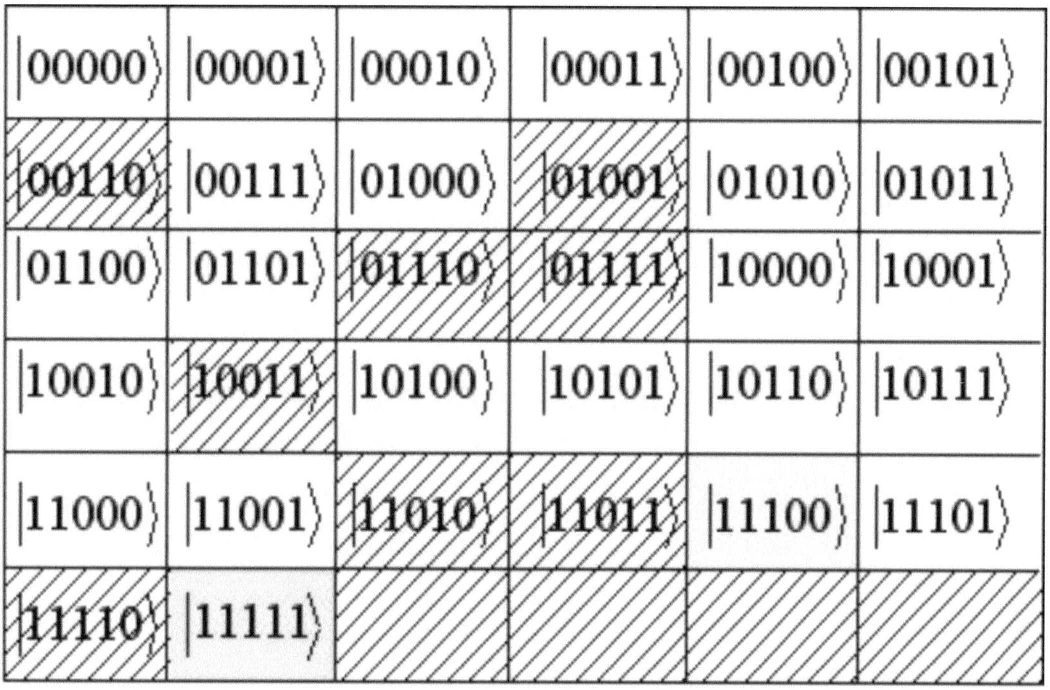

Fig. 8. The grid representation for the quantum control problem of a five-qubit system

Therefor we first fill the eigenstates of five-qubit system in a grid room and they can be described as shown in Fig. 8. Every eigenstate is arranged in a corresponding grid and the hatched grid indicates that the corresponding state can not be attained. The two states with a common side are mutually reachable through one-step control and other states can not directly reach each other through one-step control. Now the task of the quantum learning system is to find an optimal control sequence which will let the five-qubit system transform from $|11100\rangle$ to $|11111\rangle$. Using the QRL method proposed previously, we get the results as shown in Fig. 9. And more experimental results are shown in Fig. 10 to demonstrate its performance with different learning rates. From the results, it is obvious that the control system can robustly find the optimal control sequence for the five-qubit system through learning and the optimal control sequences are shown in Fig. 11. We can easily obtain two optimal control sequences from Fig. 11:

$$Sequence\_1 = \{\hat{U}_{74}^{-1}, \hat{U}_{54}^{-1}, \hat{U}_{34}^{-1}, \hat{U}_{14}^{-1}, \hat{U}_{03}^{-1}, \hat{U}_{02}^{-1}, \hat{U}_{12}, \hat{U}_{21}^{-1}, \hat{U}_{31}, \hat{U}_{40}^{-1}, \hat{U}_{50}, \hat{U}_{70}, \hat{U}_{80}, \hat{U}_{91}\} \quad (44)$$

$$Sequence\_2 = \{\hat{U}_{74}^{-1}, \hat{U}_{54}^{-1}, \hat{U}_{34}^{-1}, \hat{U}_{14}^{-1}, \hat{U}_{03}^{-1}, \hat{U}_{02}^{-1}, \hat{U}_{01}^{-1}, \hat{U}_{11}, \hat{U}_{31}, \hat{U}_{40}^{-1}, \hat{U}_{50}, \hat{U}_{70}, \hat{U}_{80}, \hat{U}_{91}\} \quad (45)$$

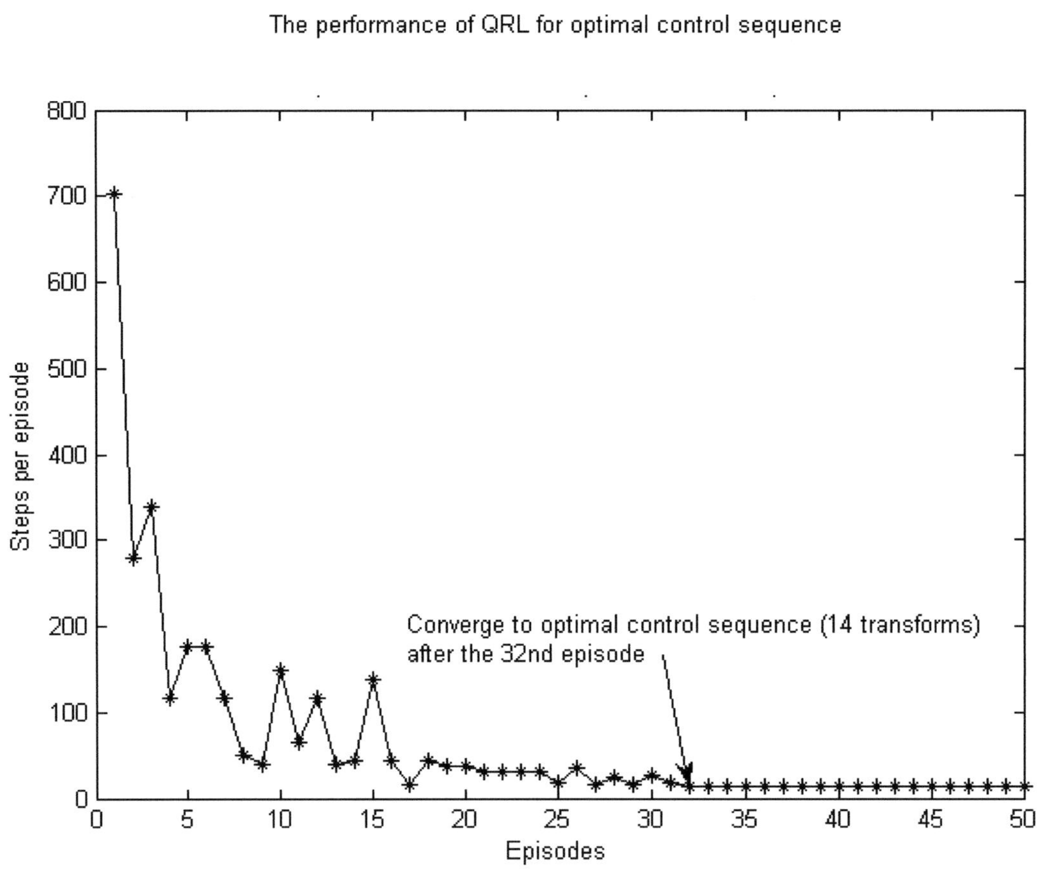

Fig. 9. The performance of QRL for optimal control sequence

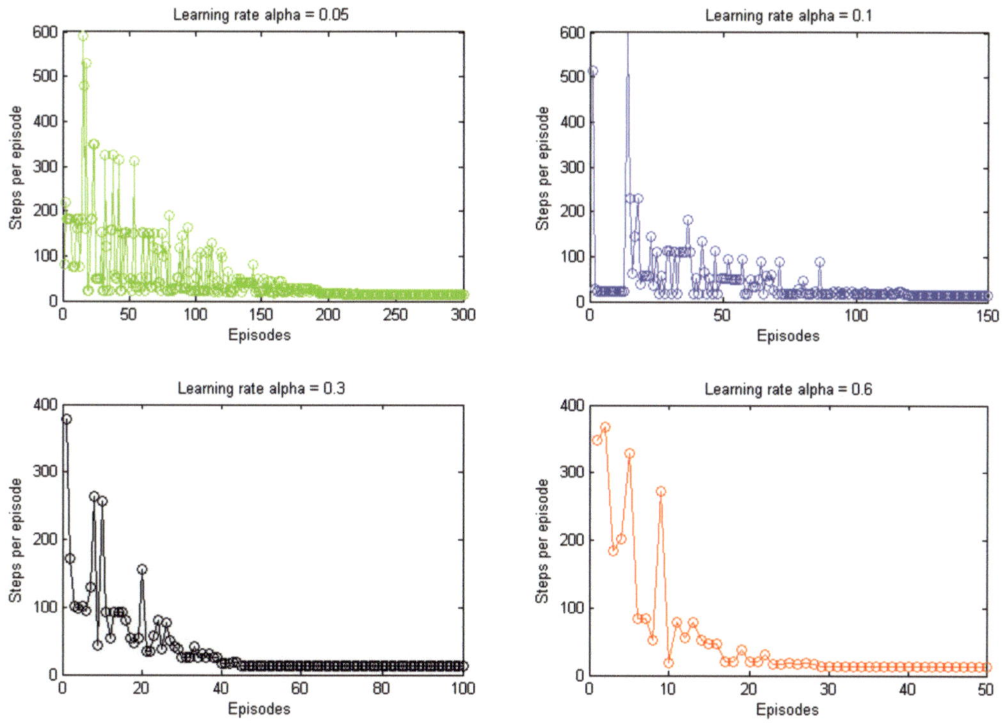

Fig. 10. The performance of QRL with different learning rates

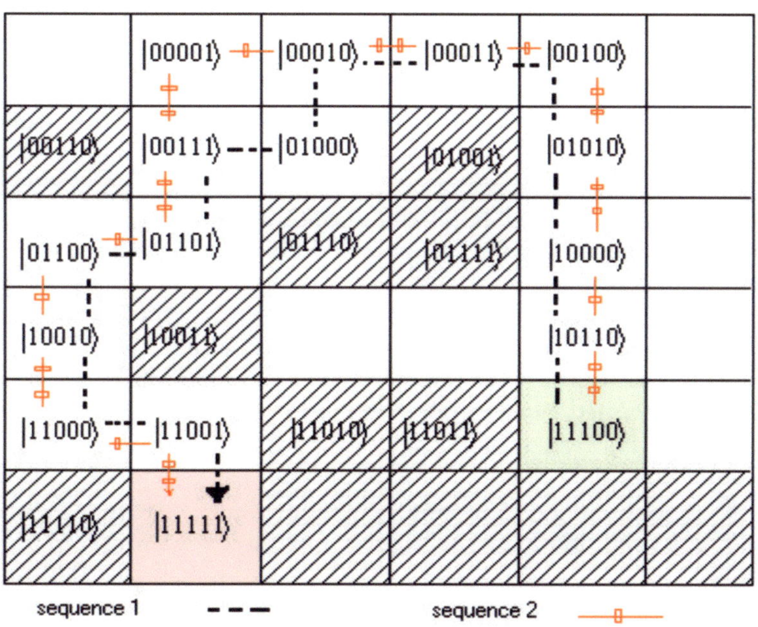

Fig. 11. The control paths for the control of a five-qubit system

5. Conclusion

According to the existing problems in RL area, such as low learning speed and tradeoff between exploration and exploitation, SIRL and QRL methods are introduced based on the theory of RL and quantum computation in this chapter, which follows the developing roadmap from the superposition-inspired methods to the RL methods in quantum systems. Just as simulated annealing algorithm comes from mimicking the physical annealing process, quantum characteristics also broaden our mind and provide alternative approaches to novel RL methods.

In this chapter, SIRL method emphasizes the exploration policy and uses a probabilistic action selection method that is inspired by the state superposition principle and collapse postulate. The experiments, which include a puzzle problem and a mobile robot navigation problem, demanstrate the effectiveness of SIRL algorithm and show that it is superior to basic TD algorithm with ε -greedy policy. As for QRL, the state/action value is represented with quantum superposition state and the action selection is carried out by observing quantum state according to quantum collapse postulate, which means a QRL system is designed for the real quantum system although it can also be simulated on a traditional computer. The results of simulated experiments verified its feasibility and effectiveness with two examples: Prisoner's Dilemma and the control of a five-qubit system. The contents presented in this chapter are mainly the basic ideas and methods related to the combination of RL theory and quantum computation. More theoretic research and applictions are to be investigated in the future.

6. References

Barto, A.G. & Mahadevan, S. (2003). Recent advances in hierarchical reinforcement learning, *Discrete Event Dynamic Systems: Theory and applications,* Vol. 13, pp. 41-77

Bertsekas, D.P. & Tsitsiklis, J.N. (1996). *Neuro-Dynamic Programming,* Athena Scientific, Belmont, MA

Chen, C.L. & Chen, Z.H. (2005). Reinforcement learning for mobile robot: from reaction to deliberation. *Journal of Systems Engineering and Electronics,* Vol. 16, No. 3, pp. 611-617

Chen, C.L.; Dong, D.Y. & Chen, Z.H. (2006a). Quantum computation for action selection using reinforcement learning. *International Journal of Quantum Information,* Vol. 4, No. 6, pp. 1071-1083

Chen, C.L.; Dong, D.Y. & Chen, Z.H. (2006b). Grey reinforcement learning for incomplete information processing. *Lecture Notes in Computer Science*, Vol. 3959, pp. 399-407

Chen, C.L.; Dong, D.Y.; Dong, Y. & Shi, Q. (2006c). A quantum reinforcement learning method for repeated game theory. *Proceedings of the 2006 International Conference on Computational Intelligence and Security,* Part I, pp. 68-72, Guangzhou, China, Nov. 2006, IEEE Press

Chen, C.L. & Dong D.Y. (2007). Quantum mobile intelligent system, In: *Quantum-Inspired Evolutionary Computation,* N. Nedjah, L. S. Coelho & L. M. Mourelle (Eds.), Springer, in press

Chen, Z.H.; Dong, D.Y. & Zhang, C.B. (2005). *Quantum Control Theory: An Introduction,* University of Science and Technology of China Press, ISBN 7-312-01863-7/TP. 363, Hefei (In Chinese)

Chuang I.L.; Gershenfeld N. & Kubinec M. (1998). Experimental implementation of fast quantum searching, *Physical Review Letters*, Vol. 80, pp. 3408-3411

Dong, D.Y.; Chen, C.L. & Chen, Z.H. (2005a). Quantum reinforcement learning. *Lecture Notes in Computer Science*, Vol. 3611, pp. 686-689

Dong, D.Y.; Chen, C.L.; Zhang, C.B. & Chen, Z.H. (2005b). An autonomous mobile robot based on quantum algorithm. *Lecture Notes in Artificial Intelligence*, Vol. 3801, pp. 394-399

Dong, D.Y.; Chen, C.L.; Zhang, C.B. & Chen, Z.H. (2006a). Quantum robot: structure, algorithms and applications. *Robotica*, Vol. 24, No.4, July 2006, pp. 513-521

Dong, D.Y.; Chen, C.L.; Chen, Z.H. & Zhang, C.B. (2006b). Quantum mechanics helps in learning for more intelligent robots. *Chinese Physics Letters*, Vol. 23, No. 7, pp. 1691-1694

Dong, D.Y.; Chen, C.L.; Chen, Z.H. & Zhang, C.B. (2006c). Control of five-qubit system based on quantum reinforcement learning. *Proceedings of the 2006 International Conference on Computational Intelligence and Security*, Part I, pp. 164-167, Guangzhou, China, Nov. 2006, IEEE Press

Dong, D.Y.; Chen, C.L. & Li, H.X. (2007a). Reinforcement strategy using quantum amplitude amplification for robot learning. *Proceedings of the 26th Chinese Control Conference*, Part VI, pp. 571-575, Zhangjiajie, China, Jul. 2007, IEEE Press

Dong, D.Y.; Chen, C.L.; Li, H.X. & Tarn, T.J. (2007b). Quantum reinforcement learning. IEEE *Transaction on System, Man, and Cybernetics B,* under review

Ekert, A. & Jozsa, R. (1996). Quantum computation and Shor's factoring algorithm, *Reviews of Modern Physics*, Vol. 68, pp. 733-753

Grover, L. K. (1996). A fast quantum mechanical algorithm for database search, *Proceedings of the 28th Annual ACM Symposium on the Theory of Computation*, pp. 212-219, New York, 1996, ACM Press

Grover, L. K. (1997). Quantum mechanics helps in searching for a needle in a haystack, *Physical Review Letters*, Vol. 79, pp. 325-327, 1997

Guo, M.Z.; Liu, Y. & Malec, J. (2004). A new Q-learning algorithm based on the metropolis criterion, *IEEE Transactions on Systems, Man and Cybernetics, Part B: Cybernetics,* Vol. 34, No. 5, pp. 2140-2143

He, P. & Jagannathan, S. (2005). Reinforcement learning-based output feedback control of nonlinear systems with input constraints, *IEEE Transactions on Systems Man and Cybernetics, Part B-Cybernetics,* Vol. 35, No. 1, pp. 150-154

Jones, J.A. (1998a). Fast searches with nuclear magnetic resonance computers, *Science,* Vol. 280, pp. 229

Jones, J.A.; Mosca, M. & Hansen R.H. (1998b). Implementation of a quantum Search algorithm on a quantum computer, *Nature,* Vol. 393, pp. 344-346

Kaelbling, L.P.; Littman, M.L. & Moore, A.W. (1996). Reinforcement learning: a survey, *Journal of Artificial Intelligence Research,* Vol. 4, pp. 237-287

Kondo, T. & Ito, K. (2004). A reinforcement learning with evolutionary state recruitment strategy for autonomous mobile robots control, *Robotics and Autonomous Systems,* Vol. 46, pp. 111-124

Kwiat, P.G.; Mitchell, J.R.; Schwindt, P.D.D. et al. (2000). Grover's search algorithm: an optical approach, *Journal of Modern Optics*, Vol. 47, pp. 257-266

Morimoto, J. & Doya, K. (2001). Acquisition of stand-up behavior by a real robot using hierarchical reinforcement learning, *Robotics and Autonomous Systems,* Vol. 36, pp. 37-51

Nielsen, M.A. & Chuang, I.L. (2000). *Quantum Computation and Quantum Information,* Cambridge University Press, Cambridge, England

Preskill, J. (1998). Physics 229: *Advanced Mathematical Methods of Physics--Quantum Information and Computation.* California Institute of Technology, 1998. Available electronically via http://www.theory.caltech.edu/people/preskill/ph229/

Scully, M.O. & Zubairy, M.S. (2001). Quantum optical implementation of Grover's algorithm, *Proceedings of the National Academy of Sciences of the United States of America,* Vol. 98, pp. 9490-9493

Shor, P. W. (1994). Algorithms for quantum computation: discrete logarithms and factoring, *Proceedings of the 35th Annual Symposium on Foundations of Computer Science,* pp. 124-134, Los Alamitos, CA, IEEE Press

Sutton, R. & Barto A.G. (1998). *Reinforcement Learning: An Introduction,* MIT Press, Cambridge, MA

Sutton, R.; Precup, D. and Singh, S. (1999). Between mdps and semi-mdps: a framework for temporal abstraction in reinforcement learning, *Artificial Intelligence,* Vol. 112, pp. 181-211

Vandersypen, L.M.K.; Steffen, M.; Breyta, G. et al. (2001). Experimental realization of Shor's quantum factoring algorithm using nuclear magnetic resonance, *Nature,* Vol. 414, pp. 883-887

Watkins, J.C.H. and Dayan, P. (1992). Q-learning, *Machine Learning,* Vol. 8, pp. 279-292

5

An Extension of Finite-state Markov Decision Process and an Application of Grammatical Inference

Takeshi Shibata[1] and Ryo Yoshinaka[2]
[1] *the University of Tokyo*
[2] *Hokkaido University*
Japan

1. Introduction

In this chapter, we introduce the notion of **simple context-free decision processes**, which are an extension of episodic finite-state Markov decision processes (MDPs). Intuitively, a simple context-free decision process can be thought of as an episodic finite-state MDP with a stack. In fact, many reinforcement learning methods can be applied to the class of simple context-free decision processes with natural modification on their equations.

On the other hand, in grammatical inference area, some non-regular subclasses of simple grammars, such as very simple grammars and **right-unique simple grammars**, have been found to be efficiently identifiable in the limit from positive data. Especially, the class of right-unique simple decision processes, which are simple context-free processes based on right-unique simple grammars, is a superset of the class of episodic finite-state MDPs.

Because episodic states histories are regarded as positive data, one might expect that those positive results in grammatical inference area could be applied to reinforcement learning directly.

However, one should note that grammars generating the same language can generate different probabilistic languages. While it is enough to find a process representing the target language in the scheme of identification in the limit, in reinforcement learning, one has to find a process representing the target probabilistic language.

Therefore, we need to modify the results in grammatical inference area for applying them to reinforcement learning. Actually, a grammar can be more general than another in the sense that it generates all the probabilistic languages generated by the other. Hence, finding a most general grammar gives a solution to this problem. This chapter however shows that both classes of simple grammars and right-unique simple grammars do not admit most general grammars.

Besides, we show that there is an intermediate class between right-unique simple grammars and simple grammars that admits an algorithm computing a most general grammar from any two grammars whose languages coincide.

We present an algorithm that learns the optimal actions under right-unique simple context-free processes, by concatenating the algorithm learning right-unique simple grammars from positive data, the one computing a most general grammar and the modified update equations of some usual reinforcement learning methods.

2. Notation and definitions

Before we give the definition of simple context-free MDPs, we write some standard notation and definitions and introduce subclasses of simple grammars and probabilistic grammars.
A **context-free grammar** (CFG) is a quadruple denoted by $<V, \Sigma, R, S>$, where V is a finite set of nonterminal symbols, Σ is a finite set of terminal symbols, $R \subset V\times(V\cup\Sigma)^*$ is a finite set of production rules, and $S \in V$ is the start symbol. Let $G=<V, \Sigma, R, S>$ be a CFG. We write $XAZ \Rightarrow_G XYZ$ if there is a rule $A\rightarrow Y$. When G is clearly identified, we write simply $\Rightarrow$ instead of $\Rightarrow_G$. $\Rightarrow^*$ denotes the reflective and transitive closure of $\Rightarrow$. G is said to be reduced if and only if, for all A in V, there are some x,y,z in Σ^* such that $S \Rightarrow^* xAz \Rightarrow^* xyz$. $L(G, X)$ denotes a language derived from X, i.e., $\{x \in \Sigma^* \mid X \Rightarrow_G^* x\}$. $L(G)=L(G,S)$ is called the language of G. Let ε denote the empty sequence. If x is a sequence, let $|x|$ denote the length of x. Let $|A|$ for a set A denote the cardinality of A, and $|G|$ denote $\sum_{A\rightarrow X\in R}|A|+|X|$.
In order to be easy to read, terminal symbols and nonterminal symbols are denoted by $a,b,c,\ldots$ and $A,B,C,\ldots$ respectively, and finite sequence of terminal symbols and nonterminal symbols are denoted by $\ldots,x,y,z$ and $\alpha,\beta,\gamma,\ldots$ respectively.
CFGs $G=<V, \Sigma, R, S>$ and $H=<V', \Sigma, R', S'>$ are equivalent modulo renaming of nonterminal symbols when there is a bijection $\varphi: V\rightarrow V'$ such that $A\rightarrow X$ is in R if and only if $\varphi(A)\rightarrow\varphi^*(X)$ is in R', and $\varphi(S)=S'$. φ^* is a homomorphism $(V\cup\Sigma)^* \rightarrow (V\cup\Sigma)^*$ defined recursively: $\varphi^*(\varepsilon)=\varepsilon$, $\varphi^*(aX)=a\varphi^*(X)$ and $\varphi^*(AX)=\varphi(A)\varphi^*(X)$.
Definition 1. Let $G=<V, \Sigma, R, S>$ be a CFG. G is called a **simple grammar** (SG) if and only if

- G is in Greibach normal form, that is, for each rule of G is written as $A \rightarrow a\alpha$.
- $A \rightarrow a\alpha \in R$ and $A \rightarrow a\beta \in R$ imply $\alpha=\beta$.

The subclasses of SGs which will appear in this chapter are defined below.
Definition 2. Let $G=<V, \Sigma, R, S>$ be an SG. G is called a **right-unique simple grammar** (RSG) if and only if

- $A \rightarrow a\alpha \in R$ and $B \rightarrow a\beta \in R$ imply $\alpha=\beta$.

Definition 3. Let $G=<V, \Sigma, R, S>$ be an SG. G is called a **very simple grammar** (VSG) if and only if

- $A \rightarrow a\alpha \in R$ and $B \rightarrow a\beta \in R$ imply $A=B$ and $\alpha=\beta$.

From definitions, a VSG is an RSG, and an RSG is an SG.
Let $G=<V, \Sigma, R, S>$ be an SG. A **probability assignment** P on G is a map from R to [0,1] such that $\sum_{r\in R(A)}P(r)=1$ for all A in V, where $R(A)=\{A\rightarrow X\in R\}$. A **probabilistic simple grammar** (PSG) is a pair of G and P, where P is probability assignment on an SG G. Let G(P) be a PSG. All of sequences of production rules that are used in the left-most derivation of $S \Rightarrow_G^* x$, where $x \in L(G)$, is called the **left Szilard language** of G. When G is an SG, every x in $L(G)$ has a unique sentence in the left Szilard language of it. Let us denote that sentence by $r(G,x,1)$, ..., $r(G,x,|x|)$. Then, the **probabilistic language** of G(P), $\Pr[\cdot \mid G(P)] : Pow(\Sigma^*) \rightarrow [0,1]$ is defined as $\Pr[x \mid G(P), S]$, where

$$\Pr[x \mid G(P), X] = \begin{cases} \prod_{i=1}^{|x|} P(r(G,X,x,i)) & \text{if } x \in L(G,X), \\ 0 & \text{otherwize.} \end{cases}$$

$r(G,X,x,1),\ldots,r(G,X,x,|x|)$ are the sequence of rules used in the derivation $X \Rightarrow_G^* x$. $G(P)$ is called **consistent** if and only if $\sum_{x \in L(G)} \Pr[x \mid G(P)] = 1$. In order that $\Pr[\cdot \mid G(P)]$ is regarded as a probability on Σ^*, $G(P)$ is required to be consistent. A sufficient condition of consistency is known (Wetherell, C. S., 1980). Let $M(G(P))$ be a $(|V|,|V|)$ matrix whose element $m_{ij}(G(P))$ represents the expectation of the number of the occurrences of the nonterminal symbol A_j derivable in one step from A_i. $G(P)$ is consistent if $\rho(M(G(P))) < 1$, where $\rho(M)$ is the spectral radius of M.

3. An extension of finite-state Markov decision processes

3.1 A representation of episodic finite-state MDPs with grammatical formalism

In this section, first, we describe the notion of the simple context-free Markov decision processes, by using a simple example of an episodic finite-state MDP. After that, the definition of simple context-free Markov decision process will be given.

Fig.1 is an episodic finite-state MDP, which contains 5 states, {*a, b, c, d, e*}. '*S*' indicates the initial state, and double circles indicate end states ({*a, e*}). The actions the robot can take are '*L*' and '*R*'. Reward given to the robot is -1 for every step, and if the robot gets in the end state '*e*', 1 is given. In this case, it is obvious that, if the robot takes '*R*' action for every state, the best policy is acquired.

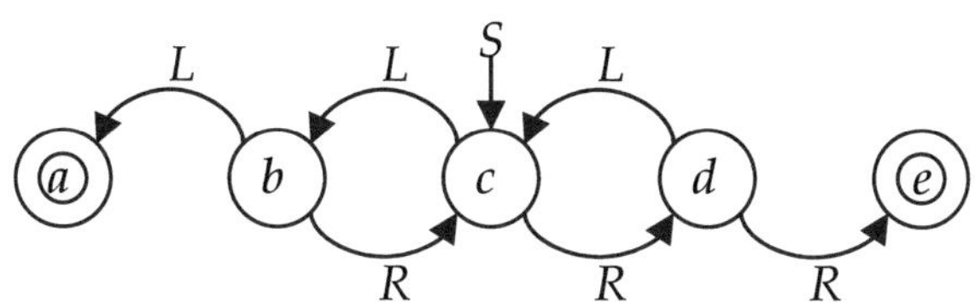

Fig. 1. An episodic finite-state MDP

A possible history of states is a sequence of states representing the transition of the robot from the initial state to an end state, such as {*cba, cde, cbdba, …* }. Let us call the set of possible histories the language generated by the finite-sate MDP in Fig. 1. While this language is a regular language, some regular languages cannot be generated by any finite-state MDPs. For example a singleton {*aae*} cannot be the language of any MDP, because each letter identifies one state. The fact that *aae* is a possible history implies that the robot may translate from the state a to a. Thus, $a^n e$ is also a possible history for any $n > 0$.

Therefore, the possible histories can be also described as a language for some regular grammar G, and its language class is not required to include the class of regular languages.

The class of simple grammars is one of the subclasses of CFGs such that all languages generated by finite-state MDPs are generated by them. For example, a CFG whose rules are $\{S \to cC,\ C \to bB,\ B \to a,\ B \to cC,\ C \to dD,\ D \to e,\ D \to cC\}$ generates the language of the MDP in Fig.1. The derivation of '*cbcde*' is written as $S \Rightarrow cC \Rightarrow cbB \Rightarrow cbcC \Rightarrow cbcdD \Rightarrow cbcde$. That CFG is a simple grammar, and a regular grammar, if nonterminal symbols are regarded as states (Fig. 2).

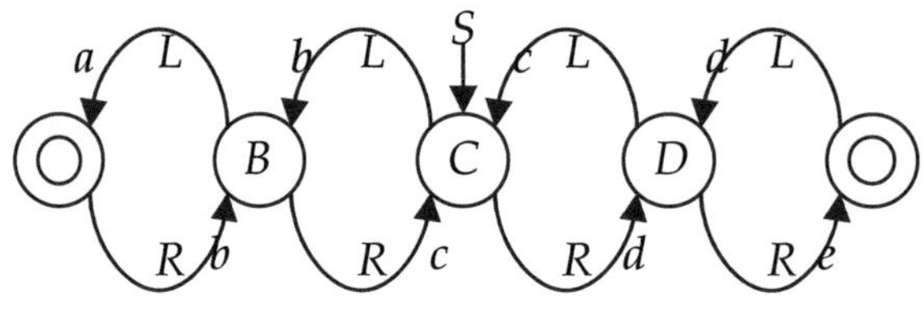

Fig. 2. Expressing the MDP in fig.1 by a regular grammar or simple grammar

A probabilistic CFG is defined by assigning a non-negative real number to every rule, where $\sum_{r\in R(A)} P(r)=1$ and $R(A)=\{A\to X\in R\}$. In a finite-state MDP, if a policy is decided, the probabilities of histories (the measure on the language) are determined. On the MDP in Fig. 1, let us suppose that the policy is chosen as the probability of choice of '*R*' or '*L*' is assigned to 0.5 for every state. In that case, the probability of a sentence '*w*' in the language is $2^{-|w|}$. The pair of a language and a measure on it is called a probabilistic language. When a policy which is taken by a robot is changed, the probabilistic language of MDP changes correspondingly.

Every context-free grammar generates various probabilistic languages by assigning various probabilities to each rule of it. The set of all probabilistic languages generated from a CFG G by assigning a probability to each rule of it is called the probabilistic generality of G. The probabilistic generality of G is a subset of $\{L(G)\to[0,1]\}$. For instance, suppose that G is a CFG whose rules are {*S*→*aS*, *S*→*b*}. The probabilistic generality of it is written as follows:

$$\{P:\{a*b\}\to[0,1]\mid P(a^n b)=q^n(1-q), q\in[0,1]\}.$$

It is clear that the fact that grammars *A* and *B* generate the same language does not imply its probabilistic generalities of them are the same. Suppose that *H* is a CFG that has rules {*S*→*aA*, *S*→*b*, *A*→*aA*, *A*→*b*}. Obviously, *L*(*G*) = *L*(*H*). But the generality of *H* is

$$\{P:\{a*b\}\to[0,1]\mid P(b)=1-q, P(aa^n b)=qr^n(1-r), q\in[0,1]\}.$$

So generalities of them are different from each other.

3.2 Simple context-free Markov decision processes

Simple context-free MDP is formally defined as follows

Definition 4. Let G be an simple grammar. *G*(*U*,*P*,*C*) =<*V*,*Σ*,*R*,*S*,*U*,*P*,*C*> is a **simple context-free decision process** if and only if *U*, *P* and *C* are the following set and functions.

- *U* is a finite set of actions.
- $P: R\times U\to[0,1]$ is a probabilistic assignment. For all (*A*,*u*) in *V*×*U*, $\sum_{r\in R(A)} P(r,u)=1$
- $C:\Sigma\to(-\infty,\infty)$ is a reward function.

In the following, when G is in a subclass of SGs, we call the simple context-free decision process *G*(*U*,*P*,*C*) [the name of the subclass]-DP.

Corresponding to a given SG-DP, a sequence of discrete random variables *X*(1), *Y*(1), *X*(2), *Y*(2), ... is given as follows. *X*(1) =*S*, the domain of *X*(*i*) is *Σ***V** and the domain of *Y*(*i*) is *U*.

$$\Pr[X(t) = x_t\alpha_t \mid X(1) = S, Y(1) = u_1, ..., X(t-1) = x_{t-1}\alpha_{t-1}, Y(t-1) = u_{t-1}]$$
$$= \Pr[X(t) = x_t\alpha_t \mid X(t-1) = x_{t-1}\alpha_{t-1}, Y(t-1) = u_{t-1}]$$
$$= \begin{cases} P(r, u_{t-1}) & \text{if} \quad x_{t-1}\alpha_{t-1} \Rightarrow x_t\alpha_t \text{ with the rule } r, \\ 1 & \text{if} \quad x_{t-1}\alpha_{t-1} = x_t\alpha_t = x_{t-1} = x_t, \\ 0 & \textit{otherwise.} \end{cases}$$

Clearly, *X* and *Y* are an infinite-state MDP. Every episodic finite-state MDP is equivalent to some SG-DP as we have discussed in the beginning of this section. In fact, an episodic finite-state MDP whose states are $a_1, \cdots, a_{n+k}$ and end states are $a_{n+1}, \cdots, a_{n+k}$ for some n >0 and k >=0, can be represented by the form of SG-DP <*V*,*Σ*,*R*,*S*,*U*,*P*,*C*>:

$$V = \{A_1(=S), ..., A_n\},$$
$$\Sigma = \{a_1, ..., a_{n+k}\},$$
$$R = \{A \to a_j A_j \mid A \in V, 1 \le j \le n\} \cup \{A \to a_j \mid A \in V, n+1 \le j \le n+k\}$$

$P(A_i \to a_j A_j)$ equals to the transition probability from *i* to *j*, and $P(A_i \to a_{n+j})$ equals to the transition probability from *i* to *n+j*, where *n+j* is an end state. *U* is the same set of actions as the MDP, and C is also the same.

Policies, value-function, optimal value function, etc. are introduced below in analogues to those of MDPs. Let *G*(*U*,*P*,*C*) = <*V*, *Σ*, *R*, *S*,*U*,*P*,*C*> be an SG-DP.

Definition 5. A **policy** of *G*(*U*,*P*,*C*) is a map $V \to U$.

One of the main purposes of reinforcement learning is to determine a policy μ so as to maximise the expectation of the total reward from *S*.

Definition 6. A **value function** of *G*(*U*,*P*,*C*) under a policy μ, $J_\mu : V \to (-\infty, \infty)$, is defined as

$$J_\mu(A) = \sum_{x \in L(G,A)} \Pr[x \mid G(P_\mu), A] \sum_{i=1}^{|x|} C(a_i),$$

where $x = a_1 a_2 \cdots a_{|x|}$ and P_μ is the probability assignment of *G* under μ, namely, for $A \to a\alpha \in R$, $P_\mu(A \to a\alpha) = P(A \to a\alpha, \mu(A))$.

When $\rho(M(G(P_\mu))) < 1$ for any policy μ, all value functions of G(U,P,C) are finite.

Definition 7. The **optimal value function** of *G*(*U*,*P*,*C*) denoted as $J_* : V \to (-\infty, \infty)$ is defined as

$$J_*(A) = \sup_{\mu \in \pi} J_\mu(A),$$

where π is the set of all policies.

There exists some policy μ_* such that $J_{\mu_*}(A) = J_*(A)$.

Definition 8. μ_* is called an **optimal policy**.

Definition 9. The **optimal action-value function** $Q_* : V \times U \to (-\infty, \infty)$ is defined as

$$Q_*(A,u) = \sum_{A \to aB_1 \cdots B_k \in R(A)} P(A \to aB_1 \cdots B_k, u) \left(C(a) + \sum_{i=1}^{k} J_*(B_i) \right).$$

Definitions 5 - 9 are a natural extension of the usual definitions on reinforcement learning for finite-state MDPs, whose discounting factor equals 1. Most of well known reinforcement learning methods, such as Q-learning, TD(λ) can be applied to SG-DPs corresponding to the above definitions. In the following theorem, an extended Q-learning for SG-DPs is introduced and its convergence to the optimal action-value is established. A proof is in (Shibata et al., 2006).

Theorem 1. Assume that $\rho(M(G(P_\mu))) < 1$ for any policy μ. A sequence of V×U×[0,1], $(A_1,u_1,k_1),(A_2,u_2,k_2),\cdots$ is supposed to satisfy the following conditions for all (A,u) in V×U.

$$\sum_{(A_t,u_t)=(A,u)} k_t = \infty \text{ and } \sum_{(A_t,u_t)=(A,u)} k_t^{\,2} < \infty .$$

The sequence of random variables $Q_1,Q_2,\cdots$ defined by the following iteration (the **extended Q-Learning**) converges to the optimal action-value function of $G(U,P,C)$ as $t \to \infty$ with probability 1.

$$Q_{t+1}(A_t,u_t) = (1-k_t)Q_t(A_t,u_t) + k_t\left(C(a) + \sum_{i=1}^{m} \max_{v\in U} Q_t(B_i,v) \right),$$

where the sequence $B_1 \cdots B_m$ is randomly chosen with probability $P(A_t \to aB_1\cdots B_m,u_t)$.

4. Identification in the limit of right-unique simple grammars from positive data

4.1 Learning simple grammars

A most rigid theoretical model for learning concepts would be identification in the limit proposed by Gold (1967). Because episodic states histories are regarded as positive data, one might expect that fruits of grammatical inference on identification in the limit from positive data could be directly applied to reinforcement learning. As simple context-free decision processes are a generalization of finite Markov decision processes, we should refer to results on grammatical inference of simple grammars. It is known that however simple languages are not identifiable in the limit from positive data, because every regular language with an endmarker is a simple language and the class of whole regular languages is not identifiable in the limit from positive data (Gold 1967).

On the other hand, Yokomori (2003, 2007) has shown that very simple grammars, which form a small subset of simple grammars, are polynomial-time identifiable in the limit from positive data. A very simple grammar is a simple grammar such that each terminal symbol has exactly one production rule in which it occurs. Therefore, the grammar has exactly the same number of production rules as terminal symbols. Decision processes constructed on very simple grammars are, however, too restricted and they are no longer able to cover finite Markov decision processes.

Thus we need another richer subclass of simple grammars that should give an extension of finite Markov decision processes and at the same time it should be efficiently identifiable in the limit from positive data. Here we introduce a new class of grammars, called right-unique simple grammars, which is located between simple grammars and very simple grammars. This class still defines a small proper subclass of simple languages, but actually it satisfies the two desired properties mentioned above.

In this section, we show the efficient learnability of right-unique simple grammars.

4.2 Identification in the limit from positive data

First we let the reader recall the notion of identification in the limit from positive data established by Gold (1967). A **positive presentation** of a language L_* is an infinite sequence of strings where all and only elements of L_* appear. Each string appearing in a positive presentation is called a positive example of L_*. A **learning algorithm** $\mathcal{A}$ is an algorithm which takes a positive presentation $w_1, w_2, \ldots$ as input, and outputs some infinite sequence of grammars $G_1, G_2, \ldots$, i.e., $\mathcal{A}$ infinitely repeats the cycle where $\mathcal{A}$ receives w_i and outputs G_i for $i = 1, 2, \ldots$. A learning algorithm $\mathcal{A}$ **converges** to G on a presentation $w_1, w_2, \ldots$ if for all but finitely many i, $G_i = G$ holds. $\mathcal{A}$ **identifies** a class $\mathcal{L}$ of languages in the limit from positive data if for every positive presentation of every $L_* \in \mathcal{L}$, $\mathcal{A}$ converges to a grammar G generating the exact language L_*.

Usually learning algorithms are supposed to output a grammar consistent with the given positive examples, i.e., the conjectured grammar generates all the examples. Moreover, they do not change the conjecture unless the current conjecture is inconsistent with the newly given example. Our learning algorithm, which will be presented in Sec. 3.4, also has this standard property.

4.3 Right-unique simple grammars

Our learning target here is **right-unique simple languages** defined by right-unique simple grammars. A simple grammar $G = \langle V, \Sigma, R, S \rangle$ is called a right-unique simple grammar (RSG) if whenever both $A \to a\alpha$ and $B \to a\beta$ are rules of the grammar with $a \in \Sigma$ and $\alpha, \beta \in V^*$, $\alpha = \beta$ holds. We note that G is a very simple grammar if moreover we have $A = B$ in addition to $\alpha = \beta$.

Let us see an example of an RSG. The grammar consisting of the following rules is an RSG:

$$S \to \neg S \mid \vee SS \mid \exists US \mid pT \mid qTT,\ T \to fT \mid gTT \mid a \mid b \mid x \mid y,\ U \to x \mid y,$$

where S,T,U are nonterminal symbols and $\neg, \vee, \exists, p, q, f, g, a, b$ are terminal symbols. The generated language is a set of formulae of first-order logic in Polish notation.

The definition of RSGs allows us to define the function $\sharp_G$ for each RSG G, called **the shape** of G, that assigns an integer to each terminal symbol as

$$\sharp_G(a) = |\alpha| - 1 \quad \text{if } G \text{ has a rule } A \to a\alpha \text{ for some } A.$$

This function is homomorphically extended so that $\sharp_G(xy) = \sharp_G(x) + \sharp_G(y)$ for any $x, y \in \Sigma^*$ ($\sharp_G(\varepsilon) = 0$ for the empty string ε). It is easy to see that whenever $\alpha \Rightarrow_G^* x\beta$ with $x \in \Sigma^*$ and $\alpha, \beta \in V^*$, we have $|\beta| = |\alpha| + \sharp_G(x)$. Moreover we have $|\alpha| + \sharp_G(x') \geq 1$ for any proper prefix x' of x, because $\alpha \Rightarrow_G^* x'\gamma \Rightarrow_G^+ x\beta$ entails $\gamma \neq \varepsilon$. Particularly for $w \in L(G)$, we have $\sharp_G(w) = -1$ and $\sharp_G(w') \geq 0$ for any proper prefix w' of w. In this way, the function $\sharp_G$ strongly characterizes the derivations and the language of G. In general, we let us call any function $\sharp$ from Σ^* to $\mathbb{Z}$ a **shape** if it holds that $\sharp(a) \geq -1$ and $\sharp(x) + \sharp(y) = \sharp(xy)$ (homomorphism) for all $a \in \Sigma$ and $x, y \in \Sigma^*$.

We also say that a shape $\sharp$ is **compatible with** a language L if $\sharp(w) = -1$ and $\sharp(w') \geq 0$ for all $w \in L$ and any proper prefix w' of w. Consequently, $\sharp_G$ is always compatible with $L(G)$. Here we note that any language L admits a finite number of compatible shapes. This is because, if $\sharp$ is compatible with L and $xay \in L$, then

$$\sharp(a) = \sharp(xay) - \sharp(x) - \sharp(y) \leq -1 - 0 + |y|,$$

because x is a proper prefix of xay and $\sharp(b) \geq -1$ for any $b \in \Sigma$. Therefore, a language L admits at most $\prod_{a\in\Sigma} \ell_a$ compatible shapes, where $\ell_a = \min\{\, |ay| \mid xay \in L \,\}$.

To simplify our discussion, here we introduce a special form of RSGs, called **canonical form**. Every RSG can be transformed into canonical form with preserving the language and the shape. The set of nonterminal symbols of an RSG G in canonical form of shape $\sharp$ is exactly

$$V_\sharp = \{S_0\} \cup \{\, [a,i] \mid a \in \Sigma,\ 0 \leq i \leq \sharp(a) \,\}$$

and every rule has the form

$$A \to a[a,0]\ldots[a,\sharp(a)]$$

for some $A \in V_\sharp$. For instance, an RSG G consisting of the rules

$$S \to aSA, \quad S \to bA, \quad A \to c$$

is converted into G' in canonical form with the rules

$$\begin{array}{lll} S_0 \to a[a,0][a,1], & S_0 \to b[b,0], & [a,1] \to c, \\ [a,0] \to a[a,0][a,1], & [a,0] \to b[b,0], & [b,0] \to c. \end{array} \quad (1)$$

Here the start symbol S of G is divided into S_0 and $[a,0]$ in G' and A is divided into $[a,1]$ and $[b,0]$. Therefore, it is allowed to consider only RSGs in canonical form. Actually our learning algorithm for RSGs computes its conjecture in canonical form.

4.4 Learning algorithm

By definition, each shape has a finite number of RSGs in canonical form. Together with the fact that any language admits a finite number of compatible shapes, we see that there is a finite number of RSLs consistent with the given positive examples. This property is known as **finite thickness**. Angluin (1980) has shown that every class of languages with finite thickness is identifiable in the limit from positive data. Thus RSGs are identifiable in the limit from positive data.

Our learning algorithm outputs an RSG that generates a minimal language among all the RSLs containing the given positive examples. This strategy ensures that the algorithm finally converges to a grammar representing the target language. If the current conjecture G does not generate the target language L_*, we never have $L_* \subsetneq L(G)$, because of the minimality of the conjecture. Thus there is $w \in L_* - L(G)$, which will appear in the positive presentation of L_*. Then the algorithm eventually abandons the conjecture G and the times changing the conjecture is finite by the finite thickness of the class of RSLs. Finally the conjecture converges to a grammar generating the target language.

To enable us to analyze the efficiency of the learning task, we present a concrete learning algorithm for RSGs. The learning method for RSGs is basically same as Yokomori's (2003, 2007) algorithm for very simple grammars. The first step of our algorithm for learning RSGs is to find shapes compatible with the given positive examples. Then the algorithm computes consistent RSGs in canonical form whose shapes are those found at the first step. At last a minimal (with respect to its language) grammar among those candidate RSGs is picked up. Fig. 3 represents this learning strategy.

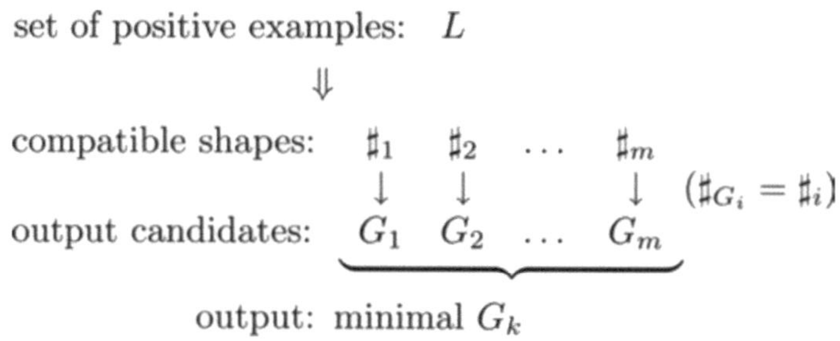

Fig. 3. Flow of our learning algorithm.

To enumerate all the compatible shapes for a given set L of positive examples, it is enough to check the compatibility of shapes $\sharp$ satisfying that $-1 \leq \sharp(a) < \ell_a - 1$ with $\ell_a = \min\{\, |ay| \mid xay \in L \,\}$. Deciding the compatibility of a shape with a finite language is trivially done in linear time. Therefore, the enumeration of compatible shapes is done in $O(\ell^{|\Sigma|})$ time simply by the brute-force search where $\ell = \max\{\, |w| \mid w \in L \,\}$. This upper bound is polynomial if we fix Σ. It would be natural to ask whether a more efficient algorithm that finds a compatible shape in polynomial time in $|\Sigma|$ is possible. Concerning this question, it is known that deciding whether or not a finite language admits a compatible shape is NP-complete if we regard $|\Sigma|$ as a variable.

Once we obtain a compatible shape, one can straightforwardly construct the minimum RSG in canonical form of that shape that is consistent with the given positive examples. For a given set L of examples and a shape $\sharp$ compatible with L, the algorithm picks up the least rules from the set

$$\{\, A \to a[a,0] \ldots [a, \sharp(a)] \mid A \in V_\sharp,\ a \in \Sigma \,\}$$

so that the resultant grammar generates all the elements of L. For instance, when two positive examples *aabccc*, *bc* are given, the only compatible shape $\sharp$ is such that $\sharp(a) = 1$, $\sharp(b) = 0$, $\sharp(c) = -1$. To derive those two strings, exactly the rules in (1) are needed. Thus, the output of the learning algorithm is G'. This procedure can be done in almost linear time in $\|L\|$ where $\|L\|$ is the sum of the lengths of all the positive examples.

In general, multiple compatible shapes would be computed. In that case, we will compute grammars as many as the compatible shapes and have to choose one among those as the conjecture. The criterion is to choose a minimal grammar with respect to the language. That is, we have to solve the inclusion problem of RSGs. This procedure would be rather purely an issue of formal language theory and thus we relegate this subroutine to (Yoshinaka 2006), where it is shown that inclusion of two RSGs computed as output candidates is decidable in polynomial time in $\|L\|$. Let us write the upper bound of the running time of this subroutine as $p(\|L\|)$ for a polynomial p. In order to pick up a minimal RSG among m output candidates, we execute this subroutine $m-1$ times. Recall that we have $m \leq \ell^{|\Sigma|}$ where ℓ is the length of a longest positive example. Therefore, our algorithm updates its conjecture in $O(p(\|L\|)\ell^{|\Sigma|})$ steps.

Let us see an example. Suppose that the first positive example is *abbc*. There are two compatible shapes $\sharp_1$ and $\sharp_2$:

$$\sharp_1 = \{\, a \mapsto 0,\ b \mapsto 0,\quad c \mapsto -1 \,\},$$

$$\sharp_2 = \{\, a \mapsto 2,\ b \mapsto -1,\ c \mapsto -1 \,\}.$$

The minimum consistent RSGs G_1 and G_2 constructed on $\sharp_1$ and $\sharp_2$, respectively, have the following production rules:

$$G_1 : S_0 \rightarrow a[a,0],\ [a,0] \rightarrow b[b,0],\ [b,0] \rightarrow b[b,0],\ [b,0] \rightarrow c,$$

$$G_2 : S_0 \rightarrow a[a,0][a,1][a,2],\ [a,0] \rightarrow b,\ [a,1] \rightarrow b,\ [a,2] \rightarrow c.$$

We have $L(G_2) = \{abbc\} \subsetneq L(G_1) = \{\, ab^n c \mid n \geq 1 \,\}$. Therefore our algorithm outputs G_2.

5. Probabilistic generality of subclasses of simple grammars

5.1 Probabilistic generalities and unifiablity

Definition 10. The **Probabilistic generality** of an SG G is defined as

$$\Gamma(G) = \{\Pr[\cdot \mid G(P)] \mid P \text{ is a probability assignment on } G\}.$$

An SG H is more general than G if and only if $\Gamma(G) \subset \Gamma(H)$.

The following lemma establishes requirements for $\Gamma(G) \subset \Gamma(H)$.

Lemma 1. Let $G = \langle V,\Sigma,R,S \rangle$ and $H = \langle V',\Sigma,R',S' \rangle$ be reduced SGs. $\Gamma(G) \subset \Gamma(H)$ if and only if $L(G) = L(H)$ and there is some map $\psi : V'_{\geq 2} \rightarrow V_{\geq 2}$ that satisfies the following condition, where $V_{\geq 2} = \{A \in V \| R(A) |\geq 2\}$. For all A in $V'_{\geq 2}$ and all x in Σ^*, $S' \Rightarrow_H^* xA\alpha$ implies $S \Rightarrow_G^* x\psi(A)\beta$.

Suppose that C is a subclass of SGs. In the following, we will discuss whether C has a more general grammar than arbitrary two grammars that generate the same language.

Definition 11. Let C and D be subclasses of SGs. C is **unifiable within** D if and only if, for all G, H in C such that $L(G) = L(H)$, there is I in D such that $\Gamma(G) \cup \Gamma(H) \subset \Gamma(I)$.

The main result of this section is construction of an SG G^* that is more general than a finite number of given RSGs whose languages are equivalent. However, neither the class of SGs nor the class of RSGs is unifiable within itself, as we see in what follows. The proofs for all of them use Lem. 1. In the following, we say that C is **unifiable** when C is unifiable within C itself.

Theorem 2. The class of SGs is not unifiable.

A proof of Theorem 2 is written in (Shibata et al., 2006). The class of RSGs is also not unifiable. This fact is showed by considering the finite language $L= (a\,|\,b)(c\,|\,d)(e\,|\,f)$ = $\{ace,acf,ade,adf,bce,bcf,bde,bdf\}$. On the other hand, the class of VSGs is unifiable. For any VSGs G and H, $L(G)=L(H)$ implies $\Gamma(G)=\Gamma(H)$. Suppose that $S \Rightarrow^*_G xA\alpha$ and $S \Rightarrow^*_G yB\beta$. $A=B$ if and only if $xA\alpha \Rightarrow_G xa\alpha'$ and $yB\beta \Rightarrow_G ya\beta'$ from the definition of a VSG. If H is a VSG such that $L(G)=L(H)$, $S \Rightarrow^*_G xA\alpha \Rightarrow xa\alpha'$ if and only if $S' \Rightarrow^*_H xC\gamma \Rightarrow xa\gamma'$. Thus, there is a bijection $\psi : V \rightarrow V'$, and $S \Rightarrow^*_G xA\alpha$ if and only if $S' \Rightarrow^*_H x\psi(A)\gamma$. From Lemma 1, $\Gamma(G)=\Gamma(H)$.

5.2 A unifiable subclass of simple grammars

In this subsection, we will introduce **unifiable simple grammars**. The class of USGs is unifiable and is a superclass of the class of RSGs. This implies that the class of RSGs is unifiable within the class of USGs. Because the proof of unifiability for the class of USGs is constructive, the algorithm that unifies a finite number of RSGs whose languages are equal is also given.

Let G = $<V,\Sigma,R,S>$ be an SG. Let $\sigma_G(A)=\{a \in \Sigma \mid A \rightarrow a\alpha \in R\}$. The relation between A and B given by $\sigma_G(A)=\sigma_G(B)$ is an equivalence relation, thus let $\overline{A}$ denote the equivalence class containing A. $\overline{A}=\{A' \in V \mid \sigma(A)=\sigma(A')\}$. We also introduce the notation $\overline{U}=\{A' \in V \mid \exists A \in U, \sigma(A)=\sigma(A')\}$ and $\overline{A_1 \cdots A_m}=\overline{A_1}\cdots\overline{A_m}$.

Definition 12. An SG G is a **unifiable simple grammar** (USG) if and only if

- $\overline{A}=\overline{B}$, $A \rightarrow a\alpha \in R$ and $B \rightarrow a\beta \in R$ imply $\overline{\alpha}=\overline{\beta}$.

Neighbourhood pairs introduced below play the most important role in constructing the proof of the unifiability of the class of USGs. Before we define neighbourhood pairs, it is necessary that two new notions are introduced.

Definition 13. For a subset U of V, $\mathrm{up}(U)=\{A \in V \mid \exists B \in U, A \Rightarrow^* xB\}$ is called the **upstream** of U.

Definition 14. Let T and U be subsets of V. W(T,U) denotes $(V\text{-}T \mid TU)^*$.

The upstream of U is easy to compute from R. Using the above definitions, we define a neighbourhood pair as follows.

Definition 15. Let $<T,U>$ be a pair of subsets of V. $<T,U>$ is called a **neighbourhood pair** if and only if the following conditions hold.

1. $T \cap U = \phi$.
2. For some A in V, $U=\overline{A}$.
3. For some B in V, $T=\mathrm{up}(\overline{B})$.
4. For all x, $S \Rightarrow^* x\alpha$ implies $\alpha \in \mathrm{W}(T,U)$.

An intuitive meaning of a neighbourhood pair can be seen in the fourth condition of Definition 15. If a nonterminal symbol $A \in T$ appears in α such that $S \Rightarrow^* x\alpha$, some $B \in U$ is adjoining on the right side of A. Fig. 4 is an algorithm to find a neighbourhood pair. The computational cost required to find a neighbourhood pair from G is $O(|G|\,|V|)$.

```
NeighbourhoodPair find(USG G=<V,Σ,R,S >) {
  for(each A ∈ V and B ∈ V − {S} ){
    T = up(B̄);
    U = Ā;
    for (each B → aα ∈ R ) {
      if ((B ∈ T and αC ∉ W(T,U) for some C ∈ U )
          or (B ∉ T and α ∉ W(T,U))) {
        < T,U > is not a neighbourhood pair, so break this and continue the 1st loop;
      }
    }
    return < T,U >;
  }
  return no_neighbourhood_pair ;
}
```

Fig. 4. Finding a neighbourhood pair

We explain only the abstract of the proof, which is constructing a unified USG from two arbitrary USGs. For the complete proof of it, refer to (Shibata et al., 2006).
First, we find and eliminate all neighbourhood pairs from both USGs. While some neighbourhood pair is found, we eliminate it keeping the generality of the grammar.

```
USG transform(USG G) {
  while ( There exists an neighbourhood pair <T,U> in G ) {
    G = Φ(G, <T,U>) ;
  }
  return G;
}
```

Fig. 5. Transformation of USGs

In Fig. 5, $\Phi(G, <T,U>)$ denotes the USG obtained by eliminating a neighbourhood pair keeping the generality. $\Phi(G, <T,U>)$ is a USG obtained by eliminating useless nonterminal symbols and rules from a USG $<V',\Sigma,R',S>$ where

$$V' = (V - T) \cup (T \times U),$$

$$R' = \{A \to a\varphi(\alpha) \mid A \to a\alpha \in R, A \in V - T\} \cup \{(A,B) \to a\varphi(\alpha B) \mid A \to a\alpha \in R, (A,B) \in T \times U\}.$$

The above map φ from V^* to V'^* is defined recursively as the following.

- $\varphi(\varepsilon) = \varepsilon$.
- $\varphi(A\beta) = \begin{cases} (A,B)\varphi(\gamma) & \text{if } A \in T \text{ and } \beta = B\gamma, \\ A\varphi(\beta) & \text{othewize.} \end{cases}$

$\Phi(G, <T,U>)$ is more general than G.

Let G/σ denote a USG $<V/\sigma,\Sigma,R/\sigma,S>$, where

$$V/\sigma = \{\bar{A} \mid A \in V\},$$

$$R/\sigma = \{\bar{A} \to a\bar{\alpha} \mid A \to a\alpha \in R\}.$$

Definition 16. USGs G and H are **σ-isomorphic** if and only if G/σ and H/σ are equivalent modulo renaming of nonterminal symbols.

When neither a USG G nor a USG H has neighbourhood pair, $L(G) = L(H)$ implies that G is σ-isomorphic to H. If G and H are σ-isomorphic, it is easy to unify them. In fact, let $G=< V,\Sigma,R,S >$ and $H=< V',\Sigma,R',S' >$ be σ-isomorphic. A USG defined as $G \otimes H$ is obtained by eliminating useless nonterminal symbols and rules from a USG $< V \otimes V', \Sigma, R \otimes R', (S,S') >$, where

$$V \otimes V' = \{(A,B) \in V \times V' \mid \sigma(A) = \sigma(B)\},$$

$$R \otimes R' = \{(A,B) \to a\alpha \otimes \beta \mid A \to a\alpha \in R \text{ and } B \to a\beta \in R'\},$$

$$A_1 \cdots A_m \otimes B_1 \cdots B_m = (A_1,B_1) \cdots (A_m,B_m).$$

Thus we have the following theorem.

Theorem 3. The class of USGs is unifiable.

As a finite language admits a finite number of compatible shapes, any RSL has a finite number of compatible shapes. This entails that any RSL is generated by only a finite number of RSGs in canonical form. In fact, for any RSG G, we can compute all the RSGs in canonical form generating the same language. It is easy to see that if G is an RSG and H is the canonical form of G, i.e., $L(G)=L(H)$, $\#_G = \#_H$ and H is in canonical form, then H is more general than G. Since we have proven Theorem 3 in a constructive manner we obtain the following theorem.

Theorem 4. For every RSG G, we can construct a USG G^* which satisfies the following property. For any RSG H such that $L(H) = L(G)$, $\Gamma(H) \subset \Gamma(G^*)$.

Fig. 6 shows a unification algorithm of RSGs whose languages are equivalent.

```
USG unify(RSGs G_1,...,G_m) {
  Confirm that all languages of G_1,...,G_m equal;
   return transform(G_1) ⊗ ... ⊗ transform(G_m);
}
```

Fig. 6. Unification of USGs

We finally describe only the result of the order of $|G^*|$. The time complexity of the algorithm is mainly dominated by $|G^*|$. $|G^*|$ is $O(m(G)^{2\,\mathrm{amb}(G)})$, where

$$m(G) = \max\{|H| \mid H \text{ is an RSG and } L(H) = L(G)\}$$

and amb(G) is the number of the equivalence classes with respect to σ-isomorphism whose languages equal to $L(G)$, that is,

$$\mathrm{amb}(G) = |\{H/\sigma \text{ modulo renaming nonterminals} \mid H \text{ is an RSG and } L(H) = L(G)\}|.$$

6. Implementation and experiments

6.1 Implementation of the learning algorithm for RSGs and the extension of QL

In the following, we assume that environments are RSG-DPs. The class of RSG-DPs is sufficiently large and includes the class of episodic finite-state MDPs, as we have described in Section 3. Those are the reasons why we assume that environments are RSG-DPs. For instance, let us consider other classes described in this chapter. The class of VSG-DPs does not include the class of episodic finite-state MDPs. If we assume the class of SG-DPs in stead of RSG-DPs as the class of environments, it is too large to learn, that is, the class of SGs is not learnable from positive data. The class of USGs is learnable theoretically, but efficient learning method is not known yet.

Although sequences of observations can be identified as positive data of grammars and we have an efficient learning algorithm for RSGs, we cannot apply a technique of reinforcement learning with assuming that the environment is constructed on the grammar obtained by the learning algorithm in Section 4. As discussed in Section 5, it is possible that any RSG-DP based on the grammar output by the learning algorithm does not generate the same probabilistic language as the environment, though both define the same (nonprobabilistic) language. In this case, actually the RSG that bases the environment must be one candidate computed in the learning algorithm, though it is not chosen as the output by the nondeterministic choice. Here, we modify the learning algorithm in Section 4 so that it outputs all the RSGs generating the same language as the grammar output by the original algorithm. By applying the unification algorithm in Section 5 to obtained RSGs, we get a USG that is more general than the RSG that bases the environment.

Combining the learning algorithm and the unification algorithm with an extended Q-learning, we obtain the algorithm in Fig. 7. Let us call that algorithm RSG-QL. RSG-QL does not require any grammar which bases the environment to be given. Only the set of actions and the set of observations (= terminal symbols) are given.

Fig. 7 shows update of the RSG-QL for one episode, or sentence. At first, a USG G, which intends to represent the environment, is set to an episodic finite-state MDP. This is just a tentative one, and when a USG is computed from the learning algorithm and the unification algorithm, it is substituted for G. If G cannot derive a prefix x given by the environment, the algorithm abandon updating Q until the episode ends. After the episode ends, it is added to the set of histories, and new USG is computed.

There are two new external functions in Fig. 7. Those are the same things in the ordinary reinforcement learning. environ(x,u) returns an observation (= terminal symbol) when a prefix of the sequence of observations is x and the action that the learning robot takes is u. Suppose that the environment is identified with an RSG-DP $H(U,P,C)$, then environ(x,u) randomly returns a with the probability $P(A \rightarrow a\alpha, u)$, where $S \Rightarrow_H^* xA\beta$. environ($x,u$) itself is not controlled by the learning algorithm directly. It is controlled by the selection of actions.

The other function is strategy(Q,G,x). strategy(Q,G,x) is the function that decides which action the learning robot takes. It can be arbitrarily chosen within the condition of Theorem 1. Actually, famous strategies such as eps-greedy and soft-max are often chosen (Sutton & Barto 1998).

For an implementation of the function enumRSGs(positive_data), i.e., the learning algorithm of RSGs from positive data, we introduce the way to save computational cost (Yokomori

2003, 2007). Suppose that input positive data is $w_1,\cdots,w_t$, and terminal symbols which occurs in positive data at least once are $a_1,\cdots,a_n$. Let M_t be a matrix whose element m_{ij} is the number of a_j in w_i. As we have seen in Section 4, each compatible shape $\vec{s}=(\#(a_1),\cdots,\#(a_n))^{\mathrm{T}}$ satisfies $M_t\vec{s}=\overrightarrow{-1}$. This implies that the number of independent variables is dimker(M_t) if other conditions to be compatible are ignored. In addition, any elements of $\vec{s}$ is not less than -1. Thus the number of candidates of compatible shapes is $O\left((\max_i |w_i|)^{\dim\ker(M_t)}\right)$.

$\lim_{t\to\infty}\dim\ker(M_t)$ is constant for any positive data of G, so we denote it as dim(G). If an upper bound of dim(G) is known, the algorithm can wait for enumeration of candidates until dimker(M_t) becomes less than it.

```
G = <V,Σ,R,S> is a USG, initially, an episodic finite-state MDP.
Q = a map from V×U to (−∞,∞).
RSG-QL () {
  x = ε;
  u = strategy (G,Q,ε);
  while ((a = environ (x,u)) ≠ ε ) {
    if (S ⇒*_G xAα ⇒ xaβα ){
      Q(A,u) = (1−k)Q(A,u) + k( C(a) + Σ_{i=1}^{m} max_{v∈U} Q(B_i,v) ), where β = B_1···B_m ;
    }
    x = xa;
    u = strategy (G,Q,x);
  }
  history = history ∪ {x};
  if (x ∉ L(G)){
    minimals = enumRSGs (history);
    if(minimals != null) H = unifyRSGs(minimals);
  }
}
```
Fig. 7. RSG-QL for one episode

Now let us see how our learning algorithm works through an example. Let G be an RSG whose rules are

$S\to a[a,0][a,1][a,2]$, $S\to b[b,0][b,1]$, $\{[a,0],[b,0],[e,0]\}\to c[c,0]$,
$\{[a,2],[c,0]\}\to d$, $[c,0]\to e[e,0][e,1][e,2]$, $[e,0]\to f$,
$[a,1]\to g$, $[b,1]\to h[h,0]$, $\{[a,2],[e,1],[h,0]\}\to i$,
$[e,2]\to j$.

Positive data from G is, for instance, {*bcefijhi, bcecdijhi, bcdhi, acefijgi, bcdhi, acececefijijijgi, ...*}. Fig. 8 shows the transition of dimker(M_t), the number of appeared terminal symbols $|\Sigma_t|$ and the number of compatible shapes for t sentences from some positive data.
We assumed that $\dim\ker(G) \leq 5$. When dimker(M_t) is less than 5, candidates of possible shapes are enumerated.

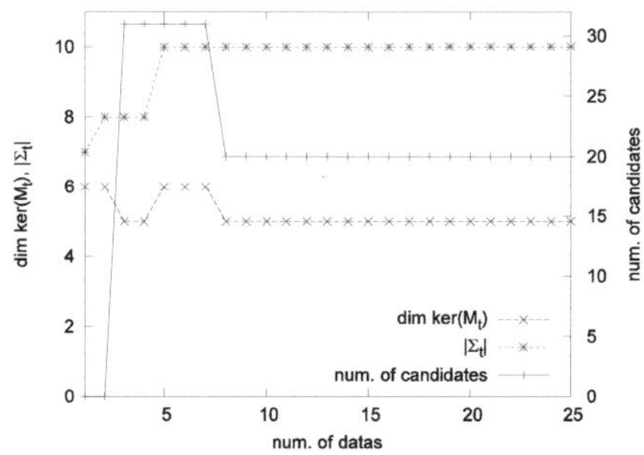

Fig. 8. dimker(M_t) and the number of candidates for possible shapes

After 100 sentences were input, the algorithm output the grammar *H* whose rules are

$S \to a[a,0][a,1]$, $S \to b[b,0][b,1]$, $\{[a,0],[b,0],[e,0]\} \to c[c,0]$,
$\{[a,2],[c,0]\} \to d$, $[c,0] \to e[e,0][e,1][e,2]$, $[e,0] \to f$,
$[a,1] \to g[g,0]$, $[b,1] \to h[h,0]$, $\{[e,1],[g,0],[h,0]\} \to i$,
$[e,2] \to j$.

L(G)=L(H) although *G* and *H* have different shapes. While there are 15 candidates for possible shape, recall that all of them do not give the same minimal language. The ambiguity of *G* is usually less than it. In this case, the ambiguity of *G* is 4.

6.2 An experiment for RSG-QL

Finally, as an experiment for RSG-QL, we consider the problem of maximizing total reword in a maze (Fig. 9).
A robot starts from the position st=(1,2) on the map of Fig. 9 and moves towards the goal gl=(9,2). The robot observes the position where it is. The robot can take four kinds of actions, left, right, up or down. The robot is given a reward -1 per single step.

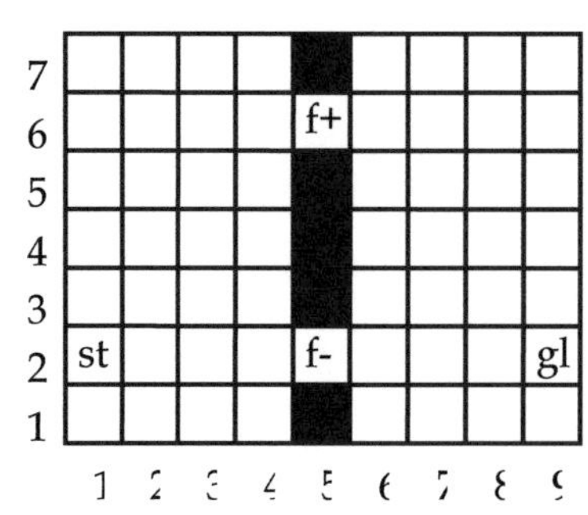

Fig. 9. The map of the maze.

The difference from ordinary maze problems is the way to give reward after the goal. The robot is allowed to occupy a location either f+=(5,6) or f-=(5,2) at most once. If the robot arrives at the goal, the robot is given two different kinds of reward that depend on its path. If the robot has passed through f+, it observes h+ with probability 0.9 and h- with 0.1. On the other hand, if the robot has passed through f-, it observes h+ with 0.1 and h- with 0.9. The reward corresponding to observation of h+ is 100, and of h- is 50. So, the best action of the robot is to pass through f+.
Formally, the RSG G=<V,Σ,R,S> representing the environment is written as follows.

$$\Sigma = \mathrm{MAP} \cup \{\mathrm{h+}, \mathrm{h-}\}.$$

$$V = \{[a,0] \mid a \in \mathrm{MAP},\ a \neq \mathrm{gl}\} \cup \{[\mathrm{f+},0], [\mathrm{f-},0], S\}.$$

$$\begin{aligned} R = &\{[a,0] \rightarrow b[b,0] \mid a \triangleright b,\ b \neq \mathrm{gl}, \mathrm{f+}, \mathrm{f-}\} \\ &\cup \{[a,0] \rightarrow \mathrm{f+}[\mathrm{f+},0][\mathrm{f+},1] \mid a \triangleright \mathrm{f+}\} \\ &\cup \{[a,0] \rightarrow \mathrm{f-}[\mathrm{f-},0][\mathrm{f-},1] \mid a \triangleright \mathrm{f-}\} \\ &\cup \{[a,0] \rightarrow \mathrm{gl} \mid a \triangleright \mathrm{gl}\} \\ &\cup \{[\mathrm{f+},1] \rightarrow \mathrm{h+},\ [\mathrm{f+},1] \rightarrow \mathrm{h-},\ [\mathrm{f-},1] \rightarrow \mathrm{h+},\ [\mathrm{f-},1] \rightarrow \mathrm{h-},\ S \rightarrow \mathrm{st}[\mathrm{st},0]\}, \end{aligned}$$

where MAP = {(i,j) | (i,j) is a reachable position on the map in Fig. 9}, and $a \triangleright b$ if and only if the robot can move from a to b in one step. $a \triangleright b \triangleright c$ denotes $a \triangleright b$ and $b \triangleright c$. For instance, $(4,6) \triangleright \mathrm{f+} \triangleright (6,6)$, $(6,6) \ntriangleright \mathrm{f+}$ and $\mathrm{gl} \ntriangleright$ anywhere.
There is another H=<V',Σ,R',S> such that $L(G) = L(H)$, where V' and R' are as follows.

$$V' = \{[a,0] \mid a \in \mathrm{MAP}\} \cup \{S\}.$$

$$\begin{aligned} R' = &\{[a,0] \rightarrow b[b,0] \mid a \triangleright b\} \\ &\cup \{[\mathrm{gl},0] \rightarrow \mathrm{h+},\ [\mathrm{gl},0] \rightarrow \mathrm{h-},\ S \rightarrow \mathrm{st}[\mathrm{st},0]\}. \end{aligned}$$

Fig.10 shows the shapes of G and H for gl, f+ and f-. the RSG-DP based on G cannot identified with any finite-state MDP, while the one on H is identified with an episodic finite-state MDP.

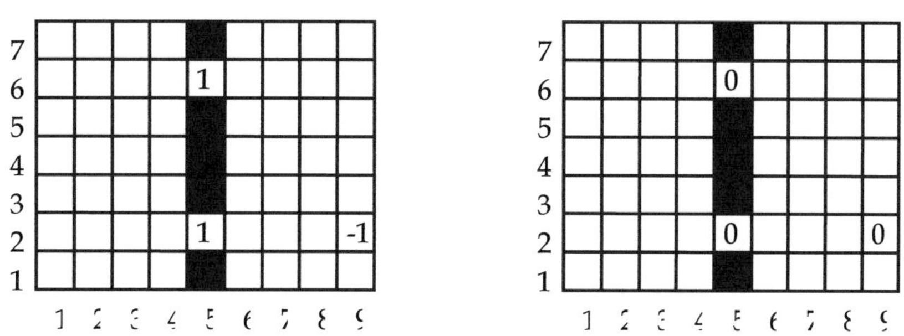

Fig. 10. (Left) The shape of G (Right) The shape of H

G and H are all the RSGs in canonical form whose languages are equivalent to $L(G)$. Thus both G and H, and only G and H are enumerated by the learning algorithm for RSGs from positive data.
The USG G^*=<V^*,Σ,R^*,S> which is the result of unifyRSG(G,H), i.e. the algorithm in Fig. 6, is as follows.

$$V^* = \{[a,0] \mid a \in \mathrm{WEST}\} \cup \{[a,0]+,[a,0]- \mid a \in \mathrm{EAST}\} \cup \{[\mathrm{f}+,0]+,[\mathrm{f}-,0]+,[\mathrm{f}+,0]-,[\mathrm{f}-,0]-,S\}.$$

$$\begin{aligned} R^* = & \{[a,0] \to b[b,0] \mid a \rhd \mathrm{b},\ b \in \mathrm{WEST}\} \\ & \cup \{[a,0]+ \to b[b,0]+,\ [a,0]- \to b[b,0]- \mid a \rhd \mathrm{b}, b \in \mathrm{EAST}\} \\ & \cup \{[a,0]+ \to \mathrm{gl}[\mathrm{f}+,1],\ [a,0]- \to \mathrm{gl}[\mathrm{f}-,1] \mid a \rhd \mathrm{gl}\} \\ & \cup \{(4,6) \to \mathrm{f}+[\mathrm{f}+,0]+,\ (4,2) \to \mathrm{f}-[\mathrm{f}-,0]-\} \\ & \cup \{[\mathrm{f}+,1] \to \mathrm{h}+,\ [\mathrm{f}+,1] \to \mathrm{h}-,\ [\mathrm{f}-,1] \to \mathrm{h}+,\ [\mathrm{f}-,1] \to \mathrm{h}-,\ S \to \mathrm{st}[\mathrm{st},0]\}, \end{aligned}$$

where WEST denotes the left half of MAP, that is, $\{(i,j) \in \mathrm{MAP} \mid i \le 4\}$, and EAST denotes the right half of MAP, that is, $\{(i,j) \in \mathrm{MAP} \mid i \ge 6\}$.

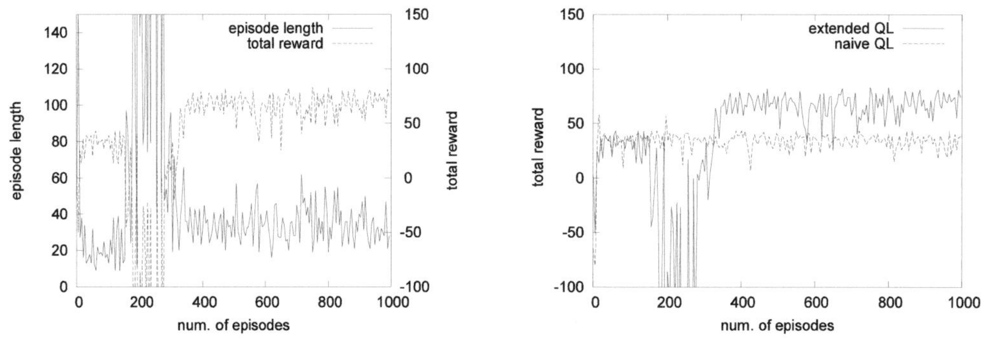

Fig.11. (Left) Total reward and episode length of RSG-QL, (Right) Comparison of naive QL and RSG-QL

Note that G^* is not an RSG. Because the SG-DP based on G^* is not an RSG-DP, it is not identified with any episodic finite-state MDP.

The optimal length of episode of this problem is 16 when the robot passes f+, and thus the maximum total reward is 79. The left side of Fig. 11 shows a result of the experiment of the SG-QL algorithm in Fig. 7 on the above maze problem. The algorithm converges to one USG as the basis of the environment at approximately the 200th episode. The result demonstrates that the robot approaches the optimal path and obtains maximum total reward after the completion of the inference. In the right side of Fig. 11, our method is compared to the naive Q-Learning method, in which the environment is assumed to be an episodic finite MDP (the same thing as *H*). The total reward obtained by the naive Q-Learning method is approximately 40, indicating that the robot is passing through f- and failing to maximize total reward.

7. Conclusion

In this chapter, we presented two new notions. One is an extension of episodic finite-state MDPs from the point of view of grammatical formalism. We can extend well-known methods of reinforcement learning and apply them to this extension easily. The other is the probabilistic generalities of grammars and unifiability of them. This notion plays an important role to apply the recent results of grammatical inference area. The difficulty with applying them is the need of consideration for the probabilistic generality of grammars. The reason is that, if the languages of two grammars are equivalent, it is not necessary that the generalities of them are also equivalent. We presented the idea of unifiability and a method to unify grammars in some grammar class to overcome the difficulty.

Episodic finite-state MDPs can be extended by using the class of SGs and its subclasses; VSG, RSG, USG and SG itself. Although the class of SG-DPs is enough large to contain all episodic finite-state MDPs, the class of SGs is neither learnable from positive data nor unifiable. The class of VSGs is efficiently learnable in the limit from positive data, but the class of VSG-DPs does not include the class of episodic finite-state MDPs. The class of USG-DPs contains all episodic finite-state MDPs and the class of USGs is unifiable, but no efficient learning algorithm for it is known yet. In the four subclasses of simple grammars, the class of RSGs is the only class that satisfies efficient learnability and unifiablity and contains all episodic finite-state MDPs at the same time. The class of RSGs is not unifiable within itself, but it is unifiable within the class of USGs.

Finally, we presented the method RSG-QL for RSG-DPs, combining the extended Q-learning with the learning algorithm and the unification algorithm. Using a maximize-reward problem in a simple maze, we demonstrated that RSG-QL learns the best answer, but the naive QL does not, when the environment is regarded as an RSG-DP. The advantage of RSG-QL is that it is applicable for the wider class of environment with requiring no prior knowledge except that the environment is regarded as an RSG-DP. On the other hand, RSG-QL requires the environment to be precisely identified with some RSG-DP, otherwise the learning algorithm for RSGs from positive data does not work well. In future work, it is required to find algorithms that are stronger for errors. That might be established by using statistical learning methods for grammatical inferences.

8. References

Angluin, D. (1980). Inductive inference of formal languages from positive data, *Information and Control 45,* pp.117-135.

Angluin, D. (1982). Inference of reversible languages, *Journal of the Association for Computing Machinery 29,* pp. 741-765.

Barto, A. G. & Mahadevan, S. (2003). Recent advances in hierarchical reinforcement learning, *Discrete Event Dynamic Systems: Theory and Applications 13,* pp.41-77.

Bertsekas, D. P. & Tsitsiklis, J. N. (1996). *Neuro-dynamic Programming,* Athena Scientific, Sec. 5.6.

Gold, E. M. (1967). Language identification in the limit, *Information and Control 10-5,* pp.447-474.

Hirshfeld, Y., Jerrum, M. & Moller, F. (1996). A polynomial algorithm for deciding bisimilarity of normed context-free processes, *Theoretical Computer Science 158,* pp. 143-159.

Kobayashi, S. (2000). Iterated transductions and efficient learning from positive data: A unifying view, *Proceedings of the 5th International Colloquium on Grammatical Inference, Lecture Notes in Computer Science 1891,* pp. 157-170.

Kaelbling, L. P. , Littman, M. L. & Cassandra, A. R. (1998). Planning and acting in partially observable stochastic domains, *Artificial Intelligence 101* pp.99-134.

Sakakibara, Y. (1997). Recent advances of grammatical inference. *Theoretical Computer Science 185,* pp. 15-45.

Shibata, T., Yoshinaka, R. & Chikayama, T. (2006). Probabilistic Generalization of Simple Grammars and Its Application to Reinforcement Learning, *Proceedings of the 17th International Conference on Algorithmic Learning Theory, Lecture Notes in Computer Science 4264*, pp.348-362.

Sutton, R. S. & Barto, A. G. (1998). *Reinforcement Learning: An Introduction,* MIT Press

Wakatsuki, M., Teraguchi, K. & Tomita, E. (2004). Polynomial time identification of strict deterministic restricted one-counter automata in some class from positive data, *Proceedings of the 7th International Colloquium on Grammatical Inference, Lecture Notes in Computer Science 3264* pp.260-272.

Wetherell, C. S. (1980). Probabilistic languages: A review and some open questions, *Computing Surveys 12-4,* pp.361-379.

Yokomori, T. (2003). Polynomial-time identification of very simple grammars from positive data, *Theoretical Computer Science 298*, pp.179-206.

Yokomori, T. (2007). Polynomial-time identification of very simple grammars from positive data, Theoretical Computer Science 377(1-3), pp.282-283.

Yoshinaka, R. (2006). Polynomial-Time Identification of an Extension of Very Simple Grammars from Positive Data, *Proceedings of the 8th International Colloquium on Grammatical Inference, Lecture Notes in Computer Science 4201*, pp.45-58.

6

Interaction Between the Spatio-Temporal Learning Rule (Non Hebbian) and Hebbian in Single Cells: A Cellular Mechanism of Reinforcement Learning

Minoru Tsukada
Tamagawa University
Japan

1. Long term potentiation(LTP), depression(LTD) and Hebbian type learning rule

Hebb (1949) formulated the idea that modification is strengthened only if the pre- and post-synaptic elements are activated simultaneously (Fig.1). Experimentally, long term potentiation (LTP) and long term depression (LTD) are generally considered to be the cellular basis of learning and memory. Bliss & Lømo (1973) first found that high- frequency electrical stimulation ("tetanus," 100-500 Hz) effectively produced LTP in the hippocampal

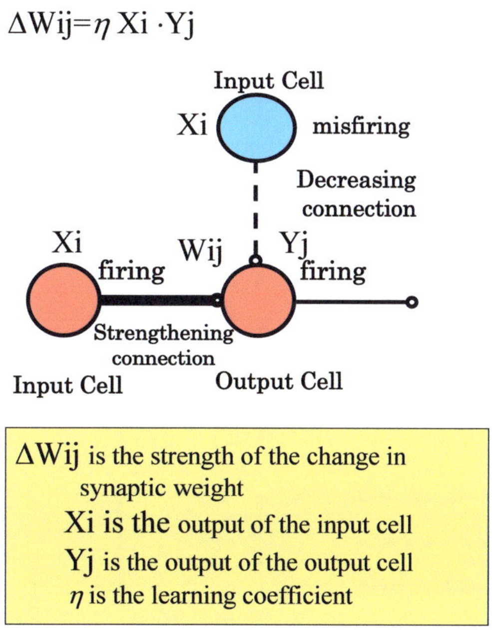

Fig. 1. The Hebbian Learning Rule

CA1 pyramidal cells. Recently, a series of experiments provided direct empirical evidence of Hebb's proposal (Markram et al., 1997; Magee & Johnston, 1997; Zhang et al., 1998; Feldman, 2000; Boettiger & Doupe, 2001; Sjostrom, 2001; Froemke & Dan, 2002). These reports indicated that synaptic modification can be induced by repetitive pairing of EPSP and back-propagating action potentials (BAPs). Pre-synaptic spiking within tens of milliseconds before postsynaptic spiking induced LTP whereas the reverse order resulted in LTD. This spike-timing-dependent LTP/LTD has been confirmed by using pyramidal cell pairs in hippocampal cultures, in which they found an asymmetric profile of LTP and LTD in relation to the relative timing between EPSPs and BAPs (Debanne & Thompson, 1998; Bi & Poo, 1998).

The influence of location dependency of synaptic modification along dendritic trees was examined in the CA1 area of rat hippocampal slices (Tsukada et al., 2005). A pair of electrical pulses was used to stimulate the Schaffer-commissural collaterals (SC) and stratum oriens (SO). Then we estimated the profile of LTP and LTD at a layer specific location from the proximal to distal region of the stratum radiatum.

Figure 2 shows the optical imaging results of LTP and LTD induced by a series of different spike timing (τ). The widest and strongest LTP was observed when simultaneous stimuli (τ= 0 ms) were applied. LTP decreased rapidly in space and time as the absolute value of relative timing increased to 15 ms on both sides. Accordingly, LTP was induced when back-propagating spikes (*Stim B*) were applied within a time window of 15 ms before and after the onset of *Stim A*, whereas LTD was induced on both sides at |τ| = 20 ms. Outside the 50 ms time window, synaptic modification disappeared. These instances of LTP and LTD showed a globally symmetric window of spike timing similar to a "Mexican hat function."

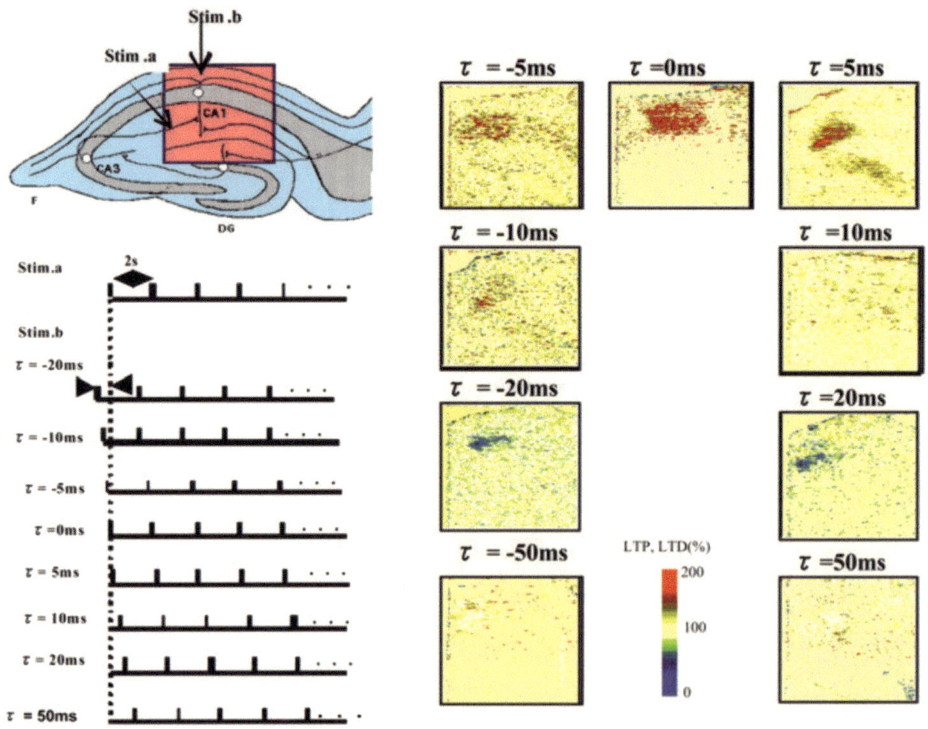

Fig. 2. Input-Output Timing Dependent LTP/LTD

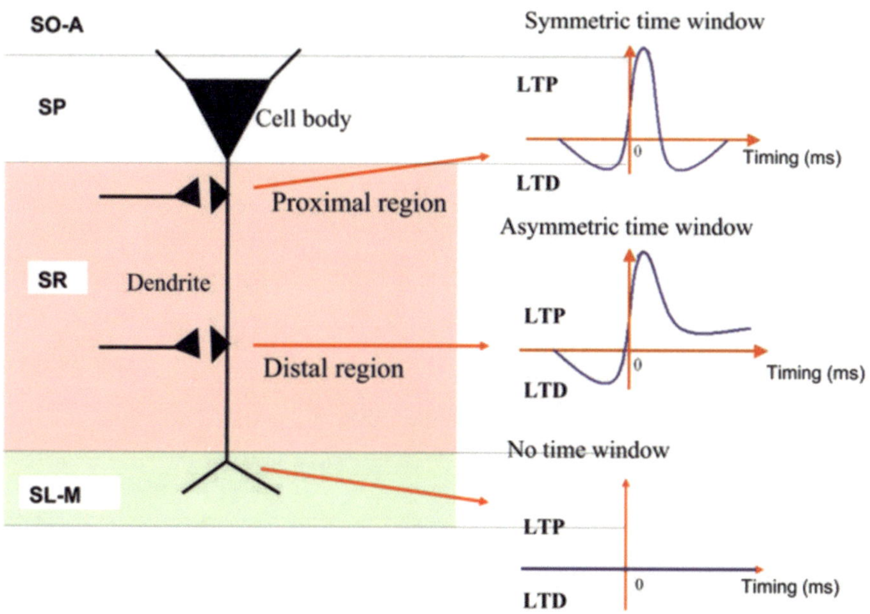

Fig. 3. Layer-specific profiles of LTP and LTD

We tested the location dependence of synaptic modification along dendritic trees. A symmetric window was obtained at the proximal region of the SR where GABAergic interneurons are projected, while an asymmetric window was obtained at the distal region of the SR where there is no projection of GABAergic interneurons (Fig 3).

The region-specific profiles of LTP/LTD depend on the network with or without the inhibitory projection on the layer of SR. Two factors of "after hyperpolarization" of spikes and "region-specific projection of inhibitory interneurons", which organize "lateral inhibition" for timing τ, underlie the "symmetric" profile for timing τ, while one factor of "after hyperpolarization" of spikes serves to organize the "asymmetric" profile. The "symmetric" profile, with a sharp window for τ, works as a coincidence detector between the input of CA3 Shaffer collaterals and the output of CA1 pyramidal cells. The time window corresponds to the time interval of a gamma cycle under the assumption that sequence information is processed in a time scheme of several gamma cycles (local) in a theta cycle (global) (Lisman, 1989; Aihara et al., 2000). On the other hand, the "asymmetric" profile, with a broad time window after τ= 0 ms, is able to integrate sequence information ("temporal summation") or to code phase information. This difference between the distal region and the proximal region of SR was seen in the results of temporal-pattern-dependent LTP using optical imaging of CA1 area in hippocampal slices (Aihara et al., 1997; Aihara et al., 2005). The sensitivity of LTP to the temporal pattern is even higher in the distal region than in the proximal region (Aihara et al., 2005). These results suggest an important function of memory processing depending on the synaptic localization on dendrites of CA1 pyramidal cells.

2. Spatio-temporal learning rule (non Hebbian)

The spatiotemporal learning rule (STLR), proposed as a non-Hebbian type by Tsukada et al. (1996) consisted of two defining factors: (a) cooperative plasticity (Input-Input timing coincidence) without a postsynaptic spike and (b) temporal summation (Fig 4).

Cooperative activity

$$\Delta W_{ij}(t) = \eta \cdot h\left(\sum_{m=0}^{n} I_{ij}(t_m) e^{-\lambda_2(t-t_{n-m})} - \theta\right)$$

Time history

$$I_{ij}(t) = w_{ij}(t)x_i(t)\sum_{k\neq i}\left(w_{kj}(t)x_k(t)\right)$$:Cooperative activity

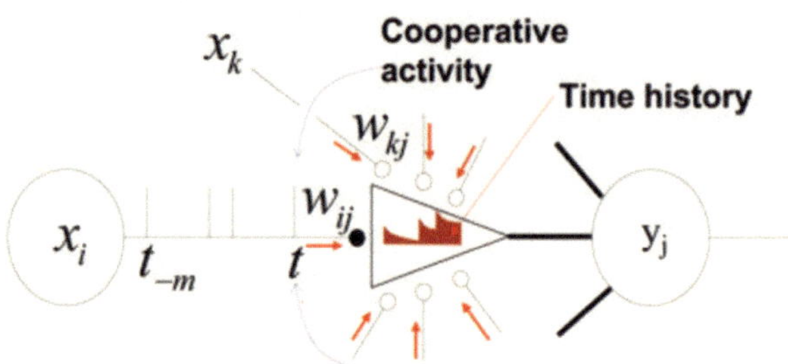

Fig. 4. Spatio-Temporal Learning Rule (STLR)

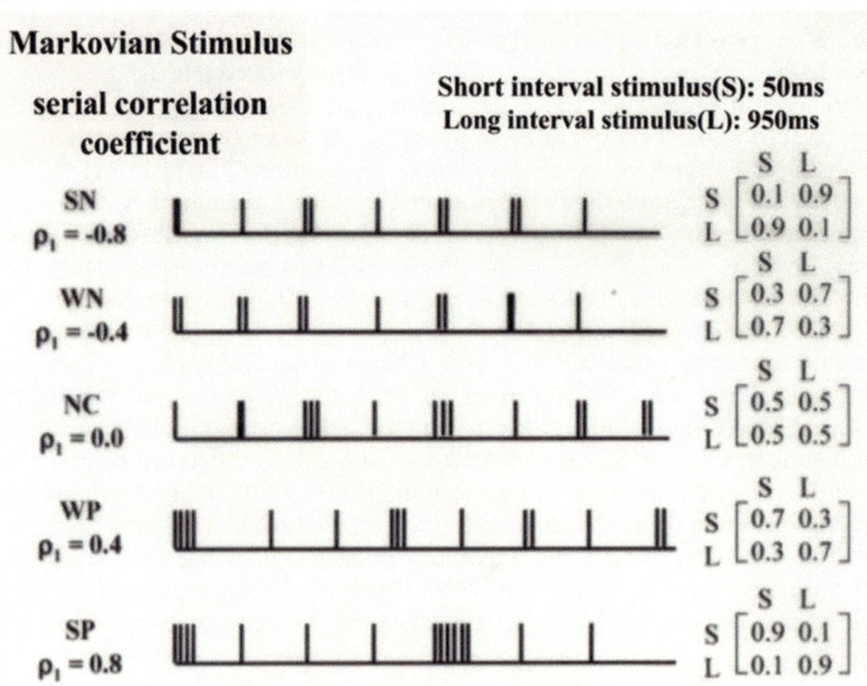

Fig. 5a. Temporal Pattern Stimuli

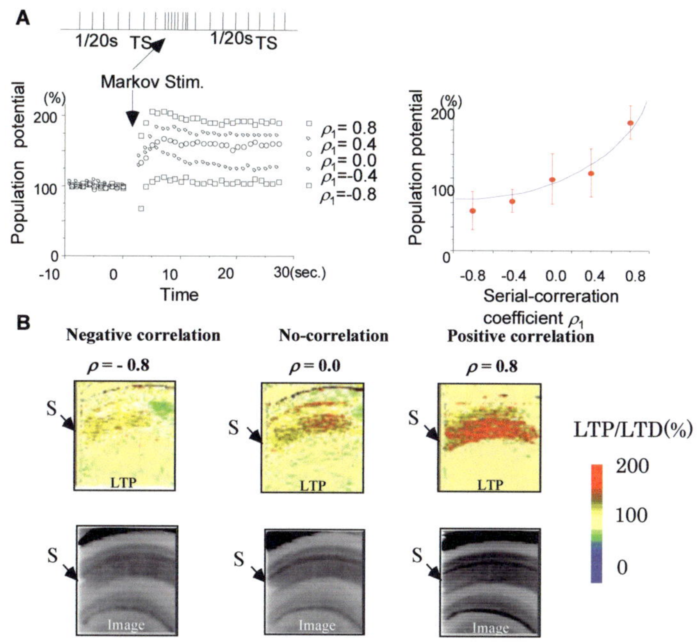

Fig. 5b. Temporal Sequence Pattern Dependent LTP/LTD - Effects of Markov Chain Stimulus -

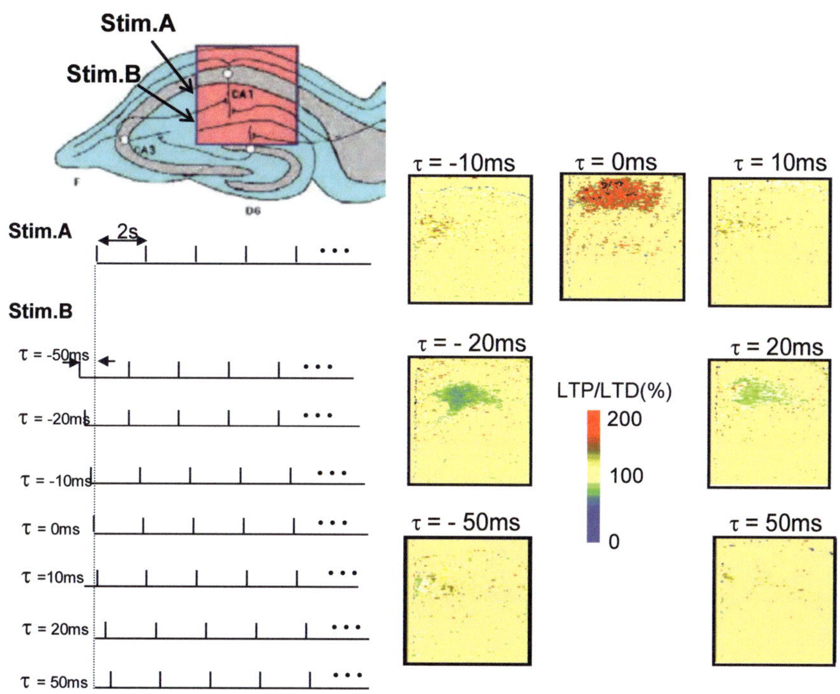

Fig. 6. Input-Input Timing-Dependent LTP/LTD

The neurophysiological evidence of "temporal summation" was obtained by applying temporal stimuli (Markov chain stimuli) to Schaffer collaterals of CA3 (Tsukada et al., 1994; 1996; Aihara et al., 2000) (Fig 5a,b). The cooperative plasticity (Fig 6) was measured by using two stimulus electrodes to stimulate the Schaffer-commissural collaterals (SC). First, electrode A was stimulated at 2 s intervals, but this did not produce any change in the synapse. Electrode B was then stimulated at a range of -50ms to 50ms with respect to electrode A. When the stimuli from both electrodes were simultaneous (relative timing $\tau=0$), an extremely large plasticity appeared, but when it was shifted by 10 ms, there was almost no activity, and if it shifted another 10 ms, LTD appeared instead of LTP. When the relative timing was shifted 50 ms, it returned to normal. These data show that a time window exists in response to the relative timing τ. That is, the existence of a Mexican hat-shaped time window at the range of $\tau=\pm50$ms. The coincidence of spike timing of Schaffer-collateral-paired stimulation of CA3 played a crucial role in inducing associative LTP (Tsukada et al., 2007). However it remains to be clarified whether the associative LTP is independent of back-propagated action potentials (BAPs) or not.

Only local dendritic depolarization at synaptic sites, such as theta-burst stimulation, can induce homosynaptic LTP evoked in the conditioning pathway by application of the associative pairing protocols to Schaffer collaterals even in the absence of BAP (in the presence of low TTX) (Golding et al., 2002). Robust homosynaptically induced LTP is observed in both the absence and presence of low TTX in the conditioning pathway (Fig.7a ; Tsukada et al., 2007). These results suggest that homosynaptic LTP by the present pairing protocol is induced under the condition of inhibiting activation of dendritic Na^+ channels.

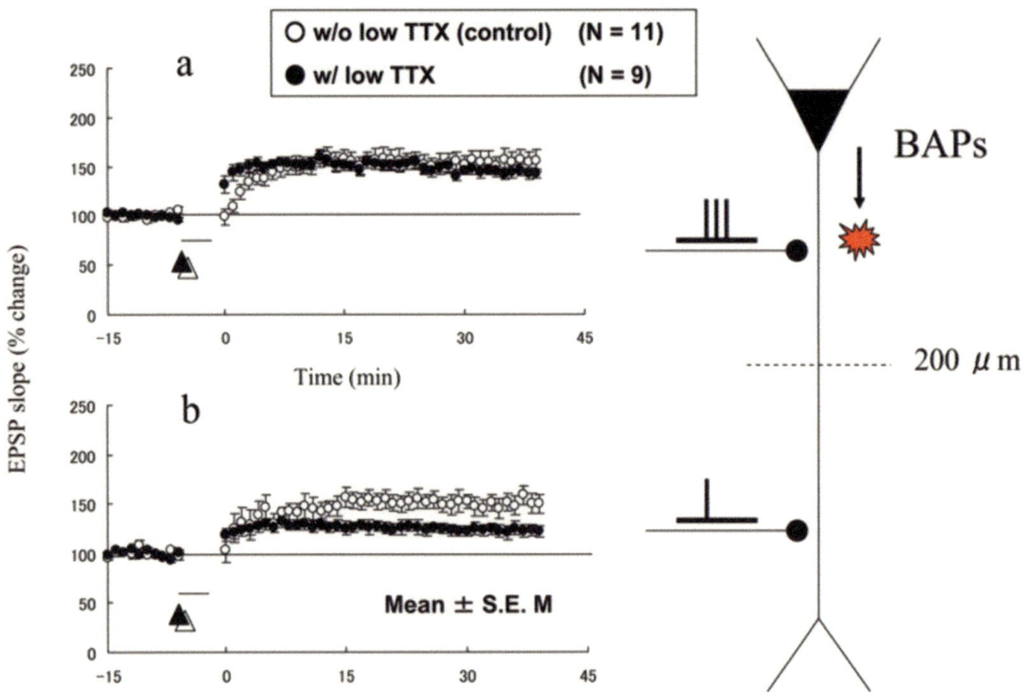

Fig. 7a/b. Input-input timing-dependent LTP can be induced independent of backpropagating action potentials (BAPs)

However, in the same preparation, the magnitude of the heterosynaptically induced LTP in association with conditioning bursts is reduced, while a considerable amount of the LTP was preserved in the presence of low TTX (Fig.7b). Homo-synaptic and hetero-synaptic associative LTP can be induced under conditions of inhibited BAPs, even in the absence of a cell spike. If the two inputs synchronize at the dendritic synapse of CA1 pyramidal cells, then the synapse is strengthened, and the functional connection is organized on the dendrite. If the two inputs are asynchronous then the connection is weakened. A schematic representation was drawn in Fig.8. The functional connection/disconnection depends on the input-input timing dependent LTP (cooperative plasticity). This is different from the Hebbian learning rule, which requires coactivity of pre- and post-cell. However, the magnitude LTP is also influenced by BAPs. From these experimental results, it can be concluded that the two learning rules, STLR and HEBB, coexist in single pyramidal neurons of the hippocampal CA1 area.

STLR (non-Hebbian) incorporates two dynamic processes: fast (10 to 30 ms) and slow (150 to 250 ms). The fast process works as a time window to detect spatial coincidence among various inputs projected to a weight space of the hippocampal CA1 dendrites, while the slow process works as a temporal integrator of a sequence of events. In a previous paper in which parameters were fitted to the physiological data of LTP's time scale (Aihara et al., 2000), the decay constant of fast dynamics was identified as 17 ms, which matches with the period of hippocampal gamma oscillation. The decay constant of the slow process is 169 ms, which corresponds to a theta rhythm. This suggests that cell assemblies are synchronized at two time scales in the hippocampal- cortical memory system, and this is closely related to the memory formation of spatio-temporal context.

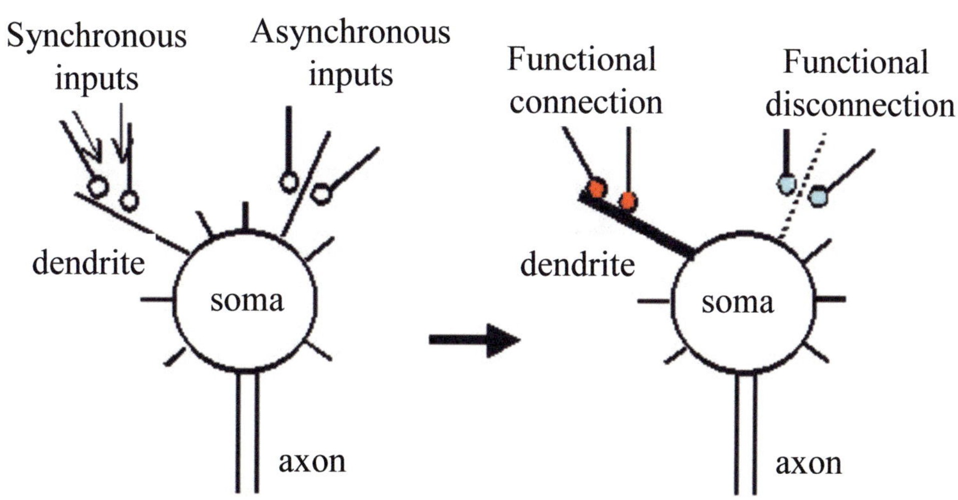

Fig. 8. A schematic presentation of synaptic potentiation or depression by the synchronous or asynchronous inputs

3. The functional differences between STLR and HEBB

Two rules are applied to a single-layered feed-forward network with random connections (Fig 9a) and their abilities to separate spatiotemporal patterns are compared with those of other rules, including the Hebbian learning rule and its extended rules (Tsukada & Pan, 2005). The elements of input patterns are connected to each neuron through a separate weight w_{ij} (i =1,2,...,N, j =1,2, ...,N). The potential of each neuron depends both on a weighted sum of the simultaneously provided inputs (spatial summation) and inputs arrived in the near past (temporal summation).
The above mentioned functions are expressed in the following equations.

Spatial summation:

$$p_i(t_n) = \sum_{j=1}^{N} w_{ij}(t_n)x_j(t_n) \tag{1}$$

Temporal summation:

$$y_i(t_n) = \sum_{m=0}^{n} p_i(t_m)e^{-\lambda_1(t_n - t_m)} \tag{2}$$

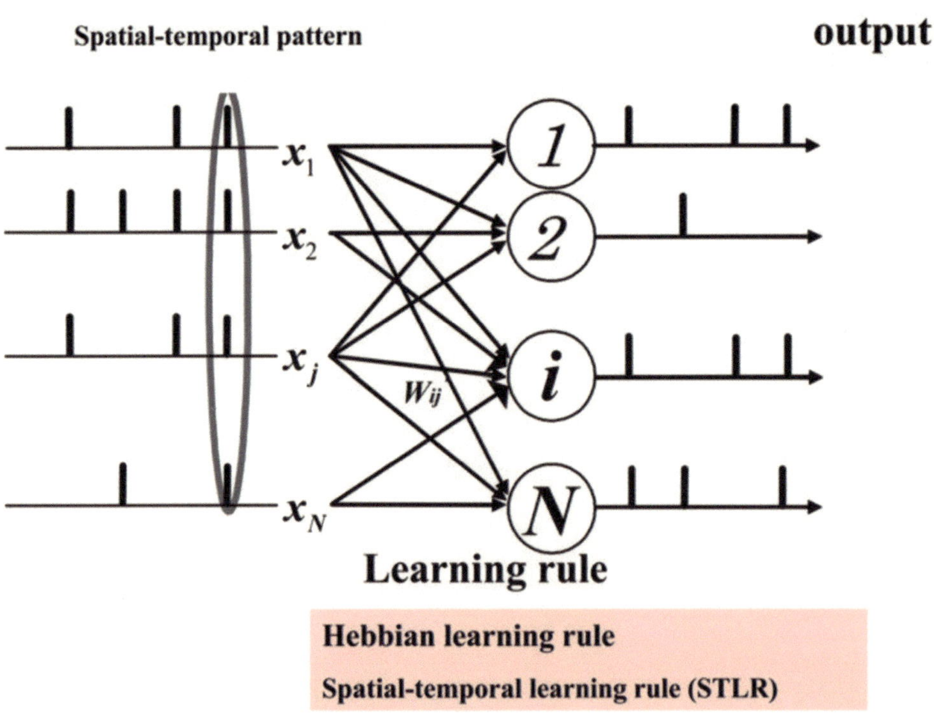

Fig. 9a. All Connected 1 Layer Neural Network

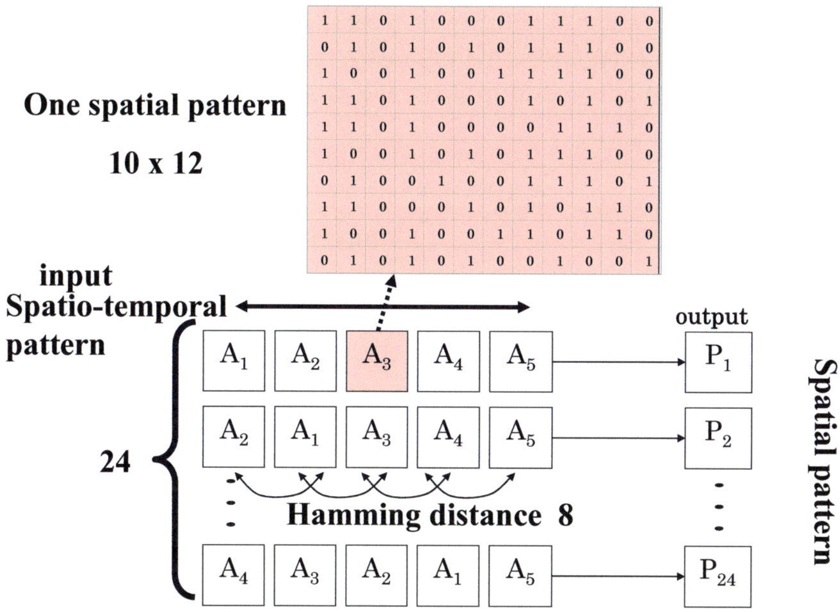

Fig. 9b. The Spatio-Temporal Pattern of Inputs

And the output of the neuron:

$$r_i(t_n) = f(y_i(t_i) - \theta_1) \tag{3}$$

where a set of label x_1, x_2, ..., x_N are inputs to neurons, $x_i(t_n)$ is an input to i neuron at time t_n (n=1,2, ..., n), $w_{ij}(t_n)$ is a synaptic weight from neuron j to neuron i at time t_n, $y_i(t_n)$ is the potential of neuron i at time t_n. $r_i(t_n)$ is its output, λ_1 is time decay constant of temporal summation, θ_1 is threshold. The output function of neurons is defined as:

$$f(u) = \begin{cases} 1 & u > 0 \\ 0 & u \le 0 \end{cases} \tag{4}$$

The spatiotemporal pattern used in this simulation consists of 5 frames of spatial patterns (Fig. 9b), i.e., A_1, A_2, A_3, A_4, A_5 (A_i is a spatial frame).

Every frame consists of N elements (N=120) and each element is chosen as "1" or "0" randomly, but the total number of "1"s is maintained throughout the various spatial patterns (in this simulation, half of the elements in one spatial frame are "1", and the other half are "0"). The Hamming distance (HD) between every two spatial patterns is 8 bits (if not specified in the simulation). In some cases it is 2 or 24 bits (mentioned). Calculating all of the permutations of 4 spatial patterns, 24 spatiotemporal patterns were grouped as a training set. The last frame of each spatiotemporal pattern is the same (A_5). During the learning process, the 24 spatiotemporal patterns in the training set were learned by each neural network under the same initial conditions. After finishing the learning course, a test pattern (same as the learned pattern) was applied to the networks to attain an output-pattern (for each learning rule, the threshold of neurons θ_1 is set so that about half of the elements in the output-pattern are "1"). We compared HDs between output-patterns for each learning rule. The averaged HD is often adopted to compare the ability of discriminating spatiotemporal patterns, which is defined as:

$$\text{averaged HD} = \frac{\sum(\text{number of pairs} * \text{HD of this pair})}{\sum \text{number of pairs}}$$

Three learning algorithms were used to train each of 24 spatiotemporal input patterns in single-layer neural network models. Each of the neural networks had the same initial condition. The differentiation of output-patterns represented in learned networks was analyzed by their Hamming distances (Fig.10a). HEBB produced the same output pattern, with a Hamming distance of zero, for all of the different spatiotemporal input patterns (Fig. 10a). This proves that the Hebbian learning rule cannot discriminate different spatiotemporal input patterns. Covariant Hebbian rule showed a slight improvement in their pattern separation ability (Fig.10a). The spatiotemporal learning rule had the highest efficiency in discriminating spatiotemporal pattern sequences (Fig.10a). The novel features of this learning rule were induction of cooperative plasticity without a postsynaptic spike and the time history of its input sequences. According to the Hebbian rule, connections strengthen only if the pre- and post-synaptic elements are activated simultaneously, and thus, the Hebbian rule tends to map all of the spatio-temporal input patterns with identical firing rates into one output pattern. HEBB has a natural tendency to attract analogous firing patterns into a representative one, in the simple word "pattern completion". In contrast, the spatio-temporal rule produces different output patterns depending on each individual input pattern. From this, the spatiotemporal learning rule has a high ability in pattern separation, while the Hebbian rule has a high ability in pattern completion. Finally, the network trained by the spatiotemporal learning rule produced the widest bimodal-distribution of Hamming distance (Fig10b), which shows that it has the highest efficiency in pattern separation.

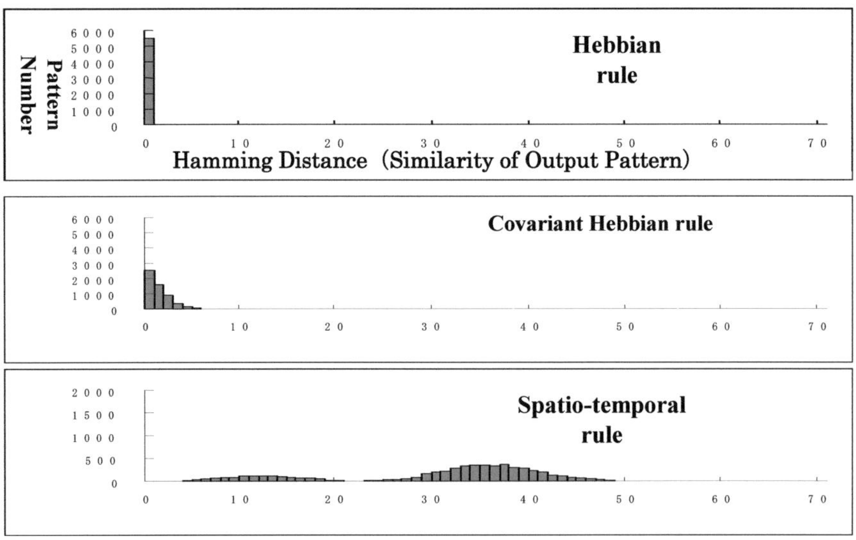

Fig. 10a. Output Pattern Distribution

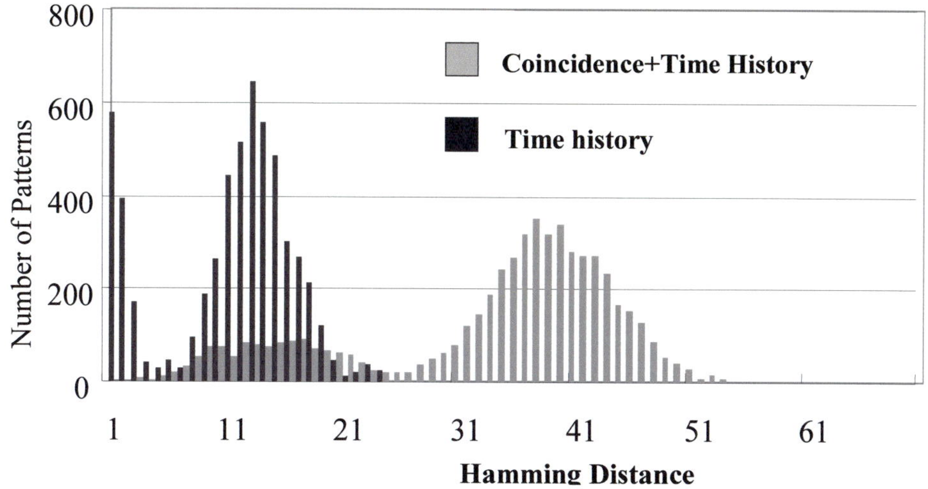

Fig. 10b. The Effect of Input Timing-Coincidence on Output Distribution

The two factors responsible for the high efficiency in pattern separation are spatial coincidence and temporal summation. The network trained by the learning rule without spatial coincidence produced the one-modal distribution. From this fact, we can conclude that the distribution in the longer range of the bimodal distribution (Fig.10b) in the histogram is generated by the spatial coincidence factor while the distribution in the short range is generated by the spatiotemporal summation. Thus, the ability of separating patterns in the network can be improved by introducing two factors: spatiotemporal summation and spatial coincidence, but the latter is more important.

4. Interaction of both rules in a dendrites-soma system

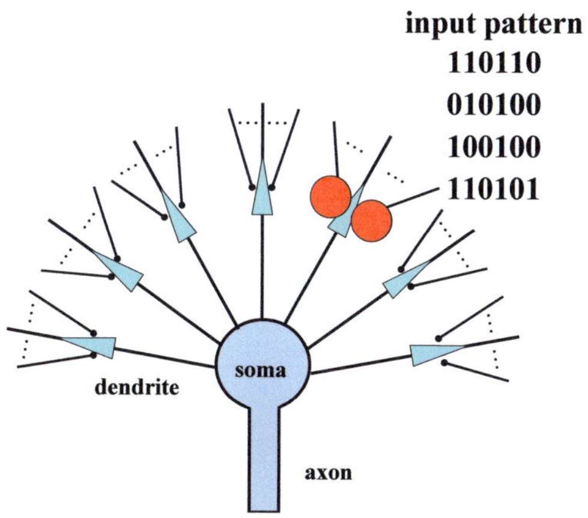

Fig. 11a. The Change in Synaptic weight according to Hebbian Learning Rule

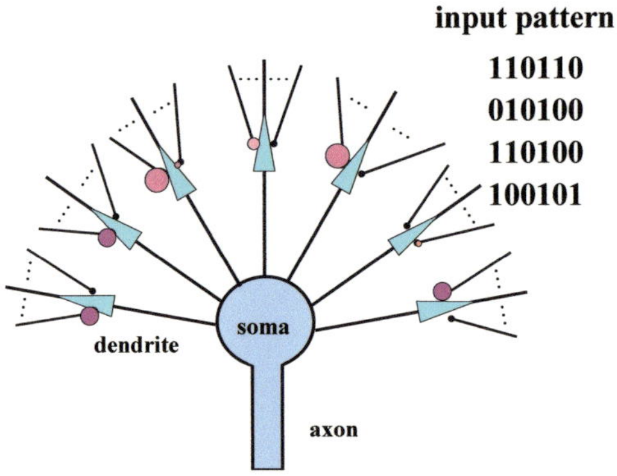

Fig. 11b. The Change in Synaptic Weight according to the Spatio-temporal Learning Rule

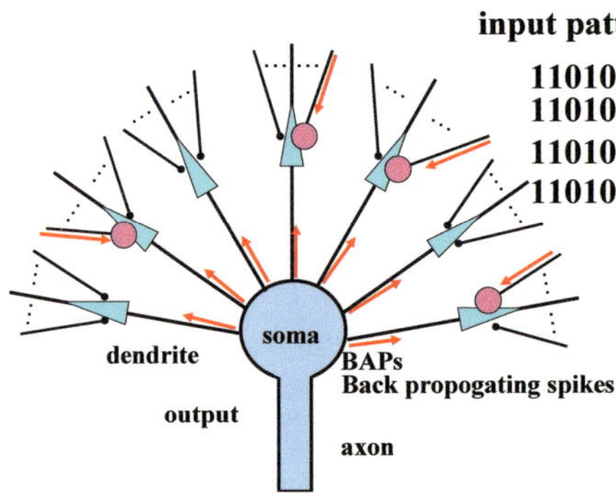

Fig. 11c. The Function of Local (dendrite) -Global (soma) Interaction and the Role of Back Propagating Spikes (BAPs)

The extension of the theoretical simulation results imply that this phenomenon occurs in a dendrites-soma system in a single pyramidal cell with many independent local dendrites in the CA1 area of the hippocampus. This system includes a spine structure, NMDA receptors, and sodium and calcium channels. The pyramidal cell integrates all of these local dendrite functions. The spatiotemporal learning rule and the Hebbian rule coexist in single pyramidal neurons of the hippocampal CA1 area (Tsukada et al., 2007). The Hebbian rule leads to the pattern completion and the spatiotemporal learning rule leads to the pattern separation.

Schematic illustrations were drawn in Figure-11abc. HEBB leads to pattern completion (Fig.11a). In contrast, STLR leads to pattern separation (Fig.11b). In the spatiotemporal learning rule, synaptic weight changes are determined by the "synchrony" level of input neurons and its temporal summation (bottom-up) whereas in the Hebbian rule, the soma fires by integrating dendritic local potentials or by top-down information such as environmental sensitivity, awareness, and consciousness. The coexistence of the spatiotemporal learning rule (local information) and the Hebbian rule (global information) on the neuronal level may support this dynamic process that repeats itself until the internal model fits the external environment (Fig 11c). The dendrite-soma interaction (Fig 11c) in pyramidal neurons of the hippocampal CA1 area can play an important role in the context formation of policy, reward, and value in reinforcement learning.

5. Mechanisms of reinforcement learning in single cells

The role of soma spiking in relation to top-down information raises a number of interesting computational predictions. Hippocampal theta is one of the candidates of top-down information which is driven by the medial septum (Buzsaki et al.,1983). The theta stimulation of adult rat hippocampal synapses can induce LTP (Thomas et al.,1998). Another candidate is extrinsic modulation by acetylcholine, serotonin, norepinephrine and dopamine. They can alter neuronal throughput and BAPs (so-called "meta-plasticity") in such a way that these transmitters diffuse broadly.

6. References

Aihara, T.; Tsukada, M.; Crair, MC. & Sinomoto, S. (1997). Stimulus-Dependent Induction of Long-Term Potentiation in CA1 Area of the Hippocampus: Experiment and Model. *Hippocampus* 7, p.416-426.

Aihara, T.; Tsukada, M. & Matsuda, H. (2000). Two dynamic processes for the induction of long-term in hippocampal CA1 neurons. *Biol. Cybern.* 82: 189-195.

Aihara, T.; Kobayashi, Y. & Tsukada, M. (2005). Spationtemporal visualization of long-term potentiation and depression in the hippocampal CA1 area. *Hippocampus* 15: 68-78.

Bi, G. & Poo, M. (1998). Synaptic modifications in cultured hippocampal neurons; dependence on spike timing, synaptic strength, and postsynaptic type. *J. Neurosci* 18:10464-10472.

Bliss, TP. & Lømo, T. (1973). Long-lasting potentiation of synaptic transmission in the dentate area of the anesthetized rabbit following stimulation of perforant path, *The Journal of Physiology,* 232: 331-356.

Boettiger, CA. & Doupe, AJ. (2001). Developmentally restricted synaptic plasticity in a songbird nucleus required for song learning. *Neuron* 31: 809-818.

Buzsaki, G.; Leung, L. & Vanderwolf, CH. (1983). Celluler bases of hippocampal EEG in the behaving rat. *Brain Res. Rev.* 6: 169-171.

Debanne, D. & Thompson, SM. (1998). Associative long-term depression in the hippocampus in vitro. *Hippocampus* 6:9-16.

Feldman, DE. (2000). Timing based LTP and LTD at vertical inputs to layer II/III pyramidal cells in rat barrel cortex. *Neuron* 27:45-56.

Froemke, RC. & Dan, Y. (2002). Spike-timing-dependent synaptic modification induced by natural spike trains. *Nature* 416:433-438.

Golding, NL.; Staff, NP. & Spruston, N. (2002). Dendritic spikes as a mechanism for cooperative long-term potentiation. *Nature* 418(6895):326-31.

Hebb, DO. (1949). *The organization of behavior.* John Wiley, New York

Lisman, J. (1989). A mechanism for Hebb and the anti-Hebb processes underlying learning and memory. *Proc Natl Acad Sci USA* 86: 9574-9578.

Magee, JC. & Johnston, D. (1997). A synaptically controlled, associative signal for Hebbian plasticity in hippocampal neurons. *Science* 275(5297):209-13.

Markram, H.; Lubke, J.; Frotscher, M. & Sakmann, B.(1997). Reguration of synaptic efficacy by coincidence of postsynaptic Aps and EPSPs. *Science* 275:213-215.

Sjostrome, PJ. (2001). Rate timing, and cooperativity jointly determine cortical synaptic plasticity. *Neuron* 32:1149-1164.

Thomas, MJ.; Watabe, AM.; Moody, TD.; Makhinson, M. & O'Dell, TJ. (1998). Postsynaptic complex spike bursting enables the induction of LTP by theta frequency synaptic stimulation. *J Neurosci* 18(18):7118-26.

Tsukada, M.; Aihara, T.; Mizuro, M.; Kato, H. & Ito, K. (1994). Temporal pattern sensitivity of long-term potentiation in hippocampal CA1 neurons. *Biol. Cybern.* 70: 495-503.

Tsukada, M.; Aihara, T.; Saito, H. & Kato, H. (1996). Hippocampal LTP depends on spatial and temporal correlation of inputs. *Neural Networks* 9: 1357-1365.

Tsukada, M. & Pan, X. (2005). The spatiotemporal learning rule and its efficiency in separating spatiotemporal patterns. *Biol. Cybern.* 92: 139-146.

Tsukada, M.; Aihara, T.; Kobayashi, Y. & Shimazaki H. (2005). Spatial analisis of spike-timing-dependant LTP and LTD in the CA1 area of hippocampal slices using optical imaging. *Hippocampus* 15: 104-109.

Tsukada, M.; Yamazaki, Y. & Kojima, H. (2007). Interaction between the Spatio-Temporal Learning Rule (STLR) and Hebb type (HEBB) in single pyramidal cells in the hippocampal CA1 Area. *Cognitive Neurodynamics* 1: 157-167.

Zhang, LI.; Tao, HW.; Holt, CE.; Harris, WA. & Poo, M. (1998). A critical window for cooperation and competition among developing retino-tectal synapses. *Nature* 395: 37-44.

7

Reinforcement Learning Embedded in Brains and Robots

Cornelius Weber[1], Mark Elshaw[2], Stefan Wermter[3], Jochen Triesch[1] and Christopher Willmot[3]

[1] Frankfurt Institute for Advanced Studies, [2]University of Sheffield, [3]University of Sunderland

[1] Germany, [2,3] UK

1. Introduction

In many ways and in various tasks, computers are able to outperform humans. They can store and retrieve much larger amounts of data or even beat humans at chess. However, when looking at robots they are still far behind even a small child in terms of their performance capabilities. Even a sophisticated robot, such as ASIMO, is limited to mostly pre-programmed behaviours (Weigmann, 2006). The reliance on robots that must be carefully programmed and calibrated before use and thereafter whenever the task changes, is quite unacceptable for robots that have to coexist and cooperate with humans, especially those who are not necessarily knowledgeable about robotics. Therefore there is an increasing need to go beyond robots that are pre-programmed explicitly towards those that learn and are adaptive (Wermter, Weber & Elshaw, 2004; Wermter, Weber, Elshaw, Panchev et al., 2004). Natural, dynamic environments require robots to adapt their behaviour and learn using approaches typically used by animals or humans.

Hence there is a necessity to develop novel methods to provide such robots with the learning ability to deal with human competence. Robots shall learn useful tasks, i.e. tasks in which a goal is reached, if executed successfully. Reinforcement learning (RL) is a powerful method to develop goal-directed action strategies (Sutton & Barto, 1998). In RL, the agent explores a 'state space' which describes his situation within the environment, by taking randomized actions that take him from one state to another. Crucially, a reward is received only at the final goal state, in case of successful completion. Over many trials, the agent learns the value of all states (in terms of reward proximity), and how to get to higher-valued states to reach the goal.

In Section 2 we will review RL in the brain, focusing on the basal ganglia, a group of nuclei in the forebrain implicated in RL.

Section 3 presents algorithms for RL and describes their possible relation to the basal ganglia. In its canonical formulation, RL maps discretely defined states to discrete actions. Its application to robotics is challenging, because sensors, such as a camera, deliver high-dimensional input that does not define a state in a way suitable for most tasks. Furthermore, several actions are to be learnt in different contexts with different reward types being given.

In Section 4 we will address how a neural network performing RL can be embedded in a larger architecture in which other modules follow different processing and learning principles. Taking inspiration from the brain, the sensory cortex may extract meaning from sensory information that may be suitable for defining a state as it is used for RL by the basal ganglia (Weber, Muse, Elshaw & Wermter, 2005). The motor cortex on the other hand may store movement primitives that may lead from one state to the next. Moreover, the basal ganglia might delegate learnt movement primitives to the motor cortex, so to focus on the learning of other, in particular higher-level, actions (Weber, Wermter & Elshaw, 2006).
Section 5 addresses vision, an untypical field for RL. We posit that visual stimuli can act as reinforcers for saccade learning (Weber & Triesch, 2006) and gaze following, leading to the emergence of mirror neuron like representations in motor cortex (Triesch, Jasso & Deák, 2007), and altering neuron properties in visual cortical areas (Roelfsema & Ooyen, 2005; Franz & Triesch, 2007). Together, this encourages a view in which RL acts at the core, while unsupervised learning establishes the interface to a complex world.
Section 6 discusses whether experiments are based on oversimplifying assumptions.

2. Anatomy and physiology

Our focus will be reinforcement learning in the basal ganglia. However, since the basal ganglia's main outputs are inhibitory, and since they are not yet connected in neonates (Humphries, Gurney& Prescott, 2005), there must be more fundamental brain substrates for behaviour/action initiation.

2.1 Reticular formation

The brain's reticular formation (RF) has been proposed as such a device for action selection (Humphries et al., 2005; Kilmer, 1997). The RF's giant neurons receive input from many brainstem nuclei, enabling them to sample from all sensory systems, and their axons bifurcate to project downward to the spinal cord as well as upward to the midbrain, enabling the production of motor behaviour and the control of higher-level brain centers.
The RF contains several specialized circuits. A potent example are the giant neurons in the caudal pontine RF which respond at very short latency to acoustic stimuli, and which are hypothesized to elicit the startle response to a loud and unexpected acoustic stimulus (Lingenhöhl & Friauf, 2004). The paramedian pontine RF is involved in the control of horizontal eye movements, and the midbrain RF in vertical eye movements (Sparks, 2002; Weber & Triesch, 2006).

Model of Behaviour Generation

Kilmer (1997) proposed a "command computer" model of the RF which outputs one behaviour, given as input several vectors of recommended behaviours, originating from several sensory systems. The RF model computes the winning behaviour using a relatively small number of connections and a distributed representation. Humphries et al. (2005) optimized the originally randomized connectivity by a genetic algorithm. In a robotic demonstration involving the behaviours 'wander', 'avoid obstacle' and 'recharge energy', the genetic algorithm augmented the model's behaviour selection from near-chance levels to achieving very long survival times.

The RF is rarely implicated in learning (see Bloch and Laroche (1985) for a counter-example), but rather seems "pre-programmed" at birth. Other brain structures are needed to allow adaptation to beneficial circumstances in the environment.

2.2 Basal ganglia

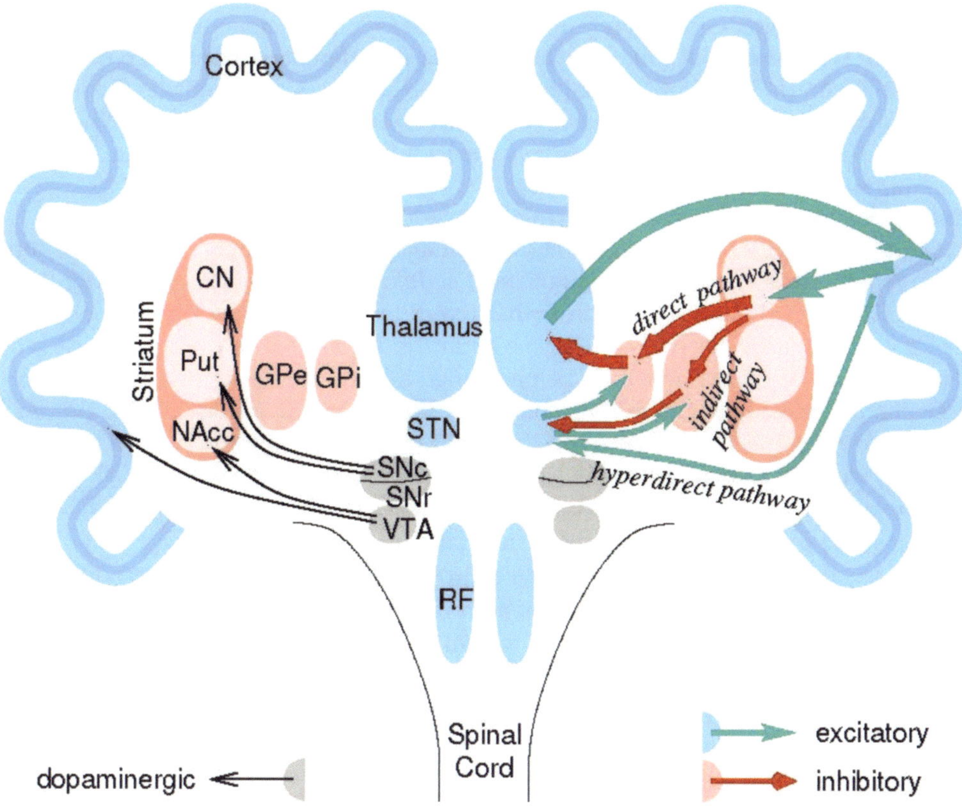

Fig. 1. Selected brain areas and connections. The thick arrows denote the primary basal ganglia (BG) → thalamus → cortex loop. This includes the direct pathway through the BG via striatum and GPi. The indirect and hyperdirect pathways are via STN, GPe and GPi. The SNr has a similar connectivity as the GPi (not shown for simplicity), so one often refers to "GPi/SNr". Dopaminergic nigro-striatal projections from SNc reach the CN and Put which make the dorsal striatum. Meso-limbic projections from VTA reach the NAcc which is part of the ventral striatum. Meso-cortical projections are from VTA to regions in the prefrontal and cingular cortex. Abbreviations: Inside the BG: CN = caudate nucleus; Put = putamen; NAcc = nucleus accumbens; GPe/i Globus pallidus externus/internus; STN = subthalamic nucleus; SNc/r = Substantia nigra pars compacta/reticulata. Outside of the BG: VTA = ventral tegmental area; RF =reticular formation.

Figure 1 shows the relevant areas and their abbreviations related to the basal ganglia (BG). The main input nucleus of the BG is the striatum which receives its main input from motor and prefrontal cortex, but also from intralaminar thalamic nuclei (not shown in Figure). The striatum accounts for approximately 95% of the total neuron population of the BG in the rat (Wood, Humphries & Gurney, 2006). The dorsal striatum (neostriatum) consists of the putamen and the caudate nucleus. The ventral striatum consists of the nucleus accumbens (core and shell) and the olfactory tubercle (not shown in Figure). The principal neurons of the dorsal striatum, the medium spiny neurons, are inhibitory GABAergic projection neurons. They emit collaterals to neighbouring spiny neurons before they project to output stages of the BG, namely to either GPi or SNr (Houk et al., 2007).

According to Shepherd (2004), the cortical and thalamic afferents to the BG have a cruciform axodendritic pattern. This implies that individual axons cross the dendritic fields of many neurons in the neostriatum, but make few synapses with any particular cell (Wilson, 2004). The opposite is also true. Any particular neostriatal neuron can synapse (sparsely) with a large number of afferents.

Optimal Decision Making

Based on the connectivity of the BG, Bogacz and Gurney (2007) propose a model of optimal decision making that implements the statistical *multihypothesis sequential probability ratio test* (MSPRT). The underlying assumption is that the different regions of the cortex each send evidence y_i for a particular decision i to the striatum. A problem of passing this directly to the thalamus is that the action would be performed as soon as the accumulated evidence in a given channel reaches a certain threshold. This is not optimal, because in the presence of noise, a wrong channel could first reach threshold (not to mention the "technical" problem of defining when to start to integrate, as addressed in Stafford and Gurney (2007)). Rather should the difference between the favored channel and the other channels reach a threshold. Mathematically, $y_i - \ln \Sigma_j e^{y_j}$ is better sent to the thalamus.

Bogacz and Gurney (2007) identify the first term y_i with the *direct pathway*: the striatum inhibits the GPi/SNr which then disinhibits a corresponding thalamic region so to perform the action. The positive sign is because the tonically spiking inhibitory GPi/SNr neurons are silenced. The second term $-\ln \Sigma_j e^{y_j}$ represents the *indirect (hyperdirect) pathway*. It has a negative sign because the cortical afferents excite the STN (the only excitatory nucleus of the BG) which then excite the GPi/SNr neurons' inhibitory activity. Diffuse STN → GPi/SNr connections implement the sum over all channels.

This model is minimal in terms of its mechanisms, and encourages additional functionality to be implemented in the same structures. For example, the number of hypotheses y_i in the input is the same as the number of outputs; however, the BG has a much larger input structure (striatum) than output structure (GPi/SNr), which suggests a transformation to take place, such as from a sensory to a motor representation. For example, the GPi/SNr might extract a low-dimensional subspace from the high-dimensional cortical and striatal representations by a principle component analysis (PCA) algorithm (Bar-Gad, Havazelet-Heimer, Goldberg, Ruppin & Bergman, 2000). Learning, not only action selection, becomes important.

Rewards

Dopamine neuron activity in SNc and VTA is known to be correlated with rewards, learning and also with addictive behaviour. Dopamine neurons are active during delivery of an unexpected reward. If a stimulus predicts a future reward, then they will instead become active at the onset of the reward-predicting stimulus (Fiorillo, Tobler & Schultz, 2003). Dopamine neuron firing in the VTA is suppressed by aversive stimuli (Ungless, Magill & Bolam, 2004). These neurons (SNc borders the SNr, an output nucleus of the BG) project dopaminergic axon fibres into the input nuclei (Fischer, 2003): the *nigro-striatal* projection is from the substantia nigra to the dorsal striatum; the *meso-limbic* projection is from the VTA to the ventral striatum; there is also a *meso-cortical* projection from the VTA to prefrontal and cingular cortex (Fig. 1). Consequentially, during the delay period of delayed-response tasks neurons in striatum were found to be selective for the values of individual actions (Samejima, Ueda, Doya & Kimura, 2005), and in orbitofrontal (a part of prefrontal) cortex neural activity represents the value of expected reward (Roesch & Olson, 2004). There may be a finer grain resolution of the reward delivery system, as Wilson (2004) suggests that any local region of the neostriatum may receive its dopaminergic innervation from a relatively small number of dopaminergic neurons.

The concept of a reward is however wider. Unexpected, biologically salient stimuli elicit a short-latency, phasic response in dopaminergic neurons (Dommett, Coizet, Blaha, Martindale & Lefebvre, 2005). If not reinforced, responses to novel stimuli become habituated rapidly, and the responses to rewarding stimuli also decline if stimuli can be predicted.

D1 and D2 Receptors

Dopamine has varying effects on neurons, because different neurons have different dopamine receptors. Lewis and O'Donnell (2000) state "D1 receptors may enhance striatal neuron response to [excitatory] NMDA receptor activation, where as D2 receptors may decrease responses to non-NMDA [e.g. inhibitory] receptors". Vaguely interpreted, D1 supports direct excitatory responses and D2 supports later decisions by limiting inhibition. This correlates with the findings of Hikosaka (2007) who make use of the fact that saccades to highly rewarded positions are initiated earlier than saccades to less rewarded positions. Injections of dopamine D1 receptor antagonist delayed the early, highly rewarded saccades. Injections of D2 antagonist delayed even more the later, less rewarded saccades.

The models of Brown, Bullock and Grossberg (2004) and Hazy, Frank and O'Reilly (2007) (Section 4) feature 'Go' cells which have the D1 receptor and project along the *direct pathway* to facilitate an action, and 'NoGo'/'Stop' cells which have the D2 receptor and which project to the *indirect pathway* to suppress an action.

In addition to facilitating activation, dopamine directly facilitates learning by increasing the number of synaptic receptors (Sun, Zhao & Wolf, 2005). As an example of dopamine-modulated Hebbian learning, Reynolds, Hyland and Wickens (2001) showed that synapses between the cortex and the striatum could be potentiated only with concurrent stimulation of the substantia nigra.

BG-Thalamo-Cortical Loops

The function of the basal ganglia as a learning action selection device makes sense only in the context of its main input, the cortex and its main output, the thalamus. Wilson suggests that the striatum contains a functional re-mapping of the cortex. For example, motor and somatosensory cortical representations of a single body part specifically converge on a particular region of the putamen (Flaherty & Graybiel, 1991), which is implicated in sensory guided movements.The other part of the neostriatum, the caudate nucleus, receives input from more anterior cortical areas and is implicated in memory-guided movement (Houk et al., 2007). Posterior cortical areas (such as the lower visual system) seem to be less connected with the BG. Specificity is preserved throughout the projection target of the BG which are the 50-60 nuclei of the thalamus (Herrero, Barcia & Navarro, 2002) and which project back to specific areas of the cortex.

3. Theory of reinforcement learning

The canonical reinforcement learning network (Sutton & Barto, 1998) has an input layer on which the activity of exactly one unit codes the state s of the agent and an output layer on which the activity of one unit codes the action a the agent is going to choose given the input. Fig. 2. a) shows the architectures of two algorithm classes, TD-learning and SARSA. Input and output layers are termed state and actor in both implementations. A critic may be used only to guide learning. Given a random initial state (position) of the agent within the limited state space, and another state at which a reward r is consistently given, the agent learns to maneuver directly to the rewarded state.

In the case of TD-learning all states are assigned goodness values v that represent the sum of discounted future rewards and are kept by the critic in a lookup table V. A distant reward will be discounted in that it keeps only a proportion, e.g. $\gamma \approx 0.9$, of its original value for each step required to get it. So if the reward r will be reached in n steps, then the current state will be worth $v = r\,\gamma^n$.

Standard reinforcement learning lacks a "working memory" to backtrack recently visited states when a reward is given. Instead, a state value v is updated from the value v' of the neighbor state that is visited in the next step. Since then one step is done, the reward was further away in the previous state, hence $v = \gamma\, v'$. If the reward is given, instead $v = r + \gamma\, v'$. This equation will be inconsistent for neighbouring states during early learning. Step (5) of the algorithm in Fig. 2c) quantifies this error which is then used in steps (6) to update the value v of the previous state. The difference in time between the new estimate $r + \gamma\, v'$ and old estimate v taken in step (6) bestows this class of algorithms the name Temporal Difference (TD) learning.

The actor-critic architecture employs a dedicated neuron, the critic, to encode the expected future reward - or the values v - in its connections V. The connections Q to the actor which encode the action policy are separate[1]. The critic influences the actor update, step (7) in Fig. 2, through its prediction error δ. Vice versa, the current action policy determines which states the agent will visit next, and this feeds back into the update of the critic's value v.

SARSA[2] encodes the value of state-action pairs (s, a) instead of the value of states. It may be implemented with a critic neuron that is connected to all state units and all action units. Fig. 2, right, shows an implementation without a critic, using only the weights from the state units to the action units. These store the state-action values Q and are also used to choose the action in step (3). However, computation of v and v' involves state units j, j' and action units i, i', hence, crosstalk involving some lateral connections must exist.

The state values V (or Q in case of SARSA) depend on the action strategy, because that influences the number of steps required to reach the reward. The action strategy is implemented in step (3) of the algorithm. Note the stochastic choice of actions. A deterministic agent may select a long path with a gradual increase of value rather than a short path on which it hasn't yet assigned any value to some states. The stochasticity allows for exploration of new states over exploitation of a previously thought optimal strategy. During learning, weights Q and hence the inputs h in step (3) become larger and so the character of action choice becomes more deterministic.

---

[1] These connections are sometimes called "P" to denote action preferences.

[2] SARSA computes the values from (s, a, r, s0, a0), hence the name.

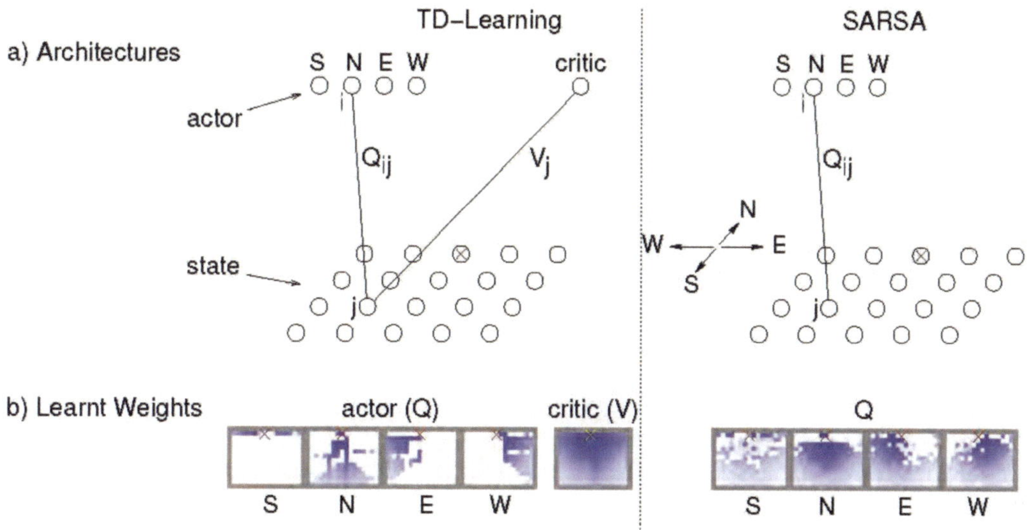

c) Algorithms

	TD-Learning	SARSA
Initialize to new starting position		
(i1) Read old state	$s_j = 1$ if in state j, else $s_j = 0$	
(i2) Choose action	$\text{Prob}(a_i = 1) = \frac{e^{2h_i}}{\sum_k e^{2h_k}}$ where $h_i = \sum_l Q_{il} s_l$	
(i3) Value	$v = \sum_l V_l s_l = V_j$	$v = \sum_{k,l} Q_{kl} a_k s_l = Q_{ij}$
Repeat until trial ends successfully (or out of valid area)		
(1) Act; Read new state	$s'_{j'} = 1$ if in state j', else $s'_{j'} = 0$	
(2) Read reward	r	
(3) Choose action	$\text{Prob}(a'_{i'} = 1) = \frac{e^{2h_{i'}}}{\sum_k e^{2h_k}}$ where $h_{i'} = \sum_l Q_{i'l} s'_l$	
(4) Value	$v' = \sum_l V_l s'_l = V'_{j'}$	$v' = \sum_{k,l} Q_{kl} a'_k s'_l = Q'_{i'j'}$
(5) Prediction error	$\delta = r + \gamma v' - v$	
(6) Critic weight update	$\Delta V_j \propto \delta s_j$	—
(7) Actor weight update	$\Delta Q_{ij} \propto \delta a_i s_j$	
(8) New becomes old	$s \leftarrow s', a \leftarrow a', v \leftarrow v'$	

Fig. 2. TD-learning vs. SARSA. a) Architectures. The actor-critic architecture used in TD-learning has weights from all state space units to all action units and to the critic. SARSA is missing these critic weights, but there is additional information flow via links that are not shown. b) Trained weights for a toy problem. Dark blue denotes strong positive weights. The rewarded position is indicated by a "×" in the 16×12 state space. c) Algorithms. Actor-critic learning assigns a value to a state s, SARSA to a state-action pair (s, a). Note: (i) The value in step (4) reduces to a single weight because only state unit j′ and action unit i′ have activation 1, others are 0. (ii) In TD-learning, step (3) may be done after (7).

Relation to Basal Ganglia

The lateral inhibition in the striatum might ensure that neurons will be active only in a small focused region which directly represents the state, just like a single active neuron denotes the state in the models. In such a localist - as opposed to a distributed - code, a neuron does not participate in the coding of several completely different states. Thereby an assignment of reward to all active units will not interfere with other states, which is important in the critic-and actor update steps (6), (7) in Fig. 2. In accordance with this demand, the striatum is known as a 'silent structure', in which only a small percentage of the dominant neuron type, the spiny projection neurons, is strongly active at any one time[3].

If the striatum encodes the state s_j, and if the GPi/SNr encode actions a_i, then the δ could modulate learning by dopaminergic projections to either striatum or GPi/SNr neurons to form the multiplicative factor in the actor update, step (7).

Dopaminergic neurons are mainly found in the VTA and the SNc, and they do not have spatial or motor properties (Morris, Nevet, Arkadir, Vaadia & Bergman, 2006). Corresponding to the value δ, dopaminergic neurons exhibit bursts of activity in response to unexpected rewarding stimuli or conditioned stimuli associated with those rewards (Ungless et al., 2004). Their firing correlates with expected reward values, i.e. probability times magnitude of the reward (Tobler, Fiorillo & Schultz, 2005). While dopamine neurons generally respond briefly to unexpected reward delivery, trained neurons will respond briefly to the cue that predicts an upcoming reward, but not to the expected reward itself, and their baseline firing will be suppressed, when an expected reward fails to be delivered (Schultz, Dayan & Montague, 1997).

Biological Support for SARSA

When monkeys choose to reach one of two levers, one paired with a frequent reward and the other with a less frequent reward, they do not always choose the more frequently rewarded action, even if overtrained. Instead, they adopt "probability matching", a suboptimal strategy in which the distribution of responses is matched to the reward probabilities of the available reward. This allows neural activations to be measured, when deciding for the lesser rewarded action (Niv, Daw & Dayan, 2006; Morris et al., 2006). Within just 200 msec after stimulus presentation dopamine neurons fire in proportion to the reward associated with the lever that they will reach at later, even if the reach is performed seconds later. In particular, they will fire less if the monkey is going to choose the poor reward. These results seem to contradict the actor-critic models in which the value v of a state is independent of the next action[4]. They are in accordance with SARSA, in which the value depends on the state and the action that is chosen (but not yet executed).

Multiple Tasks During Learning

Rothkopf and Ballard (2007) hint at a problem that arises in realistic scenarios when multiple reinforcement strategies are learning concurrently. Since there is only one dopamine reward signal, not only the successful strategy, but all active strategies would receive it. Their solution is to share it: each strategy consumes an amount of the reward that is proportional to the reward that it expects from the current state transition, the

[3] Brown et al. (2004) suggest that feedforward inhibition causes such sparse firing, because recurrent (feedback) inhibition would require significant activation of many neurons to be effective.

[4] However, a predictive (cortical) input to the basal ganglia could denote already the next state.

difference of the corresponding values. Unfortunately, a strategy would not receive any amount of the reward if the reward comes completely unexpected under this strategy. This might be remedied by taking into account confidence values to each strategy's prediction. In any case, the different parallel loops need to communicate, possibly via the indirect pathway of the basal ganglia.

Exploration – Exploitation

Sridharan, Prashanth and Chakravarthy (2006) address the problem that a RL network has to produce randomness in some controllable fashion, in order to produce stochastic action choices. For this purpose they implement an oscillatory circuit via reciprocal excitatory-inhibitory connections. The indirect pathway (see Fig. 1) represents a suitable oscillatory circuit in that the STN excites the GPe and in turn receives inhibition. Together with short-range lateral inhibition the model produces chaotic oscillatory activity that becomes more regular only with stronger input from the cortex (Sridharan et al.,2006). They propose that, in case of weak or novel sensory input, the irregular firing causes an agent to behave more randomly and thereby to explore the state space. A biological manifestation of randomness could be in the pauses by which GPe neurons randomly and independently of each other interrupt their otherwise regular high-frequency firing (Elias et al., 2007). These pauses last approximately half a second and happen on average every 5 seconds with Poissonian interpause intervals. There are less pauses during high motor activity, indicating less randomness during performance.

4. Implementations

A central idea about 'lower' and 'higher' parts of the brain is that lower centers "swap out" functions that they cannot perform themselves. At the lowest level we might find distributed control circuits such as in some inner organs, as well as spinal cord reflex mechanisms. Since they function autonomously we may not actually cast them into a hierarchy with other brain structures.

The reticular formation at a very low level is mature at birth and regulates the choice of basic behaviours such as eat, fight or mate. As a centralized structure it can coordinate these behaviours, which the distributed control circuits would not be able to do (Prescott, 2007). Yet it lacks sophisticated learning capabilities and cannot cope with a complex and changing environment.

The basal ganglia implement a memory of successful actions in performing stimulus-response mappings that lead to rewards based on experiences of previous stimulus-response performance. Whether any reward is of interest may be set by a currently active basic behaviour (a thirsty animal will appreciate water but not food). So the reticular formation may have control over the basal ganglia, in selecting sub-circuits for different types of reward and strategies.

But the sensory stimuli from a complex environment are not necessarily suitable as a 'state' in reinforcement learning. A situation like "food is behind the door" is hardly represented suitably. Suitable state representations are unlikely to be learnt from reinforcement learning, and unsupervised learning is a better candidate. The basal ganglia may "swap out" such functionality to the cortex. To learn useful representations, unsupervised learning in the cortex may be guided by rewards and attentional selection (see Section 5).

The cortex features various functionalities despite its homogeneous structure. (i) Preprocessing in low hierarchical levels in the posterior cortex. The purpose is to transform light or sound into meaningful entities like objects, words or locations. (ii) Working memory in higher hierarchical levels in more anterior cortex. An example usage is for task setting: the strategy to use, or the reward to expect, is dependent on an initial stimulus that must be held in memory. The cortex may thereby determine which part of the basal ganglia to use, possibly overriding influence from the reticular formation. (iii) Motor primitives, presumably on a middle hierarchical level, in the motor cortex. For example, an action like "press the left lever" is a coordinated temporal sequence of muscle activations. Such action primitives reside in the motor cortex, and also the cerebellum, which we do not address further, is involved.

Architectural Choices

Tiered architectures are common in robotics. They allow to implement short-term reactive decisions while at the same time pursuing long-term goals. They also allow for computer programs to be implemented in modules with minimal inter-modular communication.

Brooks' subsumption architecture is an early example (Brooks, 1986). From the robot's lowest control layer to the highest layer, actions are for example: "avoid an object" — "wander around" — "explore the world" — "create a map", the latter of which may be the ultimate goal of a particular robotic application. The layers of such an architecture are however not directly identifiable with brain structures such as reticular formation — basal ganglia — cortex.

Unlike structured computer programs the 'modules' of the brain are highly inter-dependent. Computations involve multiple brain structures, and actions are often redundantly executed in parallel. For example saccades are destroyed by a combined lesion of the midbrain superior colliculus (SC) and the cortical frontal eye field (FEF), but not by a lesion of either of the two (Sparks, 2002). Another design principle of the brain is recurrence - connections form loops within and between brain structures.

Several models which mainly focus on the basal ganglia implement a larger loop structure. The basic loop (Fig. 1) is Striatum → GPi/SNr → Thalamus → Cortex → Striatum. This loop is topographic in the sense that there are separate parallel loops, each for a specific feature, thought or action (Houk et al., 2007). Action on the level of the GPi/SNr activates the entire corresponding loop that includes slices of the thalamus and cortex as well.

Robot Action Selection

Prescott, Stafford and Gurney (2006) use a basal ganglia model for basic behaviour selection in a Khepera robot. The robot removes cylinders from its arena using five action patterns in the natural order: cylinder-seek, cylinder-pickup, wall-seek, wall-follow, cylinder-deposit. Scalar salience signals for each of these actions, which depend on perception and motivation, are the input to the basal ganglia. These are implemented with standard leaky integrator neurons and hand-set parameters to select coherent sequences of actions. A sophisticated embedding architecture complements the basal ganglia model: perceptual sub-systems (e.g. visual cortex) and motivational sub-systems (e.g. reticular formation) for computation of the salience signals; stereotyped, carefully timed "fixed action patterns" (e.g. motor cortex) for action execution. A "busy signal" prevents currently performed actions from being interrupted by other action bids. In the model of Brown et al. (2004), such a suppression of lingering actions is done via the STN which sends diffuse excitation to the inhibitory BG output nuclei GPi/SNr.

Working Memory Control

Hazy et al. (2007) generalize action selection to the selection of working memory representations in the pre-frontal cortex (PFC). This tackles the temporal credit assignment problem in trace conditioning where there is a gap between the conditioned stimulus and the reward. The working memory capacity of the PFC bridges this gap and delivers sustained input to the basal ganglia. Working memories with different time spans in parallel loops allow for the execution of nested tasks. Their example application is the 1-2-AX task, in which a subject after seeing a '1' must identify the consecutive letters 'A-X', but after seeing a '2' must identify the sequence 'B-Y'. The numbers '1', '2' are memorized for a longer duration in an 'outer' loop. An 'inner' loop identifies the desired letter sequence within a short duration. A third loop elicits the motor response. While the basal ganglia resolve only these loops, the much larger cortex distinguishes also the contents within the loops. In the 1-2-AX task these are the values of the numbers and the digits. The model PFC stores them in hypercolumn-like "stripes" with one of several entries in a stripe being active in a winner-take-all fashion. Gating is nevertheless accomplished in the basal ganglia that does not need to reflect the individual features within a stripe.

Basal Ganglia Mediate Cortical Control on Superior Colliculus

The superior colliculus (SC) is a phylogenetically old structure eliciting reactive saccades from direct retinal input. Planned saccades are elicited on the SC only via direct cortical input and concurrent disinhibition by the basal ganglia. This suggests that planned saccades are driven by expected reward (Hikosaka, 2007). Brown et al. (2004) implement such an extensive circuit and simulate saccade tasks which involve target selection and timing.

Their model takes into account the cortical layer structure. 'Planning' cells in cortical layer 3 with sustained activity send preparatory bids to the basal ganglia, while associated 'executive' cells in layer 5 generate phasic outputs if and when their basal ganglia gate opens. Planning cells are modulated by layer 6 cells which possibly reside in higher-level cortical area (PFC) that is in control. These same cells of cortical layer 6 are a source of excitation to the thalamic cells whose disinhibition allows plans to execute.

A hypothesis of Brown et al. (2004) is that thalamo-striatal connections (not shown in Fig. 1) become active in trials during which premature release of a movement leads to non-reward; this shall lead to a learned activation of the indirect channel and therefore guide the learning of 'STOP' responses.

Basal Ganglia Instruct Cortex

There appear to be two positions related to the association between the prefrontal cortex (PFC) and basal ganglia. The conventional view is that the PFC drives the learning of the basal ganglia. This is mainly based on the fact that the striatum neurons require numerous synchronous inputs from cortex (and thalamus) to become active. An alternative view is that while the dopamine system 'teaches' the striatum, the basal ganglia teaches the cortex through the basal ganglia-thalamo-cortical loop (Laubach, 2005; Graybiel, 2005). Our model of Weber et al. (2006) utilises this alternative.

Areas of the motor cortex execute action primitives; on the other hand, the basal ganglia are well equipped for learning these actions by reinforcement learning in the first place. In our model an action that has been acquired by the basal ganglia is then imitated by the motor cortex. Thereby the resources used for reinforcement learning, such as the large state space that may reside in the striatum, would be available for further learning. See Section 5 for a description of this visually guided robot docking action (Weber, Wermter & Zochios, 2004). Both of these levels of neural processing have been implemented on a PeopleBot robot.

In our model of Weber et al. (2006) the motor cortex reads the visual input and motor output of the basal ganglia. It establishes an internal representation of these input-output pairs by unsupervised self-organization (Hinton, Dayan, Frey & Neal, 1995). With 'incomplete' input in which vision is present but the action missing, the network will find a 'complete' internal code from which it will generate an appropriate action. Horizontal hetero-associator weights on the internal layer associate the current representation with a future representation one time step ahead, and thereby perform prediction, allowing for mental simulation of an action.

Experimental evidence supports our model. During associative learning, Pasupathy and Miller (2005) found earlier changes of neural activity in the striatum than in the PFC. In their study, primates were rewarded if they made saccades to a certain direction, dependent on the appearance of a complicated cue shown at the fixation point. The primate learnt the rewarded direction by trial and error. Once the relationships were learned the input-response pairs where reversed. When relearning the appropriate behaviour to the input, the striatum was found to have direction-specific firing almost straight away. In contrast, the PFC only gained direction selectivity following 15 correctly performed trials. This is consistent with the striatum training the PFC.

Jog, Kubota, Connolly, Hillegaart and Graybiel (1999) trained rats to make a left-right decision in a T-maze task. Striatal neurons which were initially active at the point of the junction became less active when the task had been learnt. Instead, they increased their activities at the beginning and at the end of the task. This suggests that the striatum might be putting together sequences of known behaviours that, once learned, are executed elsewhere.

Task Switching

Representing actions on the cortex might also make them easier to control by other cortical areas. Prelimbic and infralimbic regions of rat prefrontal cortex were shown to remember different strategies and aid in switching between learnt strategies (Rich & Shapiro, 2007). In an extension of our model of the motor cortex (Weber et al., 2006) we therefore showed that language input to another cortical area can influence which motor sequence on the motor cortex representation to recall (Wermter, Weber, Elshaw, Gallese & Pulvermüller, 2005). These cortical learning principles can lead to language-guided neural robots in the future.

5. Visual system

The actor-critic model of reinforcement learning has been used to perform various robot actions, such as camera-guided robot docking (Martínez-Marín & Duckett, 2005). In our approach (Weber et al., 2004), we first trained the peripheral vision so that it can supply a visually obtained state as input to the action selection network.

Overall, there are three processing steps and associated training phases involved in the learning of the docking behaviour (see Fig. 3). First, training the weights between the visual input and the "what" area by unsupervised learning. The learning paradigm is that of a generative model (hence the feedback connections in Fig. 3) in which the color image is reconstructed from sparse activations of neurons in the "what" area. Second, training the lateral weights within and between the "what" and the "where" areas by supervised learning. For this purpose, a supervisor placed a blob of activation onto the position on the "where" area which corresponded to the correct position of the object within the image. After learning, an attractor network covering the "what" and the "where" areas creates the "where"representation by pattern completion if only the "what" representation is supplied as input.

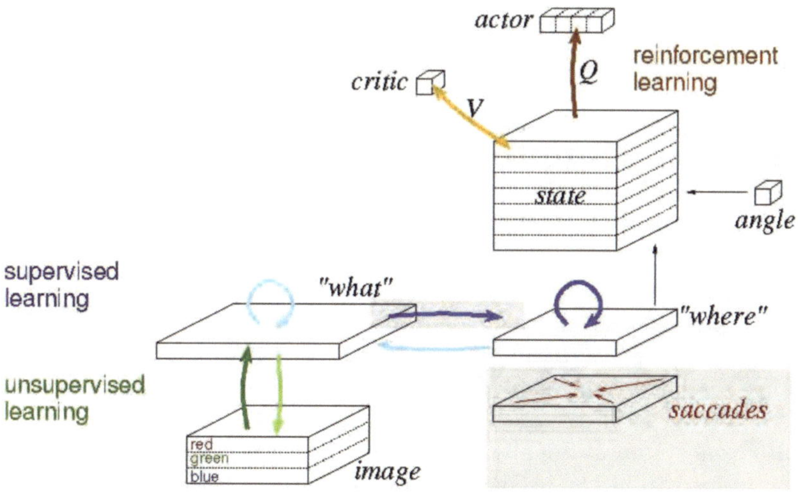

Fig. 3. Neural architecture for visual pre-processing and reinforcement-learnt action. Thick arrows denote trained weights. Only the ones depicted dark are used during performance while those depicted bright are involved in training. The area on shaded background labelled 'saccades' is assumed to perform saccades to bring the object from any location on the 'where' area to its center, as indicated by the arrows pointing to the middle. Saccades can be used here to replace supervised learning of the "what" → "where" connections (shaded background) by reinforcement learning (see Section 5.1).

The robot needed to approach the table at a right angle. For the final step therefore the visual "where" representation of the object was augmented by the robot angle w.r.t. the table, here discretized into just seven angle values. This outer product yielded the state space, a 3-dimensional block in which one unit's activity denoted the visual object position and the robot angle; in other words, seven layers of the visual space, one for every possible robot angle. Finally, the weights from this state space to the critic and the four actor units, denoting 'forward', 'backward', 'turn left' and 'turn right', were trained by TD-learning.

The critic weights assign each state a value v which is initially zero. For each trial the robot is initialized to a random starting position and the steps of Fig. 2 are followed until the reward is obtained. The reward signal is given when the target is perceived in the middle of the lower edge of the visual field (hence at the grippers) and when the robot rotation angle is zero. When the robot hits the table or looses the object out of sight, then a new trial is started without a reward. During learning, states that lead quickly to the goal will be assigned a higher value v by strengthening their connections V to the critic unit. The weights Q to the motor units which have been activated simultaneously are also increased, if the corresponding action leads to a better state.

In short, we have used a simple 'what-where' visual system as a preprocessing module, supplying suitable input to a state space for reinforcement learning. In-line with the classical view, this simplified visual system learns from visual data irrespective of the use of vision for action and reward-seeking.

5.1 Reward in the visual system

In recent years evidence is accumulating that even the lower visual system such as the primary visual cortex V1 is sensitive to reward learning. Shuler and Bear (2006) repeatedly presented rats a light flash to one eye followed by a reward given after two seconds. V1 neurons acquired reward-dependent responses such as sustained responses after visual stimulus offset, or increasing responses until the time of the (expected) reward. Schoups, Vogels, Qian and Orban (2001) trained monkeys to discriminate oriented bars (such as distinguishing 45° from 43° orientations), after the presentation of which they had to respond with saccades to a certain direction to receive a juice reward. After training, the slopes of the orientation tuning curves were increased in V1 neurons tuned to orientations near the trained orientation[5]. On the other hand, no modifications of the tuning curves were observed for orientations that had been shown as often but which were not decision relevant.

But learning in the adult visual system is not always reward dependent. Furmanski, Schluppeck and Engel (2004) trained subjects to detect very low-contrast oriented patterns, following which they indicated a decision, but which did not incur a reward. This fMRI study revealed increased V1 responses for practiced orientations relative to control orientations. However, Vessel (2004) conjectures that stimuli that make sense and are richly interpretable on a higher level are 'rewarding' and perceived as pleasurable. He recalls that there is an increasing number of opiate receptors as one traverses up the visual hierarchy. Hence, mere neuronal activation might be regarded as reward and be utilized in learning algorithms.

Saccade Learning

In Weber and Triesch (2006) we have trained saccades using a reward signal made only from visually-induced activation. The model exploits the fact that the fovea (the center of the retina) is over-represented in visual areas. Saccades to an object are rewarded dependent on the resolution increase of the object – a value that is higher the closer the object is brought to the fovea. Motor units which code for a certain saccade length, and which become active in a noisy competition, compete via limited afferent connections. A motor unit that brings the object closest to the fovea will learn with the highest reward modulation and ultimately win. Since there is evidence for a different learning mechanism for horizontal saccades, we applied this algorithm for the learning of vertical saccades in combination with a different algorithm for horizontal saccades.

When saccades have been learnt, we can assume that neurons in higher visual areas of the "where" pathway exist which code for saccades of a certain direction and amplitude, as indicated in the shaded area of Fig. 3. These are then akin to action units. With the algorithm of Weber and Triesch (2006) we can then learn the "what" $\rightarrow$ "where" connections by reward-based learning instead of by supervised learning.

---

[5] Neurons which adapted their tuning curves were found only in supra- and infragranular layers of V1 where there are dense intra- and inter-area horizontal connections as well as inter-area top-down connections. Neurons in layer IV which receive bottom-up input from retina/thalamus did not adapt.

Gaze Following

The potential of a purely visual stimulus as a reward is also used in a RL model of how infants learn to follow the gaze of the mother (Triesch et al., 2007), a skill which infants learn only after 18 months of age. The model assumes an infant's tendency to look frequently at the mother's face. It assumes further that the mother then looks to the left or the right, and that there is an interesting (rewarding) stimulus where the mother looks. The infant initially cannot make use of the mother's gaze direction, but after making (initially random) sample eye movements, it will find out that rewarding stimuli can be found in the line of sight of the mother. The model predicts a mirror-neuron like premotor representation with neurons that become activated either when the infant plans to look at a certain location or when the infant sees the mother looking in the direction of that location.

5.2 Attention-gated reinforcement learning

Attention-Gated Reinforcement Learning (AGREL) (Roelfsema & Ooyen, 2005) is a link between supervised and reinforcement learning for 1-of-n classification tasks. In supervised learning of such tasks the teacher's learning signal is 1 for the correct output unit and 0 for the other output units, and is given for every data point. The rules of reinforcement learning are that if the network - of which the output will be stochastic winner-take-all - guesses correctly, then a reward signal is given, else not. AGREL gives learning rules which in this case lead to the same average weight changes as supervised backpropagation learning, albeit learning is slower due to insufficient feedback when the network guesses incorrectly.

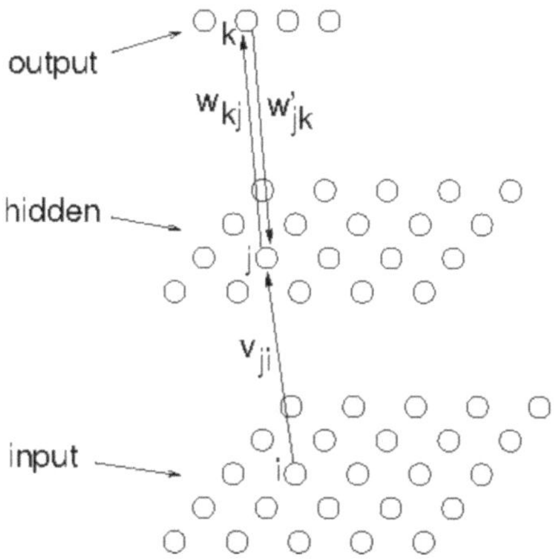

Fig. 4. Architecture of AGREL. One-in-n of the output units is active at a time, just like in TD-learning and SARSA. The input and hidden layers, however, may have a distributed code.

The AGREL architecture is that of a multilayer perceptron and shown in Fig. 4. An input unit i conveys its activation x_i via weight v_{ji} to the activation y_j of hidden layer unit j which has a logistic transfer function

$$y_j = \frac{1}{1+\exp(-h_j)} \quad \text{with} \quad h_j = \sum_i v_{ji} x_i$$

Activations are then conveyed to an output unit k, while the output units compete via a softmax function:

$$e_k := \mathrm{Prob}(z_k = 1) = \frac{\exp(h_k)}{\sum_{k'} \exp(h_{k'})} \quad \text{with} \quad h_k = \sum_j w_{kj} y_j.$$

The actual, binary output z_k of the neuron follows the probability e_k of being active, which is thus the average activation.

Learning

In order to understand AGREL, lets first consider error backpropagation[6]. The average update of a weight w_{kj} from a hidden unit j to an output unit k is:

$$E(\Delta w_{kj}) \propto (t_k - e_k)\, y_j, \tag{1}$$

where t_k is the teacher signal and e_k is, in backpropagation, the continuous activation on output neuron k. Unlike supervised backpropagation, AGREL considers only the winning output neuron, k = s, for learning. Now we apply Eq. 1 for reinforcement learning in which we distinguish two cases, unrewarded and rewarded trials. For unrewarded trials, which means $t_s = 0$, Eq. 1 becomes

$$E(\Delta w_{sj}) \propto -e_s\, y_j =: f(\delta)\, e_s\, y_j,$$

and for rewarded trials, where $t_s = 1$, Eq. 1 becomes (defining $\delta := t_s - e_s$)

$$E(\Delta w_{sj}) \propto \underbrace{(1 - e_s)}_{\delta}\, y_j = \delta\, y_j \underbrace{\frac{e_s}{1-\delta}}_{1} =: f(\delta)\, e_s\, y_j.$$

In order to make both weight update steps consistent, one defines

$f(\delta) := -1$ for unrewarded trials, and $f(\delta) := \dfrac{\delta}{1-\delta}$ for rewarded trials.

To complete our brief treatment of AGREL,the top-down feedback weights w_{jk} to the hidden layer learn with the same rule as the w_{kj}. A weight v_{ji} from an input unit i to a hidden layer unit j is updated according to:

$$\Delta v_{ji} \propto x_i\, y_j\, (1 - y_j)\, w'_{js}\, f(\delta).$$

Hence, learning of the weights from the input to hidden unit j scales with the weight w_{js} that this unit receives from the only active output unit s. The term $f(\delta)$ depends on whether the winning unit equals the correct output.

Applications

AGREL works only with immediate rewards and does not build up action strategies as TD-learning does. While TD-learning requires that only one input unit is active at a time, AGREL accepts a distributed code as input. Applications are therefore in the sensory system where a classification of a stimulus needs to be made, and where some kind of reward signal is promptly available.

For example, monkeys had previously been trained to categorize faces, and it emerged that neurons in the inferotemporal cortex preferentially encode diagnostic features of these faces, i.e. features by which categories can be distinguished, as opposed to features that vary irrespective of categories. Roelfsema and Ooyen (2005) showed that neurons of the hidden layer

---

[6] Here we outline chapter "4.1 Average Weight Changes in AGREL" of Roelfsema and Ooyen (2005) from back to front.

in AGREL also learn preferentially to code for diagnostic features. This explains that feature representations in the sensory cortex are not merely dependent on the (statistics of) sensory input, but are tailored to decisions, and thereby aimed at rewards.
Another example is the simulation of the abovementioned experiments of Schoups et al. (2001): orientation selective neurons in V1 (AGREL's hidden layer) adjust their tuning curves to distinguish orientations that are being classified, while neurons that are as often activated, but without action relevance, do not adjust their tuning curves.
In Franz and Triesch (2007), vergence eye movements were trained using AGREL so to fixate an object with both eyes in depth. No external reward was given, but a successful focusing of both eyes on a single point in space led to binocular zero-disparity cells having a particularly high activation, which was regarded as a reward. The model predicts a variety of disparity tuning curves observed in the visual cortex and thereby presents additional evidence that purely visually-induced activation can constitute a reward signal.

6. Beyond behaviourism

Reinforcement learning (RL) theory has probably been the most influential outcome of behaviourist psychology, and neuroscientific support for it continues to grow. It seems very likely that there is RL in the basal ganglia, complemented by unsupervised learning in the cortex and supervised learning in the cerebellum (Doya, 1999), possibly building upon genetic 'learning' in the reticular formation.
However, the brain still resists a unifying description. Baum (2004) argues that either cognitive behaviour can be described in a compressed way using a few theories like RL. Or it has been reasonably well optimized by evolution, and theories which are simple enough to comprehend inevitably miss out a lot of significant detail. In attempting to uncover simple psychological principles, the behaviourists have left a legacy in which the same theories which illuminate brain activity, can render us blind to other significant aspects.

6.1 Experimental conditions

In the early 1970's, every psychology department still had a "rat lab". The researchers did what they could to control the experimental conditions. But a rat swimming in a water maze is still aware that light glistens off the water in subtly different ways according to its direction, and although the walls were white and high, the sounds of birdsong outside the window or footsteps in the corridor were still there, providing good orientation cues. While human beings are often only vaguely aware of their surroundings, animals are highly attuned to their environment. A neuroscientist recounts how simply wearing a different lab coat can radically change an animal's behaviour (Panksepp,1998, p.18).
Also, the fashion at the time was to write up experiments on living animals in the same formal manner that has proven so useful when dealing with non-living subject matter. Conceptual analysis, a view of the world in stimulus-response terms, left no place for context (either external or internal). An observer at the time might see that the written accounts of the experiments were patently not portraying what was happening. They were merely reporting how the researchers interpreted what they saw, suppressing often more interesting behaviours as "irrelevant". The purpose of the experimental conditions was to

effectively deprive the animals of every possible natural behaviour apart from the sought-for response. Much of the time, the animals would do anything except the behaviour under test.

The first legacy of the behaviourists has been an oversimplified account of the experimental conditions under which RL was investigated. We have attempted to demonstrate that the maths of RL can be formulated under assumptions that are also supported by the behaviour of animals in their natural environment. Oversimplification can be avoided with a careful, honest eye on neuroscientific results and the use of robots to test the theories in a practical context.

6.2 Embedded behaviours

The founder of ecology, Konrad Lorenz, identifies adaptation (including RL) as merely one of nine types of cognitive behaviour (Lorenz, 1996). He claims RL is a phylogenetically significant information acquiring system, but one which requires sophisticated subsystems for its operation. For example, *both* stimulus recognition and adaptive modifiability must be attuned to the message of success or failure coming from the activities terminating the whole action, which also must be capable of appraising significance. Mechanisms which enable the organism to distinguish reliably between biological success and failure are rarely as simple as the binary or scalar values used by RL.

Innate behaviours such as eat, fight and flee[7] have been described as mutually incompatible modes of vertebrate behaviour (Kilmer et al., 1969), and the candidate brain system for selecting between these kinds of action is the reticular formation in the brainstem. Without a cortex (and basal ganglia), electrical stimulation in the brainstem can induce complex and coordinated behaviours, including eating, grooming and attack (Berntson & Micco, 1976). These behaviours are modifiable in complex ways. Very little is understood concerning emotion or motivation, yet these are clearly crucial to a full understanding of RL in animals.

Lorenz's cognitive behaviours include exploratory behaviour. This requires coherent activity concerning something which has not been learned, by definition. Yet it also has a rationale and a logic which is adaptive, distinguishing it from the blind randomness of behaviourists' descriptions, and of the standard RL protocols.

But just as the study of adaptation has grown significantly since the behaviourists' first formulations, so has RL. For some time, neuroscientific evidence has implicated the basal ganglia in RL. Panksepp (1998) (ch.8) revisits the literature on self-stimulation reinforcement and concludes that dopamine activity does not reinforce *consumatory* but *anticipatory* behaviours. So it is more akin to "the joy of the hunt". If this is the case, the old view of a specific stimulus becoming linked to a response via some general reinforcer seems unlikely. A better interpretation is that a stimulus set (which includes what is relevant in the wide-ranging context) is linked to the response via a reinforcer that is appropriate given that context

Hence, the second legacy of the behaviourists has been to encourage the widening of the scope of behaviours we study. It is inadequate to describe primitive behaviours as merely "innate" as this fails to account for the variety of their expression. Likewise, RL is not a

---

[7] Kilmer, McCulloch and Blum (1969) list the following: sleep, eat, drink, fight, flee, hunt, search / explore, urinate, defecate, groom, mate, give birth, mother the young, build a nest, and special speciesdependent forms of behaviour such as migrate, hibernate, gnaw, and hoard.

single, monolithic mechanism. What counts as a "stimulus" can range from a single neuron's activation to widely distributed patterns. Dopamine is unlikely to be the only reinforcer and the "response" can be as varied as any animal behaviour.

6.3 Neuroconstructivism

Lorenz has also criticized the assumption that the human mind, before any experience, was a tabula rasa, and the equivalent assumption that "learning" must "enter into" any physiological behaviour process whatever. The most common response to this is to claim that anything not learned must be innate. But this is an artificially narrow choice which follows from the philosophical assumptions science has inherited from Plato and Descartes. Science proceeds on the assumption that the only things that count are ideas which can be considered independent of anything else: objects which can be observed. This has served us well for centuries, and will continue to do so. But as psychology has already found out, studying cognitive behaviour in the same way leads to a number of difficulties. Inevitably, this will also become a problem for RL too, at some point.

Fortunately, there is an alternative viewpoint which promises to avoid many of the problems inherited from Cartesianism. Rather than assuming that things can be "atomic" as Plato suggested, Heidegger (1927/1962) emphasizes that all behaviour is executed in some context. We are thrust into a rich, pre-existing world and are actively living out our purposes in it from the start. There is no such thing as an object which has no context. Attempts to isolate things like "stimuli" and "responses" involve very high-level, sophisticated abstractions which Heidegger called *present-at-hand*, that is, we can examine them.

The neuroconstructivism of Mareschal et al. (2007) is typical of this more modern approach. They still expect all science to rest upon processes in the physical world, but this is in terms of a "coherent account". Components are intelligible as contributory constituents of the whole which gives them meaning. The system in turn is defined in terms of its components and their mutual relationships. One advantage of this formulation is that it simultaneously avoids the behaviourists' narrowness and the equally beguiling trap of modularity[8]. It is simply inappropriate in the real world to consider a "stimulus" as a single entity. Their conceptualization of "response" is equally sophisticated. According to neuroconstructivism, the outcome of almost every event is a distributed set of *partial representations* which are inevitably *context dependent*. All living systems (including cells) are considered *proactive* in the sense that they can be seen to be "active on their own behalf". This leads to an *interactive* interdependence between components, characterized by processes of cooperation and competition.

---

[8] Mareschal et al. cite Marr (1982) as their straw man here. According to them, Marr distinguishes independent computational, algorithmic and implementational levels. "For example, the same algorithm can be implemented in different technologies, or the same goals can be reached via different representational formats and transformations. The implication is that one can study and understand cognitive information processing without reference to the substrate in which it is implemented." Mareschal et al. (2007) (p.209) radically reject this view as an intelligent system must function in real time. Any sub-task is constrained not only by its functional definition but also by how it works, as it mustn't take too long. The implementation level cannot therefore be independent of the algorithmic.

6.4 Perception is an active process

Constructivists like Piaget (1953); Glasersfeld (1995) and Bickhard (2000) have emphasized that perception is essentially an *active* process. Psychological and physiological evidence (Gibson, 1979; Jeannerod, 1997; Noë, 2004) seems to indicate this is a viable theory. Although the basal ganglia are closely linked to action selection, there is a strong link with attention as well (Fielding, Georgiou-Karistianis & White, 2006). It is natural for researchers to focus on the most visible aspect of selected behaviour, the movement. But an action which has been selected is also being attended to. The implication of basal ganglia deficiencies in Attention Deficit Hyperactivity Disorder, following Teicher et al. (2000), confirms this compound nature of attention and action, as does the equitable treatment of sensory and motor basal ganglia afferents.

The model of Brown et al. (2004) illustrates this broader view of RL. It approximates the thousands of millions of interconnecting neurons in a model of less than 100 units, and tackles the complexity of the brain in a modular architecture[9]. It is sufficiently complex to take motivation and attention into account, as well as "learning". Indeed, the ability of the basal ganglia model to select between competing afferents may well provide a basis for choice - that element which distinguishes psychological learning from mere adaptation. In their words, "The basal ganglia interact with the laminar circuits in the frontal cortex and the superior colliculus to help satisfy the staging requirements of conditional voluntary behaviour." In the process they demonstrate that RL establishes stimulus control over *plans*, not responses, and provide a coherent alternative model of working memory.

The complexity of the basal ganglia, and their sensitivity to *context*, suggest a broadening of the simple stimulus-response view. Previous research becomes a special case. Stimuli become more natural and responses can be more than some action, as perception and attention are implicated in basal ganglia processing too.

The Heideggerian view that context is primary and conceptual data[10] is derivative, finds newfound support here and opens new possibilities. Many of the difficulties faced by Artificial Intelligence are the direct result of the Cartesian viewpoint that all context must be constructed from nothing. The recent success of embodied-embedded robotics research supports Heidegger's proposal that context is "given" (Wheeler, 2005). We have indicated above that the basal ganglia architecture seems to especially facilitate the processing of context alongside RL.

The understanding of RL has also widened. The change from a generally applicable pleasure-or-pain (with no clear cognitive implication) to a much more specific "sought-for" success (the cognitive link predicted by Interactivism (Bickhard, 1999)) means that RL is poised to address specific instances in a realistic way. RL, therefore, has much more in

---

[9] The assumption of modularity helps us conceptualize what is going on and formulate testable hypotheses, but it must be borne in mind that modularity is a function of our worldview, supported by its success in fields like computing and business systems. Writers like Braitenberg and Schüz (1998) go to great lengths to convey the messiness of the cortex. Overviews like Shepherd (2004) and Kandel, Schwartz and Jessell (2000) always indicate that, while neural pathways are a convenient way of getting to grips with the material, there are always exceptions and complications. Modularity is more an artefact of our scientific understanding than it is an aspect of the subject matter being explored.

[10] Heidegger would class this as "present-at-hand" - the stuff of scientific theories, or the disembodied "ideas" of Plato. Also the Cartesian view that things may be conceived of in isolation (that things-inthemselves are primary) is undermined by the same neuroscientific evidence.

common with the natural world and the variety of animal behaviour indicated by Lorenz (1996) than is warranted by the behaviourist evidence alone. This wider view places RL alongside other modern developments in philosophy and robotics. Such a combination must surely be grounds for hope that we will continue to see more robust and successful developments in artificial intelligence.

7. Acknowledgements

This work has been funded partially by the EU project MirrorBot, grant IST-2001-35282, and NEST-043374 coordinated by SW. CW, JT and AF are supported by the Hertie Foundation, and the EU projects PLICON, grant MEXT-CT-2006-042484, and Daisy, grant FP6-2005-015803. Urs Bergmann provided feedback on the manuscript.

8. References

Bar-Gad, I.; Havazelet-Heimer, G.; Goldberg, J.; Ruppin, E. & Bergman, H. (2000). Reinforcement-driven dimensionality reduction–a model for information processing in the basal ganglia. *J Basic Clin Physiol Pharmacol, 11*(4), 305-20.

Baum, E. (2004). *What is thought?* MIT Press / Bradford. Berntson, G. & Micco, D. (1976). Organization of brainstem behavioral systems. *Brain Research Bulletin, 1* (5), 471-83.

Bickhard, M. H. (1999). Interaction and representation. *Theory and Psychology, 9* (4), 435-458.

Bickhard, M. H. (2000). Motivation and emotion: An interactive process model. InR. D. Ellis& N. Newton (Eds.), *The cauldron of consciousness: Motivation, affect and self-organization* (pp. 161–178). John Benjamins, Amsterdam.

Bloch, V. & Laroche, S. (1985). Enhancement of long-term potentiation in the rat dentate gyrus by post-trial stimulation of the reticular formation. *J Physiol, 360*, 215-31.

Bogacz, R.& Gurney, K. (2007). The basal ganglia and cortex implement optimal decision making between alternative actions. *Neur Comp, 19*, 442-77.

Braitenberg, V. & Schüz, A. (1998). *Cortex: Statistics and geometry of neuronal connectivity* (2nd ed.). Springer Verlag.

Brooks, R. (1986). A robust layered control system for a mobile robot. *IEEEJ Robotics and Automation, RA-2*, 14-23.

Brown, J.; Bullock, D. & Grossberg, S. (2004). How laminar frontal cortex and basal ganglia circuits interact to control planned and reactive saccades. *Neural Networks, 17*, 471–510.

Dommett, E.; Coizet, V.; Blaha, C.; Martindale, J. & Lefebvre, V. (2005). How visual stimuli activate dopaminergic neurons at short latency. *Science, 307*(5714), 1476-9.

Doya, K. (1999). What are the computations of the cerebellum, the basal ganglia and the cerebral cortex? *Neural Networks, 12*, 961-74.

Elias, S.; Joshua, M.; Goldberg, J.; Heimer, G.; Arkadir, D.; Morris, G. et al. (2007). Statistical properties of pauses of the high-frequency discharge neurons in the external segment of the globus pallidus. *J Neurosci, 27*(10), 2525-38.

Fielding, J.; Georgiou-Karistianis, N. & White, O. (2006). The role of the basal ganglia in the control of automatic visuospatial attention. *Journal of the International Neuropsychological Society, 12*, 657–667.

Fiorillo, C.; Tobler, P. & Schultz, W. (2003). Discrete coding of reward probability and uncertainty by dopamine neurons. *Science, 299*, 1898-902.

Fischer, T. (2003). *Charakterisierung des dopaminergen Systems bei transgenen Ratten mit einem Antisensekonstrukt gegen die m-RNA der Tryptophanhydroxylase.* Unpublished doctoral dissertation, Humboldt-University, Berlin.

Flaherty, A. W. & Graybiel, A. M. (1991). Corticostriatal transformations in the primate somatosensory system. projections from physiologically mapped body-part representations. *Journal of Neurophysiology, 66,* 1249–1263.

Franz, A. & Triesch, J. (2007). Emergence of disparity tuning during the development of vergence eye movements. In *Proceedings of the 6th IEEE International Conference on Development and Learning.*

Furmanski, C.; Schluppeck, D. & Engel, S. (2004). Learning strengthens the response of primary visual cortex to simple patterns. *Curr Biol, 14,* 573-8.

Gibson, J. J. (1979). *The ecological approach to visual perception.* Houghton Mifflin, Boston, MA.

Glasersfeld, E. von. (1995). *Radical constructivism: A way of knowing and learning.* London: Falmer Press.

Graybiel, A. (2005). The basal ganglia: learning new tricks and loving it. *Curr Opinion in Neurobiol, 15,* 638-44.

Hazy, T.; Frank, M. & O'Reilly, R. (2007). Towards an executive without a homunculus: computational models of the prefrontal cortex/basal ganglia system. *Phil.Trans. R. Soc.B.*

Heidegger, M. (1927/1962). *Being and time.* SCM Press, London. (Originally published as Sein und Zeit, Gesamtausgabe Volume 2; translated by John MacQuarrie and Edward Robinson)

Herrero, M.; Barcia, C. & Navarro, J. (2002). Functional anatomy of thalamus and basal ganglia. *Child's Nerv Syst, 18,* 386-404.

Hikosaka, O. (2007). Basal ganglia mechanisms of reward-oriented eye movement. *Ann N.Y. Acad Sci, 1104,* 229-49.

Hinton, G.E.; Dayan, P.; Frey, B. J. & Neal, R. (1995). The wake-sleep algorithm for unsupervised neural networks. *Science, 268,* 1158-1161.

Houk, J.; Bastianen, C.; Fansler, D.; Fishbach, A.; Fraser, D.; Reber, P. et al. (2007). Action selection and refinement in subcortical loops through basal ganglia and cerebellum. *Phil.Trans.R. Soc.B.*

Humphries, M.; Gurney, K. & Prescott, T. (2005). Is there an integrative center in the vertebrate brain-stem? A robotic evaluation of a model of the reticular formation viewed as an action selection device. *Adaptive Behavior, 13*(2), 97-113.

Jeannerod, M. (1997). *The cognitive neuroscience of action.* Blackwell, Oxford.

Jog, M.; Kubota, Y.; Connolly, C.; Hillegaart, V. & Graybiel, A. (1999). Building neural representations of habits. *Science, 286,* 1745-9.

Kandel, E. R.; Schwartz, J. H. & Jessell, T. M. (2000). *Principles of neural science.* McGraw-Hill.

Kilmer, W. (1997). A command computer for complex autonomous systems. *Neurocomputing, 17,* 47-59.

Kilmer, W.; McCulloch, W. & Blum, J. (1969). A model of the vertebrate central command system. *International Journal of Man-Machine Studies, 1,* 279-309.

Laubach, M. (2005). Who's on first? What's on second? The time course of learning in corticostriatal systems. *Trends in Neurosci, 28*(10), 509-11.

Lewis, B. & O'Donnell, P. (2000).Ventral tegmental area afferents to the prefrontal cortex maintain membrane potential 'up' states in pyramidal neurons via D1 dopamine receptors. *Cerebral Cortex, 10*(12), 1168-75.

Lingenhöhl, K. & Friauf, E. (2004). Giant neurons in the caudal pontine reticular formation receive short latency acoustic input: An intracellular recording and HRP-study in the rat. *J Comparative Neurology, 325*(4), 473-92.

Lorenz, K. (1996). Innate bases of learning. InK.H. Pribram & J.King (Eds.), *Learning as self organization* (pp. 1–56). Lawrence Erlbaum.

Mareschal, D.; Johnson, M.; Sirois, S.; Spratling, M.; Thomas, M.& Westermann, G. (2007). *Neuroconstructivism: Perspectives and prospectives (volume i)*. Oxford University Press.

Marr, D. (1982). *Vision*. Freeman, San Francisco.

Martínez-Marín, T. & Duckett,T. (2005). Fast reinforcement learning for vision-guided mobile robots. In *Proc IEEE International Conference on Robotics and Automation (ICRA 2005).*

Morris, G.; Nevet, A.; Arkadir, D.; Vaadia, E. & Bergman, H. (2006). Midbrain dopamine neurons encode decisions for future action. *Nature Neurosci, 9*(8), 1057-63.

Niv,Y.; Daw, N. & Dayan, P. (2006). Choice values. *Nature Neurosci, 9*(8), 987-8.

Noë, A. (2004). *Action in perception*. MIT Press.

Panksepp, J. (1998). *Affective neuroscience*. New York: Oxford University Press.

Pasupathy, A. & Miller, E. (2005). Different time courses of learning-related activity in the prefrontal cortex and striatum. *Nature, 433*, 873-6.

Piaget, J. (1953). *The origin of intelligence in the child*. Routledge and Kegan Paul.

Prescott, T. (2007). Forced moves or good tricks in design space? Landmarks in the evolution of neural mechanisms for action selection. *Adaptive Behavior*, (to appear).

Prescott, T.; Stafford, T. & Gurney, K. (2006).A robot model of the basal ganglia: Behavior and intrinsic processing. *Neural Networks, 19*, 31-61.

Reynolds, J.; Hyland, B. & Wickens, J. (2001). A cellular mechanism of reward-related learning. *Nature, 413*, 67-70.

Rich, E. & Shapiro, M. (2007). Prelimbic/infralimbic inactivation impairs memory for multiple task switches, but not flexible selection of familiar tasks. *JNeurosci, 27*(17), 4747-55.

Roelfsema, P. & Ooyen, A. van. (2005). Attention-gated reinforcement learning of internal representations for classification. *Neur Comp, 17*, 2176-214.

Roesch, M. & Olson, C. (2004). Neuronal activity related to reward value and motivation in primate frontal cortex. *Science, 304*(5668), 307-10.

Rothkopf, C.& Ballard, D. (2007). Credit assignment with Bayesian reward estimation. In *COSYNE -Computational and Systems Neuroscience.*

Samejima, K.; Ueda, Y.; Doya, K. & Kimura, M. (2005). Representation of action-specific reward values in the striatum. *Science, 310*(5752), 1337-40.

Schoups, A.; Vogels, R.; Qian, N.& Orban, G. (2001). Practising orientation identification improves orientation coding in V1 neurons. *Nature, 412*, 549-53.

Schultz,W.; Dayan, P. & Montague,P. (1997). A neural substrate of prediction and reward. *Science, 275*, 1593-9.

Shepherd, G. M. (Ed.). (2004). *The synaptic organization of the brain*. Oxford University Press.

Shuler, M. & Bear, M. (2006). Reward timing in the primary visual cortex. *Science, 311*, 1606-9.

Sparks, D. (2002). The brainstem control of saccadic eye movements. *Nat Rev Neurosci, 3*, 952-64.

Sridharan, D.; Prashanth, P. & Chakravarthy, V. (2006). The role of the basal ganglia in ex ploration in a neural model based on reinforcement learning. *Int J Neur Syst, 16*(2), 111-24.

Stafford, T. & Gurney, K. (2007). Biologically constrained action selection improves cognitive control in a model of the stroop task. *Phil.Trans.R. Soc.B.*

Sun, X.; Zhao, Y. & Wolf, M. (2005). Dopamine receptor stimulation modulates AMPA receptor synaptic insertion in prefrontal cortex neurons. *J Neurosci, 25*(32), 7342-51.

Sutton, R. & Barto, A. (1998). *Reinforcement learning: An introduction.* Cambridge, MA: MIT Press.

Teicher, M.H.; Anderson, C.M.; Polcari, A.; Glod, C.A.; Maas, L.C. & Renshaw, P.F. (2000). Functional deficits in basal ganglia of children with attention-deficit/hyperactivity disorder shown with functional magnetic resonance imaging relaxometry. *Nature Medicine, 6*, 470–473.

Tobler, P.; Fiorillo, C. & Schultz, W. (2005). Adaptive coding of reward value by dopamine neurons. *Science, 307*(5715), 1642-5.

Triesch, J.; Jasso, H. & Deák, G. (2007). Emergence of mirror neurons in a model of gaze following. *Adaptive Behavior, 15*(2), 149–65.

Ungless, M.; Magill, P. & Bolam, J. (2004). Uniform inhibition of dopamine neurons in the ventral tegmental area by aversive stimuli. *Science, 303*, 2040-2.

Vessel, E. (2004). *Behavioral and neuralinvestigation of perceptual affect.* Unpublished doctoral dissertation, University of Southern California.

Weber, C.; Muse, D.; Elshaw, M. & Wermter, S. (2005). Reinforcement learning in MirrorBot. In *Proceedings of 15th international conference on artificial neural networks* (p. 305-10). Springer-Verlag Berlin Heidelberg.

Weber, C. & Triesch, J. (2006). A possible representation of reward in the learning of saccades. In *Proceedings of the 6th international workshop on epigenetic robotics* (pp. 153–60). Lund University Cognitive Studies.

Weber, C.; Wermter, S. & Elshaw, M. (2006). A hybrid generative and predictive model of the motor cortex. *Neural Networks, 19*(4), 339–53.

Weber, C.; Wermter, S. & Zochios, A. (2004). Robot docking with neural vision and reinforcement. *Knowledge-Based Systems, 17*(2-4), 165-72.

Weigmann, K. (2006). Robots emulating children. *EMBO Report, 7*(5), 474-6.

Wermter, S.; Weber, C. & Elshaw, M. (2004). Associative neural models for biomimetic multi-modal learning in a mirror neuron-based robot. In A. Cangelosi, G. Bugmann & R. Borisyuk (Eds.), *Modeling language, cognition and action* (p. 31-46).

Wermter, S.; Weber, C.; Elshaw, M.; Gallese, V. & Pulvermüller, F. (2005). Biomimetic neural learning for intelligent robots. In S. Wermter, G. Palm & M. Elshaw (Eds.), (p. 162-81). Springer.

Wermter, S.; Weber, C.; Elshaw, M.; Panchev, C.; Erwin, H. & Pulvermüller, F. (2004). Towards multimodal neural robot learning. *Robotics and Autonomous Systems, 47*(2-3), 171-5.

Wheeler, M. (2005). *Reconstructing the world.* MIT Press.

Wilson, C. J. (2004). Basal ganglia. In *The synaptic organization of the brain* (pp. 361–415). Oxford University Press.

Wood, R.; Humphries, M. & Gurney, K. (2006). A large scale biologically realistic model of the neostriatum. In *Computational Neuroscience meeting (CNS).*

8

Decentralized Reinforcement Learning for the Online Optimization of Distributed Systems

Jim Dowling and Seif Haridi
Swedish Institute of Computer Science
Sweden

1. Introduction

Distributed reinforcement learning is concerned with what action an agent should take, given its current state and the state of other agents, so as to minimize a system cost function (or maximize a global objective function). In this chapter, we give an overview of distributed reinforcement learning and describe how it can be used to build distributed systems that can adapt and optimize their operation to a dynamic environment. In particular, we focus on decentralized systems, where an agent has only a partial view of the system and does not have access to the system cost (or reward) function, that is, an agent does not have full observability of the state of all other agents in the system and system utility (performance) is not directly measurable in real-time.

Theoretical results that establish convergence and optimality guarantees for single-agent reinforcement learning algorithms do not hold for distributed (multi-agent) systems. This is because distributed environments are inherently non-stationary: agents can independently learn, adapt, and initiate new tasks. In fact, Bernstein et al. have shown that the problem of optimizing agent behavior in such a decentralized multi-agent system has non-deterministic exponential time-complexity (Bernstein et al., 2002). Thus, most existing approaches use approximate algorithms for distributed reinforcement learning.

In order for agents to learn globally good policies, we assume the need for agents to cooperate. This is because greedy policies at agents, based only on local state at the agent, do not necessarily improve global utility; in fact, they can even decrease global utility, as demonstrated in the "tragedy of the commons" problem. Another key property of distributed reinforcement learning is scalability; learning algorithms will cause message passing between agents and the algorithms need to make efficient use of the network.

Examples of distributed systems that perform online optimization using distributed reinforcement learning include packet routing in MANETs (Dowling, 2005), information-directed routing in Sensor Networks (Ghasemaghaei et al, 2007; Zhang et al, 2006), and optimization of application configurations in pervasive computing environments (Rigole, 2006). Although these systems all employ different variants of distributed reinforcement learning, they are all cooperative; agents selflessly contribute towards a common goal.

We see distributed reinforcement learning having similar potential to function approximation with reinforcement learning (RL). In both cases, the theoretical foundation that RL adopts from dynamic programming no longer applies, but that does not prevent the development of useful systems. From a RL perspective, the potential advantages of adding distribution to reinforcement learning algorithms include the ability to handle larger state spaces by partitioning the state space over agents, an increased rate of learning through parallel learning over more computational hardware, and the ability to build more robust systems using redundant agents. For distributed systems, distributed reinforcement learning is an approach that can be used to build robust, self-managing and self-optimizing systems.

In the next sections, we address these questions, describe existing and related approaches to distributed reinforcement learning and decentralized control, and, finally, we present our work on collaborative reinforcement learning, and show how it can be used to build an adaptive load-balancing system.

2. Challenges of physical aspects of distributed systems

Physical aspects of distributed systems should be accounted for in any distributed reinforcement learning algorithm. For example, agents communicate by message passing over a network, but messages may be lost and message delivery is typically not guaranteed within a fixed time bound. Message passing is required in distributed reinforcement learning algorithms to enable agents to collaborate to solve distributed problems and to enable agents to collectively learn improved policies by sharing their local information with one another. Care must be taken when designing distributed reinforcement learning algorithms, to ensure that collective learning strategies do not generate excessive amounts of network traffic, flooding the system. Techniques for improving network utilization should also be considered, such as the caching of recent data received from neighbors, asynchronous message passing, and sending batches of messages.

Given that accounting for the network is crucial to distributed reinforcement learning, there are a number of related issues that must be taken into account when designing distributed reinforcement learning algorithms. These include:

- *degree of centralization*: centralization of system state or cost (reward) signals introduces both a bottleneck and a single point of failure in a system. However, distribution of system state and cost functions requires adapting the Markov Decision Process (MDP) framework to a distributed (multi-agent) system.
- *non-stationary environments*: distributed systems cannot be modeled as strict MDPs, as they may have non-Markovian aspects such as multiple, concurrent decision-making agents and history dependence (Tesauro, 2007). However, RL is only guaranteed to work in stationary (or almost stationary) environments. Network connections, however, are non-stationary, but in practice may be stable for long enough periods to enable learning or at least be amenable to modeling. Learning algorithms should not just guarantee eventual convergence on a near-optimal policy, but also guarantee *timely convergence* to ensure that real-time distributed system constraints are met. Realistic experimentation plays an important role in validating the timeliness of convergence of algorithms.
- *agent and network dynamism*: in the system of interest, will the number of agents be fixed or limited, and will there be any form of control on how and when agents join the system? Can agents adapt their connections to change their neighbors at runtime, thus

changing the system topology? We must assume there is no control over agents leaving the system, as hosts (and, therefore, agents) can fail arbitrarily.

- *message passing costs*: what events in the learning algorithms cause message passing? We need to modify learning algorithms so that message passing costs are included when calculating the costs of actions that induce message passing. In general, acquiring experience in distributed systems is costly, as it affects system performance.
- *agent views*: do agents collaborate to solve system problems? How is an agent's local view of the system represented? What update strategies are used to update an agent's view? Are update strategies synchronous or asynchronous to the execution of the agent's learning algorithm?
- *model-based learning*: model-free learning is generally not useful where acquiring real-world experience is more expensive than computation. How do we integrate model-based learning into distributed reinforcement learning algorithms?
- *approximating the system cost signal*: how can agents approximate the system cost signal, given that the global utility of a distributed system is not directly measurable at runtime? Solutions need to address the *spatial credit assignment problem*: how agents determine which other agents and states were responsible for taking good actions. Solutions must quickly and efficiently propagate changes to relevant agents. Solutions may also address non-linear system cost functions, where a small action, relative to the size of the system, by one agent can produce large changes in system utility.

3. Distributed reinforcement learning problem definition

Goldman and Zilberstein characterize multi-agent reinforcement learning as a decentralized control problem for stochastic systems (Goldman and Zilberstein, 2004). In decentralized control systems, agents take decisions without complete state information with the goal of optimizing some system performance measure. The general distributed learning problem can be characterized as how an agent can learn a policy, using partially-observable state information that minimizes a partially-observable system cost function in the presence of other independent agents, who are also learning a policy under the same conditions.

We now formulate the problem in terms of discrete-time stochastic control problems, based on (Cogill et al, 2006). The system has a finite state space S, and a finite set A of actions available at each time step. A cost $g(s,a) \rightarrow \Re$ is incurred when an action $a \in A$ is taken while in state $s \in S$. At the time step after an action a is taken in state S, the system state transitions with probability $p(s'|s,a)$ to $s' \in S$. The goal of the system is to learn a policy for choosing actions that minimizes the overall cost incurred over a given time period, where costs may be geometrically discounted over time. (The alternative, equivalent formulation is to maximize accumulated rewards; we minimize costs to explicitly model the cost of message passing over a network). A policy $\pi : S \rightarrow A$ describes which action is chosen by the system, based on the current system state. Here we consider the problem of choosing a policy to minimize the *expected total discounted cost*

$$V^{\pi}(s) = E\left[\sum_{t=0}^{\infty} \gamma^t g(s_t, \pi_t(s_t)) \middle| s_0 = s\right] \tag{1}$$

where $0 \leq \gamma < 1$. For a policy π, we can compute the total cost V^{π} from state s by solving:

$$V^{\pi}(s) = g(s, \pi(s)) + \gamma \sum_{s' \in S} p(s' \mid s, \pi(s)) V^{\pi}(s') \tag{2}$$

For the expected total discounted cost, there is a unique optimal value function, $V^*(s)$, which minimizes the total cost for all initial states:

$$V^*(s) = \min_{a \in A}\left(g(s,a) + \gamma \sum_{s' \in S} p(s' \mid s, a) V^*(s') \right) \tag{3}$$

A closely related function is the optimal action-value function, $Q^*(s, a)$, given by

$$Q^*(s,a) = g(s,a) + \gamma \sum_{s' \in S} p(s' \mid s, a) V^*(s') \tag{4}$$

An optimal policy π^*, not necessarily unique, is obtained from Q^* by taking $\pi^* = \arg\min_a Q^*(s,a)$.

The above equations describe an optimal policy for a system with globally observable state and system actions, independent of whether a single agent controls the policy or many agents collaboratively control the policy. In some versions of distributed reinforcement learning system, many agents use local actions and message passing to control the evolution of the single system MDP.

Decentralized reinforcement learning is a different decentralized control model, where many independent RL agents learn their local policy using both local state, and a model of neighboring agents built using message passing (Schneider et al, 1999; Dowling et al, 2005). In *decentralized reinforcement learning,* an agent has a model for its neighbors, called its *view* of the system. There is no global state identifying the current state of the system and no global actions. The desired system behavior must be realized by providing agents with actions to affect their local environment, as well as the ability to both collaborate and communicate with other agents. At this point, we can no longer model the system as a single MDP, and formally reason about the system's optimal policy. The system still has a cost function that should be minimized, although its representation is now distributed.

For problems that can be factored, agents can often *approximate* the system cost function, by knowing that the agent and its neighbors make a linear contribution to the system cost. Here, an agent learns a policy that minimizes the cost of its actions based both on its local state and its view, where a view is the agent's set of neighboring agents. This way, local cost functions at agents can, over time, converge on a good approximation of the system cost. The policy will only be approximate, because other agents are simultaneously learning local policies (and may execute conflicting actions that reduce system utility), and the agent's view is typically not always fully consistent with the actual state of neighbors (as it would be overly expensive to maintain synchronized views of neighbors). Also, agents may need to learn about costs at remote parts of the system, not represented in their local view. In this case, it is important that the view model enables estimated costs to propagate over multiple views to reach the relevant agents in the system.

We now present our simplified model for decentralized reinforcement learning. A decentralized reinforcement learning agent n_i is described by the tuple

$$n_i = (S_i, A_i, v_i) \tag{5}$$

, where $n_i \in N$ is an agent from the set of all agents in the system N, S_i is the set of local states at n_i, A_i is the set of local actions at n_i, $v_i \subset N$ is the set of neighboring agents of n_i. The global state the system is a function of all local states at all agents in the system. A neighbor relation is defined from one agent to another agent, if one agent can send messages directly to the other agent. An agent may have a local representation of its set of neighbors, $v_i = (v_0, \ldots, v_{N-1})$, defined as the agent's *view* of the system. The set of all agents and their neighbors defines the *topology* of the system as a graph; where agents are the vertices and neighbor relations are the directed edges. Typically, an agent has much fewer neighbors than there are agents in the system. Finally, the behavior of the system containing *K* agents is defined as a set of policies, one for each of the agents, $\pi_i : S_i \rightarrow A_i$ for i = 1, . . . ,K-1. The decentralized reinforcement learning problem is defined as how the set of policies minimizes a system cost function.

4. Related work on distributed reinforcement learning

In distributed reinforcement learning, actions by individual agents can potentially influence any other agent in the system. However, a naïve approach to action selection where agents are required to reach full consensus on the best action for the system does not scale, due to the excessive message passing required to reach consensus. In this section we cover some of the existing distributed reinforcement learning models that reduce the amount of system knowledge that an agent requires to select an action that is approximately optimal for the system. We also discuss Ant Colony Optimization (ACO), a multi-agent learning model not directly related to RL, but which addresses the same problem of decentralized control.

4.1 Coordination graphs for the collaborative multi-agent control of a system MDP

A multi-agent RL system can be modeled as the collaborative multi-agent control of a single MDP (Guestrin et. al, 2003). In this model, the distributed control problem involves the online or offline computation of a coordinated action for a group of *n* agents. Each agent *i* selections a local action $\mathrm{a_i}$ and the joint action of all *n* agents is $\mathrm{a} = (\mathrm{a_0}, .., \mathrm{a_{n-1}})$. The joint action generates a cost $\mathrm{g(a)}$ for the group of agents, where the optimal joint action is $a^* = \arg\min_a g(a)$. The goal of the agents is to select actions that minimize the received costs over a sequence of actions. However, if agents have full observability of the system, the size of the joint action space increases exponentially in the number of agents in the system.

One way to reduce the size of the joint action space is to enable agents to exclude those states that do not need to be estimated when computing joint actions. This approach is viable for problems that can be *factored*. Factored problems can be sub-divided, solved separately by agents and the overall result can be calculated as a linear combination of the results of the sub-problems. Guestrin introduced a coordination graph (CG) as a model for representing factored problems (Guestrin et. al, 2003), where the global coordination problem is approximated as a set of local coordination problems involving a smaller number of agents. In a CG, the global cost function, **g**(a), is decomposed into a sum of local cost functions, f_i, calculated independently at each agent using every possible action combination within the agent's neighborhood:

$$g(a) = \sum_{1}^{n} f_i(a_i) \tag{6}$$

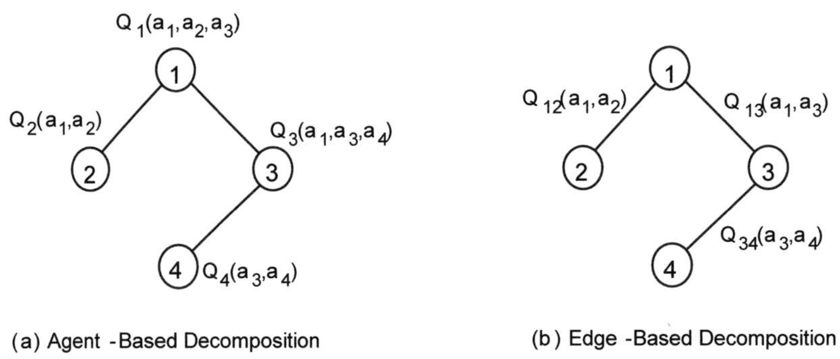

Fig. 1. The global Q-function for a 4-agent problem can be modeled in a coordination graph (Kok and Vlassis, 2006).

Although Guestrin's CG model was designed for off-line approximation, Kok and Vlassis adapted the model for online learning. In both models, the global Q-function is factored in a CG. In *Fig. 1*, we can see how Guestrin decomposes the global Q-function using an agent's set of neighbors, called agent-based decomposition (Guestrin et. al, 2002), while Kok and Vlassis decompose the global Q-function using connections between pairs of agents, called edge-based decomposition (Kok and Vlassis, 2006). In edge-based decomposition, an edge from agent i to agent j is represented as a Q-function, $Q_{i,j}$, where the sum of all edges (Q-functions) defines the global Q-function. Local Q-functions are updated based on the local Q-functions of the pair of agents that form the edge. This compares to agent-based decomposition where local Q-functions are updated based on the local Q-functions of all neighbors. In order to calculate the best joint action, agents in Kok and Vlassis' model use an approximate algorithm called max-plus, while agents in Guestrin's model use an exact algorithm called variable-elimination. The edge-based decomposition approach scales linearly to the width of the CG, while the agent-based decomposition approach scales exponentially (Kok and Vlassis, 2006).

The main problem with applying coordination graphs to online optimization of distributed systems is that it is often communication constraints that determine the topology of distributed systems, not problem constraints as in coordination graphs. The approach also assumes that problems can be factored, and does not explicitly account for the possibility of agent failure.

4.2 Independent learners

An alternative to selecting joint actions is to allow agents take individual actions, with the goal that the collective behavior of the agents will minimize the system cost function (Kok and Vlassis, 2007). Experiments by Claus and Boutilier with groups of independent Q-learning agents showed the need for agent cooperation to ensure that local agent actions are globally good (Claus and Boutilier, 1998). Agent's that are unaware of other agents can choose actions which are suboptimal for the system, as they use local Q-values that are incorrectly assumed to be independent of the actions selected and rewards received by the other agents. Another approach to building an independent learner model, where agents are unaware of one another, is Wolpert's Collective Intelligence (COIN) model (Lawson and Wolpert, 2002). In the COIN model, problems are structured such that independent agents' local cost models are adapted to approximate the system cost model, ensuring that actions that are locally good are always globally good. This approach, however, has limited applicability.

4.3 Distributed value functions

Schneider et al., 2002, have designed a distributed reinforcement learning algorithm where independent agents coordinate learning by sharing value functions between one another. Agents define a weight function *f(i,j)* that defines an agent's fixed set of neighbors (through weights being zero to non-neighbors, and non-zero for neighbors), and the weight of the Q-values from neighbors that should be contributed to updates to Q-values. The weight function is quite a general, as it defines both the static topology of the system and how value information is transferred over the network to a state-action pair from a successor state. As it is an approximate algorithm, they do not provide any convergence guarantees. The update function is defined as:

$$Q_i(s_i,a_i)=(1-\alpha).Q_i(s_i,a_i)+\alpha\left[R_i(s,a)+\gamma\sum_{neighbours}f(i,j)\max_{a_j}\ Q_j(s'_j,a'_j)\right] \quad (7)$$

However, the weight function assumes that agents can exchange information about their local values at no cost and that the environment is stationary. Also, the model does not provide support for reducing network utilization, such as caching data and asynchronous or batched message passing.

4.4 DEC-POMDP-Com

Goldman and Zilberstein address an offline version of the decentralized reinforcement learning problem for independent agents. They firstly assume that agents have probabilistic observations of the state space (noisy observations), that is, agents are described locally by a partially observable Markov Decision Process (POMDP). A group of agents is defined as a decentralized POMDP (DEC-POMDP). They also provide agents with an explicit language of communication, consisting of an alphabet of messages, to develop a communication policy. Communication policies model agent communications and its associated costs and the complete model of decentralized POMDPs with communication support is called a DEC-POMDP-Com. With this model, a joint policy can be defined over agents as a set of local policies, where each policy is composed of the communication and action policies for each agent. The result is a complex model, which eschews a potentially simpler approach of integrating messaging costs into reward functions. As their model is an off-line approach, it is unsuitable for online learning in distributed systems.

4.5 Ant colony optimization

The distributed control problem is also addressed by Ant-Colony Optimization (ACO), a non-reinforcement learning based approach, best described as a meta-heuristic for producing approximate solutions to combinatorial optimization problems (Dorigo and Stuetzle, 2004). Combinatorial optimization problems involve finding the minimum cost solution from a set of possible solutions, and problems are defined as

$$\Pi = \left(S, f, \Omega\right) \tag{8}$$

, where S is the set of candidate solutions, f is the objective function that assigns a value $f(s)$ to each candidate solution, $s \in S$, and Ω is a set of constraints (Dorigo and Stuetzle, 2004). ACO can be used to solve both static and dynamic combinatorial problems, where dynamic problems have non-stationary stochastic dynamics. Dynamic problems are defined as a function of some quantities whose value is set by the dynamics of an underlying system.

In order solve dynamic combinatorial optimization problems, ACO algorithms construct a problem with the following structure (Curran, 2003):

- a set of *components* $C = \{c_1, \ldots, c_M\}$, which correspond to agents with a single state in RL;
- a set of L *connections* among C, which correspond to neighbor relationships between agents;
- a *connection cost* function, $J : L \times R \rightarrow \Re$ defined over the connections, and parameterized by time. $J(l, t)$ corresponds loosely to the expected cost $g(s,a)$;
- ACO defines a *solution* to a combinatorial optimization problem as the lowest cost feasible path through the topology, that is, the graph of components and connections, which satisfies the set of problem requirements;
- In ACO a *solution cost* function is typically a summation of the connection cost over the connections that the solution contains. This is similar to factoring the system cost function in factored MDPs, as it is also a linear combination of the cost of the sub-problems.

ACO works by a population of agents, called ants, finding minimum cost paths (solutions) in the component graph by exploring, measuring the cost of edges as it traverses them, and storing estimated path costs at components as a *pheromone trail*. Components represent the environment of the agents, and pheromone trails store path costs from the current component c_i to another (often the terminal) component c_M. The pheromone trail at c_i can be observed by other agents as they traverse component c_i, in a form of indirect communication, known as stigmergy. Other agents can use the pheromone trail as a partial solution to their (potentially different) optimization problem.

Similar to agent action selection in RL, ants choose a connection in the graph using a probabilistic decision rule, and must balance exploration and exploitation to ensure that good quality solutions are found in reasonable time. However, an ant also has a memory of the path it has traversed that can be used in decision making, for example, to prevent loops in paths. When an ant has reached its termination conditions, it generally uses its memory to retrace its path and update the pheromone trails to reflect the cost of the solution found. This process of sending backward ants is very similar to multi-step backups in RL. Also, the backup approach in ACO naturally factors optimization problems by only attempting to update some subset of the states in the system, those states traversed by the ant from the start state. This is similar to approaches in RL used to reduce the amount of states updated after an action is taken, such as coordination graphs and prioritized sweeping (Sutton and Barto, 1998).

An important difference with RL is ACO's *pheromone trail decay*, in which the value of the pheromone trails decreases automatically over time. Decaying discovered solutions over time prevents too early convergence on sub-optimal solutions and increases exploration. Decay also helps adaptation from old solutions to new solutions in response to changes in the environment. Later, in collaborative reinforcement learning, we show how the similar mechanisms of decaying of estimated costs in RL can be used by agents learning in non-stationary environments.

ACO problems can be viewed as a subset of RL problems (Curran, 2003). In particular, ACO is applicable to problems where:

- agents are independent learners;
- states are discrete and all paths eventually terminate, that is, absorbing Markov Decision Processes in RL;
- there are *start states*, which are those where optimization is initiated, and whose value must be optimized.

A significant difference between ACO and RL are connection costs in ACO which may be time-varying, enabling adaptation to a non-stationary environment. RL has no time-based model for decaying discovered solutions.

5. Collaborative reinforcement learning

The rest of this chapter concerns our work on collaborative reinforcement learning (CRL), (Dowling et al, 2005; Dowling, 2004). CRL's system model defines a decentralized reinforcement learning system as a set of independent, collaborative learner agents. Similar to ACO, collaborative reinforcement learning models system optimization problems as a set of discrete optimization problems (DOP), that can be initiated at any agent and solved at any agent in the system. A DOP is defined as the combinatorial optimization problem, see Equation 8, of finding the agent from a discrete set of agents (the system) that can solve a particular problem with lowest cost. The ACO-like notion of a DOP as the problem to be solved by an agent can also be viewed as a task from traditional RL literature.

In CRL, a system is modeled as a graph, $G(V,E)$, where agents are vertices and views of neighbors, defined later in Equation 10, define the edges in the graph. From the agent-perspective the goal of CRL is to solve a DOP at the lowest cost agent in the system. From a system perspective, the goal of CRL is to minimize the total cost of solving all DOPs in the system. Each agent is an independent learner with its own local MDP; there is no global MDP or any joint actions defined over agents. Agents have only local actions and local states, but may collaborate with neighbors to solve DOPs and share estimated costs of solving DOPs with one another.

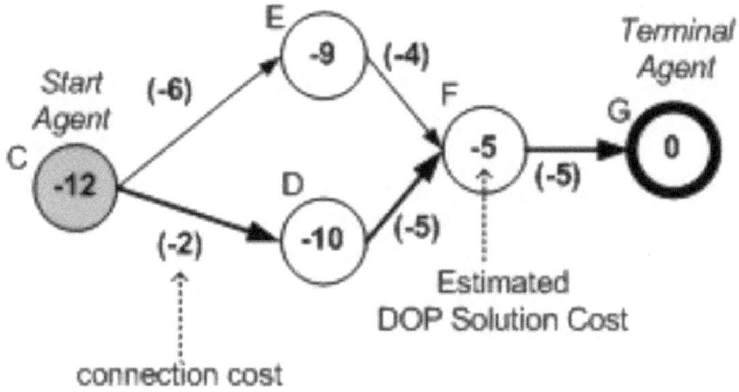

Fig. 2. A Discrete Optimization Problem (DOP) in CRL involves agents finding the lowest cost path from a Start Agent to a Terminal Agent that can solve the DOP.

In CRL, a DOP is solved as a sequential decision making problem, where the objective is to solve the DOP at lowest cost at some agent in the system (see

Fig. 2). This system problem can be viewed as an absorbing MDP (although no system MDP is explicitly represented) where the agents are states, that is, the DOP is guaranteed to enter a terminal state after a finite amount of time. Each agent has at least one state, an *initial state,* where the solution to the DOP is started, and at least one (and possibly all) agent(s) have a *terminal state,* where the DOP is solved.

There are three types of action that are supported in CRL for an agent to solve a DOP: a *local action* that contributes to solving the DOP at the current agent, a *delegation action* that forwards the DOP to a neighbor, and a *discovery action* that attempts to find a new neighbor (that may be able to solve the DOP at lower cost). Discovery actions are necessary for system bootstrap, when an agent does not have any neighbors, and for discovering new neighbors online. The three action types are illustrated in

Fig. 3, where it is shown how a MDP can be started either by an application at the agent's host or by a neighbor delegating the DOP to it. In distributed systems, delegation actions map to message passing over a network and discovery actions map to some form of underlying service or host discovery protocol. A discovery action that finds a new neighbor adds a new delegation action for the neighbor and a new Q-Value entry in its lookup table for the relevant state(s). For delegation actions, CRL provides a *connection cost* as an explicit model for the cost of using a network link. Agents attempt to learn a policy that solves DOPs with minimal cost, treating all three types of action equally, and attempting to select the action with the minimal estimated cost, given the agent's current state.

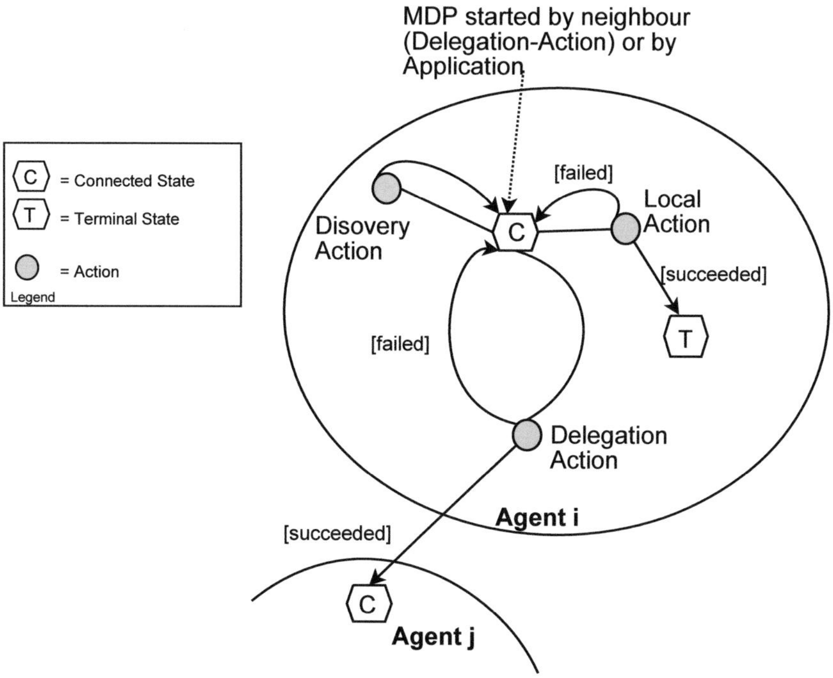

Fig. 3. Agent i has two states and three actions (a delegation, local and discovery action). The connected state is an initial state for the MDP at agent i and when the terminal state is reached at some agent the DOP has been solved. These are the three main types of action in CRL: local actions attempt to solve the DOP at the agent, delegation actions attempt to forward the DOP to a neighbor, and discovery actions try to find new neighbors. DOPs can be started by either an application or a neighbor; delegation and local actions may fail.

5.1 CRL system model

We now present the system model for Collaborative Reinforcement Learning (CRL). An agent n_i is described by the tuple

$$n_i = (S_i, A_i, v_i, C_i) \tag{9}$$

, where S_i is its set of local states, A_i is the set of local actions, $v_i \subset N$ is the set of neighboring agents of n_i , and C_i is the *cache*, a set of all *cached views* of neighbors of n_i . A cached view is defined as a pair containing a Q-function $Q_i(s_i, a_j)$ at n_i , where a_j is a delegation-action, and a V-value $V_j(s_v)$ for a state s_v at a neighboring agent n_j, for which a state transition is possible from s_i at agent n_i to s_j at agent n_j ,

$$(Q_i(s_i, a_j), V_j(s_v)) \in C_i, \ if \ P(s_v | s_i, a_j) > 0 \tag{10}$$

, where $s_i \in S_i$, $a_j \in A_i$, $s_v \in \bigcup_{j=0}^{|v_i|} S_j, S_j \in v_i$, and $V_j(s_v) \in \Re$. A state transition from a state s_i at n_i to a state s_j at n_j is realized by the termination of the local MDP at n_i and the initiation of a new MDP at n_j. The state s_j is called a connected state as it represents the connection of the MDPs at the two different agents. On a successful state transition state s_i to state s_j, a backup of $V_j(s_v)$ is made to its entry in the cache at agent n_i. A cached view of a neighbor, thus, represents a directed connection from agent n_i to agent n_j for the delegation of DOPs and the backup of V-value information. Model-based Q-learning algorithms can use the cached V-values to reason about the cost of delegation actions to neighbors, without having to send messages to those neighbors; thus helping improve network utilization. As we will see, the cached V-values can also be updated asynchronously by neighbors, using advertisements, and over time, by decay of the cache.

5.2 Advertisement of estimated DOP costs between agents

When an agent executes a delegation action to successfully forward a DOP to a neighbor, it receives an instantaneous cost (backup) from its neighbor that is used to update the agent's cached V-value. However, agents can also asynchronously advertise to their neighbors updates to the V-values of their connected states. This asynchronous advertisement enables agents to learn about remote parts of the system without executing actions.

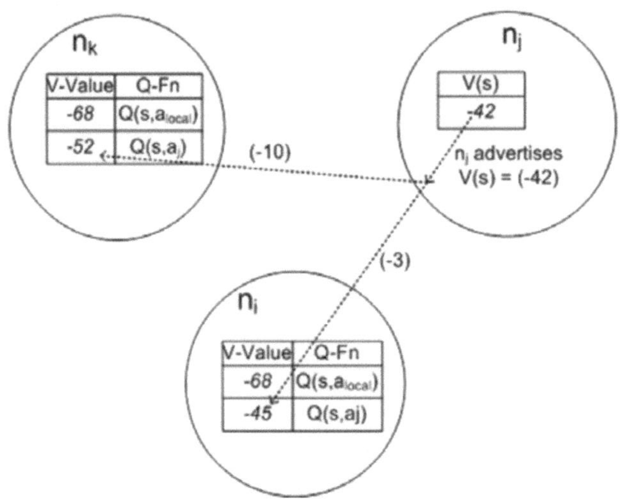

Fig. 4. Agent j advertises its V-value for state s to neighbors k and i. Advertisement enables agents to collectively learn about the state space by agents sharing updated V-values; agents do not have to take actions to learn about changes in the state space.

In *Fig. 4*, we can see how agent n_j sends its updated V-value to neighboring agents n_i and n_k. In this example, at agent *k* the V-value for a local action is -68, whereas its estimated cost of its neighbor agent *j* solving it is -52 (of which -10 is the estimated connection cost to *j*). Agent *k* will, therefore, have a higher probability of delegating a DOP to agent *j* than attempting to solve it locally. In this example, the advertisement may be caused by a local action at n_j or possibly by an advertisement received by n_j. Advertisements can cause cascading changes in MDPs at many agents caused by a change in a MDP at a single agent.

Implementation strategies for advertisement of V-values include broadcasting (useful in wireless networks where the network medium is shared), gossiping values periodically, conditional notification, and return values from delegation actions. Advertisements should be sent regularly to neighbors to indicate the agent's availability and refresh any cached V-values.

5.3 Decaying of cached Q-values for connected states

In the absence of advertisements, agents *decay* the V-values in their cache over time. The decay model allows agents to remove non-contactable agents from their set of neighbors when a cost threshold is reached. Decay enables agents to adapt their policies to a dynamic set of neighbors, as neighbors that were lower cost in the past are gradually forgotten over time in the absence of advertisements from them, for example, because they left the system. The rate of decay of costs in the cache is configurable, with higher rates more appropriate for more dynamic networks. Cached V-values for connected states are decayed using the following equation:

$$Decay(V(s)) = V(s).\rho^{td} \tag{11}$$

where *td* is the amount of time elapsed since the last received advertisement for $V(s)$ from a neighbor, $V(s) \in \Re$, and ρ is a scaling factor that sets the rate of decay.

5.4 CRL learning algorithm

The CRL learning algorithm is a *distributed model-based reinforcement learning algorithm* with a cost model for network connections. In CRL, agents maintain a model of the state transition probabilities, $P_i(s'|s,a)$, which is particularly useful for state transitions to connected states, as they represent network links between agents. Even a simple statistical model based on recent observations of the network link can be a powerful predictor of whether it will function or not (Dowling et al., 2005).

Executing actions in CRL returns a cost signal, $g_i(s,a)$ from the agent's local environment. However, delegation actions receive an additional connection cost, $D_i(s'|s,a)$, that provides the estimated network cost of delegating the DOP from the local agent to a neighboring agent. Our distributed model-based reinforcement learning algorithm *for delegation actions* is

$$Q_i(s,a) = g_i(s,a) + \sum_{s' \in S_i} P_i(s'|s,a).(D_i(s'|s,a) + V_j(s')) \tag{12}$$

, where s is the current state, a the action to be executed from the set of possible actions, and s' is the next state from the set of possible next states. $V_j(s')$ is the estimated cost of the

neighbor *j* solving the DOP, that is, it is the value function for agent *j*'s connected state s'. The value, $V_j(s')$, is retrieved from the local cache at agent *i*, and no message needs to be sent to agent *j* to calculate it. $P_i(s'|s,a)$ is calculated from the local state transition model, as the probability of the next state being s' after action *a* was executed in state s.
If, however, the action is not a delegation action, the connection cost, $D_i(s'|s,a)$, becomes zero. Thus, the distributed model-based reinforcement learning algorithm *for local actions and discovery actions* is:

$$Q_i(s,a) = g_i(s,a) + \sum_{s' \in S_i} P_i(s'|s,a)\left(V_j(s')\right) \tag{13}$$

The pseudo-code for the algorithm that a CRL agent executes at each time-step is outlined in Fig. 5. In this version, advertisement and decay are implemented as synchronous activities in the single thread; an alternative implementation would be to execute them asynchronously in a second thread.

```
Thread 1
1.  repeat forever
2.  listen for a DOP/advertisement from a neighbor/application;
3.  if (no DOP) execute asynchronous advertisements; update/decay cache;

4.  repeat
5.    observe the local environment's current state s,
6.    select and execute some legal action (local, delegation or discovery action) in state s
        using a probabilistic action selection strategy;
7.    receive a cost g followed by an observed transition to a state s';
8.    update the state transition model;
9.    execute the model-based distributed learning algorithm;
10.   execute asynchronous advertisements;
11.   decay cached delegation costs;
12. until DOP solved locally or DOP delegated
```

Fig. 5. Pseudo-Code for the CRL algorithm.

5.5 System optimization in CRL

The system optimization problem in CRL involves minimizing the cost of solving all DOPs in the system, that is, terminating all MDPs at all CRL agents. The system optimization problem is defined as minimizing the total cost of solving all DOPs

$$\sum_{i=0}^{K-1} \sum_{j=0}^{Mi-1} g(n_i, DOP_j) \tag{14}$$

, where K is the number of agents in the system and Mi is the number of DOPs to be solved at agent i. When DOPs are not competing for finite resources in the system and the network environment is stable, the DOPs can be optimized using local information and cached views of neighbors. However, when there are several agents attempting to solve DOPs concurrently at neighboring agents or the network environment is dynamic, the local estimated DOP solution cost at agent i quickly becomes stale, and agents need feedback from their neighbors to improve the quality of their local models.

5.6 Non-Markovian aspects in CRL

There are several heuristics in CRL that seek to overcome non-Markovian properties of distributed systems. For example, the DOP can have a local memory with information such as the list of currently visited agents, and a timeout value for when the DOP becomes invalid due to real-time constraints. The DOP memory can ensure that DOPs do not traverse loops, something MDP cannot prevent. The timeout value for a DOP could be added to an agent's MDP state space, although it could reduce the potential for collective learning of advertised V-Values, as the advertised values would now include a timeout value.

6. Load balancing experiments using CRL

We now define the load balancing problem for CRL. These experiments extend some previous work on load balancing using CRL (Dowling, 2004). We define the load balancing problem as a set J of n loads, and a set M of m hosts, where the goals are to store all load in the system (maximize resource utilization) in as short a time as possible (minimize the number of messages sent when storing the load), as well as to balance load equally among agents in the system. These last two goals can conflict, as storing loads as quickly as possible may not equalize load in the system. In our problem, we assume that any load can be potentially stored at any agent, subject to available local storage at the agent. We simplify the network cost problem by assuming that all network connections have equal latency. The loads have an entry point at some host (or hosts) in system; a load is routed from an entry point to a host that handles the load, constrained by the network topology of the system, which may contain cycles.

In our experiments, we define two different cost models for CRL that only differ by their cost models: in the *discrete cost model*, a successful store action for a load has no cost and an unsuccessful store action has some fixed high cost; in the *gradient cost model*, a successful store action has a cost that is a function of the spare capacity at the agent and an unsuccessful store action has some fixed high cost. In both models, we assigned a fixed connection cost for forwarding a load to a neighboring agent (in a real network, the connection cost could be measured from the underlying network message sending cost). The purpose of these two different CRL models is to show how the algorithm can be tuned exploit the first available space at agents (discrete model will prefer the first agent with spare capacity), or to exploit space at higher capacity agents (gradient cost model will prefer agents with higher spare capacity).

We ran our experiments in a discrete event simulator written in Java. The experiments define a topology of agents with connections between them, and a set of DOPs, where each DOP is a load storage problem. The unit of time in the experiments corresponds to a step in the simulator, where a step involves the execution of an action (storage, delegation or discovery) by an agent.

6.1 Experiment 1: Grid topology: Balancing of load over 48 homogenous agents and 2 server agents

The goal of this experiment is to evaluate whether agents can exploit their total load capacity (maximize resource usage), and minimize the amount of messages sent between agents (minimize time required to store all load). Sub-goals include evaluating how the different CRL policies exploit the higher load capacity at two servers in topology, and how well load is equalized among agents in the system. The topology in this experiment is a Grid; there are 48 agents with a capacity of 20 units, and 2 server agents with a capacity of 200 units. Each agent has 10 neighbors, where each agent *i* is connected to neighbors ((i+1) mod 50, … , (i+9) mod 50). The servers are placed at positions 47 and 48 in the grid, with the starting position at 0. Load units are sent into the system via the agent at position 0. We compare the two different CRL policies (CRL-discrete and CRL-gradient) with both a random policy (that selects a random action), and a dynamic programming (DP) solution that performs a breadth-first balancing of the load from the entry point. The CRL policies use a Boltzmann action selection strategy with a temperature parameter used to control the ratio of explorative to exploitative actions (Sutton and Barto, 1998). The results for the CRL and random policies were averaged over 5 experimental runs. The configuration parameters for the CRL policies are given in *Table 1*, below.

Parameter	**Value**
initial Q-Values for storage/discovery actions	-3
initial Q-Values for delegation actions	(-3*numNeighbours) + connection cost
connection cost	-10
MinQValue	-200
MaxQValue	0
delegation success reward	-2
cache decay rate	0.01
action store success reward for CRL-gradient	(MinQValue / (2 * (Capacity – CurrentLoad))
action store success reward for CRL-discrete	0
action store failure CRL-gradient/CRL-discrete	MinQValue
Temperature	0.9

Table 1. CRL-gradient and CRL-discrete configuration parameters.

As illustrated in

Fig. 6, all the policies successfully exploit the available capacity in the system. The random policy eventually finished after ~120,000 time steps. The dynamic programming (DP) policy is near optimal with respect to the number of time steps (i.e., actions executed) required to store the load. The CRL-discrete policy is also near optimal, as it is an exploitative policy that favors storing load over delegating load until an agent has reached its maximum capacity. The CRL-gradient policy is also near optimal until there is roughly 5% capacity left in the system, after which it performs similar to the random policy. This is because, at 5% spare capacity, the advertised V-Values from neighbors with a spare capacity reach the MinQValue, and DOPs effectively have to do a random walk to find the agents with spare capacity. This effect can be seen in Fig. 9.

In *Figures 7-10*, we can see how long the different policies take to discover and exploit the servers. Fig. 11 shows how well the loads are equalized among agents. The CRL and DP policies are more exploitative and tend to fill agents capacities sequentially from agent 0, leading to suboptimal load equalization, but they still compare favorably with the Random policy. The measure we used to determine load equalization is the standard deviation of agent loads from the mean agent load (in terms of percentage of capacity used) at agents.

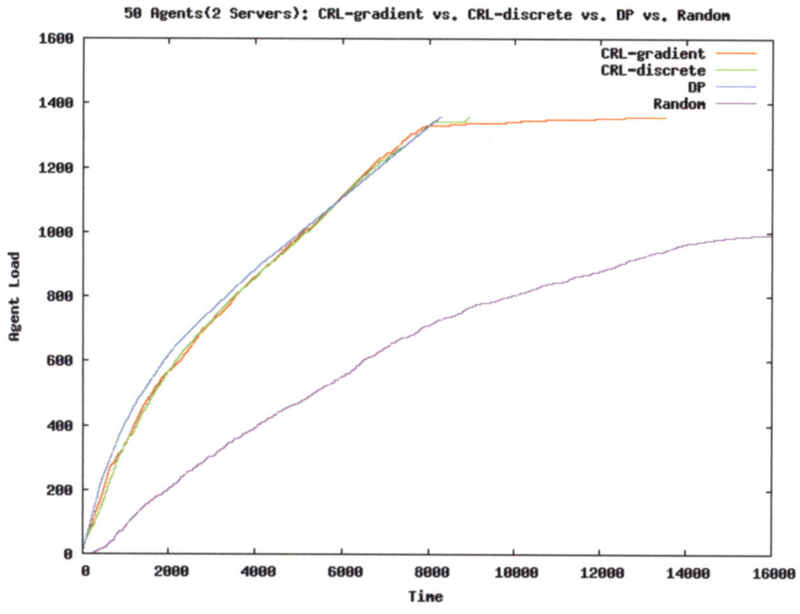

Fig. 6. Grid Topology: Load Balancing in a static topology with 48 agents and 2 servers (at positions 48, 49 in the grid) with CRL-gradient, CRL-discrete, Dynamic Programming and a random policy. Resource utilization is eventually maximized by all policies, while message passing is near-optimally minimized in both DP and CRL-Discrete.

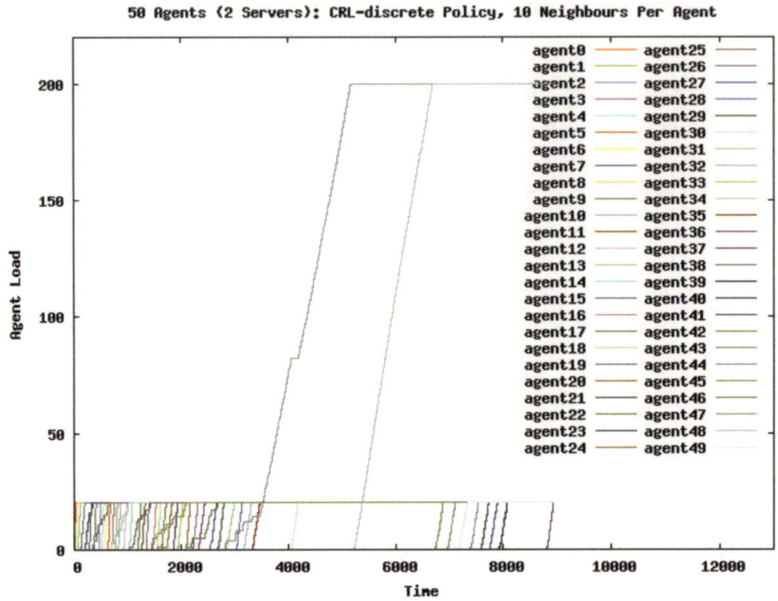

Fig. 7. Grid Topology: CRL-Discrete Policy. This exploitative policy favors storage actions at agents that are not fully loaded. Notice how agents are filled almost sequentially from the source of the load, agent 0.

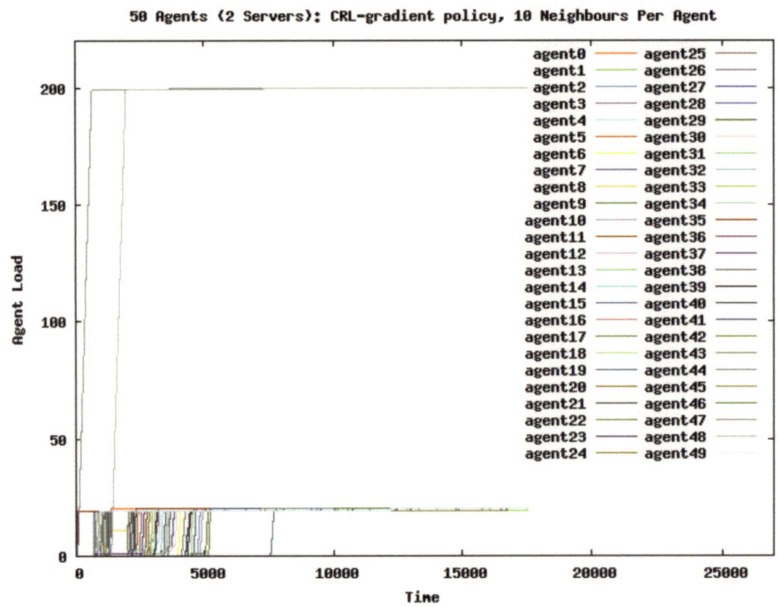

Fig. 8. Grid Topology: CRL-Gradient Policy. This policy favors storage actions on servers, but becomes random when agents are almost fully loaded. Notice how quickly the server agents are almost discovered and exploited, even though they are 3 hops from agent 0.

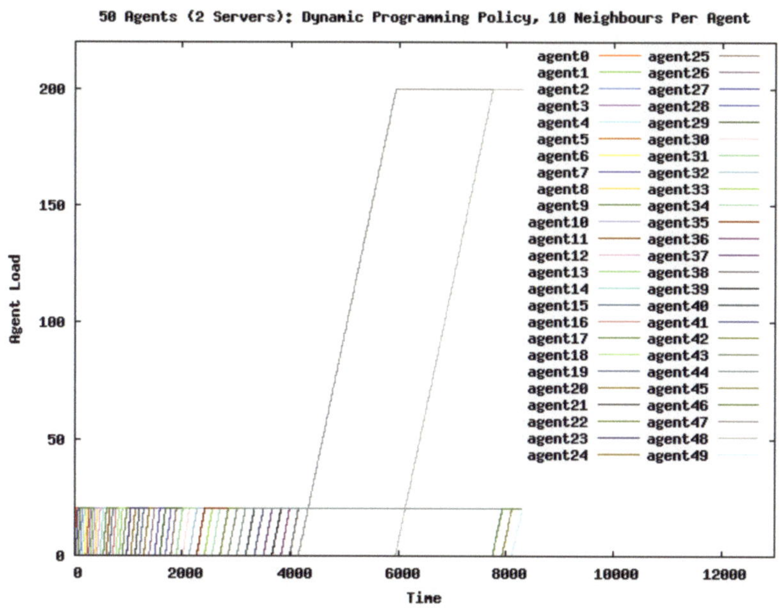

Fig. 9. Grid Topology: Dynamic Programming policy. Notice the similarity of this exploitative policy to the CRL-Discrete Policy.

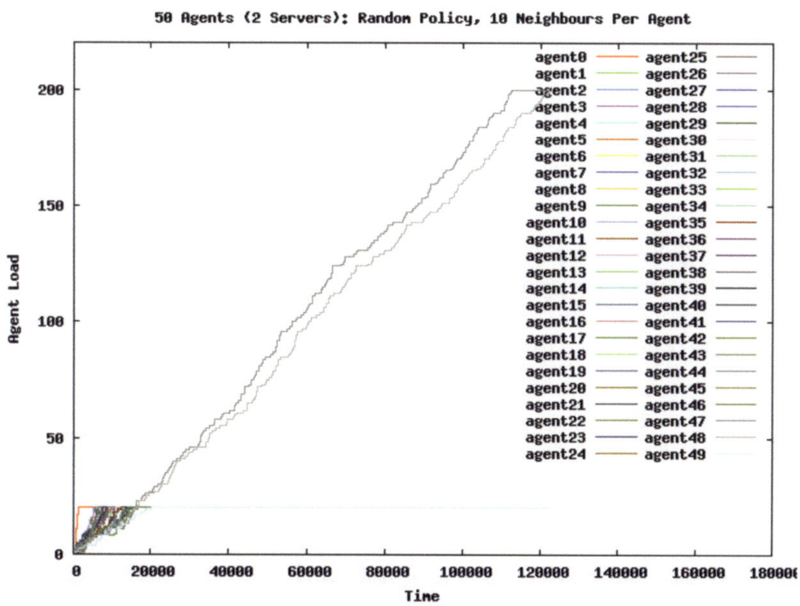

Fig. 10. Grid Topology: The random policy took over 15 times longer than the DP and CRL-Discrete policies to store all the load.

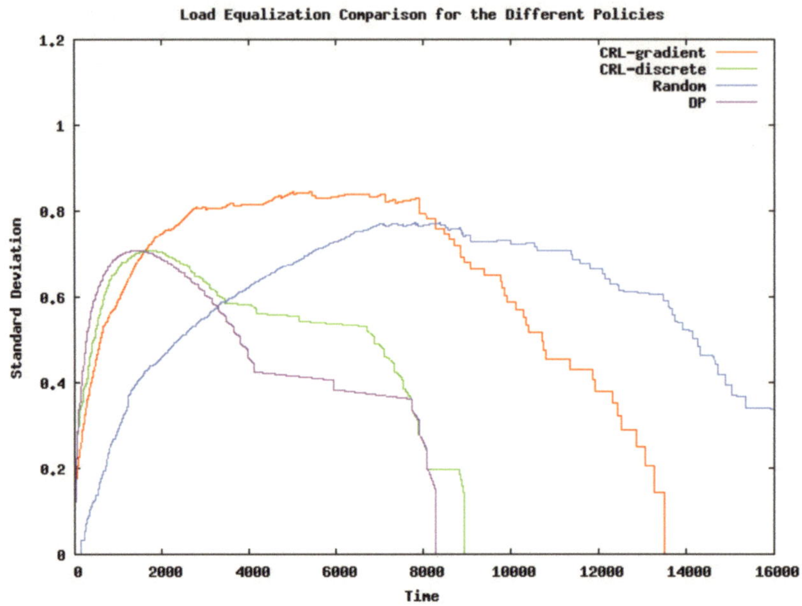

Fig. 11. Grid Topology: Standard Deviation of the Percentage of Load Capacity used at Agents for DP, CRL-Discrete, CRL-Gradient and Random Policies.

6.2 Experiment 2: Random topology: Balancing of load over 48 homogenous agents and 2 server agents

The goal of this experiment is, again, to maximize resource usage, and minimize message overhead, but this time in a random graph topology. In this topology, there are 48 agents with a capacity of 20 units, and 2 server agents with a capacity of 200 units. Each agent has 10 different neighbors, randomly distributed from the set of available agents, but where an agent cannot be a neighbor to itself. The servers are placed at positions more than 1-hop away from the starting position at 0. Load units are sent sequentially into the system via the agent at position 0. The same random topology was used to evaluate all policies, and the results were averaged over 5 experimental runs.

Again, we compare the two different CRL policies (CRL-discrete and CRL-gradient) with a random policy (that randomly selects an action from the local store action and the set of delegation actions), but the DP policy was not included as it does not finish, due to the presence of cycles in the topology. The CRL configuration parameters were the same as in experiment 1, with the exception of the Temperature, which was set to 0.85 for slightly increased exploration.

In *Fig. 12*, we can see that the CRL-Discrete policy is very effective at exploiting all available load in the system, while the CRL-Gradient policy again becomes a roughly random policy for the last ~5% spare capacity in the system. The Random Policy took an increased amount of time, over the grid topology, and terminated at time step ~150,000.

In another experiment, we added some dynamism to the environment by adding an extra server to the system when the system's load capacity was full (see *Fig. 13*). At the same time step, we added a discovery action to the 1-hop neighbors from agent 0 to enable them to discover the server (located at a 2-hop distance from the source agent 0). As can be seen, the

CRL-discrete policy quickly discovers and exploits the new server, while the CRL-gradient policy takes a longer time to do so. There was also quite high variation in how long the CRL-gradient policy took to discover the new server, indicating a high level of randomness in its exploration. The upward spike near the end of CRL-gradient policy was a point where collaborative feedback (that is, advertisements) from the new server eventually influenced reached the origin agent 0.

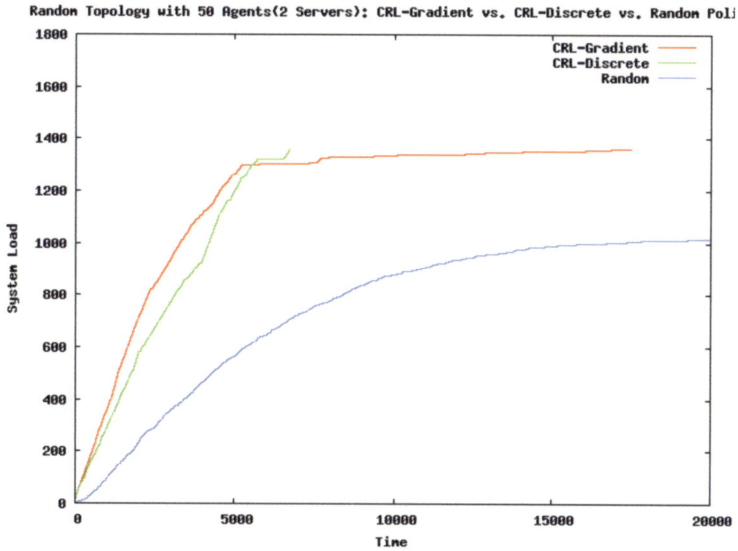

Fig. 12. Random Graph: Load Balancing for CRL-gradient, CRL-discrete and Random Policies.

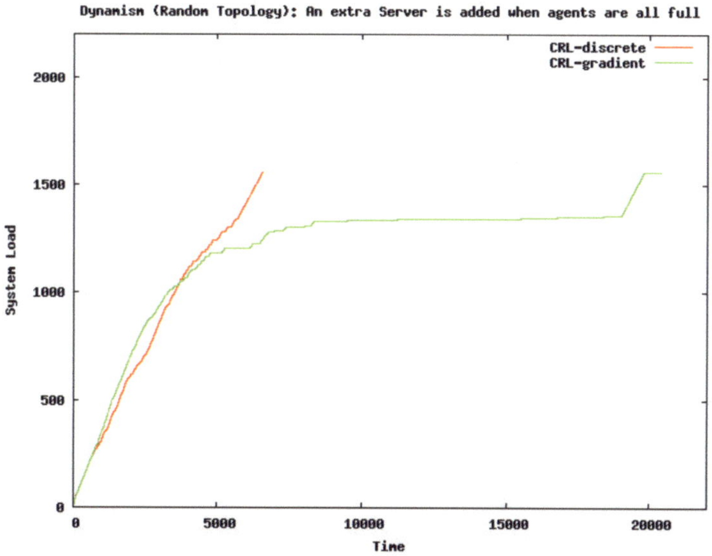

Fig. 13. Dynamism in the Random Topology: a new server was added, when the 50 agents were full, and was quickly exploited by the CRL-Discrete policy, less so by CRL-Gradient.

6.3 Discussion of experiments and CRL

The experiments show how CRL can be used to build a system that adapts to a dynamic environment. Agents interact with their local environment by storing loads and receiving feedback on available local storage capacity. Agents interact with their neighbors by delegating load storage to them, receiving estimated costs for neighbors' storing loads. Through delegating load and locally storing load, agents collaboratively provide a load balancing service that is robust, adaptive, and can learn about and exploit new agents introduced into the system. The experiments could easily be extended to improve performance by adding asynchronous advertisements and adding heuristics, for example, adding memory to the DOP of the list of agents already visited prevent DOPs entering network loops.

CRL, itself, is an approximate approach to online, decentralized reinforcement learning. It has similarities with population-based techniques such as ACO, particle swarm intelligence (Kennedy and Eberhart, 2001) and evolutionary computing: the system takes a diverse set of DOPs as input, and it reinforces the selection of agents that were successful at solving the DOPs given the state of the system environment; this process improves system utility for a stable environment and can also adapt a system to better match its changing environment. Rather than having agents die and be replaced by fitter agents, CRL agents decay their solutions to purge the system of stale information and use collaborative feedback to cooperatively learn new solutions.

7. Future of distributed reinforcement learning

Distributed reinforcement learning is an emerging field that offers the promise of enabling the construction of distributed systems that can adapt and optimize their operation online.

Existing approaches to distributed reinforcement learning include multi-agent control of a single MDP that describes system behavior, and decentralized approaches where agents are independent learners that collaborate to provide system services and collectively learn from one another to build local policies that improve system utility.

Designers of distributed reinforcement learning algorithms should give careful consideration to real-world properties of distributed systems, such as the high cost of message passing, and the possibility of failure for both agents and network connections. As a proof of concept, in this chapter, we showed how collaborative reinforcement learning can be used to build a load balancing system that can adapt to a dynamic environment.

In the future, we anticipate that distributed reinforcement learning algorithms will be increasingly applied in a variety of domains, from large-scale grid computing systems, to optimize resource usage, to small-scale wireless and sensor networks, where power usage and radio transmission usage should be minimized. In both cases, the goal of distributed reinforcement learning will be to replace existing parametric models with online learning models that can demonstrate improved adaptation to dynamic environments.

8. Acknowledgements

This research was supported by a Marie Curie Intra-European Fellowship within the 6th European Community Framework Programme. The authors would like to thank Jan Sacha for an implementation of CRL in Java on which the experiments in this paper are based.

9. References

Bernstein, D.; Zilberstein, S.; Immerman, N. (2002). The Complexity of Decentralized Control of Markov Decision Processes. *Proceedings of the Conference on Uncertainty in Artificial Intelligence,* pp. 32-27, Morgan Kaufmann Publishers Inc., San Francisco.

Bowling, M.; Veloso, M.. (2000). An Analysis of Stochastic Game Theory for Multiagent Reinforcement Learning. Technical Report, Carnegie Mellon University, (CMU-CS-00-165), January 2000.

Chang, Y-H; Ho, T; Kaebling, L. (2003). All learning is local: Multi-agent learning in global reward games , *Advances in Neural Information Processing Systems,* MIT Press, ISBN .

Cogill, R; Rotkowitz, M; Van Roy, B.;Lall, S. (2006). An Approximate Dynamic Programming Approach to Decentralized Control of Stochastic Systems, *Control of Uncertain Systems,* pp. 243–256, LNCIS 329, Springer-Verlag, Berlin.

Claus, C.; Boutilier, C. (1998). The Dynamics of Reinforcement Learning in Cooperative Multiagent Systems, *In Proceedings of the Fifteenth National Conference on Artificial Intelligence,* pp. 746-752. American Association for Artificial Intelligence.

Curran, E. (2003). Swarm: Cooperative Reinforcement Learning for Routing Ad-hoc Networks, *MSc. Thesis,* Dept. of Computer Science, Trinity College Dublin, October 2003.

Dorigo, M; Stützle, T. (2004). Ant Colony Optimization, MIT Press, ISBN-10: 0262042193.

Dowling, J.; Curran, E.; Cunningham, R.; Cahill, V. (2005). Using Feedback in Collaborative Reinforcement Learning to Adaptively Optimise MANET Routing, *IEEE Transactions on Systems, Man and Cybernetics (Part A), Special Issue on Engineering Self-Orangized Distributed Systems,* pp. 360-372, Vol. 35, No. 3, ISSN 0018-9472.

Dowling, J. (2004). The Decentralised Coordination of Self-Adaptive Components for Autonomic Distributed Systems, *PhD Thesis,* Dept of Computer Science, Trinity College Dublin.

Ghasemaghaei, R.; Rahman, Md. A.; Gueaieb, W.; El Saddik, A. (2007). Ant Colony-Based Reinforcement Learning Algorithm for Routing in Wireless Sensor Networks. *In Proceedings of IEEE Conference on* Instrumentation and Measurement Technology Conference, pp. 1-6, Warsaw, Poland, ISBN 1-4244-0588-2.

Goldman, C.; Zilberstein, S. (2004). Decentralized Control of Cooperative Systems: Categorization and Complexity Analysis, *Journal of Artificial Intelligence Research,* pp. 143-174, Vol. 22, ISSN 11076 - 9757.

Guestrin, C; Koller, D.; and Parr, R.; (2002). Multiagent Planning with Factored MDPs, *In Advances in Neural Information Processing Systems,* pp. 1523-1530, Vancouver, Canada.

Guestrin, C.; Koller, D.; Parr, R.; Venkataraman, S. (2003). Efficient Solution Algorithms for Factored MDPs, *Journal of Artificial Intelligence Research,* pp. 399-468, Vol. 19, ISSN 11076 - 9757.

Hu, J; Wellman, M. (2003). Nash q-learning for general-sum stochastic games, *Journal of Machine Language Research,* pp. 1039-1069, vol. 4, MIT Press (Cambridge), ISSN 1533-7928.

Kennedy, J; Eberhart, R. (2001). Swarm Intelligence, Morgan Kaufman, ISBN:1-55860-595-9.

Kok, J.; Vlassis, N. (2006). Collaborative Multiagent Reinforcement Learning by Payoff Propagation, *Journal of Machine Language Research,* pp. 1789-1828, Vol. 7, MIT Press, ISSN 1533-7928.

Lauer, M.; Riedmiller, M. (2000). *An Algorithm for Distributed Reinforcement Learning in Cooperative Multi-Agent Systems*. In Proceedings of the 17th International Conf. on Machine Learning, pp. 535-54, Morgan Kaufmann Publishers Inc., San Francisco.

Lawson, J.; Wolpert, D. (2002). The Design of Collectives of Agents to Control Non-Markovian Systems, *In Proceedings of the National Conference on Artificial intelligence*, pp. 332-337, American Association for Artificial Intelligence, ISBN: 0-262-51129-0.

Martin, J.A.;De Lope, H. (2007). A Distributed Reinforcement Learning Architecture for Multi-Link Robots, *4th International Conference on Informatics in Control, Automation and Robotics*, pp. 192-197, INSTICC Press 2007, ISBN 978-972-8865-82-5.

Ng, A; Kim, H-J.; Jordan, M.; Sastry, S. (2004). Autonomous helicopter flight via reinforcement learning, *Advances in Neural Information Processing Systems*, MIT Press, ISBN 0-262-20152-6.

Peshkin, L.; Kim, K.; Meuleau, N.; Kaelbling, L. (2000). Learning to Cooperate via Policy Search. *Proceedings of the 16th Conference on Uncertainty in Artificial Intelligence*, pp. 489-496, Morgan Kaufmann Publishers Inc., San Francisco.

Rigole, P; (2006). Task- and resource-aware component deployment in ambient intelligence environments, *Ph.D. Thesis*, Department of Computer Science, K.U. Leuven, Leuven, Belgium, November, 2006.

Schneider, J.; Wong. W; Moore, A.; Riedmiller, M. (1999). Proceedings of the Sixteenth International Conference on Machine Learning, pp. 371-378, Morgan Kaufmann Publishers Inc., San Francisco, ISBN:1-55860-612-2.

Shoham, Y. ; Powers, R.; Grenager, T. (2003). Multi-agent reinforcement learning: a critical survey, Technical report, Computer Science Department, Stanford University.

Sutton, R.; Barto, A. (1998). Reinforcement Learning: An Introduction, *MIT Press*, ISBN 0-262-19398, Cambridge MA.

Tesauro, G. (2007). Reinforcement Learning in Autonomic Computing: A Manifesto and Case Studies, *IEEE Internet Computing*, pp. 22-30, Vol. 11, No. 2, ISSN 1089-7801.

Tsitsiklis, J; Athans, M.. (1985). On the complexity of decentralized decision making and detection problems," *IEEE Trans. Automatic Control*, vol. 30, no. 5, pp. 440–446.

Van Renesse, R., Birman, K., Vogels, W. 2003. Astrolabe: A robust and scalable technology for distributed system monitoring, management, and data mining. *ACM Transactions on Computing Systems*, pp.164–206, Vol. *21*, No. 2, ISSN: 0734-2071.

Zhang, Y; Liu, J.; Zhao, F. (2006). Information-Directed Routing in Sensor Networks Using Real-Time Reinforcement Learning, In Combinatorial Optimization in Communication Networks, pp. 259-289, Kluwer Academic Publishers.

9

Multi-Automata Learning

Verbeeck Katja[1], Nowe Ann[2], Vrancx Peter[2] and Peeters Maarten[2]
[1]*MiCC-IKAT Maastricht University, The Netherlands*
[2] *COMO Vrije Universiteit Brussel, Belgium*

1. Introduction

It is well known that Reinforcement Learning (RL) techniques are able to solve Markovian stationary decision problems (MDP) with delayed rewards. However, not much is known yet about how these techniques can be justified in non-stationary environments. In a non-stationary environment, system characteristics such as probabilities of state transitions and reward signals may vary with time. This is the case in systems where multiple agents are active, the so called Multi-Agent Systems (MAS). The difficulty in a MAS is that an agent is not only subject to external environmental changes, (like for instance load changes in a telecommunication network setting) but, also to the decisions taken by other agents, with whom the agent might have to cooperate, communicate or compete. So a key question in multi-agent Reinforcement Learning (MARL) is how multiple reinforcement learning agents can learn optimal behavior under constraints such as high communication costs. In order to solve this problem, it is necessary to understand what optimal behavior is and how can it be learned.

In a MAS rewards are sensed for combinations of actions taken by different agents, and therefore agents are actually learning in a product or joint action space. Moreover, due to the existence of different reward functions, it usually is impossible to find policies which maximize the expected reward for all agents simultaneously. The latter is possible in the so-called team games or multi-agent MDP's (MMDP's). In this case, the MAS is purely cooperative and all agents share the same reward function. In MMDP's the agents should learn how to find and agree on the same optimal policy. In general, an equilibrium point is sought; i.e. a situation in which no agent on its own can change its policy to improve its reward when all other agents keep their policy fixed.

In addition, agents in a MAS face the problem of incomplete information with respect to the action choice. One can assume that the agents get information about their own choice of action as well as that of the others. This is the case in what is called joint action learning, (Littman, 2001),(Claus & Boutilier, 1998), (Hu & Wellman, 2003). Joint action learners are able to maintain models of the strategy of others and explicitly take into account the effects of joint actions. In contrast, independent agents only know their own action. The latter is often a more realistic assumption since distributed multi-agent applications are typically subject to limitations such as partial or non observability, communication costs, asynchronism and stochasticity.

Our work in MARL is mainly motivated by the early results achieved by simple learning automata (LA) that can be interconnected in games, networks and hierarchies. A learning

automaton describes the internal state of an agent as a probability distribution according to which actions should be chosen. These probabilities are adjusted with some reinforcement scheme according to the success or failure of the actions taken. Important to note is that LA are updated strictly on the basis of the response of the environment, and not on the basis of any knowledge regarding other automata, i.e. nor their strategies, nor their feedback. As such LA agents are very simple. Moreover, LA can be treated analytically, from a single automaton model acting in a simple stationary random environment to a distributed automata model interacting in a complex environment.
The past few years, a substantial amount of research has focused on comprehending (Tuyls & Nowé 2005) and solving single-stage multi-agent problems, modeled as normal form games from game theory e.g. joint-action learners (Claus & Boutilier, 1998); ESRL (Verbeeck et al, 2007 (b)) or Commitment Sequences (Kapetanakis et al, 2003). Recently, more researchers focus on solving the more challenging multi-stage game or sequential games where the agents have to take a sequence of actions. These can be modeled as Markov Games (Shapley, 1953). Many real-world problems are naturally translated into multi-stage problems. The expressiveness of multi-stage games allows us to create more realistic simulation models with less abstraction. This brings us closer to the application level. Moreover, we argue that multi-stage games help to improve the scalability of an agent system.
Here we present a summary of current LA-based approaches to MARL. We especially focus on multi-stage multi-agent decision problems of the following type : ergodic Markov Games, partial observable ergodic Markov Games and episodic problems that induce tree-based Markov games. We describe both their analytical as well as their experimental results, and we discuss their contributions to the field. As in single agent learning, we consider the different updating mechanisms relevant to sequential decision making; i.e. using global reward signals for updating called Monte Carlo updating, versus using intermediate rewards to update strategies, the so-called Bootstrapping methods.
First we start with a short description of the underlying mathematical material for analyzing multi-agent, multi-stage learning schemes.

2. Markov decision processes and Markov games

In this section we briefly explain the formal frameworks used in single and multi-agent learning.

2.1 The Markov property

A Stochastic process $\{X(t) \mid t \in T\}$ is a system that passes from one state to another governed by time. Both the state space S as the index set (time) T can be either discrete or continuous. A Markov process is a stochastic process that satisfies the *Markov property*. This property states that the future behavior of the process given its path only depends on its current state. A Markov process whose state space is discrete is also called a Markov chain, whereas a discrete-time chain is called stationary or homogenous when the probability of going from one state to another in a single step is independent of time. So, if the current state of the

Markov chain at time t is known, transitions to a new state at time $t + 1$ are independent of any of the previous states.

One of the most important questions in the theory of Markov chains is how the chain will be distributed among the states after a long time. In case the Markov chain is ergodic, a unique stationary probability distribution exists. However the process can also be absorbed into a closed set of states. An absorbing state is a state from which there is a zero probability of exiting. An absorbing Markov system is a Markov system that contains at least one absorbing state, and possesses the property that it is possible to get from each non-absorbing state to some absorbing state in one or more time-steps. More information on the properties of Markov processes can be found in (Puterman, 1994).

2.1 Definition of an MDP

A Markov Decision Process (MDP) is a discrete-time Markov process characterized by a set of states; each having several actions from which a decision maker must choose. The decision maker earns a reward for each state visited. The problem of controlling an MDP for which transition probabilities and rewards are unknown can be stated as follows. Let $S= \{s_1, \dots, s_N\}$ be the state space of a finite Markov chain $\{X_t\}_{t\geq 0}$ and $A_i = \{a_{i1}, \dots, a_{il}\}$ the action set available in state s_i. Each starting state s_i, action choice $a_i \in A_i$ and ending state s_j has an associated transition probability $T_{i\text{->}j}(a_i)$ and reward $R_{i\text{->}j}(a_i)$. The overall goal is to learn a policy α, or a set of actions, $\alpha = (a_1, \dots, a_N)$ with $a_j \in A_j$ so that the expected average reward for policy α : $J(\alpha)$ is maximized:

$$J(\alpha) \equiv \lim_{l\to\infty} \frac{1}{l} E\left[\sum_{t=0}^{l-1} R^{x(t)x(t+1)}(\alpha)\right] \quad (1)$$

The policies we consider, are limited to stationary, nonrandomized policies. Under the assumption that the Markov chain corresponding to each policy α is ergodic, it can be shown that the best strategy in any state is a pure strategy, independent of the time at which the state is occupied (Wheeler & Narendra, 19986). Assume the limiting distribution of the Markov chain to be $\pi(a) = (\pi_1(a), \dots, \pi_N(a))$ with forall i, $\pi_i(a) > 0$ as $n \to \infty$. Thus, there are no transient states and the limiting distribution $\pi(a)$ can be used to rewrite Equation 1 as:

$$J(\alpha) \equiv \sum_{i=1}^{N} \pi_i(\alpha) \sum_{j=1}^{N} T^{ij}(\alpha) R^{ij}(\alpha) \quad (2)$$

2.2 Definition of a Markov game

An extension of single agent Markov decision problems to the multi-agent case is straightforward and can be defined by Markov Games (Shapeley, 1953). In a Markov Game, actions are the joint result of multiple agents choosing an action separately. Note that $A_{i,k} = \{a_{i,k1}, \dots, a_{i,kl}\}$ is now the action set available in state s_i for agent k, with $k: 1 \dots n$, n being the total number of agents present in the system. Transition probabilities $T_{i\text{->}j}(a_i)$ and rewards $R_{i\text{->}j}(a_i)$ now depend on a starting state s_i, ending state s_j and a joint action a_i from state s_i, i.e. $a_i = (a_{i1}, \dots, a_{in})$ with $a_{ik} \in A_{i,k}$. The reward function $R_{i\text{->}j}(a_i)$ is now individual to each agent k, indicated as R_k^{ij}. Different agents can receive different rewards for the same state transition. Since each agent k has its own individual reward function, defining a solution concept becomes non-trivial.

Again we will only treat non-randomized policies and we will assume that the Markov Game is ergodic in the sense that there are no transient states present and a limiting distribution on the joint policies exists. We can now use Equation 2 to define the expected reward for agent k, for a given joint policy α.

$$J_k(\alpha) \equiv \sum_{i=1}^{N} \pi_i(\alpha) \sum_{j=1}^{N} T^{ij}(\alpha) R_k^{ij}(\alpha) \tag{3}$$

Due to the existence of different reward functions, it is in general impossible to find an optimal policy for all agents simultaneously. Instead, equilibrium points are sought. In an equilibrium, no agent can improve its reward by changing its policy if all other agents keep their policy fixed. In the case of single state multi-agent problems, the equilibrium strategies coincides with the Nash equilibria of the corresponding normal form game. In the case of multi stage problems, limiting games can be used as analysis tool. The limiting game of a corresponding multi-agent multi-state problem can be defined as follows: each joint agent policy is viewed as a single play between players using the agent's policies as their individual actions. The payoff given to each player is the expected reward for the corresponding agent under the resulting joint policy. Analyzing the multi state problem now boils down to explaining the behaviour of the multi-agent learning technique in terms of Nash equilibriums in this limiting game.

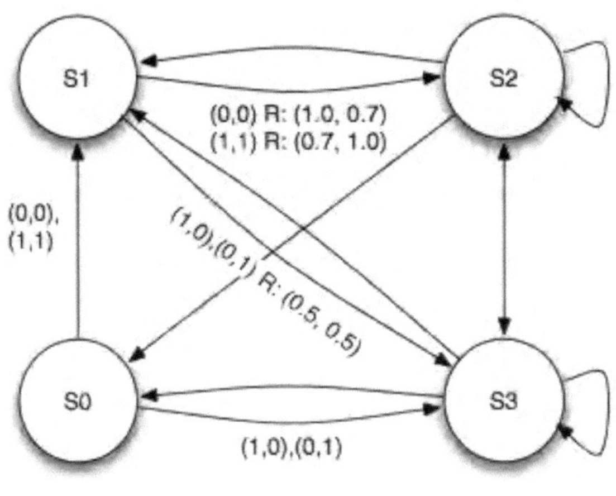

		Agent 2			
		(0,0)	(0,1)	(1,0)	(1,1)
Agent 1	(0,0)	**0.29, 0.20**	0.17, 0.17	0.14, 0.12	0.08, 0.08
	(0,1)	0.17, 0.17	**0.20, 0.29**	0.08, 0.08	0.12, 0.14
	(1,0)	0.14, 0.12	0.08, 0.08	**0.29, 0.20**	0.17, 0.17
	(1,1)	0.08, 0.08	0.12, 0.14	0.17, 0.17	**0.20, 0.29**

Fig. 1. A Markov Game Problem and its corresponding limiting game

Figure 1 shows an example Markov game with 4 states and 2 agents. States s_0 and s_1 are the only action states, with 2 possible actions (*0* and *1*) for each each agent. Joint actions and nonzero rewards (R) associated with the state transitions are indicated in the figure. All transitions are deterministic, except in the non-action states s_2 and s_3 where the process goes to any other state with equal probability (1/4). The corresponding limiting game for this problem is shown in the accompanying table. Equilibria in this game are indicated in bold.
In a special case of the general Markov game framework, the so-called team games or multi-agent MDP's (MMDP's) (Boutilier, 1999) optimal policies are proven to exist. In this case, the Markov game is purely cooperative and all agents share the same reward function. This specialization allows us to define the optimal policy as the joint agent policy, which maximizes the payoff of all agents. An MMDP can therefore also be seen as an extension of the single agent MDP to the cooperative multi-agent case.

3. Learning automata as simple policy iterators

The study of learning automata started in the 1960's by Tsetlin and his co-workers (Tsetlin, 1973). The early models were examples of fixed-structure stochastic automata. In its current form, LA are closely related to a Reinforcement Learner of the policy iteration type. Studying learning automata theory is very relevant for multi-agent reinforcement learning, since learning is treated analytically not only in the single automaton setting, but also in the case of distributed interconnected automata and hierarchies of automata interacting in complex environments (Narendra & Thathachar, 1989) . In this section, we only discuss the single automaton case in stationary environments. More complicated LA models and their behaviour will be discussed in the following sections.
A variable structure learning automaton formalizes a general stochastic system in terms of actions, action probabilities and environment responses. The action probabilities, which make the automaton mathematically very tractable, are updated on the basis of the environment input. Formally, the automata can be defined as follows: a quadruple $\{A, r, p, U\}$ for which : $A = \{a_1, \ldots, a_l\}$ is the action or output set of the automaton, $r(t)$ is an element of the set $\{0,1\}$ and denotes the environment response at instant t, $p(t) = (p_1(t), \ldots, p_l(t))$ is the action probability vector of the automaton, with $p_i(t) = Prob(a(t) = a_i)$ and which satisfies the condition that $\Sigma^l_{i=1} p_i(t)=1$ for all t and U is called the learning algorithm and denotes the schema with which the action probabilities are updated on the basis of the environment input. The output a of the automaton is actually the input to the environment. The input r of the automaton is the output of the environment. In general the environment refers to all external conditions and influences affecting life and development of an organism. In the P-model learning automaton, the output $r(t)$ of the environment is considered to be binary. The output set of the environment is the set $\{0,1\}$ so that output signal $r = 0$ is identified with a failure or an unfavourable response, while $r = 1$ denotes a success or a favourable response. Static environments are characterized by penalty probabilities c_i . They represent the probability that the application of action a_i will be successful or not, i.e. $Prob(r = 0 \mid a = a_i) = c_i$. Knowing c_i , the reward probability d_i for action a_i is given by: $d_i = 1 - c_i$. Other environment models exist, depending on the nature of the environment response. In the Q-model the environment response is an element of a discrete, finite set of possible responses which has more than 2 elements, while in the S-model the environment response r is a real number in the interval $[0,1]$.
Important examples of linear update schemes are linear reward-penalty, linear

reward-inaction and linear reward-ε-penalty. The philosophy of those schemes is essentially to increase the probability of an action when it results in a success and to decrease it when the response is a failure. The general algorithm is given by:

$$\begin{aligned} p_m(t+1) &= p_m(t) + \alpha_r(1-\beta(t))(1-p_m(t)) - \alpha_p\beta(t)p_m(t) \\ &\quad \text{if } a_m \text{ is the action taken at time } t \\ p_j(t+1) &= p_j(t) - \alpha_r(1-\beta(t))p_j(t) + \alpha_p\beta(t)\left[(r-1)^{-1} - p_j(t)\right] \\ &\quad \text{if } a_j \neq a_m \end{aligned} \tag{4}$$

with l the number of actions of the action set A. The constants α_r and α_p are the reward and penalty parameters respectively. When $\alpha_r = \alpha_p$ the algorithm is referred to as linear reward-penalty $L_{R\text{-}P}$, when $\alpha_p = 0$ it is referred to as linear reward-inaction
$L_{R\text{-}I}$ and when α_p is small compared to α_r it is called linear reward-ε-penalty $L_{R\text{-}\varepsilon P}$. In the above, it is assumed that c_i and d_i are constants. This implies that the environment is stationary and that the optimal action a_m can be identified. The goal of the learning automaton is to find this optimal action, without knowing the environments' reward or penalty probabilities. The penalty probability c_m of the optimal action has the property that $c_m = min_i\ \{ c_i \}$. Optimality of the learning automaton can then be defined using the quantity $M(t) = E[r(t) = 0 \mid p(t)]$ which is the average penalty for a given action probability vector. Consider for instance a pure-chance automaton, i.e. the action probability vector $p(n)$ is given by: $p_i(n) = 1/l$ for all i: 1, … , l. Then $M(t)$ is a constant (denoted by M_0) and given by:

$$M_0 = 1/l\sum_{i=1}^{l} c_i$$

Definition 1

A learning automaton is called optimal if $\lim_{t\to\infty} E[M(t)] = c_m$

While optimality is desirable in stationary environments, practically it may not be achieved in a given situation. In this case, ε-optimality may be reached. So, put differently, the objective of the learning scheme is to maximize the expected value of reinforcement received from the environment, i.e. $E[r(t) \mid p(t) = p]$ by searching the space of all possible action probability vectors. Stated as above, a learning automata algorithm can be viewed as a policy iteration approach.

In arbitrary environments and for arbitrary initial conditions, optimality or ε-optimality may be hard to reach. Some form of desired behaviour in these cases can be specified by expediency and absolute expediency.

Definition 2

A learning automaton is called expedient if it performs better than a pure-chance automaton, i.e. $\lim_{t\to\infty} M(t) < M_0$

Definition 3

A learning automaton is said to be absolutely expedient if $E[M(t+1)|p(t)] < M(t)$

Absolute expediency imposes an inequality on the conditional expectation of $M(t)$ at each instant. In (Narendra & Thathachar, 1989) it is shown that in stationary environments absolute expediency implies ε-optimality.

The reinforcement learning algorithms given above, i.e. the $L_{R\text{-}P}$, $L_{R\text{-}I}$ and $L_{R\text{-}\varepsilon P}$ schemes show the following asymptotic behaviour: the $L_{R\text{-}I}$ scheme is proved to be absolutely

expedient and thus ε-optimal in stationary environments. The L_{R-P} scheme is found to be expedient, while the $L_{R-\varepsilon P}$ scheme is also ε-optimal, (Narendra & Thathachar, 1989).
Another classification used for reinforcement schemes is made on the basis of the properties of the induced Markov process $\{p(t)\}_{\{t>0\}}$. If the penalty probabilities c_i of the environment are constant, the probability $p(t+1)$ is completely determined by $p(t)$ and hence $\{p(t)\}_{\{t>0\}}$ is a discrete-time homogeneous Markov process. The L_{R-P} and $L_{R-\varepsilon P}$ schemes result in Markov processes that are ergodic, the action probability vector $p(t)$ converges in distribution to a random variable p^*, which is independent of the initial conditions. In case of the $L_{R-\varepsilon P}$ scheme, the mean value of p^* can be made as close as desired to the optimal unit vector by choosing α_r and α_p sufficiently small. The Markov process generated by the L_{R-I} scheme is non-ergodic and converges to one of the absorbing states with probability *1*.
Choosing parameter α_r sufficiently small can make the probability of convergence to the optimal action as close to *1* as desired. More on the convergence of learning schemes can be found (Narendra & Thathachar, 1989).

4. Interconnected learning automata for ergodic Markov games

It is well known that Reinforcement Learning techniques (Sutton & Barto, 1998) are able to solve single-agent Markovian decision problems with delayed rewards. In the first subsection we focus on how a set of interconnected LA is able to control an MDP (Wheeler & Narendra, 1986) . In the next subsection, we show how to extend this result to the multi-agent case in a very natural way.

4.1 Control of MDP's

The problem of controlling a Markov chain can be formulated as a network of automata in which control passes from one automaton to another. In this set-up every state in the Markov chain has a LA that tries to learn the optimal action probabilities in that state with learning scheme given in Equation 4. Only one LA is active at each time step and transition to the next state triggers the LA from that state to become active and take some action. LA LAi active in state si is not informed of the one-step reward Ri->j(ai) resulting from choosing action ai ЄAi in si and leading to state sj. However when state si is visited again, LAi receives two pieces of data: the cumulative reward generated by the process up to the current time step and the current global time. From these, LAi computes the incremental reward generated since this last visit and the corresponding elapsed global time. The environment response or the input to LA^i is then taken to be:

$$\beta^i(t_i+1)=\frac{\rho^i(t_i+1)}{\eta^i(t_i+1)} \tag{5}$$

where $\rho_i(t_i + 1)$ is the cumulative total reward generated for action a_i in state s_i and $\eta_i(t_i + 1)$ the cumulative total time elapsed. The authors in (Wheeler & Narendra, 1986) denote updating scheme as given in Equation 4 with environment response as in Equation 5 as learning scheme T1. The following results were proved:
Lemma1 *(Wheeler & Narendra, 1986)*
The Markov chain control problem can be asymptotically approximated by an identical payoff game of N automata.

Theorem 1 *(Wheeler & Narendra, 1986)*
Let for each action state s_i of an N state Markov chain, an automaton LA^i using the Monte Carlo updates as described above and having r_i actions be associated with. Assume that the Markov Chain, corresponding to each policy α is ergodic. Then the decentralized adaptation of the LA is globally ε-optimal with respect to the long-term expected reward per time step, i.e. J(α).
The principal result derived is that, without prior knowledge of transition probabilities or rewards, the network of independent decentralized LA controllers is able to converge to the set of actions that maximizes the long-term expected reward (Narendra & Thathachar, 1989). Moreover instead of one agent visiting all states and keeping a model for all the states in the system as in traditional RL algorithms such as Q-learning; in this model there are some non-mobile LA agents who do not move around the state space but stay in their own state waiting to get activated and learn to take actions only in their own state. The intelligence of one mobile agent is now distributed over the states of the Markov chain, more precisely over the non-mobile LA agents in those states.

4.2 Control of Markov games

In a Markov Game the action chosen at any state is the joint result of individual action components performed by the agents present in the system. The LA network of the previous section can be extended to the framework of Markov Games just by putting a simple learning automaton for every agent in each state (Vrancx et al., 2007) Instead of putting a single learning automaton in each action of the system, we propose to put an automaton $LA^{i,k}$ in each state s_i with $i: 1 \ldots N$ and for each agent k, $k: 1 \ldots n$. At each time step only the automata of one state are active; a joint action triggers the LA from that state to become active and take some joint action.
As before, LA $LA^{i,k}$ active for agent k in state s_i is not informed on the one-step reward $R_{i\text{->}j,k}(a_i)$ resulting from choosing joint action $a_i = (a_{i1}, \ldots, a_{in})$ with $a_{ik} \in A_{i,k}$ in s_i and leading to state s_j. When state s_i is visited again, all automata $LA^{i,k}$ with $k: 1 \ldots n$ receive two pieces of data: the cumulative reward generated for agent k by the process up to the current time step and the current global time. From these, all $LA^{i,k}$ compute the incremental reward generated since this last visit and the corresponding elapsed global time. The environment response or the input to $LA^{i,k}$ is exactly the same as in Equation 6. The following result was proven in (Vrancx et al., 2007) :
Theorem **2** *(Vrancx et al, 07)*
The Learning Automata model proposed for ergodic Markov games with full state observability is able to find an equilibrium point in pure strategies for the underlying limited game.
The behaviour of the LA learning model on the sample problem described in section 2.2 is demonstrated in Figure 2. We show the average reward over time for both agents. Since we are interested in the long term convergence we show a typical run, rather than an average over multiple runs. To demonstrate convergence to the different equilibria, we use a single very long run in which the automata are allowed to converge and are then restarted. After every restart the automata are initialized with random action probabilities in order to allow them to converge to different equilibria.

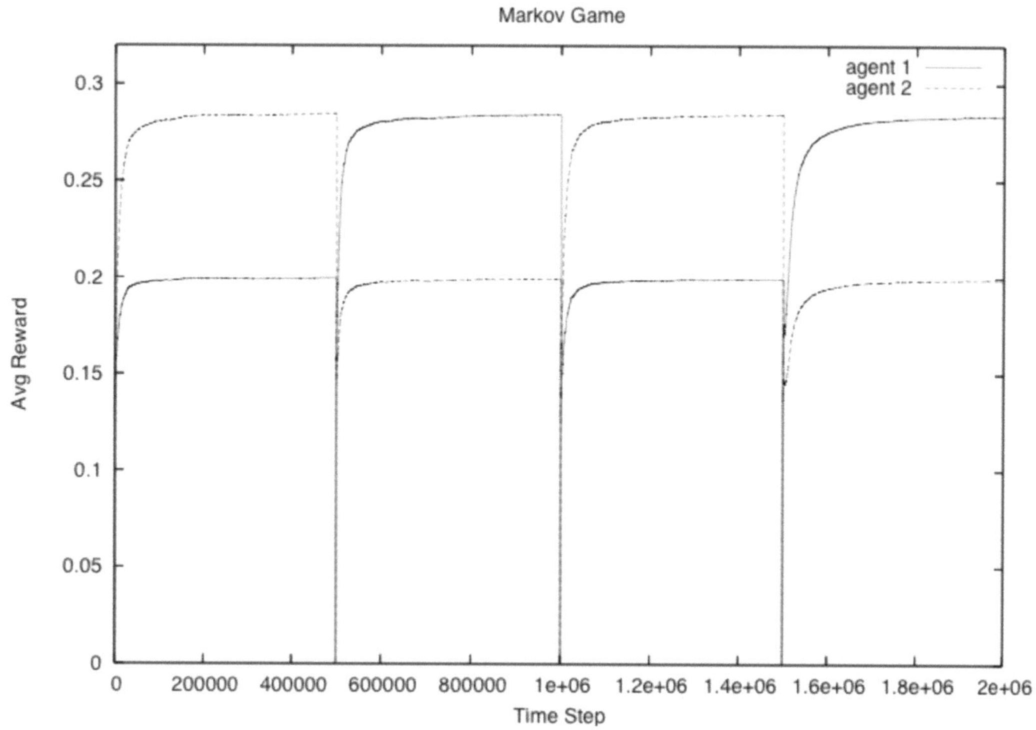

Fig. 2. Experimental results on the example Markov game of Figure 1.

5. Interconnected learning automata for partially observable ergodic Markov games

The main difference with the previous setup for learning Markov games (Vrancx et al., 2007) is that here we do not assume that agents can observe the complete system state. Instead, each agent learns directly in its own observation space, by associating a learning automaton with each distinct state it can observe. Since an agent does not necessarily observe all state variables, it is possible that it associates the same LA with multiple states, as it cannot distinguish between them. For example, in the 2-state problem of Figure X, an agent associates a LA with each location it can occupy, while the full system state consists of the joint locations of all agents. As a consequence, it is not possible for the agents to learn all policies. For instance in the 2-state problem, the automaton associated by agent x with location *L1* is used in state $s_1 = \{L1,L1\}$ as well as state $s_2 = \{L1,L2\}$. Therefore it is not possible for agent x to learn a different action in state s_1 and s_2. This corresponds to the agent associating actions with locations, without modelling the other agents.

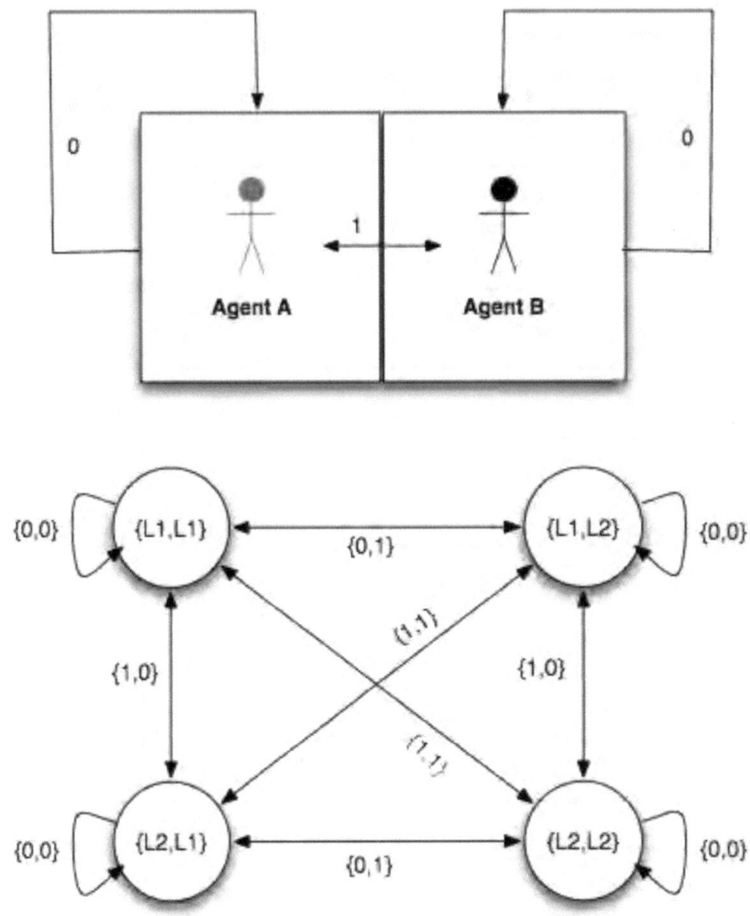

Fig. 3. A 2-location grid-world problem and its corresponding Markov game.

So the definition of the update mechanism here is exactly the same as in the previous model, the difference is that here agents only update their observable states which we will call locations to differentiate with the notion of a Markov game state. This will give the following: a LA $LA^{i,k}$ active for agent k in location L_i is not informed on the one-step reward $R_{i\text{->}j,k}(a_i)$ resulting from choosing joint action $a_i = (a_{i1}, \ldots, a_{in})$ with $a_{ik} \in A_{i,k}$ in s_i and leading to state L_j. Instead, when location L_i is visited again, automaton $LA^{i,k}$ receives two pieces of data: the cumulative reward generated for agent k by the process up to the current time step and the current global time. From these, automaton $LA^{i,k}$ compute the incremental reward generated since this last visit and the corresponding elapsed global time.
The environment response or the input to $LA^{i,k}$ is then taken to be: $\beta_{i,k}(t_i + 1) = \rho_{i,k}(t_i + 1) / \eta_{i,k}(t_i + 1)$ where $\rho_{i,k}(t_i + 1)$ is the cumulative total reward generated for action $a_{i,k}$ in location L_i and $\eta_{i,k}(t_i + 1)$ the cumulative total time elapsed. We still assume that the Markov chain of system states generated under each joint agent policy a is ergodic. In the following we will show that even when the agents have only knowledge of their own location, in some situations it is still possible to find an equilibrium point of the underlying limiting game.

		Agent 2			
		(0,0)	(0,1)	(1,0)	(1,1)
Agent 1	(0,0)	0.38	0.28	0.48	0.38
	(0,1)	0.48	0.14	**0.82**	0.48
	(1,0)	0.28	**0.42**	0.14	0.28
	(1,1)	0.38	0.28	0.28	0.38

Table 1. Limiting game for the 2-location grid world experiment of Figure 3.

***Theorem** 3 (Verbeeck et al, 2007(a))*

The network of LA that was proposed here for myopic agents in Markov Games, converges to a pure equilibrium point of the limiting game provided that the Markov chain of system states generated under each joint agent policy is ergodic and agents' transition probabilities do not depend on other agents' activities.

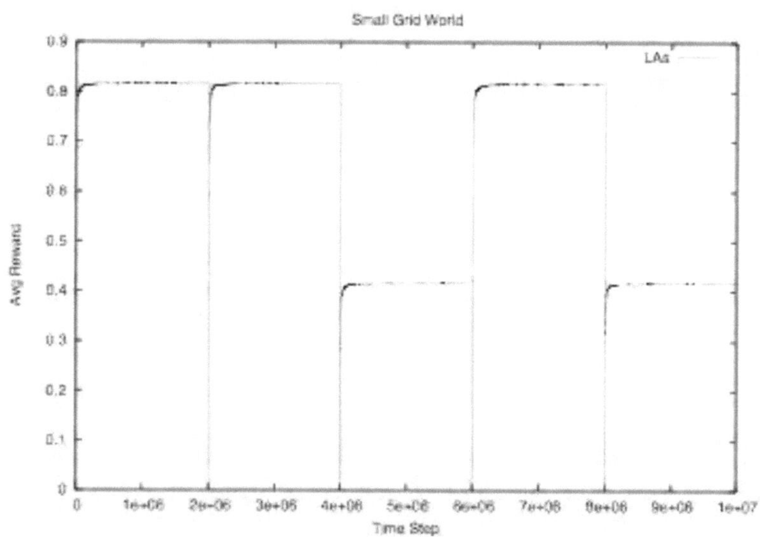

Fig. 4. Average Reward for the 2-location grid-world problem of Figure 3 .

Figure 4 shows experimental results of the LA network approach on the grid world problem of Figure 3. In these experiments both agents were given an identical reward based on their joint location after acting. The agents receive rewards *1.0* and *0.5* for joint locations *{L1,L2}* and *{L2,L1}* respectively and reward *0.01* when both agents are in the same location. The resulting limiting game matrix for this reward function is shown in Table 1. In Figure 4 we show the average reward over time for both agents, during a single long run of the algorithm, in which agents are allowed to converge and are then randomly re-initialised. We can observe that the agents move to either the optimal or the suboptimal equilibrium of the underlying limiting game, depending on their initialisation.

6. Hierarchical learning automata for episodic problems

Until now we only considered ergodic Markov games, which excludes problems that have a periodic nature or absorbing states such as finite episodic tasks. To this end we study agents constructed with hierarchical learning automata. An agent here is more complex than a simple learning automaton in the sense that the agents' internal state is now a hierarchy of learning automata. The idea is that in each step of the episode the agent chooses to activate an automaton of the next level of its hierarchy. The numbers of steps of the episodic task defines the size of the internal LA hierarchy. In (Narendra & Parthasarathy, 1991), hierarchical learning automata were introduced for multi-objective optimization. A simple problem of consistently labelling images was given. At a first stage, the object had to be recognized and in a second stage the background of the image was determined.
When several hierarchical agents play an episodic multi-agent task a corresponding Markov game can be determined as follows: at each time step, there is a new state available for each joint action possible. The resulting state space is then a tree, so no loops or joining branches are allowed. Similar to the previous section,, it is the case that learning automata can belong to different states, and we could call this setting an POMarkov game (in analogy with POMDP's). Note that in this section we only consider cooperative tasks.

6.1 Hierarchical LA agents

Learning automata can be combined into more complex structures such as hierarchies. Figure 5 shows an interaction between such hierarchies.

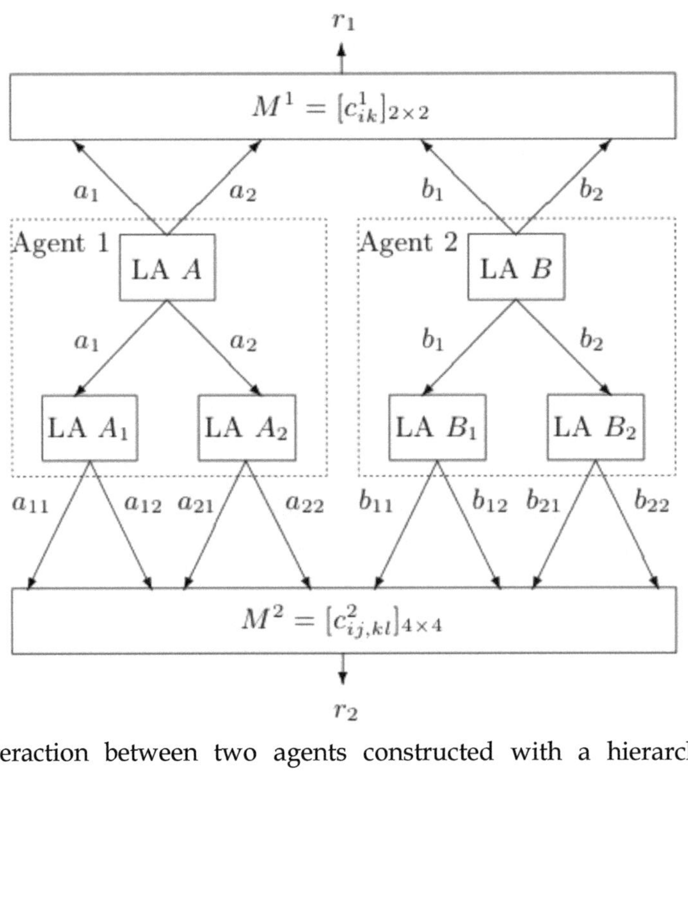

Fig. 5. An interaction between two agents constructed with a hierarchy of learning automata.

A hierarchical LA works as follows. The first automaton that is active is the root at the top of the hierarchy: LA *A* This automaton selects one of its *l* actions. If, for example, the automaton selects action *2*, the learning automaton that will become active is learning automaton LA *A2*. Then this active learning automaton is eligible for selecting an action. Based on this action, another learning automaton at the next level will become active. This process repeats itself until one of the learning automata at the bottom of the hierarchy is reached.
The interaction of the two hierarchical agents of Figure 5 goes as follows. At the top level (or in the first stage) Agent *1* and Agent 2 meet each other in a game with stochastic rewards. They both take an action using their top level learning automata, respectively *A* and *B*. Performing actions a_i by *A* and b_k by *B* is equivalent to choosing automata A_i and B_k to take actions at the next level. The response of environment $E_1 : r_t \in \{0,1\}$, is a success or failure, where the probability of success is given by c^1_{ik} . At the second level the learning automata A_i and B_k choose their actions a_{ij} and b_{kl} respectively and these will elicit a response from the environment E_2 of which the probability of getting a positive reward is given by $c^2_{ij,kl}$. At the end of the episode all the automata that were involved in one of the games, update their action selection probabilities based on the actions performed and the responses of the environments.

6.2 Monte Carlo updating

In the Monte Carlo method, the updating of the probabilities is based on the averaged sample returns. This averaged return is usually generated at the end of an episode. Each time such a clear end state is reached, an averaged return is generated by calculating a weighted sum of all the returns obtained. This sum is then given to all learning automata that were active during the last episode in order to update their action probabilities. Thus when we reach an end stage at time step *t* we generate the following sum: $R = \theta_1 r_1 + \theta_2 r_2 + \ldots + \theta_t r_t$ where r_i is the reward generated at time step *i*. Note that the weights θ_i should sum up to 1 and $0 \leq \theta_i \leq 1$ for all θ_i.
Theorem 4 *(Narendra & Parthasarathy, 1991)*
If all the automata of the hierarchical learning automata update their action probabilities at each stage using the L_{R-I} *update scheme and if the composite reward is constructed as a Monte Carlo reward and at each level the step sizes of the automata are chosen sufficiently small then the overall system is absolutely expedient.*
Stated differently, this means that the overall performance of the system will improve at each time step and convergence is assured toward a local optimum. The optima of the dynamical system under consideration, are the pure equilibrium points of the corresponding limiting single stage game.
Using a careful exploration strategy called exploring selfish reinforcement learning which is used in combination with hierarchical LA, it was shown in (Verbeeck et al., 2007) that the optimal equilibrium path can be learned.

7. Monte Carlo updating versus bootstrapping

Standard single agent reinforcement learning techniques, such as Q-learning (Watkins & Dayan, 1992), which are by nature designed to solve sequential decision problems, use the mechanism of bootstrapping to handle non-episodic tasks. Bootstrapping means that values or estimates are learned on the basis of other estimates (Sutton & Barto, 1998). The use of

next state estimates allows reinforcement learning to be applied to non-episodic tasks. Another advantage of bootstrapping over Monte Carlo methods include the fact that the former can be naturally implemented in an on-line, fully incremental fashion. As such, these methods can learn from each transition, which can sometimes speed-up learning time.
For instance the Q-learning algorithm, which is a value iteration method (see (Sutton & Barto, 1998); (Tsitsiklis, 1994)) bootstraps its estimate for the state-action value $Q_{t+1}(s,a)$ at time $t+1$ upon the estimate for $Q_t(s',a')$ with s' the state where the learner arrives after taking action a in state s :

$$Q_{t+1}(s,a) \leftarrow (1-\alpha)Q_t(s,a) + \alpha\left(r_t + \gamma \max_{a'} Q_t(s',a')\right) \tag{6}$$

With a the usual step size parameter, $\gamma \in [0,1]$ a discount factor and r_t the immediate reinforcement received at time step t. Non-bootstrapping evaluation methods such as Monte Carlo methods update their estimates based on actual returns. For instance the every-visit Monte Carlo method updates a state-action value $Q(s,a)$ at time $t+n$ (with n the time for one episode to finish) based on the actual return R_t and the previous value:

$$Q_{t+n}(s,a) \leftarrow (1-\alpha)Q_t(s,a) + \alpha(R_t) \tag{7}$$

With $R_t = r_{t+1} + \gamma\, r_{t+2} + \gamma^2 r_{t+3} + \ldots + \gamma^{n-1} r_n$ and t is the time at which (s,a) occurred.
Methods that learn their estimates, to some extend, on the basis of other estimates, i.e. they bootstrap are called Temporal Difference Learning Methods. The Q-learning algorithm seen in Equation 7 can be classified as a TD(0) algorithm. The back-up for each state is based on the immediate reward, and the estimation of the remaining rewards which is given by the value of the next state. One says that Q-learning is therefore a one-step TD method. However, one could also consider backups based on a weighted combination as follows:

$$R_t = r_{t+1} + \gamma r_{t+2} + \gamma^2 r_{t+2} + \cdots + \gamma^{k-1} r_{t+k} + \gamma^k V_{t+k+1}(s_{t+k+1}) \tag{8}$$

In the limit, all real rewards up-until-termination are used, meaning there is no bootstrapping, this is the Monte Carlo method. So, there is a spectrum ranging from using simple one-step returns to using full-backup returns. Some of them were implemented in the set-up of section 5. The Monte Carlo technique, which was described there and which is commonly used in a LA setting, is compared with the following variations: intermediate rewards, one-step updating, n-step updating.

7.1 Intermediate rewards

In (Peeters et al., 2006) an update mechanism based on Intermediate Rewards was introduced. With this technique the learning automata at level l only get informed about the immediate reward and the rewards on the remainder of the path. The LA does not get informed about the rewards that are given to automata on the levels above because the learning automaton at this level has no direct influence over rewards depending on higher level actions and they would clutter up its combined reward. In (Van de Wege, 2006) a theoretical proof that hierarchical learning automata using only the rewards of the remainder of the path will converge to an equilibrium path in an identical pay-off multi-stage game (under the same conditions we described above for the traditional Monte Carlo technique) is given. The complete algorithm can be found in Figure 6. Because the learning automata get updated at the end of an episode, the intermediate rewards technique is still an off-line algorithm.

All the learning automata: initialise action probabilities: $\forall a \in A : p_0(a) = \frac{1}{|A|}$
for each trial **do**
  Activate the top LA of the hierarchies
  for each level l in hierarchy h **do**
    The active learning automata take action $a_t^l(h)$
      $\Rightarrow$ joint-action $\mathbf{a} = [a_t^l(1), \ldots, a_t^l(h), \ldots]$
    Store immediate reward r_t (team reward based on **a**)
  end for
  for each level l in hierarchy h **do**
    Compute combined reward: $R^l(h) = \theta_t r_t + \theta_{t+1} r_{t+1} + \ldots + \theta_T r_T$
    Update the automaton that was active at level l in hierarchy h with reward $R^l(h)$
  end for
end for

Fig. 6. The pseudo code of the Intermediate Rewards algorithm.

7.2 One-step returns

In the One-Step Estimates technique, introduced in (Peeters et al., 2007), the updating of the learning automata will no longer take place at an explicit end-stage. The automata get informed immediately about the local or immediate reward they receive for their actions. In addition each automaton has estimates about the long term reward for each of its actions. These estimates are updated by combing the immediate rewards with an estimate of possible rewards that this action might give on the remainder of the path, similar to TD(0) methods. The behavior of the algorithm is controlled by three parameters: α, γ and ρ. Here, α is the step size parameter from the LR-I update scheme (Equation 8), γ is the discount factor as used in traditional bootstrapping (Equation 9), and ρ controls the influence of the difference between the combined reward and the old-estimate on the new-estimate (Note: in standard Q-learning notation this parameter is denoted by α).

7.3 n-step returns

The 1-step algorithm described above can easily be extended to the general n-step case. This creates a whole range of updating algorithms for multi-stage games, similar to the range of algorithms that exist for the single agent case. Figures 7 to 9 show the general n-step updating algorithm for pursuit learning automata. The parameters α, γ and ρ are equivalent to those of the *1*-step algorithm, described above.

All the learning automata: Initialise action probabilities: $\forall a \in A : p_0(a) = \frac{1}{|A|}$
Initialise the estimates of all the actions: $\forall a \in A : myEstimates(a) = 0$ (estimates for all the actions, meaning: what is the long term reward associated with this action)
Initialise estimates for the learning automata at level n $\forall a \in A : nStepEstimates_0(a) = 0$ (for each action this learning automaton has, keep an estimate of the automata at level $n + 1$ of the branch connected to the action)
for each trial **do**
    Activate the top LA of the hierachies
    for each level l in hierarchy h **do**
        Take action $a_t^l(h)$
            $\Rightarrow$ joint-action $\mathbf{a} = [a_t^l(1), \ldots, a_t^l(h), \ldots]$
        Observe immediate reward r_{t+1} (reward based on **a**) and store it for later use
        Propagate r_{t+1} up to the parent $\Rightarrow$ *see Figure 8: Compute the n-step reward.*
    end for
end for

Fig. 7 Pseudo code of the n-step algorithm. This part of the n-step algorithm shows how to handle immediate rewards.

if r_x is the nth reward I receive **then**
    Compute the n-step truncated return: $R_t^{(n)} = r_t + \gamma r_{t+1} + \ldots + \gamma^{n-1} r_{t+n} + \gamma^n \; nStepEstimates(a_t^l(h))$
    Update $myEstimates(a_t^l(h)) = myEstimates(a_t^l(h)) + \rho[R_t^{(n)} - myEstimates(a_t^l(h))]$
    Update action probability **p** using $myEstimates(a_t^l(h))$ as the reward for the L_{R-I} scheme
    Propagate $myEstimates(a_t^l(h))$ up to parent $\Rightarrow$ *see Figure 9: Propagating estimates.*
else
    if this wasn't the nth reward, this reward also needs to go to the parent: Propagate r_x up to the parent $\Rightarrow$ *Apply this part of the algorithm recursively.*
end if

Fig. 8 Pseudo code of the n-step algorithm. This part of the n-step algorithm computes the complete n-step reward and shows how to update the estimates.

if this estimate comes from the $n + 1^{th}$ level **then**
    $nStepEstimates(a_t^l(h)) \leftarrow nStepEstimates(a_t^l(h)) + \rho(\kappa - nStepEstimates(a_t^l(h)))$
else
    Keep propagating est_x up in the hierarchy $\Rightarrow$ *Apply this part of the algorithm recursively.*
end if

Fig. 9 Pseudo code of the n-step algorithm. This part of the n-step algorithm handles the updating of the estimates of the parents in the hierarchy.

The interaction between the hierarchies remains the same as for the Monte Carlo case (and the 1-step case). The learning automata at the top of the hierarchies start by selecting an action. Based on this joint-action the environment generates a reward and this reward is handed to the automata. Since this is the immediate reward, the automata cannot yet

generate the n-step truncated return (if $n > 1$) instead they propagate this reward to their parents (Figure 7 line 10). The automata that receive this reward check whether this is the nth reward they have received (Figure 8 line 1). If so, they compute the n-step truncated return (Figure 8 line 2), update the estimates of the long term reward of their own actions (Figure 8 line 3), update their probabilities (Figure 8 line 4) and keep their n^{th}-level-grandparents up to date by providing them with the updated estimates (Figure 8 line 5). If the parents didn't receive the nth reward yet (thus they can't compute the n-step reward yet), they just propagate the reward to their parents (Figure 8 lines 6 and 7).
In addition to propagating the immediate rewards, the automata also propagate their updated estimates. The parents receiving an estimate from their children check whether it is the estimate they need to compute the n-step truncated return (i.e. the estimate coming from level $(n+1)^{th}$ and they adjust the estimates of their n^{th}-level-grandchildren if necessary. This process continues for each level that gets activated in the hierarchies.

7.4 Empirical results

For the Monte Carlo updating and the Intermediate Rewards method, there are theoretical proofs guaranteeing that the learning automata converge to an equilibrium path in any multi-stage game. This can be proved under the assumptions that the learning automata use the L_{R-I} update scheme and the step sizes are chosen small enough. We have however no guarantee that the automata will converge to the optimal equilibrium path. Therefore it is useful the compare the practical performance of the different update techniques. A thorough comparison can be found in Peeters et al. 2007 (b).
Here we show experiments of a series of *1000* Random Games. For each value of the learning rate we considered in our experiments, we averaged the obtained reward over *1000* randomly generated games. Thus after each of the 1000 runs, we reset the values of the reward matrices to a random number in *[0,1]*. In the experiment we used *2* hierarchies of *8* levels, with *2* actions per automaton. This gives a total of $(2^8)^2 = 65.563$ solution paths. Figure 10 shows the results for the Monte Carlo algorithm and the *4*-step reward.
The average reward when using the Monte Carlo algorithm is systematically lower compared to the average reward of any of the n-step algorithms (the plot shown is for the *4*-step algorithm, but this is observed for the whole tested range of *1*-step to *8*-step, although the performance differs). All of our results demonstrate that the performance increases when the hierarchical learning automata use an n-step updating algorithm.

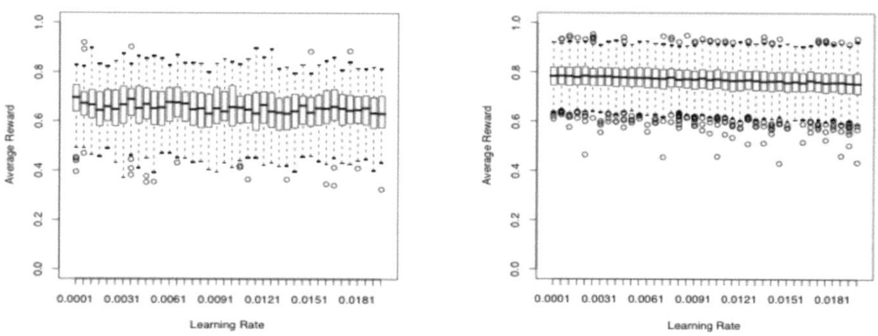

Fig. 10 The average reward using Monte Carlo (left) and the *4*-step rewards for various learning rates. The rewards are averaged over 1000 runs.

In general, using the Intermediate Reward technique, the average reward increases, compared to the Monte Carlo approach, however the variance of the rewards to which the hierarchies converge, remains the same (these results are not shown here). The results of the n-step algorithm show that the average convergence can remain at the same high level (compared to Monte Carlo updating) while the variance of the solution-paths is much less. This means that if the hierarchies converge to a sub-optimal solution, they are more likely to converge to a sub-optimal solution with an average reward that is almost as good as the optimal.

8. Conclusion

In this chapter we have demonstrated that Learning Automata are interesting building blocks for multi-agent Reinforcement learning algorithms. LA can be viewed as policy iterators, that update their action probabilities based on private information only. Even in multi-automaton settings, each LA is updated using only the environment response, and not on the basis of any knowledge regarding the other automata, i.e. nor their strategies, nor their feedback.

As such LA based agent algorithms are relatively simple and the resulting multi-automaton systems can still be treated analytically. Convergence proofs already exist for a variety of settings ranging from a single automaton model acting in a simple stationary random environment to a distributed automata model interacting in a complex environment.

The above properties make LA attractive design tools for multi-agent learning applications, where communication is often expensive and payoffs are inherently stochastic. They allow to design multi-agent learning algorithms with different learning objectives. Furthermore, LA have also proved to be able to work in asynchronous settings, where the actions of the LA are not taken simultaneously and where reward comes with delay.

We have demonstrated this design approach in 2 distinct multi-agent learning settings. In ergodic markov games each agent defers its action selection to a local automaton, associated with the current system state. Convergence to an equilibrium between agent policies can be established by approximating the problem by a limiting normal form game. In episodic multi-stage learning problems agents were designed as tree-structured hierarchies of automata, mimicking the structure of the environment. Convergence of this algorithm can again be established based on existing automata properties. By using Intermediate Rewards instead of Monte Carlo rewards, the hierarchical learning automata are shown (both empirically and theoretically) to have a faster and more accurate convergence by even using less information. However, the Intermediate Rewards update mechanism is still an off-line algorithm in which the updating happens at explicit end-states. The general n-step algorithm solves this problem by handing immediate rewards to the automata which use bootstrapping to compensate for the absence of reward of the remainder of the path. Empirical experiments show that the n-step rewards (with an appropriate value for n) outperform both the Monte Carlo technique as well as the Intermediate Rewards.

9. References

Claus, C; Boutilier, C. (1998). The dynamics of reinforcement learning in cooperative multiagent systems, *Proceedings of the 15th National Conference on Artificial*

Intelligence, pp. 746 - 752, ISBN: 978-1-57735-258-7, Madison, Wisconsin, July 1998, AAAI Press

Boutilier, C; Sequential Optimality and Coordination in Multiagent Systems. *Proceedings of the 16th International Joint Conference on Artificial Intelligence,* pp. 478-485, ISBN 1- 55860-613-0, Stockholm, Sweden, August 1999, Morgan Kauffman

Hu, J.; Wellman, M. (2003). Q-learning for General-Sum stochastic Games, *Journal of Machine Learning Research,* 4, (November 2003) pp. 1039-1069, ISSN 1533-7928

Kapetanakis, S.; Kudenko, D., & Strens, M. (2003) Learning to coordinate using commitment sequences in cooperative multi-agent systems, In: *Adaptive Agents and Multi-Agent Systems II,* D. Kudenko et al. (Ed.), pp. 106-118 , Springer LNAI 3394 , ISBN 978-3-540-25260-3, Berlin/Heidelberg

Littman, M.; (2001). Friend-or-foe Q-learning in general-sum games, *Proceedings of the 18th International Conference on Machine Learning,* pp. 322-328, ISBN 1-55860-556-8, July 2001, Williamstown, MA, USA, Morgan Kaufmann Publishers, San Francisco.

Narendra, K; Parthasarathy, K. (1991). Learning Automata Approach to Hierarchical Multiobjective Analysis. *IEEE Transactions on Systems, Man and Cybernetics,* 21, 1, pp 263-272, ISSN 0018-9472.

Narendra, K.; Thathachar, M. (1989). *Learning Automata: An Introduction,* Prentice-Hall International Inc, ISBN 0-13-485558-2 , Upper Saddle River, NJ, USA.

Peeters, M.; Verbeeck, K.; Nowé A. (2006). Bootstrapping versus Monte Carlo in a Learning Automata Hierarchy. In *Proceedings of the Sixth Adaptive Learning Agents and Multi-Agent Systems Symposium,* pp. 61-71, Brussels, April 2006.

Peeters, M.; Verbeeck, K.; Nowé A. (2007) (a). The effect of bootstrapping in multi-automata reinforcement learning. *IEEE Symposium on Approximate Dynamic Programming and Reinforcement Learning,* ISBN 1-4244-0698-6, April 2007, Honolulu, Hawaii, USA.

Peeters, M,; Verbeeck, K.; Nowé A. (2007) (b). Solving Multi-Stage Games with Hierarchical Learning Automata that Bootstrap. To appear LNAI.

Puterman, M; (1994) *Markov Decision Processes: Discrete Stochastic Dynamic Programming* John Wiley & Sons, ISBN 0471727822, Inc. New York, NY, USA.

Ramakrishnan, K.R. (1982. Hierarchical systems and cooperative games of learning automata. Ph.D. thesis, Indian Institute of Science, Bangalore, India.

Shapley, L; (1953) Stochastic games. *Proceeding of the National Academy of Sciences USA,* 39, October 1953, pp. 1095-1100, ISSN 1091-6490

Sutton, R; Barto, A. (1998) *Reinforcement Learning: An Introduction.* MIT Press, ISBN 0-262-19398-1 , Cambridge, MA

Thathachar, M.A.L.; Ramakrishnan, K.R. (1981). A Hierarchical System of Learning Automata. *IEEE Transactions on Systems, Man and Cybernetics,* 11, 3, pp 236-241, ISSN 0018-9472.

Thathachar , M.A.L.; Sastry, P.S. (1985). A new approach to the design of reinforcement schemes for learning automata. *IEEE Transactions on Systems, Man and Cybernetics,* 15, 168–175, ISSN 0018-9472.Tsetlin, M; (1973) *Automaton Theory and Modeling of biological Systems.* Academic Press New York.

Tsitsiklis, J. (1994). Asynchronous Stochastic Approximation and Q-learning. *Machine Learning,* 16, pp 185-202, ISSN 0885-6125.

Tuyls, K.; Nowé, A. (2005). Evolutionary Game Theory and Multi-Agent Reinforcement Learning. *The Knowledge Engineering Review*, 20, 01, March 2005, pp 63–90, ISSN 0269-8889.

Van de Wege, L. (2006). Learning Automata as a Framework for Multi-Agent Reinforcement Learning. Masters thesis.

Verbeeck K.; Vrancx P., Nowé A., (2007) (a). Networks of Learning Automata and Limiting Games, *Proceedings of the 7th ALAMAS Symposium*, pp. 171-182 , ISSN 0922-8721, April 2007, Maastricht, The Netherlands, number 07-04, Maastricht University.

Verbeeck, K; Nowé, A., Parent, J., & Tuyls, K. (2007) (b). Exploring Selfish Reinforcement Learning in Repeated Games with Stochastic Rewards. *The Journal of Autonomous Agents and Multi-Agent Systems*, 14, 3, June 2007, pp. 239–269, ISSN 1387-2532 .

Vrancx, P; Verbeeck, K. & Nowé, A. (2007). Decentralized Learning in Markov Games, Tech Report Vrije Universiteit Brussel Mei 2007, Submitted.

Watkins C; Dayan P. (1992). Q-learning. *Machine Learning*, 8, 3, pp 279-292, ISSN 0885-6125.

Wheeler, R; Narendra, K. (1986). Decentralized Learning in Finite Markov Chains. *IEEE Transactions on Automatic Control*, 31, 6, 1986, pp. 519 - 526, ISSN 0018-9286

10

Abstraction for Genetics-Based Reinforcement Learning

Dr Will Browne, Dan Scott and Charalambos Ioannides
University of Reading
UK

1. Introduction

Abstraction is a higher order cognitive ability that facilitates the production of rules that are independent of their associations.

In standard reinforcement learning it is often expedient to directly associate situations (states) with actions in order to maximise the environmental reward signal. This may lead to problems including a lack of generalisation and not utilising higher order patterns in complex domains. Thus standard Q-learning has been developed to include models or genetics-based search (Learning Classifier Systems), which improve learning speeds and generality. In order to extend reinforcement learning techniques to higher-order rules, abstraction is considered here.

The process of abstraction can be likened to Information Processing Theory (a branch of Learning Theory) (Miller, 1956), which suggests that humans have the ability to recognize patterns in data and chunk these patterns into meaningful units. The individual patterns do not necessarily remain in a memory store due to the holistic nature of the individual patterns. However, the chunks of meaningful information remain, and become a basic element of all subsequent analyses.

The need for abstraction arose from the data-mining of rules in the steel industry through application of the genetics-based machine learning technique of Learning Classifier Systems (Holland, 1975), which utilise a Q-learning type update for reinforcement learning. It was noted that many rules had similar patterns. For example, there were many rules of the type 'if side guide setting < width, then poor quality product' due to different product widths. This resulted in a rule-base that was unnecessarily hard to interpret and slow to learn. The initial development of the abstraction method was based on the known problem of Connect4 due to its vast search space, temporal nature and available patterns.

The contribution of this chapter is that the novel method of abstraction is described and shown to be effective on a large search space test problem. Abstraction enabled higher order rules to be learned from base knowledge, which mimic important aspects of human cognition. Tests showed that the abstracted rules were more compact, had greater utility and assisted in developmental learning. The emergence of abstracted rules corresponded with escaping from local minima that would have otherwise trapped basic reinforcement learning techniques, such as standard Q-learning.

2. Background

During the application of the Genetics-Based Machine Learning technique of Learning Classifier Systems (LCS) to data-mine rules in the steel industry, Browne noted that many rules had similar patterns (Browne 2004). For example, there were many rules of the type 'if side guide setting < width, then poor quality product' due to different product widths. This resulted in a rule-base that was unnecessarily hard to interpret and slow to learn. A method is sought to generate higher order (abstracted) rules from the learnt base rules.
A novel Abstraction algorithm has been proposed (see figure 1) to improve the performance of a reinforcement learning genetics-based machine learning technique in a complex multi-step problem (Browne & Scott, 2005). It is hoped that this algorithm will help reinforcement learning techniques identify higher-order patterns inherent in an environment.

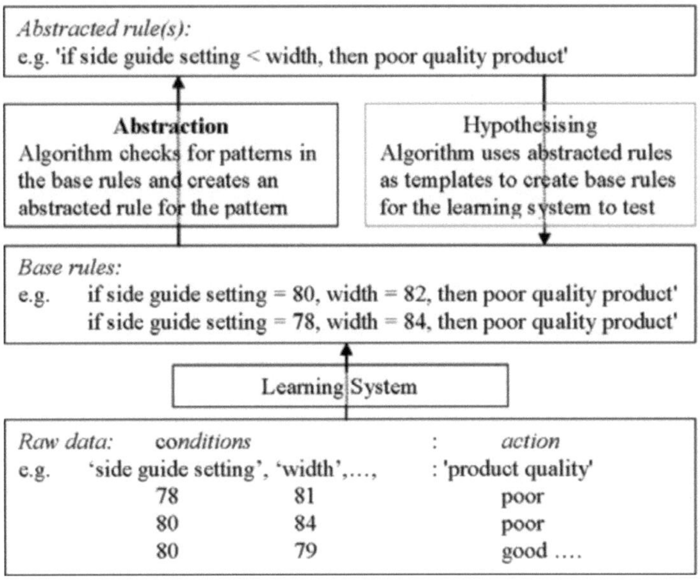

Fig. 1. Abstraction from data to higher order rules.

2.1 Test domain

Connect 4 is a turn-based game between two players, each trying to be the first to achieve four counters in a row (horizontally, vertically or diagonally). The game takes place on a 7 * 6 board; players take it in turns to drop one of their counters into one of the seven columns. The counters will drop to the lowest free space in the column. Play continues until the board is full or one player gets four in a row, see figure 2. Optimum strategies exist (Allis, 1988; Watkins, 1989), so the problem is both known and bounded.
A client-server program of Connect 4 was written in Java, as Java Applets can easily be viewed on the internet, allowing a website to be constructed for this project [please visit: http://sip189a.rdg.ac.uk].
A Q-Learning (Sutton & Barto, 1998) approach to the problem is implemented in order to provide benchmark learning performance. Two different approaches were taken to training the Q-Learning system. The first progressively trained the algorithm against increasingly hard opponents, whilst the second trained for the same number of games, but against the hardest opponent from the outset.

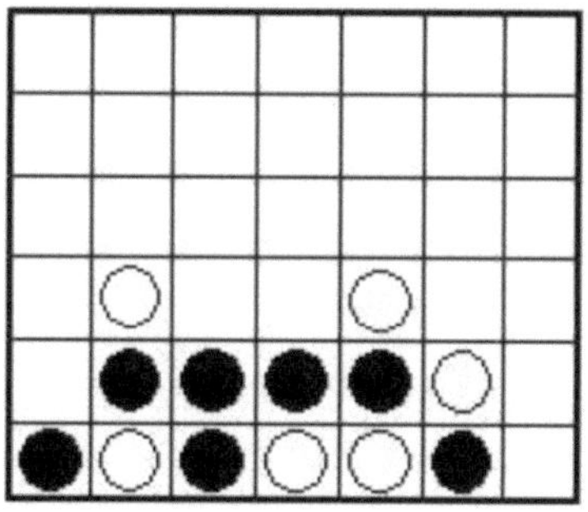

Fig. 2. Connect 4 board, black horizontal win

The Abstraction algorithm requires rules in order to perform abstraction. A well-known LCS, XCS (Butz, 2004) was implemented to create rules and provide a second benchmark learning performance.

3. Biological inspiration for abstraction

The human brain has inspired artificial intelligence researchers, such as the development of Artificial Neural Networks that model aspects of low-level neuronal activity. Higher-level functional modelling has also been undertaken, see ACT-R and SOAR architectures (Anderson et al, 2004; Laird et al, 1987). Behavioural studies suggest that pattern recognition, which includes abstraction, is important to human cognition. Thus this section considers how the brain abstracts. This includes using the common neuroscience technique of studying subjects with liaisons to specific brain areas.

It has been observed in cases of autism that there is a lack of abstraction. A well studied case is that of Kim Peek -due to his Savant abilities and popularity as the inspiration for the main character in the film Rain Man. He was born with macrocephaly (an enlarged head), an encephalocele (part of one or more of the skull plates did not seal) and agenesis of the corpus callosum (the bundle of nerves that connects the two hemispheres of the brain is missing). Brain studies, such as MRI, show that the there is also no anterior commissure and damage to the cerebellum.

Kim has the ability to analyse certain types of information in great detail, e.g. Kim's father indicates that by the age of 16-20 months Kim was able to memorize every book that was read to him. It is speculated that neurons have made other connections in the absence of a corpus callosum, resulting in the increased memory capacity (Treffert & Christensen, 2005). However, Kim has difficulty with motor skills, such as buttoning a shirt, which is likely to be caused by the damaged cerebellum as it normally coordinates motor activities. His general IQ is well below normal, but he scores very highly in some subtests.

An absent corpus callosum (ACC) does not regenerate as no new callosal fibers emerge during an infant's development. Although people with ACC lead productive and meaningful lives there are common developmental problems that may occur with disorders of the corpus callosum (DCC). The National Organization for Disorders of the Corpus Callosum states:

> Behaviorally individuals with DCC may fall behind their peers in social and problem solving skills in elementary school or as they approach adolescence. In typical development, the fibers of the corpus callosum become more efficient as

children approach adolescence. At that point children with an intact corpus callosum show rapid gains in abstract reasoning, problem solving, and social comprehension. Although a child with DCC may have kept up with his or her peers until this age, as the peer-group begins to make use of an increasingly efficient corpus callosum, the child with DCC falls behind in mental and social functioning. In this way, the behavioral challenges for individuals with DCC may become more evident as they grow into adolescence and young adulthood.

Behavioural characteristics related to DCC difficulties on multidimensional tasks, such as using language in social situations (for example, jokes, metaphors), appropriate motor responses to visual information (for example, stepping on others' toes, handwriting runs off the page), and the use of complex reasoning, creativity and problem solving (for example, coping with math and science requirements in middle school and high school, budgeting) (NODCC, 2007).

The connection between the left and right half of the brain is important as each hemisphere tends to be specialised on certain tasks. The HERA model asserts that the left pre-frontal cortex is associated with semantic (meaning) memory, whilst the right is associated with episodic (temporal) memory (Tulving et al., 1994). Memories themselves are associated with the hippocampus, which assists in transforming short to long term memory. This is intact in many savants, such as Kim Peek. Thus, it is postulated here that a link is needed between the separated episodic and semantic memory areas in order for abstract, higher order, knowledge to form -it is not sufficient just to create long-term generalised memories.

A caveat of the above analysis is that even with modern behavioural studies, functional MRI, PET scans and other neurological analysis, the brain/mind is highly complex, plastic and still not fully understood.

4. Learning classifier systems

This section outlines the architecture of XCS, including the required adjustments for the Connect 4 domain, so that it may train against a pre-coded expert system. A standard XCS (Butz, 2004, available from www-illigal.ge.uiuc.edu/) was implemented with the Abstraction algorithm (see section 5). Following these results tests were also conducted with a modified version of XCS (mXCS) that had its reinforcement learning component adjusted to complement the Abstraction algorithm.

4.1 Setup and board representation

The board representation formed an important part of the LCS. Each space on the board could be one of three possible states, red, yellow or empty, however it was considered useful to further split down the empty squares into two categories, playable and unplayable (unplayable squares are above the playable squares and become playable in the future as the game progresses).

A two character representation for each space was chosen, leading to an 84 character long string representing the board (running from top row to bottom row). The encoding for a red was chosen as "11" and a yellow was "10", a playable space was "00" whilst an unplayable was "01". Mutation may only generalize by replacing specific characters with a "#"; where hashes can stand for either a "1" or a "0".

4.2 Gameplay and reward

LCS must decide upon the best move to play at its turn without knowing where its opponent will play in the subsequent turn. An untrained LCS will often play randomly as it attempts to learn the best moves to play. After each move has been played by the opponent, the LCS attempts to match the state of the board to its rules. Attached to each of these classifiers are three pieces of information: the move that should be played, the win score (the higher this is the more likely a win will occur) and the accuracy score (accuracy of the win score). Win scores of less than 50 indicate a predicted loss, greater than 50 is a projected win. After matching, an action must be selected through explore, exploit or coverage. Exploring (which is most likely to happen) uses a weighted roulette wheel based on accuracy to choose a move. Exploiting chooses the move that has the greatest win score and is used for performance evaluation. Coverage generates a new rule by simply selecting a random move to play for the current board position.

θ_{GA} the GA threshold was set to 1000 games, the GA would run after a set of 1000 games had been played and the maximum population size was set to 5000. χ, the crossover possibility was set to generate 500 random crossovers every time the GA is run. Of the 500 crossovers generated, approximately 100 in every GA run passed validity checks and were inputted into the new population. μ, the mutation rate was set at a 1% chance to receive a mutation and then a 2% that each character in that rule would receive a mutation. Deletion θ probabilities (θ_{del}) were based upon tournament selection of rule fitness and the number of rules deleted was chosen to keep the population size at 5000.

The standard reinforcement update for LCS is the Widrow-Hoff update (Butz & Wilson, 2002), which is a recency weighted average. A Q-learning type update is used within the LCS technique for multistep decision problems (Lanzi, P-L., 2002).

5. Abstraction algorithm

The Abstraction algorithm was designed to work upon generated rules, e.g. by the LCS. Abstraction is independent of the data itself. Other methods, such as the standard coverage operator, depend directly on the data. Crossover and mutation depend indirectly on the data as they require the fitness of the hypothesized rules, which is dependent on the data. Abstraction is a higher order method, as once good rules have been discovered; it could function without the raw data being available.

The abstraction attempts to find patterns in the rules that performed best within the LCS. Having found a pattern common to two or more of the LCS rules, the Abstraction algorithm is to generate a new rule in the abstracted population based solely on this pattern. This allows the pattern to be matched when it occurs in any state, not just the specific rules that exist within the LCS.

Not all of the rules generated by the LCS are worthwhile and therefore the Abstraction algorithm should not be run upon all of the rules within the LCS. The domain is noiseless, so the parameters chosen to govern the testing of rules for abstraction were the conditions that a rule must have a 100% win score and a 100% accuracy. Therefore the rules abstracted by the Abstraction algorithm should only be rules that lead to winning situations.

The main mechanism that allowed the abstraction to perform was a windowing function that was used in rule generation as well as rule selection (when it came to choosing an abstracted rule to play). The windowing function acted as a filter that was passed over the 'good' rules generated by the LCS. This filter would compare two rules at a time for similarities that could lead to abstracted rules.

The windowing function worked in all directions on the board, horizontally, vertically and in both diagonal directions. The window size was set to 4 space/counters (8 characters in terms of the board representation). However code allowed for a window size of between 4 and 6 spaces/counter (8 - 12 characters in terms of the board representation), any greater than a window size of 6 and the vertical and diagonal windows no longer fit on the board.

Any match that is found is turned into an abstracted rule, each rule had 8 characters (assuming a window size of 4) to represent the pattern occurring on the board. Each rule also had to be assigned a move to play whenever that rule was used. The move assigned was always chosen from one of the playable spaces within the pattern. An example rule is '10,10,10,00:11', which translate to 'if three red counters in a row and payable space in the next position, then play in the next position'. All rules entered the abstracted population with a win and accuracy of 50.

Several limitations were placed upon what was considered a valid match for the Abstraction algorithm, including ignoring all unplayable areas. A valid pattern had to contain at least one playable space and no more than 2 playable spaces. Patterns without a playable space are useless because rules as they offer nowhere for a move to be played. The second limitation placed upon the abstraction process was that a valid rule could have a maximum of one unplayable space. This helps limit the generation of "empty" rules. Figure 3 shows an example of two windowing functions finding a match and generating an abstracted rule.

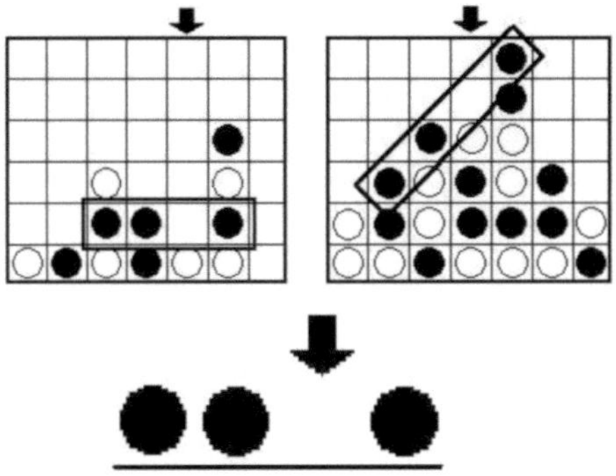

Fig. 3. Example of Abstraction Algorithms generating a new rule.

5.1 Base rule discovery

As with the LCS, the Abstraction algorithm also had a GA that was run upon the population to generate new rules. It had a single point crossover and mutation; however it had no deletion algorithm as all the abstraction rules were kept. Duplication was prevented through a duplication check that was made each time a rule was to be inserted into the rule-base, including those generated by crossover and mutation.

A LCS can function alone, but the Abstraction algorithm cannot function without a rule-base to work on; hence it needs an LCS to function alongside it. How the two are combined and work together is detailed in this section.

When the LCS with abstraction needs to play a move, the system searches the board for any matches within its abstracted rule set. The board is searched by passing the windowing function over the board (horizontally vertically and diagonally). A rule is then chosen out of

all matched rules. When exploiting the rule with the best win score is chosen, whilst when exploring a roulette wheel based upon accuracy is used.
The chosen abstracted rule also has a move associated with it, however unlike the LCS rules the move does not relate directly to the board. With a window size of 4 counters the rule could occur anywhere on the board, horizontally, vertically or diagonally. Therefore an extra calculation is required to translate the abstracted rules' move into the corresponding move on the actual board.
If no abstracted rule is found after the initial search of the board state, then control of playing the move is handed to the base LCS.

6. Results

The following section details the results found during the trials of the LCS and Abstraction algorithm. Initial trials investigated the difficulty of the problem domain with standard Q-learning and XCS techniques. Preliminary tests of the Abstraction algorithm with XCS were followed by tests of the Abstraction algorithm with a modified XCS (mXCS) where the reinforcement learning complemented the abstraction. The use of abstraction as the training progressed was investigated. During these tests, each system was trained for 20,000 games against an opponent that played randomly. Finally, the robustness of the Abstraction algorithm to changes in the domain was tested by increasing the difficulty of the opponent.

6.1 Q-Learning and standard XCS

The Q-Learning Algorithm performed well in the initial 20,000 games (see figure 4), achieving an average win percentage of 69%. However, there was no progress in the wins as the 20,000 games progressed, with the win percentage always remaining at around 69%. This exhaustive search nature of the algorithm meant it took several weeks of computation on a 3GHz PC. Ideally, each test would have been repeated 10 times and the average results taken, but this was impractical due to time constraints.
The XCS performance trend was similar, with an average win percentage of 62% reached quickly, but no further improvements. Analysis of the rules showed that they had become trapped in local optima. A few specific strategies had been learnt, such as initially trying to build a column of counters in a given column. However, if this column happened to be blocked, then the overall strategy failed.

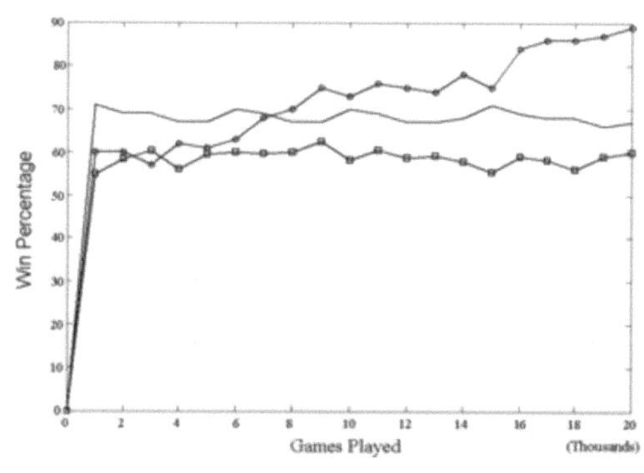

Fig. 4. Graphs of win percentages for the 3 algorithms Solid Line -Q-Learning Algorithm, square -XCS Algorithm, circle -mXCS with Abstraction.

When the Abstraction algorithm is added it produces a similar trend until 6000 trials. A significant improvement is noted after 8000 trials as the performance increases to 90%. This compares favorably with both Q-learning (69%) and standard XCS (62%).

During testing the rules that the Abstraction algorithm produced were observed and an interesting pattern arose in the order in which the abstractions were discovered. In early generations no abstracted rules are found, whilst mXCS attempts to establish a set of good rules that have a win and accuracy of 100. The first abstracted rules found are not rules for a direct win (i.e. 3 in a row and play in the fourth). The first rules that emerge are those rules that cause a 3 in a row situation with an empty playable fourth space.

Learning to form 3 in a row followed by learning to form 4 in a row is a novel example of incremental learning. Intuitively, it could be expected that learning to form 4 in a row, which is closer to obtaining the reward, would be achieved first. Incremental learning is hypothesized to be an important cognitive ability (Butz, 2004).

Whilst there is no direct feedback from the abstraction rule-base to the mXCS rule-base, it is possible to see them evolve together and there is a definite dependency between the two. With the introduction of abstracted rules to make 3 in a row, this is likely to occur far more often (as abstracted rules take preference over mXCS rules). With 3 in a row occurring more often, mXCS has more opportunities to conceive of rules that directly give a win. Therefore, with more winning rules the Abstraction algorithm is more likely to come up with abstracted rules that lead to a direct win, greatly bolstering the winning ability of the algorithm.

6.2 Effect of abstraction

The use of abstracted rules as training progresses can be monitored, see figure 5. As outlined in section 5, the combined system always plays a matching abstracted rule in preference to a matching base rule. After 8000 trials the base rules were accurate enough to allow abstraction to start. Once abstraction had started, the performance of the system continued to improve beyond that of standard XCS and Q-learning (see figure 4). A further 8000 trials occur where the system uses a combination of both base and abstracted rules. After this period the system just uses abstracted rules in its decision-making. Small improvements in performance occurred due to the action of the genetic algorithm in the abstracted population.

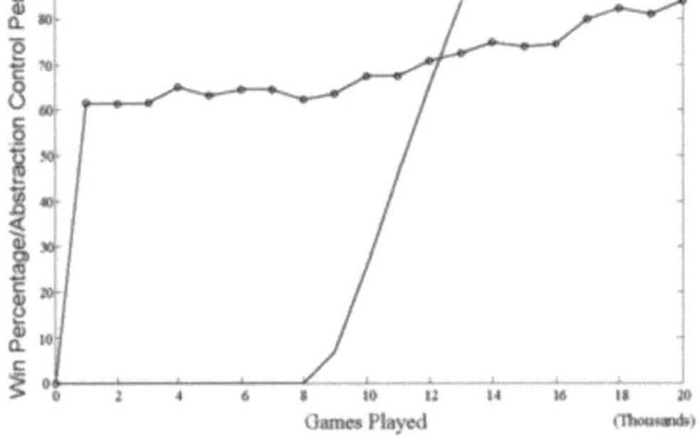

Fig. 5. Graph of percentage base rules versus abstracted rules (solid line) as training progresses (circle line).

The random opponent still defeats the system in 10% of the games when it chances upon a good strategy. As there are multiple positions for good strategies to occur in, the system is rarely presented with them, which makes them difficult to learn. In order to determine the robustness and scalability of the techniques the difficulty of the opponent was increased.

6.3 Robustness of the systems

The opponent could now block a potentially winning three in a row state. The system has to learn to create multiple win situations. This is a significantly harder problem, especially as the opponent could win either randomly or in the act of blocking, which halts the game. All algorithms perform poorly as all win percentages are under 20%. If no good base rules are found, then the Abstraction algorithm will not start.

Instead of training from the start with the harder opponent, it was decided to train first with the simple opponent and then switch to the harder opponent, see figure 6. After the switch, standard XCS performed better than the Q-Learning Algorithm, achieving a win percentage of 15%, it should be noted that the performance was less than the Q-Learning algorithm during the first 20000 games. Analysis of the Q-Learning algorithm testing showed that progressive training, from the easiest to the hardest opponent, caused it to get stuck in a local optimum with a win percentage of only 11%. The generality and adaptability of the standard XCS algorithm enables it to switch opponent without as great a penalty.

The performance of the Abstraction algorithm was significant. Not only did it outperform standard XCS and Q-learning (53%, compared with 15% and 11% respectively), but it performed significantly better then when it had been trained only on the harder opponent (53% compared with 19%). This is a good example of incremental learning, where it is necessary to build up the complexity of the problem domain.

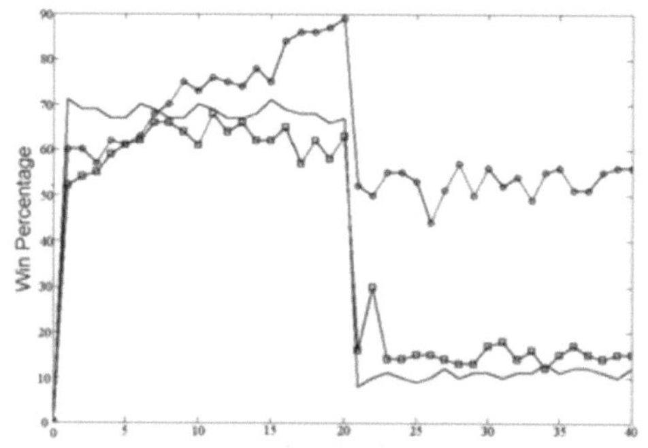

Fig. 6. Change in opponent at 20x103 games played (Solid Line -Q-Learning Algorithm, square -XCS, circle -mXCS with Abstraction).

The concept of abstraction has been applied to the alternative domain of the Multiplexer problem (Browne & Ioannides, 2007). This was to test if a different representation (alphabet) could be used between the initial population (e.g. binary alphabet) and the abstracted population (e.g. s-expression alphabet). Result showed on hypothesised base data that abstraction is capable of scaling well on the formed rules (max length 1034 bits compared with 84 bits for the Connect4 domain). A significant advantage was the compacting of the rule-based, see figure 7 and see table 1, compared with a bit string of 1034. Abstraction also selected the most appropriate functions within the s-expressions for the domain (two from a possible 10).

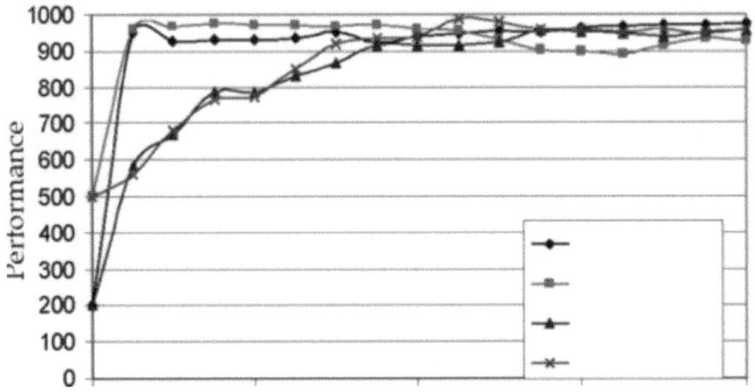

Fig. 7. Abstracted XCS with hypothesised base rules on 3-MUX ♦, 6-MUX ■, 135-MUX ▲, 1034-MUX **x** problem

MUX	Condition	Length
3	VALUEAT OR 2 2	4
3	VALUEAT AND 2 2	4
3	VALUEAT ADDROF 2 2	4
3	VALUEAT AND 2 POWEROF 1	5
3	VALUEAT OR POWEROF 2 2	5
3	VALUEAT OR POWEROF 1 2	5
6	VALUEAT ADDROF 4 5	4
6	VALUEAT ADDROF 5 4	4
6	VALUEAT ADDROF 4 POWEROF 5	5
6	VALUEAT ADDROF POWEROF 3 4	5
6	VALUEAT ADDROF POWEROF 5 4	5
135	VALUEAT ADDROF 128 134	4
135	VALUEAT ADDROF 134 128	4
135	VALUEAT ADDROF POWEROF 22 128	5
135	VALUEAT ADDROF 128 PLUS 133 134	6
1034	VALUEAT ADDROF 1033 1024	4
1034	VALUEAT ADDROF PLUS 1029 1029 1024	6
1034	VALUEAT ADDROF MULTIPLY 1025 324 1024	6
1034	VALUEAT ADDROF PLUS 1029 1024 1024	6
1034	VALUEAT ADDROF MULTIPLY 1029 324 1024	6
1034	VALUEAT ADDROF PLUS 1033 1033 1024	6

Table 1. Abstracted rules on 3-MUX, 6-MUX, 135-MUX & 1034-MUX problem

7. Discussion

Abstraction may appear a trivial task for humans and the positive results from this work intuitive, but abstraction has not been routinely used in genetics-based reinforcement learning. One reason is that the time each iteration requires is an important consideration and abstraction increases the time for each iteration. Typically XCS takes 20 minutes to play 1000 games (and remains constant), mXCS with abstraction takes 20 minutes for 100 games (although this can vary greatly depending on the choice of parameters) and the Q-Learning algorithm ranges from 5 minutes for 1000 games initially to 90 minutes for 1000 games after 100,000 games training. However, given a fixed amount of time to train all three algorithms mXCS with abstraction would perform the best, once the initial base rules were found.

The Q-Learning algorithm has to visit every single state at least once in order to form a successful playing strategy. Whilst the Q-Learning system would ultimately play a very good game, weeks of computation failed to achieve the level of success the Abstraction algorithm had in a very short space of time (hours rather than weeks). Although better Q-learning algorithms (including generalization capabilities) exist (Sutton & Barto, 1998) this choice of benchmark algorithm showed the scale of the problem, which is difficult to calculate.

The improvement in abstraction performance from standard XCS to the modified XCS was due to using simpler reinforcement learning. The Widrow-Hoff delta rule converges much faster, which for simpler domains that can be solved easily is beneficial. However, slower and more graceful learning may be required in complex domains when interacting with higher level features.

The abstracted rules allow the system to play on states as a whole, including those that have not been encountered, where these states contain a known pattern. This is useful in data-mining, but with the inherent dangers of interpolation and extrapolation. The abstracted rule-base is also compact as an abstracted rule covers more states than either a generalized LCS rule or a Q-learning state. Unique states may still be covered by the base rules.

Abstraction has been shown to give an improvement in a complex, but structured domain. It is anticipated that the Abstraction algorithm would be suited to other domains containing repeated patterns.

8. Future work

Instead of the current linear filters in the Abstraction algorithm, it is possible to vary the size and shape in order to represent and hopefully discover advantageous multi-win situations. The abstraction method is static and determined a priori, which is successful for this structured domain. The next stage is to evolve the abstracted rules and/or filters thus reducing the searching time.

A process termed 'hypothesizing' is proposed (see figure 1) where the abstracted rules form a template in order to produce new rules for the base population, with the worth of the abstracted rule being determined by the success of their hypothesized rules.

9. Conclusion

A novel Abstraction algorithm has been developed to successfully improve the performance of a genetics-based machine learning technique in a complex multi-step problem. It is hoped that this algorithm will help to fulfill the intended use of the LCS technique as a test bed for artificial cognitive processes.

10. Acknowledgements

Our thanks to the Nuffield Foundation for their support through grant NUF-URB04.

11. References

Allis, V. (1988). *A Knowledge Based Approach of Connect 4*. Masters Thesis, Vrije Universiteit, Netherlands.

Anderson, JR.; Bothell, D.; Byme, MD.; Douglass, S.; Lebiere C. & Qin Y (2004). An integrated theory of the mind. *Psychological Review* 111 4, pp. 1036-1060.

Browne, WN. & Scott, D. (2005). An abstraction agorithm for genetics-based reinforcement learning. *GECCO 2005*, editors Hans-Georg Beyer et al. Washington D. C., USA, pp. 1875-1882.

Browne, WN. & Ioannides, C. (2007) Investigating Scaling of an Abstracted LCS Utilising Ternary and S-Expression Alphabets. *International Workshop on Learning Classifier Systems*, London

Browne, WN. (2004). The development of an industrial learning classifier system for data-mining in a steel hot strip mill. *Applications of Learning Classifier Systems*. Bull, L. (Ed.), pp. 223-259, Springer, Berlin.

Butz, M. & Wilson, SW. (2002). An algorithmic description of XCS. *Soft Computing: a fusion of foundations, methodologies and applications*, 6 pp. 162-170.

Butz, M. (2004). *Rule-base evolutionary online learning systems: learning bounds, classification and prediction*. PhD thesis University of Illinois, Illinois.

Holland, JH. (1975). *Adaptation in natural and artificial systems*. Ann Arbor, MI: University of Michigan press.

Laird, J.; Newell, A. & Rosenbloom, P. (1987) Soar -An architecture for general intelligence. *Artificial Intelligence* 33 pp. 1-64.

Lanzi, P-L. (2002). Learning classifier systems from a reinforcement learning perspective. *Soft Computing: a fusion of foundations, methodologies and applications*, 6 pp. 162-170.

Miller, GA. (1956). The magical number seven, plus or minus two; Some limits on our capacity for processing information. *Psychological Review*, 63, pp. 81-97.

NODCC. (2007) National Organization for Disorders of the Corpus Callosum http://www.nodcc.org

Sutton, RS. & Barto, AG. (1998). *Reinforcement learning: An introduction*. MIT Press, Cambridge, MA.

Treffert, DA. & Christensen, DD. (2005) Inside the Mind of a Savant *Scientific American* pp. 50-55.

Tulving, E.; Kapur, S.; Craik, FIM.; Moscovitch, M. & Houle. S. (1994) Hemispheric encoding/retrieval asymmetry in episodic memory: positron emission tomography findings. Proc. Natl. Acad. Sci. U. S. A. 91, pp. 2016–2020

Watkins, CJCH. (1989). *Learning from Delayed Rewards*. PhD thesis, King's College, Cambridge, England.

11

Dynamics of the Bush-Mosteller Learning Algorithm in 2x2 Games

Luis R. Izquierdo[1] and Segismundo S. Izquierdo[2]
[1]*University of Burgos*
[2]*University of Valladolid*
Spain

1. Introduction

Reinforcement learners interact with their environment and use their experience to choose or avoid certain actions based on the observed consequences. Actions that led to satisfactory outcomes (i.e. outcomes that met or exceeded aspirations) in the past tend to be repeated in the future, whereas choices that led to unsatisfactory experiences are avoided. The empirical study of reinforcement learning dates back to Thorndike's animal experiments on instrumental learning at the end of the 19th century (Thorndike, 1898). The results of these experiments were formalised in the well known 'Law of Effect', which is nowadays one of the most robust properties of learning in the experimental psychology literature:

"*Of several responses made to the same situation those which are accompanied or closely followed by satisfaction to the animal will, other things being equal, be more firmly connected with the situation, so that, when it recurs, they will be more likely to recur; those which are accompanied or closely followed by discomfort to the animal will, other things being equal, have their connections to the situation weakened, so that, when it recurs, they will be less likely to occur. The greater the satisfaction or discomfort, the greater the strengthening or weakening of the bond.*" (Thorndike, 1911, p. 244)

Nowadays there is little doubt that reinforcement learning is an important aspect of much learning in most animal species, including many phylogenetically very distant from vertebrates (e.g. earthworms (Maier & Schneirla, 1964) and fruit flies (Wustmann, 1996)). Thus, it is not surprising that reinforcement learning -being one of the most widespread adaptation mechanisms in nature- has attracted the attention of many scientists and engineers for decades. This interest has led to the formulation of various models of reinforcement learning and -when feasible- to the theoretical analysis of their dynamics. In particular, this chapter characterises the dynamics of one of the best known stochastic models of reinforcement learning (Bush & Mosteller, 1955) when applied to decision problems of strategy (i.e. games).

The following section is devoted to explaining in detail the context of application of our theoretical analysis, i.e. 2-player 2-strategy games. Section 3 is a brief review of various models of reinforcement learning that have been studied in strategic contexts. Section 4 presents the Bush-Mosteller reinforcement learning algorithm. Section 5 describes two types of critical points that are especially relevant for the dynamics of the process: self-reinforcing-equilibria (SREs) and self-correcting-equilibria (SCEs). Sections 6 and 7 detail the relevance of these equilibria. Section 8 analyses the robustness of the model to "trembling-hands" noise and, finally, section 9 presents the conclusions of this chapter. The reader can replicate all the simulation runs reported in this chapter using an applet available at http://www.luis.izquierdo.name/papers/rl-book; we have also placed the source code used to create every figure in this chapter at the same web address.

2. Decision problems of strategy

At the heart of any learning algorithm we always find the problem of choice: learning is about making better decisions. At the most elementary level, decision problems can be classified according to the factors that may influence the outcome of the problem. Following that criterion we can distinguish, in ascending order of generality, the following categories (Colman, 1995):

1. Individual decision-making problems of *skill*. In this category there is no uncertainty involved: a single individual makes a decision, and the outcome of the problem depends solely on that decision (e.g. the problem of distributing a fixed production generated in various factories over several consumption centres, each with a given demand, in order to minimise transportation costs).
2. Individual decision-making problems under *risk*. In these problems, the solitary decision maker does not know with certainty the consequences of each of the possible options available to her, but she can meaningfully attach probabilities to each of the outcomes that may occur after each of her possible choices (e.g. the decision of buying a lottery ticket or not).
3. Individual decision-making problems under *uncertainty*. In this type of problem, as in the previous case, even though the consequences of a decision cannot be known with certainty at the time of making the decision, the range of possible consequences for each decision can be roughly identified in advance. However, unlike in decisions under risk, in decisions under uncertainty probabilities cannot be meaningfully attached to each of those consequences (e.g. deciding what to order in a new restaurant).
4. Decision problems of *strategy*. These problems involve many decision makers, and each of them has only partial control over which outcome out of a conceivable set of them will actually occur. Decision makers may have the ability to adapt to each other's decisions (e.g. setting prices in an oligopoly with the aim of maximising individual profit).
5. Decision problems under *ignorance*, or structural ignorance (Gilboa & Schmeidler, 1995 and 2001). This category is characterised by the fact that it is not possible to meaningfully anticipate the set of potential consequences that each of the possible choices may have (e.g. deciding whether to give the go-ahead to genetically modified crops).

Problems of skill have been extensively studied in several branches of mathematics. In decision-making under risk, compelling solutions have been derived using the theory of probability and expected utility theory. Expected utility theory, however, has not been so successful in the study of decision-making under uncertainty and strategic decision-making, which is the competence of game theory. Finally, understandably so, the formal study of decision problems under ignorance has not developed much.

In this chapter we formally study social interactions that can be meaningfully modelled as decision problems of strategy and, as such, using game theory as a framework. Game theory is a branch of mathematics devoted to the formal analysis of decision making in social interactions where the outcome depends on the decisions made by potentially several individuals. A game is a mathematical abstraction of a social interaction where (Colman, 1995):

- there are two or more decision makers, called *players*;
- each player has a choice of two or more ways of acting, called actions or (*pure*) *strategies*, such that the outcome of the interaction depends on the strategy choices of all the players;
- the players have well-defined preferences among the possible outcomes (Hargreaves Heap & Varoufakis, 1995). Thus, *payoffs* reflecting these preferences can be assigned to all players for all outcomes. These payoffs are very often numerical (Fig. 1)

		Player 2	
		Player 2 chooses LEFT	Player 2 chooses RIGHT
Player 1	Player 1 chooses UP	3 , 3	0 , 4
	Player 1 chooses DOWN	4 , 0	1 , 1

Fig. 1. Normal form or payoff matrix of a 2-player, 2-strategy game.

A normal (or strategic form) game can be defined using a function that assigns a payoff to each player for every possible combination of actions. For games with only two players this function is commonly represented using a matrix (see Fig. 1). The example shown in Fig. 1 is a 2-player 2-strategy game: there are two players (player 1 and player 2), each of whom must select one out of two possible (pure) strategies. Player 1 can choose Up or Down, and player 2 simultaneously decides between Left or Right. The payoffs obtained by each player are represented in the corresponding cell of the matrix. Player 1 obtains the first payoff in the cell (coloured in red) and player 2 gets the second (coloured in blue). As an example, if player 1 selects Down and player 2 selects Left, then player 1 gets a payoff of 4 and player 2 obtains a payoff of 0. This chapter deals with 2×2 (2-player 2-strategy) games, which can be represented using a matrix like the one shown in Fig. 1.

Game theory is a useful framework to accurately and formally describe interdependent decision-making processes. Furthermore, it also provides a collection of solution concepts that narrow the set of expected outcomes in such processes. The most widespread solution concept in game theory is the Nash equilibrium, which is a set of strategies, one for each player, such that no player, knowing the strategy of the other(s), could improve her expected payoff by unilaterally changing her own strategy (e.g. the unique Nash equilibrium of the game represented in Fig. 1 is the combination of strategies Down-Right). The Nash equilibrium has been tremendously influential in the social sciences, especially in economics, partly because it can be interpreted in a great number of meaningful and useful ways (Holt & Roth, 2004). Unfortunately, as a prediction tool, the concept is formally valid only when analysing games played by rational players with common knowledge of rationality[1] under the assumption of consistently aligned beliefs (Hargreaves Heap & Varoufakis, 1995). Such assumptions are clearly not appropriate in many social contexts, where it might not be clear at all that the outcome of the game should be a Nash equilibrium. In particular, if players are assumed to adapt their decisions using a reinforcement learning algorithm, it is often the case that the final outcome of their repeated interaction will not be a Nash equilibrium -as will be shown below.

3. Reinforcement learning in strategic contexts

In strategic contexts in general, empirical evidence suggests that reinforcement learning is most plausible in animals with imperfect reasoning abilities or in human subjects who have no information beyond the payoff they receive and may not even be aware of the strategic nature of the situation (Duffy, 2005; Camerer, 2003; Bendor et al., 2001a; Roth & Erev, 1995; Mookherjee & Sopher, 1994). In the context of experimental game theory with human subjects, several authors have used simple models of reinforcement learning to successfully explain and predict behaviour in a wide range of games (McAllister, 1991; Roth & Erev, 1995; Mookherjee & Sopher, 1994; Mookherjee & Sopher, 1997; Chen & Tang, 1998; Erev & Roth, 1998; Erev et al., 1999). In general, the various models of reinforcement learning that have been applied to strategic contexts tend to differ in the following, somewhat interrelated, features:

- Whether learning slows down or not, i.e. whether the model accounts for the 'Power Law of Practice' (e.g. Erev & Roth (1998) vs. Börgers & Sarin (1997)).
- Whether the model allows for avoidance behaviour in addition to approach behaviour (e.g. Bendor et al. (2001b) vs. Erev & Roth (1998)). Approach behaviour is the tendency to repeat the associated choices after receiving a positive stimulus; avoidance behaviour is the tendency to avoid the associated actions after receiving a negative stimulus (one that does not satisfy the player). Models that allow for negative stimuli tend to define an aspiration level against which achieved payoffs are evaluated. This aspiration level may be fixed or vary endogenously (Bendor et al., 2001a; Bendor et al., 2001b).
- Whether "forgetting" is considered, i.e. whether recent observations weigh more than distant ones (Erev & Roth, 1998; Rustichini, 1999; Beggs, 2005).
- Whether the model imposes inertia - a positive bias in favour of the most recently selected action (Bendor et al., 2001a; Bendor et al., 2001b).

Laslier et al. (2001) present a more formal comparison of various reinforcement learning models. Each of the features above can have important implications for the behaviour of the particular model under consideration and for the mathematical methods that are adequate for its analysis. For example, when learning slows down, theoretical results from

[1] Common knowledge of rationality means that every player assumes that all players are instrumentally rational, and that all players are aware of other players' rationality-related assumptions (this produces an infinite recursion of shared assumptions).

the theory of stochastic approximation (Benveniste et al., 1990; Kushner & Yin, 1997) and from the theory of urn models can often be applied (e.g. Ianni, 2001; Hopkins & Posch, 2005; Beggs, 2005), whereas if the learning rate is constant, results from the theory of distance diminishing models (Norman, 1968; Norman, 1972) tend to be more useful (e.g. Börgers & Sarin, 1997; Bendor et al., 2001b; Izquierdo et al., 2007). Similarly, imposing inertia facilitates the analysis to a great extent, since it often ensures that a positive stimulus will be followed by an increase in the probability weight on the most recently selected action at some minimal geometric rate (Bendor et al., 2001b).

Two of the simplest and most popular models of reinforcement learning in the game theory literature are the Erev-Roth (ER) model (Roth & Erev, 1995; Erev & Roth, 1998) and the Bush-Mosteller (BM) model (Bush & Mosteller, 1955). Both models are stochastic: players' strategies are probabilities or propensities to take each of their possible actions. In the ER model, playing one action always increases the probability of playing that action again (i.e. only positive stimulus are considered), and the sensitivity of players' strategies to a new outcome decreases as the game advances (Power Law of Practice). On the other hand, the BM model is an aspiration-based reinforcement learning model where negative stimuli are possible and learning does not fade with time.

A special case of the BM model where all stimuli are positive was originally considered by Cross (1973), and analysed by Börgers & Sarin (1997). In this chapter we characterise the dynamics of the BM model in 2×2 games where aspiration levels are fixed, but not necessarily below the lowest payoff (i.e. negative stimuli are possible). The dynamics of this model were initially explored by Macy & Flache (2002) and Flache & Macy (2002) in 2×2 social dilemma games using computer simulation, and their work was formalised and extended for general 2×2 games by Izquierdo et al. (2007). This chapter follows closely the work conducted by Izquierdo et al. (in press), who analysed the BM model using a combination of computer simulation experiments and theoretical results. Most of the theoretical results used in this chapter derive from Izquierdo et al. (2007).

4. The BM reinforcement learning algorithm

The model we analyse here is an elaboration of a conventional Bush-Mosteller (1955) stochastic learning model for binary choice. In this model, players decide what action to select stochastically: each player's strategy is defined by the probability of undertaking each of the two actions available to them. After every player has selected an action according to their probabilities, every player receives the corresponding payoff and revises her strategy. The revision of strategies takes place following a reinforcement learning approach: players increase their probability of undertaking a certain action if it led to payoffs above their aspiration level, and decrease this probability otherwise. When learning, players in the BM model use only information concerning their own past choices and payoffs, and ignore all the information regarding the payoffs and choices of their counterparts.

More precisely, let $I = \{1, 2\}$ be the *set of players* in the game, and let Y_i be the *pure-strategy space* for each player $i \in I$. For convenience, and without loss of generality, later we will call the actions available to each of the players C (for Cooperate) and D (for Defect). Thus $Y_i = \{C, D\}$. Let u_i be the *payoff functions* u_i that give player i's payoff for each profile $\boldsymbol{y} = (y_1, y_2)$ of pure strategies, where $y_i \in Y_i$ is a pure strategy for player i. As

an example, u_i(C, D) denotes the payoff obtained by player i when player 1 cooperates and player 2 defects. Let $Y = \times_{i \in I} Y_i$ be the space of pure-strategy profiles, or possible outcomes of the game. Finally, let p_{i,y_i} denote player i's probability of undertaking action y_i.
In the BM model, strategy updating takes place in two steps. First, after outcome $\boldsymbol{y}^n = (y_1^n, y_2^n)$ in time-step n, each player i calculates her stimulus $s_i(\boldsymbol{y}^n)$ for the action just chosen y_i^n according to the following formula:

$$s_i(\boldsymbol{y}) = \frac{u_i(\boldsymbol{y}) - A_i}{\sup_{k \in Y} | u_i(\boldsymbol{k}) - A_i |}$$

where A_i is player i's aspiration level. Hence the stimulus is always a number in the interval [-1, 1]. Note that players are assumed to know $\sup_{k \in Y} | u_i(\boldsymbol{k}) - A_i |$. Secondly, having calculated their stimulus $s_i(\boldsymbol{y}^n)$ after the outcome $\boldsymbol{y}^n$, each player i updates her probability p_{i,y_i} of undertaking the selected action y_i as follows:

$$p_{i,y_i}^{n+1} = \begin{cases} p_{i,y_i}^n + l_i \cdot s_i(\boldsymbol{y}^n) \cdot (1 - p_{i,y_i}^n) & \text{if } s_i(\boldsymbol{y}^n) \geq 0 \\ p_{i,y_i}^n + l_i \cdot s_i(\boldsymbol{y}^n) \cdot p_{i,y_i}^n & \text{if } s_i(\boldsymbol{y}^n) < 0 \end{cases}$$

where p_{i,y_i}^n is player i's probability of undertaking action y_i in time-step n, and l_i is player i's learning rate ($0 < l_i < 1$). Thus, the higher the stimulus magnitude (or the learning rate), the larger the change in probability. The updated probability for the action not selected derives from the constraint that probabilities must add up to one. Note that the state of the game can be fully characterized by a two-dimensional vector $\boldsymbol{p}$ = [p_1 , p_2], where p_i is player i's probability to cooperate (i.e. $p_i = p_{i,C}$). We will refer to such vector $\boldsymbol{p}$ as a *strategy profile*, or a *state of the system*.
In the general case, a 2×2 BM model parameterisation requires specifying both players' payoff function u_i, aspiration level A_i, and learning rate l_i. Our analysis is based on the theoretical results derived by Izquierdo et al. (2007), which are valid for any 2×2 game, but –for illustrative purposes– we focus here on systems where two players parameterised in exactly the same way ($A_i = A$ and $l_i = l$) play a symmetric Prisoner's Dilemma game. The Prisoner's Dilemma is a two-person game where each player can either cooperate or defect. For each player i, the payoff when they both cooperate (u_i(C, C) = R_i, for *Reward*) is greater than the payoff obtained when they both defect (u_i(D, D) = P_i, for *Punishment*); when one cooperates and the other defects, the cooperator obtains S_i (*Sucker*), whereas the defector receives T_i (*Temptation*). The dilemma comes from the fact that, individually, each player is better off defecting given any of her counterpart's choices ($T_i > R_i$ and $P_i > S_i$; i = 1, 2), but they both obtain a greater payoff when they both cooperate than when they both defect ($R_i > P_i$; i = 1, 2). Symmetry implies that $T_i = T$, $R_i = R$, $P_i = P$ and $S_i = S$. Figure 1 shows an example of a symmetric Prisoner's Dilemma. A certain parameterisation of this type of system will be specified using the template [T , R , P , S | A | l][2].
The following notation will be useful: A parameterised model will be denoted **S**, for System. Let $\boldsymbol{P}_n$(**S**) be the state of a system **S** in time-step n. Note that $\boldsymbol{P}_n$(**S**) is a random variable and a strategy profile $\boldsymbol{p}$ is a particular value of that variable. The sequence of random variables

$\{P_n(S)\}_{n\geq 0}$ constitutes a discrete-time Markov process with potentially infinite transient states.

5. Attractors in the dynamics of the system

Macy & Flache (2002) observed and described two types of attractors that govern the dynamics of the BM model: self-reinforcing equilibria (SRE), and self-correcting equilibria (SCE). These two concepts are not equilibria in the static sense of the word, but strategy profiles which act as attractors that pull the dynamics of the simulation towards them. The original concepts of SRE and SCE were later formalised and refined by Izquierdo et al. (2007).

SREs are absorbing states of the system (i.e. states $\boldsymbol{p}$ that cannot be abandoned) where both players receive a positive stimulus (Izquierdo et al., 2007). An SRE corresponds to a pair of pure strategies (p_i is either 0 or 1) such that its certain associated outcome gives a strictly positive stimulus to both players (henceforth a *mutually satisfactory outcome*). For example, the strategy profile [1 , 1] is an SRE if both players' aspiration levels are below their respective $R_i = u_i(\text{C, C})$. Escape from an SRE is impossible since no player will change her strategy. More importantly, SREs act as attractors: near an SRE, there is a high chance that the system will move towards it, because there is a high probability that its associated mutually satisfactory outcome will occur, and this brings the system even closer to the SRE. The number of SREs in a system is the number of outcomes where both players obtain payoffs above their respective aspiration levels.

The definition of the other type of attractor, namely the SCE, is related to the expected motion function of the system. The Expected Motion (**EM**) of a system **S** in state $\boldsymbol{p}$ for the following iteration is given by a function vector $\mathbf{EM}^{\mathrm{S}}(\boldsymbol{p})$ whose components are the expected change in the probabilities to cooperate for each player. Mathematically,

$$\mathbf{EM}^{\mathrm{S}}(\boldsymbol{p}) \equiv [\,\mathrm{EM}_1^{\mathrm{S}}(\boldsymbol{p}),\mathrm{EM}_2^{\mathrm{S}}(\boldsymbol{p})\,] \equiv \mathbf{E}(\Delta \boldsymbol{P}_n(\mathrm{S}) \mid \boldsymbol{P}_n(\mathrm{S}) = \boldsymbol{p})$$

$$\mathrm{EM}_i^{\mathrm{S}}(\boldsymbol{p}) = \Pr\{\mathrm{CC}\}\cdot \Delta p_i\big|_{\mathrm{CC}} + \Pr\{\mathrm{CD}\}\cdot \Delta p_i\big|_{\mathrm{CD}} + \Pr\{\mathrm{DC}\}\cdot \Delta p_i\big|_{\mathrm{DC}} + \Pr\{\mathrm{DD}\}\cdot \Delta p_i\big|_{\mathrm{DD}}$$

where {CC, CD, DC, DD} represent the four possible outcomes that may occur.

For instance, for a Prisoner's Dilemma parameterised as $[\,4 , 3 , 1 , 0 \mid 2 \mid l\,]^2$, the function $\mathbf{EM}(\boldsymbol{p})$ is

$$[\mathbf{EM}_1(\boldsymbol{p}),\mathbf{EM}_2(\boldsymbol{p})] = l\,[p_1p_2 \quad p_1(1-p_2) \quad (1-p_1)p_2 \quad (1-p_1)(1-p_2)]\begin{bmatrix}(1-p_1)/2 & (1-p_2)/2\\ -p_1 & -p_2\\ -p_1 & -p_2\\ (1-p_1)/2 & (1-p_2)/2\end{bmatrix}$$

This Expected Motion function is represented by the arrows shown in figure 2.

Consider now differential equation (1), which is the continuous time limit approximation of the system's expected motion:

$$\dot{f} = \mathbf{EM}^{\mathrm{S}}(f) \tag{1}$$

or, equivalently,

$$\left.\begin{aligned} \frac{df_1(t)}{dt} &= \mathrm{EM}_1^{\mathrm{S}}(f(t)) \\ \frac{df_2(t)}{dt} &= \mathrm{EM}_2^{\mathrm{S}}(f(t)) \end{aligned}\right\}$$

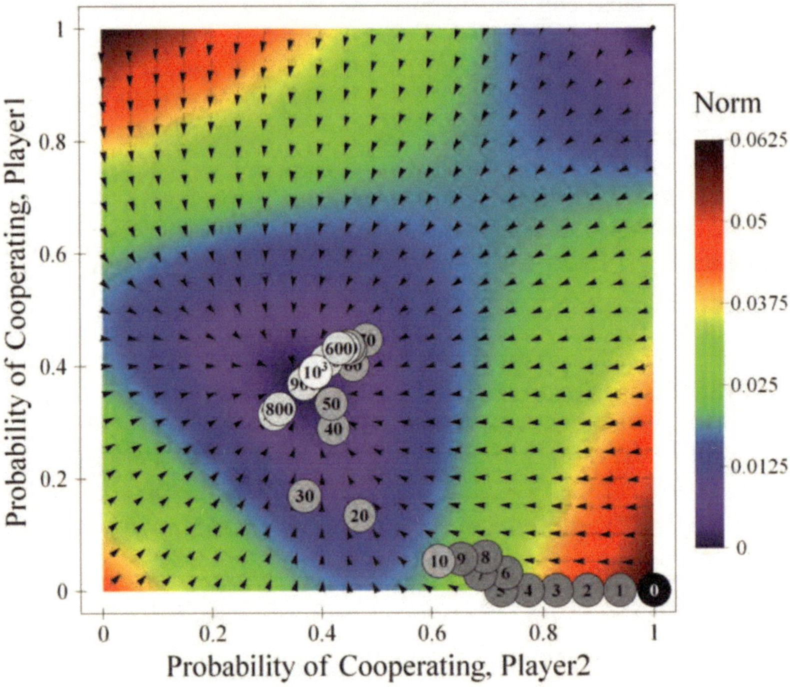

Fig. 2. Expected motion of the system in a Prisoner's Dilemma game parameterised as [4 , 3 , 1 , 0 | 2 | 2^{-4}]^2, together with a sample simulation run (1000 iterations). The arrows represent the expected motion for various states of the system; the numbered balls show the state of the system after the indicated number of iterations in the sample run. The background is coloured using the norm of the expected motion. For any other learning rate the size of the arrows (i.e. the norm of the expected motion) would vary but their direction would be preserved.

Thus, for the Prisoner's Dilemma parameterised as [4 , 3 , 1 , 0 | 2 | l]^2, the associated differential equation is

$$\left[\frac{df_1}{dt}, \frac{df_2}{dt}\right] = l\left[f_1 f_2 \quad f_1(1-f_2) \quad (1-f_1)f_2 \quad (1-f_1)(1-f_2)\right] \begin{bmatrix} (1-f_1)/2 & (1-f_2)/2 \\ -f_1 & -f_2 \\ -f_1 & -f_2 \\ (1-f_1)/2 & (1-f_2)/2 \end{bmatrix}$$

Some trajectories of this differential equation are shown in figure 3. The expected motion at any point $\boldsymbol{p}$ in the phase plane is a vector tangent to the unique trajectory to which that point belongs. Having explained the expected motion of the system and its continuous time limit approximation we can now formally define SCEs.

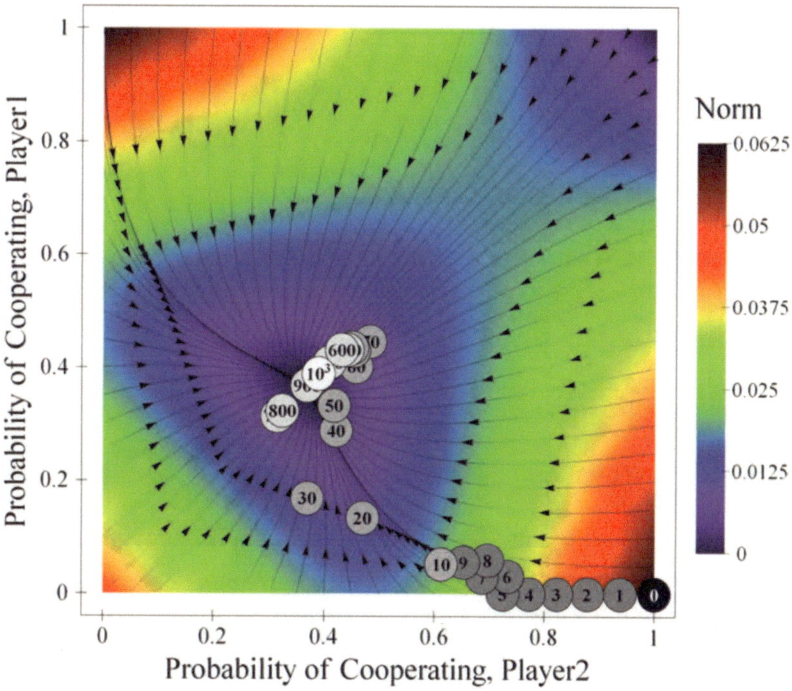

Fig. 3. Trajectories in the phase plane of the differential equation corresponding to the Prisoner's Dilemma game parameterised as [4 , 3 , 1 , 0 | 2 | l]^2, together with a sample simulation run ($l = 2^{-4}$). The background is coloured using the norm of the expected motion. This system has an SCE at [0.37 , 0.37].

An SCE of a system **S** is an asymptotically stable critical point (Mohler, 1991) of differential equation (1) (Izquierdo et al., 2007). Roughly speaking this means that all trajectories in the phase plane of Eq. (1) that at some instant are sufficiently close to the SCE will approach the SCE as the parameter t (time) approaches infinity and remain close to it at all future times. Note that, with these definitions, there could be a state of the system that is an SRE and an SCE at the same time. Note also that $\mathbf{EM}^{\mathbf{S}}(SCE) = \mathbf{0}$ and $\mathbf{EM}^{\mathbf{S}}(SRE) = \mathbf{0}$. In particular, the Prisoner's Dilemma represented in figure 3 exhibits a unique SCE at [0.37 , 0.37] and a unique SRE at [1 , 1].

Let $f_x(t)$ denote the solution of differential equation (1) for some initial state $\boldsymbol{x}$. Figure 4 shows $f_x(t)$ for the Prisoner's Dilemma game parameterised as [4 , 3 , 1 , 0 | 2 | l]^2 for different (and symmetric) initial conditions $\boldsymbol{x} = [x_0 , x_0]$. For this particular case and settings, the two components of $f_x(t) = [f_{1,x}(t) , f_{2,x}(t)]$ take the same value at any given t, so the representation in figure 4 corresponds to both components of $f_x(t)$. Convergence to the SCE at [0.37 , 0.37] can be clearly observed for every initial condition x, except for x = [1, 1], which is the SRE.

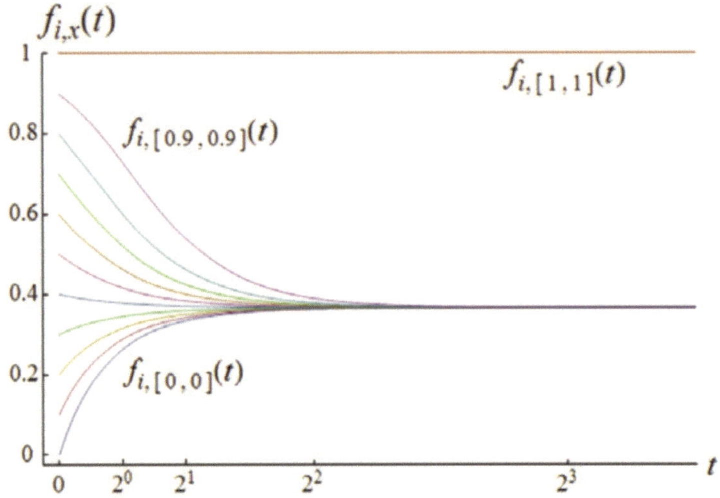

Fig. 4. Solutions of differential equation (1) for the Prisoner's Dilemma game parameterised as [4 , 3 , 1 , 0 | 2 | l]^2 with different (and symmetric) initial conditions $x = [x_0 , x_0]$. This system has a unique SCE at [0.37 , 0.37] and a unique SRE at [1 , 1].

The use of expected motion (or mean-field) approximations to understand simulation models and to design interesting experiments has already proven to be very useful in the literature (e.g. Huet et al., 2007; Galán & Izquierdo, 2005; Edwards et al., 2003; Castellano et al., 2000). Note, however, that such approaches are approximations whose validity may be constrained to specific conditions: as we can see in Figure 3, simulation runs and trajectories will not coincide in general. Later in this chapter we show that trajectories and SCEs are especially relevant for the transient dynamics of the system, particularly with small learning rates, but, on the other hand, the mean-field approximation can be misleading when studying the asymptotic behaviour of the model.

6. Attractiveness of SREs

Macy and Flache's experiments (Macy & Flache, 2002; Flache & Macy, 2002) with the BM model showed a puzzling phenomenon. A significant part of their analysis consisted in studying, in a Prisoner's Dilemma in which mutual cooperation was mutually satisfactory (i.e. $A_i < R_i = u_i(\mathrm{C}, \mathrm{C})$), the proportion of simulation runs that "locked" into mutual cooperation. Such "lock-in rates" were reported to be as high as 1 in some experiments. However, starting from an initial state which is not an SRE, the BM model specifications guarantee that after any finite number of iterations any outcome has a positive probability of occurring (i.e. strictly speaking, lock-in is impossible)[2]. To investigate this apparent

[2] The specification of the model is such that probabilities cannot reach the extreme values of 0 or 1 starting from any other intermediate value. Therefore if we find a simulation run that

contradiction we conducted some qualitative analyses that we present here to familiarise the reader with the complex dynamics of this model. Our first qualitative analysis consisted in studying the expected dynamics of the model. Figure 5 illustrates the expected motion of a system extensively studied by Macy & Flache: the Prisoner's Dilemma game parameterised as [4 , 3 , 1 , 0 | 2 | 0.5]^2. As we saw before, this system features a unique SCE at [0.37 , 0.37] and a unique SRE at [1 , 1]. Figure 5 also includes the trace of a sample simulation run. Note that the only difference between the parameterisation of the system shown in figure 2 and that shown in figure 5 is the value of the learning rate.

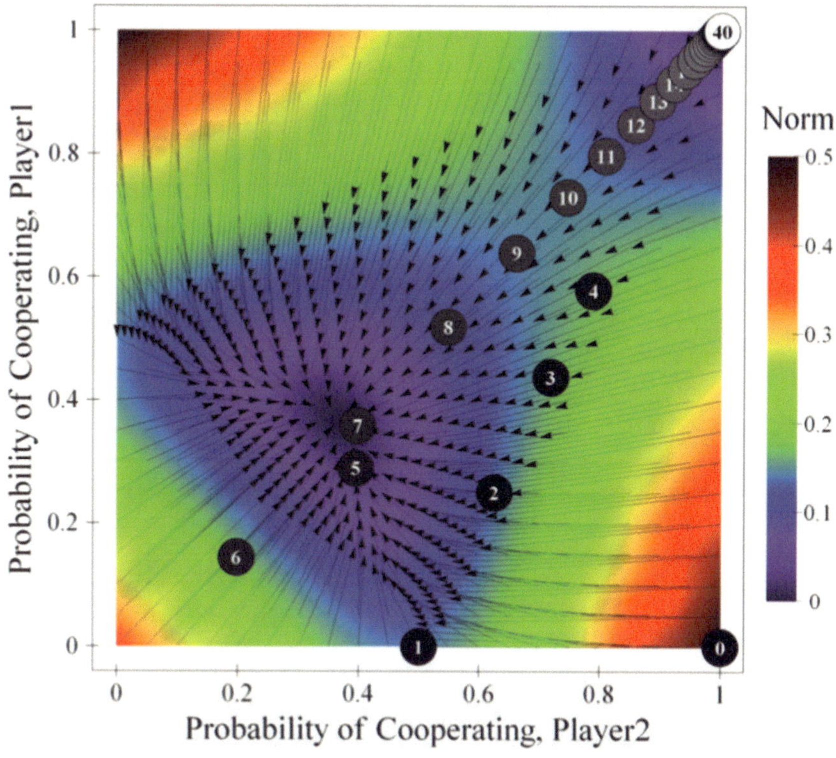

Fig. 5. Expected motion of the system in a Prisoner's Dilemma game parameterised as [4 , 3 , 1 , 0 | 2 | 0.5]^2, with a sample simulation run.

Figure 5 shows that the expected movement from any state is towards the SCE, except for the only SRE, which is an absorbing state. In particular, near the SRE, where both probabilities are high but different from 1, the distribution of possible movements is very peculiar: there is a very high chance that both agents will cooperate and consequently move

has actually ended up in an SRE starting from any other state, we know for sure that such simulation run did not follow the specifications of the model (e.g. perhaps because of floating-point errors). For a detailed analysis of the effects of floating point errors in computer simulations, with applications to this model in particular, see Izquierdo and Polhill (2006), Polhill and Izquierdo (2005), Polhill et al. (2006), Polhill et al. (2005).

a small distance towards the SRE, but there is also a positive chance, tiny as it may be, that one of the agents will defect, causing both agents to jump away from the SRE towards the SCE. The improbable, yet possible, leap away from the SRE is of such magnitude that the resulting expected movement is biased towards the SCE despite the unlikelihood of such an event actually occurring. The dynamics of the system can be further explored analysing the most likely movement from any given state, which is represented in Figure 6.

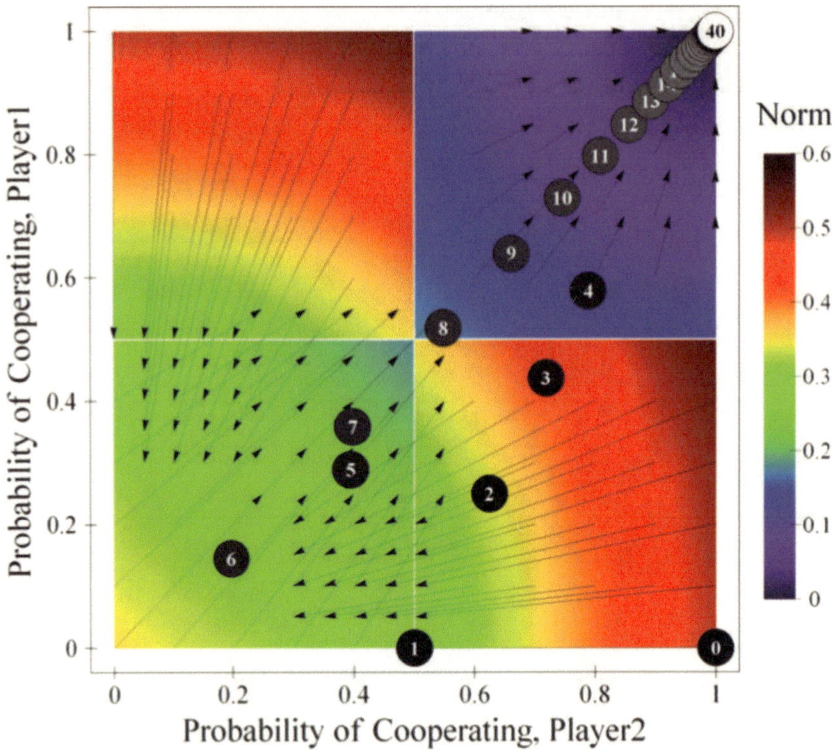

Fig. 6. Figure showing the most likely movements at some states of the system in a Prisoner's Dilemma game parameterised as $[\,4\,,3\,,1\,,0 \mid 2 \mid 0.5\,]^2$, with a sample simulation run. The background is coloured using the norm of the most likely movement.

Figure 6 differs significantly from Figure 5; it shows that the most likely movement in the upper-right quadrant of the state space is towards the SRE. Thus, the walk towards the SRE is characterised by a fascinating puzzle: on the one hand, the most likely movement leads the system towards the SRE, which is even more likely to be approached the closer we get to it; on the other hand, the SRE cannot be reached in any finite number of steps and the expected movement as defined above is to walk away from it (see figure 5).

It is also interesting to note in this game that, starting from any mixed (interior) state, both players have a positive probability of selecting action D in any future time-step, but there is also a positive probability that both players will engage in an infinite chain of the mutually satisfactory event CC forever, i.e., that neither player will ever take action D from then onwards (see Izquierdo et al., in press).

The probability of starting an infinite chain of CC events depends largely on the value of the learning rate l. Figure 7 shows the probability of starting an infinite chain of the mutually satisfactory outcome CC in a Prisoner's Dilemma game parameterised as $[\ 4\ ,\ 3\ ,\ 1\ ,\ 0\ |\ 2\ |\ l\ ]^2$, for different learning rates l, and different initial probabilities to cooperate x_0 (the same probability for both players). For some values, the probability of immediately starting an infinite chain of mutual cooperation can be surprisingly high (e.g. for l = 0.5 and initial conditions $[\ x_0\ ,\ x_0\ ] = [\ 0.9\ ,\ 0.9\ ]$ such probability is approximately 44%).

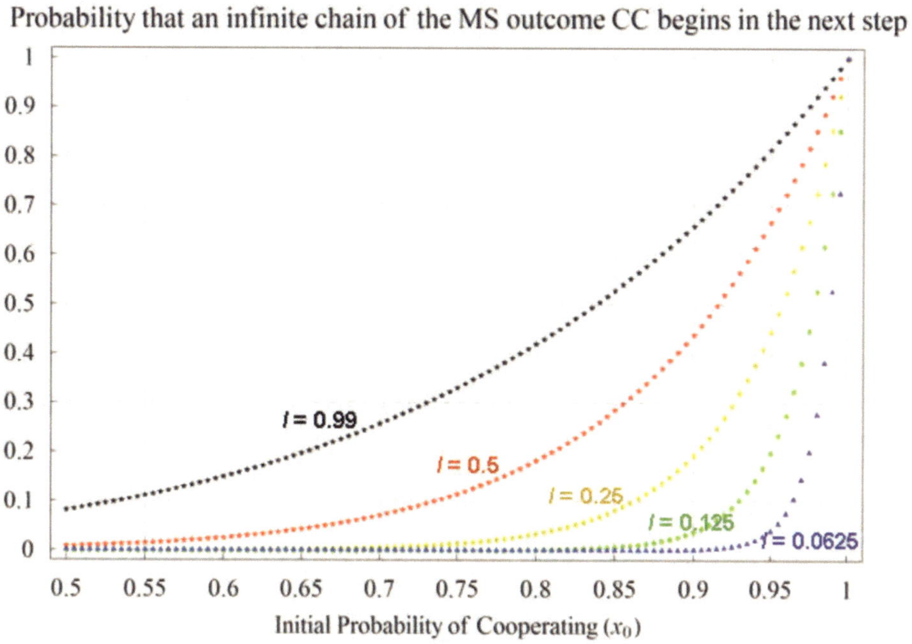

Fig. 7. Probability of starting an infinite chain of the Mutually Satisfactory (MS) outcome CC in a Prisoner's Dilemma game parameterised as $[\ 4\ ,\ 3\ ,\ 1\ ,\ 0\ |\ 2\ |\ l\ ]^2$. The 5 different (coloured) series correspond to different learning rates l. The variable x_0, represented in the horizontal axis, is the initial probability of cooperating for both players.

In summary, assuming that aspirations are different from payoffs (see Izquierdo et al., 2007), a BM process that starts in an initial state different from an SRE will never reach an SRE in finite time, and there is always a positive probability that the process leaves the proximity of an SRE. However, if there is some SRE, there is also a positive probability that the system will approach it indefinitely (i.e. forever) through an infinite chain of the mutually satisfactory outcome associated to the SRE.

7. Different regimes in the dynamics of the system

This section illustrates the dynamics of the BM model for different learning rates. Most of the theoretical results that we apply and summarise in this section are valid for any 2×2 game and can be found in Izquierdo et al. (2007). The analysis is presented here in a somewhat qualitative fashion for the sake of clarity and comprehensibility, and illustrates the behaviour of the BM model using the Prisoner's Dilemma shown in figure 1.

In the general case, the dynamics of the BM model may exhibit three different regimes: medium run, long run, and ultralong run. The terminology used here is borrowed from Binmore & Samuelson (1993) and Binmore et al. (1995), who reserve the term short run for the initial conditions.

"By the ultralong run, we mean a period of time long enough for the asymptotic distribution to be a good description of the behavior of the system. The long run refers to the time span needed for the system to reach the vicinity of the first equilibrium in whose neighborhood it will linger for some time. We speak of the medium run as the time intermediate between the short run [i.e. initial conditions] *and the long run, during which the adjustment to equilibrium is occurring."* (Binmore et al., 1995, p. 10)

Binmore et al.'s terminology is particularly useful for our analysis because it is often the case in the BM model that the *"first equilibrium in whose neighborhood it* [the system] *will linger for some time"*, i.e. the long run, is significantly different from the asymptotic dynamics of the system. Whether the three different regimes (medium, long, and ultralong run) are clearly distinguishable in the BM model strongly depends on the players' learning rates. For high learning rates the system quickly approaches its asymptotic behaviour (the ultralong run) and the distinction between the different regimes is not particularly useful. For small learning rates, however, the three different regimes can be clearly observed. Since the ultralong run is the only regime that is (finally) observed in every system, we start our description of the dynamics of the BM model characterising such regime (for details see Propositions 2 and 3 in Izquierdo et al., 2007). Assuming players' aspirations are different from their respective payoffs ($u_i(\boldsymbol{y}) \neq A_i$ for all i and $\boldsymbol{y}$):

- If players' aspirations are below their respective *maximin*[3], the BM system converges to an SRE with probability 1 (i.e. the set formed by all SREs is asymptotically reached with probability 1). If the initial state is completely mixed, then every SRE can be asymptotically reached with positive probability.
- If players' aspirations are above their respective *maximin*:
  - if there is any SRE then the BM system converges to an SRE with probability 1. If the initial state is completely mixed, then every SRE can be asymptotically reached with positive probability.
  - If there are no SREs then the process is ergodic, so the states of the system present an asymptotic distribution which is independent of the initial conditions.

In the context of the Prisoner's dilemma game described above, this implies that if players' aspirations are above the payoff they receive when they both defect ($A_i > u_i(\text{D, D}) = P_i$), which is their *maximin*, then the ultralong run is independent of the initial state. Under such conditions, there is an SRE if and only if mutual cooperation is satisfactory for both players (i.e. $A_i < u_i(\text{C, C}) = R_i$) and, if that is the case, the process converges to certain mutual cooperation (i.e. the unique SRE) with probability 1. As an example, note that the ultralong-run behaviour of the systems shown in figures 2, 3, 5 and 6 is certain mutual cooperation.

---

[3] Maximin is the largest possible payoff players can guarantee themselves in a single-stage game using pure strategies.

7.1 Learning by large steps (fast adaptation)

As mentioned above, when learning takes place by large steps, the system quickly reaches its ultralong-run behaviour. To explain why this is the case we distinguish between two possible classes of systems:

- In systems where there is at least one SRE, the asymptotic behaviour is quickly approached because SREs are powerful attractors (e.g. see figures 5 and 6). The reason for this is that, if an SRE exists, the chances of a mutually satisfactory outcome not occurring for a long time are low, since players update their strategies to a large extent to avoid unsatisfactory outcomes. Whenever a mutually satisfactory outcome occurs, players update their strategy so the chances of repeating such a mutually satisfactory outcome increase. Since learning rates are high, the movement towards the SRE associated with such a mutually satisfactory outcome takes place by large steps, so only a few coordinated moves are sufficient to approach the SRE so much that escape from its neighbourhood becomes very unlikely. In other words, with fast learning the system quickly approaches an SRE, and is likely to keep approaching that SRE forever (this is the system's ultralong-run behaviour). As an example, consider figure 7 again: starting from any initial probability to cooperate x_0, the occurrence of a mutually satisfactory outcome CC would increase both players' probability to cooperate (the updated probability can be seen as the following period's x_0), which in turn would increase the probability of never defecting (i.e. the probability of starting an infinite chain of CC). Thus, if learning rates are large, a few CC events are enough to take the state of the system into areas where the probability of never defecting again is large.
- In the absence of SREs, the fact that any outcome is unsatisfactory for at least one of the players[4] and the fact that strategy changes are substantial, together imply that at least one player will switch between actions very frequently -i.e. the system will indefinitely move rapidly and widely around a large area of the state space.

7.2 Learning by small steps (slow adaptation)

The behaviour of the BM process with low learning rates is characterised by the following features (Izquierdo et al., 2007; Proposition 1):

- For low enough learning rates, the BM process with initial state x tends to follow the trajectory $f_x(t)$ in the phase plane of Eq. (1), i.e. the trajectory that corresponds to $f(0) = x$ (e.g. see figure 3).
- For low enough learning rates l, the BM process in time-step n tends to be concentrated around a particular point of the mentioned trajectory: the point $f_x(n \cdot l)$ (e.g. see figure 4).
- If trajectories get close to an SCE (as t increases), then, for low learning rates, the BM process will tend to approach and linger around the SCE; the lower the learning rate, the greater the number of periods that the process will tend to stay around the SCE.
- Eventually the system will approach its asymptotic behaviour, which -as explained above- is best characterised by the SREs of the system.

When learning takes place by small steps the transient regimes (i.e. the medium and the long run) can be clearly observed, and these transient dynamics can be substantially different from the ultralong-run behaviour of the system. For sufficiently small learning

---

4 Recall that each player's aspiration level is assumed to be different from every payoff the player may receive.

rates and number of iterations n not too large ($n \cdot l$ bounded), the medium-run dynamics of the system are best characterised by the trajectories in the phase plane of Eq. (1), which can follow paths substantially apart from the end-states of the system (see figure 8, where the end-state is [1 , 1]). Under such conditions, the expected state of the system after n iterations can be estimated by substituting the value $n \cdot l$ in the trajectory that commences at the initial conditions (see figure 4). The lower the learning rates, the better the estimate, i.e. the more tightly clustered the dynamics will be around the corresponding trajectory in the phase plane (see figure 8).
When trajectories finish in an SCE, the system will approach the SCE and spend a significant amount of time in its neighbourhood if learning rates are low enough and the number of iterations n is large enough (and finite)[5]. This latter regime is the long run. The fact that trajectories are good approximations for the transient dynamics of the system for slow learning shows the importance of SCEs -points that "attract" trajectories within their neighbourhood- as attractors of the actual dynamics of the system. This is particularly so when, as in most 2×2 games, there are very few asymptotically stable critical points and they have very wide domains of attraction.

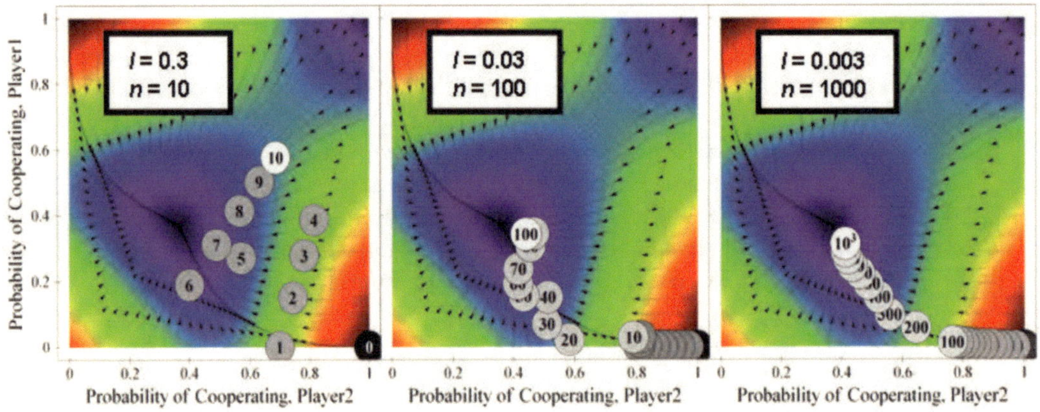

Fig. 8. Three sample runs of a system parameterised as [4 , 3 , 1 , 0 | 2 | l]^2 for different values of n and l. The product $n \cdot l$ is the same for the three simulations; therefore, for low values of l, the state of the system at the end of the simulations tends to concentrate around the same point.

Remember, however, that the system will eventually approach its asymptotic behaviour, which in the systems shown in figures 2, 3, 4, 5, 6, 7 and 8 is certain mutual cooperation. Having said that, as Binmore et al., (1995) point out, approaching the asymptotic behaviour may require an extraordinarily long time, much longer than is often meant by long run, hence the term ultralong run.
To illustrate how learning rates affect the speed of convergence to asymptotic behaviour, consider once again the Prisoner's Dilemma game parameterised as [4 , 3 , 1 , 0 | 2 | l]^2, a system extensively studied by Macy & Flache (2002). The evolution of the probability to cooperate with initial state [0.5 , 0.5] (with these settings the probability is identical for both

[5] Excluded here is the trivial case where the initial state is an SRE.

players) is represented in the rows of figure 9 for different learning rates l. The top row shows the evolution for $l = 0.5$, and the bottom row shows the evolution for $l = 2^{-7}$.

For $l = 0.5$, after only $2^9 = 512$ iterations, the probability that both players will be almost certain to cooperate is very close to 1, and it remains so thereafter. For $l = 2^{-4}$ and lower learning rates, however, the distribution is still clustered around the SCE even after $2^{21} = 2097152$ iterations. With low learning rates, the chain of events that is required to escape from the neighbourhood of the SCE is extremely unlikely, and therefore this long run regime seems to persist indefinitely. However, given sufficient time, such a chain of coordinated moves will occur, and the system will eventually reach its ultralong-run regime, i.e. almost-certain mutual cooperation. The convergence of the processes to the appropriate point in the trajectory $f_x(n \cdot l)$ as $l \to 0$ and $n \cdot l$ is kept bounded can be appreciated following the grey arrows (which join histograms for which $n \cdot l$ is constant).

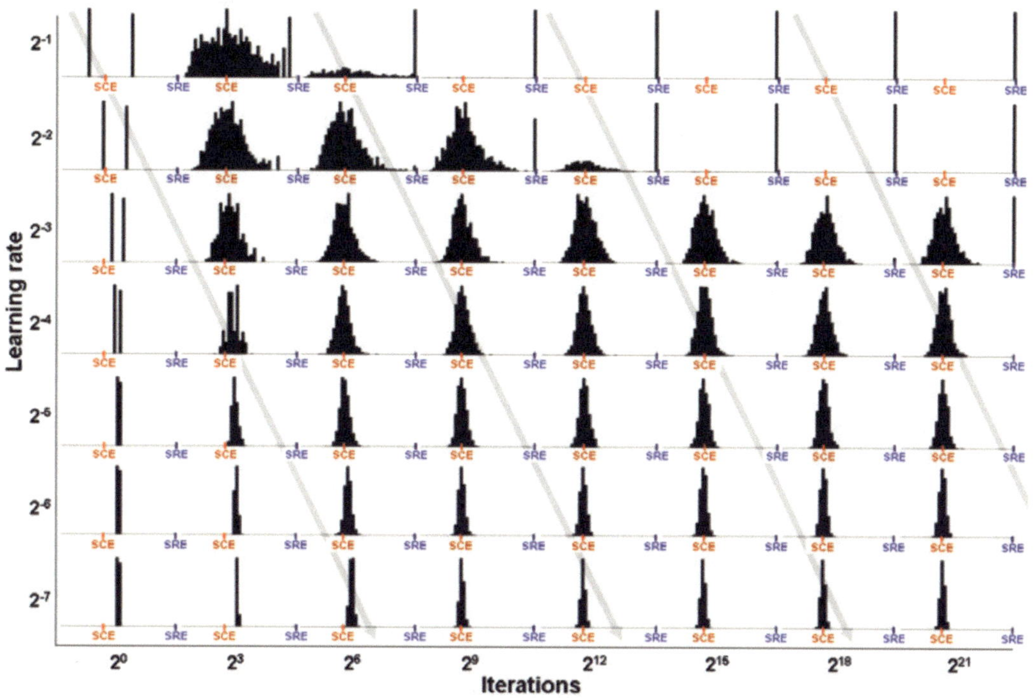

Fig. 9. Histograms representing the probability of cooperating for one player (both players' probabilities are identical) after n iterations for different learning rates l in a Prisoner's Dilemma game parameterised as $[\,4, 3, 1, 0 \mid 2 \mid l\,]^2$, each calculated over 1,000 simulation runs. The initial probability for both players is 0.5. The grey arrows join histograms for which $n \cdot l$ is constant.

8. Trembling hands process

To study the robustness of the previous asymptotic results we consider an extension of the BM model where players suffer from 'trembling hands' (Selten, 1975): after having decided which action to undertake, each player *i* may select the wrong action with some probability $\varepsilon_i > 0$ in each iteration. This noisy feature generates a new stochastic process, namely the *noisy process* N_n, which can also be fully characterized by a 2-dimensional vector ***prop*** = [$prop_1$, $prop_2$] of *propensities* (rather than probabilities) to cooperate. Player *i*'s actual probability to cooperate is now $(1 - \varepsilon_i) \cdot prop_i + \varepsilon_i \cdot (1 - prop_i)$, and the profile of propensities ***prop*** evolves after any particular outcome following the rules given in section 4. Izquierdo et al. (2007) prove that the noisy process N_n is ergodic in any 2×2 game[6]. Ergodicity implies that the state of the process presents an asymptotic probability distribution that does not depend on the initial state.

The noisy process has no absorbing states (i.e. SREs) except in the trivial case where both players find one of their actions always satisfactory and the other action always unsatisfactory - thus, for example, in the Prisoner's Dilemma the inclusion of noise precludes the system from convergence to a single state. However, even though noisy processes have no SREs in general, the SREs of the associated unperturbed process (SREUPs, which correspond to mutually satisfactory outcomes) do still act as attractors whose attractive power depends on the magnitude of the noise: *ceteris paribus* the lower the noise the higher the long run chances of finding the system in the neighbourhood of an SREUP (see Figure 10). This is so because in the proximity of an SREUP, if ε_i are low enough, the SREUP's associated mutually satisfactory outcome will probably occur, and this brings the system even closer to the SREUP. The dynamics of the noisy system will generally be governed also by the other type of attractor, the SCE (see figure 10).

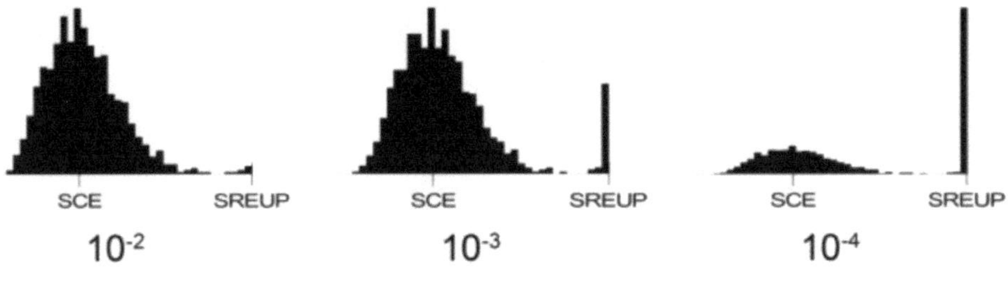

Fig. 10. Histograms representing the propensity to cooperate for one player (both players' propensities are identical) after 1,000,000 iterations (when the distribution is stable) for different levels of noise ($\varepsilon_i = \varepsilon$) in a Prisoner's Dilemma game parameterised as $[\,4\,,3\,,1\,,0\mid 2\mid 0.25\,]^2$. Each histogram has been calculated over 1,000 simulation runs.

Figures 11 and 12, which correspond to a Prisoner's Dilemma game parameterised as $[\,4\,,3\,,1\,,0\mid 2\mid l\,]^2$, show that the presence of noise can greatly damage the stability of the (unique) SREUP associated to the event CC. Note that the inclusion of noise implies that the probability of an infinite chain of the mutually satisfactory event CC becomes zero.

---

[6] We exclude here the meaningless case where the payoffs for some player are all the same and equal to her aspiration ($T_i = R_i = P_i = S_i = A_i$ for some *i*).

The systems represented on the left-hand side of figure 11, corresponding to a learning rate $l = 0.5$, show a tendency to be quickly attracted to the state [1 , 1], but the presence of noise breaks the chains of mutually satisfactory CC events from time to time (see the series on the bottom-left corner); unilateral defections make the system escape from the area of the SREUP before going back towards it again and again. The systems represented on the right-hand side of figure 11, corresponding to a lower learning rate ($l = 0.25$) than those on the left, show a tendency to be lingering around the SCE for longer. In these cases, when a unilateral defection breaks a chain of mutually satisfactory events CC and the system leaves the proximity of the state [1 , 1], it usually takes a large number of periods to go back into that area again.

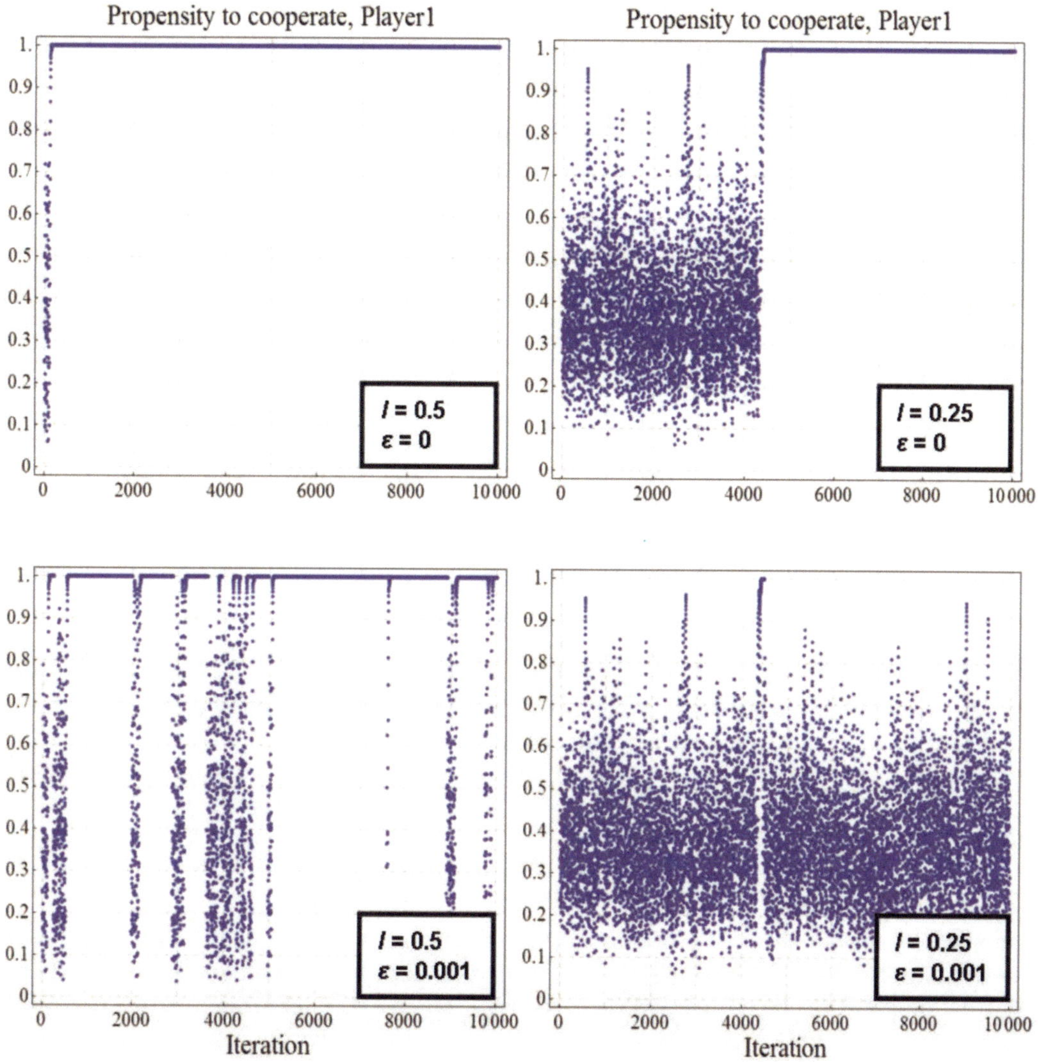

Fig. 11. Representative time series of player 1's propensity to cooperate over time for the Prisoner's Dilemma game parameterised as $[4 , 3 , 1 , 0 \mid 2 \mid 0.5]^2$ (left) and [4 , 3 , 1 , 0 | 2

| 0.25]^2 (right), with initial conditions [x_0 , x_0] = [0.5 , 0.5], both without noise (top) and with noise level $\varepsilon_i = 10^{-3}$ (bottom).

Figure 12 shows that a greater level of noise implies higher destabilisation of the SREUP. This is so because, even in the proximity of the SREUP, the long chains of reinforced CC events needed to stabilise the SREUP become highly unlikely when there are high levels of noise, and unilateral defections (whose probability increases with noise in the proximity of the SREUP) break the stability of the SREUP.

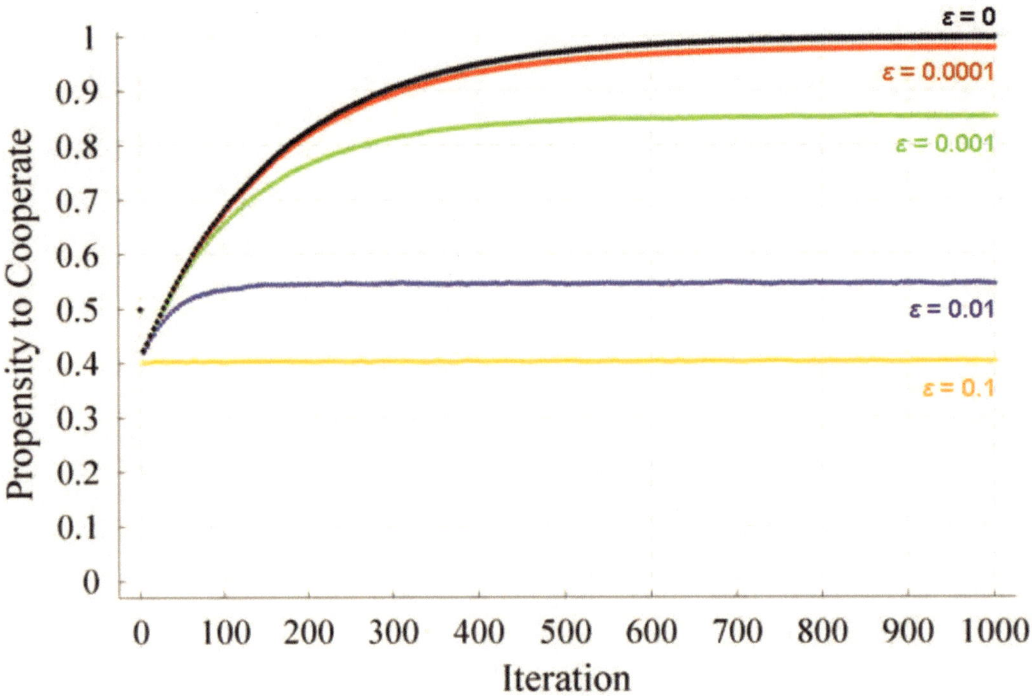

Fig. 12. Evolution of the average probability / propensity to cooperate of one of the players in a Prisoner's Dilemma game parameterised as [4 , 3 , 1 , 0 | 2 | 0. 5]^2 with initial state [0.5, 0.5], for different levels of noise ($\varepsilon_i = \varepsilon$). Each series has been calculated averaging over 100,000 simulation runs. The standard error of the represented averages is lower than $3 \cdot 10^{-3}$ in every case.

8.1 Stochastic stability

Importantly, not all the SREs of the unperturbed process are equally robust to noise. Consider, for instance, the system [4 , 3 , 1 , 0 | 0.5 | 0. 5]^2, which has two SRES: [1 , 1] and [0 , 0]. Using the results outlined in section 7 we know that the set formed by the two SREs is asymptotically reached with probability 1; the probability of the process converging to one particular SRE depends on the initial state; and if the initial state is completely mixed, then the process may converge to either SRE. Simulations of this process show that, almost in every case, the system quickly approaches one of the SREs and then remains in its close vicinity. Looking at the line labelled "ε = 0" in figure 13 we can see that this system with initial state [0.9 , 0.9] has a probability of converging to its SRE at [1 , 1] approximately equal to 0.7, and a probability of converging to its SRE at [0 , 0] approximately equal to 0.3. However, the inclusion of (even tiny levels of) noise may alter the dynamics of the system dramatically. In general, for low enough levels of "trembling hands" noise we find an ultralong-run (invariant) distribution concentrated on neighbourhoods of SREUPs. The lower the noise, the higher the concentration around SREUPs. If there are several SREUPs, the invariant distribution may concentrate on some of these SREUPs much more than on others. In the limit as the noise goes to zero, it is often the case that only some of the SREUPs remain points of concentration. These are called stochastically stable equilibria (Foster & Young, 1990; Young, 1993; Ellison, 2000). As an example, consider the simulation results shown in figure 13, which clearly suggest that the SRE at [0 , 0] is the only stochastically stable equilibrium even though the unperturbed process converges to the other SRE more frequently with initial conditions [0.9 , 0.9]. Note that whether an equilibrium is stochastically stable or not is independent on the initial conditions.

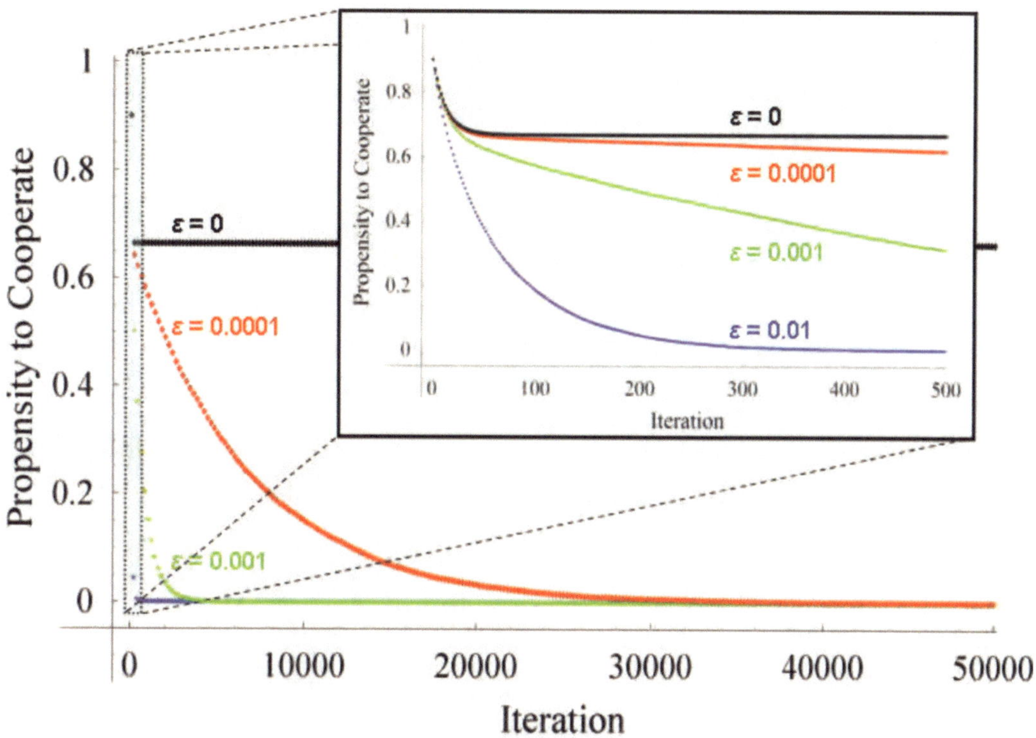

Fig. 13. Evolution of the average probability / propensity to cooperate of one of the players in a Prisoner's Dilemma game parameterised as [4 , 3 , 1 , 0 | 0.5 | 0. 5]^2 with initial state [0.9 , 0.9], for different levels of noise ($\varepsilon_i = \varepsilon$). Each series has been calculated averaging over 10,000 simulation runs. The inset graph is a magnification of the first 500 iterations. The standard error of the represented averages is lower than 0.01 in every case.

Intuitively, note that in the system shown in figure 13, in the proximities of the SRE at [1 , 1], one single (possibly mistaken) defection is enough to lead the system away from it. On the other hand, near the SRE at [0 , 0] one single (possibly mistaken) cooperation will make the system approach this SRE at [0 , 0] even more closely. Only a coordinated mutual cooperation (which is highly unlikely near the SRE at [0 , 0]) will make the system move away from this SRE. This makes the SRE at [0 , 0] much more robust to occasional mistakes made by the players when selecting their strategies than the SRE at [1, 1], as illustrated in figures 14 and 15.

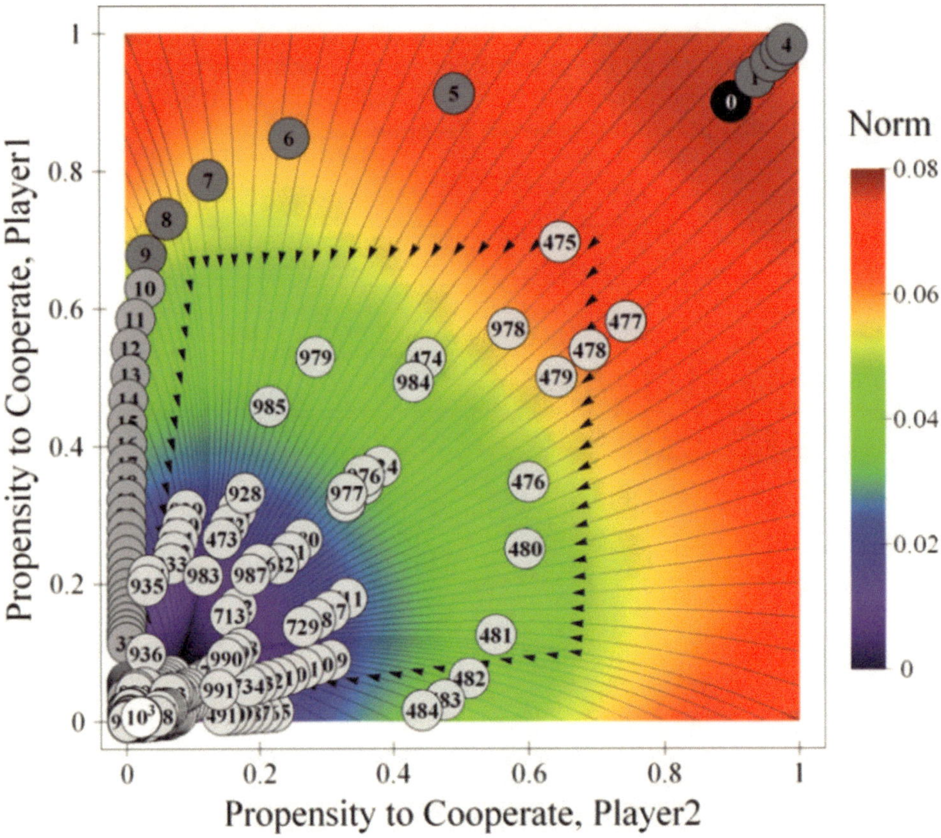

Fig. 14. One representative run of the system parameterised as [4 , 3 , 1 , 0 | 0.5 | 0. 5]^2 with initial state [0.9 , 0.9], and noise $\varepsilon_i = \varepsilon = 0.1$. This figure shows the evolution of the system in the phase plane of propensities to cooperate, while figure 15 below shows the evolution of player 1's propensity to cooperate over time for the same simulation run.

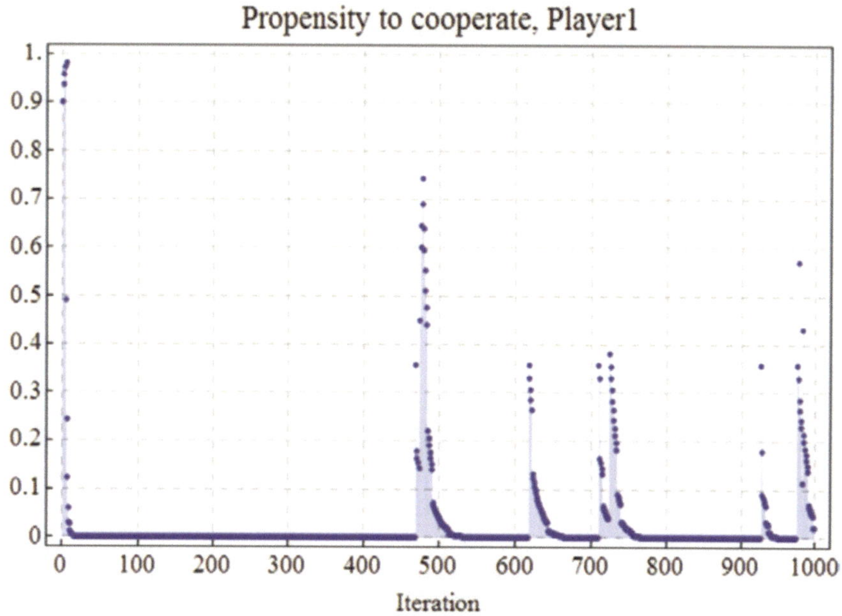

Fig. 15. Time series of player 1's propensity to cooperate over time for the same simulation run displayed in figure 14.

9. Conclusions

This chapter has characterised the behaviour of the Bush-Mosteller (Bush & Mosteller, 1955) aspiration-based reinforcement learning model in 2x2 games. The dynamics of this process depend mainly on three features:

- The speed of learning.
- The existence of self-reinforcing equilibria (SREs). SREs are states which are particularly relevant for the ultralong-run or asymptotic behaviour of the process.
- The existence of self-correcting equilibria (SCEs). SCEs are states which are particularly relevant for the transient behaviour of the process with low learning rates.

With high learning rates, the model approaches its asymptotic behaviour fairly quickly. If there are SREs, such asymptotic dynamics are concentrated on the SREs of the system. With low learning rates, two transient distinct regimes (medium run and long run) can usually be distinguished before the system approaches its asymptotic regime. Such transient dynamics are strongly linked to the solutions of the continuous time limit approximation of the system's expected motion.

The inclusion of small quantities of noise in the model can change its dynamics quite dramatically. Some states of the system that are asymptotically reached with high probability in the unperturbed model (i.e. some SREs) can effectively lose all their attractiveness when players make occasional mistakes in selecting their actions. A field for further research is the analytical identification of the asymptotic equilibria of the unperturbed process that are robust to small trembles (i.e. the set of stochastically stable equilibria).

10. Acknowledgements

We are grateful to the Spanish Ministry of Education and Science (Projects DPI2004-06590 and DPI2005-05676 -SIGAME-) and the University of Burgos for providing financial support to conduct this piece of research. We are also very grateful to Jörgen W. Weibull for deriving a mathematical result that we used to produce figure 7, and to Alexandre Eudes, Alexis Revue and Vincent Barra, for helping to implement the applet provided at http://www.luis.izquierdo.name/papers/rl-book.

11. References

Beggs, AW. (2005). On the Convergence of Reinforcement Learning. *Journal of Economic Theory* 122, 1-36.

Bendor, J.; Mookherjee, D. & Ray, D. (2001a). Aspiration-Based Reinforcement Learning In Repeated Interaction Games: An Overview. *International Game Theory Review* 3(2-3), 159-174.

Bendor, J.; Mookherjee, D. & Ray, D. (2001b). Reinforcement Learning in Repeated Interaction Games. *Advances in Theoretical Economics* 1(1), Article 3.

Benveniste, A. ; Métivier, M. & Priouret, P. (1990). *Adaptive Algorithms and Stochastic Approximations*. Springer-Verlag, Berlin.

Binmore, K. & Samuelson, L. (1993). An Economist's Perspective on the Evolution of Norms. *Journal of Institutional and Theoretical Economics* 150, 45-63.

Binmore, K.; Samuelson, L. & Vaughan, R. (1995) Musical Chairs: Modeling Noisy Evolution. *Games and Economic Behavior* 11(1), 1-35.

Börgers, T. & Sarin, R. (1997). Learning through Reinforcement and Replicator Dynamics. *Journal of Economic Theory* 77, 1-14.

Bush, R. & Mosteller, F. (1955). *Stochastic Models of Learning*. John Wiliey & Son, New York.

Camerer, CF. (2003). *Behavioral Game Theory: Experiments in Strategic Interaction*. Russell Sage Foundation, New York.

Castellano, C.; Marsili, M. & Vespignani, A. (2000). Nonequilibrium phase transition in a model for social influence. *Physical Review Letters*, 85(16), pp. 3536-3539.

Chen, Y. & Tang, F. (1998). Learning and Incentive-Compatible Mechanisms for Public Goods Provision: An Experimental Study. *Journal of Political Economy* 106, 633-662.

Colman, AM. (1995). *Game theory and its applications in the social and biological sciences*. 2nd edition. Butterworth-Heinemann, Oxford, UK

Cross, JG. (1973). A Stochastic Learning Model of Economic Behavior. *Quartertly Journal of Economics* 87, 239-266.

Duffy, J. (2005). Agent-Based Models and Human Subject Experiments. In: Judd, K. L., Tesfatsion, L. (Eds.), *Handbook of Computational Economics II: Agent-Based Computational Economics*. Amsterdam: Elsevier.

Edwards, M.; Huet, S.; Goreaud, F. & Deffuant, G. (2003). Comparing an individual-based model of behaviour diffusion with its mean field aggregate approximation. *Journal of Artificial Societies and Social Simulation*, 6(4)9 http://jasss.soc.surrey.ac.uk/6/4/9.html.

Ellison, G. (2000). Basins of Attraction, Long-Run Stochastic Stability, and the Speed of Step-by-Step Evolution. *Review of Economic Studies*, 67, 17-45.

Erev, I. & Roth, AE. (1998). Predicting How People Play Games: Reinforcement Learning in Experimental Games with Unique, Mixed Strategy Equilibria. *American Economic Review* 88(4), 848-881.

Erev, I.; Bereby-Meyer, Y. & Roth, AE. (1999). The effect of adding a constant to all payoffs: experimental investigation, and implications for reinforcement learning models. *Journal of Economic Behavior and Organization* 39(1), 111-128.

Flache, A. & Macy, MW. (2002). Stochastic Collusion and the Power Law of Learning. *Journal of Conflict Resolution* 46(5), 629-653.

Foster, D. & Young, HP. (1990). Stochastic Evolutionary Game Dynamics. *Theoretical Population Biology*, 38, 219-232.

Galán, JM. & Izquierdo, LR. (2005). Appearances Can Be Deceiving: Lessons Learned Re-Implementing Axelrod's 'Evolutionary Approach to Norms'. *Journal of Artificial Societies and Social Simulation*, 8(3)2. http://jasss.soc.surrey.ac.uk/8/3/2.html.

Gilboa I, Schmeidler D (1995) Case-Based Decision Theory. *The Quarterly Journal of Economics*, 110, 605-639.

Gilboa I, Schmeidler D (2001) *A Theory of Case-Based Decisions*. Cambridge University Press, Cambridge, UK

Hargreaves Heap, SP. & Varoufakis, Y. (1995). *Game theory: a critical introduction*. Routledge, London

Holt, CA. & Roth, AE. (2004). The Nash equilibrium: A perspective. *Proceedings of the National Academy of Sciences USA* 101(12), 3999–4002.

Hopkins, E. & Posch, M. (2005). Attainability of Boundary Points under Reinforcement Learning. *Games and Economic Behavior* 53 (1), 110-125.

Huet, S.; Edwards, M. & Deffuant, G. (2007). Taking into Account the Variations of Neighbourhood Sizes in the Mean-Field Approximation of the Threshold Model on a Random Network. *Journal of Artificial Societies and Social Simulation* 10(1)10 http://jasss.soc.surrey.ac.uk/10/1/10.html.

Ianni, A. (2001). Reinforcement Learning and the Power Law of Practice. *Mimeo*, University of Southampton.

Izquierdo, LR.; Izquierdo, SS.; Gotts, NM. & Polhill, JG. (2007). Transient and Asymptotic Dynamics of Reinforcement Learning in Games. *Games and Economic Behavior* 61(2), 259–276.

Izquierdo, SS.; Izquierdo, LR. & Gotts, NM. (in press). Reinforcement Learning Dynamics in Social Dilemmas. *Journal of Artificial Societies and Social Simulation.*

Izquierdo, LR. & Polhill, JG. (2006). Is Your Model Susceptible to Floating-Point Errors?. *Journal of Artificial Societies and Social Simulation* 9(4)4, http://jasss.soc.surrey.ac.uk/9/4/4.html.

Kushner, HJ. & Yin, GG. (1997). *Stochastic Approximation Algorithms and Applications.* Springer-Verlag. New York.

Laslier J.; Topol, R. & Walliser, B. (2001). A Behavioral Learning Process in Games. *Games and Economic Behavior* 37, 340-366.

Macy, MW. & Flache, A. (2002). Learning Dynamics in Social Dilemmas. *Proceedings of the National Academy of Sciences USA* 99(3), 7229-7236.

Maier, NRF. & Schneirla, TC. (1964). *Principles of Animal Psychology.* Dover Publications, New York.

McAllister, PH. (1991). Adaptive approaches to stochastic programming. *Annals of Operations Research* 30, 45-62.

Mohler, RR. (1991). *Nonlinear Systems, Volume I: Dynamics and Control*. Prentice Hall, Englewood Cliffs.

Mookherjee, D. & Sopher, B. (1994). Learning Behavior in an Experimental Matching Pennies Game. *Games and Economic Behavior* 7, 62-91.

Mookherjee, D. & Sopher, B. (1997). Learning and Decision Costs in Experimental Constant Sum Games. *Games and Economic Behavior* 19, 97-132

Norman, MF. (1968). Some Convergence Theorems for Stochastic Learning Models with Distance Diminishing Operators. *Journal of Mathematical Psychology* 5, 61–101.

Norman, MF. (1972). *Markov Processes and Learning Models*. Academic Press, New York.

Polhill, JG. & Izquierdo, LR. (2005). Lessons learned from converting the artificial stock market to interval arithmetic. *Journal of Artificial Societies and Social Simulation*, 8 (2)2, http://jasss.soc.surrey.ac.uk/8/2/2.html

Polhill, JG.; Izquierdo, LR. & Gotts, NM. (2005). The ghost in the model (and other effects of floating point arithmetic). *Journal of Artificial Societies and Social Simulation*, 8 (1)5, http://jasss.soc.surrey.ac.uk/8/1/5.html

Polhill, JG.; Izquierdo, LR. & Gotts, NM. (2006). What every agent based modeller should know about floating point arithmetic. *Environmental Modelling and Software*, 21 (3), March 2006. pp. 283-309.

Roth, AE. & Erev, I. (1995). Learning in Extensive-Form Games: Experimental Data and Simple Dynamic Models in the Intermediate Term. *Games and Economic Behavior* 8, 164-212.

Rustichini, A. (1999). Optimal Properties of Stimulus–Response Learning Models. *Games and Economic Behavior* 29, 244-273.

Selten, R. (1975). Re-examination of the Perfectness Concept for Equilibrium Points in Extensive Games. *International Journal of Game Theory* 4, 25-55.

Thorndike, EL. (1898). *Animal Intelligence: An Experimental Study of the Associative Processes in Animals* (Psychological Review, Monograph Supplements, No. 8). MacMillan, New York.

Thorndike, EL. (1911). *Animal Intelligence*. New York: The Macmillan Company.

Young, HP. (1993). The evolution of conventions. *Econometrica*, 61(1): 57–84

Wustmann G.; Rein K.; Wolf R. & Heisenberg M. (1996). A New Paradigm for Operant Conditioning of Drosophila Melanogaster. *Journal of Comparative Physiology [A]* 179, 429-436.

12

Modular Learning Systems for Behavior Acquisition in Multi-Agent Environment

Yasutake Takahashi and Minoru Asada
Osaka University
Japan

1. Introduction

There has been a great deal of research on reinforcement learning in multirobot/agent environments during last decades[1]. A wide range of applications, such as forage robots (Mataric, 1997), soccer playing robots (Asada et al., 1996), prey-pursuing robots (Fujii et al., 1998) and so on, have been investigated. However, a straightforward application of the simple reinforcement learning method to multi-robot dynamic systems has a lot of issues, such as uncertainty caused by others, distributed control, partial observability of internal states of others, asynchronous action taking, and so on. In this paper we mainly focus on two major difficulties in practical use :

- unstable dynamics caused by policy alternation of other agents
- curse of dimension problem

The policy alternation of others in multi-agent environments may cause sudden changes in state transition probabilities of which constancy is needed for behavior learning to converge. Asada et al. (Asada et al., 1999) proposed a method that sets a global learning schedule in which only one agent is specified as a learner with the rest of the agents having fixed policies to avoid the issue of the simultaneous learning. As a matter of course, they did not consider the alternation of the opponent's policies. Ikenoue et al. (Ikenoue et al., 2002) showed simultaneous cooperative behavior acquisition by fixing learners' policies for a certain period during the learning process. In the case of cooperative behavior acquisition, no agent has any reason to change policies while they continue to acquire positive rewards as a result of their cooperative behavior with each other. The agents update their policies gradually so that the state transition probabilities can be regarded as almost fixed from the viewpoint of the other learning agents. Kuhlmann and Stone (Kuhlmann and Stone, 2004) have applied a reinforcement learning system with a function approximator to the keep-away problem in the situation of the RoboCup simulation league. In their work, only the passer learns his policy is to keep the ball away from the opponents. The other agents (receivers and opponents) follow fixed policies given by the designer beforehand.

The amount of information to be handled in multi-agent system tends to be huge and easily causes the curse of dimension problem. Elfwing et al. (Elfwing et al., 2004) achieved the cooperative behavior learning task between two robots in real time by introducing the

[1] For example, a survey (Yang and Gu, 2004) is available.

macro action that is an abstracted action code predefined by the designer. However, only the macro actions do not seem sufficient to accelerate the learning time in a case that more agents are included in the environment. Therefore, the sensory information should be also abstracted to reduce the size of the state space. Kalyanakrishnan et al. (Kalyanakrishnan et al., 2006) showed that the learning rate can be accelerated by sharing the learned information in the 4 on 5 game task. However, they still need long learning time since they directly use the raw sensory information as state variables to determine the situation that the learning agent encounters.

Keys for cooping with the above difficulties are to divide a whole complex situation into several ones in which state transition can be regarded as stable enough, and to keep exploration space as small as possible based on abstracted task specific information instead of the row sensory information. A modular learning system might be a practical solution for those difficulties.

This chapter briefly introduces examples of application of modular learning systems for cooperative/competitive behavior acquisition in scenarios of RoboCup Middle Size League. A modular learning system is successfully applied for adaptation to the policy alternation of others by switching modules each of which corresponds to different situation caused by the policy alternation of the other. Introduction of macro actions enables reduction of exploration space and simultaneous multi-agent behavior learning. The experimental results of 2 on 3 passing task are shown. Furthermore, in order to attack the problem of curse of dimension, a state abstraction method based on state value function of a behavior learning module is proposed and applied to the 4 on 5 passing task. A player can acquire cooperative behaviors with its teammates and competitive ones against opponents within a reasonable learning time. Finally, conclusions and future work are shown.

2. Modular learning system for policy alternation of others

In this section, a modular learning system for behavior acquisition in the multiagent environment is introduced. A multi-module learning system for even single agent learning in a multi-agent environment is shown difficult when we straightforwardly apply it. A simple learning scheduling is introduced in order to make it relatively easy to assign modules automatically. Second, macro actions are introduced to realize simultaneous learning in multi-agent environments in which each agent does not need to fix its policy according to some learning schedule. More detailed description was given in (Takahashi et al., 2005).

2.1 3 on 1 game

Before describing the modular learning system in details, a task in the RoboCup middle size league context is introduced as a testbed to evaluate the learning system. The game is like a three-on-one involving one opponent and three other players. The player nearest to the ball becomes a passer who passes the ball to one of its teammates (receivers) while the opponent tries to intercept it. Fig.2 shows the viewer of our simulator for the robots and the environment and a situation the learning agents are supposed to encounter. Fig.1 shows a mobile robot we have designed and built. The robot has an omni-directional camera system. A simple color image processing is applied to detect the ball, the interceptor, and the receivers on the image in real-time (every 33ms.) The left of Fig.2 shows a situation a learning agent can encounter while the right images show the simulated ones of the normal and omni vision systems. The mobile platform is an omni-directional vehicle (roration and translation in any direction on the plane are possible at any moment).

Fig. 1. A real Robot

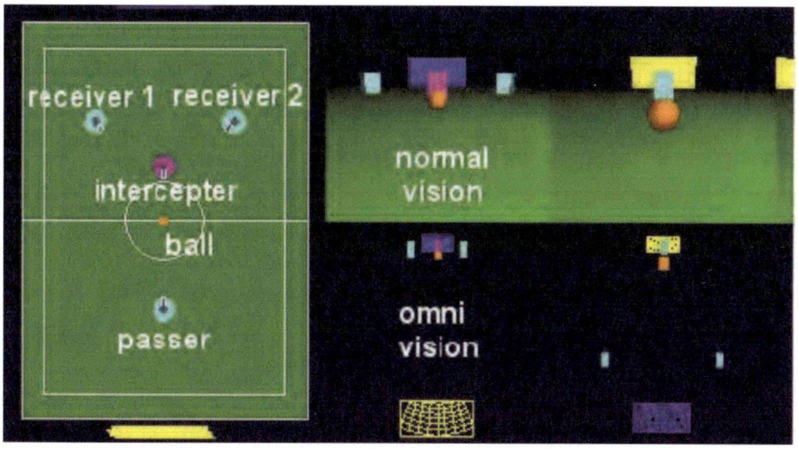

Fig. 2. A 3 on 1 game (left) and the viewer of the game simulator (right)

2.1 Modular learning system

The basic idea is that the learning agent could assign one behavior learning module to one situation which reflects another agent's behavior and the learning module would acquire a purposive behavior under the situation if the agent can distinguish a number of situations, each in which the state transition probabilities are almost constant. We introduce a modular learning approach to realize this idea (Fig.3). A module consists of both a learning component that models the world and an action planner. The whole system follows these procedures:

- select a module in which the world model is estimated best among the modules;
- update the model in the module; and
- calculate action values to accomplish a given task based on the estimated model using dynamic programming.

Fig. 3. Adaptive behavior selection based on Multi-module learning system

As an experimental task, we suppose ball passing with the possibility of being intercepted by the opponent (Fig.2). The problem for the passer (interceptor) here is to select one module of which model can most accurately describe the interceptor's (passer's) behavior from the viewpoint of the agent and then to take an action based on the policy which is planned with the estimated model.

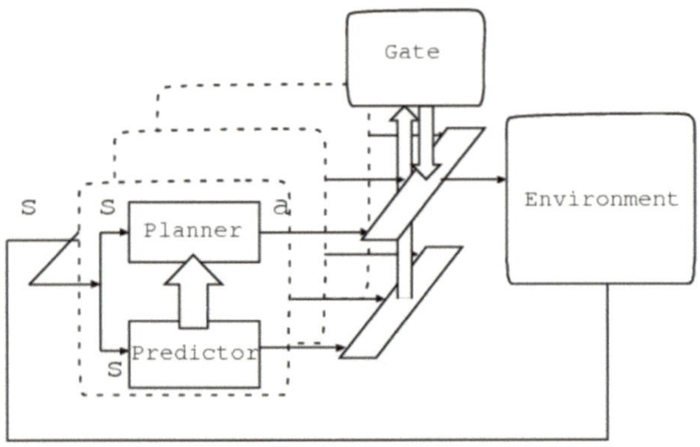

Fig. 4. A multi-module learning system

Fig. 4. shows a basic architecture of the proposed system, i.e., a modular reinforcement learning system. Each module has a forward model (predictor) which represents the state transition model and a behavior learner (action planner) which estimates the state-action value function based on the forward model in a reinforcement learning manner. This idea of a combination of a forward model and a reinforcement learning system is similar to the H-DYNA architecture (Singh, 1992) or MOSAIC (Doya et al., 2000). The system selects one module which has the best estimation of a state transition sequence by activating a gate signal corresponding to the module while deactivating the gate signals of the other modules; the selected module then sends action commands based on its policy.

2.3 Behaviors acquisition under scheduling

First, we show how it is difficult to directly introduce the proposed multi-module learning system in the multi-agent system. A simple learning scheduling is introduced in order to make it relatively easy to assign modules automatically.

The initial positions of the ball, passer, interceptor, and receivers are shown in Fig. 2. The opponent has two kinds of behaviors: it defends the left side or right side. The passer agent has to estimate which direction the interceptor will defend and go to the position so as to kick the ball in the direction the interceptor does not defend. From the viewpoint of the

multi-module learning system, the passer will estimate which situation of the module is going on and select the most appropriate module as its behavior. The passer acquires a positive reward when it approaches the ball and kicks it to one of the receivers.
A learning schedule is composed of three stages to show its validity. The opponent fixes its defending policy as a right-side block at the first stage. After 250 trials, the opponent changes the policy to block the left side at the second stage and continues this for another 250 trials. Finally, the opponent changes the defending policy randomly after one trial.

2.4 Configuration

The state space is constructed in terms of the centroid of the ball on the image, the angle between the ball and the interceptor, and the angles between the ball and the potential receivers (see Figs. 9 (a) and (b)). The action space is constructed in terms of the desired three velocity values (xd, yd, wd) to be sent to the motor controller (Fig. 6). The robot has a pinball-like kick device which allows it to automatically kick the ball whenever the ball comes within the region to be kicked. It tries to estimate the mapping from sensory information to appropriate motor commands by the proposed method.

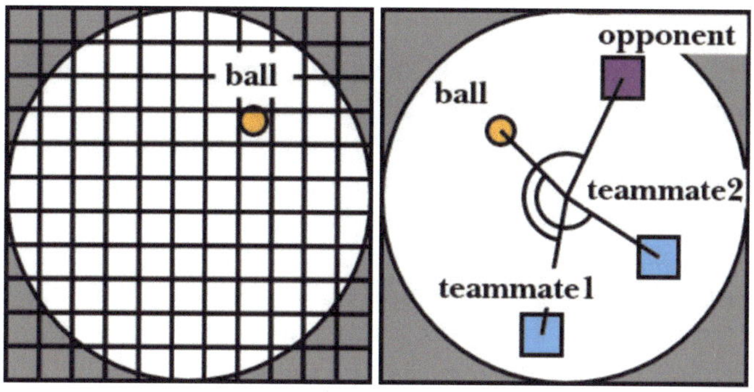

Fig. 5. State variables : Left : (a) state variables (position) Right: (b) state variables (angle)

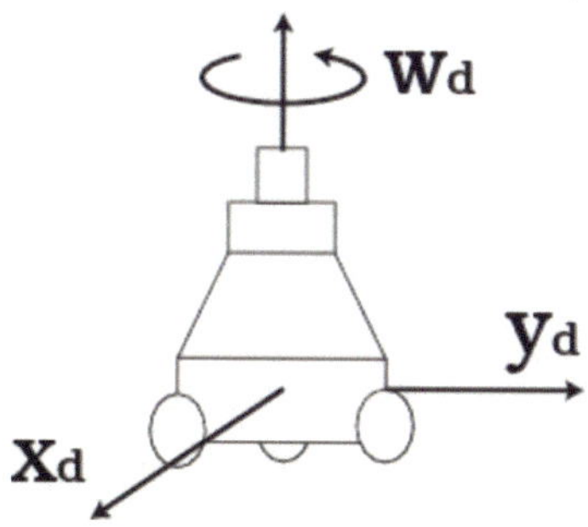

Fig. 6. Action variables

2.5 Simulation results

We have applied the method to a learning agent and compared it with only one learning module. The performances between the methods with and without the learning scheduling are compared as well. Fig.7 shows the success rates of those during the learning process. "success" indicates the learning agent successfully kicked the ball without interception by the opponent. The success rate shows the number of successes in the last 50 trials. The "mono. module" in the figure means a "monolithic module" system which tries to acquire a behavior for both policies of the opponent.

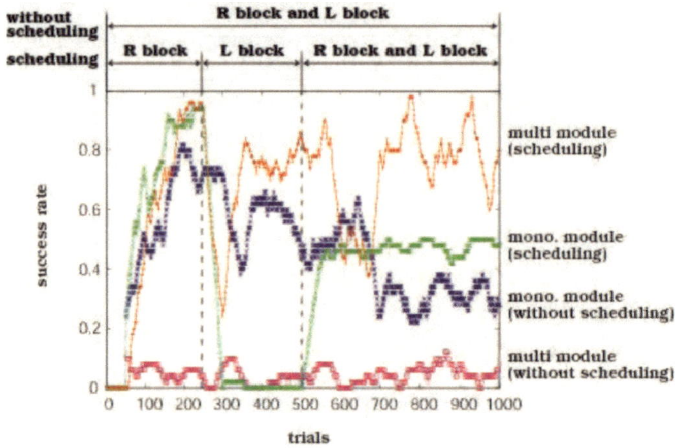

Fig. 7. Success rates during the learning

The multi-module system with scheduling shows a better performance than the one-module system. The monolithic module with scheduling means we applied the learning scheduling mentioned in 2.3 even though the system has only one learning module. The performance of this system is similar to the multi-module system until the end of the first stage between the fist and the 250th trials; however, it goes down at the second stage because the obtained policy is biased by the experiences at the first stage and cannot follow the policy change of the opponent. Because the opponent uses one of the policies at random in the third stage, the learning agent obtains about 50% of the success rate.

The term "without scheduling" means we do not apply learning scheduling and the opponent changes its policy at random from the beginning. Somehow the performance of the monolithic module system without learning scheduling gets worse after 200 trials. The multi-module system without a learning schedule shows the worst performance in our experiments. This result indicates it is very difficult to recognize the situation at the early stage of the learning process because the modules have too few experiences to evaluate their fitness; thus, the system tends to select the module without any consistency. As a result, the system cannot acquire any valid policies.

3. Simultaneous learning with macro actions

The exploration space with macro actions becomes much smaller than the one with primitive actions; therefore, the macro action increases the possibility of creating cooperative/competitive experiences and leads the two agents to find a reasonable solution in a realistic learning time frame. Here, macro actions are introduced in order to realize simultaneous learning in a multi-agent environment in which each agent does not need to fix its policy according to some learning schedule. In this experiment, the passer and the interceptor learn their behaviors simultaneously. The passer learns behaviors for different situations caused by the alternation of the interceptor's policies, i.e., blocking to the left side or the right. The interceptor also learns behaviors for different situations caused by the alternation of the passer's policies, i.e., passing a ball to a left receiver or a right one.

3.1 Macro actions and state spaces

Fig. 8 shows the macro actions of the passer and the interceptor. The macro actions by the interceptor are blocking the pass way to the left receiver and the right one. On the other hand, the macro action by the passer are turning left, turning right around the ball, and approaching the ball to kick it. A ball gazing control is embedded in both learners. The number of the actions is 2 and 3, respectively.

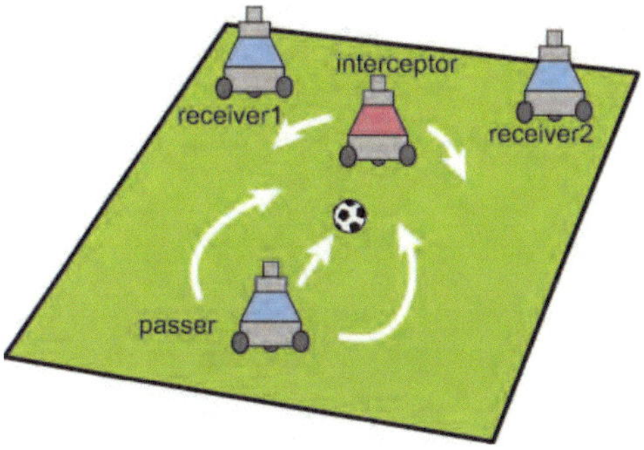

Fig. 8. Macro actions

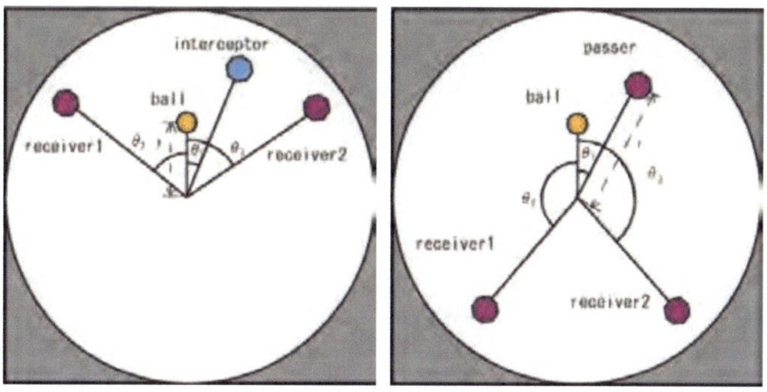

Fig. 9. State variables Left : (a) passer Right : (b) interceptor

The state space for the passer is constructed in terms of the y position of the ball on the normal image, the angle between the ball and the centers of interceptor, and the angles between the balls and the two receivers on the image of omni-directional vision. The number of the states is reduced because the set of macro actions enable us to select a smaller number of state variables and coarser quantization. The state space for the interceptor is constructed in terms of the y position of the passer on the image of normal vision system, the angle between the ball and the passer, and the angles between the ball and the two receivers on the image of omni-directional vision.

3.2 Experimental results

We have checked how the simultaneous learning of the passer and interceptor works on our computer simulation. Both agents start to learn their behaviors from scratch and have 1500 trials without any scheduling. To check whether both learners acquired appropriate behaviors against the opponent's behaviors, we fixed one agent's policy and checked to see if the other could select an appropriate behavior, then determined its success rate. Table 1 shows these results.

Passer	Interceptor	Passer's success rate [%]	Interceptor's success rate [%]	Draw rate [%]
LM0, LM1	LM0	59.0	23.0	18.0
LM0,LM1	LM1	52.7	34.3	13.0
LM0	LM0,LM1	25.6	55.0	19.4
LM1	LM0,LM1	26.0	59.3	14.7
LM0,LM1	LM0,LM1	27.6	37.3	25.1

Table 1. Success rates for a passer and an interceptor in different cases

Both players have two modules and were assigned to appropriate situations by themselves. LM and the digit number right after the LM indicate the Learning Module and the index number of the module, respectively. For example, if the passer uses both LM0 and LM1 and the interceptor uses only LM0, then the passer's success rate, interceptor's success rate, and draw rate are 59.0 %, 23.0%, and 18.0%, respectively. Apparently, the player with multi-modules switching achieves a higher success rate than the opponent using only one module. These results demonstrate the multi-module learning system works well for both.

The same architecture is applied to the real robots. Fig. 10 shows one example of behaviors by real robots. First, the interceptor tried to block the left side, then the passer approached the ball with the intention of passing it to the right receiver. The interceptor found it was trying to block the wrong side and changed to block the other (right) side, but it was too late to intercept the ball and the passer successfully passed the ball to the right receiver.

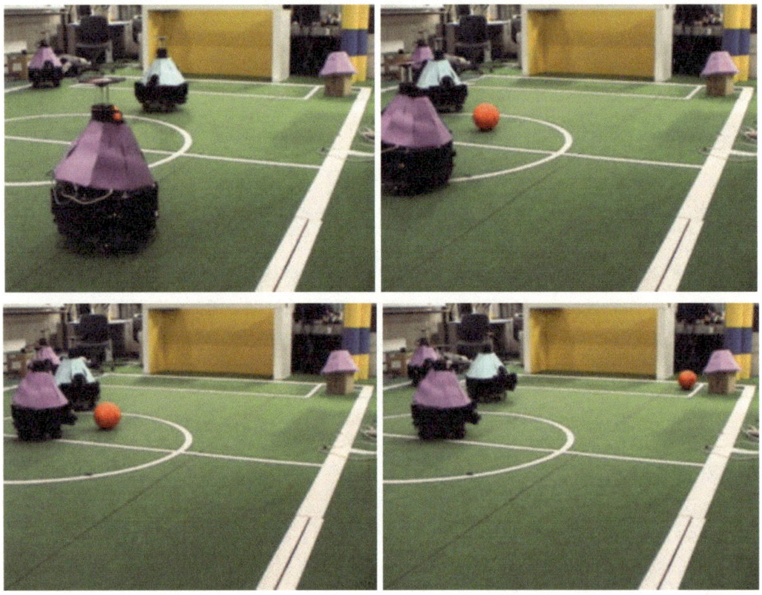

Fig. 10. A sequence of a behavior of passing a ball to the right receiver while

4. Cooperative/competitive behavior learning with other's state value estimation modules

Conventional approaches, including ones described in the previous sections, have been suffering from the curse of dimension problem when they are applied to multiagent dynamic environments. State/action spaces based on sensory information and motor commands easily become too huge for a learner to explore. In the previous section, macro actions are introduced to reduce the exploration space and enable agents to learn purposive competitive behaviors according to the situation caused by the opponent. As the next step, state space should be constructed as small as possible to enable cooperative/competitive behaviour learning in practical time. The key ideas to resolve the issue are as follows. First, a two-layer hierarchical system with multi learning modules is adopted to reduce the size of the sensor and action spaces. The state space of the top layer consists of the state values from the lower level, and the macro actions are used to reduce the size of the physical action space. Second, the state of the other to what extent it is close to its own goal is estimated by observation and used as a state value in the top layer state space to realize the cooperative/competitive behaviors. The method is applied to 4 (defense team) on 5 (offense team) game task, and the learning agent successfully acquired the teamwork plays (pass and shoot) within much shorter learning time. Here, the method is briefly introduced. More detailed description was given in (Noma et al., 2007).

Fig.11 shows a basic architecture of the proposed system, i.e., a two-layered multi-module reinforcement learning system. The bottom layer consists of two kinds of modules: behavior modules and other's state value estimation ones. The top layer consists of a single gate module that learns which behavior module should be selected according to the current state that consists of state values sent from the modules at the bottom layer. The gate module acquires a purposive policy to select an appropriate behavior module based on reinforcement learning.

The role of the other's state value estimation module is to estimate the state value that indicates the degree of achievement of the other's task through observation, and to send this value to the state space of the gate module at the top layer. In order to estimate the degree of achievement, the following procedure is taken.

1. The learner acquires the various kinds of behaviors that the other agent may take, and each behavior corresponds to each behavior module that estimates state value of the behavior.
2. The learner estimates the sensory information observed by the other through the 3-D reconstruction of its own sensory information.
3. Based on the estimated sensory information of the other, each other's state value estimation module estimates the other's state value by assigning the state value of the corresponding behavior module of its own.

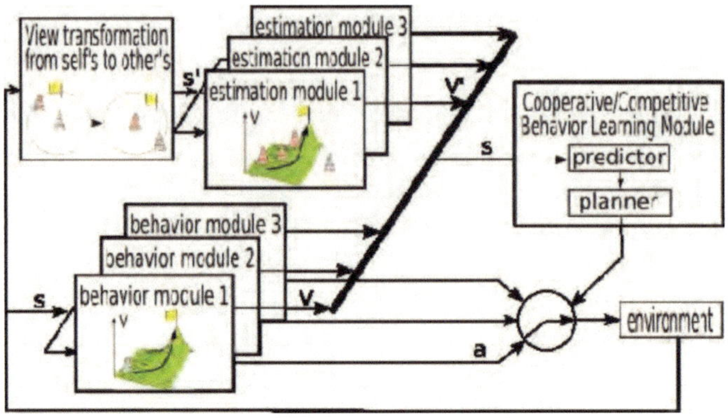

Fig. 11. A multi-module learning system

4.1 5 on 4 game

The game consists of the offense team (five players and one of them can be the passer) and the defense team (four players attempt to intercept the ball). The offense player nearest to the ball becomes a passer who passes the ball to one of its teammates (receivers) or shoot the ball to the goal if possible while the opposing team tries to intercept it (see Fig. 12).

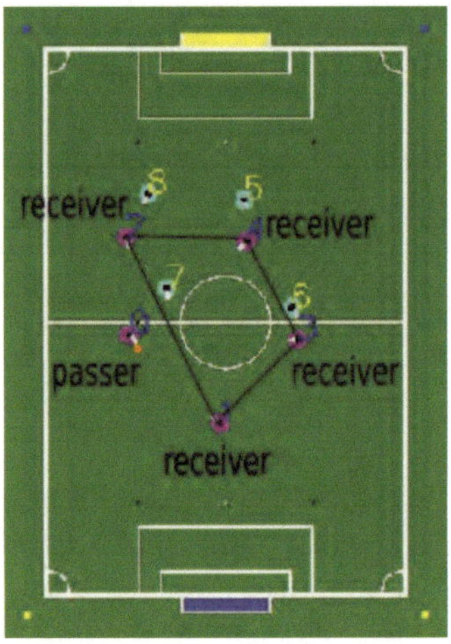

Fig. 12. A passer and the defense formation

Only the passer learns its behavior while the receivers and the defense team members take the fixed control policies. The receiver becomes the passer after receiving the ball and the passer becomes the receiver after passing the ball. After one episode, the learned information is circulated among team members through communication channel but no communication during one episode. The behavior and the state value estimation modules are given a priori. The offense (defense) team color is magenta (cyan), and the goal color is blue (yellow) in the following figures.

The passer who is the nearest to the ball passes the ball to one of four receivers or dribble-shoots the ball to the goal. After its passing, the passer shows a pass-and-go behavior that is a motion to the goal during the fixed period of time. The receivers face to the ball and move to the positions so that they can form a rectangle by taking the distance to the nearest

teammates (the passer or other receivers) (see Fig. 12). The initial positions of the team members are randomly arranged inside their territory.
The defense team member who is nearest to the passer attempts to intercept the ball, and each of other members attempts to "block" the nearest receiver. "Block" means to move to the position near the offense team member and between the offense and its own goal (see Fig. 12). The offense team member attempts to catch the ball if it is approaching. In order to avoid the disadvantage of the offense team, the defense team members are not allowed inside the penalty area during the fixed period of time. The initial positions of the team members are randomly arranged inside their territory but outside the center circle.

4.2 Structure of the state and action spaces

The passer is only one learner, and the state and action spaces for the lower modules and the gate one are constructed as follows. The action modules are four passing ones for four individual receivers, and one dribble-shoot module. The other's state value estimation modules are the ones to estimate the degree of achievement of ball receiving for four individual receivers, that is how easily the receiver can receive the ball from the passer. These modules are given in advance before the learning of the gate module.
The action spaces of the lower modules adopt the macro actions that the designer specifies in advance to reduce the size of the exploration space without searching at the physical motor level. The state space **S** for the gate module consists of the following state values from the lower modules:

- four state values of passing behavior modules corresponding to four receivers,
- one state value of dribble-shoot behavior module, and
- four state values of receiver's state value estimation modules corresponding to four receivers.

In order to reduce the size of the whole state space, these values are binarized, therefore its size is $2^4 \times 2 \times 2^4 = 512$.
The rewards are given as follows:

- 10 when the ball is shot into the goal (one episode is over),
- -1 when the ball is intercepted (one episode is over),
- when the ball is successfully passed,
- when the ball is dribbled.

When the ball is out of the field or the pre-specified time period elapsed, the game is called "draw" and one episode is over.

4.3 Experimental results

The success rate is shown in Fig. 13(a) where the action selection is 80% greedy and 20% random to cope with new situations. Around the 900th trial, the learning seems to have converged at 30% success, 70% failure, and 10% draw. Compared to the results of (Kalyanakrishnan et al., 2006) that has around 30% success rate with 30,000 trials, the learning time is drastically improved (30 times quicker). Fig. 13(b) indicates the number of passes where it decreases after the 350 trials that means the number of useless passes decreased.
In cases of the success, failure, and draw rates when 100% greedy and 100% random are 55%, 35%, 10%, and 2%, 97%, 1%, respectively. The reason why the success rate in case of

100% greedy is better than in case of 80% greedy seems that the control policies of the receivers and the defense players are fixed, therefore not so new situations happened.
An example of acquired behavior is shown in Fig. 14 where a sequence of twelve top views indicates a successful pass and shoot scene.

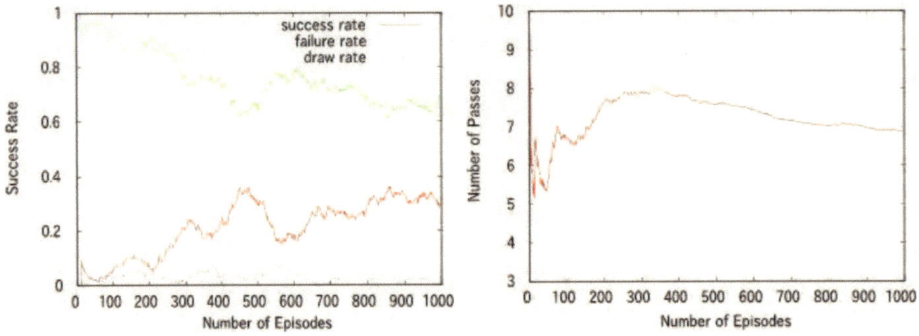

Fig. 13. (a) Success rates and (b) the number of passes

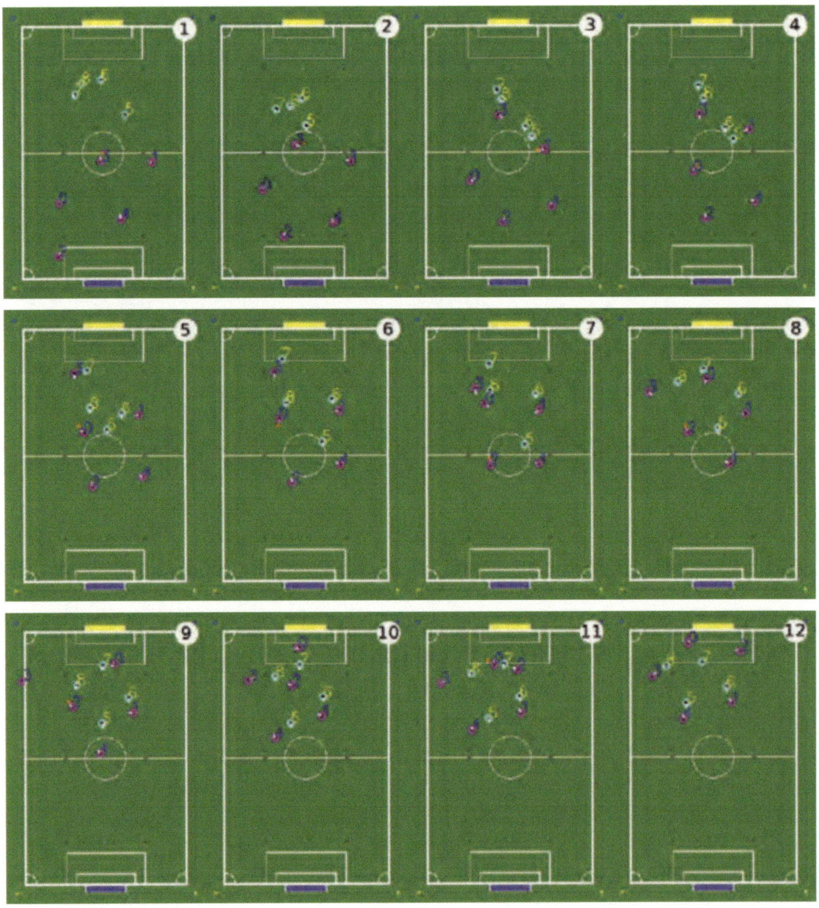

Fig. 14. An example of the acquired behavior in 5 on 4 game

Although we have not used the communication between agents during one episode, the receiver's state value estimation modules seem to take the similar role. Then, we performed the learning without these modules. Fig. 15 shows the success rate, and we can see that the converged success rate is around 21% that is close to 23% of the success rate of the result of the existing method (Kalyanakrishnan et al., 2006).

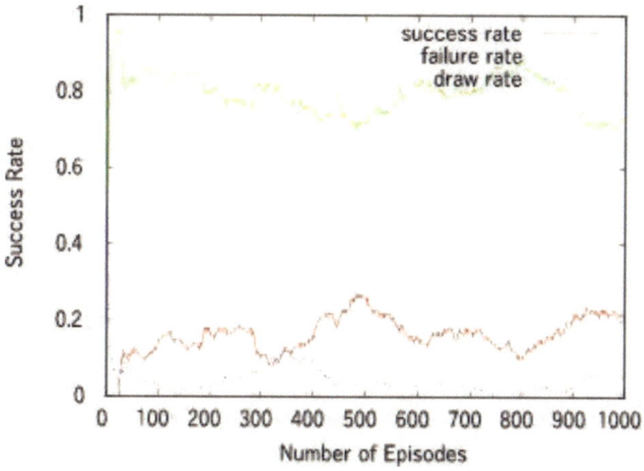

Fig. 15. Success rate without the receiver's state value estimation modules

5. Conclusion

In this chapter, we have showed a method by which multiple modules are assigned to different situations caused by the alternation of the other agent's policy so that an agent may learn purposive behaviors for the specified situations as consequences of the other agent's behaviors.

Macro actions are introduced to realize simultaneous learning of competitive behaviors in a multi-agent system. Results of a soccer situation and the importance of the learning scheduling in case of none-simultaneous learning without macro actions, as well as the validity of the macro actions in case of simultaneous learning in the multi-agent system, were shown.

We have also showed another learning system using the state values instead of the physical sensor values and macro actions instead of the physical motor commands, and adopted the receiver's state value estimation modules that estimate how easy for each receiver to receive the ball in order to accelerate the learning. The state and action space abstraction (the use of state values and macro actions) contributes to the reduction of the learning time while the use of the receiver's state value estimation modules contributed to the improvement of the teamwork performance.

6. References

Asada, M., Noda, S., Tawaratumida, S., and Hosoda, K. (1996). Purposive behavior acquisition for a real robot by vision-based reinforcement learning. *Machine Learning*, 23:279–303.

Asada, M., Uchibe, E., and Hosoda, K. (1999). Cooperative behavior acquisition for mobile robots in dynamically changing real worlds via vision-based reinforcement learning and development. *Artificial Intelligence*, 110:275–292.

Doya, K., Samejima, K., ichi Katagiri, K., and Kawato, M. (2000). Multiple model-based reinforcement learning. Technical report, Kawato Dynamic Brain Project Technical Report, KDB-TR-08, Japan Science and Technology Corporatio.

Elfwing, S., Uchibe, E., Doya, K., and Christensen1, H. I. (2004). Multi-agent reinforcement learning: Using macro actions to learn a mating task. In *Proceedings of 2004 IEEE/RSJ International Conference on Intelligent Robots and Systems*, pages CD–ROM.

Fujii, T., Arai, Y., Asama, H., and Endo, I. (1998). Multilayered reinforcement learning for complicated collision avoidance problems. In *Proceedings of the 1998 IEEE International Conference on Robotics and Automation*, pages 2186–2198.

Ikenoue, S., Asada, M., and Hosoda, K. (2002). Cooperative behavior acquisition by asynchronous policy renewal that enables simultaneous learning in multiagent environment. In *Proceedings of the 2002 IEEE/RSJ Intl. Conference on Intelligent Robots and Systems*, pages 2728–2734.

Kalyanakrishnan, S., Liu, Y., and Stone, P. (2006). Half field offense in robocup soccer: A multiagent reinforcement learning case study. In Lakemeyer, G., Sklar, E., Sorrenti, D., and Takahashi, T., editors, *RoboCup 2006 Symposium papers and team description papers*, pages CD–ROM.

Kuhlmann, G. and Stone, P. (2004). Progress in learning 3 vs. 2 keepaway. In Polani, D., Browning, B., Bonarini, A., and Yoshida, K., editors, *RoboCup- 2003: Robot Soccer World Cup VII*. Springer Verlag, Berlin.

Mataric, M. J. (1997). Reinforcement learning in the multi robot domain. *Autonomous Robots*, 4(1):77–83.

Noma, K., Takahashi, Y., and Asada, M. (2007). Cooperative/competitive behavior acquisition based on state value estimation of others. In Visser, U., Ribeiro, F., Ohashi, T., and Dellaert, F., editors, *Proceedings of the RoboCup2007 Symposium*, pages CD–ROM.

Singh, S. P. (1992). Reinforcement learning with a hierarchy of abstract models. In *National Conference on Artificial Intelligence*, pages 202–207.

Takahashi, Y., Edazawa, K., Noma, K., and Asada, M. (2005). Simultaneous learning to acquire competitive behaviors in multi-agent system based on a modular learning system. In *Proceedings of the 2005 IEEE/RSJ International Conference on Intelligent Robots and Systems*, pages 153–159.

Yang, E. and Gu, D. (2004). Multiagent reinforcement learning for multi-robot systems: A survey. Technical report, University of Essex Technical Report CSM-404.

13

Optimising Spoken Dialogue Strategies within the Reinforcement Learning Paradigm

Olivier Pietquin
Ecole Supérieure d'Electricité (Supélec)
France

1. Introduction

Human-Computer Interfaces are now widely studied and become one of the major interests among the scientific community. More and more electronic devices surround people in their day-to-day life. This exponential incursion of electronics in homes, cars and work places is not only due to its ability to ease the achievement of common and boring tasks or the continuously decreasing prices but also because the increasing "user-friendliness" of interfaces makes it easier to use.

Being studied for more than fifty years, speech and natural language processing knew major progresses during the two last decades. It is now feasible to build real Spoken Dialogue Systems (SDS) interacting with human users through voice-enabled interactions. Speech often appears as a natural way to interact for a human being and it provides potential benefits such as hand-free access to machines, ergonomics and greater efficiency of interaction. Yet, speech-based interfaces design has been an expert job for a long time. It necessitates good skills in speech technologies and low-level programming. Moreover, rapid design and reusability of previously designed systems are almost impossible. For these reasons, but not only, people are less used to interact with speech-based interfaces which are therefore thought as less intuitive.

Designing and optimizing a SDS is not only the combination of speech and language processing systems such as Automatic Speech Recognition (ASR) (Rabiner & Juang 1993), Spoken Language Understanding (SLU) (Allen 1998), Natural Language Generation (NLG) (Reiter & Dale 2000), and Text-to-Speech (TTS) synthesis (Dutoit 1997) systems. It also requires the development of dialogue strategies taking at least into account the performances of these subsystems (and others), the nature of the task (e.g. form filling (Pietquin & Dutoit 2006a), tutoring (Graesser *et al* 2001), robot control, or database querying (Pietquin 2006b)), and the user's behaviour (e.g. cooperativeness, expertise (Pietquin 2004)). The great variability of these factors makes rapid design of dialogue strategies and reusability across tasks of previous work very complex. Most often, such a design is a cyclic process composed of strategy hand-coding, prototype releases and expansive and time consuming user tests. In addition, there is also no guarantee that hand-crafted strategies developed by experts are anything close to optimal. Because it provides data-driven methods and objective clues about performances, statistical learning of optimal dialogue strategies became a leading domain of research (Lemon & Pietquin, 2007). The goal of such approaches is to reduce the number of design cycles (Fig. 1).

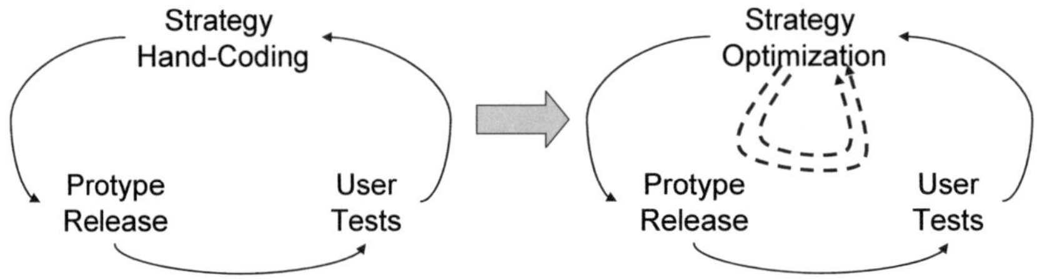

Fig. 1. Optimization for minimizing the number of design cycles

Supervised learning for such an optimization problem would require examples of ideal (sub)strategies which are typically unknown. Indeed, no one can actually provide an example of what would have objectively been the perfect sequencing of exchanges after having participated to a dialogue. Humans have a greater propensity to criticize what is wrong than to provide positive proposals. In this context, reinforcement learning using Markov Decision Processes (MDPs) (Levin *et al* 1998, Singh *et al* 1999, Scheffler & Young 2001, Pietquin & Dutoit 2006a, Frampton & Lemon 2006) and Partially Observable MDP (POMDPs) (Poupart *et al* 2005, Young 2006) has become a particular focus.

2. Formalism

2.1 Definitions

In the rest of this chapter, a *dialogue* will be referred to as an interaction between two *agents* based on sequential turn taking. In most of the cases, this interaction is *goal-directed* and both agents cooperate in order to achieve an aim (or accomplish a task). In the case of a man-machine dialog, one of the agents is a human *user* while the other is a computer (or system). In the particular case in which the interaction uses speech as the main communication mean, the computer implements a *Spoken Dialogue System* (SDS) while a system using several means of communication is referred to as a *Multimodal Dialogue System* (MMDS). When the man-machine dialog is dedicated to the realisation of a particular task (or set of tasks) it is called a *task-oriented* dialogue system. When one of the agents is an SDS, the dialogue consists of a sequence of *utterances* exchanged at each turn. A *spoken utterance* is the acoustic realisation of the *intentions* or *concepts* or *dialog acts* one of the agents wants to communicate to the other and is expressed as a *word* sequence.

2.2 Formal description of man-machine spoken dialog

A man-machine spoken dialog can be considered as a sequential process in which a human user and a Dialog Manager (DM) are communicating using speech through speech and language processing modules (Fig. 2). The role of the DM is to define the sequencing of spoken interactions and therefore to take decisions about what to do at a given time (providing information, asking for information, closing the dialog, etc.). A Spoken Dialog System is often meant to provide information to a user; this is why it is generally connected to a Knowledge Base (KB) through its DM. The dialog is therefore regarded as a turn-taking process in which pieces of information are processed sequentially by a set of modules and perform a cycle going from the DM to the user and back. At each turn t the DM generates a communicative act set a_t according to its internal state s_t and corresponding to its decision about what to do in that state. Dialogue communicative acts (shortly dialogue acts) can be of different kind such as greeting the user, ask a constraining question to the user, provide information to the user, ask for confirmation about some information to the user, query a database, close the dialogue. This act set is then transformed into a linguistic representation lt (generally a text) by a natural language processing module. The textual representation lt serves as an input to a text-to-speech synthesizer to produce a system spoken output syst. The TTS and the NLG modules are therefore spoken output generation modules. To this spoken solicitation, the user answers by a new spoken utterance ut according to what he could understand from syst, to his/her knowledge kt (about the task, the interaction history, the world in general) and to the goal gt s/he is trying to achieve by interacting with the system. Both spoken utterances syst and ut can be mixed with some background noise nt. The noisy user utterance is in turn processed by an automatic speech recognition system, which produces a written word sequence wt as a result and a confidence measure CLASR about this result. A natural language understanding module subsequently tries to extract communicative acts (or concepts) ct from wt (possibly helped by CLASR). The NLU module also provides some confidence measure CLNLU about this processing. The NLU and ASR sub-systems are speech input processing modules. The set {ct, CLASR, CLNLU} composes an observation ot which can be considered as the result of the processing of the DM communicative acts a_t by its *environment*. The dialogue manager then computes a new internal state s_{t+1} according to this observation.

The following paragraphs will use this description of a man-machine dialog as a base to build a probabilistic model.

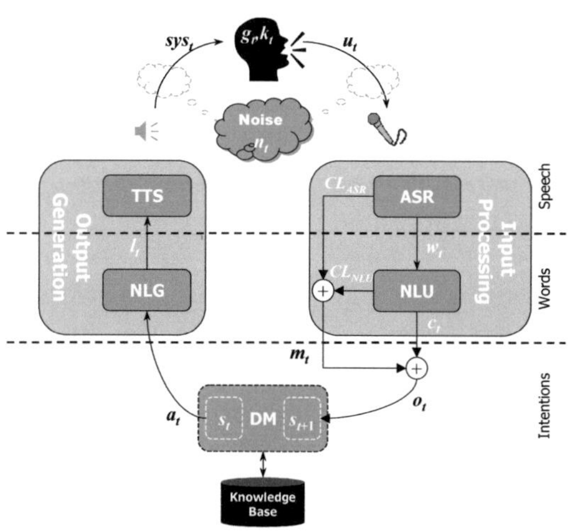

Fig. 2. Man-Machine Spoken Communication

2.3 MDP and reinforcement learning

In our vision of the MDP formalism, a discrete-time system interacting with its stochastic environment through actions is described by a finite or infinite number of states $\{s_i\}$ in which a given number of actions $\{a_j\}$ can be performed. To each state-action pair is associated a transition probability $\mathcal{T}$ giving the probability of stepping from state s at time t to state s' at time $t+1$ after having performed action a when in state s. To this transition is also associated a reinforcement signal (or reward) r_{t+1} describing how good was the result of action a when performed in state s. Formally, an MDP is thus completely defined by a 4-tuple $\{S, A, \mathcal{T}, \mathcal{R}\}$ where S is the state space, A is the action set, $\mathcal{T}$ is a transition probability distribution over the state space and $\mathcal{R}$ is the expected reward distribution. The couple $\{\mathcal{T}, \mathcal{R}\}$ defines the dynamics of the system:

$$\mathcal{T}_{ss'}^{a} = P(s_{t+1} = s' \mid s_t = s, a_t = a) \tag{1}$$

$$\mathcal{R}_{ss'}^{a} = E[r_{t+1} \mid s_t = s, a_t = a, s_{t+1} = s'] \tag{2}$$

These last expressions assume that the Markov property is met, which means that the system's functioning is fully defined by its one-step dynamics and that its behavior from state s will be identical whatever the path followed before reaching s. To control a system described as an MDP (choosing actions to perform in each state), one would need a *strategy* or *policy* π mapping states to actions: $\pi(s) = P(a \mid s)$ (or $\pi(s) = a$ if the strategy is deterministic). In this framework, a RL *agent* is a system aiming at optimally mapping states to actions, that is finding the best strategy π^* so as to maximize an overall return R which is a function (most often a discounted return is used i.e. a weighted sum of immediate rewards) of all the immediate rewards r_t.

$$R^{\pi} = E\left[\sum_{t=0}^{\infty} \gamma^t r_t \mid s_0 = s, a_t = \pi(s_t)\right] \tag{3}$$

$$\pi^* = \underset{\pi}{arg\,max}\left[E\left[\sum_{t=0}^{\infty} \gamma^t r_t \mid s_0 = s, a_t = \pi(s_t)\right]\right] \tag{4}$$

If the probabilities of equations (1) and (2) are known, an analytical solution can be computed by dynamic programming, otherwise the system has to learn the optimal strategy by a trial-and-error process. RL is therefore about how to optimally map situations to actions by trying and observing environment's feedback. In the most challenging cases, actions may affect not only the immediate reward, but also the next situation and, through that, all subsequent rewards. Trial-and-error search and delayed rewards are the two main features of RL. Different techniques are described in the literature, in the following the Watkin's Q(λ) algorithm (Watkin 1989) will be used.

3. Human-machine dialogue and Markov decision process

From the point of view of the dialogue manager, the interaction can probabilistically be described by the joint probability of the signals a_t, o_t and s_{t+1} given the history of the interaction (Pietquin 2005):

$$\begin{aligned} P(s_{t+1}, o_t, a_t \mid s_t, n_t, a_{t-1}, s_{t-1}, n_{t-1}, \ldots, a_0, s_0, n_0) = \underbrace{P(s_{t+1} \mid o_t, a_t, s_t, n_t, a_{t-1}, s_{t-1}, n_{t-1}, \ldots, a_0, s_0, n_0)}_{\text{Task Model}} \cdot \\ \underbrace{P(o_t \mid a_t, s_t, n_t, a_{t-1}, s_{t-1}, n_{t-1}, \ldots, a_0, s_0, n_0)}_{\text{Environment}} \cdot \underbrace{P(a_t \mid s_t, n_t, a_{t-1}, s_{t-1}, n_{t-1}, \ldots, a_0, s_0, n_0)}_{\text{DM}} \end{aligned} \tag{5}$$

In (5), the first term stands for the *task model* that helps building a new dialogue manager internal state thanks to the perceived observation, the second term stands for the response of the environment to the dialogue manager stimulation, and the third stands for the dialogue manager decision process.

3.1 Markov property and random noise

In the case of a SDS, the Markov Property is met if the dialogue manager choice about the action a_t to perform at time t and the according transition probability for stepping to state s_{t+1} at time t+1 are only conditioned by the state s_t at time t and not of previous states and actions. From now on, the Markov Property will be assumed. It can anyway be met by a judicious choice of the DM state representation, which should embed the history of the interaction into the current state. Such a state representation is said *informational.*

Let's illustrate this on a train ticket booking system. When accessing such a system a customer can book a ticket by providing information about the cities of departure and arrival and a desired time of departure. Like in a 3-slot-filling application, three bits of information (sometimes called *attributes*) should therefore be transferred from the user to the system. A very simple way to build the state space is to represent the dialogue state as a vector of three Boolean values (e.g. [dep arr time]) set to *true* if the corresponding attribute is supposed to be known by the system and to *false* otherwise. An ideal dialogue for such an application and the corresponding dialogue state evolution is shown in Table 1.

Speaker	Spoken Utterance	Dialogue state
System	Hello, how may I help you?	[*false false false*]
User	I'd like to go to Edinburgh.	
System	What's your departure city?	[*false true false*]
User	I want to leave from Glasgow.	
System	When do you want to go from Glasgow to Edinburgh ?	[*true true false*]
User	On Saturday morning.	
System	Ok, seats are available in train n° xxx …	[*true true true*]

Table 1. Ideal dialogue in a train ticket booking application

To meet the Markov property with such a state representation, we have to assume that the system behaves the same whatever the order in which the slots where filled (and by the way, whatever the values of the attributes). The Markov assumption is also made about the environment; that is the user behaves the same whatever the filling order as well. These are of course strong assumptions but we will see later that they lead to satisfactory results.

Finally, most often the noise is considered as being random so as to have independence between n_t and n_{t-1}. Eq. (5) then simplifies as follow:

$$P(s_{t+1},o_t,a_t \mid s_t,n_t) = \underbrace{P(s_{t+1} \mid o_t,a_t,s_t,n_t)}_{\text{Task Model}} \cdot \underbrace{P(o_t \mid a_t,s_t,n_t)}_{\text{Environment.}} \cdot \underbrace{P(a_t \mid s_t,n_t)}_{\text{DM}} \tag{6}$$

3.2 Dialogue management as an MDP

As claimed in paragraph 0 and depicted on Fig. 2, a task-oriented (or goal-directed) man-machine dialogue can be seen as a turn-taking process in which a human user and a dialogue manager exchange information through different channels processing speech inputs and outputs (ASR, TTS ...). In our problem, the dialogue manager's action (or dialogue act) selection *strategy* has to be optimized, the dialogue manager should thus be our learning *agent.*

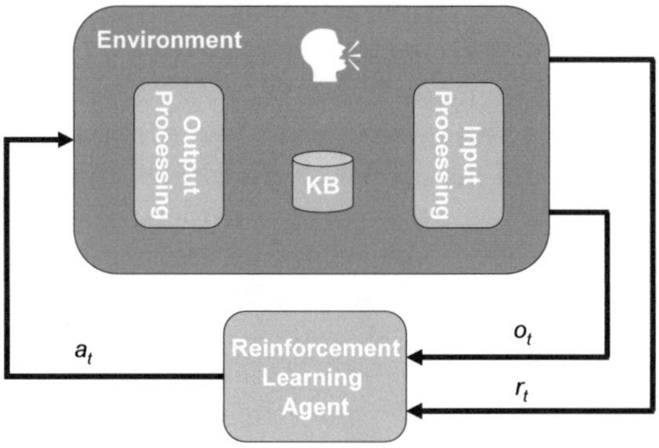

Fig. 3. Dialogue management as an MDP

As shown on Fig. 3, the *environment* modeled by the MDP comprises everything but the dialogue manager, i.e. the human user, the communication channels (ASR, TTS …), and any external information source (database, sensors etc.). In this context, at each turn t the dialogue manager has to choose an *action* a_t according to its interaction *strategy* so as to complete the task it has been designed for. The RL agent has therefore to choose an action among greetings, spoken utterances (constraining questions, confirmations, relaxation, data presentation etc.), database queries, dialogue closure etc. They result in a response from the DM environment (user speech input, database records etc.), considered as an observation o_t, which usually leads to a DM *internal state* update according to the task model (Eq. 6).

3.3 Reward function

To fit totally to the MDP formalism, a *reinforcement signal* r_t is required. In (Singh *et al* 1999) it is proposed to use the contribution of an action to the user's satisfaction. Although this seems very subjective, some studies have shown that such a reward could be approximated by a linear combination of the task completion (TC) and objective measures c_i related to the system performances (Walker *et al* 1997):

$$r_t = \alpha \cdot \mathcal{N}(TC) - \sum_i w_i \cdot \mathcal{N}(c_i), \tag{7}$$

where N is a Z-score normalization function that normalises the results to have mean 0 and standard deviation 1 and w_i are non-zero weights. This way, each weight (α and w_i) expresses the relative importance of each term of the sum in the performance of the system. The task completion can for example be measured by the kappa (κ) coefficient (Carletta 1996):

$$\kappa = \frac{P(A) - P(E)}{1 - P(E)}, \tag{8}$$

where $P(A)$ is the proportion of correct interpretations of user's utterances by the system and P(E) is the proportion of correct interpretations occurring by chance. One can see that κ

= 1 when the system performs perfect interpretation (P(A) = 1) and $\kappa = 0$ when the only correct interpretations were obtained by chance (P(A) = P(E)). In order to compute weights α and wi, a large number of users are asked to answer a satisfaction survey after having used the system while costs ci are measured during the interaction. The questionnaire comprises around 9 statements on a five-point Likert scale and the overall satisfaction is computed as the mean value of collected ratings. A Multivariate Linear Regression is then applied using the results of the survey as the dependent variable and the weights as independent variables. In practice, the significant performance measures ci are mainly the duration of the dialogue and the ASR and NLU performances.

3.4 Partial observability

If a direct mapping between observations and system (or dialogue) states exists, the process is completely observable and the task model (see Eq. 6) can easily be built. Yet, it is rarely the case that the observations are directly linked to the dialogue state. Indeed, the real dialogue state at time *t* is related to the information the user intended to transmit to the system until time *t* during the interaction. This information being transmitted through error prone statistical speech recognition and understanding systems, it can occur that the observation doesn't contain only the information meant by the user but a probability distribution over a set of possible bits of information. Indeed, the output of a speech recognition system is usually a list of N word sequences (named N-bests list), each of them being associated with a confidence level that can be considered as a probability of the word sequence being correct given the spoken utterance (and maybe the context). This N-bests list serves as an input to the natural language understanding module which in turn provides a list of concept sequences associated to confidence levels.

This is typically what happens in partially observable environments where a probability distribution is drawn over possible states given the observations. For this reason, emerging research is focused on the optimization of spoken dialogue systems in the framework of Partially Observable Markov Decision Processes (POMDPs) (Poupart *et al* 2005, Young 2006)

4. Learning dialogue policies using simulation

Using the framework described previously, it is theoretically possible to automatically learn spoken dialogue policies allowing natural conversation between human users and computers. This learning process should be realised online, through real interactions with users. One could even imagine building the reinforcement signal from direct queries to the user about his/her satisfaction after each interaction (Fig. 4).

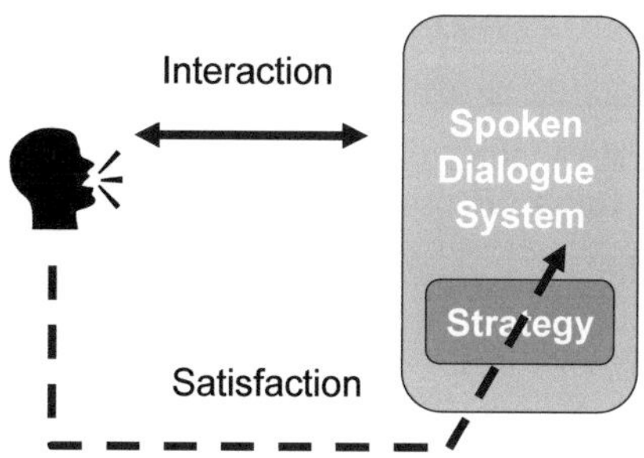

Fig. 4. Ideal learning process

For several reasons, direct learning through interactions is made difficult. First, a human user would probably react badly to some of the exploratory actions the system would choose since they might be completely incoherent. Anyway a very large number of interactions are required (typically tens of thousands of dialogues for standard dialogue systems) to train such a system. This is why data driven learning as been proposed so as to take advantage of existing databases for bootstrapping the learning process. Two methods were initially investigated: learning the state transition probabilities and the reward distribution from data (Singh *et al*, 1999) or learning parameters of a simulation environment mainly reproducing the behaviour of the user (Levin *et al* 2000). The second method is today preferred (Fig. 5). Indeed, whatever the data set available, it is unlikely that it contains every possible state transitions and it allows exploring the entire state and policy space. Dialogue simulation is therefore necessary for expanding the existing data sets and learning optimal policies. Most often, the dialogue is simulated at the intention level rather than at the word sequence or speech signal level, as it would be in the real world. An exception can be found in (Lopez Cozar *et al* 2003). Here, we regard an intention as the minimal unit of information that a dialogue participant can express independently. Intentions are closely related to concepts, speech acts or dialogue acts. For example, the sentence "I'd like to buy a desktop computer" is based on the concept buy(desktop). It is considered as unnecessary to model environment behavior at a lower level, because strategy optimization is a high level concept. Additionally, concept-based communication allows error modeling of all the parts of the system, including natural language understanding (Pietquin & Renals 2002, Pietquin & Dutoit 2006b). More pragmatically, it is simpler to automatically generate concepts compared with word sequences (and certainly speech signals), as a large number of utterances can express the same intention while it should not influence the dialogue manager strategy. Table 2 describes such a simulation process. The intentions have been expanded in the last column for comprehensiveness purposes. The signals column refers to notations of section 0.

Signals	Intentions	Expanded Intentions
$\mathbf{sys_0}$	greeting	*Hello! How may I help you?*
$\mathbf{u_0}$	arr_city = 'Paris'	I'd like to go to Paris.
$\mathbf{sys_1}$	const(arr_time)	*When do you prefer to arrive?*
$\mathbf{u_1}$	arr_time = '1.00 PM'	I want to arrive around 1 PM.
$\mathbf{sys_2}$	rel(arr_time)	*Don't you prefer to arrive later?*
$\mathbf{u_2}$	rel = *false*	No.
$\mathbf{sys_3}$	conf(arr_city)	*Can you confirm you want to go to Paris?*
$\mathbf{u_3}$	conf = *true*	Yes !
...	...	...
...	...	...

Table 2. Simulated dialogue at the intention level ('const' stands for constraining question, 'rel' for relaxation and 'conf' for confirmation)

This approach requires modelling the environment of the dialogue manager as a stochastic system and to learn the parameters of this model from data. It has been a topic of research since the early 2000's (Levin et al 2000, Scheffler & Young 2001, Pietquin 2004). Most of the research is now focused on simulating the user (Georgila et al 2005, Pietquin 2006a, Schatzmann et al 2007a) and assessing the quality of a user model for training a reinforcement learning agent is an important track (Schatzmann et al 2005, Rieser & Lemon 2006, Georgila et al 2006). Modelling the errors introduced by the ASR and NLU systems is also a major topic of research (Scheffler & Young 2001, Lopez Cozar et al 2003, Pietquin & Beaufort 2005, Pietquin & Dutoit 2006b).

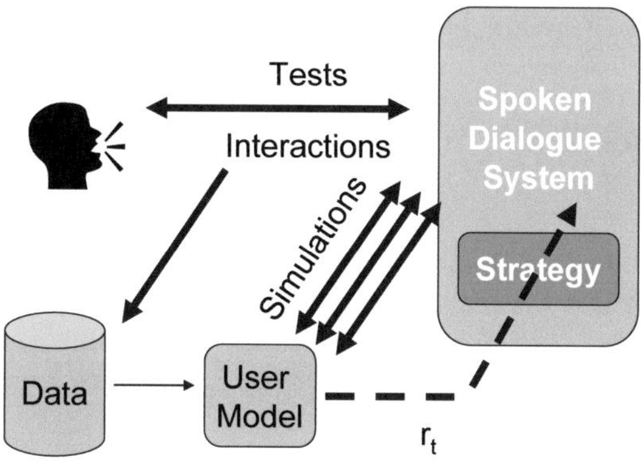

Fig. 5. Learning via simulation

5. Speech-based database querying

We will illustrate reinforcement learning based dialogue optimization on the particular task of a speech-based database querying system. In such an application, the user wants to extract from a database one or a list of records selected according to specific features provided by a user through speech-based interactions.

In the following, several experiments made on a database containing 350 computer configurations are described. The database is split into 2 tables (for notebooks and desktops), each of them containing 6 fields: pc_mac (pc or mac), processor_type, processor_speed, ram_size, hdd_size and brand. The goal of the dialogue system is therefore to extract one or a short list of computer configurations from the database and to present it the user. To do so, the system will have to gather information about which computer features the user wants. In the following, the application is described in terms of actions, states and rewards so as to be mapped to the Markov decision processes paradigm.

5.1 Action set

The task involves database querying. Therefore possible systems actions do not only imply interactions with the user (such as spoken questions, confirmation requests or assertions) but also with the database (such as database querying). The action set contains 8 generic actions:

- greet: greeting (e.g. "How may I help you ?").
- constQ(*arg*): ask to constrain the value of *arg*.
- openQ: ask an open ended question.
- expC(*arg*): ask to confirm the value of *arg*.
- allC: ask for a confirmation of all the arguments.
- rel(*arg*): ask to relax the value of *arg*.
- dbQ([*args*]): perform a database query thanks to retrieved information.
- close: present data and close the dialogue session.

The value of *arg* may be the table's type (notebook or desktop) or one of the 6 table fields. Notice that there is no data presentation action because it will be considered that the data presentation is included in the 'close' action. This means that, when the dialogue is closed by the dialogue manager, it systematically presents to the user the content of the last retrieved recordset.

5.2 State space

The way the state space is built is very important and several state variables can be envisioned for describing the same task. Yet, some general considerations might be taken into account:

1. The state representation should contain enough information about the history of the dialogue so as to assume the Markov property to be met.
2. State spaces are often considered as informational in that sense that they are built thanks to the amount of information the DM could retrieve from the environment until it reached the current state.
3. The state representation must embed enough information so as to give an accurate representation of the situation to which an action has to be associated (it is not as obvious as it sounds).
4. The state space must be kept as small as possible since the reinforcement learning algorithms converge in linear time with the number of states of the underlying Markov decision process.

According to these considerations and the particular task of database querying, two slightly different state spaces where built to describe the task as an MDP so as to illustrate the sensitivity of the method to the state space representation. In the first representation, referred to as S_1 in the following, each state is represented by two features.

- A vector of 7 boolean values (one for each value of *arg*). Like in the example of paragraph 0, each of these values is set to *true* if the corresponding value of *arg* is known (for example if the user specified to search in the notebooks table, the fist value is set to *true*). This is a way to meet the Markov property (informational state).
- Information about the Confidence Level (CL) of each value set to *true*. The confidence level is usually a real number ranging between 0 and 1 computed by the speech and/or language analysis subsystems (ASR and NLU) and providing information about the confidence of the system in the result of its processing. To keep the size of the state space reasonable, we only considered 2 possible values for the confidence level: *High* or *Low* (i.e. *High* means $CL \geq 0.8$ and *Low* means $CL < 0.8$).

Notice that 'dbQ' actions will only include values with a *High* confidence level. For each value of *arg*, there are 3 different possibilities for the corresponding slot in the state representation: {value = *false*, *CL* = *undef*}, {value = *true*, *CL* = *Low*}, {value = *true*, *CL* = *High*}. This leads to 3^7 possible states.

The second way to represent the state space is built on the same basis but an additional state variable *NDB* is added to take the number of records returned by the last database query into account. This variable can also take only two values (*High* or *Low*) and is set according to the comparison of the query result size and a predefined threshold. If no 'dbQ' action has been performed, the *NDB* variable is initialized with the *High* value (an empty query would provide the whole database as a result). This state space representation will be referred to as S_2 in the following.

5.3 Reward function

Once again, there is not a unique way to build the reward function and slight differences in the choices can result in large variations in the learned strategy. To illustrate this, some simple functions will be described in the following. According to (Walker *et al*, 1997), the reward function (which is here a cost function that we will try to minimize) should rely on an estimate of the dialogue time duration (D), the ASR performances (ASR) and the task completion (TC) so as to approximate the user's satisfaction using objective measures:

$$R = w_D \cdot D - w_{ASR} \cdot ASR - w_{TC} \cdot TC \tag{9}$$

In this last expression, the w_x factors are positive weights. Considering the estimate of the time duration, two values are actually available: the number of user turns $D = N_U$ (the number of turns perceived by the user) and the number of system turns $D = N_S$ (including database queries as well).
On another hand, the task completion is not always easy to define. The *kappa* coefficient defined in (Carletta 1996) and section 0 is one possibility but didn't always prove to correlate well with the perceived task completion. For the purpose of this experiment, two simple task completion measures will be defined:

$$TC_{max} = \max_{R_i}\left(\#\left(G_U \cap R_i\right)\right) \tag{10}$$

$$TC_{av} = average\left(\#\left(G_U \cap R_i\right)\right) \tag{11}$$

In these last expressions, $\#(G_U \cap R)$ is the number of common values in the user's goal G_U (the user goal is supposed to have the same structure as an existing database record and is set before the dialogue begins) and one of the records R presented to the user at the end of a dialogue. When a value is not present in the user goal it is considered as common (if a field is not important to the user, it is supposed to match any value). The first task completion measure TC_{max} indicates how close the closest record in the presented results is. The second TC_{av} measures the mean number of common values between the user's goal and each presented record.
Finally, the ASR performance measures will be provided by the confidence levels (CL) computed by the ASR system after each speech recognition task.

6. Experiments

The number of required interactions between a RL agent and its environment is quite large (10^4 dialogues at least in our case). So, it has been mandatory to simulate most of the dialogues for reasons explained in section 0. An intention-based simulation environment has therefore been built as described in (Pietquin & Dutoit 2006a). It simulates ASR errors using a constant Word Error Rate (WER). It generates confidence levels as real numbers ranging between 0 and 1 according to a distribution measured on a real system. If the system has to recognize more than one argument at a time, the CL is the product of individual CLs obtained for each recognition task (so it usually decreases). Other ASR simulation models can be considered (Pietquin & Beaufort 2005) but it is out of the scope of this introduction to the technique.
Several experimental results obtained with different settings of the state space and the

reward function will be exposed in the following. These settings are obtained by combining in three different ways the parameters S_1, S_2, N_U, N_S, TC_{max}, TC_{av} mentioned before. Results are described in terms of average number of turns (user and system turns), average task completion measures (TC_{max} and TC_{av}) for the performance and action occurrence frequency during a dialogue session to get a clue about the learned strategy. These results are obtained by simulating 10,000 dialogues with the learned strategy.

6.1 First experiment: S_1, N_U, TC_{max}

The first experiment is based on the smaller state space S_1 (without any information about the number of retrieved records). The dialogue cost is computed thanks to the number of user turns N_U as a measure of the time duration and the TC_{max} value as the task completion measure. Results are shown in the following tables.

N_U	N_S	TC_{max}	TC_{av}
2.25	3.35	6.7	1.2

Table 3. Performances of the learned strategy for the {S_1, N_U, TC_{max}} configuration

greet	constQ	openQ	expC	AllC	rel	dbQ	close
1.00	0.06	0.0	0.14	0.0	0.05	1.10	1.00

Table 4. Learned strategy for the {S_1, N_U, TC_{max}} configuration

When looking at the three first columns of the performance table (Table 4), the learned strategy doesn't look so bad. It actually has a short duration in terms of user turns as well as in system turns and has a very high task completion rate in terms of TC_{max} measure. Yet the TC_{av} shows a very low mean value.

When looking to the average frequency of actions in table, one can see that the only action addressed to the user that happens frequently during a dialogue is the greeting action. Others almost never occur. Actually, the learned strategy consists in uttering the greeting prompt to which the user should answer by providing some arguments. Then the system performs a database query with the retrieved attributes and presents the results to the user. Sometimes, the user doesn't provide any attribute when answering to the greeting prompt or the value is not recognized at all by the ASR model (very low *CL* value), so the strategy is to perform a constraining question (and not an open-ended question) that will provide an argument with a better *CL*. Sometimes the provided arguments have still a poor *CL* and an explicit confirmation is requested. Sometimes the provided arguments don't correspond to any valid record in the database so the strategy is to ask for relaxation of one argument (this also explains why the number of database queries is greater than 1). The value of TC_{max} is not maximal because sometimes the dialogue fails.

This results in presenting almost the whole database when the user only provides one argument when prompted by the greeting. This is why there is a so big difference between TC_{max} and TC_{av}. The desired record is actually in the presented data (TC_{max} is high) but is very difficult to find (TC_{av} is low). The learned strategy is definitely not suitable for a real system, specially if the record set have to be presented vocally. An example of dialogue is shown in Table 5, where the signal column refers to signals used on Fig. 2 and in section 0.

Signals	Intentions	Expanded Intentions
$a_0 \rightarrow sys_0$	greeting	*Hello! How may I help you?*
u_0	Table= 'Notebook'	I'd like to buy a Notebook.
o_0	Table = 'Notebook' CL = *high*	
a_1	dbQ	
o_1	DB = 97 (*high*)	
$a_2 \rightarrow sys_2$	As = close	*Ok, here are the computers corresponding to your request: (proposes the 97 Notebooks in the DB) ...*

Table 5. Dialogue sample for the {S_1, N_U, TC_{max}} configuration

6.2 Second experiment: S_2, N_U, TC_{av}

Here, the same settings are used except that the *NDB* variable is added to the state variables and the task completion is measured with TC_{av}.

N_U	N_S	TC_{max}	TC_{av}
5.75	8.88	6.7	6.2

Table 6. Performances of the learned strategy for the {S_2, N_U, TC_{av}} configuration

greet	constQ	openQ	expC	AllC	rel	dbQ	close
1.00	0.87	1.24	0.31	1.12	0.21	3.13	1.00

Table 7. Learned strategy for the {S_2, N_U, TC_{av}} configuration

Results shows that TC_{max} and TC_{av} are close to each other, so the presented results are more accurate but the number of turns has increased. The number of system turns particularly exhibits higher values. This is obviously explained by the increase of database queries. Looking at Table 7 one can see that the learned strategy tries to maximize the TC_{av} value while minimizing the number of user turns and maximizing recognition performance. To do so, it systematically performs a database query after having retrieved information from the user. The number of results being among the state variables, the agent learned not to present the results when in a state with a high *NDB* value. If this value is too high after the greeting, the learner tries to reach a state where it is lower. Thus it almost systematically performs an 'openQ' action after the greeting so as to get as much information as possible in a minimum of turns (this explains the 1.24 value). Yet, this often results in lower CL values, thus it also performs a confirmation of all the fields before presenting any result. Sometimes, more information is provided after the greeting and only a constraining question is required to gather enough information to reach a state with less result. A constraining question is preferred in this case because it leads to better recognition results.

The mean number of user turns shows that only 5.75 turns are usually needed to reach an accurate result set because the computer configurations are sufficiently different so as not to need too much attributes in the database query to provided accurate results. Thus, the system doesn't ask for all the attribute values to the user. Further investigations would show that the system takes advantage of the structure of the database and asks for attributes allowing extracting the desired records as fast as possible.

Signals	Intentions	Expanded Intentions
$a_0 \rightarrow sys_0$	greeting	*Hello! How may I help you?*
u_0	Table = 'Notebook'	I'd like to buy a Notebook.
o_0	Table = 'Notebook' CL = *high*	
a_1	dbQ	
o_1	DB = *high*	
$a_2 \rightarrow sys_2$	openQ	*Do you have any other preference?*
u_2	pc_mac = 'PC' proc_type = 'Pentium III'	I'd rather like a PC with a Pentium III processor.
o_2	pc_mac = 'PC' proc_type = 'Pentium III' CL = *high*	
a_3	dbQ	
o_3	DB = *high*	
$a_4 \rightarrow sys_4$	constQ(ram)	*How much memory would you like?*
u_4	ram = 128	128 MB.
a_5	dbQ	
o_5	DB = *low*	
$a_6 \rightarrow sys_6$	allC	*You asked for a PC Notebook with a Pentium III processor and 128 MB memory.*
u_6	conf_table = *true* ...	Yes.
$a_7 \rightarrow sys_7$	close	*Ok, here are the computers corresponding to your request: (proposes the 3 results of the DB query) ...*

Table 8. Dialogue sample for the $\{S_2, N_U, TC_{av}\}$ configuration

6.3 Third experiment: S_2, N_S, TC_{av}

The same experiment as the previous one has been performed but replacing the N_U measure of time duration by the N_S measure. It actually makes sense since in a real application, the database could be much larger than the one used here. Thus, the database queries could be much more time consuming.

N_U	N_S	TC_{max}	TC_{av}
6.77	7.99	6.6	6.1

Table 9. Performances of the learned strategy for the $\{S_2, N_S, TC_{av}\}$ configuration

greet	constQ	openQ	expC	AllC	rel	dbQ	close
1.00	1.57	1.24	0.33	1.32	0.31	1.22	1.00

Table 10. Learned strategy for the $\{S_2, N_S, TC_{av}\}$ configuration

This obviously results in a decrease of the number of database queries involving a proportional decrease of the number of system turns N_S. Yet, an increase of the number of user turns N_U is also observed. By examining the action frequencies, one can notice that the number of constraining questions increased resulting in an increase of N_U. Indeed, the learned strategy implies gathering enough information from the user before performing a database query. This explains why the systems ask more constraining questions.
This last strategy is actually optimal for the considered simulation environment (constant word error rate for all tasks) and is suitable for using with this simple application.

7. Conclusion

This chapter described a formal description of a man-machine spoken dialogue suitable to introduce a mapping between man-machine dialogues and (partially observable) Markov decision processes. This allows data-driven optimization of a dialogue manager's interaction strategy using the reinforcement learning paradigm. Yet, such an optimization process often requires tenths of thousands of dialogues which are not accessible through real interactions with human users because of time and economical constraints. Expanding existing databases by means of dialogue simulation is a solution to this problem and several approaches can be envisioned as discussed in section 0. In this context, we described the particular task of speech-based database querying and its mapping into the MDP paradigm in terms of actions, states and rewards. Three experiments on a very simple task have shown the influence of parameterization of the MDP on the learned conversational strategy. From this, one can say first that the state space representation is a crucial point since it embeds the knowledge of the system about the interaction. Second, the reward function is also of major importance since it measures how well the system performs on the task by simulating the perception of the dialogue quality from the users' point of view. Performance measure is a key of RL. The three experiments described in the last section showed the influence of these parameters on the learned strategy and concluded that a correctly parameterized RL algorithm could result in an acceptable dialogue strategy while little changes in the parameters could lead to silly strategies unsuitable for use in real conditions.

8. Future works

Data-driven optimization of spoken dialogue strategies is an emerging area of research and lots of problems still remain. One of the first is to find tractable algorithms to train real size dialogue systems. Indeed, the standard RL algorithms are suitable for small tasks as described in section 0 but real applications can exhibit up to several million of states, possibly with continuous observations (Williams *et al* 2005). The curse of dimensionality is therefore of particular interest in the area of spoken dialogue systems. Several attempts to tackle this problem in the framework of spoken dialogue systems can be found in the literature by scaling up MDPs using supervised learning (Henderson *et al* 2005) and hierarchical learning (Cuayáhuitl *et al* 2007). Also algorithms for tractable solutions to the optimization of spoken dialogue systems via the POMDP paradigm can be found in (Poupart *et al* 2005, Young 2006). This preliminary work in the field of generalisation and hierarchical learning shows the interest of the community in these techniques. Another problem to tackle is the development of realistic user models, easily trainable from data and suitable for training RL-based dialogue managers. Different approaches are being studied such as the recently proposed agenda-based user model (Schatzmann *et al* 2007b) that can be trained by an Expectation-Maximisation algorithm from data, or user models based on dynamic Bayesian networks (Pietquin & Dutoit 2006a). Assessing such user models in terms of quality of the trained strategies and similarity with real user behavior is of course primordial (Schatzmann *et al* 2005, Georgila *et al* 2006, Rieser & Lemon 2006). On another hand, it might be interesting to see how to use learned strategies to help human developers to design optimal strategies. Indeed, the solution may be in computer-aided design more than fully automated design (Pietquin & Dutoit 2003). Finally, designing a complete dialogue system using an end-to-end probabilistic framework, from speech recognition to speech synthesis systems automatically trained on real data, is probably the next step (Lemon & Pietquin 2007).

9. Acknowledgement

The research presented in this chapter has been funded by the 'First Europe' program of the Belgian Walloon Region, the SIMILAR European Network of Excellence and the French Lorraine Region.

10. References

Allen, J. (1994) *Natural Language Understanding*, Benjamin Cummings, 1987, Second Edition, 1994.

Carletta J. (1996), Assessing Agreement on Classification Tasks: the Kappa Statistic. *Computational Linguistics*, 22(2), 1996, 249-254.

Cuayáhuitl, H.; Renals, S.; Lemon, O. and Shimodaira, H. (2007) Hierarchical Dialogue Optimization Using Semi-Markov Decision Processes, in *Proceedings of International Conference on Speech Communication (Interspeech'07)*, Anvers (Belgium), 2007.

Dutoit, T., *An Introduction to Text-To-Speech Synthesis*. Kluwer Academic Publishers, Dordrecht, ISBN 0-7923-4498-7, 1997.

Frampton, M. & Lemon O. (2006). Learning more effective dialogue strategies using limited dialogue move features, in *Proceedings of ACM*, 2006.

Georgila, K.; Henderson, J. and Lemon, O. (2005). Learning User Simulations for Information State Update Dialogue Systems, in *Proceedings of International Conference on Speech Communication (Interspeech'05)*, Lisbon (Portugal) 2005.

Georgila, K.; Henderson, J. and Lemon, O. (2006) User simulation for spoken dialogue systems: Learning and evaluation, in *Proceedings of International Conference on Speech Communication (Interspeech'06)*, Pittsburgh, 2006.

Graesser, A.; VanLehn, K.; Rosé, C.; Jordan, P. & Harter, D. (2001) Intelligent Tutoring Systems with Conversational Dialogue. in *AI Magazine* vol. 22(4) , 2001, pp. 39-52.

Henderson, J.; Lemon, O. and Georgila, K. (2005) Hybrid Reinforcement/Supervised Learning for Dialogue Policies from COMMUNICATOR data, in *Proceedings of the IJCAI workshop on Knowledge and Reasoning in Practical Dialogue Systems*, 2005, pp. 68–75.

Lemon, O. & Pietquin, O. (2007). Machine learning for spoken dialogue systems, in *Proceedings of the European Conference on Speech Communication and Technologies (Interspeech'07)*, Anvers (Belgium), August 2007.

Levin, E.; Pieraccini, R. & Eckert, W. (1997). Learning dialogue strategies within the Markov decision process framework, in *Proceedings of the International Workshop on Automatic Speech Recognition and Understanding* (ASRU'97), December 1997.

Levin, E.; Pieraccini, R. and Eckert, W. (2000). A stochastic model of human-machine interaction for learning dialog strategies, in *IEEE Transactions on Speech and Audio Processing*, vol. 8, no. 1, pp. 11–23, 2000.

Lopez-Cozar, R.; de la Torre, A.; Segura, J. and Rubio, A. (2003) Assesment of dialogue systems by means of a new simulation technique, in *Speech Communication*, vol. 40, no. 3, pp. 387–407, May 2003.

Pietquin, O. and Renals, S. (2002). Asr system modelling for automatic evaluation and optimization of dialogue systems, in *Proceedings of the IEEE International Conference on Acoustics, Speech and Signal Processing (ICASSP'02)*, Orlando, (USA, FL), May 2002.

Pietquin, O. and Dutoit, T. (2003). Aided Design of Finite-State Dialogue Management Systems, in *Proceedings of the IEEE International Conference on Multimedia and Expo (ICME 2003)*, Baltimore (USA, MA), 2003.

Pietquin, O. (2004). *A Framework for Unsupervised Learning of Dialogue Strategies*, Presses Universitaires de Louvain, ISBN : 2-930344-63-6, 2004.

Pietquin, O. (2005). A probabilistic description of man-machine spoken communication, in *Proceedings of the IEEE International Conference on Multimedia and Expo (ICME'05)*, Amsterdam (The Netherlands), July 2005.

Pietquin, O., Beaufort, R. (2005). Comparing ASR Modeling Methods for Spoken Dialogue Simulation and Optimal Strategy Learning. In *Proceedings of Interspeech/Eurospeech 2005*, Lisbon, Portugal (2005)

Pietquin, O. (2006a) Consistent goal-directed user model for realistic man-machine task-oriented spoken dialogue simulation, in *Proceedings of the IEEE International Conference on Multimedia and Expo (ICME'06)*, Toronto, Canada, July 2006.

Pietquin, O. (2006b). Machine learning for spoken dialogue management : an experiment with speech-based database querying, in *Artificial Intelligence : Methodology, Systems and Applications*, J. Euzenat and J. Domingue, Eds., vol. 4183 of Lecture Notes in Artificial Intelligence, pp. 172–180. Springer Verlag, 2006.

Pietquin, O. & Dutoit, T. (2006a). A probabilistic framework for dialog simulation and optimal strategy learning, in *IEEE Transactions on Audio, Speech and Language Processing*, vol. 14, no. 2, pp. 589–599, March 2006.

Pietquin, O. and Dutoit, T. (2006b). Dynamic Bayesian networks for NLU simulation with applications to dialog optimal strategy learning, in *Proceedings of the IEEE International Conference on Acoustics, Speech and Signal Processing (ICASSP'06)*, May 2006.

Poupart, P.; Williams, J. & Young, S. (2006). Partially observable Markov decision processes with continuous observations for dialogue management, in *Proceedings of the SigDial Workshop (SigDial'06)*, 2006.

Rabiner, L. & Juang, B.H. (1993). *Fundamentals of Speech Recognition*, Prentice Hall, Signal Processing Series, 1993.

Reiter, E. & Dale, R. (2000) *Building Natural Language Generation Systems*, Cambridge University Press, Cambridge, 2000.

Rieser, V. and Lemon, O. (2006) Cluster-based user simulations for learning dialogue strategies and the super evaluation metric, in *Proceedings of Interspeech/ICSLP*, 2006.

Schatzmann, J.; Georgila, K. and Young, S. (2005) Quantitative evaluation of user simulation techniques for spoken dialogue systems, in *Proceedings of the SIGdial'05 Workshop*, September 2005.

Schatzmann, J.; Weilhammer, K.; Stuttle, M. and Young, S. (2007a) A survey of statistical user simulation techniques for reinforcement-learning of dialogue management strategies, in *Knowledge Engineering Review* 21(2): 97-126, 2007.

Schatzmann, J.; Thomson, B. and Young., S. (2007b). Statistical User Simulation with a Hidden Agenda. In *Proceedings of the 8th SigDIAL Workshop*, Antwerp, 2007.

Scheffler, K. & Young, S. (2001). Corpus-based dialogue simulation for automatic strategy learning and evaluation, in *Proc. NAACL Workshop on Adaptation in Dialogue Systems*, 2001.

Singh, S.; Kearns, M.; Litman, D. & Walker, M. (1999), Reinforcement learning for spoken dialogue systems, in *Proceedings of NIPS'99*, 1999.

Young, S. (2006). Using POMDPs for dialog management, in *Proceedings of the 1st IEEE/ACL Workshop on Spoken Language Technologies (SLT'06)*, 2006.

Young, S.; Schatzmann, J.; Weilhammer, K. & Ye, H. (2007). The hidden information state approach to dialog management, in *Proceedings of the International Conference on Acoustics, Speech and Signal Processing (ICASSP'07)*, April 2007.

Walker, M.; Litman, D.; Kamm, C. & Abella, A. (1997). PARADISE: A Framework for Evaluating Spoken Dialogue Agents. in *Proceedings of the 35th Annual Meeting of the Association for Computational Linguistics*, Madrid, Spain (1997) 271-280.

Watkins, C. (1989). *Learning from delayed rewards*. PhD thesis, Psychology Department, Cambridge University, Cambridge, England, 1989.

Williams, J. & Young, S. (2005). Scaling up POMDPs for dialogue management: the summary POMDP method, in *Proceedings of the IEEE workshop on Automatic Speech Recognition and Understanding (ASRU'05)*, 2005.

Williams, J.; Poupart, P. and Young, S. (2005). Partially Observable Markov Decision Processes with Continuous Observations for Dialogue Management, in *Proceedings of the 6th SigDial Workshop*, Lisbon (Portugal), 2005.

14

Water Allocation Improvement in River Basin Using Adaptive Neural Fuzzy Reinforcement Learning Approach

Abolpour B.[1], Javan M.[2] and Karamouz M.[3]
[1] *Iranian Agricultural Engineering Research Institute, Shiraz,*
[2]*Department of Water Engineering, Shiraz University, Shiraz,*
[3]*Department of Environmental and Civil Eng., Amir-Kabir University, Tehran, Iran*

1. Introduction

Optimal use of water is an important objective of water resource development projects all over the world. An integrated approach toward better water resources management in river basins for irrigation planning is needed to find optimal water use policies. In the past, researchers used variables affecting crop pattern and reservoir releases as decision variables (Yeh, 1985). Labadie, 1993, found discrepancies in simulation and optimization models which are important factors in non-adaptive and weak system managements in river basins. These models become more complicated considering conflicting objectives, stochastic hydrology behavior, and uncertain consumptive water use. Labadie, 1993, presented a combined simulation-optimization strategy for river system management. In his studies, decision variable was reservoir release and objective function was maximization of power generation. However, the objective of his study was to assess directly the optimal water use.
The other group of studies is concerned with indirect optimization of water use by selecting the best strategies or alternatives in the river basin or even on the farms. Multi-objective methods have been widely used in different water resource projects. Bogardi & Nachtnebel, 1994, used multicriteria decision analysis in the study of water resources management. Other applications of this group can be found in the works of.Karamouz et al., 1992, and Owen et al., 1997.
The theory of fuzzy logic provides a mechanism to represent the degree of satisfaction of reservoir objective through the use of fuzzy membership function measures that can be combined in an integrated fashion. The fuzzy approach, alluding to the vagueness or imprecision inherent in problems of this type, has found increasing application in many fields. Fontane et al., 1997, applied reservoir operation based on Fuzzy Logic concept in order to deal with imprecise objectives for the reservoirs located in the monographic area on the Cache la Poudre river basin in the northern Colorado. Sasikumar and Mujumdar, 1998, developed a Fuzzy Waste-Load Allocation Model (FWLAM) for water quality management of a river system using fuzzy multiple objective optimization. Dubrovin et al., 2002, used a new methodology for fuzzy inference and compared it with a traditional (Sugeno style) method, for multipurpose real-time reservoir operation. In these researches, it is implicitly

assumed that current decisions are independent of future events and decisions beyond the planning horizon. Besides, stochastic nature of hydrologic parameters, imprecise water demand, uncertainty of relationship between variables in groundwater and surface water resources, can not be completely incorporated into membership functions (Tilmant et al., 2002, and Karamouz and Mousavi, 2003).

Molden and Gates, 1990, Gates and Ahmed, 1995, developed an approach for assessing the alternative strategies for improving irrigation water delivery system in the context of multiple planning criteria. Alternatives that involve structural, managerial and policy changes have also been discussed. The model takes into account the parameter of uncertainty on both supply and demand sides of the system resulting from temporal and spatial variability and inadequate data. The objective of adequacy, efficiency, dependability and equity of water delivery were used to evaluate system performance under each alternative considered. Techniques of Multicriterion Decision Making (MCDM) were also presented. The part of historical data is created by the decisions of experts, users (farmers), designers, and managers and is defined as "Human effects" (Belaineh et al, 2003). In these researches, the effects are not completely incorporated into membership functions and the results of this method are in conflict by application of this approach. This approach has also problems in defining objectives, constraining functions or implementing models.

Increasing demands for agricultural products with limited water resources lead to water allocation and management problems. In addition, the conflicting objectives of individual monetary benefits and social benefits make the problems rather more complex. For efficient and scientific solutions of these problems, groundwater is also to be optimally extracted and combined with surface water to meet the requirements. On the other hand, uncertainty, vagueness and random factors make water allocation problems more complex in the form of unexpected droughts and floods, uncertainty in conjunctive use of surface and ground water, vagueness in water use efficiency and variation of inflows from month to month. As control problems become more complex in these applications, the use of traditional control techniques requiring mathematical models of the plant becomes more difficult to apply. Intelligent controllers have several important advantages, such as shorter development time, and less assumption about the dynamical behavior of the plant, that makes them attractive for application to these problems. Fuzzy set theory provides a mathematical framework for modeling vagueness and imprecision. Neural networks have the ability to learn complex mappings, generalize information, and classify inputs. Hybrid controllers utilize the advantages of each, as well as other novel techniques, creating a powerful tool for intelligent control (Sasaki and Gen, 2003).

The methodology that can be used in selecting the optimum decision of water allocation for each sub-basin from the previous decisions (historical data) is the basic modeling approach in this study. This method includes two steps: the first step is to prepare the simulation models of water use, and the second step is development of the optimization models of water allocation for each sub-basin. Usually, these steps are separated in the literature. In this study, models of each step are not only obtained based on compatible methodologies, but the results of each optimization model are also obtained based on the optimal values of input predictor variables which are selected from the results of simulation models over historical data. Therefore, the output values of the simulation models remain constant. In other words, the simulation models learn to minimize the error between the output and real values (observed values) by using Adaptive Neural Fuzzy Inference System (ANFIS) method. The optimization models are reinforcement learning that seeks to maximize the values of the input predictor variables subject to the fixed output values of simulation models.

For all sub-basins, river outflow was the sole prediction variable for the all simulation models. ANFIS method used different sets of input predictor variables for each sub-basin as dictated by the hydrologic factors. For example, if groundwater extraction occurred, this variable was also used as an input predictor variable, as well as decision variable.

The abilities and advantages of presented method can be explained as: 1) The direct effects of uncertain, vague and random factors over water resources system, water demand estimated and hydrological regime can be incorporated into membership function that are considered in developing the simulation and optimization models. 2) The Human effects are incorporated into membership functions, and the results of this approach will not be conflicted in the future conditions. Therefore, these effects can be quantified by using the reliabilities of previous and optimum conditions of the decision variables in this study. 3) This method does not have problems like MCDM or Economical methods in defining objectives, constraining functions or implementing models.

2. Methods

2.1 Adaptive neural fuzzy inference system

An adaptive network is a network structure consisting of a number of nodes connected through direct links. Each node represents a process unit, and the links between nodes specify the causal relationship between the connected nodes. All or parts of the nodes are adaptive, which means the outputs of theses nodes depend on modifiable parameters pertaining to these nodes. The learning rule specifies how these parameters should be updated to minimize a prescribed error measure, which is a mathematical expression that measures the discrepancy between the network's actual output and a desired output (Papadrakakis and Lagaros, 2003). Neuro-fuzzy systems are multi-layer feed forward adaptive networks that realize the basic elements and functions of traditional fuzzy logic systems (Oh et al., 2002). Since it has been shown that fuzzy logic systems are universal approximators, neuro-fuzzy control systems, which are isomorphic to traditional fuzzy logic control systems in terms of their functions, are also universal approximators. Adaptive Neural Fuzzy Inference System (ANFIS), developed by Jang et al., 1997, is an extension of the Takagi, Sugeno, and Kang (TSK) fuzzy model (Li et al., 2001). The TSK fuzzy model was known as the first fuzzy model that was developed to generate fuzzy rules from a given input-output data set. This model allows the fuzzy systems to learn the parameters using adaptive backpropagation learning algorithm. In general, ANFIS is much more complicated than fuzzy inference systems (Li et al., 2001). A fuzzy inference system (FIS) can be considered to be a parameterized nonlinear map or a crisp function in a consequence called f , namely:

$$f(x) = \frac{\sum_{l=1}^{m} y^l \left(\prod_{i=1}^{n} \mu_{A_i^l}(x_i)\right)}{\sum_{l=1}^{m} \left(\prod_{i=1}^{n} \mu_{A_i^l}(x_i)\right)} \tag{1}$$

Where y_l is a part of output if Mamdani reasoning is applied or a constant if Sugeno reasoning is applied (Jang et al., 1997). The membership function $\mu_{A_i^l}(x_i)$ corresponds to the input $x = [x_1,\ldots,x_n]$ of the rule l and m is the number of fuzzy rules. For the ith input predictor variable, x_i is the real data (for example- the measured values of inflow and storage volume) in one point from the set of observed values. The output values, $f(x)$ are the estimated values (for example- the estimated value of release) of simulation function within the range of input set. The center of gravity method is used for defuzzification. This can be further written as:

$$f(x)=\sum_{l=1}^{m} w_l\, b_l(x) \tag{2}$$

Where $w_l=y^l$ and

$$b_l(x)=\frac{\prod_{i=1}^{n}\mu_{A_i^l}(x_i)}{\sum_{l=1}^{m}\left(\prod_{i=1}^{n}\mu_{A_i^l}(x_i)\right)} \tag{3}$$

If F_S is a set of continuous estimated value functions on domain D, then f can approximate F_S to any desired accuracy. Let F_S be a bounded function on $[a,b]$ and $D=\{x^1,\ldots,x^h\}$ a set of points in $[a,b]$. Then there exists the Least Squares Polynomial of degree $\leq$ r between F_S and Q^h, which minimizes the following expression:

$$\sum_{j=1}^{h}\left|F_S(x^j)-Q(x^j)\right|^2 \tag{4}$$

Overall polynomial's degree is equal to or less than r. Where Q^h is real data of output values over h^{th} point of input set (For each input predictor variable $i=1,2,\ldots,n$ and for each point of real world data $j=1,2,\ldots,h$).

Simulation model. In the Mamdani type of fuzzy system, the real data of the output values can be classified into classes such that the length of each class is equal to $[a,b]$. But in the Sugeno type, the length of $[a,b]$ is only determined over input data set (D), and f can be approximately equal to F_S; hence, F_S is the output values of simulation model. Consider a Sugeno type of fuzzy system, the following rule base is developed:

1. If x_1 is A_1^1 and x_2 is A_2^1, … , and x_n is A_n^1, Then $f_1= p_0^1 + p_1^1 x_1 + p_2^1 x_2 + \ldots + p_n^1 x_n$.
2. If x_1 is A_1^2 and x_2 is A_2^2, … , and x_n is A_n^2, Then $f_2= p_0^2 + p_1^2 x_1 + p_2^2 x_2 +\ldots + p_n^2 x_n$.

⋮ ⋮ ⋮

m. If x_1 is A_1^m and x_2 is A_2^m, … , and x_n is A_n^m, Then $f_m= p_0^m + p_1^m x_1 + p_2^m x_2 + \ldots + p_n^m x_n$.

If the membership function of fuzzy sets (*i=1,2,…,m, l=1,2,…,n*) is μ_i^l , *m* is the number of rules and *n* is the number of variables. In the water resources system, μ_i^l can be the numeral value of membership function of input predictor variable such as agricultural water demand. Also, A_i^l is the real world data where the agricultural water demand is one of the input predictor variables. Using product for *T-norm* or logical and, evaluation of the rules can be written as (Jang et al., 1997):

1. Evaluating the rule premises results in

$$w_l = \mu_{A_1^l}(x_1)\cdot\mu_{A_2^l}(x_2)\cdot\ldots\cdot\mu_{A_n^l}(x_n) \tag{5}$$

2. Evaluating the implication and the rule consequences gives

$$f(x_1,x_2,\ldots,x_n)=\frac{w_l(x_1,x_2,\ldots,x_n)f_l(x_1,x_2,\ldots,x_n)+\ldots+w_m(x_1,x_2,\ldots,x_n)f_m(x_1,x_2,\ldots,x_n)}{w_l(x_1,x_2,\ldots,x_n)+w_2(x_1,x_2,\ldots,x_n)+\ldots.+w_m(x_1,x_2,\ldots,x_n)} \tag{6}$$

This can be separated to phases by defining

$$\overline{w}_l = \frac{w_l}{w_l + w_2 + \ldots.. + w_m} \tag{7}$$

Then,

$$f(x_1,x_2,\ldots,x_n)=\overline{w}_l(x_1,x_2,\ldots,x_n)f_l(x_1,x_2,\ldots,x_n)+\ldots+\overline{w}_m(x_1,x_2,\ldots,x_n)f_m(x_1,x_2,\ldots,x_n) \tag{8}$$

$$F_S \cong f(x_1,x_2,\ldots,x_n)=\sum_{l=1}^{m}\overline{w}_l(x_1,x_2,\ldots,x_n)f_l(x_1,x_2,\ldots,x_n) \tag{9}$$

w_l is the connection weights and is updated only after presentation of the entire data set. This process is called "Learning", (Jang et al., 1997).

2.2 Adaptive neural fuzzy reinforcement learning

On the traditional optimization models of reservoir operation and river basin systems, net benefit has been maximized or costs have been minimized. Applications can be found in the work of Jacobs and Vogel, 1998, and Malek, 1998. Most of the operation models are not consistent in dealing with the objectives of the group of farmers, designers, and decision makers with conflicting points of views. Multiobjective uses of water, different strategies and natural factors have added complexity to these models. The natural factors can be included by considering drought or spring periods. Because of these factors, in recent years, efforts are devoted to the development of objective functions and optimization methods of water use on large river basins. Main objectives in this research include distributed water, excess water in the sub-basins, and allocated water in downstream sub-basins.

Reinforcement Learning (RL) is one of the major approaches to solve Markov decision problems with unknown transition probabilities. RL, one of the most studied reinforcement learning algorithms, maintains estimates of the average reward ρ and of the relative value function $R(s,x)$ of choosing decision x in state s, from which an optimal strategy can be derived (Jouffe, 1998). It is assumed that the reinforcement learning agent obtains inputs from a continuous state space S of dimension N^S and may perform actions taken from a continuous action space X of dimension N^X. The sets of dimensions of the state space and the action space will be denoted as $D^S := \{1,..,N^S\}$ and $D^X := \{1,...,N^X\}$, respectively. Considering, for each state $s \in S$ and each action $x \in X$, $\tilde{h}(t|s,x)$, there is a probability density function giving the distribution of the successor state t if action x is executed in state s. Furthermore, let $\tilde{f}(s,x,t) \in R$ be the (unknown) reward the agent gets for executing action x in state s if the action causes a transition to state t. The agent is supposed to select actions at discrete points in time.

The goal of the learning task then is to find a stationary policy $\mu : S \rightarrow X$,i.e. a mapping from states to actions, such that the expected sum of future rewards

$$\tilde{J}^{\mu}(s) := \underset{N \to \infty}{Lim} E\left\{ \sum_{k=0}^{N} w^k \tilde{f}(s_k, \mu(s_k), s_{k+1}) | s_0 = s \right\} \quad , \quad w \in [0,1) \tag{10}$$

is maximized for each $s \in S$, where s_{K+1} is determined from s_K using $\tilde{h}(s_{K+1}|s_K, \mu(s_K))$.

Let

$$\tilde{Q}^{\mu}(s,x) := \int_{\in S} \tilde{h}(t;s,x)\left(\tilde{f}(s,x,t) + w\tilde{J}^{\mu}(t)\right)dt, \tag{11}$$

be the sum of discounted future rewards the agent may expect if it executes action x in state s and behaves according to the policy μ afterwards. Then, the optimal Q-values, $\tilde{Q}^{\mu^*}(s,x)$, are given by the fixed-point solution of the Bellman equation

$$\tilde{Q}^{\mu^*}(s,x) = \int_{\in S} \tilde{h}(s;x,t)\left(\tilde{f}(s,x,t) + w \max_{y \in X} \tilde{Q}^{\mu^*}(t,y) \right)dt, \tag{12}$$

and the optimal policy μ^* is to execute in each state s the action x that maximizes these Q-values (Apple and Brauer, 2000):

$$\mu^*(s) := arg \max_{x \in X} \tilde{Q}^{\mu^*}(s,x). \tag{13}$$

Optimization model. In this study, the optimal values of decision variables are obtained by combining Fuzzy Reinforcement Learning and Adaptive Neural Fuzzy Inference Systems (ANFIS). Simulation model is developed based on ANFIS method and input predictor variables (observed values) xi. Optimization model is developed based on two groups of variables. First group is known variables and their values can be obtained from the sets of input data (historical data). Second group is decision variables that have been unknown in the optimization process and will be estimated at the end of optimization process. Hence, fl for each rule is written as:

$$f_l(x_1, x_2, ..., x_n) = P_0^l + \sum_{i=1}^{m} P_i^l x_i = P_0^l + \sum_{i=1}^{k} P_i^l x_i + \sum_{i=k}^{n} P_i^l x_i \tag{14}$$

Where l=1,2,...,m is the number of rules, i=1,2,..,k is number of input predictor variables which m, n and k are the numbers of rules, decision variables, and known variables, respectively. p_i^l is the modifiable parameter for each rule and the input predictor variables that were obtained from ANFIS method. In the first step, it is assumed that w_l is constant, independent of $\mathbf{x_i}$ and can be estimated based on the known variables. Substituting Eq. 14 into Eq. 9 results in:

$$F_O = \sum_{l=1}^{m} \overline{w}_l \left[P_0^l + \sum_{i=1}^{k} P_i^l x_i + \sum_{i=k}^{n} P_i^l x_i \right] \tag{15}$$

Where F_O is the estimated values of objective function in optimization model. Defining $\boldsymbol{C_l}$ for independent values of decision variables for each rule, Eq.15 can be written as:

$$F_O = \sum_{l=1}^{m} \overline{w}_l P_0^l + \sum_{l=1}^{m} \sum_{i=1}^{k} \overline{w}_l P_i^l x_i + \sum_{l=1}^{m} \sum_{i=k}^{n} \overline{w}_l P_i^l x_i \tag{16}$$

$$F_O = C_l + \sum_{l=1}^{m} \sum_{i=k}^{n} \overline{w}_l P_i^l x_i \tag{17}$$

In this study, Gaussian membership function is used in the simulation and optimization process. It is written as (Harris, 2000, and Odhiambo et al., 2001):

$$\mu_{A_i^l}(x) = e^{-\frac{(x-\phi)^2}{2\sigma^2}} \tag{18}$$

Where $\mu_{A_i^l}(x)$ is the membership value for fuzzy set, x is the input predictor variables (for example- inflow and storage volume in the sub-basin No. 4), ϕ describes the 'center' of the membership function, and σ is the spread of the membership function. Also by using this equation the value of variable x can be obtained assuming that $\mu_{A_i^l}(x)$ is known.

$$x = \phi \pm \left(-2 \ln \mu_{A_i^l}(x)\right)^{0.5} \sigma \tag{19}$$

Equation 17 is the objective function and the value of F_O (for example- release from the dam) in Eq. 16 depends on the value of decision (for example- inflow) and known variables (for example- storage volume) x_i. If the goal with the membership function (μ_G) is to find maximum value of F_O based on the known variables and given modifiable parameters, then value of decision variables can be obtained based on maximizing the objective function. This process will be completely adjusted with Reinforcement Learning method (Eq. 12). But, in this study, it is assumed that value of F_S is fixed and can be given by the sets of input data (historical data) or it can be the set of decision-makers (in the future). In other words, the goal is to estimate the best values of decision variables that have been obtained from given value of F_S. Therefore, the optimal value of decision variables must be found based on objective function and simulation model. The objective function and constraints can be written as:

$$\text{Max } F_O \tag{20}$$

Subject to:

$$x_i \leq \phi_i^l \pm \left(-2 \ln \mu_{A_i^l}\right)^{0.5} \sigma_i^l \tag{21}$$

$$C_l + \sum_{l=1}^{m} \sum_{i=k}^{n} \overline{w}_l P_i^l x_i \leq F_S \tag{22}$$

Equation 22 is developed by fuzzy rule base system that can be derived by ANFIS method using historical observation data (the sets of input data in simulation process). Equation 22 can be used for control value of F_S, and will be divided into rule base number $\boldsymbol{l}$ and input predictor variables number $\boldsymbol{i}$.

In the first step, it is assumed that w_l is constant and independent of $\boldsymbol{x_i}$, but these connection weights (w_l) are not constant and depend on x_i, as can be seen in Equations 5 and 7. Therefore, using trial and error methods, these parameters are found in the presented method using fuzzy linear programming with crisp objective function developed by Zimmermann, 1996, for solving equations 20 to 22. An algorithm was developed based on combining ANFIS method and fuzzy linear programming. The state variables are the values of membership function for each decision variable ($\mu_{A_i^l}(x_i)$). In this study, this algorithm and solution process is called "ANFRL" method, and equations 20 to 22 are the basic modeling approach in this method. The optimal values of these variables can be found by the solution process, subject to minimizing the error of the estimated value of membership function for each decision variable, which is computed by simulation and optimization phases. The parameters of membership function (σ and ϕ) are the constraints in the optimization process. Figure 1 shows the algorithm of solution process, which is presented in Appendix I.

Quantifiable parameter for method results justification. Reliability is defined as the probability that a state of the system z_r is in satisfactory state Z (Hashimoto et al., 1982).

$$\gamma = h(z_r \in Z) \tag{23}$$

In this paper, there are two satisfactory states. First, in each month, the water resources discharge is equal to water demand in downstream sub-basin. The water resources discharge includes the release from dam or the excess water of upstream sub-basin, groundwater pumping and drainage water reused in the downstream sub-basin. Second, in each month, the residual storage volume is equal or greater than inflow. The two satisfactory states were chosen so as to reflect concerns on how the system will satisfy the two major purposes such as water supply and flood control. Hence, the reliability of the first satisfactory state for the primary water resources management is obtained based on water resources discharge toward water demand. The reliability of the second satisfactory state is obtained based on the residual storage volume toward inflow. The reliability for the results of each optimization model is computed too.

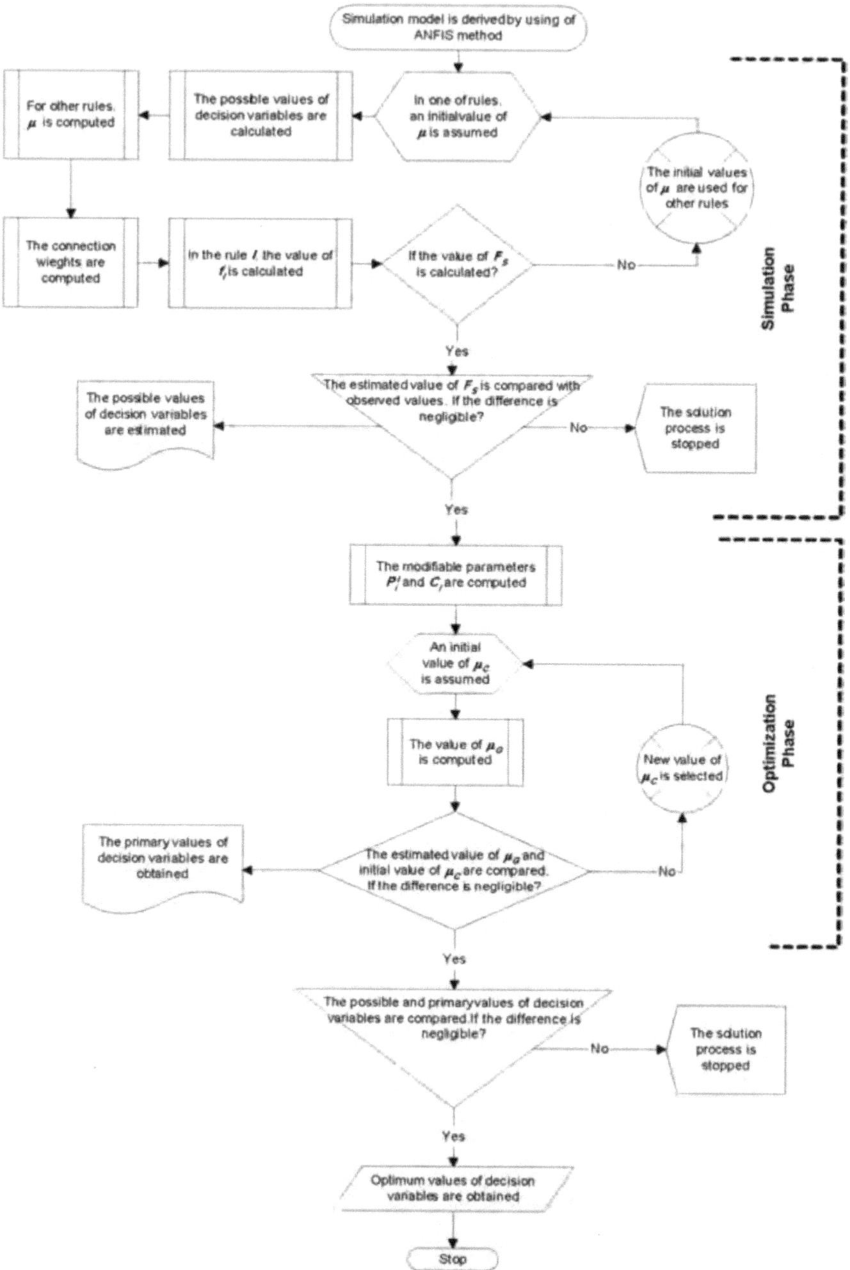

Fig. 1. The algorithm of the solution process (ANFRL method) based on combined ANFIS and fuzzy linear programming.

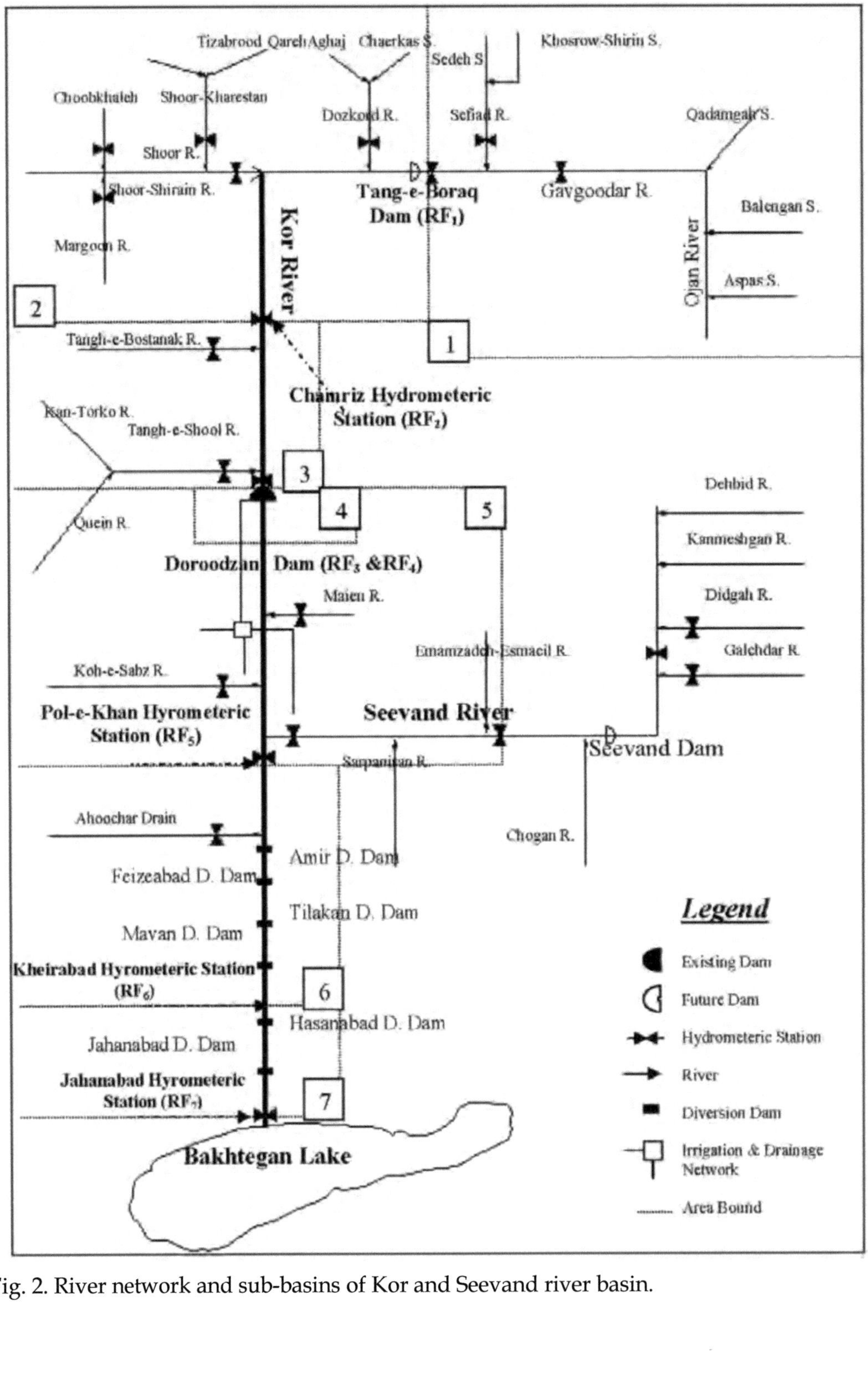

Fig. 2. River network and sub-basins of Kor and Seevand river basin.

3. Case study: the Kor and Seevand river basin

General features. The Kor and Seevand river basin is located in the northern part of Fars province in Iran and lies between 51o, 45′ to 54o, 30′ eastern latitude and 29o, 01′ to 31o, 15′ northern longitude. Total river basin area is 31511 km2 with 16630 km2 of mountains and 14881 km2 of plains and lakes. Kor river with two branches called Kor and Seevand are the artery of this river basin. These two branches join in Marvdasht area and form the main Kor River. The downstream reach flows into Bakhtegan Lake and is called Korbal river. River network of Kor and Seevand basin is shown in Fig. 2. Doroodzan Dam with 993 million cubic meters of capacity is located on Kor river. This dam supplies irrigation demands of Ramjerd and Marvdasht plains, domestic water for Shiraz City, and hydropower generation.

Sub-basins characteristics. In this study, the river basin is divided into seven sub-basins. Six diversion dams are built on Korbal reach. Some of these ancient diversion dams like Feizeabad and Amir are currently under rehabilitation program and play an important role in the distribution of irrigation water system. In the future, there will be two more storage dams. One will be located near Tang-e-Boraq hydrometeric station on the Kor river (Mollasadra Dam), and the other will be located near Ghaderabad hydrometeric station on Seevand river (Seiboyeh Dam).

Sub-basin No. 4 is Doroodzan Lake that is the only available reservoir in Kor and Seevand river basin. This sub-basin is considered as a single basin because there is a balance between inflow, release, and volume of reservoir that can be evaluated well for periods during which observed data are available. Sub-basin No.5 is located between Doroodzan Dam and Pol-e-Khan hydrometeric station, the irrigation and drainage network lie in this area, too. In this sub-basin, there are different water resources such that it is a complete water resource system. The amount of water required in this sub-basin is used for agricultural, domestic, industrial, and hydropower uses. Release from Doroodzan Dam supplies such demands in two downstream sub-basins (No. 6 and No. 7). These water demands have not been included in the water demands of sub-basin No. 5 (DEM_5). These demands would be input predictor variables in the developing simulation models and known variables in the optimization analysis of sub-basins No. 5 and No. 6.

Simulation data characteristics. Simulation of a large-scale river basin can often be very difficult considering different factors affecting the hydrologic characteristics of the basin. This is mainly due to the fact that water use and water resource systems characteristics can significantly vary in different parts of the basin. Therefore, the simulation methods of water resources are used on small-scale basin (sub-basin). The simulation models developed for this river basin are capable of simulating each sub-basin, separately. The basic modeling approach is included in seven simulation models for each sub-basin so that this river basin could be simulated by combination of these models. For all sub-basins, the monthly values of river flows at each of the downstream hydrometer station are estimated by using the simulation models that were developed from the ANFIS method. Hence, seven models are obtained in the step of developing simulation models. Observed monthly values were used to develop the simulation models from October 1975 to September 2001 that were the sets of input data (real world data). The accuracy of the results of each simulation model with the real world data is evaluated in another step that is called " verification modeling". Each simulation model is verified by using observed value of years 1982-83, 1995-96, and 1999-2000 (36 months). These three years were selected based on normal, dry, and spring periods.

Since Doroodzan Dam became operational on October 1975, this date was selected as the starting date for all of the analysis in this study. Some observed or measured values were incorrect; therefore, these input data were omitted from the analysis. Table 1 shows the simulation results in Kor and Seevand river basins obtained from ANFIS methods.

Sub- Basin No.	**1**	**2**	**3**	**4**	**5**	**6**	**7**
Name	Aspas	Tang-e-Boraq	Kamfirooz	Doroodzan	Doroodzan	Korbal up	Korbal Down
Simulated Data (Month)	295	269	246	246	271	120	96
Verified Data (Month)	36	36	36	36	36	0	0
Input predictor Variables	SW_1 DEM_1 GW_1	SW_2 RF_1	SW_3 DEM_3 RF_2	RF_3 VOL	SW_5 DEM_5 RF_3 VOL RF_4 GW_5 DW_5	DEM_6 RF_5 GW_6 DW_6	DEM_7 RF_6
River Flow at H.S.* (Output values)	RF_1	RF_2	RF_3	RF_4	RF_5	RF_6	RF_7
RMSE**	9.85	12.44	23.19	29.08	10.85	10.81	14.00
R^2	0.78	0.94	0.9	0.71	0.88	0.86	0.89
Slope***	1.03	0.98	0.95	0.89	0.995	0.98	0.95
Fuzzy Rules	5	4	7	8	7	6	6

Table 1. Properties and ANFIS method based simulation results in the Kor and Seevand river basin. (*Hydrometeric Station; **Root Mean Square Error; *** Slope of Regression Line).

3.1 Developing simulation models

Cross validation. In order to attain statistically significant results, a 10-fold cross validation was carried out in the sub-basin No. 5 such that ten different splitting of the data set could be considered. The data set had 271 monthly data of input predictor variables that ninety percent of the set is the training set and 10% of the set is the test set for each fold. The process of the developing simulation model was repeated ten times, for each fold, with different rules number and variform membership functions. The six, seven and eight rules respectively with the one of membership function shapes like Gaussian, Bell and Pi Shaped were assumed for each time. The Gaussian Combination Shaped for membership function with seven rules was also assumed in the 10th time. For all folds, the prediction ability of each model was evaluated both on the training set and the test set in terms of Root Mean Squared Error (RMSE). For example in the 5th fold, assuming Gaussian membership function for each input predictor variables and 6, 7 and 8 rules, RMSE for training set equal 17.68, 10.81 and 14.86 for 17680, 22800 and 31386 Epoch, respectively.

Fold	1	2	3	4	5	6	7	8	9	10	Mean
Error on Training Set	10.83	10.14	11.53	10.17	11.03	11.58	10.20	11.42	11.64	11.07	10.96
Error on Test Set	29.83	27.50	10.02	20.64	13.67	10.01	24.58	11.56	13.58	13.98	17.54

Table 2 . RMSE of the 10th simulation model identified from each fold.

Results of such experiments can be summarized in a table, in which 10 rows are identified as errors of 10 simulation models for each fold and the 10 columns are identified errors on the 10 fold for each simulation model. The average of RMSE in each row is reported, as an estimate of the prediction capability of each simulation model. For example, the RMSE of the 10th simulation model is identified for each fold and is shown in Table 2. The averages of RMSE equal 10.96 and 17.54 for training and test data in this simulation model. There is not a statistically significant difference between the means or distributions of error on the training and test data at the 99.0 % confidence level. For all simulation models (in each row), these means or distributions have not statistically significant differences either. However, at this confidence level in each fold there is a statistically significant difference between the means of error on the training and test data of each simulation model (in each column). On the other hand, the process of developing simulation model is independent of splitting the data set, and is dependent on rules number and membership function shape. Therefore, Gaussian membership function with seven rules is the best setting of simulation model and has the minimum error on training and test data. Note that 10-fold cross validation is only considered in the sub-basin No. 5, and results, which have been presented in Table 1, are the simulation results in Kor and Seevand river basin for the entire text of this paper.

Sub-basins simulation models. For all sub-basins, the parameters of membership function (σ,ϕ) and the modifiable parameters (p_i^l) in the Sugeno type of fuzzy system for each model are obtained by using water resources factors (input data) that are only shown in Table 3 for the sub-basin No. 5. For example in sub-basin No. 7, the excess water of sub-basin No. 6 (RF_6) and agricultural water demand (DEM_7) in this sub-basin are the input predictor variables for estimating the river flow at Jahanabad hydrometeric station (RF_7). The unit of these variables is million cubic meters per month (MCMM) for all sub-basins. The river flow can be estimated by using these parameters as follows, that is one of the ANFIS models in this study:

Rule	Parameter	Constant	RF_3 MCMM	RF_4 MCMM	SW_5 MCMM	DEM_5 MCMM	GW_5 MCMM	DW_5 MCMM	VOL MC
1	P_i^1	-1272.08	-2.34	-1.06	-0.65	4.31	-55.00	12.01	1.70
2	P_i^2	6.75	-0.26	0.21	1.43	-0.04	0.68	1.38	-0.02
3	P_i^3	-143.20	-0.03	0.31	1.78	-0.31	-1.13	-0.61	0.17
4	P_i^4	31.80	0.12	0.27	2.65	0.13	-0.77	-0.18	-0.03
5	P_i^5	-30.04	0.52	0.83	1.08	-1.06	3.08	-1.13	-0.01
6	P_i^6	-135.80	0.49	0.58	-0.31	-5.03	26.20	4.04	0.39
7	P_i^7	-224.50	0.22	-0.04	-0.35	0.38	1.45	0.06	0.17
1	σ	-----	105.79	95.25	40.32	32.63	5.28	18.19	191.68
	ϕ	-----	50.93	38.51	0.00	0.00	0.00	36.12	624.00
2	σ	-----	115.37	114.93	5.67	69.63	32.98	34.13	144.33
	ϕ	-----	30.89	99.00	9.83	112.77	19.07	12.66	708.61
3	σ	-----	117.22	110.57	25.91	42.03	4.91	38.28	140.79
	ϕ	-----	47.63	116.21	21.47	116.79	36.77	11.97	930.54
4	σ	-----	117.04	111.16	41.14	36.43	11.07	32.47	130.98
	ϕ	-----	26.51	110.80	5.51	92.79	34.22	3.34	472.35
5	σ	-----	94.15	122.23	28.32	20.37	21.05	47.40	150.73
	ϕ	-----	131.74	21.29	23.19	0.00	0.00	28.17	908.11
6	σ	-----	144.14	118.62	33.98	44.53	33.36	26.48	187.31
	ϕ	-----	78.37	6.32	12.96	9.49	0.00	16.92	369.40
7	σ	-----	117.20	112.53	39.35	39.22	6.75	35.31	139.34
	ϕ	-----	39.20	141.80	8.39	182.00	59.91	13.51	868.42

Table 3. The estimated values of the modifiable parameters (P_i^l) and the membership function parameters (ϕ and σ) obtained from ANFIS simulation method in the sub-basin No. 5. The unit of membership function parameters is million cubic meters per month (MCMM) and the modifiable parameters are linear coefficient.

Rule 1. If x_1 is RF_6 over the input set with σ=12.03, ϕ=45.7 (membership function parameters); and x_2 is DEM_7 over the input set with σ=0.7, ϕ=16.06; then f_1= -0.15 + 1.07RF_6 - 2.04DEM_7.

⋮ ⋮ ⋮

Rule 6. If x_1 is RF_6 over the input set with σ=11.76, ϕ=47.18; and x_2 is DEM_7 over the input set with σ=0.64, ϕ=10.87; then f_6= 122.98 + 1.06RF_6 – 12.95DEM_7.

The simulation of sub-basin No. 5 is achieved by using relationship between input predictor variables and river flow of Pol-e-Khan hydrometeric station or spilled water in this sub-basin (RF_5). Input predictor variables were demand (DEM_5), release (RF_4), inflow to the dam (RF_3), storage volume (VOL), groundwater pumping (GW_5), surface water (SW_5), and drainage water reused (DW_5). In the sub-basin No.4, release values (RF_4) are simulated using inflow (RF_3) and volume of stored water in the lake (VOL). The detailed overview and the type of input predictor variables for other sub-basins are listed in Table 1. Other simulation models can be rewritten similar to the presented approach in sub-basin No. 7. Abolpour, 2005, presented more detail of simulation models in the case study.

Sub- Basin No.	1	2	3	4			5					6					7
ANFRL Model No.	1	1	1	1	2	3	1	2	3	4	5	1	2	3	4	5	1
DEM_j	Kn.*	----	Kn.	----	----	----	Kn.	Kn.	Kn.	Kn.	Kn.	Kn.	Kn.	Kn.	Kn.	Kn.	Kn.
DW_j	----	----	----	----	----	----	Kn.	Kn.	De.	Kn.	De.	Kn.	Kn.	De.	Kn.	De.	----
GW_j	De.*	----	----	----	----	----	Kn.	De.	Kn.	De.	De.	Kn.	De.	Kn.	De.	De.	----
SW_j	Kn.	Kn.	Kn.	----	----	----	Kn.	Kn.	Kn.	Kn.	Kn.	----	----	----	----	----	----
RF_1	Kn.	De.	----	----	----	----	----	----	----	----	----	----	----	----	----	----	----
RF_2	----	Kn.	De.	----	----	----	----	----	----	----	----	----	----	----	----	----	----
RF_3	----	----	Kn.	De.	Kn.	De.	Kn.	Kn.	Kn.	Kn.	Kn.	----	----	----	----	----	----
RF_4	----	----	----	Kn.	Kn.	Kn.	De.	Kn.	Kn.	De.	De.	----	----	----	----	----	----
RF_5	----	----	----	----	----	----	Kn.	Kn.	Kn.	Kn.	Kn.	De.	Kn.	Kn.	De.	De.	----
RF_6	----	----	----	----	----	----	----	----	----	----	----	Kn.	Kn.	Kn.	Kn.	Kn.	De.
RF_7	----	----	----	----	----	----	----	----	----	----	----	----	----	----	----	----	Kn.
VOL	----	----	----	Kn.	De.	De.	Kn.	Kn.	Kn.	Kn.	Kn.	----	----	----	----	----	----
Length of real world data (Month)	295	269	246	246	246	246	271	271	271	271	271	120	120	120	120	120	96
Length of total data (Month)	300**	324	273	288	288	288	288	288	288	288	288	300	300	300	300	300	300
Number of optimum values	106	223	151	160	182	121	160	204	165	153	164	148	115	183	132	174	171

Table 4. Known and decision variables in each optimization scenario for all sub-basins, and optimization results in the Kor and Seevand river basin. (*Known and decision variable, and j is sub-basin index.; ** Including real world data , for example 295 months of observed data, and predicted values, for example 5 months of simulated data by using ANFIS method).

Membership function properties. A property of ANFIS method is the development of membership functions for each input predictor variable (Jang et al., 1997). These membership functions can be used for the evaluation of input predictor variables. For example, in the downstream of Doroodzan dam (sub-basin No. 5), membership functions are developed for each input predictor variables. In this sub-basin, for each of seven input predictor variables, seven membership functions are obtained. Because the values of the input and output variables are vague or uncertain over time and / or space, they are classified into classes (e.g. low, mean, very high, etc.) for seven different climate season (e.g. Drought - Spring) using fuzzy membership functions. Based on 10-fold cross validation in the ANFIS process, the historical data follows the seven formulated fuzzy rules. Each rule pertains to a single climate season, adaptively adjusting the midpoints and ranges of the membership functions so as to minimize the prediction error. By using these fuzzy membership functions, the water resources management policies could be evaluated in the real time operation of the system and the results can be compared with the historical records of water supply in the study area (Abolpour , 2005, Abolpour & Javan, 2007).

3.2 Using optimization methods for different scenarios

The ANFRL method is used to develop optimization models for each sub-basin that has obtained the optimum values of decision variables. These models are conducted with simulation models developed by using ANFIS method. The membership function parameters (σ,ϕ) and the modifiable parameters (P_i^l) in optimization models are the same values of the simulation models. But, the input predictor variables for each simulation models are divided into the known and unknown variables where unknown variables are the decision variables in the optimization models. Also, the output values in simulation models are one of the known variables in the optimization models. In some of sub basins, the ANFRL method may develop several optimization models for each scenario so that they are only conducted with one of the simulation models. Therefore, the total number of optimization models is 17 in this study and their properties are presented in Table 4.

In each sub-basin, the optimization models find the optimum values of decision variables for the period of past 25 years. The values of known variables are obtained from the sets of input data (real world data) that have been used in the process of developing simulation models. If the values of known variables that are output values (river flow) in simulation models do not exist in the sets of input data, then the predicted values of these variables are used in the optimization models. The predicted values are estimated by using the results of simulation models. In this manner, the optimization models can be completely implemented in each month of the period. For all sub-basins, known and decision variables in each optimization scenario are presented in Table 4. The length of real world data is the number of input data (historical data) that are used to develop simulation models. The length of total data includes the length of real world data and predicted values, which are estimated by using ANFIS method. The number of optimum values is the results of optimization models that yield the optimal values by using the ANFRL method. The lengths of real world data, total data, and the number of optimum values are shown in Table 4, too.

As an introduction to the problem, we will consider representative sub-basin No. 4, which has a surface water reservoir. For this portion of the river basin, we must balance reservoir inflows (RF_3), outflows (release from dam - RF_4), and storage volumes (VOL). The ANFIS method uses the formulated fuzzy rule system to predict the single output variable, outflow, in response to the two input predictor variables, reservoir inflow and storage volume. A different set of decision variables is used for three different optimization scenarios, and they are 1) inflow into dam; 2) reservoir storage volume; 3) both inflow and storage volume. In the optimization model of scenario No. 1, the inflow value is one of the input data and the release value (downstream of this sub-basin) is the output value in the simulation process. In the optimization process, the inflow value is decision variable and the optimal value of this variable must be found subject to a fixed release value.

Because the release values are fixed in the modeling of the optimization process, this variable is defined as "known" variable. The values of storage volume (input data) are used to develop the simulation model; hence, the specified value of this variable is required in using the optimization model of scenario No. 1. Therefore, the sets of input data (observed values) are used to find the given values of release and storage volume, and these variables are defined as "known" variables (Table 4). The values of inflows that are used as decision variables in the process of optimization modeling are called "unknown" variables (Table 4). The state variable is the value of membership function for each decision variable and is obtained from ANFIS method from simulation process over monthly management periods (Table 3). Therefore, in this sub-basin, three optimization models are used and the results of optimization model No. 1 and 2 are shown in Fig. 3.

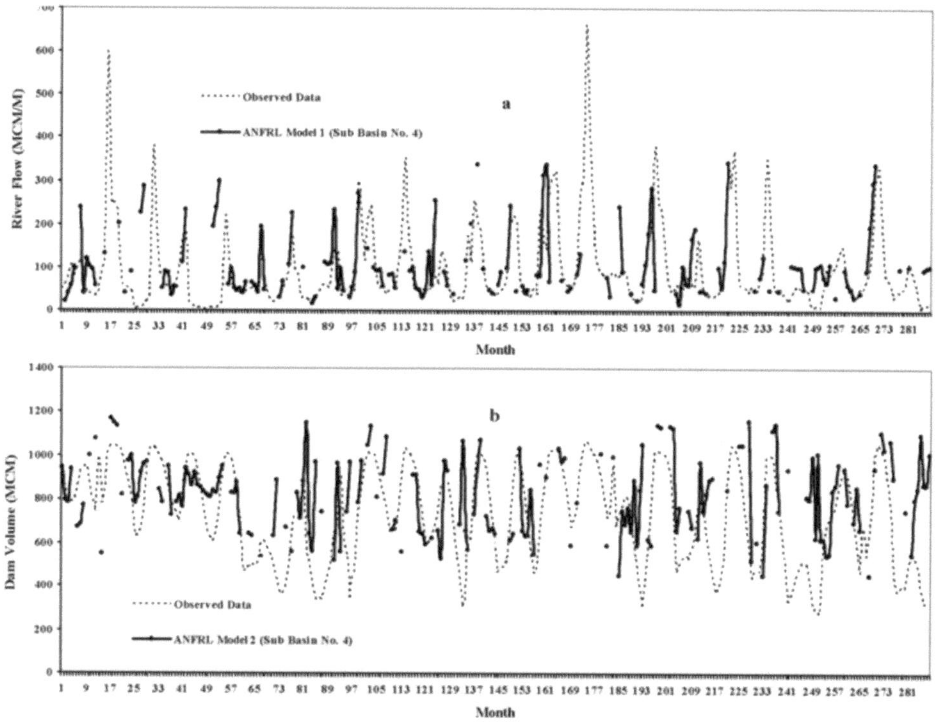

Fig. 3. Results of optimization models in sub-basin No. 4. Optimal and observed data of inflow (a-RF_3) and storage volume (b-VOL) in Doroodzan Dam.

Optimization models in sub-basin No.5 are developed under five scenarios. In all models, objective functions are defined so that they optimize river flows at Pol-e-Khan hydrometeric station (RF_5), using ANFRL method. Optimization model No.1 is developed for condition in which release of dam (RF_4) is the decision variable. In this model, surface water (SW_5), water demand (DEM_5), inflow (RF_3), storage volume (VOL), groundwater pumping (GW_5) and drainage water reused (DW_5), are the known variables. Properties of other optimization models are presented in Table 4. All areas in this sub-basin have been under cultivation during the past 25 years and no new development plans are available for this area. There have been a considerable number of dry and spring periods with different severity during the past 25 years. Therefore, the results of optimization models can definitely be used for future conditions. The results of optimization model No. 1, 2 and 3 are shown in Fig. 4. For the other sub-basins, the characteristics of optimization models are presented in Table 4, but the optimum values of decision variables are not shown.

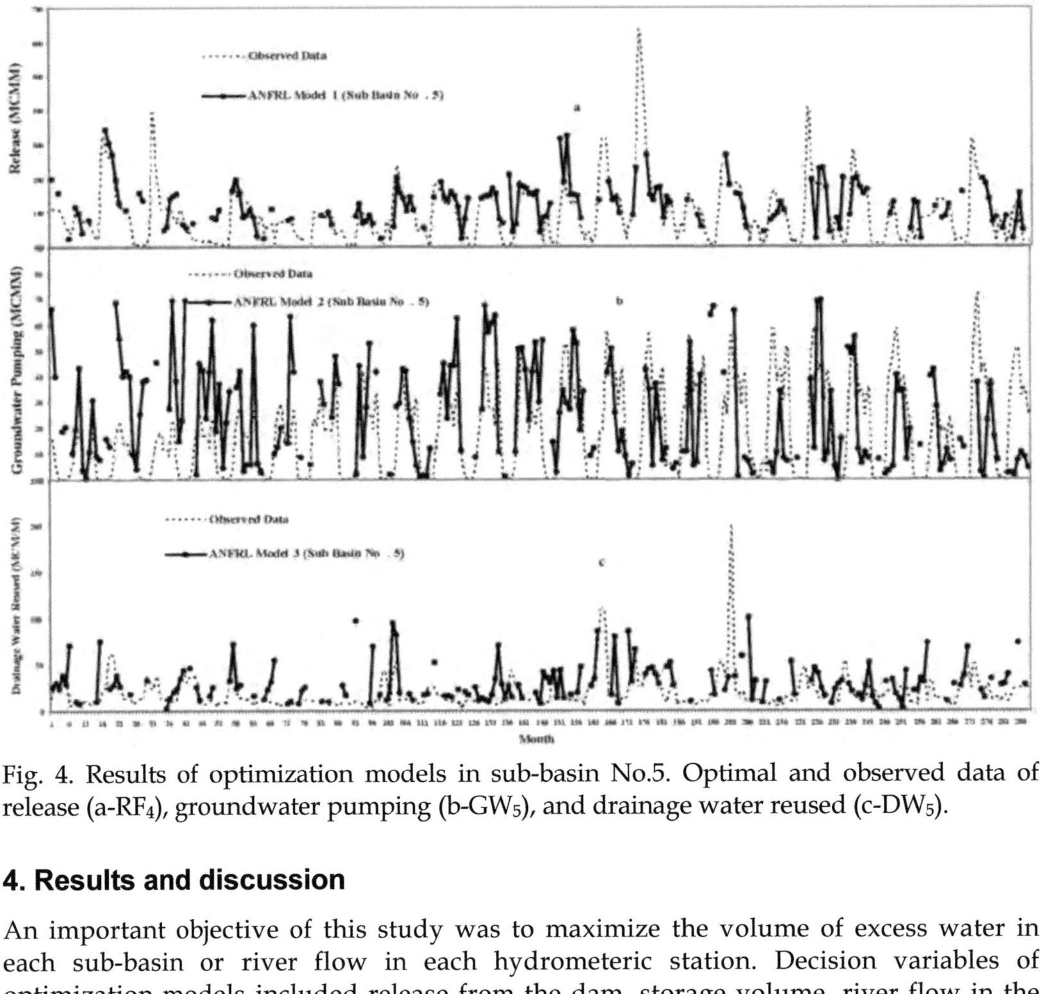

Fig. 4. Results of optimization models in sub-basin No.5. Optimal and observed data of release (a-RF_4), groundwater pumping (b-GW_5), and drainage water reused (c-DW_5).

4. Results and discussion

An important objective of this study was to maximize the volume of excess water in each sub-basin or river flow in each hydrometeric station. Decision variables of optimization models included release from the dam, storage volume, river flow in the upstream sub-basin, and groundwater pumping or drainage water reused. Results of these models are presented in Table 4. In some months, optimum values of decision variables could not be found. Optimum values of decision variables were found from the algorithm presented in Fig. 1. This process consists of two phases. In the simulation phase, the possible values of decision variables are determined from simulation models of the ANFIS method. If the possible values for decision variables could be found from simulation model, these values would be compared with the primary values obtained from optimization phases. If simulation model had a better correlation with real world data, the possible values of variables could be obtained for more months. If the values of known variables were out of range for the physical conditions of sub-basin, then optimization phase would not yield reasonable values for decision variables. Therefore, as it can be seen in Figures 3 and 4, the results of the optimization model are only presented for the month in which the model yields the optimum value.

For all sub-basins, the ANFRL based numerical results are the optimal values of decision variables such as excess water, release from dam, groundwater pumping and drainage water reused. The justification of applying these values instead of primary water resources management should be considered by using a quantifiable parameter. Hence, the reliabilities of previous and optimum conditions of the decision variables are obtained based on the observed data and the results of optimization models (Eq. 23). In the sub-basin No. 4, the storage volume used in computing flood control reliability for observed data and the optimal value, is the decision variables in the upstream Doroodzan Dam. In sub-basin No. 5, the release from dam, groundwater pumping and drainage water reused are the decision variables, used in computing water supply reliability for observed data and the optimal value. The reliabilities of previous and optimum conditions for each month are shown in Table 5.

In sub-basin No.5, the annual water supply reliability equals 0.42 based on the observed data of release form dam, groundwater pumping and drainage water reused in the past 25 years. Also, the variation range of monthly reliability is 0.19 to 0.75 (Table 5). The decision variable is the release from dam, groundwater pumping and drainage water reused in scenarios No. 1, 2 and 3, respectively. The annual reliability equals 0.44, 0.45 and 0.40 based on the results of scenarios No. 1, 2 and 3, respectively. In scenario No. 4 (Model-4), the decision variables are release from dam and groundwater pumping. The annual reliability equals 0.47 based on the results of this scenario. The release from dam, groundwater pumping and drainage water reused are the decision variables in scenario No. 5. The water supply reliability, which is based on this scenario result equals 0.5 for each year. Therefore, the optimization model results obtained based on the scenarios Nos. 1, 2, 4 and 5 yields reliability increment of about 4, 9, 13, and 21 percent respectively (Table 5).

For each month, the variation range is 0.18 to 1.0 in the optimization model No. 5 whose average is equal to 0.5 has been greater than what was obtained from other optimization models. The maximum value of the reliability increment can be related to the integration management that is obtained in scenario No. 5. Besides, in this study, the reliability is defined based on the satisfactory state that the water resources discharge is only equal to water demand. This satisfactory state is created by assuming that the water demand is determinate. Hence, the present approach for developing simulation and optimization models can enable us to consider the effects of uncertainty, vague and random factors over water resources discharge. For example in sub-basin No. 5, these effects are 21 percent that are considered in developing models of scenario No. 5.

The reason of considering the agent non-increment of the reliability more than 0.5 is that, the water supply reliability recalculated based on another satisfactory state. At this state the water resources discharge is equal or greater than water demand and these reliability are shown in Table 5. In this way, the satisfactory state is created by assuming that the water demand is not determinate. The annual water supply reliability in sub-basin No. 5 is equal to 0.86 based on the observed data for the period of the past 25 years. For all scenarios, the variation range of the annual reliability of water supply is 0.86 to 0.96 and is very close to one.

Month	P. W.R.M.	Scenario No.				
		1	2	3	4	5
October	0.53	0.60	0.50	0.69	0.25	0.32
November	0.40	0.15	0.34	0.04	0.24	0.18
December	0.19	0.33	0.22	0.21	0.36	0.50
Jane	0.66	0.83	0.71	0.68	1.00	1.00
February	0.75	0.95	0.86	0.90	1.00	1.00
March	0.38	0.60	0.59	0.47	0.75	0.82
April	0.19	0.13	0.18	0.06	0.06	0.32
May	0.34	0.32	0.46	0.36	0.55	0.62
Jun	0.44	0.52	0.61	0.44	0.63	0.39
July	0.42	0.30	0.39	0.32	0.26	0.27
August	0.46	0.27	0.43	0.33	0.38	0.41
September	0.25	0.23	0.16	0.29	0.19	0.22
Annaul	**0.42**	**0.44**	**0.45**	**0.40**	**0.47**	**0.50**
Increasing (%)	**-----**	**4.34**	**9.02**	**0.00**	**13.50**	**20.86**
October	0.57	0.75	0.55	0.69	0.95	0.82
November	0.78	0.95	0.84	0.97	1.00	1.00
December	0.98	1.00	1.00	1.00	1.00	1.00
Jane	0.99	1.00	1.00	1.00	1.00	1.00
February	1.00	1.00	1.00	1.00	1.00	1.00
March	1.00	1.00	1.00	1.00	1.00	1.00
April	0.86	0.95	0.77	0.97	0.99	0.82
May	0.88	0.93	0.86	0.90	0.90	0.62
Jun	0.73	0.77	0.70	0.69	0.78	0.73
July	0.83	0.85	0.84	0.92	0.93	0.87
August	0.84	0.87	0.84	0.86	0.93	0.95
September	0.88	0.93	0.89	0.91	1.00	1.00
Annaul	**0.86**	**0.92**	**0.86**	**0.91**	**0.96**	**0.90**
Increasing (%)	**-----**	**6.37**	**0.00**	**0.93**	**11.07**	**4.56**
October	1.00	1.00	-----	1.00	-----	-----
November	0.97	0.88	-----	0.90	-----	-----
December	0.96	0.88	-----	1.00	-----	-----
Jane	0.89	0.94	-----	1.00	-----	-----
February	0.84	1.00	-----	1.00	-----	-----
March	0.82	0.92	-----	1.00	-----	-----
April	0.75	0.82	-----	0.58	-----	-----
May	0.80	1.00	-----	0.75	-----	-----
Jun	0.95	0.87	-----	0.75	-----	-----
July	1.00	0.91	-----	0.86	-----	-----
August	1.00	0.94	-----	1.00	-----	-----
September	0.97	0.99	-----	0.99	-----	-----
Annaul	0.91	0.93	-----	0.90	-----	-----
Increasing (%)	-----	1.86	-----	0.00	-----	-----
Wet Months	**0.79**	**0.91**	**-----**	**0.77**	**-----**	**-----**
Increasing (%)	**-----**	**15.35**	**-----**	**0.00**	**-----**	**-----**

Table 5. The water resources and flood control reliabilities for each scenario in the sub-basins No. 4 and No. 5.

In scenario No. 4, the decision variables are release from the dam and groundwater pumping. The increment of the water supply reliability is about 11 percent based on the results of this scenario and is greater than what was obtained from other scenarios. The annual release from the dam in this scenario is equal to 1070 MCMM that is the maximum value of discharge compared to other scenarios. Therefore, in the previous and optimum conditions of water resources management, water resources discharge is usually more than water demand. This is due to the existence of the effects of the uncertainty and imprecise factors such as irrigation efficiency on estimated water demand. Hence, the present approach for developing simulation and optimization models can enable us to consider these effects which are about 11 percent in sub-basin No. 5.

In sub-basin No. 4, the annual flood control reliability is equal to 0.91 based on the observed data of storage volume for the period of the past 25 years (Table 5). The annual reliability is equal to 0.93 based on the results of scenario No. 1, and this optimal value of decision variables is only obtained for storage volume. In scenario No. 3 (Model-3), the decision variables are storage volume and inflow, and the annual reliability is equal to 0.90 based on the results of this scenario. In this case study, most of the previous floods occurred during March to May. The residual storage volume is very important during these months, and the flood control reliability must be obtained for these months. The variation range of the flood control reliability is 0.75 to 0.82 form March to May, and the average value is equal to 0.79 during this period (Table 5). In scenario No. 1, the variation range is 0.82 to 1.0 whose average is equal to 0.91. This value has more than what was obtained from other optimization models. In this scenario, the reliability increment is about 15 percent by considering the effects of random factors over hydrological regime in the upstream sub-basin.

5. Summary and conclusions

In recent years, fuzzy logic has become a strong tool in water resources studies. The main objective of this study is to use this approach in the optimization of water use in river basins. An approach is presented for considering spatial and temporal variation in allocating water on a large-scale river basin. Using simulation models is very important in developing an optimization model in this study. The simulation model used for this purpose consisted of smaller multi-process simulation models. The ability of fuzzy control systems or fuzzy rule based on water resources systems have been presented in the previous studies (Nguyen and Prasad, 1999, Oldhiambo et al., 2001, and Dubrovin, 2002). ANFIS method is a modified form of these methods that can simulate uncertainty, vagueness and other factors affecting the input predictor variables. Although this method is not a complete reasoning model, the development ability of Gaussion membership functions based on the conjunction of univariate fuzzy sets which is defined on the individual components of the input domain, is the reason of the application of this method. Monthly data for developing simulation model has been used in this study. The selection of these time interval and input predictor variables, which had the suitable effects on water balance in each sub-basin, may have impact on the quality of model results in this application. However, ANFIS and Fuzzy Reinforcement Learning concepts are combined to derive the ANFRL method for developing the optimization models.

Water Balance (WB), Linear Regression (LR), Autoregressive Integrated Moving Average (ARIMA), and ANFIS methods are used to simulate seven interconnected sub-basins in this case study. By using the quantitative parameters like modeling efficiency, the accuracy of the ANFIS methodology was considered in the simulation of the behavior of complex river basin systems within the context of uncertainty. Although, WB and ARIMA methods were better methods in upstream sub-basins, ANFIS model was the only method that could be used for simulation of all sub-basins (Abolpour, 2005, Abolpour & Javan 2007).

The presented approach offers two important advantages. First, this method can analyze the direct effects of uncertain, vague, conflicting, and random nature variables and parameters in a water resources system. In sub-basins No. 4 and 5, the present approach for developing simulation and optimization models have the ability of considering the effects of uncertainty factors over water resources system, imprecise factors over water demand estimated and random factors over hydrological regime. The quantitative values of these effects are 21,11 and 15 percent, respectively. The average value is about 16 percent, which can be considered as water allocation improvement in these sub-basins. Second, this method does not show any problem in defining the objective or constraint functions, and the solution process is simpler in comparison with other methods like Genetic Algorithm or Multi-Criteria Decision Making (MCDM). However, two important disadvantages in using this approach are: First, this method requires relatively long periods of historical data for deriving a robust rule set. Second, if the ANFIS model cannot yield suitable estimation of water resources variability then the results of ANFRL model will not be accurate.

Moreover, multi-processes optimization models for each sub-basin on a large scale river basin are developed too. Combination of the results of these optimization models can yield the spatial and temporal optimum values for allocating water. For example, in the Kor and Seevand river basins, the manager of water resources system can find the optimum value for allocating water in each sub-basin. The results obtained from this analysis enable the manager to allocate water for river flow, environmental needs of Bakhtegan Lake and other uses in the sub-basin. In the future, this analysis will be performed by using the expected values of monthly input data obtained from historical record based on Markov chain approach. The analysis could start from anywhere in the sub-basin. Therefore, if the expected value of each input predictor variable is given for each sub-basin, the optimum value of decision variables could be determined in any other part of the sub-basins.

The results of ANFIS method were obtained based on the assumption of simulating primary water resources management. The results obtained from ANFRL method were based on the assumption of selecting optimum strategies from primary water resources management. Therefore, if the results of ANFIS method are only used, the sixteen percent improvement in water allocation will not be attained for the same conditions in the future. The ANFRL, Stochastic Programming Problems with Recourse (SPPR) and Fuzzy Stochastic Dynamic Programming (FSDP) methods are used to optimize water allocation in these sub-basins. The results of ANFRL method based on utilization of conjunctive use strategy of surface and ground water, showed that about 100 percent improvement in water supply reliability as compared to the previous decision of water resources management during dry periods (Abolpour, 2005, Abolpour & Javan, 2007). The imprecise factors like random, vague an uncertainty does not only affect the balance variables of water resources in each sub-basin, but are also related to each other. Therefore, if the simulation models based on ANFIS method could accurately simulate the relationships between factors and their effects on water use modeling in each river basin, the optimization models based on ANFRL method could also achieve the same goal in other case study.

6. Acknowledgments

The research leading to this paper was conducted at the Shiraz University, Iran. The measured data were collected by Fars Regional Water Authority - Iran, and Fars Agricultural Research Center - Iran. The authors are grateful to Dr. B. Zahraie from University of Tehran, Sh. Araghi - Nejhad and Reza Karachian Ph. D. Candidates of Amir Kabir University. Water and Environment Research and Development (WE-R&D) office is also greatly appreciated.

7. References

Abolpour, B. & Javan, M. (2007). Optimization model for allocating water in a river basin during a drought, *Journal of Irrigation and Drainage Engineering.*, ASCS, 133(6) 559-572.

Abolpour, B. (2005). Simulation and optimization water allocation in Kor and Seevand river basins, *Ph. D. Thesis, Department of Water Eng., University of Shiraz, Shiraz, Iran.*

Apple, M. & Brauer, W. (2000). Fuzzy model-based reinforcement learning, In: *Proc. ESIT2000, European Symposium on Intelligent Techniques,* Aachen, Germany, 212-218.

Belaineh, G. & Peralta, R. C. & Hughes, T. C. (2003). Simulation/optimization modeling for water resources management, *J. Water Resour. Plann. Manage.* 125 (3) (1999) 154-161.

Bogardi, J. H. & Nachtnebel, P. (1994). Multicriteria decision analysis in water resources management. International Hydrological Program, *UNESCO, Paris.*

D. Molden, J. & Gates, T. K. (1990). Performance measures for evaluation of irrigation water delivery systems, *J. Irriga. Drain. Eng.,* 116 (6) 804-823.

Dubrovin, T. & Jolma, A. & Turunen, E. (2002). Fuzzy model for real-time reservoir operation, *J. Water Resour. Plann. Manage* 128 (1) 66-73.

Fontane, D. G. & Gates., T. K. & Moncada, E. (1997). Planning reservoir operations with imprecise objectives, *J. Water Resour. Plann. Manage.* 123 (3) 154-163.

Gates, T. K. & Ahmed, S. I. (1995). Sensitivity of predicted irrigation delivery performance to hydraulic and hydrologic uncertainty, *J. Agri. Water Manage.,* 27 267-282.

Harris, J. (2000). An introduction to fuzzy logic applications: microprocessor-based and intelligent systems engineering, *Kluwer Academic Publishers.*

Hashimoto, T. & Stedinger, J. R. & Loucks, D. P. (1982). Reliability, resiliency, and vulnerability criteria for water resource system performance evaluation, *J. Water Resour. Res.,* 18 (1) 14–20.

J. Jang, S.-R. & Sun, C. & Mizutani, T. E. (1997). Neuro-fuzzy and soft computing, *Prentice-Hall, International,* Inc.

Jacobs, J. M. & Vogel, M. (1998). Optimal allocation of water withdrawals in a river basin, *J. Water Resour. Plann. Manage.* 124 (6) 357-363.

Jouffe, L. (1998). Fuzzy inference system learning by reinforcement methods, *IEEE Transaction on Systems, Man and Cybernetics Part C,* 28 (3) 338-355.

Karamouz, M. & Houck, M.H. & Delleur, J.W. (1992). Optimization and simulation of multiple reservoir systems with an implicitly stochastic scheme, *J. Water Resour. Plann. Manage.* 118 (1) 71-81.

Karamouz, M. & Mousavi, S. & Uncertainty J. (2003). based operation of large-scale reservoir systems, *J. of American Water Resour.* Ass.

Labadie, J. W. (1993). Combining simulation and optimization in river basin management, In: J. B. Marco et al., ed., Stochastic Hydrology and its Use in Water Resources Systems Simulation and Optimization, *Kluwer Academic Publishers,* 345-370.

Li, H. G. & Chen, L.-P. & Huang, H. P. (2001). Fuzzy neural intelligent systems: mathematical foundation and the applications in engineering *CRC, Press.*

Malek, M. E. (1998). Irrigation planning: integrated approach, *J. Water Resour. Plann. Manage,* 124 (5) 272-279.

Nguyen, H. T. & Prasad, N. R. (1999). Fuzzy modeling and control: selected works of sugeno, *CRC press.*

Odhiambo, L. O. & Yoder, R. E. & Yoder, D. C. & Hines, J. W. (2001). Optimization of fuzzy evapotranspiration model through neural training with input-output examples, *Trans. ASAE* 44 (6) 1625-1633.

Oh, S. K. & Pedrycz, W. T. & Ahn, C. (2002). Self-organizing neural networks with fuzzy polynomial neurons, *Applied Soft Computing,* 2 1-10.

Owen, W. & Gates,T. K. & Flug, M. (1997). Variability in perceived satisfaction of reservoir management objectives, *J. Water Resour. Plann. Manage.* 123 (3) 147-153.

Papadrakakis, M. & Lagaros, N. D. (2003). Soft computing methodologies for structural optimization, *Applied Soft Computing,* 3 283-300.

Sasaki, M. & Gen, M. (2002). Fuzzy multiple objective optimal system design by hybrid genetic algorithm, *Applied Soft Computing,* 2 189-196.

Sasikumar, K. & Mujumdar, P. P. (1998). Fuzzy optimization model for water quality management of a river system, *J. Water Resour. Plann. Manage.* 124 (2) (1998) 79-87.

Tilmant, A. & Faouzi, E.H. & Vanclooster, M. (2002). Optimal operation of multipurpose reservoirs using flexible stochastic dynamic programming, *Applied Soft Computing,* 2 61-74.

Yeh, W. W.-G. (1985). Reservoir management and operations models: a state of the art review, *Water Resour. Res.* 21 (12) 1797-1818.

Zimmermann, H. J. (1996). Fuzzy set theory and its applications, Third Edition, *Kluwer Academic Publishers.*

Appendix I. Solution Process

The solution process of ANFRL method can be summarized as follows:

1. Simulation model is derived by using ANFIS method and observed data.
2. Simulation phase which consists of:
   - 2.1. An initial value of $\mu_{A_i^l}$ is assumed for input predictor variables in one of the rules. These are decision variables in optimization phase.
   - 2.2. The values of decision variables are calculated by using Gussian equation (Eq. 19) and are the possible values of decision variables.
   - 2.3. In other rules, a value of $\mu_{A_i^l}$ is computed based on possible value of decision variables.

2.4. The values of connection weights w_l and $\overline{w}_l$ are computed for each rule (Equations 5 and 7).
2.5. In the rule l, the estimated value of crisp function (f_l) is calculated based on the possible values of decision and known variables (Eq. 8).
2.6. The estimated value of output function F_S is computed by using Eq. 9.
2.7. The initial values of $\mu_{A_i^l}$ are used for other rules and steps 2.1 to 2.6 are also repeated.
2.8. The estimated values of F_S are compared with observed values, for selecting the possible values of decision variables, which are calculated in the simulation phase.

3. Optimization phase which consists of:
3.1. The modifiable parameters p_i^l, and C_l are computed by using the results of simulation phase.
3.2. The constraints are formulated by assuming the initial value of μ_c (Equations 21 and 22).
3.3. Fuzzy linear programming with crisp objective function is used to compute the estimated value of membership functions of goal (μ_G).
3.4. The estimated value of μ_G and the initial value of μ_c are compared. If the difference is negligible, the primary values of decision variables are estimated. Otherwise, another value of μ_c is used and steps 3.2 to 3.3 are also repeated.
3.5. The possible and primary values of decision variables are compared. If the difference is negligible, then optimum value is obtained and the solution process is stopped.

Appendix II. NOTATION

A_i^l = Fuzzy set of i th input variable for rule l.
$b_l(x)$ = Relative value (connection weights) of membership function for rule l.
CONS = Constant value of simulation model.
DEM_j = Water demand variable in sub-basin No. j.
DW_j = Drainage water reused in sub-basin No. j.
F_S = The output values of simulation model in ANFIS method.
F_O = The estimated values of objective function in optimization model (ANFRL method).
$\tilde{f}(s,x,t)$ = The reward the agent gets for executing action x in state s if the action causes a transition to state t.
GW_j = Groundwater pumping in sub-basin No. j.
$\tilde{h}$ = A probability density function.

$\widetilde{J}^{\mu}(s) =$ The value of expected sum of discounted future rewards for state s corresponding to μ.

P_i^l = The modifiable parameters for each rules and variables that are obtained from ANFIS method.

Q^h = The real value of output variable over h th point of input set.

$\widetilde{Q}^{\mu}$ = Q-value in reinforcement learning algorithms corresponding to μ.

$\widetilde{Q}^{\mu^*}$ = The optimal Q-value corresponding to μ^*.

RF_1 = River flow at Tang-e-Boraq Hydrometeric Station (Spilled water of sub-basin No.1).
RF_2 = River flow at Chamriz Hydrometeric Station (Spilled water of sub-basin No.2).
RF_3 = Inflow of Doroodzan Dam (Spilled water of sub-basin No.3).
RF_4 = Releases from Doroodzan Dam (Spilled water of sub-basin No.4).
RF_5 = River flow at Pol-e-Khan Hydrometeric Station (Spilled water of sub-basin No.5).
RF_6 = River flow at Kheirabad Hydrometeric Station (Spilled water of sub-basin No.6).
RF_7 = River flow at Jahanabad Hydrometeric Station (Spilled water of sub-basin No.7 or discharged into Bakhtegan Lake).
SW_j = Surface water in sub-basin No. j.
VOL = Storage volume of Doroodzan Dam for each month.

$\overline{w}_l$ = The connection weights of membership function for l^{th} fuzzy rule system.

x_i = The real value of ith input predictor variables in simulation analysis, and the values of known or unknown variables in the optimization analysis.
y^l = A place of output , which is a constant value in rule l.
z_r = A state of the system.
Z = Satisfactory state.

$\mu_{A_i^l}(x_i)$ = The membership function of i th input predictor variable in rule l on fuzzy set A.

μ^* = The optimal value of membership function.
ϕ = The " center" of membership function.
σ = The spread of the membership function.

15

Reinforcement Learning for Building Environmental Control

Konstantinos Dalamagkidis[1] and Dionysia Kolokotsa[2]
[1]University of South Florida,[2] Technical Educational Institute of Crete
[1]USA,
[2]Greece

1. Introduction

During the last few decades, significant changes have been made in the area of building construction and management, especially regarding climate control and energy conservation.

A significant turning point was reached in the early 70s with the oil crisis driving a movement for airtight buildings to minimize energy consumption. Unfortunately this turn resulted in a significant deterioration of the indoor air quality, raising health concerns around the world. This started a more involved study of human comfort with respect to air quality, lighting and temperature among other factors.

There has been a drive in recent years to enhance current Building Environmental Management Systems (BEMS) with decision logic that takes into account all of the aforementioned issues namely thermal comfort, visual comfort, air quality and energy consumption. In order to maximize performance on all of the above indexes, the BEMS controller can use among other things the mechanical HVAC system, natural ventilation through windows, artificial lighting and shading devices.

There are several aspects of the problem that make it attractive to intelligent control implementations. First of all the knowledge of the state of the indoor environment is imprecise due to several reasons. Localized phenomena can affect parameters like temperature or air velocity making it impossible to measure them accurately. Building environments are also characterized by changing dynamics due to human activity as well as equipment and building aging. Some parameters like clothing and activity type that are normally required to accurately estimate thermal comfort are difficult or even impossible to measure. Finally it should also be noted that despite the existence of mathematical models, thermal comfort remains a subjective measure and thus any such model is characterized by some error. On the other hand the action space is discrete and of small dimensionality.

The nature of the problem therefore indicates that controllers that are able to generalize can offer a good performance. This is also suggested by the numerous controllers proposed in the literature ranging from classic PD/PID to fuzzy, neural networks and their combinations.

For the reasons mentioned above, reinforcement learning is also suited for this problem, but it also has some unique features that make this approach of particular interest. Although a

specific setting of the HVAC system has an immediate impact on energy consumption, its effects on the indoor climate can endure for longer periods of time. Using reinforcement learning, it is straightforward to capture this effect through discounting, while the same would be more involved for other types of controllers. Additionally, its on-line learning capabilities allow the controller to follow gradually changing dynamics and minimize the adverse effects of abrupt changes, without need for significant reconfiguration.
This chapter will begin with a detailed presentation of the problem and prior art in the field. Controller design issues and alternatives will be discussed, although rigorous theoretical analysis will be omitted for the sake of brevity. A simple case study will be presented and the performance of the reinforcement learning controller will be compared to that of a fuzzy-PD and a typical on/off controller under various scenarios. The chapter concludes with current issues and suggestions for future research.

2. Comfort

After the emergence of the sick building syndrome and the realization that sealed indoor environments can have adverse effects on health and productivity, significant attention is now given to the comfort of buildings' occupants. Modern bioclimatic architecture dictates an exploitation of local climatic and geographic characteristics to provide a comfortable environment while minimizing energy consumption. On the other hand urban construction poses some limitations in the application of bioclimatic architecture and of course there are millions of buildings already constructed and in use. As a result the need arises for the introduction of sophisticated control systems. In order for such systems to be designed, comfort must be defined and quantified first.
When we refer to the comfort level of a building occupant, we have to consider several factors like thermal comfort, indoor air quality as well as light and noise levels. There are already published standards in the area of comfort and there are others in development. Thermal comfort is addressed in ISO 7730:1994 and ASHRAE 55. ISO 8995:1989 describes lighting demands of indoor work environments and ISO 1996-3:1987 and 1999:1990 describe noise limits and the impact of noise on human hearing. The Centre Europeen de Normalisation is also preparing prEN 15251:2006 under the title "Criteria for the indoor environment including thermal, indoor air quality, light and noise" (Olesen et al, 2006)

2.1 Thermal comfort

Thermal comfort is defined in the ISO 7730 standard as being "That condition of mind which expresses satisfaction with the thermal environment". Although this definition does not directly provide the means to measure thermal comfort, the standard proposes the use of the Fanger model. This model is based on the following equilibrium of the human body (Fanger, 1970):

$$M - W = H + E_c + C_{res} + E_{res} \tag{1}$$

Where M is the metabolic rate (provided in tables as a function of activity), W is the external work (usually considered to be zero), H is the dry heat loss, E_c the evaporative heat exchange at the skin during thermal neutrality, C_{res} the convective respiratory heat exchange and E_{res} the evaporative respiratory heat exchange. The latter four require the knowledge of the air temperature, the mean radiant temperature, the air velocity, the humidity and the clothing type in order to be evaluated.

In actual conditions several of the above parameters (air velocity, clothing type, activity) vary from occupant to occupant and as a result the task of measuring and achieving thermal comfort for all occupants is almost impossible (Olesen & Parsons, 2002). On the other hand people have some ability for self-regulation by adjusting their clothes or opening a window.

The Fanger model provides two indexes of the thermal comfort. The first is the PMV (Predicted Mean Vote) that corresponds to the average vote of a large volume of people about their thermal sensation and ranges between -3 (very cold) to +3 (very hot). The second is the PPD (Percent of People Dissatisfied) and is derived from the PMV using the following relationship (Memarzadeh & Manning, 2000):

$$PPD = 100 - 95 \exp(-0.03353\ PMV^4 - 0.2179\ PMV^2) \quad (2)$$

It should be noted that the PMV, PPD indexes are based on North American and European healthy adults in sedentary activity and the ISO standard warns against applying it to different groups.

The last decade the Fanger model has seen some criticism especially because of its inaccurate predictions for naturally ventilated buildings. This is because the model doesn't take into account the psychological adaptability that people exhibit, i.e. people living in naturally ventilated buildings are used to the large diversity and exhibit different preferences and wider tolerances (de Dear & Brager, 2002).

As an alternative to the Fanger model for fully air-conditioned buildings, the ACS or Adaptive Comfort Standard was proposed for naturally ventilated buildings. More specifically (de Dear & Brager, 2002) hypothesized that the thermal comfort temperature in the latter type buildings is a function of only the outdoor temperature:

$$T_{comfort} = 0.31\ T_{out} + 17.8 \quad (3)$$

In a similar study (Nicol & Humphreys, 2002) developed their comfort equation as a function of the monthly average temperature:

$$T_{comfort} = 0.54\ T_{out,avg} + 13.5 \quad (4)$$

Using the same methodology (McCartney & Nicol, 2002) developed comfort equations of the same type for 5 different European countries using the running mean temperature. These efforts where continued with studies for other regions like Singapore (Wong et al, 2002) and Indonesia (Feriadi & Wong, 2004)

Although it might seem that the ACS models differ significantly from study to study, its significance is still high because of its simplicity and lack of better alternatives for naturally ventilated buildings.

2.2 Air quality

It is a common misconception that the polluted air is outside, when the truth is that indoor air concentrations of various irritating, carcinogenic and mutagenic compounds can be higher than their corresponding outdoor concentrations even in industrial areas. Some of the most common pollutants found in indoor environments are radon (a carcinogenic compound that originates from the ground), CO and other pollutants from cigarette smoke,

volatile organic compounds from detergents, disinfectants, glues, paints etc and ozone from copying machines and air cleaners.
The only way to control the concentration of these pollutants is by introducing as much fresh air into the building as possible, although that is usually at some cost because the fresh air normally needs to be cooled or heated depending on the climate. As an indicator of indoor air quality it is common to use the concentration of CO_2 where such information is available. This is under the assumption that the concentrations of the other pollutants will follow similar trends, which in some cases may not be accurate.

2.3 Light requirements

Sufficient light is important in establishing a feeling of comfort and maintaining high productivity. Light comfort depends on illuminance or the adequacy of light, glare and light color (Serra, 1998). Therefore to enable people to perform visual tasks, adequate light without side glare and blinding must be provided. The required luminance levels can be reached by means of daylight, artificial light or a combination of both. For reasons of health, comfort and energy in most cases the use of daylight is preferred over the use of artificial light (Serra, 1998). The use of daylight though, depends on many factors like occupancy hours, autonomy, building location, daylight hours during summer and winter, window openings and orientation.
To make sure that for a reasonable amount of occupancy time daylight can be used, demands on the daylight penetration in the spaces meant for human occupancy have been set (CEN, 2002). Despite the fact that lighting can be controlled also by controlling shading devices, in commercial BEMS it is common to control only the artificial lighting to complement natural light when required.

2.3 Noise

Although noise can significantly affect the feeling of comfort and in some cases even have temporary or permanent health effects, unfortunately it is impossible to have any control over the noise levels via the BEMS. As a result this issue is dealt independently during the construction and operation of the building.

3. State of the art

Recent developments in BEMS have been influenced by the wider adaptation of intelligent control techniques like fuzzy systems, genetic algorithms and neural networks. Many of the controllers proposed in the literature have some provisions for thermal comfort and almost all have the reduction of energy consumption as objective function.
Starting with fuzzy systems, (Hamdi & Lachiver, 1998) designed a controller consisting of two separate fuzzy modules, one to determine the comfort zone and the other to provide the actual control. In (Salgado et al., 1997) fuzzy on/off and fuzzy-PID controllers where proposed with improved performance over their non-fuzzy counterparts. A PMV-based fuzzy controller was chosen by (Dounis & Manolakis, 2001) while (Kolokotsa et al. 2001) presented a family of fuzzy controllers that regulate also air quality and visual comfort. In (Alcala et al., 2005) the use of weighted linguistic fuzzy rule sets was proposed for controlling heating, cooling and ventilation systems. A

review of artificial intelligence in buildings with a focus on fuzzy systems is assessed by (Kolokotsa, 2006).
Genetic algorithms have been used to optimize the parameters of control systems in (Huang & Lam, 1997) as well as in (Kolokotsa et al., 2002). Similarly (Egilegor et al., 1997) used neural networks to adapt the parameters of their fuzzy-PI controller.
Neural networks have also been used independently for control as in the case of (Karatasou et al., 2006) or cooperatively with fuzzy systems as in (Yamada et al., 1999).
Some other approaches include the neurobat project by (Morel et al., 2001) for predictive control, empirical models used in (Yao et al, 2004) and decision support systems using rule sets proposed by (Doukas et al., 2007).

4. Designing a reinforcement learning controller

Despite the fact that a BEMS controller is also responsible for the artificial lighting, it is possible to delegate the lighting control to a separate slave controller, under the assumption that the two controllers are independent. This is because the output of the controller depends exclusively on the light conditions inside the building and that output only has an almost negligible effect on the thermal environment. As a result the state-action dimensionality is kept low and the controller can learn faster.
The choice of the learning algorithm is based on several factors. Since the state space is continuous and only a relatively small number of discrete actions are available, algorithms based on function approximation are particularly suitable. The authors have used with success the recursive least-squares (RLS-TD) algorithm proposed by (Xu et al., 2002) and presented in Fig. 1. Nevertheless other approaches are also available.
A very important aspect of the design of a controller that is based on reinforcement learning is the definition of a reward function. In the case of building environmental control, the reward can be based on more than one factors. To make the quantities comparable it is prudent to scale everything, so that they take values in the same range - usually [0,1].
The energy consumption can be scaled using the ratio of the current consumption that includes the heating, air conditioning and ventilation, to the maximum possible consumption. For the thermal comfort the PPD index can be chosen, since it is already in the desired range. Care should be taken to use the PPD only in the cases where it accurately models the reality, according with the guidelines of the ISO standard. Finally in order to create the indoor air quality index based on the CO_2 concentration, it is possible to use an appropriately chosen sigmoid function of the following form:

$$f(x) = 1/(1+\exp(-\alpha x+\beta)) \qquad (5)$$

The constant parameters α, β for the sigmoid function are chosen empirically based on the fact that for CO_2 concentrations close to the average outdoor concentrations, the index should take near zero values. Similarly double the average outdoor concentration should yield an index close to 1.
Since all the rewards are in the same range with zero being the best value and one the worst, it is possible to create a simple reward function based on the weighted average of all the indexes:

$$r = -(w_1\, r_{energy} + w_2\, r_{comfort} + w_3\, r_{air\_quality}) \qquad (6)$$

where the w_i are weights chosen empirically and the minus sign is because learning tries to maximize the reward.
Using the sigmoid function described above it is also possible to scale the inputs to the controller to the same range. This approach can help with simplifying the coding scheme that precedes the feature vector generation. Besides the usual inputs (temperatures, CO_2 concentrations, etc.) an additional input was given to the controller regarding the time of the year and the time of the day. Although this choice increases the dimensionality of the state space, it gives the controller sufficient information to anticipate the changes in the outdoor environment and choose better actions.
The learning parameters are chosen based primarily on experience and trial and error. Special care should be taken in the choice of the decay and discount factors. This is because their effect depends also on the timestep chosen. As an example for a timestep of 10 minutes a decay factor of 0.5-0.6 should be used so that the eligibility trace reduces significantly after 30-40 minutes. If the timestep is lowered to 5 minutes, then the decay factor should be increased to 0.7-0.8 to get the same effect and comparable results.

For a given set of basis functions $\varphi(x)$
Initialization:
    Initialize weight vector W_t randomly
    Variance matrix $P_o = \delta I$
    Eligibility traces $z_o = 0$
Loop:
    For current state x_t and chosen action a_t, observe new state x_{t+1} and reward r_t
    $K_{t+1} = P_t z_t / (1+(\varphi^T(x_t) - \gamma\, \varphi^T(x_{t+1}))\, P_t z_t)$
    $W_{t+1} = W_t + K_{t+1}(r_t - (\varphi^T(x_t) - \gamma\, \varphi^T(x_{t+1}))W_t)$
    $P_{t+1} = P_t - K_{t+1}(\varphi^T(x_t) - \gamma\, \varphi^T(x_{t+1}))P_t$
    $z_{t+1} = \gamma\lambda z_t + \varphi(x_t)$

Fig. 1. RLS-TD(λ) algorithm from (Xu et al., 2002)

5. Case study and sample results

As an example the case study of a simulated simple building will be investigated. The building is comprised of a single $35m^2$ room, with one window to the north ($1m^2$) and one to the west ($1m^2$). All the exterior walls are insulated concrete with a total thickness of 22.5cm. The sensor information available is the indoor and outdoor temperatures, the current PPD and the date and time. All these variables are used as the state input to the controller with the exception of the PPD which is used only in determining the reward function.
The inputs where scaled using sigmoid functions and then encoded using radial basis functions, to create the feature vector.
The environmental control equipment is composed of a heat pump that has a cooling and heating mode and 3 levels for each mode (low, medium, high) with specifications similar to modern AC inverter units and a ventilation unit that has a low and high setting. A window actuator is also available that can open or close the windows. As a result, all the possible combinations give a total of 42 different actions.

The reward function is given by equation 7, where the weights were chosen after trial and error to fairly balance the importance of energy conservation and thermal comfort.

$$r = -(0.4\ r_{energy} + 0.6\ r_{comfort}) \qquad (7)$$

The decay chosen was 0.5 and the discount factor was 0.85, nevertheless it should be noted that small perturbations around those values did not significantly alter the performance of the controller. The ε parameter was chosen to be 0.05 for the first two years and 0 afterwards.

The results of the first 5 years of simulation are summarized in Table 1, along with comparative results from a single year simulation of an on/off and a fuzzy-PD controller. It should be noted that the parameters of the fuzzy-PD were chosen empirically and where not optimized with training data.

	Reinforcement Learning					Fuzzy-PD	On/off
Year	**1**	**2**	**3**	**4**	**5**	**5**	**5**
Energy	19.47%	17.16%	15.82%	12.73%	12.78%	11.17%	12.89%
Avg. PPD	21.1%	15.3%	12.9%	13.7%	13.6%	15.8%	14.44%
Max PPD	100%	79.8%	65.7%	58.3%	56.4%	60.3%	62.2%

Table 1. Results from 5 years of simulated building response to the reinforcement learning controller. The energy index is given as the ratio of the integrated power consumption to the maximum possible consumption in the same period.

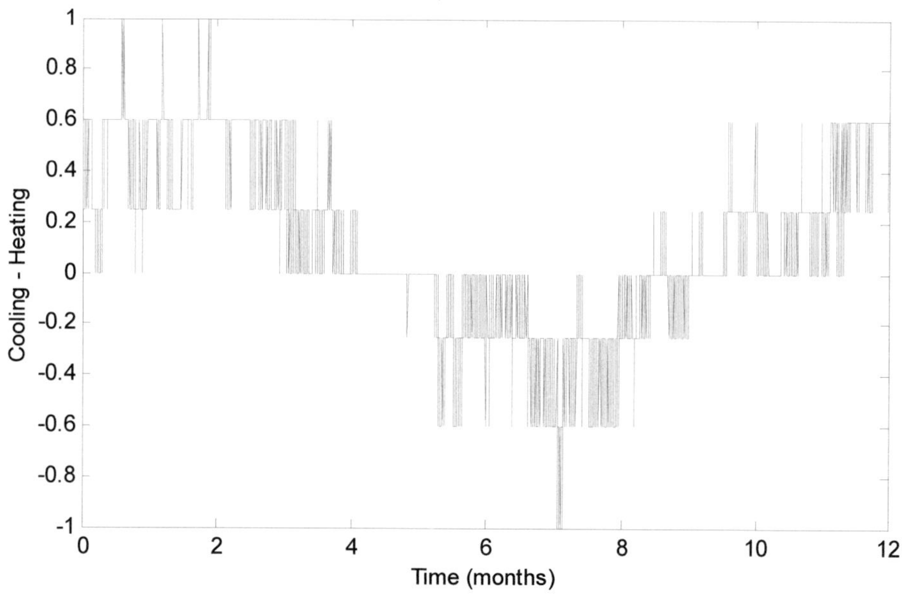

Fig. 2. A plot of cooling/heating controller signal after 4 years of simulated training (1 in 10 points are shown for better clarity).

In Fig. 2 the control signal for the heat pump is presented. It can be observed that the controller does not make significant errors and rarely chooses to use the heat pump at the high settings. Nevertheless the fact remains that the controller is still learning and its behavior still hasn't converged. Similarly Fig. 3 shows the PMV and PPD indexes in the building for the same period. Here it is more evident that the controller is still learning to maintain an acceptable PPD level throughout the simulated year. Nevertheless it is also obvious that it is able to keep the PPD under 25% more than 96% of the time. It should be noted that the PPD cannot drop below 5% by definition.

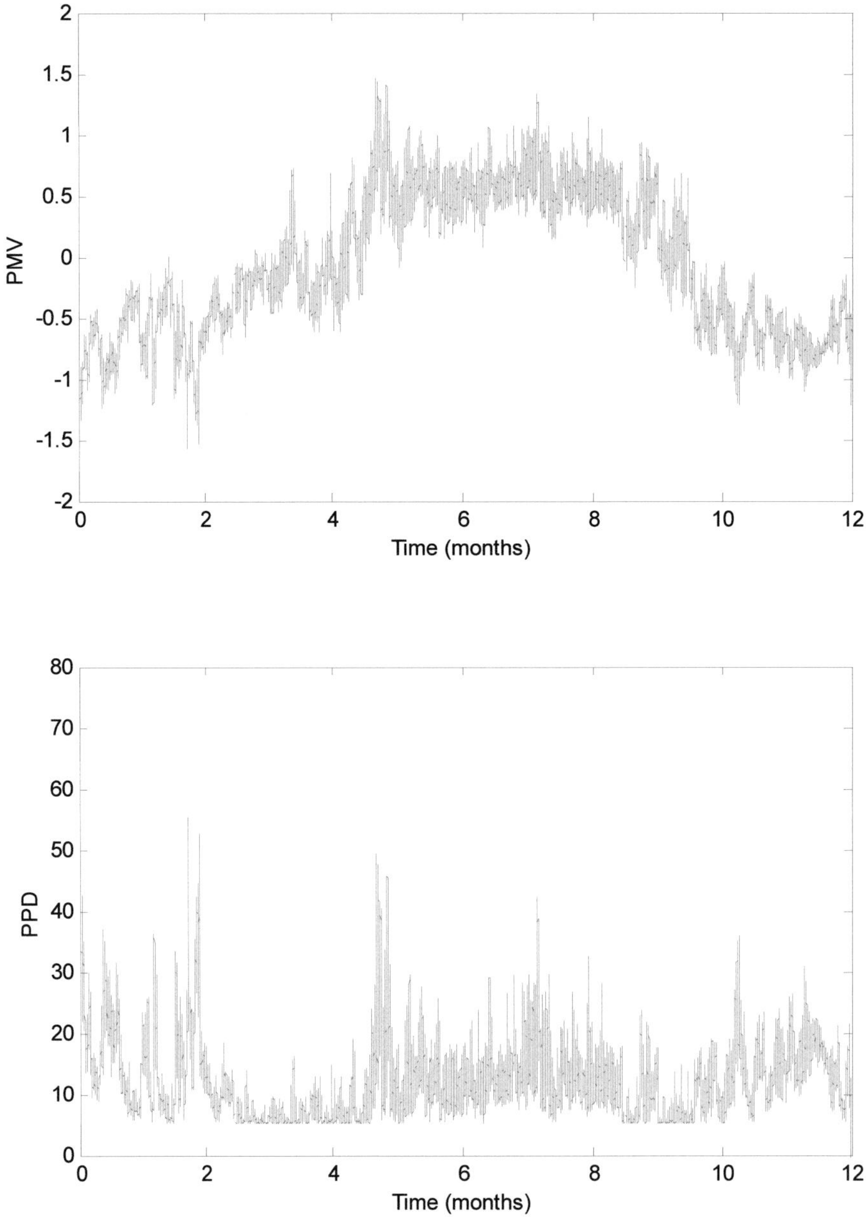

Fig. 3. The PMV and PPD indexes as a function of time, after 4 years of simulated time.

The results presented above show that the reinforcement learning controller within 4 years of simulated time has achieved performance comparable if not better than other controllers. Nevertheless even after the 4 years the controller is still changing its policy and further improvements are to be expected by more training, optimization of the training parameters and more descriptive feature vectors.

The advantage that this controller has over the other controllers is that it is possible to continually adapt the weight vector, thus allowing it to follow gradual changes in the behavior of a building. These changes can stem from equipment aging, leakages or changes in the climatic patterns in the area. On the other hand since in a real building suboptimal action selection is usually not permitted, exploration during the operation of the controller should be avoided. As a result it is necessary to exhaustively train the controller beforehand in a similar simulation environment.

6. Future research opportunities

This chapter has demonstrated the utility of reinforcement learning in the development of controllers for BEMS. It is also evident that the potential benefits both in terms of energy conservation as well as in terms of comfort are significant. Nevertheless the results presented above and earlier in (Dalamagkidis et al, 2007) signify that there is still room for improvements. Besides better fine-tuning of the parameters and further training, the authors would like to propose some other ideas for future work.

On the first order of business is the development of a better reward assignment algorithm. Although only hinted at in previous sections, the reward mechanism described in this chapter does not represent the real phenomenon with accuracy. A separation of the energy consumption related reward from the rest is suggested. This is because any control action is associated with a very specific energy consumption that occurs only while this control action is in effect. On the other hand the impact of that control action on the other comfort related factors lingers for several minutes after that action has ceased to occur.

As an example the effect of the heat pump control on the indoor temperature is presented in Fig. 4. Although most of the effect on the temperature occurs within the time that the control action was active, there is significant after-effect, that lasts almost for 40 minutes after that control action ceased. The same is true for the indoor air quality index which represents a more complicated case since it depends on the rate of air exchanges and thus depends exclusively on the window and ventilator actions.

For the case study presented earlier, it was decided to represent the complete reward as a simple weighted average of the energy and thermal comfort indexes and a decay factor was chosen that reduces the weight of the reward after 30-40 minutes. The suggested alternative solution is an n-step backup that waits until the real reward is available, with the known disadvantages presented by (Sutton & Barto, 1998). A different scheme would involve a more complicated value-updating step, which would entail an immediate update based on the energy performance and eligibility traces (perhaps even separate) for the other indexes. This mixture of TD(0) and TD(λ) of course needs to be evaluated for its convergence properties. The authors expect that an improved reward assignment algorithm could benefit both the final performance of the controller as well as the convergence speed.

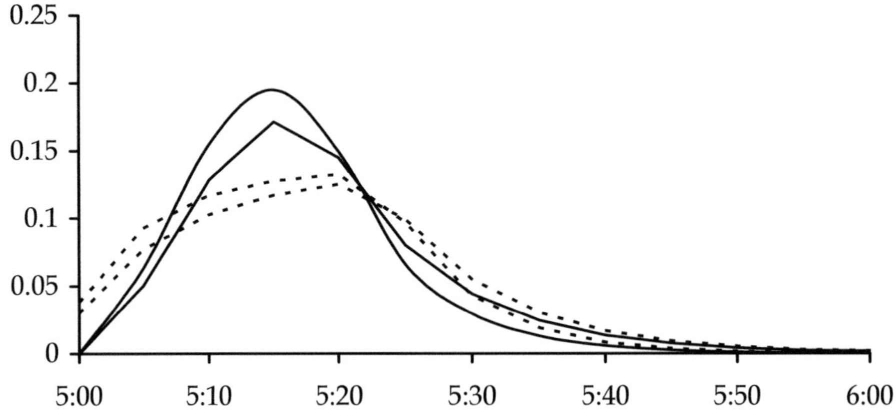

Fig. 4. A plot of the absolute temperature deviation after a control command that begun at 5:00 and lasted 20 minutes, with respect to no control. The two filled lines represent cooling for two different buildings and the dashed lines heating.

An additional method to increase the learning speed is to have two different speeds during learning. The first speed would correspond to the value function update speed which could be as frequent as every 2 or 3 minutes, while the second speed would correspond to the frequency with which a new action is selected and should be around 15 to 20 minutes. This change would require using different learning algorithms since now the controller would be operating off-policy. Additionally the learning parameters would need to be adjusted to correspond to the new temporal characteristics of the learning process.

Although the scientific literature of the last couple of decades is full with proposals of classic and intelligent controllers that claim significant savings in terms of energy and superior performance in terms of comfort, the technology mostly used today is still the basic thermostat. Besides being a simple and tried technology, the thermostat also has two features that help it retain its position. The first is that it requires only a temperature sensor that is usually incorporated in the device and the second is that it allows people to directly control their environment thus contributing to their feeling of comfort.

It is therefore the authors' opinion that in order for a modern controller to be successful and replace the installed base of controllers, it needs the aforementioned characteristics in some degree. Reducing the sensor demand of the controller can be difficult. Nonetheless it is a straightforward process. On the other hand finding ways for the occupants to interact with the controller is far more complicated. In (Dalamagkidis et al, 2007) an additional module was proposed that is trained by occupant input whenever the latter is available. This module is then used as another component in determining the reward function. Another idea is for the occupants to be able to override to a degree some of the controller's actions and the controller learning from that experience.

Regardless of the number of papers proposing new and more efficient technologies for building environmental control, the fact remains that the penetration of these technologies in the market is minimal if any. To open the doors for the introduction of more advanced controllers in BEMS, more work should be done on controllers that can efficiently replace what is already installed with little to no additional requirements.

7. References

Alcala, R.; Casillas, J.; Cordon, O.; Gonzalez, A. & Herrera, F. (2005). A genetic rule weighting and selection process for fuzzy control of heating, ventilating and air conditioning systems. *Engineering Applications of Artificial Intelligence*, Vol. 18, No. 3, April 2005, pp. 279-296

CEN, 2002. EN 12464-1:2002, Light and lighting. Lighting of work places. Indoor work places

Dalamagkidis, K.; Kolokotsa, D.; Kalaitzakis, K. & Stavrakakis, G. S. (2007). Reinforcement learning for energy conservation and comfort in buildings. *Building and Environment*, Vol. 42, No. 7, July 2007, pp. 2686-2698

De Dear, R. J. & Brager, G. S. (2002). Thermal comfort in naturally ventilated buildings: revisions to ASHRAE Standard 55. *Energy and Buildings*, Vol. 34, No. 6, July 2002, pp.549-561

Doukas, H.; Patlitzianas, K. D.; Iatropoulos, K. & Psarras, J. (2007). Intelligent building energy management system using rule sets, *Building and* Environment, Vol. 42, No. 10, October 2007, pp.3562-3569

Dounis, A. I. & Manolakis, D. E. (2001). Design of a fuzzy system for living space thermal-comfort regulation. *Applied Energy*, Vol. 69, No. 2, pp. 119-144

Egilegor, B.; Uribe, J. P.; Arregi, G.; Pradilla, E. & Susperregi, L. (1997). A fuzzy control adapted by a neural network to maintain a dwelling within thermal comfort. *Proceedings of Building Simulation 1997*, Vol. 2, September 1997, pp. 87-94

Fanger, P. O. (1970). Thermal comfort analysis and applications in environmental engineering. Mc Graw Hill, New York

Feriadi, H. & Wong, N. H. (2004). Thermal comfort for naturally ventilated houses in Indonesia. *Energy and Buildings*, Vol. 36, No. 7, July 2004, pp.614-626

Hamdi, M. & Lachiver, G. (1998). A fuzzy control system based on the human sensation of thermal comfort, In: *Fuzzy Systems, The 1998 IEEE international conference on*, Vol. 1, May 1998, pp. 487-492

Huang, W. & Lam, H. N. (1997). Using genetic algorithms to optimize controller parameters for HVAC systems. *Energy and Buildings*, Vol. 26, No.3, pp. 277-282

Karatasou, S.; Santamouris M. & Geros V. (2006). Modeling and predicting building's energy use with artificial neural networks: Methods and results. *Energy and Buildings*, Vol. 38, No. 8, August 2006, pp. 949-958

Kolokotsa, D.; Tsiavos, D.; Stavrakakis, G. S.; Kalaitzakis, K. & Antonidakis, E. (2001). Advanced fuzzy logic controllers design and evaluation for buildings' occupants thermal - visual comfort and indoor air quality satisfaction. *Energy and Buildings*, Vol. 33, No. 6, July 2001, pp. 531-543

Kolokotsa, D.; Stavrakakis, G. S.; Kalaitzakis, K. & Agoris, D. (2002). Genetic algorithms for optimized fuzzy controller for the indoor environmental management in buildings implemented using PLC and local operating networks. *Engineering Applications of Artificial Intelligence*, Vol. 15, No. 5, September 2002, pp. 417-428.

Kolokotsa, D. (2006). Artificial Intelligence in Buildings: A Review on the Application of Fuzzy Logic, *Advances in Building Energy Research*, Vol.1, pp. 29-54, James and James Publisher.

McCartney, K. J. & Nicol, J. F. (2002). Developing an adaptive control algorithm for Europe. *Energy and buildings*, Vol. 34, No.6, July 2002, pp. 623-635

Memarzadeh, F. & Manning, A. (2000). Thermal comfort, uniformity and ventilation effectiveness in patient rooms: performance assessment using ventilation indices, ASHRAE Annual Meeting, MN-00-11-3

Morel, N.; Bauer, M.; El-Khoury, M. & Krauss, J. (2001). Neurobat, a predictive and adaptive heating control system using artificial neural networks. *International Journal of Solar Energy*. Vol. 21, April 2001, pp. 161-202

Nicol, J. F. & Humphreys, M. A. (2002). Adaptive thermal comfort and sustainable thermal standards for buildings. *Energy and Buildings*, Vol. 34, No. 6, July 2002, pp. 563-572

Olesen, B. W. & Parsons, K. C. (2002). Introduction to thermal comfort standards and to the proposed new version of EN ISO 7730. *Energy and Buildings*, Vol.34, No. 6, July 2002, pp.537-548

Olesen, B. W.; Seppanen, O. & Boerstra, A. (2006). Criteria for the indoor environment for energy performance of buildings: A new European standard. *Facilities*, Vol. 24, No 11/12, pp. 445-457

Salgado, P.; Cunha, J. B. & Couto, C. (1997). A computer-based fuzzy temperature controller for environmental chambers, In: *Industrial Electronics, IEEE 1997 international symposium on*, Vol. 3, July 1997, pp. 1151-1156

Serra, R. (1998). Daylighting, In: *Renewable and sustainable energy reviews*, Vol. 2, No.1-2, June 1998, pp. 115-155

Sutton, R. S. & Barto, A. G. (1998). *Reinforcement learning: an introduction*, MIT Press, ISBN 0-262-19398-1, Cambridge, MA

Tsitsiklis, J. & Van Roy, B. (1997). An Analysis of Temporal-Difference Learning with Function Approximation. *IEEE Transactions on Automatic Control*, Vol. 42, No. 5, May 1997, pp.674-690

Wong, N. H.; Feriadi, H.; Lim, P. Y.; Tham, K. W., Sekhar, C. & Cheong K. W. (2002). Thermal Comfort evaluation of naturally ventilated public housing in Singapore. *Building and Environment*, Vol. 37, No. 12, December 2002, pp. 1267-1277

Xu, X.; He, H. G. & Hu, D. (2002). Efficient reinforcement learning using recursive least-squares methods. *Journal of Artificial Intelligence Research*, Vol. 16, pp.259-292

Yamada, F.; Yonezawa, K.; Sugarawa, S. & Nishimura, N. (1999). Development of air-conditioning control algorithm for building energy-saving, In: *Control applications, IEEE 1999 International conference on*, Vol. 2, pp. 1579-1584

Yao, Y.; Lian, Z.; Hou, Z. & Zhou, X. (2004). Optimal operation of a large cooling system based on an empirical model. *Applied Thermal Engineering*, Vol. 24, No. 16, November 2004, pp. 2303-2321

16

Model-Free Learning Control of Chemical Processes

S. Syafiie[1], F. Tadeo[1] and E. Martinez[2],
[1]*Department of Systems Engineering and Automatic Control, University of Valladolid,*
[2] *Consejo Nacional de Investigaciones Científicas y Técnicas,*
[1]*Spain,* [2]*Argentina.*

1. Introduction

Learning is the nature for human being. For example, a school-student learns a subject by doing exercise and home-work. Then, a school-teacher grades the school-student's works. From this student and teacher interaction, the ability of the student mastering the subject is a feedback that the previous teaching method is successful or failure. As a result, the teacher will change the teaching method to improve the student ability for mastering the subject. This is a picture that the reinforcement learning (RL) agent learns the environment.

Process control mainly focuses on controlling variable such as pressure, level, flow, temperature, pH, level in the process industries. However, the methodologies and principles are the same as in all control fields. The early successful application control strategy in process control is in evolution of the PID controller and Ziegler-Nichols tuning method (Ziegler and Nichols, 1942). Till nowadays, 95% of the controllers implemented in the process industries are PID-type (Chidambaram and See, 2002). However, as (i) the industrial demands (ii) the computational capabilities of controllers and (iii) complexity of systems under control increase, so the challenge is to implement advanced control algorithms.

There have been commercial successes of the intelligent control methods, but the dominating controller in process industries is still by far the PID-controller (Chidambaram and See, 2002). This stands to the fact that a simple and general purpose automatic controller (for example PID) is demanded in process industries. Therefore, designing advanced controllers are to address the industrial user demand. This is the reason that a learning method called model-free learning control (MFLC) is introduced. The MFLC algorithm is based on a well known Q-learning algorithm (Watkins, 1989).

Successful applications of RL are well documented in the recent literature, including learning to control mobile robots (Bucak and Zohdy, 2001), sustained inverted flight on an autonomous helicopter (Ng *et al.*, 2004), and learning to minimize average wait time in elevators (Crites and Barto, 1996). However, only few articles can be found regarding RL applications for process control: multi-step actions based on RL was fruitfully applied for thermostat control (Schoknecht and Riedmiller, 2003), and one of the authors successfully applied RL for modeling for optimization in bath reactors by making the most effective use of cumulative data and an approximate model (Martinez, 2000). The reason for the difference between robotics and process control is possibly the nature of the control task in each field: typically in robotics the degrees of freedom for control are significantly high whereas in process plants are much more constrained. However with the shift from regulation to optimization and supervisory control the area is entering into a set of problems where RL can become the alternative choice.

This chapter discusses novel, yet simple to implement learning system in process control based on RL algorithms. As the ability to store and process large amounts of data in computer's memory and processor increases by time, this ability has made feasible the use of learning methods in systems for business, scientific and engineering, and medical decision-making. The proposed MFLC is mainly for nonlinear, complex, and time-varying chemical processes for which the development of a first-principles model is too costly in terms of time and money. The state-action space is defined using a symbolic representation and control incremental constraints. The state space is based on length errors of the system regarding a goal state. In this chapter, the MFLC approach is discussed for process control.

This proposed technique is then tested on two laboratory plants: pH control and oxidation plants. Industrial pH control has received considerable attentions in literature (see Kalafatis *et al.*, 2005 and references therein). However, as the inherent characteristics (time-varying, nonlinear and buffer capacity) of pH process dynamic are extremely difficult to model and predict in wastewater treatment plant, then a general purpose control strategy is a very challenging problem. As result most wastewater treatment plant uses on-off pH control.

The issues are more complicated when oxidation reduction potential (ORP) is used to guarantee on-specification discharge by regulating the residence time. The ORP sensor measures the presence oxidizer or reducer in the solution and not the concentration of a given chemical species (McPherson, 1993). Many researchers find some processes are near optimal in certain ORP values (Peng *et al.*, 2002; Baeza *et al.*, 2000; Kwan, 2005). Clearly, it is a challenge to use ORP sensor for controlling the load to a wastewater oxidation process.

This chapter is organized as follows: a MFLC algorithm for designing controller for chemical process control is given in section 2. In section 3, the application for a simulated buffer tank control is discussed. Laboratory online applications are discussed in section 4 for pH and ORP control processes.

2. MFLC algorithms

From the different proposed RL algorithms (Sutton and Barto, 1998), this paper proposes a Model-Free Learning Control (MFLC) where the basic Q-learning algorithm is combined with symbolic states which are frequently visited to address process control problems related to wastewater oxidation plants. The resulting value function, which is a mapping of history of visited states and executed actions to cumulative rewards, gives a clue for the learning controller to select an action in a given state. Through this function, the agent takes into account that taking an action in the current state will provide a given cumulative future reward derived from the control task at hand. This predicted value is used by the controller policy for selecting an action from those available in each visited symbolic state. This MFLC can be seen in Figure 1. The value of the reinforcement at each time reflects the control task objectives (Sutton and Barto, 1998), in process control problem it is proposed to involve control energy costs and error tolerance. The "situation" block is used to generate the symbolic state from plant readings and control task specification.

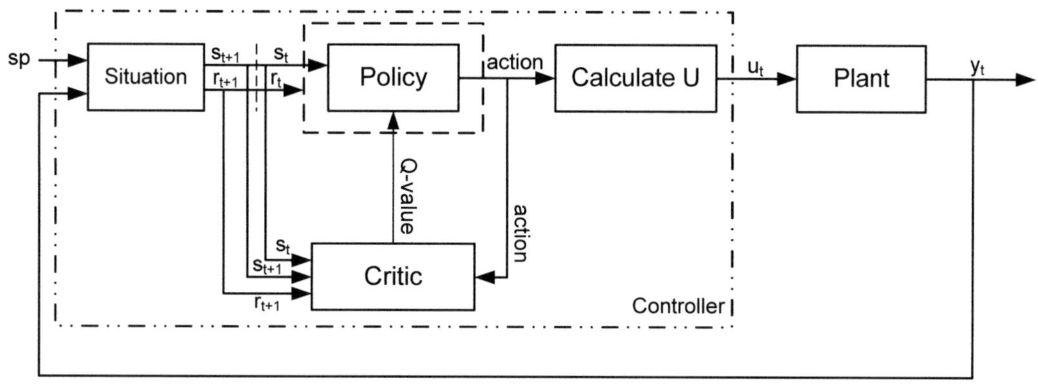

Fig. 1. MFLC architecture based on Q-Learning

A central part of RL algorithms is the estimation of the so-called *Q-function*, which gives the benefit of applying action a_t when the system is in state s_t. This function is denoted by $Q(s_t, a_t)$. To learn this Q-function it is necessary to take into account the benefit now and in the future: when action a_t has been selected and applied to the environment, the system moves to a new state, s_{t+1}, and receives a reinforcement signal, r_{t+1}; The value function for state-action pairs, $Q(s_t, a_t)$, is updated by the basic learning rule:

$$Q_\pi(s_t, a_t) \leftarrow Q_\pi(s_t, a_t) + \alpha_t \left[r_{t+1} + \gamma \max_{b \in A_{s_{t+1}}} Q_\pi(s_{t+1}, b) - Q_\pi(s_t, a_t) \right] \tag{1}$$

where:

- $A_{s_{t+1}}$ is the set of possible actions in the next symbolic state.
- The *learning rate*, $0 \leq \alpha \leq 1$, is a tuning parameter, that can be used to optimize the speed of learning (Although too small learning rates might induce slow learning, while too large learning rates might induce oscillations).
- The *discount factor*, γ, is used to weight near term reinforcements more heavily than distant future reinforcements: If γ is small, the agent learns to behave only for short-term reward; the closer γ is to 1 the greater the weight assigned to long-term reinforcements.

2.1 MFLC state-action space

A central issue in Reinforcement Learning algorithms is the definition of the states. In MFLC the states are defined based on the control objective and control constraints, as follows:
In a SISO implementation of the MFLC approach, the control task is defined as the ability to achieve and maintain a given process variable inside a specification band *r-d* and *r+d*, as shown in Figure 2. The width of this band is defined based on the tolerance of the system (which depends on measurement noise, disturbances and systems specification) and referred to as the *goal band*, and corresponds to the *goal state*, where the learning control system operates (it is now assumed, without loss of generality, that it is exactly in the middle of the working range).

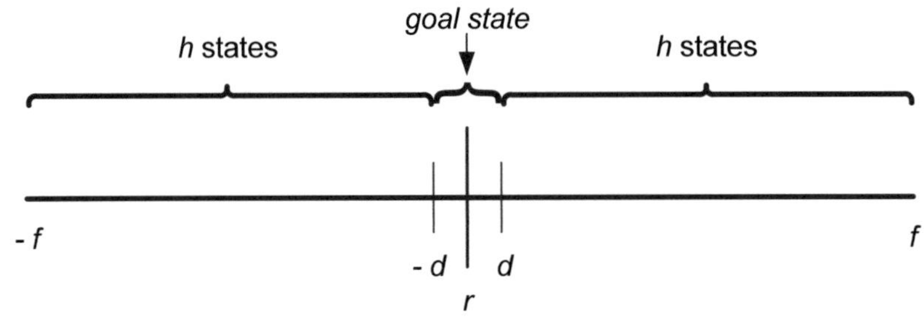

Fig. 2. Symbolic states definition in MFLC

To describe the rest of the symbolic states, it is considered that the process may be in h states from the goal state to the maximum positive or negative error of the system, f (Selecting h is a trade-off: this number must be large enough to describe all the different behaviours of the process, but small enough to reduce learning time and the size of the Q-value matrix).
If needed, the "length" of each state can be calculated as follows:

$$c = \frac{f-d}{h} \tag{2}$$

Thus, the positive bound parameter can be defined as:

$$\omega_i = d + (i-1)c, \quad i \in [1, \cdots, h] \tag{3}$$

(For negative errors, the bound parameter is trivial by changing signs).
Thus, the vector of symbolic states can be represented as follow:

$$g_j = \begin{cases} e - \omega_j & \text{if } e > \omega_j \\ \omega_j - e & \text{else} \end{cases}, \quad j \in [1, \cdots, 2h+1], \tag{4}$$

where e is the tracking error. The symbolic current state s_t, is just:

$$s_t = \arg\max(g_j) \tag{5}$$

In MFLC, the control signal u_t is calculated by varying the previous control signal in a magnitude calculated from the difference of the numerical values of the selected optimal action, a_t, with respect to the wait action, a_w (action corresponding to maintaining the previous control signal). That is,

$$u_t = u_{t-1} + k(a_w - a_t) \tag{6}$$

This gives a PI-like structure, which simplifies initialization and tuning for the end user (k is the tuning parameter defining the aggresiviness of the controller). At each state there is only a finite set of possible actions (see Figure 3). These actions are selected based on the systems description: in particular from the limitations on the minimum and maximum variations of the control signal, as follows:
Let the incremental control be bounded as:

$$\underline{\Delta u} \le \Delta u \le \overline{\Delta u}. \tag{7}$$

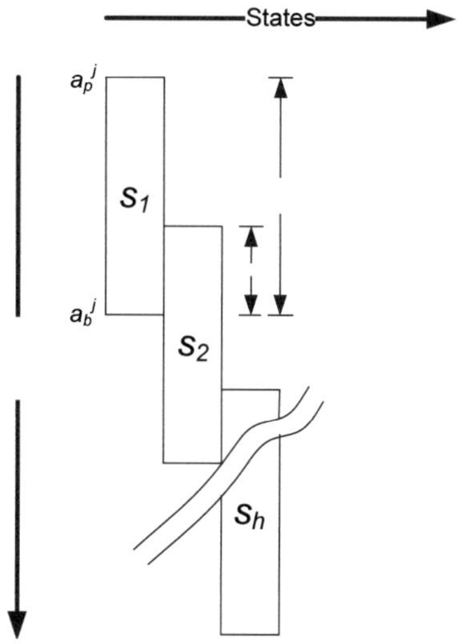

Fig. 3. Definition of the action set

The number of total actions needed to satisfy the input constraints can be calculated as follows:

$$N_a = round\left(\frac{\overline{\Delta u} - \underline{\underline{\Delta u}}}{k}\right) + 1. \tag{8}$$

From (7) and (8), the value corresponding to the wait action a_w, can be calculated as follows:

$$a_w = 1 + round\left(\frac{\overline{\Delta u}}{k}\right). \tag{9}$$

As expected, not all the actions may be available at each state: only a constrained set of the actions is available depending of the symbolic state, e.g. if the error is very small, the only actions available are those that correct a small error.

The number of action in each state is

$$N_a^s = \left(\frac{N_a}{h}\right)\rho, \tag{10}$$

where ρ is a parameter that gives the degree of overlapping with neighboring states (selected such that N_a^s is integer. Then, the available actions for every state ranges from a_p^j to a_b^j (except in the goal state, where only the wait action can be selected). The idea is presented in Figure 3. Those available actions can be calculated as

$$\begin{aligned} a_p^j &= a_p + (j-1)v, \\ a_b^j &= a_p^j + N_a^s - 1, \end{aligned} \tag{11}$$

where

$$v = \frac{N_a^h h - N_a}{h-1} - 1 \tag{12}$$

So far, the SISO implementation has been presented. For MIMO system the simplest methodology would be used several learning controllers that interact between them.
Next section discusses the application of the proposed MFLC for a buffer tank control. The application is to maintain smoothly the out flow of the tank and to keep the level of the tank to avoid overflow and empty.

3. Buffer tank control

Buffer tanks are very common in the process industry to alleviate the impact downstream of disturbances in temperature, concentration, and flow rate in important process streams (Faanes and Skogestad, 2003). In industry, buffer tanks are known under many different names, such as intermediate storage vessels, hold up tanks, surge drums, accumulators, inventories, mixing tanks, continuous stirred tank reactors (CSTR), and neutralization vessels. Typically, the buffer tank shown in Figure 4 is subject to significant and unsystematic variations in its inflow rate. For example, if the downstream is fed to a heater, fast changes in its feed give temperature variations which affect the rest of the process. Also, a buffer tank is often installed to avoid propagation of disturbances from batch operations to continuous processes. Furthermore, a buffer tank is also installed between operation units to allow a more flexible operation. Therefore, the task of controlling a buffer tank is such that the outflow rate must be changed smoothly despite significant variations in its incoming flow rate. To avoid overflow and empty, the level in the tank needs to be constantly varied within its operation minimum and maximum limits. However, the tank has a limited capacity that should be used appropriately. Thus, keeping the tank level in limitation is also an important component of the control task to be learnt.
These tanks are usually used as examples to check novel control algorithms, as they are simple to understand and easy to reproduce. For example, a neuro-fuzzy controller is proposed by Tani *et al.* (1996) for controlling a buffer tank using a predictive inductive model (neural network) and fuzzy decision rules.

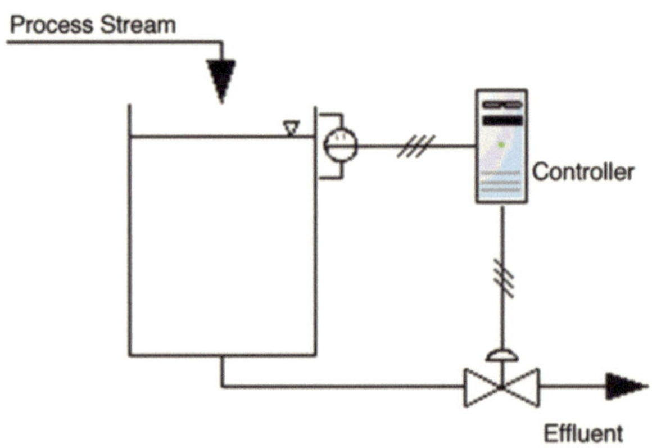

Fig. 4. Buffer tank

A very simple approach to control a buffer tanks using the proposed MFLC is now presented. For designing controller using MFLC, the designer should define how big the Q-table and reward function can be. The learner will interact online with the environment and learn providing best actions to fulfil the requirement. Once the learner's parameters are defined, they can be used for other similar processes.

3.1 Problem definition

The tank has A=100 cm^2 and a level constrain $0<h<50$ cm. Clearly, the learning system is allowed to variate the level of the tank within its minimum and maximum capacity. Another limitation is that the controller can only manipulate the valve opening in the range $0\leq u\leq 100\%$. The learning controller must comply these limitations: The agent will be punished if it generates an action that causes the system to be outside this limitation.
The main objective of the proposed MFLC is to bring the outflow inside the goal band; the process responses are allowed to ocsillate within the band. Therefore, in the case of the buffer tank control, the goal band is selected to outflow within ± 2% error of the desired outflow (reference). On the other hand, the system allows the level to vary 60% from the head of the tank: The remaining 40% is for safety.

3.2 Design parameters

In this example, the goal band is defined as ± 1 l/m from the reference. Let reference, r see Figure 2, be 50 l/m and therefore, the parameter d is 1 and f is 5 l/m. The agent also has limitation $0.1\leq\Delta u\leq 0.3$ in the variation of the manipulated variable with regard to the previous control signal. The gain controller, k, is introduced to be 1×10^{-4}. By taking $\rho = 1.5$, therefore, there are 600 available actions in every symbolic state. For each available action, the controller will receive a positive reward (see equation 13) if the next response is inside the goal band. Meanwhile, if the next response is reaching the lower and upper bound output constrains, the selected action is punished. If the next state is not in the goal state, the selection of the action will also be negatively rewarded. That is :

$$r_{t+1} = \begin{cases} 10 & \text{if } r - d < f_{out_{t+1}} < r + d, \\ -10 & \text{if } h_{t+1} \leq 0 \text{ or } h_{t+1} \geq 50, \\ -1 & \text{else.} \end{cases} \tag{13}$$

The discounted factor, γ, is set to 0.9 while the learning rate, α, is set to a value of 0.1. The policy for selecting an action is ε-greedy policy, with $\varepsilon = 0.1$. The probability for selecting an optimal action from those available in each state is 90%.

3.3 Simulation results and discussion

The inflow rate into a simulated buffer tank is introduced as in Figure 5 (a), which is a sinusoidal signal with amplitude 20, from an average value of 50 l/m. The level evolution can be seen in Figure 5(b). The control signal, which is the opening of the out-flow valve, is shown in Figure 5 (c). Clearly, the controller opens the valve widely when the system observes that the level of the tank is lower; otherwise, the opening of the valve is reduced when the level of the tank is high to maintain outflow as constant as possible. As a result, the outflow of the system remains in the defined goal band; as shown in Figure 5 (d). The noise observes in outflow is because the agent has finite-discrete action space. Thus, the controller objectives are fulfilled: the controller is capable to learn to avoid abrupt changes in the out flow.

Next section discusses the online laboratory application of the proposed MFLC to control pH and oxidation processes.

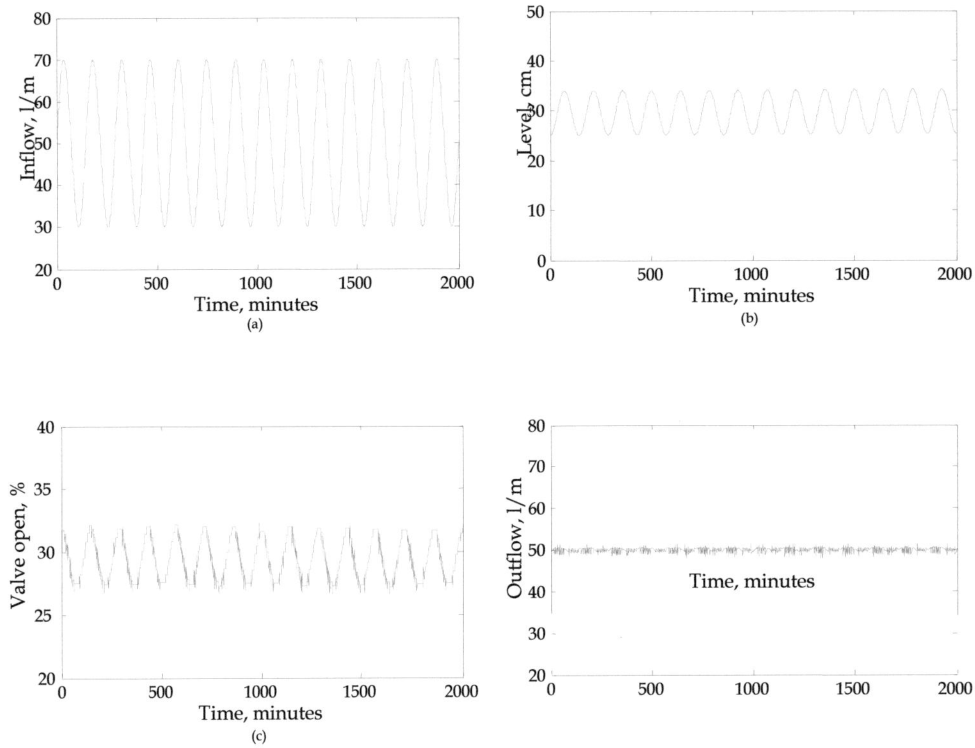

Fig. 5. Incoming and outcoming signal for learning to control buffer tank; (a) inflow signal, (b) liquid level in the tank, and (c) output manipulation flow.

4. Online laboratory assessment

The proposed algorithm has been tested for a view towards real-world applications in the laboratory plants. The first application is for controlling a pH process during wastewater treatment, which is known as a representative example of highly nonlinear, time-varying and difficult to model process plant, mainly resulting from interactions between many different chemical species. Thus, this pH process is very difficult to control using standard control techniques. Secondly, the MFLC algorithm is tested to control oxidation processes at certain ORP values corresponding to on-specification discharge.

4.1 pH control

pH control in neutralization process is a ubiquitous problem encountered many process control industry (see Kalafatis *et al.*, 2005 and references therein). For example, the pH value is controlled in chemical processes such as fermentation, precipitation, oxidation, flotation and solvent extraction process. Also, control of pH in food and beverage production (such as in bread, liquor, beer, soy sauce, cheese, and milk production) is an important issue because the enzymatic reactions are affected by the pH value of the process and each has its an optimum pH which is critical to the yield. Other parameters involved in controlling pH process are chemical equilibrium, kinetic, thermodynamic and mixing problems. Considering all these influencing factors in controller design is an overwhelming task. On the other hand, the process buffer capacity varies with time, which is unknown and dramatically changes process gain. This can be understood as, for example, if either the concentration in the inlet flow or the composition of the feed changes, the shape of the titration curve will be drastically altered. This means that the process nonlinearity becomes time dependent and the system moves among several titration curves. Other characteristics include the dissociation of weak acids and bases or their salts involved in the solution determine the number of hydrogen ions. All weak species have the property, called buffering, to resist change in pH. A weak acid, for example, is not completely dissociated, so it can absorb hydrogen ion by converting them to undissociated acid molecules. Also, due to the nonlinear dependence of the pH value on the amount of titrated reactant the process will be inherently nonlinear. Therefore, it is difficult to develop a sound mathematical model of the pH process for designing a proper controller.

Many researchers proposed control strategies based on the titration curve (see Wright and Kravaris, 1991 and references therein). Wiener models are used for controller design by Kalafatis *et al.* (2005). These types of controllers are difficult to implement due to the complexity of the resulting control structures. Also, the designed controller is not a general purpose one, namely as the acid-base system change, the controller needs to be redesigned.

Intelligent controllers have been proposed by some researchers as alternative strategies, applying fuzzy control, neural networks or different combination of intelligent and model-based methods (Edgar and Postlethwaite, 2000; Krishnapura and Jutan, 2000; Mwembeshi *et al.*, 2004; Fuente *et al.*, 2006). As discussed in these cited references, tight and robust pH control are often difficult to achieve due to the inherent uncertain, nonlinear and time varying characteristics of pH neutralization processes. Also, the controller needs a huge number training examples in order to guarantee stability and performance.

In this section, the MFLC design strategy is assessed experimentally. The experimental setup consists of a CSTR (Figure 6) where a process stream (sodium acetate) is titrated with a solution of hydrochloric acid (HCl) to maintain at a certain pH value outflow stream. The solution of process stream is prepared for various concentration levels. However, the titrating stream is prepared using 1% concentration. To have the desirable outflow pH level, the controller manipulates titrating flow into the CSTR and it is assumed that the mixing in the tank is homogeneous; therefore, the concentration in the effluent stream is similar to the concentration in the reactor.

The control variable u_t is the flowrate of the titrating stream (normalized to the maximum value), which is applied using a peristaltic pump (ISMATEC MS-1 REGLO/6-160).

The output variable, y_t, is the logarithmic hydrogen ion concentration (pH) in the reactor. The pH value in the mixture is measured using an Ag-AgCl electrode (Crison 52-00) and transmitted using a pH-meter (Kent EIL9143). The electrode dynamic response presents appreciable and asymmetric inertia. The pH measured and the control signals are transmitted through an A/D interface (ComputerBoards CIO-AD16, 0-5V). The plant is controlled and monitored with a standard PC, using Matlab and the Real-Time Toolbox for online control.

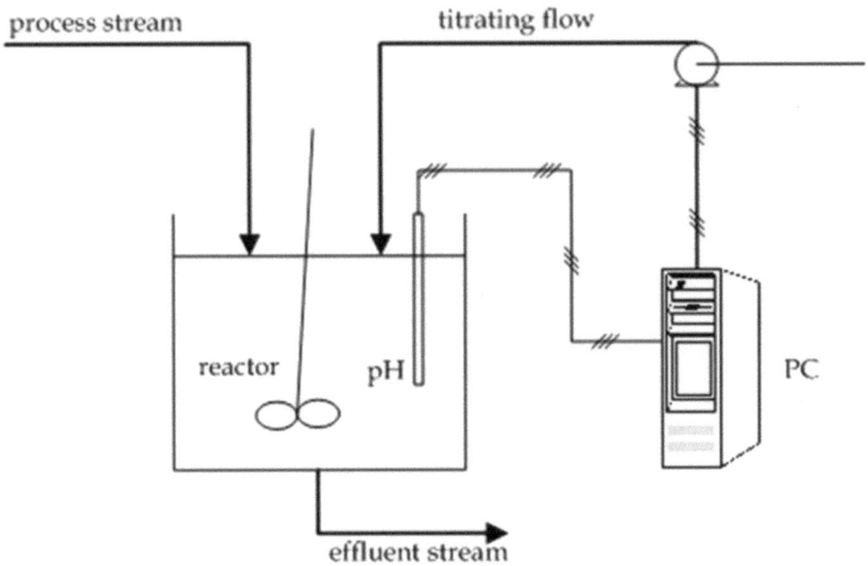

Fig. 6. Typical pH neutralization process plant.

The pH plant shown in Figure 6 is a typical laboratory set-up existing in the Department of Systems Engineering, University of Valladolid. The neutralization reactor is to overflow, hence the volume of liquid in the tank is constant (1 litter).

a) Parameters

The control objective is to bring the pH being inside a goal band with d=0.1, selected based on the level of measurement noise and the desired operating range of pH. The controller gain, k, is selected to be 2×10^{-5} and incremental control is defined as $-4.2\times10^{-4}<\Delta u<4.2\times10^{-4}$. There are 5 available states for negative or positive error. Therefore, there are 11 states. Every state has 5 available actions, except in goal state which only requires the wait action. Action 22 is the wait action.

In all the experiments the discounted factor, γ, is set to a value of 0.98 and the learning rate, α, is set 0.1. The Q-value matrix is initialized using zero entries. At every time step, the selected action is based on an ε-greedy policy, with ε=0.1, to leave enough room for the learning controller to explore state and actions. Rewards are defined using the simple assignment function

$$r_{t+1} = \begin{cases} 1 & \text{if } r-d < pH < r+d \\ -1 & \text{else} \end{cases} \tag{14}$$

b) Online Experimental Results and Discussion

Many experiments were carried out in the laboratory plant with different conditions, and with small variations in the algorithms and tuning parameters. For most cases, the application of the proposed MFLC controller to the laboratory plant showed good responses. Some responses of the plant for some changes in setpoint, compared with the responses for a PID in similar conditions can be seen in Figure 7 for the sodium acetate - hydrochloride acid system. The PID controller was tuned based on operating conditions at pH=5, where correction and proportional gains are chosen to be 0.01 and 0.001, respectively, whereas derivative and integral times are selected to be 1.

The comparison shows that the responses of the proposed MFLC algorithm settle in the reference faster than the PID controller, when a similar time is spent for the parameters: PID gives higher peaks and some oscillations due to variations from the nominal conditions.

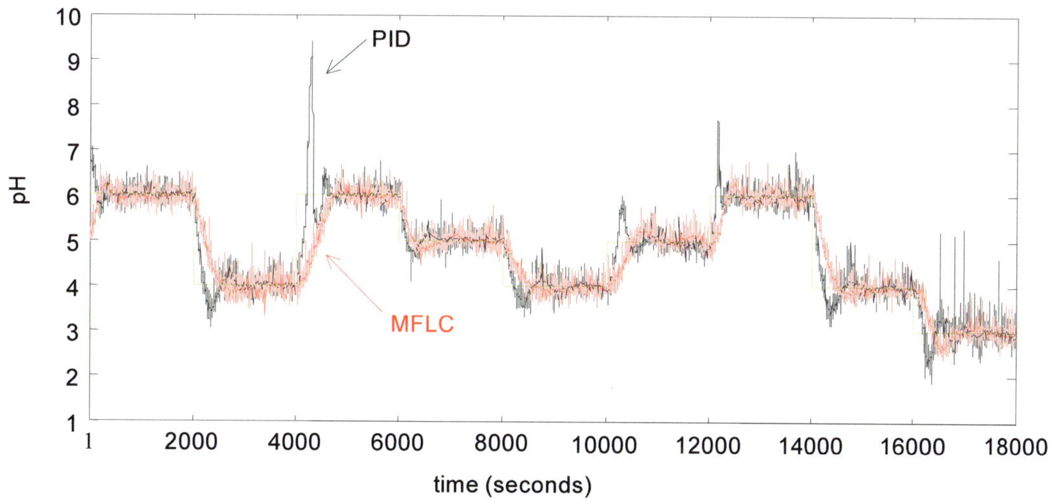

Fig. 7. Output responses of the plant for NaCH3COO-HCl.

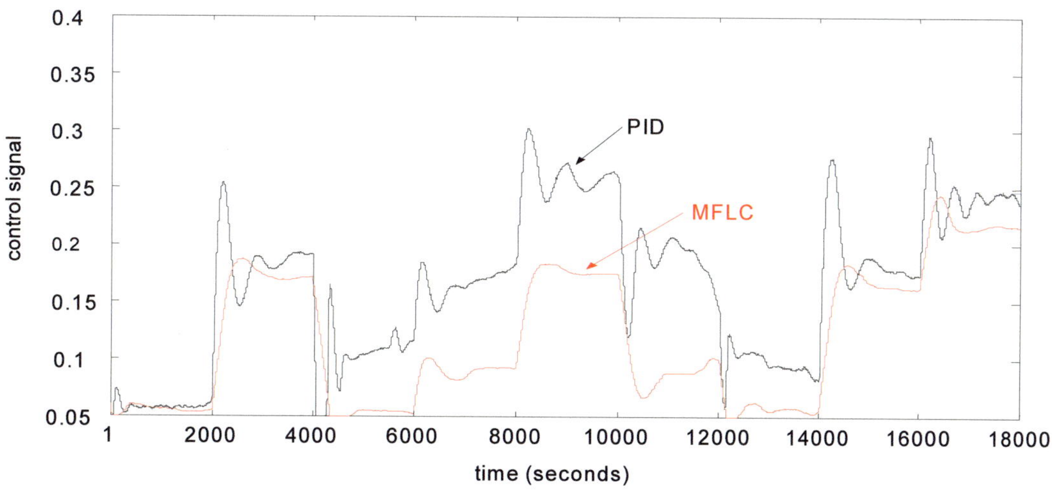

Fig. 8. Control signals for NaCH3COO-HCl.

Also the MFLC controller manipulates the actuator in a smoother than the one given by the PID controller (see Figure 8). Since MFLC allows a tolerance error of the process whenever the pH is within the control band, the control signal is very smooth when the pH is closer or within the control band, even if some exploration is carried out. The detailed discussion of the application MFLC to pH control is given in Syafiie *et al.* (2007a).

4.2 ORP control in Fenton's oxidation processes

Nowadays a central issue in the treatment of industrial wastewaters is the elimination of certain organic pollutants, which are very harmful to health even in small concentrations. Some of them are phenols, which are usually efficiently and economically eliminated through oxidation using Fenton's reagent. This Fenton's reagent refers to iron-mediated hydroxyl (•OH) production by hydrogen peroxide (H_2O_2).

The main issue is maintaining adequate values of hydroxil concentrations despite the huge number of chemical reactions involved (Laat and Gallard, 1999; Kwan, 2003). Unfortunately, it is very difficult to develop a sound mathematical model of the Fenton's oxidation processes for control purposes. Some reactions are slow rate and others are relative fast, but refractory intermediate act as a bottleneck for the complete oxidation. Also, as the process is used to decompose organic compounds, many parallel reactions are involved. For more detailed discussion, see Syafiie *et al.* (2007b).

Moreover, even if a detailed mathematical model were available (possible involving dozens of chemical reactions), it would be useless for real-time control, as it is not possible to measure in real-time the concentration of specific components ($OH^\bullet$, Fe^{3+}, Fe^{2+}, etc): the only available sensors are pH (to measure H^+ concentration) and ORP sensors to estimate the oxidizers activity (where ORP stands for oxidation-reduction potential). When using ORP for process control, it means that it is the present of the oxidizer or reducer that is being monitored, and not the chemical it is reacting with (McPherson, 1993). Thus, non-model based algorithms based on Reinforcement Learning ideas, such as the proposed MFLC algorithm would be very adequate to control this process.

A schematic of the experimental setup used to test the proposed algorithm is shown in Figure 9: For elimination of phenols, it is known that the oxidation reaction for phenol breakdown operates optimally on 550 to 600 mV of ORP value (Kwan, 2003), so the setpoint of the first MFLC agent is set to 570mV. It is also known that Fenton's reaction must be conducted on the range of temperatures between 80 to 90 ^{o}C, which is regulated using a simple thermostat, to represent industrial practice. Also, level in the buffer tank is not controlled to represent industrial practice, although there are detectors for low and high values. The reaction occurs on pH values between 3 and 5, so in the pretreatment the wastewater is titrated with hydrochloride acid.

The final part of the process is based on regulating pH to neutralize the drain (It would be dangerous for environment if the drain is released without neutralizing the pH). Therefore,. This neutralization is based on titrating the acidy stream (drain) with the base titrating flow (NaOH) to have pH around 7. Controlling pH of this strong acid-strong base system is known very difficult because the process is extremely nonlinear around the neutral pH, so it will be controlled using a second MFLC agent, designed following the methodology shown in previous section, coordinating with the first one.

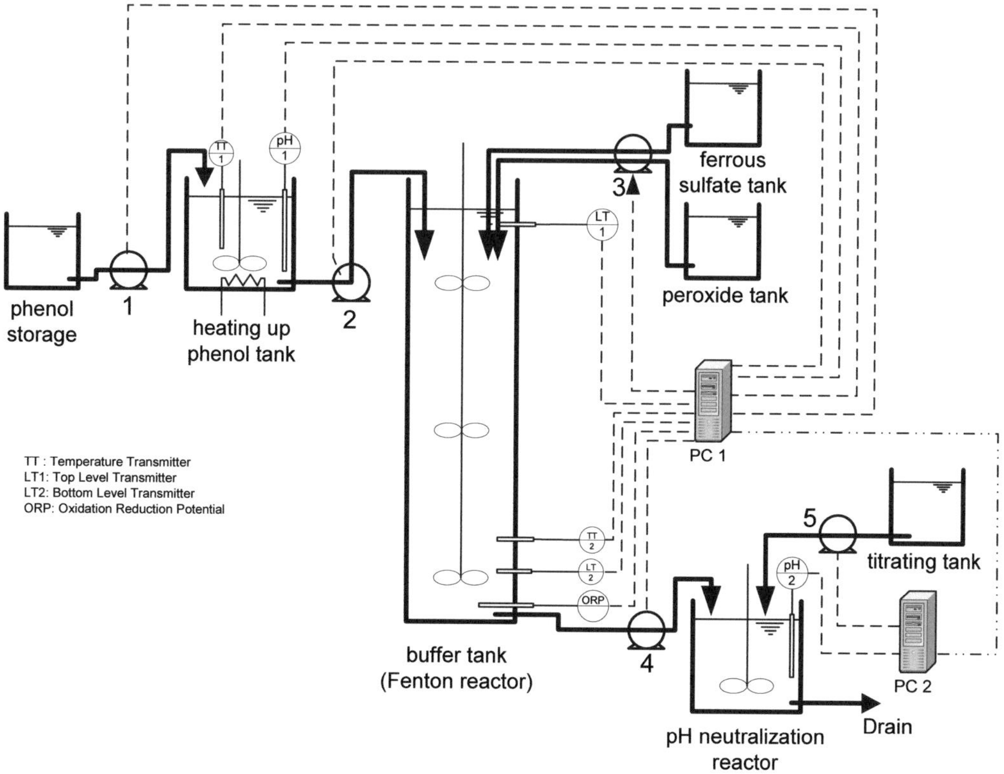

Fig. 9. Wastewater oxidation at a laboratory pilot plant

In summary, the first agent in order to handle the oxidation process receives reading of the process variables: apart from ORP value in buffer tank, temperature of inlet stream, and level and temperature in buffer tank. From this information, the agent learns to perform actions to control the oxidation process using the MFLC algorithm. For start-up of the process, first the wastewater is pretreated by heating and pH regulation. Once the temperature of the process stream reaches 80ºC, the first agent starts the process (turn on the pump 2) and starts manipulating the Fenton's reagent coming into the buffer tank (pump 3) to learn to handle the oxidation process.

a) Parameters

In this section, the selection of parameters for the MFLC agent that controls the oxidation process is discussed. The values of discounted factor γ=0.98 and learning rate a=0.1 from the previous study for pH control are maintain as the dynamics are similar. An ε-greedy policy is used, with parameter ε=0.1, to leave space for the agent to explore. To allow for sensor noise, the process goal is defined to be that the controller tolerates only d=5mV deviations from the setpoint r. In normal operation, states are defined for at most 100 mVolt for positive and negative error: thus, there are 41 states. The gain, k, is chosen to be 1×10^{-5}: Thus, every state has 20 available actions. The reinforcement signal is simple defined to be:

$$r_{t+1} = \begin{cases} 1 & \text{if } r-d < ORP < r+d \\ -1 & \text{else} \end{cases}, \tag{15}$$

The second agent, that controls the neutralization process, is the same as in the previous section, except that the controller gain is selected smaller, $k = 5\times10^{-7}$, because the process has higher gain.

b) Online Experimental Results and Discussion

Different experiments were carried out in the laboratory plant using the proposed MFLC agent. Some experiments are now shown for 1000 ppm phenol concentration, 10% $FeSO_4$, 1% NaOH, 1% HCl and 30% H_2O_2

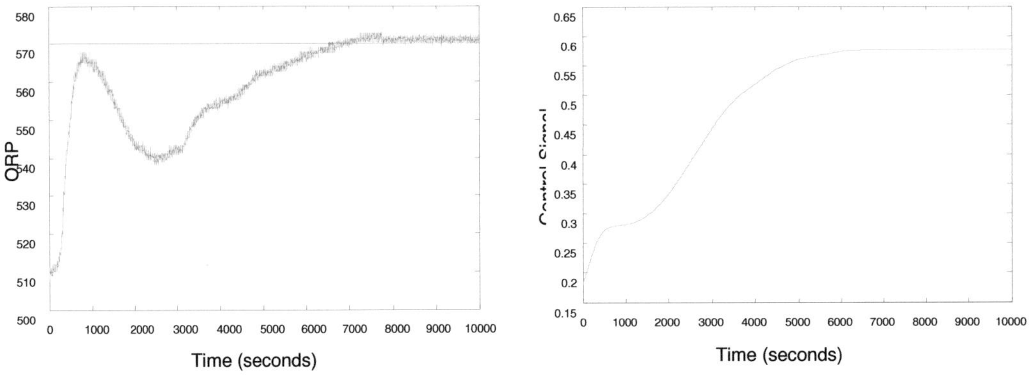

(a) (b)

Fig. 10. Oxidation control; (a) measured output, and (b) control signal

One typical response of the phenol decomposition process, controlled by the proposed MFLC agent, after learning, can be seen in Figure 10 (a): it can be seen that the MFLC controller maintains the oxidation process around the desired ORP level. This is carried out despite the complex dynamics of the system; During the first 1000 seconds, the process responses was reaching fast the reference, but then the process responses went down (until around 3000 seconds), because of the sequence of slow reactions that consumed both oxidizer and catalyst. After the balancing reaction are reached, then the responses of the process slowly returns to the goal band by increasing the control signal (see Figure 10, b). Thus, the responses of the process are most of time being on the optimal range of the reaction (550 to 600 mV), so phenols are correctly oxidized.

At the same time, the second agent manages the pH of the process on neutral range before it is discharged to environment. The responses of the neutralization process are plotted on Figure 11 (a). The second agents learns to manipulate the process to maintain it within the goal band, although there are some oscillations around the setpoint, as this is known to be a highly nonlinear process and the inlet composition changes with time, depending on the reactions in the buffer tank. The control signals (Figure 11, b) show that the agent actively manipulates the control signal when the process is outside the goal band.

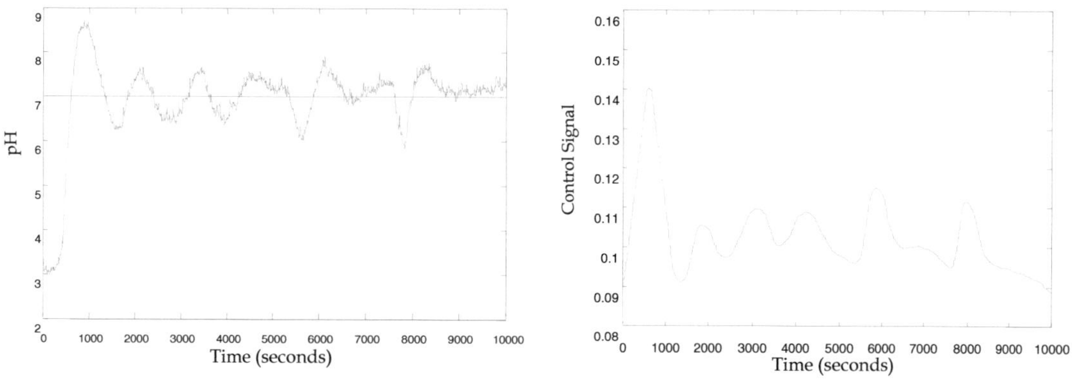

(a) (b)

Fig. 11. pH process control; (a) measured output, and (b) control signal

5. Conclusion

This chapter has presented a proposal to apply RL algorithms for process control problems. This proposal (called MFLC algorithm) is based on the well known *Q*-learning algorithm, using an specific definition of symbolic states based on specifying tolerances on the outputs and constraints on the control and its variation. Also, the propose approach uses few and simple tuning parameters to simplify the presentation of these techniques to plant operators. The technique has been presented on a simple example (buffer tank) to present the ideas behind the algorithm (in particular, the parameter selection issue) and then some experimental results in wastewater control problems have been presented to show the applicability of the proposed ideas. It is shown that the control objectives are fulfilled by the proposed MFLC agents, with smooth manipulated variables. Thus, the proposed MFLC technique is promising for increasing the degree and type of automation that can be effectively used in process control.

6. References

Baeza J. A., E. C. Ferreira and J. Lafuente (2000), Knowledge-Based Supervision and Control of Wastewater Treatment Plant: a Real-Time Implementation, *Water Science and Technology*, Vol. 14, No. 12, pp. 129-137.

Bucak I. O. and M. A. Zohdy (2001), Reinforcement learning control of nonlinear multi-link system, *Journal of Engineering Application of Artificial Intelligence*, Vol. 14, pp. 563 - 575.

Chidambaram, M. and See, R. P. (2002), A simple method of tuning PID controllers for integrator/dead-time processes, *Computer & Chemical Engineering*, Vol. 27, pp. 211-215.

Crites R. H. And Barto A. G. (1996), Improving Elevator Performance Using Reinforcement Learning, *Advances in Neural Information Processing Systems 8*, MIT Press, Cambridge MA.

De Laat, J., and H. Gallard (1999), Catalytic decomposition of hydrogen peroxide by Fe(III) in homogeneous aqueous solution: mechanism and kinetic modelling, *Environmental Science Technology*, Vol. 33 No. 16, pp. 2726-2732.

Faanes, A. & Skogestad, S. (2003), Buffer Tank Design for Acceptable Control Performance, *Industrial Engineering Chemistry Research*, Vol. 42, pp. 2198-2208.

Fuente M. J., Robles C., Casado O., Syafiie S. & Tadeo F. (2006), Fuzzy Control of a Neutralization Process, Engineering Applications of Artificial Intelligence, Vol. 19, pp. 905-914.

Kalafatis A. D., L. Wang and W. R. Cluett (2005), Linearizing feedforward-feedback control of pH process based on Wiener model, *Journal of Process Control*, Vol. 15, pp. 10 3 - 112.

Krishnapura V. G. and Jutan. A. (2000), A neural adaptive controller, *Chemical Engineering Science*, Vol. 55, pp 3803 - 3812.

Kwan, W.P. (2003), *Decomposition of Hydrogen Peroxide and Organic Compounds in the Present of Iron and Iron Oxides*, PhD Dissertation, MIT.

Martinez E. C. (2000), Batch process modelling for optimization using reinforcement learning, *Computer and chemical engineering*, Vol. 24, pp. 1187 - 1193.

McPherson L. L. (1993), Understanding ORP's in the disinfection process. *Water Engineering Management*, Vol. 140, No. 11, pp.29-31.

Mwembeshi M. M., Kent C. A., and Salhi S. (2004), A genetic algorithm based approach to intelligent modelling and control of pH in reactor, *Computer and Chemical Engineering*, Vol. 28, No. 9, pp. 1743 - 1757.

Ng A. Y., Coates A., Diel M., Ganapathi V., Schulte J., Tse B., Berger E. and Liang E.(2004), Inverted autonomous helicopter flight via reinforcement learning, In *International Symposium on Experimental Robotics, 2004.*

Peng Y.Z. Gao J. F., Wang S. Y. and Sui M. H. (2002), Use pH and ORP as fuzzy control parameters of denitrification in SBR process, *Water Science Technology*, Vol. 46, No. 4-5, pp. 131 - 137.

Ramirez, N., and Jackson H. (1999), "Application of neural networks to chemical process control", *Computers and Chemical Engineering*, Vol. 37, pp. 387-390.

Schoknecht, R. and M. Riedmiller (2003), Learning to control a multiple time scales, *Proceeding of ICANN 2003*, Istanbul Turkey, June 26 - 29, pp 479 - 487.

Sutton, R. S. & Barto, A. G. (1998), *Reinforcement Learning: an Introduction*, the MIT Press, Cambridge, MA.

Syafiie S., F. Tadeo and E. Martinez (2007a), Model-Free Learning Control of Neutralization Process Using Reinforcement Learning, *Engineering Application Of Artificial Intelligence*, Vol. 20, No. 6, pp. 767-782.

Syafiie S., F. Tadeo, and E. Martinez (2007b), Coordinated Control of Wastewater Oxidation Processes under Constrained Incremental Control, proceeding of *European Control Conference 2007*, Kos, Greece 2 - 5 Juli, 2007

Tani T., Murakoshi S. and Umano M. (1996), Neuro-fuzzy hybrid control system of tank level in petroleum plant, IEEE transactions on Fuzzy Systems, Vol. 4, No. 3, pp. 360 - 368.

Watkins C. J. C. H. (1989), *Learning from delayed rewards*, a PhD thesis at King's College, Cambridge.

Wright, R. A., and Kravaris, C.(1991), "Nonlinear Control of pH Processes Using the Strong Acid Equivalent" *Industrial and Engineering Chemistry Research*, Vol. 30, No. 7, pp. 1561-1572.

Ziegler, J. G. and Nichols, N. B. (1942), Optimum settings for automatic controllers, *Trans. ASME*, Vol. 64, pp. 759 - 765.

17

Reinforcement Learning-Based Supervisory Control Strategy for a Rotary Kiln Process

Xiaojie Zhou, Heng Yue and Tianyou Chai
Key Laboratory of Integrated Automation of Process Industry, Northeastern University
P. R. China

1. Introduction

Rotary kiln is a kind of large scale sintering device widely used in metallurgical, cement, refractory materials, chemical and environment protection industries. Its complicated working mechanism includes physical change and chemical reaction of material, procedure of combustion, thermal transmission among gaseous fluid, solid material fluid and the liner. The automation problem of such processes remains unsolved because of the following inherent complexities. A rotary kiln is a typical distributed parameter system with correlative temperature distribution of gaseous phase and solid phase along its axis direction. Limited by device rotation and technical design, sensors and actuators can be installed only at the kiln head and kiln tail, and lumped parameter control strategies are employed to deal with distributed parameter problems. Thus the rotary kiln process is a multivariable nonlinear system with strong coupling, large lag and uncertain disturbances. Moreover, the key controlled variable of burning zone temperature is measured with serious disturbances. Most of rotary kilns are still under manual control with human operator observing the burning status. As a result, the product quality is hard to be kept consistent and energy consumption remains high, kiln liner is easy to wear out, the kiln running rate and yield is low.

Although several advanced control strategies including fuzzy control (Holmblad & Østergaard, 1995) , intelligent control (Jarvensivu et al., 2001a; Jarvensivu et al., 2001b) and predictive control (Zanovello & Budman, 1999) have been introduced into process control of rotary kiln, all these researches focused on stabilizing some key controlled variables but are valid only for cases that boundary conditions do not change frequently. As a matter of fact, the boundary conditions of a rotary kiln often change. For example, the material load, water content and components of the raw material slurry vary frequently and severely. Moreover, the offline analysis data of components of raw material slurry reach the operator with large time delay. Thus conventional control strategy cannot reach automatic control and keep the product quality consistent. To deal with the complexity of operation conditions, the authors have proposed an intelligent control system based on human-machine interaction for an alumina rotary kiln in (Zhou et al., 2004; Zhou et al., 2006), in which human intervention function was design so that, if the operation condition changed largely, the human operator observing burning status can intervene the control actions when the system is in the automatic control mode to enhance the adaptability of the control system.

This chapter develops a supervisory control approach for burning zone temperature based on Q-learning, in which the signals of human intervention are viewed as the reinforcement learning signals. Section 2 makes brief descriptions of process and supervisory control system architecture. Section 3 discusses the detailed methodology of Q-learning-based supervisory control approach. The implementation and industrial applications are shown in Section 4. Finally, Section 5 draws the conclusion.

2. Process description and supervisory control system architecture

The alumina rotary kiln process is described as follows. Raw material slurry is sprayed into the rotary kiln from upper end (the kiln tail). At the lower end (the kiln head), the coal powders from the coal injector and the primary air from the air blower are mixed into bi-phase fuel flow, which is sprayed into the kiln head hood and combusts with the secondary air, which comes from the cooler. The heated gas was brought to the kiln tail by the induced draft fan, while the material moves to the kiln head via the rotation of the kiln and its self weight, in counter direction with the gas. After the material passes through the drying zone, pre-heating zone, decomposing zone, burning zone and cooling zone in sequence, soluble sodium aluminate is generated in the clinker, which is the product of the kiln process. This process aims to reach high digesting rate of alumina in the following digestion procedure.

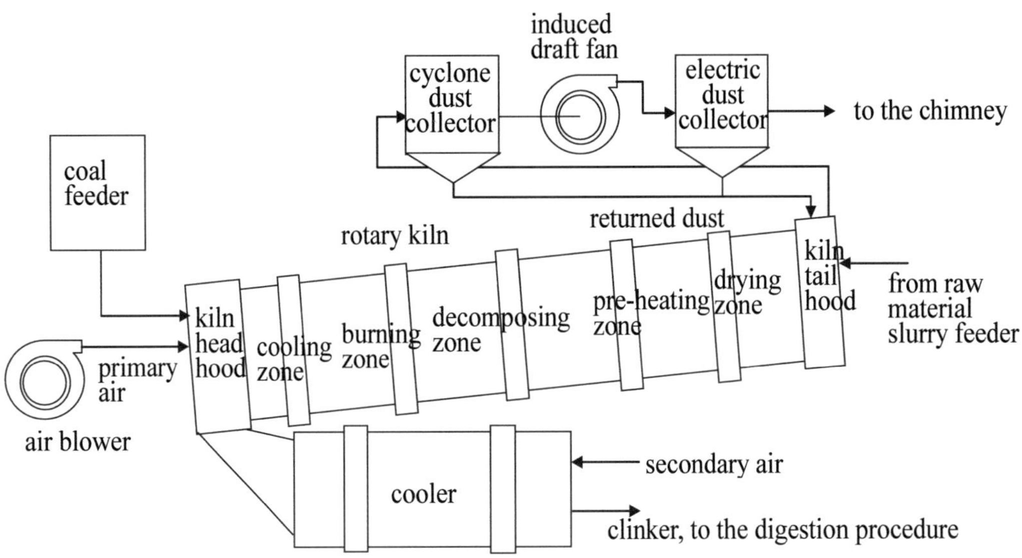

Fig. 1. Schematic diagram of the alumina rotary kiln

The control problem of quality index of kiln production is how to keep the liter weight of clinker being qualified under fluctuated boundary conditions and operating conditions. The liter weight of clinker is hard to measure online and cannot be controlled directly. This paper employs the following strategy to deal with this problem. Some online measurable technologic parameters with closed relations to the final quality index are chosen and controlled into certain ranges governed by technical requirement so that the quality index control is realized indirectly.

In the sintering process, the normal range of sintering temperature T_{sinter} of raw material depends upon components of raw material slurry. Variations of components of raw material slurry require corresponding variations of sintering temperature. Inconsistency of real sintering temperature range with requirement of raw material will results in over burning or under burning, and clinker quality is not satisfactory. Thus we conclude that components of raw material slurry and sintering temperature are the main aspects influencing clinker quality. Besides, other factors include particle size of raw material and residing time under T_{sinter}. The relationship between desired T_{sinter} and components of raw material slurry can be viewed as a unknown nonlinear function

$$T_{sinter} = f([A/S],[N/R],[C/S],[F/A]) \tag{1}$$

where [A/S] is the alumina silica ratio of raw material slurry, [N/R] is the alkali ratio, [C/S] is the calcium silica ratio, [F/A] is the iron alumina ratio. Among them, the alumina silica ratio of raw material slurry has the strongest influence on T_{sinter}, the latter must be enhanced along with the enhancement of the former.

From above analysis, one may conclude that there are two key issues about the control problem of quality index of kiln production. One is how to keep the kiln temperature distribution satisfing technical requirement under fluctuated boundary conditions and operating conditions, i.e. how to keep burning zone temperature, kiln tail temperature and residual oxygen content in combustion gas in their technical required ranges. The other is how to adjust the setpoint range of burning zone temperature so that the liter weight of clinker may be kept qualified under fluctuated boundary conditions and operating conditions.

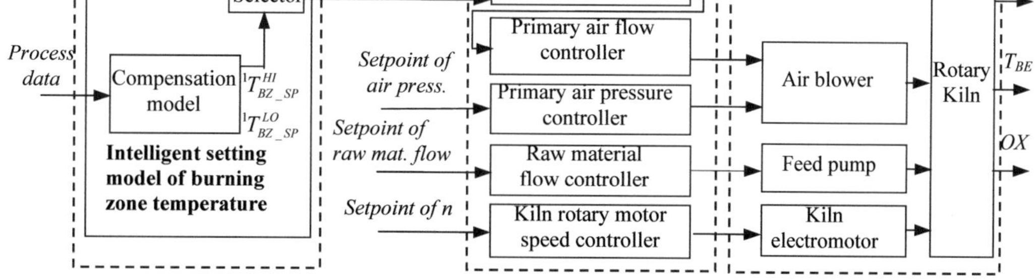

Fig. 2. General structure of the supervisory control system for rotary kiln process

This paper has constructed a supervisory control system consisting of a supervisory level and a process control level, whose general structure is shown in Fig. 2. The final target of this supervisory control system is to keep the production quality index, i.e. the clinker unit weight, being acceptable even if the boundary conditions changed. The related process control strategies in process control level include, 1) a hybrid intelligent temperature controller was designed, which coordinated the coal feeding u_1, damper position of the induced draft fan u_2, and primary air flow u_3 to make the burning zone temperature T_{BZ}, the kiln tail temperature T_{BE}, and the residual oxygen content in combustion gas OX satisfy technical requirements; T_{BZ} is indirectly measured by an infrared pyrometer located at kiln head hood, and T_{BE} is obtained through a thermocouple; 2) individual PI controllers were assigned to basic loops of primary air flow, primary air pressure and flow rate of raw material slurry; and 3) a human-machine interaction(HMI) mechanism was designed so that certain human interventions to coal feeding control from experienced operator can be introduced in the mode of automatic control when the operating conditions changed significantly. The aforementioned process control strategies were depicted in our previous study (Zhou et al., 2004).

The main part of the supervisory level is an intelligent setting model of T_{BZ}, which adjusts the setpoint range of T_{BZ} according to the variations of components of raw material slurry. The setpoints of T_{BE}, OX, primary air pressure, flow rate of raw material slurry and the kiln rotary speed n are given by the operators according to production scheduling and production experiences.

The intelligent setting model of burning zone temperature consists of a pre-setting model of burning zone temperature, a compensation model and a setting selector mechanism. The pre-setting model is to give the upper and lower limits of setpoint range of burning zone temperature, denoted by ${}^{0}T^{HI}_{BZ\_SP}$ and ${}^{0}T^{LO}_{BZ\_SP}$, calculating from the offline analysis data of components of raw material slurry. The fuzzy clustering analysis combined with case-based inference learning is employed to build up the pre-setting model of burning zone temperature. The core of the pre-setting model is a case base containing different upper and lower limits of setpoint range of burning zone temperature corresponding to different components of raw material slurry. Such case base is established through fuzzy clustering based data mining from vast process data samples under various components of raw material slurry. Details are not described in this paper.

As a matter of fact, the main problem we are facing is that the components of raw material slurry often change due to unstable raw material mixing process and the offline analysis data reach to the operator with large time delay so that the operator or the pre-setting model cannot directly adjust the setpoint of T_{BZ} duly. As a result, a single intelligent temperature controller and a single pre-setting model of T_{BZ} cannot maintain satisfactory performance. In such a case, a human operator usually rectifies the output of the temperature controller, i.e. the coal feeding, based on the experience of observing burning status through the HMI embedded in the control system. Such interventions can adapt the variation of operating conditions to a certain degree to sustain the quality of the product.

To deal with such a problem, a compensation model and a setting selector are appended. When the offline analysis data of components of raw material slurry are known and input into the system, i.e. the lth sampled time, the setting selector mechanism triggers the pre-setting model to calculated the proper setpoint range of T_{BZ}. When the components of raw material slurry are unknown, the compensation model is triggered to calculated the proper upper and lower limits of setpoint range of the burning zone temperature, denoted by ${}^{1}T_{BZ\_SP}^{HI}$ and ${}^{1}T_{BZ\_SP}^{LO}$ respectively. In the following section, a Q-learning strategy is employed to construct compensation model to learn the self-adjusting knowledge about the setpoint of T_{BZ} through online self-learning from the human intervention signals.

3. Setpoint adjustment approach based on Q-learning

3.1 Bases of Q-learning

Reinforcement learning is learning with a critic instead of a teacher. The only feedback provided by the critic is a scalar signal r called reinforcement, which can be regarded as a reward or a punishment. Reinforcement learning performs an online search to find an optimal decision policy in multi-stage decision problems.

Q-learning (Watkins & Dayan, 1992) is a reinforcement learning method where the learner builds incrementally a Q-function which attempts to estimate the discounted future rewards for taking actions from given states. The output of the Q-function for state x and action a is denoted by $Q(x,a)$ .When action a has been chosen and applied, the environment moves to a new state, x', and a reinforcement signal, r, is received. $Q(x,a)$ is updated by

$$Q_k(x,a) \leftarrow Q_{k-1}(x,a) + \alpha_k \{r + \gamma \max_{a' \in A(x')} Q_{k-1}(x',a') - Q_{k-1}(x,a)\} \tag{2}$$

where

$$\alpha_k = \frac{1}{1 + visits_k(x,a)} \tag{3}$$

where $A(x')$ is the set of possible actions in state x', γ is discount factor , α_k is the learning rate, and $visits_k(x,a)$ is the total number of times this state-action pair (x,a) has been visited up to and including the kth iteration.

3.2 Principle of setpoint adjustment approach based on Q-learning

In this section, we may design an online self-learning system based on reinforcement learning to gradually establish the optimal policy of setpoint adjustment of T_{BZ}. Although it cannot reach to the operator in time, the changes of components of raw material slurry may be indirectly reflected through certain measurements of the rotary kiln process. The measurements can be used to construct the environment state set of the learning system. Moreover, information of human interventions can be regarded as evaluations about whether the setpoint of T_{BZ} is proper or not, for human interventions often occur when the performance is unsatisfactory. Thus this kind of information can be defined as reward signal from environment.

For the learning system, the environment includes the rotary kiln process, the temperature controller and the operator. The environment provides current states and reinforcement payoffs to the learning system. The learning system produces the compensated upper and lower limits of setpoint range of T_{BZ} to temperature controller in the environment. The learning system consists of a state perceptron, a critic, a learner and an action selector, as shown in Fig. 3. The state perceptron firstly samples and processes selected measurements to construct the original state vector, and then converts the original continuous state vector into a discrete feature vector **x** based on a defined feature extraction function. The action selector employs a ε-greedy action selection strategy to produce an amendment of setpoint of T_{BZ} , i.e. ΔT_{BZ_SP} and the critic serves to calculate an internal practicable reward r relying on some heuristic rules. The learner updates value function of the state-action pair based on tabular Q-learning. The final outputs of the learning system are the compensated upper and lower limits of setpoint range of T_{BZ}, which are calculated respectively by

$$^{1}T_{BZ\_SP}^{HI}(k) = \Delta T_{BZ\_SP}(k) + {}^{1}T_{BZ\_SP}^{HI}(k-1) \tag{4}$$

$$^{1}T_{BZ\_SP}^{LO}(k) = \Delta T_{BZ\_SP}(k) + {}^{1}T_{BZ\_SP}^{LO}(k-1) \tag{5}$$

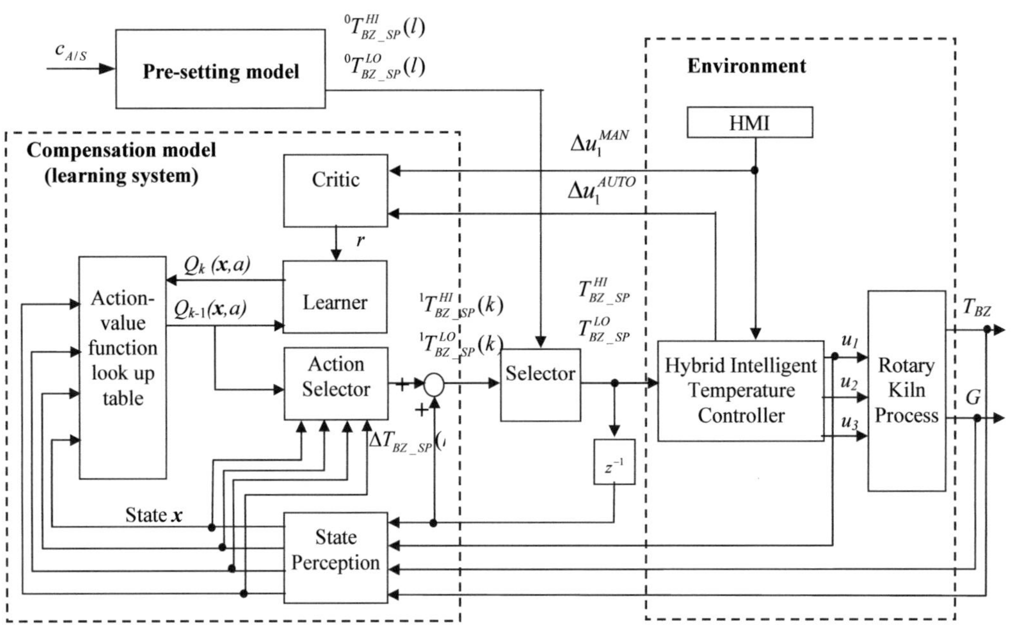

Fig. 3. Schematic diagram of setpoint adjustment approach for T_{BZ} based on Q-learning

In a Markov decision process (MDP), only the sequential nature of the decision process is relevant, not the amount of time that passes between decision stages. A generalization of this is the semi-Markov decision process (SMDP) in which the amount of time between one decision and the next is a random variable. For the learning process, we define τ_s as state perception time span for the perceptron to get the state of the environment and τ_r as reward calculation time span, also named as action execution time span, for the critic to calculate internal reward. The shortest time span from one decision to the next is $\tau = \tau_s + \tau_r$.

The design of the learning system concerns the following key issues:

1. Construction of the environment perception state set;
2. Determination of the action set;
3. Determination of the immediate reward function;
4. Determination of the learning algorithm.

3.3 Construction of the state set

When components of raw material slurry fluctuate and related offline analysis data are unavailable, we hope that the learning system can estimate the changes of the components of raw material slurry through the percepted information about the environment state. From this idea, some related variables are selected from online measurable variables of the kiln process based on human experience, with which the state vector $\mathbf{s}$ is defined to buildup the original state space $\mathbf{S}$ of the learning system, where $\mathbf{s}=[s_1,s_2,s_3,s_4,s_5]$, $\mathbf{s}\in\mathbf{S}$. s_1 is defined as the averaged burning zone temperature $\overline{T}_{BZ}$, s_2 is the averaged flow rate of raw material slurry $\overline{G}$, s_3 is the averaged coal feeding $\overline{u}_1$, s_4 and s_5 are the averaged upper and lower limit of the setpoint range of T_{BZ}, named as $\overline{T}^{HI}_{BZ\_SP}$ and $\overline{T}^{LO}_{BZ\_SP}$ respectively, all during τ_s. They are calculated from

$$\overline{T}_{BZ}=\sum_{j=1}^{J}T_{BZ}(j)/J \tag{6}$$

$$\overline{G}=\sum_{j=1}^{J}G(j)/J \tag{7}$$

$$\overline{u}_1=\sum_{j=1}^{J}u_1(j)/J \tag{8}$$

$$\overline{T}^{HI}_{BZ\_SP}=\sum_{j=1}^{J}T^{HI}_{BZ\_SP}(j)/J \tag{9}$$

$$\overline{T}^{LO}_{BZ\_SP}=\sum_{j=1}^{J}T^{LO}_{BZ\_SP}(j)/J \tag{10}$$

where $T_{BZ}(j)$, $G(j)$, $u_1(j)$, $T^{HI}_{BZ\_SP}(j)$, $T^{LO}_{BZ\_SP}(j)$ denote the jth sampling values of T_{BZ}, flow rate of raw material slurry, coal feeding, upper and lower limits of the setpoint range of T_{BZ} during τ_s respectively. J is the total number of sampling values during τ_s.

Since the state space $\mathbf{S}$ defined above is continuous, it is impossible to compute and store value functions for every possible state or state-action pair due to the curse of dimensionality. The issue is often addressed by generating a compact parametric representation, such as an artificial neural network, that approximates the value function and can guide future actions. we practically choose to use a feature extraction method (Tsitsiklis & Van Roy, 1996) to map the original continuous state space into a finite feature space, then we can employ tabular Q-learning to solve the problem.

By identifying one partition per possible feature vector, the feature extraction mapping $F(\mathbf{s}) = [f_1(s_1, s_4, s_5), f_2(s_1), f_3(s_2), f_4(s_3)]$ defines a partitioning of the original state space. The burning zone temperature biasing (from the setpoint range) level feature f_1, the temperature level feature f_2, flow rate of raw material slurry level feature f_3, the coal feeding level feature f_4 are defined respectively by

$$f_1(s_1,s_4,s_5) = \begin{cases} -2, & (\overline{T}_{BZ} - \overline{T}_{BZ\_SP}^{LO}) < -L2 \\ -1, & -L2 \le (\overline{T}_{BZ} - \overline{T}_{BZ\_SP}^{LO}) < -L1 \\ 0, & (\overline{T}_{BZ} - \overline{T}_{BZ\_SP}^{HI}) \le L1 \text{ and } (\overline{T}_{BZ} - \overline{T}_{BZ\_SP}^{LO}) \ge -L1 \\ 1, & L1 < (\overline{T}_{BZ} - \overline{T}_{BZ\_SP}^{HI}) \le L2 \\ 2, & (\overline{T}_{BZ} - \overline{T}_{BZ\_SP}^{HI}) > L2 \end{cases} \tag{11}$$

$$f_2(s_1) = \begin{cases} 0, & \overline{T}_{BZ} < 1250 \\ 1, & 1250 \le \overline{T}_{BZ} < 1280 \\ 2, & \overline{T}_{BZ} \ge 1280 \end{cases} \tag{12}$$

$$f_3(s_2) = \begin{cases} 0, & 70 \le \overline{G} < 75 \\ 1, & 75 \le \overline{G} < 80 \\ 2, & \overline{G} \ge 80 \\ 3, & else \end{cases} \tag{13}$$

$$f_4(s_3) = \begin{cases} 0, & 800 \le \overline{u}_1 < 1000 \\ 1, & 1000 \le \overline{u}_1 < 1200 \\ 2, & 1200 \le \overline{u}_1 < 1400 \\ 3, & else \end{cases} \tag{14}$$

where $L1$ and $L2$ are the thresholds scaling the burning zone temperature bias from setpoint range level.

Each feature function maps the state space $\mathbf{S}$ to a finite set $P_m, m = 1,2,3,4$. Then we associate the feature vector $\mathbf{x} = [x_1, x_2, x_3, x_4] = F(\mathbf{s})$ to each state $\mathbf{s} \in \mathbf{S}$. The resulting set of all possible feature vectors, also defined as feature space $\mathbf{X}$, is the Cartesian product of the sets P_m.

Because the compensation model for the setpoint of burning zone temperature needs only to be applicable for the normal kiln operating conditions, the design of state set needs certain filtration in the feature space $\mathbf{X}$. The appearence of $x_3 = 3$ or $x_4 = 3$ might means the abnormal operating conditions such as low load of flow rate of raw material slurry during kiln starting phase or abnormal coal components. The state set excludes such valued feature vectors.

3.4 Action set

The learning system aims to deduce the proper or best actions of setpoint adjustment of T_{BZ} from specified environment state. The problem to be handled is how to choose ΔT_{BZ_SP} according to the changes of environment state. Thus the action set can be defined as $A = \{a^1, a^2, a^3, a^4, a^5\} = \{-30, -15, 0, 15, 30\}$.

3.5 Immediate reward signal

During τ_r after the action selection based on current state judgment, the learning system determines the immediate reward signal $r = R(\Delta u_1^{MAN}, \Delta u_1^{AUTO})$, which represents the satisfactory degree of the environment about the action execution under current state, using the human intervention regulation of coal feeding Δu_1^{MAN} and temperature controller regulation Δu_1^{AUTO}.The reward signal r is determined in table 1.

r	$\lvert\Delta Coal_{AUTO}\rvert \le L3$	$\Delta Coal_{AUTO} > L3$	$\Delta Coal_{AUTO} < -L3$
$\lvert\Delta Coal_{MAN}\rvert \le L3$	0.4	0.4	0.4
$\Delta Coal_{MAN} > L3$	-0.2	0.2	-0.4
$\Delta Coal_{MAN} < L3$	-0.2	-0.4	0.2

Table 1. Definition of immediate reward function R

where $L3$ is the threshold constant, $\Delta Coal_{MAN}$ denotes the total regulation of coal feeding from human intervention during τ_r, which is calculated by

$$\Delta Coal_{MAN} = \sum_{\tau_r} \Delta u_1^{MAN} \tag{15}$$

and $\Delta Coal_{AUTO}$ denotes the total regulation from temperature controller during τ_r, which is calculated by

$$\Delta Coal_{AUTO} = \sum_{\tau_r} \Delta u_1^{AUTO} \tag{16}$$

The immediate reward function R in Table 1 is from the following heuristic rules:
During τ_r, if $|\Delta Coal_{MAN}| \le L3$, which means the operator is satisfied with the regulation action of the control system and little human intervention occurs, then a positive reward r=0.4 is returned. If $\Delta Coal_{MAN}$ and $\Delta Coal_{AUTO}$ have same regulation directions , which means the direction of regulation action of the control system fits with the operator expectation with short amplitude, then a positive reward r=0.2 is returned. If $\Delta Coal_{MAN} > L3$ or $\Delta Coal_{MAN} < -L3$, and $|\Delta Coal_{AUTO}| \le L3$, which means little regulation action of the control system occurs while large human intervention occurs, then r=-0.2. If $\Delta Coal_{MAN}$ and $\Delta Coal_{AUTO}$ have contrary regulation directions, which means the operator is not satisfied with the regulation action of the control system, then a negative reward r=-0.4 is returned.

3.6 Algorithm summary

The whole learning algorithm of the learning system under learning mode is summarized as follows:

Step 1: If it is in initialization, then the Q value table of state-action pairs is initialized according to expert experience, otherwise goto step 2 directly;

Step 2: During τ_s, the state perceptron obtains and saves measured burning zone temperature, flow rate of raw material slurry, coal feeding, upper and lower limits of the setpoint range of the burning zone temperature, and calculates related averaged values by using (6)-(10), then transfer them into related level features to construct feature vector $\mathbf{x}$ by using (11)-(14) .

Step 3: Search in the Q table to make state matching, if unsuccessful then goto step 2 to make state judgement again, if successful then go ahead;

Step 4: The action selector chooses an amendment of setpoint of T_{BZ} as its output according to ε-greedy action selection strategy (Sutton & Barto, 1998), where ε=0.1;

Step 5: During τ_r, the critic determines the reward signal r of this state-action pair according to Table 1.

Step 6: When the current τ_r finishes, entering the next τ_s, the state perceptron judges the next state $\mathbf{x}'$, state matching is made in the Q table, if unsuccessful then goto step 2 to start the next learning round, if successful then using the reward signal r, the learner calculates and updates the Q value of the last state-action pair by using (2)-(3), where $\gamma = 0.9$.

Step 7: Judge if the learning should be finished. When all evaluation values of state-action pairs in the Q table do not change obviously, it means that the Q-function have converged, and the compensation model is well trained.

The problem of Q table initialization: there is no explicit tutor signal in reinforcement learning, the learning procedure is carried out through constant interaction with environment to get the reward signals. Usually, less information from environment will results low learning efficiency of reinforcement learning. In this paper different initial evaluation values are given for different actions under same state based on expert experience so that the convergence of the algorithm has been speedup, and online learning efficiency has been enhanced.

3.7 Technical issues

The main task of the learning system is to estimate the variations of the kiln operating conditions continuously, and to adjust the setpoint range of burning zone temperature accordingly. Such adjustments should be made when the burning zone temperature is fairly controlled smooth by the temperature controller. Such a judgment signal is given out from the hybrid intelligent temperature controller. If the temperature control is in the abnormal conditions, the learning procedure must be postponed. In this case the setpoint range of the burning zone temperature is kept constant.

Moreover, setpoint adjustments should be made when the learning system make accurate judgment about the kiln operating conditions. Because of complexity and fluctuation of kiln operating conditions, accurate judgment for current state usually needs long time, and the time span between two setpoint adjustments cannot be too short, otherwise the calculated immediate reward cannot reflect the real influence of the above adjustment upon the behaviour and performance of the control system. Thus special attention should be paid to selection of τ_s and τ_r. This makes solid foundation, on which obtained environmental states and reinforcement payoffs are effective.

After long term running, large characteristic changes of components of raw material slurry, coal and kiln device may appear. The previous optimal designed compensation model for the setpoint of burning zone temperature might become invalid under new operating conditions. This needs new optimal design to keep good performance of control system for long term. In this case, the reinforcement learning system should be switched into the learning mode, and above models can be established through new learning to improve the performance, so that the control system has strong adaptability for long term running. This is an important issue drawing the attentions of the enterprise.

4. Industrial application

Shanxi Alumina Plant is the largest alumina plant in Asia with megaton production capacity. It has 6 oversize rotary kilns of φ4.5×110m. Its production employs the series parallel technology of Bayer and Sintering Processes. Such a production technology makes components of the raw material of rotary kilns often vary in large range. It is more difficult to keep a stable kiln operation than ordinary rotary kiln.

A supervisory control system has been developed in the #4 rotary kiln of Shanxi Alumina Plant based on the proposed structure and the setpoint adjustment approach of burning zone temperature. It is implemented in the I/A Series 51 DCS of Foxboro. The Q-learning-based strategy has been realized in the configuration environment of Fox Draw and ICC of I/A Series 51 DCS. Related parameters are chosen as τ_s = 30min, τ_r =120min.

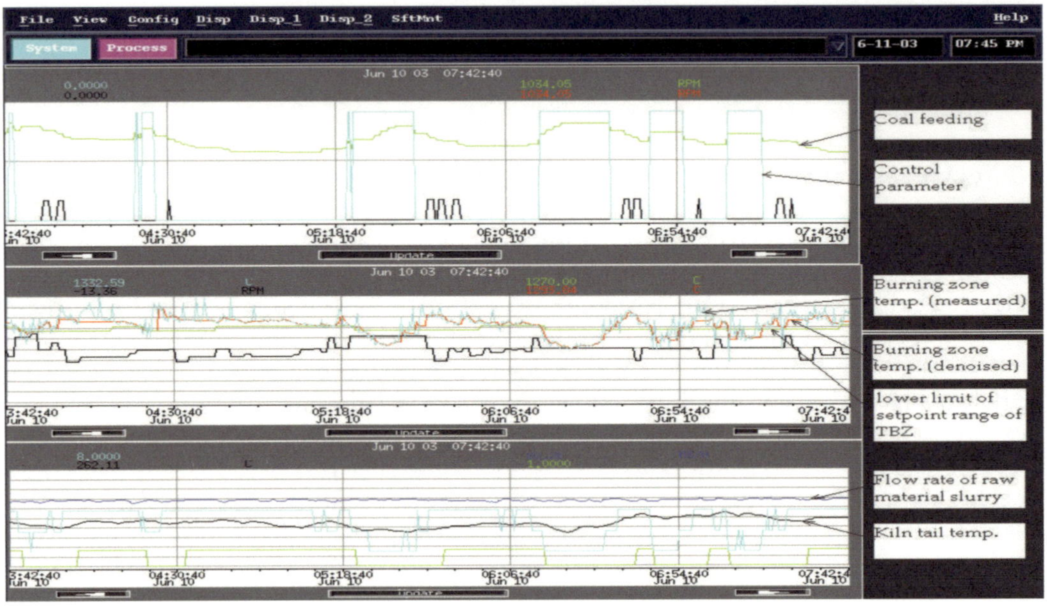

Fig. 4. The setpoint of burning zone temperature is properly adjusted after learning

Fig. 4 shows the condition that, after a period of learning, a set of relatively stable strategies of setpoint adjustment has been established so that the setpoint range of T_{BZ} can be automatically adjusted to satisfy the requirement of sintering temperature, according to the level of raw material slurry flow, the level of coal feeding, the level of T_{BZ} and the level of temperature biasing. It can be seen that the setpoint adjustment happened only when T_{BZ} is controlled smoothly. The judgment signal, denoted by "control parameter" in Fig. 4, takes value of 0 when the burning zone temperature is fairly controlled smooth, and vice versa.

The adjustment actions of the above reinforcement learning system result in satisfactory performance of the kiln temperature controller, with reasonable and acceptable regulation amplitude of coal feeding and regulation rhythm, so that the adaptability for variations of operating conditions has been significantly enhanced and the production quality index, liter weight of clinker, can be kept to reach the technical requirement even if the boundary conditions and operation conditions change. Meanwhile, human interventions become weaker and weaker since the model application has improved the system performance.

In the period of test run, the running rate of supervisory control system has been up to 90%. Negative influences on the heating and operating conditions from human factors have been avoided, rationalization and stability of clinker production has been kept, and operational life span of kiln liner has been prolonged remarkably. The qualification rate of clinker unit weight has been enhanced from 78.67% to 84.77%; production capacity in unit time per kiln has been increased from 52.95t/h to 55t/h with 3.9% increment. The kiln running rate has been elevated up to 1.5%. Through the calculation based on average 10°C reduction of kiln tail temperature and average 2% decrease of the residual oxygen content in combustion gas, it can be concluded that 1.5% energy consumption has been saved.

5. Conclusion

In this chapter, we focus on the discussion about an implementation strategy of how to employ reinforcement learning in control of a typical complex industrial process to enhance control performance and adaptability for the variations of operating conditions of the automatic control system.

Operation of large rotary kilns is difficult and relies on experienced human operators observing the burning status, because of their inherent complexities. Thus the problem of human-machine coordination is addressed when we design the rotary kiln control system, and the human intervention and adjustment can be introduced. Except for emergent operation conditions that need urgent human operation for system safety, the fact is observed that human interventions to the automatic control system usually imply human's discontent to the performance of the control system when the variation of boundary conditions occurs. From this idea, an online reinforcement learning-based supervisory control system is designed, in which the human interventions might be defined as the environmental reward signals. The optimal mapping between rotary kiln operating conditions and adjustment of important controller setpoint parameters can be established gradually. Successful application of this strategy in an alumina rotary kiln has shown that the adaptability and performance of the control system have been improved effectively.

Further research will focus on trying to improve the setting model of the burning zone temperature by introducing the offline analysis data of clinker liter weight to reject the other uncertain disturbances in the quality control of kiln production.

6. References

Holmblad, L. & Østergaard, J. (1995). The FLS application of Fuzzy logic, *Fuzzy Sets and Systems*, Vol. 70, No. 2-3, (March 1995) 135-146, ISSN: 0165-0114

Jarvensivu, M.; Saari, K. & Jamsa-Jounela, S. (2001a). Intelligent control system of an industrial lime kiln process, *Control Engineering Practice*, Vol. 9, No. 6, (June 2001) 589-606, ISSN: 0967-0661

Jarvensivu, M.; Juuso, E. & Ahava, O. (2001b). Intelligent control of a rotary kiln fired with producer gas generated from biomass, *Engineering Applications of Artificial Intelligence*, Vol. 14, No. 5, (October 2001) 629-653, ISSN: 0952-1976

Sutton, R. & Barto, A. (1998). *Reinforcement Learning: An Introduction*, MIT Press, ISBN: 0262193981, Cambridge, MA

Tsitsiklis, J. & Van Roy, B. (1996). Feature-based methods for large scale dynamic programming, *Machine Learning*, Vol. 22, No. 1-3, (Jan./Feb./March 1996) 59-94, ISSN:0885-6125

Watkins, J. & Dayan, P. (1992). Q-Learning, *Machine Learning*, Vol. 8, No. 3-4, (May 1992) 279-292, ISSN:0885-6125

Zanovello, R. & Budman, H. (1999). Model predictive control with soft constraints with application to lime kiln control, *Computers and Chemical Engineering*, Vol. 23, No. 6, (June 1999) 791-806, ISSN: 0098-1354

Zhou, X.; Xu, D.; Zhang, L. & Chai, T. (2004). Integrated automation system of a rotary kiln process for Alumina production, *Journal of Jilin University (Engineering and*

Technology Edition), Vol. 34, No. sup, (August 2004)350-353. ISSN:1671-5497(in Chinese)

Zhou, X.; Yue, H.; Chai, T. & Fang, B. (2006). Supervisory control for rotary kiln temperature based on reinforcement learning , *Proceedings of* 2006 *International Conference on Intelligent Computing*, pp. 428-437, ISBN: 3 540 37255 5, Kunming, China, August, 2006, Springer-Verlag, Berlin, Germany

18

Inductive Approaches Based on Trial/Error Paradigm for Communications Network

Abdelhamid Mellouk
LISSI/SCTIC/QoSiDiN laboratory, University Paris XII-Val de Marne
France

1. Introduction

Today, providing a good quality of service (QoS) in irregular traffic networks is an important challenge. Besides, the impressive emergence and the important demand of the rising generation of real-time Multi-service (such as Data, Voice VoD, Video-Conference, etc.) over communication heterogeneous networks, require scalability while considering a continuous QoS. This emergence of rising generation Internet required intensive studies these last years which were based on QoS routing for heterogeneous networks on the one hand and on the backbone architecture level of communication networks characterized by a high and irregular traffic on the other hand (Mellouk et al., 2007b).

The basic function of QoS routing is to find a network path which satisfies the given constraints and optimize the resource utilization. The integration of QoS parameters increases the complexity of the used routing algorithms. Thus, the problem of determining a QoS route that satisfies two or more path constraints (for example, delay and cost) is known to be NP-complete (Gravey & Jhonson, 1979). A difficulty is that the time required to solve the Multi-Constrained Optimal path problem exactly cannot be upper-bounded by a polynomial function. Hence the focus has been on the development of pseudo-polynomial time algorithms, heuristics and approximation algorithms for multi-constrained QoS paths (Kuipers & Mieghem, 2005).

At present, several studies have been conducted on QoS routing algorithms which integrate the QoS requirements problematic for the routing algorithm. (Song & Sahni, 2006) introduce heuristics to find a source-to-destination path that satisfies two or more additive constraints on edge weights. (Jaffe, 1984) has proposed a polynomial time approximation algorithm for k multi-constrained path which uses a shortest path algorithm such as Dijkstra's (Sahni, 2005). (Korkmaz & Krunz, 2001) propose a randomized heuristic that employs two phases. In the first one, a shortest path is computed for each of the k QoS constraints as well as for a linear combination of all k constraints. The second phase performs a randomized breadth-first search for a solution of k multi-constrained problem. In (Kuipers & Mieghem, 2005), authors suggest that QoS routing in realistic networks could not be NP-complete regarding to a particular class of networks (topology and link weight structure).

Due this complexity, QoS routing problems are divided on several classes according to some aspects. For example, we distinguish the single path routing problem and the multipath routing problem, where routers maintain multiple distinct paths of arbitrary costs between a source and a destination. The Multipath routing offers several advantages like good bandwidth, bounding delay variation, minimizing delay, and improved fault tolerance. So, it makes an effective use of the graph structure on a network, as opposed to single path routing which superimposes a logical routing tree upon the network topology. We find in literature many and various approaches that have been proposed to take into account the QoS requirement. The reader can refer to (Masip-Bruin et al., 2006) for an overview. Constraints imposed by QoS requirements, such as bandwidth, delay, or loss, are referred to as QoS constraints, and the associated routing is referred to as QoS routing which is a part of Constrained-Based Routing (CBR). Interest in constrained-based routing has been steadily growing in the Networks. Based on heuristics used in all of these approaches to reduce their complexity, we can classified it in three main categories:

Label Switching/Reservation Approaches- spurred by approaches like ATM PNNI, MPLS or GMPLS. With MPLS, fixed length labels are attached to packets at an ingress router, and forwarding decisions are based on these labels in the interior routers of the label-switched path. MPLS Traffic Engineering allows overriding the default routing protocol, thus forwarding over paths not normally considered. A resource reservation protocol such as RSVP must be employed to reserve the required resources. Another Architecture proposed for providing Internet QoS is the Differentiated Services architecture. Diffserv scales well by pushing complexity to network domain boundaries.

Multi-Constrained Path Approaches (MCP)- The goal of all of these approaches is to retrieve the shortest path among the set of feasible paths between two nodes. Considerable work in the literature has focused on a special case of the MCP problem known as the Restricted Shortest Path (RSP) problem. The goal is to find the least-cost path among those that satisfy only one constraint. An overview of these approaches can be found in (Kuipers et al., 2004).

Inductive approaches- To be able to make an optimal routing decision, according to relevant performance criteria, a network node requires to have a complete knowledge of the entire network state and an accurate prediction of the evolution of the networks and its dynamics. This, however, is impossible unless the routing algorithm is capable of adapting to the network state changes in almost real time. Thus, it is necessary to design intelligent and adaptive optimizing routing algorithms which take into account the network state and its evolution. We need to talk about QoS based state dependent routing algorithm.

In this chapter, we present an accurate description of the current state-of-the-art and give an overview of our work in the use of reinforcement learning concepts focused on communication networks. We focus our attention by developing a system based on this paradigm called KOCRA for K Optimal Constrained path Routing Algorithm. Basically, these inductive approaches selects routes based on flow QoS requirements and network resource availability. After developing in section 2 the concept of routing in high speed networks, we present in section 3 the family of inductive approaches. After, we present our works based on reinforcement learning approaches in three different communication networking domains: wired networks, mobile ad hoc networks, and packet router's scheduling networks. Last section concludes and gives some perspectives of this work.

2. Routing problem

As Internet is a large collection of more than 25,000 independent domains called autonomous systems (Ases), the cooperation between ASes is not optimized at the network

level, but rather it is based on the business relationships between organizations. The fully-independent management actions in each AS are expressed in terms of a policy-based routing strategy which primarily controls the outbound traffic of an AS and can include conflicting policies. A global solution for QoS routing over all the ASes must be able to handle both the differing QoS provisioning mechanisms and service specifications. This latter solution of building models of large ISP's is so complex to obtain (Quoitin & Uhlig, 2005). For this, Routing is divided onto two classes: IGP and EGP. IGP, such as OSPF or IS-IS, compute the interior paths in one AS, while EGP, such as BGP, is responsible for the selection of the interdomain paths. To fulfill application QoS requirements, many ISPs have deployed mechanisms to provide differentiated services in their networks. In fact, in the last decade, the development of none of QoS routing proposals has turned out to be sufficiently appealing to become deployed in practice. This is because ISPs have preferred to overprovision their networks rather than deliver and manage QoS (Yanuzzi et al., 2005).
In the IGP or EGP cases, a routing algorithm is based on the hop-by-hop shortest-path paradigm. The source of a packet specifies the address of the destination, and each router along the route forwards the packet to a neighbour located "closest" to the destination. The best optimal path is choosed according to given criteria. When the network is heavily loaded, some of the routers introduce an excessive delay while others are under-utilized. In some cases, this non-optimized usage of the network resources may introduce not only excessive delays but also high packet loss rate. Among routing algorithms extensively employed in the same AS routers, one can note: distance vector algorithm such as RIP and the link state algorithm such as OSPF or IS-IS (Grover, 2003).

2.1 Distance vector approach

Also known as Bellman-Ford or Ford-Fulkerson, the heart of this type of algorithm is the routing table maintained by each host. With the distance-vector (DV) routing scheme (e.g. RIP, IGRP), each node exchanges with its neighbouring nodes its distance (e.g. hop count) to other networks. The neighbouring nodes use this information to determine their distance to theses networks. Subsequently these nodes share this information with their neighbours, etc. In this way the reachability information is disseminated through the networks. Eventually each node learns, which neighbour (i.e. next hop router) to use, to reach a particular destination with a minimum number of hops. A node does not learn about the intermediate to the destination. These approaches suffers from a classic convergence problem called "count to infinity". It also does not have an explicit information collection phase (it builds its routing table incrementally). DV routing protocols are designed to run on small networks.

2.2 Link state approach

With link-state (LS) routing (e.g. OSPF or IS-IS), each node builds a complete topology database of the network. This topology database is used to calculate the shortest path with Dijkstra's algorithm. Each node in the network transmits its connectivity information to each other node in the network. This type of exchange is referred to as flooding. This way each node is able to build a complete topological map of the network. The computational complexity cost used here is lower than the DV protocol. However, LS algorithms trade off communication bandwidth against computational time.

3. Inductive approaches

Modern communication networks is becoming a large complex distributed system composed by higher interoperating complex sub-systems based on several dynamic parameters. The drivers of this growth have included changes in technology and changes in regulation. In this context, the famous methodology approach that allows us to formulate this problem is dynamic programming which, however, is very complex to be solved exactly. The most popular formulation of the optimal distributed routing problem in a data network is based on a multicommodity flow optimization whereby a separable objective function is minimized with respect to the types of flow subject to multicommodity flow constraints (Gallager, 1977; Ozdaglar & Bertsekas, 2003). In order to design adaptive algorithms for dynamic networks routing problems, many of works are largely oriented and based on the Reinforcement Learning (RL) notion (Sutton & Barto, 1997). The salient feature of RL algorithms is the nature of their routing table entries which are probabilistic. In such algorithms, to improve the routing decision quality, a router tries out different links to see if they produce good routes. This mode of operation is called exploration. Information learnt during this exploration phase is used to take future decisions. This mode of operation is called exploitation. Both exploration and exploitation phases are necessary for effective routing and the choice of the outgoing interface is the action taken by the router. In RL algorithms, those learning and evaluation modes are assumed to happen continually. Note that, the RL algorithms assigns credit to actions based on reinforcement from the environment. In the case where such credit assignment is conducted systematically over large number of routing decisions, so that all actions have been sufficiently explored, RL algorithms converge to solve stochastic shortest path routing problems. Finally, algorithms for RL are distributed algorithms that take into account the dynamics of the network where initially no model of the network dynamics is assumed to be given. Then, the RL algorithm has to sample, estimate and build the model of pertinent aspects of the environment.

Many of works has done to investigate the use of inductive approaches based on artificial neuronal intelligence together with biologically inspired techniques such as reinforcement learning and genetic algorithms, to control network behavior in real-time so as to provide users with the QoS that they request, and to improve network provide robustness and resilience. For example, we can note the following approaches:

Q-Routing approach- In this technique (Boyan & Littman, 1994), each node makes its routing decision based on the local routing information, represented as a table of Q values which estimate the quality of the alternative routes. These values are updated each time the node sends a packet to one of its neighbors. However, when a Q value is not updated for a long time, it does not necessarily reflect the current state of the network and hence a routing decision based on such an unreliable Q value will not be accurate. The update rule in Q-Routing does not take into account the reliability of the estimated or updated Q value because it depends on the traffic pattern, and load levels. In fact, most of the Q values in the network are unreliable. For this purpose, other algorithms have been proposed like Confidence based Q-Routing (CQ-Routing) or Confidence based Dual Reinforcement Q-Routing (DRQ-Routing).

Cognitive Packet Networks (CPN)- CPNs (Gelenbe et al., 2002) are based on random neural networks. These are store-and-forward packet networks in which intelligence is constructed into the packets, rather than at the routers or in the high-level protocols. CPN is then a reliable packet network infrastructure, which incorporates packet loss and delays directly into user QoS criteria and use these criteria to conduct routing. Cognitive packet networks carry three major types of packets: smart packets, dumb packets and acknowledgments (ACK). Smart or cognitive packets route themselves, they learn to avoid link and node failures and congestion and to avoid being lost. They learn from their own observations about the network and/or from the experience of other packets. They rely minimally on routers. The major drawback of algorithms based on cognitive packet networks is the convergence time, which is very important when the network is heavily loaded.

Swarm Ant Colony Optimization (AntNet)- Ants routing algorithms (Dorigo & Stützle, 2004) are inspired by dynamics of how ant colonies learn the shortest route to food source using very little state and computation. Instead of having fixed next-hop value, the routing table will have multiple next-hop choices for a destination, with each candidate associated with a possibility, which indicates the goodness of choosing this hop as the next hop in favor to form the shortest path. Given a specified source node and destination node, the source node will send out some kind of ant packets based on the possibility entries on its own routing table. Those ants will explore the routes in the network. They can memory the hops they have passed. When an ant packet reaches the destination node, the ant packet will return to the source node along the same route. Along the way back to the destination node, the ant packet will change the routing table for every node it passes by. The rules of updating the routing tables are: increase the possibility of the hop it comes from while decrease the possibilities of other candidates. Ants approach is immune to the sub-optimal route problem since it explores, at all times, all paths of the network. Although, the traffic generated by ant algorithms is more important than the traffic of the concurrent approaches.

In the following, we give an overview of our work in the use of reinforcement learning concepts focused on communication networks. We focus our attention by developing a system based on this paradigm called KOCRA for K Optimal Constrained path Routing Algorithm and present our works based on reinforcement learning approaches in three different communication networking domains: wired networks, mobile ad hoc networks, and packet router's scheduling networks.

4. KOCRA system based reinforcement learning in routing wired networks.

KOCRA is the successor of KONRS, a K Optimal Neural Routing System (Mellouk et al., 2006a).

4.1 Brief summary of KONRS

In (Mellouk et al., 2006a), we have presented an adaptive routing algorithm based on Q learning approach, the Q function is approximated by a reinforcement learning based neural network (NN). As shown in figure 1, In this approach, NN ensure the prediction of parameters depending on traffic variations. Compared to the approaches based on a Q table, the Q value is approximated by a reinforcement learning based neural network of a fixed size, allowing the learner to incorporate various parameters such as local queue size and time of day, into its distance estimation. Indeed, a neural network allows the modelling of complex functions with a good precision along with a discriminating training and a taking into account of the context of the network. Moreover, it can be used to predict non-stationary or irregular traffics. In this approach, the objective is to minimize the average packet delivery time. Consequently, the reinforcement signal which is chosen corresponds to the estimated time to transfer a packet to its destination. Typically, the packet delivery time includes three variables: The packet transmission time, the packet treatment time in the router and the latency in the waiting queue.

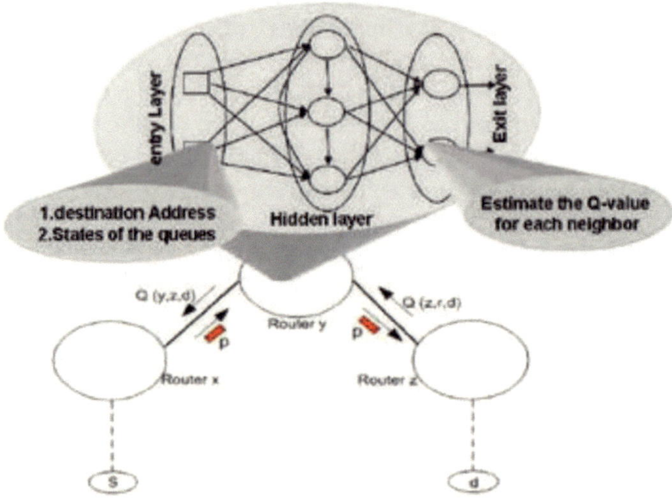

Fig. 1. Neural Net Architecture

The input cells in NN used correspond to the destination and the waiting queue states. The outputs are the estimated packet transfer times passing through the neighbours of the considered router. The algorithm derived from this architecture can be described according to the following steps:

When receiving a packet of information:
1. Extract a destination IP address,
2. Calculate Neural Network outputs,
3. Select the smallest output value and get an IP address of the associated router,
4. Send the packet to this router,
5. Get an IP address of the precedent router,
6. Create and send the packet as a reinforcement signal.

At the reception of a reinforcement signal packet:
1. Extract a Q estimated value computed by the neighbor,
2. Extract a destination IP address,
3. Neural Network updating using a retro-propagation algorithm based on gradient method,
4. Destroy the reinforcement packet.

This approach offers advantages compared to standard Distance Vector (DV) routing policy and earlier Q-routing algorithm, like the reduction of the memory space for the storage of secondary paths, and a reasonable computing time for alternative paths research. The Q value is approximated by a reinforcement learning based neural network of a fixed size. Results given in (Mellouk et al., 2006a) show better performances of the proposed algorithm comparatively to standard distance vector and Q-routing algorithms. In fact, at a high load level, the traffic is better distributed along the possible paths, avoiding the congestion of the network.

4.2 The concepts behind KOCRA

This first version of our KONRS routing system explore all the network environment and do not take into account loop problem in a way leading to large time of convergence algorithm. To address this drawback and reducing computational time, we have worked on the evolution of our earlier Q-neural routing algorithm and present the enhanced version of KONRS called "K Optimal Constrained path Routing Algorithm (KOCRA)" (Mellouk et al., 2007a). KOCRA contains three stages. The objective of the first stage is to select the K Best candidate paths according to the cost cumulative path from the source and the destination nodes (for simplicity, we consider here all link costs equal to 1). The second stage is used to integrate the dynamics of traffic. For this, a continuous end-to-end delay among the K Best selected Paths is computed using a reinforcement Q-learning function. In order to force the router to take the alternative routes regarding to the second stage, we used a third one which compute automatically a probability affected to each path based on packet delivery time obtained by the second stage and the time latency in queuing file associated for each path.

4.2.1 First stage: constructing K-best paths

First of all, in spite of exploring the entire network environment which needs large computational time and space memory (Mellouk et al., 2006a), our approach reduces this environment to K Best no loop paths in terms of cost cumulative links. Thus, each router maintains a link state database as map of the network topology. We used a label setting algorithm based on the optimality principle and being a generalization of Dijkstra's algorithm (Sahni, 2005). In order to find these K best paths, a variant of Dijkstra's algorithm proposed in (Eppstein, 1999) was used. The space complexity is $O(Kmn)$, where K is the number of paths, m (resp. n) is the number of edges (resp. the number of links). By using a pertinent data structure, the time complexity can be kept at $O(m+nlogn+K)$ (Mellouk et al., 2007a). When a network link changes its state (i.e., goes up or down, or its utilization is increased or decreased), the network is flooded with a link state advertisement (LSA) message. This message can be issued periodically or when the actual link state change exceeds a certain relative or absolute threshold. Obviously, there is tradeoff between the frequency of state updates (the accuracy of the link state database) and the cost of performing those updates. In our approach, the link state information is updated when the actual link state change. Once the link state database at each router is updated, the router computes the K optimal paths.

Let a DAG (N; A) denote a network with n nodes and m edges, where N = {1.. n}, and A ={aij/i,j€N}. N}. The problem is to find the top K paths from source s to all the other nodes. Let's define a label set X and a one-to-many projection h: N→ X, meaning that each node i€ N corresponds to a set of labels h(i), each element of which represents a path from s to i.

---

* *S the source node*
* *N –set of nodes in network*

```
* X – the label set
* Count_i – Number of paths determined from S to I
* elm – Affected number to assigned label
* P – Paths list from S to destination (D)
* K – paths number to compute
        * h – corresponding between node and affected label number
/* Initialisation */
count_i = 0 /* for all i □ K */
elem = 1
h(elem) = s
h^-1(s) = {elem}
distance_elem = 0
X = {elem}
P^K = 0
While (count_t < K and X != { })
        begin
            /* find a label lb from X, such that
            distance_lb <= distance_lb1, □ lb1 □ X*/
            X = X – {lb}
            i = h(lb)
            count_i = count_i + 1
            if (i == D) then /* if the node I is the destination node D */
                        begin
                                    p = path for 1 to lb
                                    P^K = P^K U {h(p)}
                        end
            if (count_i <= K) then
                    begin
                        for each arc(i,j) □ A
                                begin
                                 /* Verify if new label does not result in loop */
                                 v=lb
                                 While (h(v) != s)
                                  begin
                                    if (h(v) == j) then
                                       begin
                                           goto do_not_add
                                       end
                                    v = previous_v
                                  end
                            /* Save information from new label */
                            elem = elem + 1
                            distance_elem = distance_n + c_ij
                            previous_elem = lb
                            h(elem) = j
                            h^-1(j) = h^-1(j) U {elem}
```

X = X U {elem}
do_not_add:
end
end
end

4.2.2 Second stage: Q-learning algorithm for optimizing the end-to-end delay

After finding our K best Optimal Paths based on link costs, the second step is to distribute the traffic on these K candidate paths. For this, we use another criteria based on the end-to-end delay. The reinforcement signal which is chosen corresponds to the estimated time to transfer a packet to its destination. This value is computed by a variant of Q-Routing algorithm which is considered as an asynchronous relaxation of the Bellman-Ford algorithm used in distance vector protocols. Typically, the packet delivery time includes three variables: the packet transmission time, the packet treatment time in the router and the latency in the waiting queue. In our case, the packet transmission time is not taken into account. In fact, this parameter can be neglected in comparison to the other ones and has no effect on the routing process.

In this approach, each router x maintains in a Q-table a collection of values of $Q(x, y, d)$ for every destination d and for every interface y. This value reflects a delay of delivering a packet for destination d via interface s. Then, the router x forwards the packet to the best next router y determined from the Q-table. Just after receiving this packet, the router y provides x an estimate of its best Q value to reach the destination. This new information is then added in the Q-values of the router x.

The reinforcement signal T employed in the Q-learning algorithm can be defined as the minimum of the sum of the estimated $Q(x, y, d)$ sent by the router y neighbour of router x and the latency in waiting queue q_x corresponding to router x.

$$T = \min_{y \in \text{neighbof } x} \{ q_x + Q(x, y, d) \} \tag{1}$$

Where $Q(x, y, d)$, denote the estimated time by the router x so that the packet p reaches its destination d through the router y. This parameter does not include the latency in the waiting queue of the router x. The packet is sent to the router y which determines the optimal path to send this packet.

Once the choice of the next router is made, the router y puts the packet in the waiting queue, and sends back the value T as a reinforcement signal to the router x. It can therefore update its reinforcement function as:

$$\Delta Q(x, y, d) = \eta(\alpha + T - Q(x, y, d)) \tag{2}$$

α and η are the packet transmission time between x and y and the learning rate respectively. So, the new estimation $Q'(x, y, d)$ can be written as follows:

$$Q'(x, y, d) = Q(x, y, d)(1 - \eta) + \eta(T + \alpha) \tag{3}$$

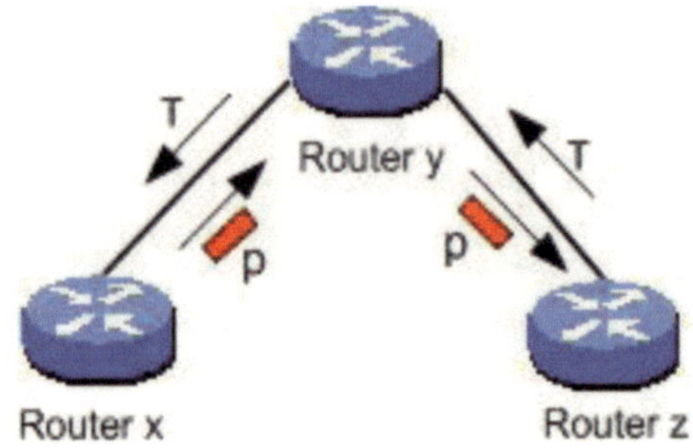

Fig. 2. Updating of the reinforcement signal.

4.2.3 Third stage: adaptive probabilistic path selection.

The goal of this stage is to distribute the traffic on K best paths in probabilistic manner. To force the router to take alternative routes find in K best paths and not only the best one, we compute a probability affected to each path automatically. We associated a maximal value P_{max} for the best path and divided the rest of probability (1- P_{max}) for the remaining (K-1) paths. The value of P_{max} is fixed by a counting process. To force the router to take the alternative routes find in the second stage and not only the best path, a uniform distributed random process is implemented in each router. This process chooses randomly a number between [0, 1]. Next, a router choose the path verifying the condition that it's probability is less than this random number. For example, in the situation characterized by K=2 (two paths), P1=0.8, P2=0.2, if the random number <=0.8, the router chooses the first path, otherwise the router takes the second one. In this manner, the flow packets reach their destination with a time close to optimal, while ensuring a good exploration of the remaining paths. Unfortunately, this kind of fixed hand probability don't take automatically into account the dynamic of the irregular traffic. We have proposed a second version of computing automatically the load balancing distribution. The process is based on the packet delivery time computed by our Q reinforcement learning and the latency in queuing file associated for each path.

Let D_i *(t)* be the packet delivery time for path *i* at time *t*. Let T_i^n *(t)* be the latency in queuing file associated to closest router *n'* in the direction of path *i* at time *t* (that is, the neighbour of router *n*). The following formula allows us to count the probability P_i^n *(t)* for the *i^th^* path in router *n* at time *t:*

$$P_i^n = \left[\left(\frac{1}{D_i}\right)^{\alpha} \cdot \left(\frac{1}{T_i^{n'}}\right)^{\beta}\right] \Big/ \left[\sum_{i=1}^{K}\left(\frac{1}{D_i}\right)^{\alpha} \cdot \left(\frac{1}{T_i^{n'}}\right)^{\beta}\right] \quad (4)$$

Where α and β are two tuneable parameters that determine respectively the influence of delay time and waited queue time. They have an equivalent influence in the case of $\alpha=\beta$. This formula associates a very small probability for paths with high delay time and/or high queue time. This is due to the fact that when delay time (respectively waited time) increase the value of $[1/D_i(t)]^{\alpha}$ (respectively $[1/T_i(t)]^{\beta}$) decreases.

4.3 Performance evaluation

To validate our results in the case of irregular traffic in wired networks, we take the results given by a well-known Djikstra's algorithm (which offers to use an existing polynomial-time path computation) used in protocols such OSPF, IS-IS or CISCO EIGRP as a reference for our study. This choice of this classical approach is argued by the fact that the majority of ISP's used actually this kind of protocols to exchange routing information in their networks. In order to do comparison with KOCRA, parameters of standard approach used here are fixed in order to optimize the delay and cost criteria simultaneously (on the rest of paper, we used the notation "Standard Optimal Multi-Path Routing Algorithm (SOMRA)" for this kind of algorithm). All algorithms have been implemented with OPNET and used the same data structure. OPNET software constitutes for telecommunications networks an appropriate modelling, scheduling and simulation tool. It allows the visualization of a physical topology of a local, metropolitan, distant or on board network. The protocol specification language is based on a formal description of a finite state automaton.

The simulations presented in this article consisted of creating a traffic merged in irregular network topology, through which the two family of algorithms (KOCRA and SOMRA) computed the best paths between two nodes. QoS measures of each of tested algorithms concerns two additive constraints: cost and delay criteria. Results given in all the figures are evaluated in terms of average packet end-to-end delivery time on both topologies. Time simulation is represented on the other axis of the figures.

4.3.1 Simulation parameters on the irregular topology.

The topology of the network is specified by a collection of routers and a set of links that bind these routers elements. The network traffic is specified in the source router by setting several parameters like: the start time, the stop time, the statistical distribution for packet inter-arrival times, the statistical distribution for packet size and the destination node.

To ensure a meaningful validation of our algorithm performance, we devised a realistic simulation environment in terms of network characteristics, communications protocols and traffic patterns. We focus on IP datagram networks with irregular topology. The topology of the network employed for simulations includes 36 interconnected nodes with essentially two parts of the network, as shown in Fig 3. This topology is the same used in (Boyan & Littman, 1994) for their Q learning approach.

We model traffic in terms of requests characterized by its source and destination. While we concern ourselves with arrival and departure of flows, we do not model the data traffic of the flows. For simplicity, we also chose not to implement a proper management of error, flow and congestion control. In act, each additional control component has a considerable impact on the network performance, making very difficult to evaluate and to study properties of each control algorithm without taking in consideration the complex way it interacts with all the other control components (Dorigo & Stüzle, 2004). Therefore, we chose to test the behavior of our algorithm such that the routing component can be evaluated in isolation.

The traffic is sent/received by four end nodes (marked in the figure noeud100, noeud101, noeud102 and noeud103).

For our simulation results, we studied the performance of the algorithms for increasing traffic load, examining the evolution of the network status toward a saturation condition, and for temporary saturation conditions. For this topology, we study the performance of our routing strategies according a Poisson Law inter-arrival times statistical distribution.

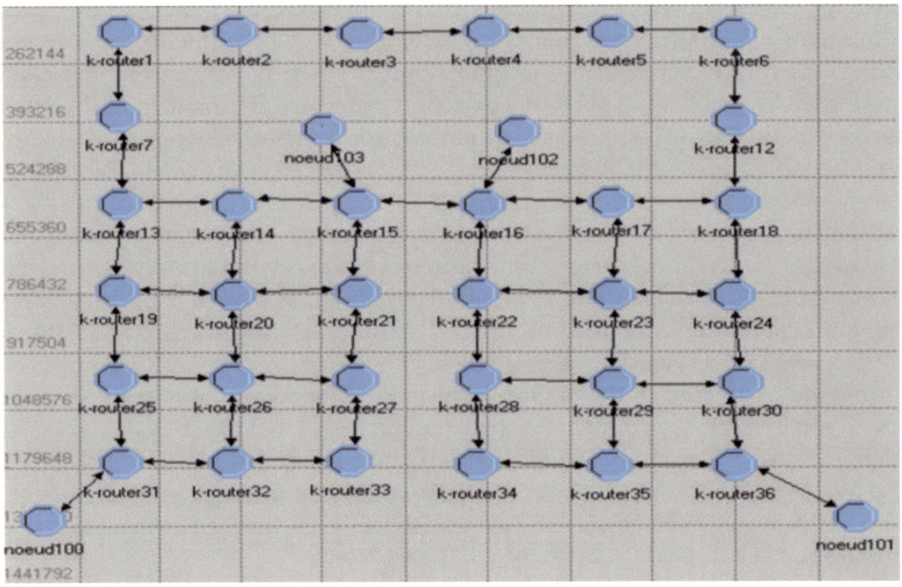

Fig. 3. Network topology.

4.3.2 Poisson distribution of model traffic.

In probability theory, the Poisson distribution is a discrete probability distribution which expresses the probability of a number of events occurring in a fixed period of time if these events occur with a known average rate, and are independent of the time since the last event. The It is represented by random variables N that count a number of discrete occurrences (called "arrivals") that take place during a time-interval of given length. The probability that there are exactly k occurrences (with k a non-negative integer, $k = 0, 1, 2, \ldots$) is:

$$P(k,\lambda) = \frac{e^{-\lambda}\lambda^{k}}{k!} \tag{5}$$

Where$\lambda$is a positive real number and is the mean number of occurrences k. The Poisson law is then defined by its mean λparameter.

In our simulations, we suppose the mean λ of the inter-arrival times is 3 s and fix the time start to 1 min and the stop time to the end of simulation is fixed to 6 h.

4.3.3 Simulation results.

As shown in Fig. 4 which represent time simulation versus the average packet delivery time, our probabilistic K Optimal Constrained path Routing Algorithm (KOCRA) give better results than the well-known N best optimal path routing Algorithm SOMRA. This is due to the fact that in our new approach, routers are able to take into account not only the average of delivery delay but also the waiting queue time. Thus, they are able to adapt their decisions very fast and in close concordance with the network dynamics. In spite of the many packages taking secondary ways, N-optimal routing does not present better performances because it rests on a probabilistic method to distribute the load of the network over the closest cost paths, and not on the degradation of the times of routing. So, in classical approach, the routers take their decisions only according to the average of delivery delay and the exploration of potentials good paths, none trivially best and that can give us betters results, is not realized. Our approach, with the introduction of a probabilistic module, responds to this inconvenience and shows better results for Poisson law distribution of traffic. Thus, mean of average packet delivery time obtained by KOCRA is reduced by 37% compared to traditional N best optimal routing Algorithm.

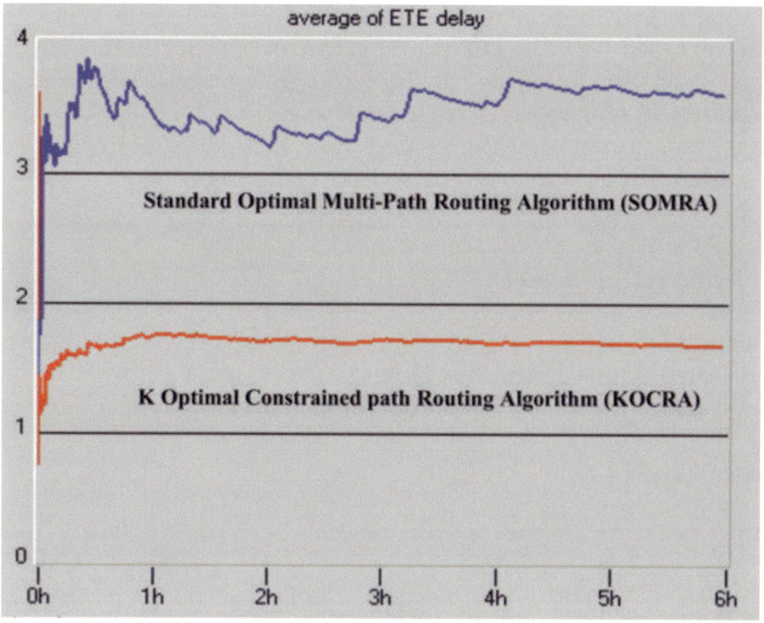

Fig. 4. Poisson law distribution simulations results

5. AMDR based reinforcement learning in mobile ad hoc networks.

AMDR (Adaptive Mean Delay Routing) is a new adaptive routing protocol based on probabilities and built around two exploration RL agents. Exploration agents gather mean delay information available at each node in their route and calculate total delay between source and destination. According to the delay value gathered, probabilistic routing tables are updated at each intermediate node. In order to deal with mobile nodes synchronisation we consider, in our protocol, delay estimation model proposed in [Naimi, 2005; Naimi & Jacquet, 2004], instead of instantaneous delay considered in the most oriented delay routing protocols.

Unlike data packets, control packets, used in adaptive routing, are sent in broadcast manner and so treated at IEEE 802.11, MAC layer differently than unicast packets. For this, we consider that trip delay of a control packet is not the same of a data packet.

In AMDR, routing function is determined by means of very complex interactions of forward and backward network exploration agents. Forward agents report network delay conditions to the backward ones. So, no node routing updates are performed by the forward agents.
AMDR uses two kinds of agents: Forward Exploration Packets (FEP) and Backward Exploration Packets (BEP). Forward agents explore the paths of the network, for the first time in reactive manner, but it continues the exploration proactively.
FEP packets create a probability distribution at each node for its neighbours. Backward agents are used to propagate the information gathered by forward agents through the network, and to adjust the routing table entries.

5.1 Forward exploration packet

When a new traffic arrives at a node *n*, periodically the node *n* generates a forward exploration packet called FEP. The FEP packet is then sent to the destination of traffic. Each FEP packet contains the following fields: *source_node_address, destination_node_address, ext_hop_address, stack_of_visiting_nodes_addresses, total_delay*.
If the entry of the current destination does not exist then a routing table entry is immediately created. The algorithm of FEP sending is the following:

```
Algorithm (Send FEP)
    At Each T_interval_secondes Do
    Begin
        Generate a FEP
        If any entry for this destination Then
                Create an entry with uniform probabilities.
      End If
        Broadcast the FEP
    End
End (Send FEP)
```

When a FEP arrives to a node *i*, it checks if the address of the node *i* is not equal to the *destination address* contained in the FEP agent then the FEP packet will be forwarded. FEP packets are forwarded according to the following algorithm:

```
Algorithm (Receive FEP)
        If any entry for this destination Then
                Create an entry with uniform probabilities.
        ELSE If my_adress ≠ dest_adress Then
            IF FEP not already received then
                    Stock address of the current node,
                    Recover the available mean delay,
                    Broadcast FEP
            ELSE
                    Send BEP
          End IF
      End IF
End (forward FEP)
```

5.2 Backward exploration packet

As soon as a forward agent FEP reaches its destination, a backward agent called BEP is generated and the forward agent FEP is destroyed. BEP inherits the stack and the total delay information contained in the forward agent. We define five options for our algorithm in order to reply to a FEP agent. The algorithm of sending a BEP packet depends on the chosen option. The five options considered in our protocol are:

Reply to All: for each FEP reception, the destination a BEP packet is generated. In this case, the delay information is not used and the overhead generated is very important.

Reply to First: Only one BEP agent is generated for a FEP packet. The mean delay module is not exploited. It's the same approach used in the AntNet. The overhead is reduced but any guarantee to have the best delay paths.

Reply to N: destination node can generate until N BEP packet for the same FEP. The overhead is reduced compared to reply to N but it is more important than the Reply to first option.

Reply to the Best: We save at each node the information of the best delay called "Node.Total_delay". When the first FEP arrives to the destination, Node.Total_delay takes the value of total delay of the FEP packet. When another FEP arrives, its total delay is compared to the node total delay, and we reply only if the FEP has a delay better or equal to the node total delay.

Reply to delay Constraint: This option focuses on Delay-Constrained-Path (DCP) unicast routing. The DCP issue is to select the path with given delay requirement. This is the case of real time applications having serious delay constraints.

Applications needs in term of delay are determined in a max delay supported "D" value. Arriving to destination, this one compares FEP *total_delay* to the application *delay_constraint* "D". If the FEP *total_delay* is equal or less than "D" then a BEP is generated and sent to the source of the FEP. We give in the following a part of BEP sending algorithm. We focus on "Reply to best" option which will be used in simulation part:

Algorithm (Send BEP)

```
Select Case Option
   Case: Reply to All
         ....
   Case: Reply to first
   If (First (FEP) ) Then
         .....
      endIf
   Case: Reply to N
   If (N>0) Then
         .......
      endIf
   Case: Reply to Best
   If (FEP.Total_Delay <= Node.Total_Delay) Then
         Genarate BEP
         BEP.Total_Delay=0,
         BEP.dest = FEP.src,
```

```
        Send BEP,
        Node.Total_Delay= FEP.Total_Delay,
    endIf
  Case: Reply to Delay Constraint (D)
  If (FEP.Total_Delay <= D) Then
      ......
    End If
End (Send BEP)
```

Backward Exploration Packet (BEP) retraces the inverse path traversed by the FEP packet. In other words, unlike FEP packets, a BEP packet is sent in a unicast manner because it must take the same path of its FEP generator. During its trip, the BEP agent calculates the total mean delay of its route and uses this new delay to adjust the probabilistic routing table of each intermediate node. The algorithm of forwarding BEP agent is the following:

```
Algorithm (Receive BEP)
    If (my_adress = BEP.dest) Then
        Update probabilistic routing table
    Else
        Update probabilistic routing table
        Forward BEP
    End If
End (Receive BEP)
```

5.3 Updating routing tables

Routing tables are updated when a BEP agent is received. The probabilities updating can take many forms, and we have chosen updating rules (6), (7), (8) and (9) described in (Baras & Mehta, 2003). As soon as, routing table is calculated, data packets are then routed according to the highest probabilities in the probabilistic routing tables.

Unlike on demand routing protocols, there is no guarantee to route all packets on the same route because of the proactive exploration. The BEP agent make changes to the probability values at the intermediate and final node according to the following update rules:

$$p_{fd} \leftarrow (p_{fd} + r)\,(1+r) \tag{6}$$

$$p_{nd} \leftarrow p_{nd} / (1+r) \tag{7}$$

$$p_{nd} \leftarrow p_{nd} - rp_{nd} \tag{8}$$

$$p_{fd} \leftarrow p_{fd} + r\,(1-p_{fd}) \tag{9}$$

In both the above cases, the reinforcement parameter r can be defined as a function of delay. Here, r=k / f(c), where k > 0 and f(c) is the cost function (Baras & Mehta, 2003).

5.4 Flooding optimization

In order to improve the performance of our routing protocol, we introduce the MPR (Nguyen & Minet, 2006) concept in the broadcast process. However, the MPR selection according to native OLSR is unable to build path satisfying a given QoS request. To avoid this problem, we propose a new algorithm for MPR selection. We keep at each node a table called MPR table containing a partial view of MPR neighbours. Our algorithm takes into account the mean delay available at each node. The MPR selection algorithm based on mean delay is the same proposed for bandwidth in (Nguyen & Minet, 2006), unlike their approach for bandwidth MPR; we define only one kind of MPR which are delay MPR. Mean delay MPR selection algorithm is composed of the following steps:

1. A node N_i selects, first, all its neighbours that are the only neighbours of a two hop node from N_i.
2. Sort the remaining one-hop delay neighbours in increasing order of mean delay.
3. Consider each one-hop neighbour in that order: this neighbour is selected as MPR if it covers at least one two-hop neighbour that has not yet been covered by the previous MPR.
4. Mark all the selected node neighbours as covered and repeat step 3 until all two-hop neighbours are covered.

With the present MPR selection algorithm, we guarantee that paths having best delays will be discovered but there are any guarantees about the overhead generated (Ziane & Mellouk, 2006).

5.5 Performance evaluation

We use NS-2 simulator to implement and test AMDR protocol. We present in this section two scenarios of simulation. In the first one, we define a static topology of 8 nodes. To compare AODV, OLSR and AMDR, we have chosen the Reply to Best option of AMDR.

5.5.1 Static scenario

The following table summarizes the simulation environment:

Routing	AODV, AMDR, OLSR
MAC Layer	802.11
Bandwidth	11Mb/s
TERRAIN	1000m,1000m
Nodes	8
Simulation time	1000 sec
Data traffic	exponential

Table 1. Simulation settings scenario 1

We injected three types of traffic in the network and compared for each simulation the file trace for each routing protocol. Figure 5 shows the comparison of end to end delay realized by AODV, AMDR and OLSR protocols. We can see that, at first OLSR realizes the best

delays when AMDR and AODV show a large initial delay, which is required for routes to be set up.
A few times after initialisation stage, AMDR shows more adaptation to changes in the network load and realizes the best end to end delay followed by AODV and at last OLSR.
On the other hand, comparing loss rate performances of the three protocols shows in figure 6, that OLSR realizes the best performances followed by AMDR and then AODV. AMDR performance is justified by keeping alternative paths used when the actual path is broken. Any additional delay is need to route waiting traffics and deliverance ratio is well improved than AODV.

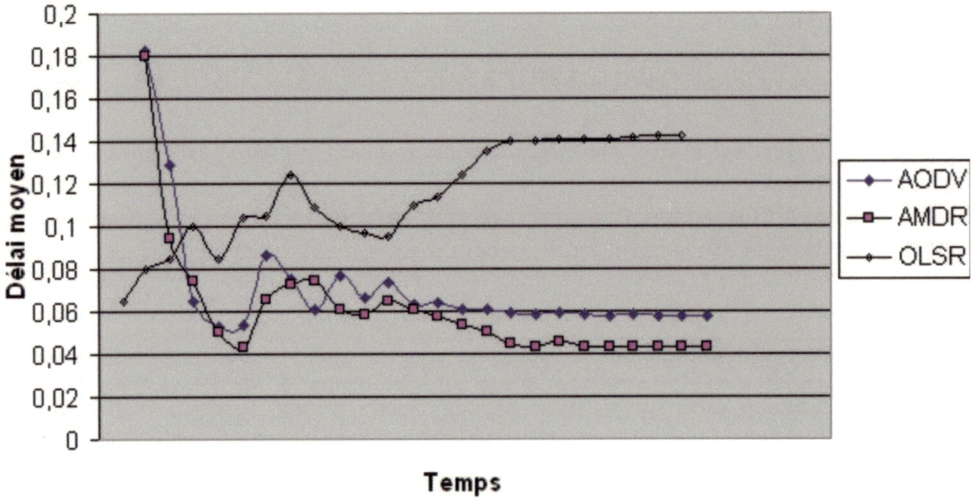

Fig. 5. Packets delay comparison in static scenario

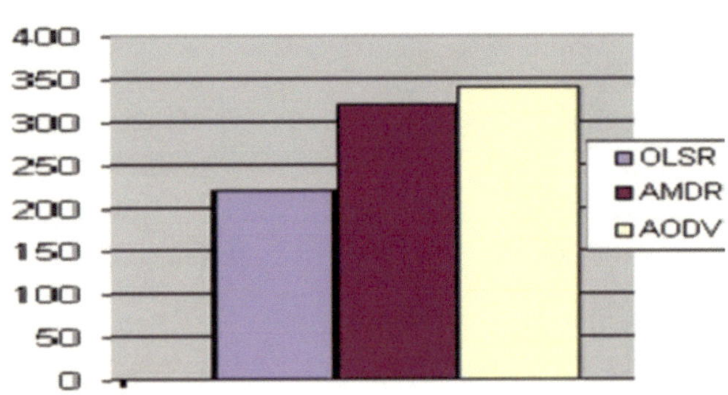

Fig. 6. Comparison of loss rate for static scenario

From the overhead comparison results, we saw that overhead generated by OLSR was the most important followed by AMDR and than AODV. This is justified by the proactive exploration process used by AMDR even a route is already established. The difference between overhead of AMDR and AODV is not very important because of optimization flooding mechanism used in AMDR.

5.5.2 Mobility scenario

In this scenario, we test the impact of mobility on AMDR and compare its performances with OLSR and AODV. We define a random topology of 50 nodes.

Traffic model	Exponential
Surface of simulation	1000m,1000m
Packets size	512 byte
Bandwidth	1Mbs
Rate of mobility	5m /s , 10m/s
Number of connections	5, 10, 15, 20, 25
Rate	5 paquets/s
Simulation duration	500 s

Table 2. Simulation settings scenario 2

Table 2 summarizes the simulation setting. We injected at first five traffics, ten, fifteen, twenty and at last twenty five traffics. After each simulation we calculate the end to end delay realized by each protocol. Figure 7 summarizes our comparison. We can observe that with low load, there is no difference in end to end delays. However, more the network is loaded more AMDR is better in term of delay. Such performance is justified by the adaptation of AMDR to changes in the network load. In the case of AODV and OLSR an additional delay is impossible to circumvent for adapting to changes.

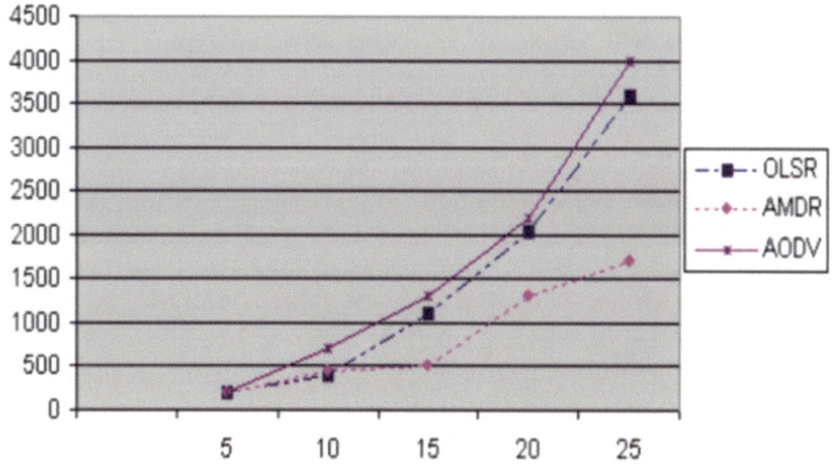

Fig. 7. Packets delay comparison for mobility scenario

Comparing loss rate performance between AODV, AMDR and OLSR, shows in figure 8 that both AMDR and OLSR have, in a low loaded network, the same performance when AODV realises the best performances. However, in a high loaded network (case of 20 or 25 connexions), AODV becomes less good than AMDR and OLSR. We justify such results by the adaptation of AMDR to load changes when AODV needs more route request function.

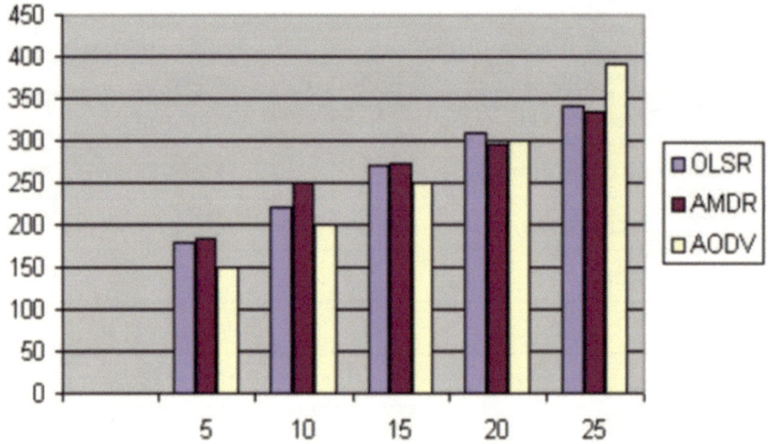

Fig. 8. Loss rate comparison for mobility scenario

6. A system based reinforcement learning in packet scheduling communications network routing.

6.1 Problem formulation

In the dynamic environment the scheduler take the actual evolution of the process into account. It is allowed to make the decisions as the scheduling process actually evolves and more information becomes available. For that, we consider at each router an agent that can make decision. This decision-maker collects information gathered by mobile agents and then decides which action to perform after learning the current situation. We will focus on dynamic technique and will formulate the packet scheduling problem through several routers as a multi-agent Markov Decision Problem (MDP). As Machine learning techniques, we use reinforcement learning to compute a good policy in a multi-agent system (Mellouk & Hoceini, 2005; Hoceini et al., 2005). Simultaneous decision making in a dynamic environment is modelled using multi-agent Markov Decision Processes (MMDPs) (Puterman, 2005). However, learning in multi-agent system suffers from several limitations such the exponential growing of number of states, actions and parameters with the number of agents. In addition, since agents carry out actions simultaneously so they have evolving behaviours, transitions are non-stationary. Since centralized MAS may be considered as a huge MDP, we work with decentralized system where each agent learns individually in environment improved with information gathered by mobile agents.

6.2 Markov decision processes

Markov decision problem (MDP) can be used for modelling the interaction of an agent with its environment. It is defined as a 4-tuple $< S, A, P, r >$ where S is a finite set of states, A is a finite set of actions, P is the transition probability function and r is the reward function. Given a state s and an action a, $P(s, a, s')$ denotes the transition probability of the system to state s' when action a is executed in state s. Hence, the dynamics of the environment can be characterized by the transition probabilities. The process is said to be Markovian when the transition function depends only on the current state and not on any previously traversed states or any previous actions. If the state and action spaces are finite, then it is called a finite

Markov decision process (FMDP). The reward function r is defined as a real function r: S x A x S → đ, where the scalar reinforcement signal r(s, a, s′) is the reward of taking action a in state s and observing state s′ as the next state. A policy π is denoted for a description of behaviours of an agent. It is a function that maps the current state s of the system into an action. The value of a state s under a policy π is the expected discounted sum of rewards obtained following this policy. The action value of a state according to the policy π noted Qπ(s, a) is the expected discounted sum of reward obtained by taking action a in state s and following policy π. We use the reward as feedback to find an optimal policy π* by iteratively refining an initial policy π0.

In a Markov decision process, the objective of the agent is to find a policy π so as to maximize the expected sum of discounted rewards, It has been proved that there exists an optimal policy π* such that for any s □ S, the following Bellman equation holds:

$$V(s, \pi^*) = \max_a\{r(s, a) + \gamma \sum_{s'} P(s, a, s')\, V(s', \pi^*)\} \tag{10}$$

where V(s, π*) is the optimal value for state s. When the transition function is unknown, the Q-learning (Watkins, 1989) is one of the algorithms most used to find an optimal policy. In Q-learning, Q*(s, a) is the total discounted reward obtained in state *s* after performing action *a* and following the optimal policy π*. Then, the above equation becomes:

$$V(s, \pi^*) = \max_a Q^*(s, a) \tag{11}$$

On basis of Q*(s, a) the optimal policy π* can be found by performing an action *a* in state *s* so as to maximise Q*(s, a).

The Q-Learning algorithm builds values of Q(s, a) for all *s* □ S and *a* □ A whose initial values may be arbitrarily chosen. If the agent, after executing an action a, moves from state *s* to *s′* and receives an immediate reward r(s, a), the current Q(s, a) values are updated using the following formula:

$$Q(s, a) \leftarrow (1-\alpha)Q(s, a) + \alpha\, [r(s, a) + \gamma \max_{a'} Q(s', a')] \tag{12}$$

where α, 0≤ α ≤1 is the learning rate. (Watkins & Dayan, 1992) proved that equation (12) converges to optimal Q*(s, a). At the end of the learning, an optimal policy π* can be derived such as $\pi^*(s) = \arg\max_a Q^*(s, a)$.

6.3 Multi-agent MDPs

The single MDP and Q-learning are defined for the case where only one action is selected with each iteration. In this case the existence of optimal policy π* is guaranteed. Nevertheless, the formalism can be extended to problems where multiple actions can be carried out simultaneously by several agents (Boutilier, 1999). In this way, we consider n agents each one of them having learned the optimal solution from its own MDP. The effort of these n agents in individual learning is combined to learn the joint optimal policy of this multi-agent MDP.

We define a multi-agent MDP as 4-tuple (S, A, P, R) where the state space is a subset of the joint state space of n agents such that $S = S^1 \times \ldots \times S^n$ in which each S^i is a discrete state space of each agent, the action space is the joint action space of n agents $A = A^1 \times \ldots \times A^n$ in which a joint action $(a^1, a^2, ..., a^n)$ corresponds to the concurrent execution of the actions a^i by each agent i. The transition probabilities and rewards are factorial and defined for all states s, s′ □ S and for all actions a □ A respectively as:

$$P^a_{ss'} = \prod_{i=1}^{n} P(s^i, a^i, s^{i\prime}) \tag{13}$$

and R is given by the function R: S × A → đ such that:

$$R = \sum_{i=1}^{n} r^i(s^i, a^i, s^{i\prime}) \tag{14}$$

where $r^i(s^i, a^i, s^{i\prime})$ is the reward obtained by agent i when it performs action a^i in state s^i and move to state $s^{i\prime}$.

However, the multi-agent MDP approach has two disadvantages. The learning is centralized, i.e. the task consisting in finding an optimal policy for the group cannot be distributed among the agents. Moreover, the need to consider all the joint actions increases considerably the complexity of learning, since the size of the space of joint actions grows in an exponential way according to the number of agents. We are interested in a decentralized MDP with communication where each agent takes into account only its actions but considers that all the other agents are part of the environment. The communication is governed by mobile agents.

6.4 Mobile agent

An important aspect of multi-agent systems is to construct intelligent agent able of achieving goals in complex environment. They address specifically the behaviour of the agent in its environment changes [Hadeli et al., 2004; Mellouk et al., 2006). Reinforcement learning provides a framework of adaptation of the agent's behaviour according to its environment. As mobile agents we consider an ants' colony. The structure of the model identifies two kinds of agents, their responsibilities, and the way they interact. The structure consists of a scheduler agent that deals with management of queues on the basis of available information (resource capacity) and a resource agent that measures the resource amount and gives this information to the scheduler.

Scheduling in this system is done as follows: Before performing action selection and then scheduling the different queues based on their QoS, each scheduler agent sends ants moving downstream to control actual situation. They gather information about the availability of the resource and then return to the sender agent with the information. On the basis of this information the scheduler agent chooses a schedule and sends ants to reserve the needed resources by deposing pheromone. After that the scheduler agent regularly sends ants to reserve the previously found best resource capacity because if the reservation is not refreshed, the pheromone evaporates after a while. From time to time, the scheduler agent sends ants to survey the possible new (and better) amount of this resource. If they find a better measurement, the scheduler agent reserves the resource that is needed for the new schedule and the old reserving information evaporates. Ants are used also to distribute information and make their current state known throughout the system. The scheduler agent is not restricted to send the ants in one direction only. The ants are sent towards various directions which are directly connected with the router containing this scheduler agent. The scheduler agent waits until all the ants arrive back with the gathered information and than decides to keep only the ant with the best information, the others terminate. Also, each agent sends ants to distribute information about its current state to the other agents. Every time an ant arrives at a scheduler agent, it gives a reward according to the information that was investigated. This reward is in form of a belief factor which will allow each scheduler agent in the multi-agent system to make update on their scheduling policies. The belief factor is a function of the synthetic pheromone concentration. It reflects the degree of confidence that an agent will consider on the information established by other agents from the same cooperating group. The belief factor might be useful in situations where the information is not reliable due to changes in the environment.

6.4.1 Combining pheromone and Q-learning

At level on each router, the scheduler agent performs a reinforcement learning to schedule the service of queues. This scheduling is done by taking account the current state of the environment provided by the ant agent. During the learning, the Q-function is updated based on the concentration of pheromone in the current state and the neighbour states. The used technique combines Q-learning (Sutton & Barto, 1998) with a synthetic pheromone introducing a belief factor into the update equation. The formula bellow describes the belief factor (Monekosso & Remagnino, 2004):

$$B(s, a) = \frac{\sum_{s \in Na} \Phi(s)}{\sum_{\sigma \in Na} \Phi_{max}(\sigma)} \tag{15}$$

where $\Phi(s)$ is a synthetic pheromone, a scalar value that integrates the basic dynamic nature of the pheromone, namely aggregation, evaporation and diffusion.
where $\Phi(s)$ is a synthetic pheromone, a scalar value that integrates the basic dynamic nature of the pheromone, namely aggregation, evaporation and diffusion.

6.5 Proposed model.

Definition: A decentralized multi-agent MDP is defined as 4-tuple (S, A^i, P^i, r^i), where S is a set of all states, A^i is the set of all actions of agent i, $P^i: S \times A^i \rightarrow \Delta(S)$ is the state transition function where $\Delta(S)$ is the set of probability distributions over the set S and $r^i: S \times A^i \times S \rightarrow$ đ is the individual reward such that $r^i(s, a^i, s')$ is the reward obtained by agent i when it performs action a^i in state s and move to state s'.

We define a local policy π^i for each agent i such that:

$$\pi^i : S \rightarrow A^i \tag{16}$$

The expected discounted value function of agent i is the following:

$$V^i(s, \pi^i) = E(\pi^i)[\, r^i \mid s_0 = s] = E(\pi^i)[\, \sum_{t=0} \gamma^t r^i_{t+1} \mid s_0 = s] \tag{17}$$

where r^i_t is the immediate reward at time step for agent i and γ is a discount factor.

We consider also Q^i as local Q-function, defined for each state-action pair as:

$$Q^{i}\pi^{i}(s, a^{i}, s') = E(\pi^{i})[\, r^{i} \mid s_0 = s, a^{i}, s'] = r^{i}(s, a^{i}, s') + \gamma\Sigma\, P(s' \mid s, a^{i})\, V^{i}(s', \pi^{i}) \qquad (18)$$

The Q-learning update equation adapted to the local decision process according the global state space and modified with synthetic pheromone is given by the following formula:

$$Q^{i}(s, a^{i}) \leftarrow Q^{i}(s, a^{i}) + \alpha\, \{R + \gamma \max_{a^{i'}} [Q^{i}(s', a^{i'}) + \xi\, B(s', a^{i'})] - Q^{i}(s, a^{i})\} \qquad (19)$$

where the parameter ξ is a sigmoid function of time periods such that $\xi \geq 0$. The value of the parameter ξ increases with the number of agents which achieve successfully the current task.

The optimal policy $\pi^{i,*}$ for each agent i can be obtained by using the modified formula (11):

$$V^{i}(s^1, \ldots\ldots, s^n, \pi^{i,*}) = \max_{a^{i}} Q^{i,*}(s^1, \ldots\ldots, s^n, a^{i}) \qquad (20)$$

The effect of one agent's action depends on the action taken by others or choosing an action by an agent may restrict actions that can be selected by others. In this case each agent should change its local learned policy in order to achieve a multi-agent global optimal policy. For any global state s = (s1, ….., sn) and any joint action a = (a1, …., an), the optimal action value function Q*of the multi-agent MDP is the sum of the optimal action value functions Qi,*learned by a decentralized multi-agent MDP for each agent. The agents could have different estimations on the optimal state-action values according to the environment. These estimations wi(s, a) can be computed as:

$$w^{i}(s, a^{i})) = \frac{\exp(h^{i}(s, a^{i})/\eta)}{\Sigma_{j=1}^{n} \exp(h^{j}(s, a^{i})/\eta)} \qquad (21)$$

where $h^{i}(s, a^{i})$ is the number of estimations' updates achieved by agent i for $(s^{1}, \ldots\ldots, s^{n}, a^{i})$ and η is an adjustable parameter. So,

$$Q^{*}(s^1, \ldots, s^n, a^1, \ldots., a^n) = \sum_{i=1}^{n} w^{i}(s, a^{i})\, Q^{i,*}(s^1, \ldots\ldots, s^n, a^{i}) \qquad (22)$$

When the learning is finished, an optimal policy can be directly derived from the optimal action value Q*(s, a) by:

$$\pi^{*}(s^1, \ldots\ldots, s^n) = \arg\max_{(a^1, \ldots., a^n)} Q^{*}(s^1, \ldots\ldots, s^n, a^1, \ldots., a^n) \qquad (23)$$

6.5.1 Learning algorithm

The model of the environment's dynamics, the transition probabilities and rewards is unknown in learning of a single agent MDP and consequently the subsequent multi-agent MDP. So, the learning of the optimal solution of a problem is done by agents through interaction with the environment.

We describe the global scheduling problem as a multi-agent MDPs in a decentralized approach. We derive a multi-agent learning algorithm from traditional reinforcement learning method based on Markov decision process to construct global solutions from

solutions to the individual MDPs. In this case, we assume that the agents work independently by making their trials in the simulated environment. The system state s is described by the space state of all agents; an action a^i describes which queue is serviced in the time slot. Therefore, the goal of scheduling is to find an optimal policy π^* such that the rewards accumulated are maximized.
The proposed algorithm converges to the optimal policy and optimal action value function for the multi-agent MDP since the difference between standard multi-agent and our decentralized multi-agent MDP model is the global states space for each action set A^i of an agent i.
The rewards may depend both on the current situation and on the selected action and express the desired optimization goal. In our approach, the global action a is a vector of single action made by distributed agents each associated with one of the n routers.
Learning here means iteratively improving the selection policy according to the maximization of the global reward. This is done by a Q-learning rule adapted to the local selection process (eq. 19). The learning rule relates the local scheduling process of agent i to the global optimization goal by considering the global reward R.
If Q^i converges the $Q^{i,*}$ predicts if the action a^i would be selected next. This action will be chosen by a policy greedy.
In a single-agent learning case, Q-learning converges to the optimal action independent of the action selection strategy. However, in a multi-agent situation, the action selection strategy becomes crucial for convergence to any joint action. A major challenge in defining a suitable strategy for the selection of actions is to make a trade-off between exploration of new policies and exploitation of existing policies.
In our research, we use a Boltzmann distribution (Katanakis & Kudenko, 2002) for the probability of choosing an action by each agent. In this strategy, each agent derive a scheduling policy from the current value of Q^i matrix and then update Q^i using the rewards from actions chosen by the current scheduling policy according to a probability distribution $\pi^i(s, a^i)$:

$$\pi^i(s, a^i) = \frac{\exp(Q^i(s, a^i) / T)}{\sum_{a^{i'} \in A^i} \exp(Q^i(s, a^{i'}) / T)} \tag{24}$$

where exp is the exponential function and T is a parameter called temperature. The value of the temperature determines the possibility for an agent to balance between exploration and exploitation. For high temperature, even when an expected value of a given action is high, an agent may still choose an action that appears less desirable. In contrast, low temperature values support more exploitation, as the agent is more expected to have discovered the true estimates of different actions. The three important settings for the temperature are the initial value, the rate of decrease and the number of steps until it reaches its lowest limit. This lower limit must be set to a value close enough to 0 to allow the learners to converge by stopping their exploration.
In our work, we start with a very high value for the temperature to force the agents to make random moves until the temperature reaches a low enough value to play a part in the

learning. This is done when the agents are gathering information about the environment or the other agents. The temperature defined as a function of iterations is given by:

$$T(x) = (e^{-sx} * T_{max}) + 1 \quad (25)$$

where x is the iteration number, s is the rate of decay and T_{max} is the starting temperature.

In this section we present an algorithm called DEMAL (Decentralized Multi-Agent Learning) that uses Q-learning and decentralization on the level of the action.

Algorithm DEMAL

Repeat

Initialize $s = (s^1, \ldots, s^n)$

Repeat

For each agent i

Choose a^i using Boltzman formula

Take action a^i, observe reward r^i and state s′

$$Q^i(s, a^i) \leftarrow Q^i(s, a^i) + \alpha\{R + \gamma \max_{a^{i\prime}} [Q^i(s', a^{i\prime}) + \xi B(s', a^{i\prime})] - Q^i(s, a^i)\}$$

$s \leftarrow s'$

until s is terminal

until algorithm converges

6.5.2 Approximation

In this model, we define the optimal policy by using optimal action value function Q*of the multi-agent MDP as the sum of the optimal action value functions $Q^{i,*}$learned by a decentralized multi-agent MDP for each agent. We can apply this learning algorithm directly to solve multi-agent MDP but this method would not be very efficient because of the state and action spaces dimension that can be huge since they increase exponentially with the number of agents. This increase influences the complexity of the learning algorithm since this one depends on the number of states and actions. In tabular methods, Q^i values were assumed to be stored in lookup tables which can be large since each one depends on the number of states and actions. In order to approximate the tabular Q^i function, a feed-forward multilayer neural network like the MLP can be used. Its structure is a three-layered model containing an input layer, a hidden layer, and an output layer. The input variables of the NN are the states of the system and the set of actions A^i for each agent, which have n and m dimensions respectively. The output of the network corresponds to the Q^i value for the current states and actions. Each node in every layer subsequently calculates its activation as the weighted sum over its inputs according to:

$$\mu_j = \sum_i x_i w_{ij} \quad (26)$$

where x_i is the ith input to node j and w_{ij} is the weight of the synapse connecting node i with node j from a higher level. A common activation function for MLPs is the sigmoidal function which is applied to the hidden layer and which will also be used for our specific implementation.

$$\sigma(y) = (1+e^{-y})^{-1} \tag{27}$$

The technique used to learn the Q-function is the back propagation algorithm [18, 19, 20]. The weight update can be expressed by gradient descent, where the weights are added, at each iteration by the value of:

$$\Delta w = -\eta \frac{\partial E}{\partial w} \tag{28}$$

where η is a small learning rate.

The network error is backpropagated through the network from output to input space, where at each node we aim to match the node's output o as closely to the target t as possible. The network error δ_k for the output nodes k, can be calculated as:

$$\delta_k \leftarrow o_k(1-o_k)(t_k-o_k) \tag{29}$$

For the hidden nodes h δ_h can be calculated as:

$$\delta_h \leftarrow o_h(1-o_h) \sum_{k \in outputs} w_{kh}\delta_k \tag{30}$$

The error terms are directly derived from the mean-squared error (MSE) which is defined according to formula:

$$E(w) = \frac{1}{2} \sum_{k \in outputs} (t_k-o_k)^2 \tag{31}$$

The approximate state-action value function Q^i is proven to converge to the optimal function $Q^{i,*}$ (and hence π^i to $\pi^{i,*}$) given certain technical restrictions on learning rates.

6.6 Performance evaluation.

We carried out our evaluation in two stages. The first stage consists to realizing the scheduling on level of one router. For that, we just consider in this stage a single agent MDP. In the second stage, we solve the whole problem which concerns the optimization of the end to end queuing delay through the global scheduling. Hence, we apply our algorithm based on the multi-agent MDP in its decentralized version. We start to describe the context of the first phase.

In each router, an agent deals with scheduling N classes of traffic, where each traffic class has its own queue q_i, for i = 1…N. Let q_N denote the queue for best-effort traffic, which has no predefined delay requirements and $R_1, R_2,\ldots,R_{N-1}$ denote the delay requirements of the remaining classes. Let $M_1, M_2,\ldots,M_{N-1}$ denote the measured delays of these classes observed over the last P packets. We assume that all packets have a fixed size. We consider also that a fixed length timeslot is required for transmitting a packet and at most one packet can be serviced at each timeslot. The arrival of packets is described by a Bernoulli process, where the mean arrival rate μ_i for q_i is represented by the probability of a packet arriving for q_i in any timeslot. Our goal is to learn a scheduling policy that ensures $M_i \leq R_i$ for i=1,…,N-1. For the simulation, we used a three queue system that is Q_1, Q_2 and the best effort queue and the parameters of this simulation are given in table 3. We have considered two cases according to the availability of resource. For investigating the case where the output link capacity of the router is sufficient we assume that this capacity is 500 Kbps. In this case, a sufficient amount of capacity is provided for each queue so our algorithm satisfied the mean delay requirements for Q_1 and Q_2 (see fig.9). We have also observed that our approach requires 1.5 x 10^4 timeslots in terms of convergence time. In the second scenario (table 4) we consider the case where the output link capacity of the router is small and equal to 300 Kbps. The result of this case is shown in fig. 10. We observe that an allocation of a share of the available bandwidth is given to the delay-sensitive class Q_1 and then to Q_2 and the best effort queue. This is carried out on the basis of information gathered by a mobile agent. Also, $\varepsilon = 0.2$; $\gamma = 0.5$.

In the second part of our evaluation, we consider a network with several routers connected to each other like in (Bourenane et al., 2007). We introduce also the mobile agents to gather and distribute necessary and complete information in order to help the agents to update their knowledge of the environment. The figures 10 and 11 show that in both scenarios, the presence of mobile agents provides a better queuing delay for all routers.

Queue	Arrival Rate (packets/timeslot)	Mean Delay Requirement	eBi Kbps
Q_1	0.30	8	64
Q_2	0.20	2	128
BE	0.40	Best-effort	Best-effort

Table 3. Simulation Parameters: Scenario 1

Queue	Arrival Rate packets/timeslot	Mean Delay Requirement	eBi Kbps
Q_1	0.30	4	128
Q_2	0.20	6	256
BE	0.40	BE	BE

Table 4. Simulation Parameters: Scenario 2

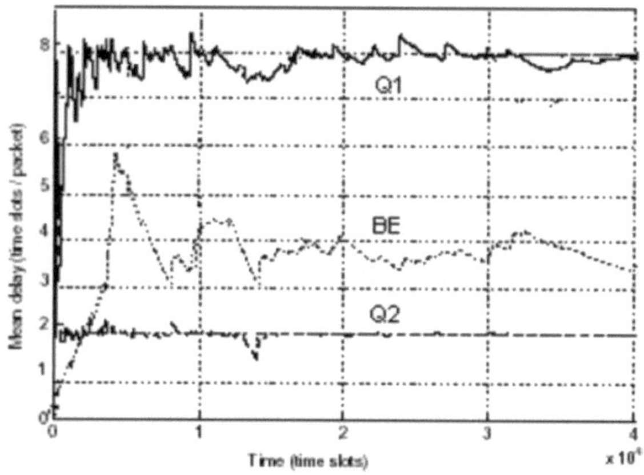

Fig. 9. Mean Delay for three classes

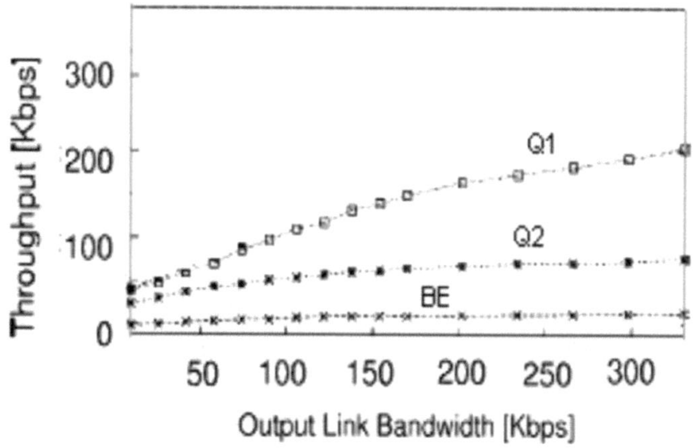

Fig. 10. Average throughput of three queues

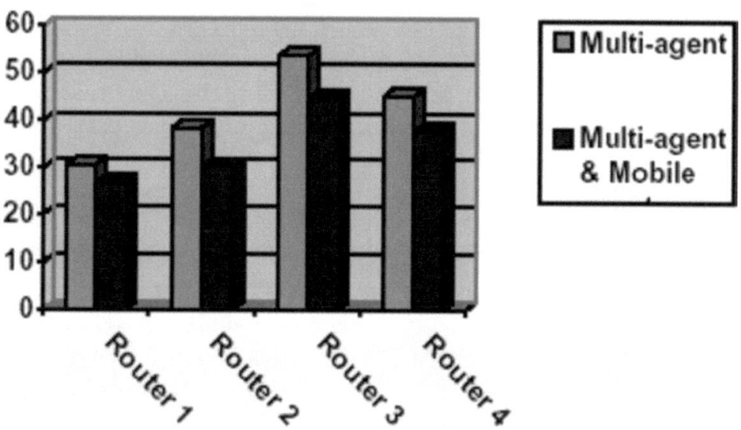

Fig. 11. Average queuing delay (scenario 1)

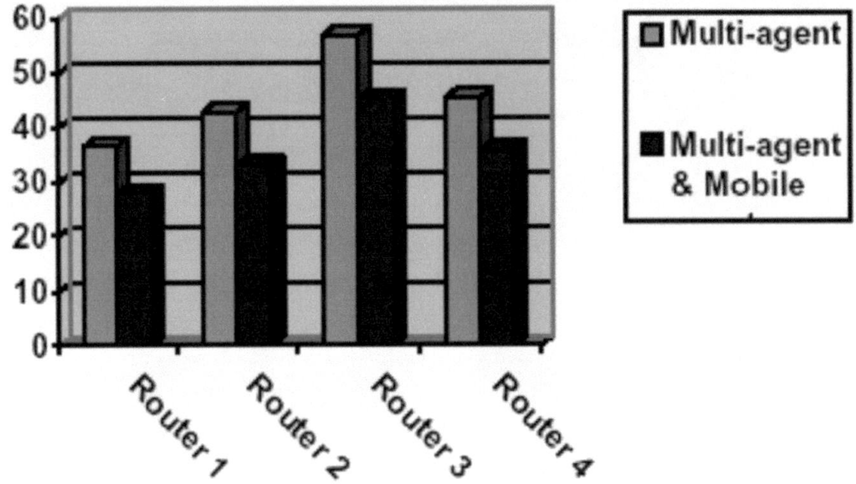

Fig. 12. Average queuing delay (scenario 2)

7. Conclusion

Due to the growing needs in telecommunications (VoD, Video-Conference, VoIP, etc.) and the diversity of transported flows, communication networks does not meet the requirements of the future integrated-service networks that carry multimedia data traffic with a high QoS. The main drivers of this evolution are the continuous growth of the bandwidth requests, the promise of cost improvements and finally the possibility of increasing profits by offering new services. First, it does not support resource reservation which is primordial to guarantee an end-to-end Qos (bounded delay, bounded delay jitter, and/or bounded loss ratio). Second, data packets may be subjected to unpredictable delays and thus may arrive at their destination after the expiration time, which is undesirable for continuous real-time media. In this context, for optimizing the financial investment on their networks, operators must use the same support for transporting all the flows. Therefore, it is necessary to develop a high quality control mechanism to check the network traffic load and ensure QoS requirements. It's clear that the integration of these QoS parameters increases the complexity of the used algorithms. Anyway, there will be QoS relevant technological challenges in the emerging hybrid networks which mixed several different types of networks (wireless, broadcast, mobile, fixed, etc.).

QoS management in networking has been a topic of extensive research in a last decade. As the Internet network is managed on a best effort packet routing, QoS assurance has always been an open issue. Because the majority of past Internet applications (email, web browsing, etc.) do not used strong QoS needs, this issue is somewhat made less urgent in the past. Today, with the development of internet real-time application and the convergence of voice and data networks, it is necessary to develop a high quality control mechanism to check the network traffic load and ensure QoS requirements. Constraints imposed by QoS requirements, such as bandwidth, delay, or loss, are referred to as QoS constraints, and the associated routing is referred to as QoS routing which is a part of Constrained-Based Routing (CBR).

Several methods have been proposed to integrate QoS constraints and to reduce their complexity. However, for a network node to be able to make an optimal routing decision, according to relevant performance criteria, it requires not only up-to-date and complete knowledge of the state of the entire network but also an accurate prediction of the network dynamics during propagation of the message through the network. This problem is naturally formulated as a dynamic programming problem, which, however, is too complex to be solved exactly. Reinforcement learning (RL) is used to approximate the value function of dynamic programming. In these algorithms, the environment is modeled as stochastic, so routing algorithms can take into account the dynamics of the network. However no model of dynamics is assumed to be given.

The second part of this chapter was devoted the study of our system based on reinforcement learning for different network communication domains.

First of all, we have focused our attention in some special kind of Constrained Based Routing in wired networks which we called QoS self-optimization Routing. Our algorithm is based on a multi-path routing technique combined with the Q-Routing algorithm and is tested for improving distribution of traffic on N-Best paths. The learning algorithm is based on founding N-Best paths in term of hops router and the minimization of the average packet delivery time on these paths. The performance of our algorithm is evaluated experimentally with OPNET simulator for different levels of traffic's load and compared to standard optimal path routing algorithms. Our approach prove superior to a classical algorithms and is able to route efficiently in networks even when critical aspects are allowed to vary dynamically. The fact that the reinforcement signal is continuously updated, parameter's adaptation of our system take into account variations of traffic.

Secondary, we study the use of reinforcement leaning in AMDR algorithm in the case of Mobile Ad Hoc Networks. It is shown from simulation results that combining proactive exploration agents with the on-demand route discovery mechanism, the AMDR routing algorithm would give reduced end-to-end delay and route discovery latency with high connectivity. This is ensured because of the availability of alternative routes in our algorithm. The alone case where our approach can provide more important delay is the first connection where any route is yet established. On the other hand, the use of delay-MPR mechanism, guarantees that the overhead generated will be reduced.

In the last part, we address the problem of optimizing the queuing delay in several routers of a network, through a global packet scheduling. We formulated this problem as a multi-agent MDP and used the decentralized version since multi-agent MDPs usually have huge state and action spaces (because they grow exponentially with the number of agents). This decentralized MDP is improved by ant-like mobile agent on the level of each router to guarantee a global view of the system's state. We presented a modified Q-learning algorithm in the decentralized approach. Our simulation shows that the proposed approach leads to better results than when the multi-agent system acts alone.

Finally, extensions of the framework for using these techniques across hybrid networks to achieve end-to-end QoS needs to be investigated, in particular on large scalable networks. Another challenging area concerns the composite metric used in routing packets (especially residual bandwidth) which is so complex and the conditioning of different models in order to take into account other parameters like the information type of each flow packet (real-time, VBR, …).

8. Acknowledgments

The work presented here is a part of QoSiDiN SCTIC LISSI research activities team, especially in the scope of the supervising Malika Bourenane, Saida Ziane and Said Hoceini PhD's thesis. I would like to thank them for their support and their suggestions.

9. References

Baras, J.S., Mehta, H. (2003). A Probabilistic Emergent Routing Algorithm (PERA) for Mobile Ad Hoc Networks, *Proceedings of WiOpt '03: Modeling and Optimization in Mobile, AdHoc and Wireless Networks*, Sophia-Antipolis, France.

Bourenane M, Mellouk A., Benhamamouche D., (2007). A QoS-based scheduling by Neurodynamic Learning. *System and Information Sciences* Journal, Vol. 2, n° 2, pp 138-144.

Boutilier C., (1999). Sequential Optimality and Coordination in Multiagent Systems, *Proceedings of IJCAI*, pp. 478-485.

Boyan, J. A., Littman, M. L., (1994). Packet routing in dynamically changing networks: A reinforcement learning approach, Advances in Neural Information Processing Systems 6, Morgan Kaufmann, San Francisco, CA, pp. 671-678.

Christopher, W. , Dayan, J.C.H., (1992). Q-learning. *Machine Learning*, vol. 3, pp. 279-292.

Dorigo, M., Stüzle, T., (2004). *Ant Colony Optimization*, MIT Press, Cambridge, MA.

Eppstein, D., (1999). Finding the K shortest paths, *SLAM J. Computing* 28:0, pp. 652-673.

Gallager, R.G. (1977). A minimum delay routing algorithm using distributed computations. *IEEE Transactions on Communications*, 25(1), 73-85.

Garey, M.R., Jhonson, D. S., (1979). *Computers and Intractability: A Guide to the Theory of NP-Completeness*, Freeman, San Francisco, 1979.

Gelenbe, E., Lent, L., Xu, Z, (2002). Networking with Cognitive Packets, *Proc. ICANN 2002*, Madrid, Spain, pp. 27-30.

Grover, W.D. (2003). *Mesh-based Survivable Transport Networks: Options and Strategies for Optical, MPLS, SONET and ATM Networking*. Ed. Prentice Hall PTR.

Hadeli, M., Valckenaers, P., Kollingbaum, M., Van Brussel, H., (2004). Multi-Agent Coordination and Control Using Stigmergy. *Computers in Industr*, vol. 53, pp. 75 – 96.

Hoceini S., Mellouk A., Amirat Y., (2005). A New QoS Routing Algorithm in Dynamic Traffic's Network : N-Best Routing Policy based on Reinforcement Learning, *International Transactions on Computer Science and Engineering (GESTS)*, vol. 8, pp 25-36.

Jaffe, J.M., (1984). Algorithms for Finding Paths with Multiple Constraints, *IEEE Networks*, Vol. 14, pp. 95-116.

Kapetanakis S., Kudenko, D., (2002). Reinforcement learning of coordination in cooperative multi-agent systems. *Proceedings of AAAI 2002*, pp 326–331.

Korkmaz, T., Krunz, M., (2001). A randomized Algorithm for Findind a Path Subject to Multiple QoS Requirements, *Computer Networks*, Vol. 36, pp. 251-268.

Kuipers, F. A., Korkmaz, T., Krunz, M., Van Mieghem, P., (2004). Performance Evaluation of Constraint-Based Path Selection Algorithms, *IEEE Network*, Vol. 18, No. 5, pp. 16-22.

Kuipers, F. A., P. Van Mieghem, (2005). Conditions that impact the Complexity of QoS Routing, *IEEE/ACM Transaction on Networking*, Vol. 13, No. 4, pp. 717-730.

Masip-Bruin X. et al., (2006). Research challenges in QoS Routing, *Computer Communications*, Vol. 29, pp. 563-581.

Mellouk, A., Hoceini S., (2005). A Reinforcement Learning Approach for QoS Based Routing Packets in Integrated Service Web Based Systems, *Lecture Notes in Artificial Intelligence*, LNAI 3528, Springer-Heidelberg GmbH, vol. 3528, pp 299-305.

Mellouk, A., Hoceini, S., Amirat, Y., (2006a). Adaptive Quality of Service Based Routing Approaches: Development of a Neuro-Dynamic State-Dependent Reinforcement Learning Algorithm, *International Journal of Communication Systems*, Ed. Wiley InterSciences, on-line september, to appear.

Mellouk A., Hoceini S., Larynouna S., (2006b). Self-Optimization Quality of Service by Adaptive Routing in Dynamic Communication Networks, *International Transactions on Systems Science and Applications*, Xiaglow UK Ed., vol. 2, n°3, pp 265-273.

Mellouk, A., Hoceini, S., Cheurfa, M., (2007a). Reinforcing Probabilistic Selective Quality of service Routes in Dynamic Heterogeneous Networks, *Journal of Computer Communication*, Elsevier Ed., to appear, on line.

Mellouk, A., Lorenz, P., Boukerche, A., Lee, M.H., (2007b). Impact of Adaptive Quality of Service Based Routing Algorithms in the next generation heterogeneous networks, *IEEE Communication Magazine*, IEEE Press, vol. 45, n°2, pp. 65-66.

Monekosso, N., Remagnino P., (2004). Analysis and performance evaluation of the pheromone-Q-learning algorithm, *Expert Systems* 21 (2), pp 80–91.

Naimi, A.M., Jacquet, P., (2004). One Hop Delay Estimation In 802.11 Ad Hoc Networks Using The OLSR Protocol. *Research Report INRIA*, N° 5327.

Naimi, A.M., (2005). *Délai et Routage dans les réseaux ad hoc 802.11*, PHD Thesis, INRIA Rocquencourt, France.

Nguyen, D.Q., Minet, P., (2006). Analysis of Multipoint Relays Selection in the OLSR Routing Protocol with and without QoS Support, *Research Report INRIA*, N° 6067.

Ozdaglar, A.E., Bertsekas, D.P. (2003). Optimal Solution of Integer Multicommodity Flow Problem with Application in Optical Networks. *Proc. Of Symposium on Global Optimisation*, June, 411-435.

Puterman, M., (2005). *Markov Decision Processes: Discrete Stochastic Dynamic Programming*, Wiley-Interscience.

Quoitin, B., Uhlig, S., (2005). Modeling the Routing of an Automous System with C-BGP, *IEEE Network*, Vol. 19, No.6, pp. 12-19.

Sahni, S., (2005). *Data Structures, Algorithms, and Applications in C++*, second Edition, Silicon Press.

Song, M., Sahni, S., (2006). Approximation Algorithms for Multiconstrained Quality-of-Service Routing, *IEEE Transaction on Computers*, Vol. 55, No. 8, pp. 1048-1056.

Sutton, R.S., Barto, A.G. (1997). *Reinforcement Learning*. Ed. MIT Press.

Sutton, R. S., Barto, A. G. (1998). *Reinforcement Learning: An Introduction*, MIT Press/Bradford Books.

Yanuzzi, M., Masip-Bruin, X., Bonaventure, O., (2005). Open Issues in Interdomain Routing : A Survey, *IEEE Network*, Vol. 19, No.6, pp. 49-56.

Ziane, S., Mellouk, A. (2006). A Swarm Quality of Service Based Multi-Path Routing Algorithm (SAMRA) for Wireless Ad Hoc Networks, *International Review on Computers and Software Journal*, Vol.1, n°1., pp. 11-20.

19

The Allocation of Time and Location Information to Activity-Travel Sequence Data by Means of Reinforcement Learning

Janssens, Wets
Hasselt University, Transportation Research Institute
Belgium

1. Introduction

In the transportation research area, activity and travel modes are critically important information, based on which the transportation demand/status are simulated or predicted. Once the sequential activity-travel combination is known, such as for instance Sleep-Eat-car-Work-Eat-Work-car-Eat-bike-Shop-bike-Leisure-bike-Sleep, it is meaningful to observe how a learning agent can allocate time and location information for given activity-travel pattern combinations in a reasonable way. Also interesting to observe is how it reacts when it is thrown off its optimal arrangement because of some unforeseeable events, such as for instance a traffic jam. Given a constrained environment, we simulate and look into a learning agent's behavior under the framework of Reinforcement Learning (Mitchell, 1997; Sutton & Barto; 1998), which is in fact a synonym for learning by interaction (Kaelbling, 1996). More specifically, the vector <activity, starting time, duration, location> denotes the agent's current state, where duration indicates how long the agent has spent on the current activity. There are two actions available for each state: Stay (continue current activity for another time slot at the same location) or Move (travel to a possible location where the agent starts to perform the next activity in the pattern). At each state, the agent will receive a reward from the environment when any possible action is chosen. By accumulating this reward information that it obtained from its trial and error search in the state space, the agent finally gets the optimal/satisfactory time and location arrangement. Previous research work in this area generally deals with only one of these two allocation problems: they either focus on the time planning of the activity patterns (Charypar et al., 2004), or search the shortest path in a dynamic programming way (Dijkstra, 1959). In reality, however, a rational person will consider the time and location arrangements simultaneously in order to achieve a total maximal reward. To the best of our knowledge, it is the first time that both problems are integrated and solved using Reinforcement Learning.

Reinforcement Learning goes back to the very first stages of Artificial Intelligence and Machine Learning and has several applications in the domain of Intelligent Knowledge Engineering Systems. Indeed, the applications of reinforcement learning are situated in the basic roots of artificial intelligence, such as for instance game playing (Littman, 1994; esauro, 1992, 1994; Thrun, 1995) and robotics (Mahadevan & Connell, 1992; Schaal, 1994). However, there are also numerous other application domains such as for instance in elevator dispatching (Crites & Barto, 1996; Barto & Sutton, 1981), production scheduling (Schneider et al., 1998), but also in a transportation-related context such as in intelligent lane selection (Moriarty, 1998) for achieving a higher traffic throughput. Within an activity-based framework, the reinforcement learning technique has been first applied by Arentze and Timmermans (Arentze & Timmermans, 2003) in the context of learning and adaptation, and only recently by Charypar et al. (Charypar et al., 2004; Charypar & Nagel, 2005) in a time allocation problem.

The current paper elaborates this latter approach by not only focusing on an optimal time allocation solution, but also on the allocation of location information. Furthermore, the time and location allocation problem were treated and integrated simultaneously, which means that the respondents' reward is not only maximized in terms of minimum travel duration, but also simultaneously in terms of optimal time allocation. With respect to the allocation of location information, the travel time between two locations (origin and destination locations) is used and is made dependent on the transport mode that has been chosen for travelling from one location to another. Indeed, travel durations between two locations are obviously not equal over different transport modes, so it is warranted to take this dimension into account.

The remainder of this paper has been organized as follows. The basic conceptions of reinforcement learning are elaborated in section 2, along with the introduction to Qlearning, one of the popular algorithms to realize reinforcement learning. In section 3, we will detail by means of artificial examples how Q-learning can be applied to the time and location allocation problem respectively, which will help us improve the understanding of reinforcement learning. Section 4 illustrates characteristics and results of activity-travel patterns being optimized in a more realistic environment. Finally, concluding remarks are given in section 5.

2. Reinforcement learning

Under a constrained environment, the learning agent can perceive a set S of distinct states, which are normally characterized by a number of dimensions, and has a set A of actions to perform at each state. Reinforcement learning tasks are generally treated in discrete time steps. At each time step t, the agent observes the current state s_t and chooses a possible action to perform, which leads to its succeeding state $s_{t+1}=\delta(s_t, a_t)$. The environment responds by giving the agent a reward $r(s_t, a_t)$. These rewards can be positive, zero or negative. It is probable that these preferable rewards come with a delay. In other words, some actions and their consequential state transitions may bring low rewards in short term, while it will lead to state-action pairs later with a much higher reward. On the contrary, an action in a given state may receive an immediate high reward, whereas it makes the agent enter into a path where a series of actions followed, have very low or even negative rewards.

Therefore, the task of the agent is to learn a policy $\pi : S \rightarrow A$, according to which the agent will achieve the maximal accumulative reward over time. Given an arbitrary policy π from an arbitrary state s_t, the accumulative reward can be formulated as follows:

$$V^{\pi}(s_t) = r_t + \gamma r_{t+1} + \gamma^2 r_{t+2} + \cdots = \sum_{i=0}^{\infty} \gamma^i r_{t+i}$$

$\gamma \in [0,1]$ is the discount factor and it also determines the relative value of immediate versus delayed reward, which indicates how far the agent looks into the future. The agent only considers the immediate reward if γ is set at zero. A parameter γ close to one means that rewards in the far future are given greater emphasis relative to the immediate rewards.
Now the agent is required to learn the optimal policy $\pi^*(s)$ that maximizes the accumulative reward:

$$\pi^* \equiv \arg\max_{\pi} V^{\pi}(s), (\forall s)$$

We refer to the optimal value function V_{π}^* as V^* for the sake of simplicity. Given a state *s*, the formula above can be extended with the immediate reward explicitly displayed, which indicates that the optimal action *a* at current state *s* should maximize the immediate reward *r*(*s*, *a*) plus the value *V**(*s*) of the succeeding state, discounted by γ:

$$Q(s,a) \equiv r(s,a) + \gamma \max_{a'} Q(\delta(s,a),a')$$

where δ (*s*, *a*) denotes the resulting state after action *a* is performed at state *s*.

2.1 Q-learning algorithm

It is natural to choose *V** as the evaluation function in order to let the algorithm determine the state and action pairs that optimize V*. Unfortunately, it is required that the perfect knowledge of immediate reward function *r* and state transition function δ are known in advance. When the agent has learned through trial and error the reward and state transition pairs responded by its environment at any state, it is able to calculate the optimal action *a* at any state *s*.
In reality, however, it is usually impossible for the agent to predict in advance the exact outcome of applying an arbitrary action to an arbitrary state. In other words, the domain knowledge is probably not perfect. Q-learning (Watkins, 1989; Watkins & Dayan, 1992) is then devised to select optimal actions even when the agent has no knowledge about the reward and state transition functions. It employs the novel evaluation function *Q*(*s*, *a*) as follows

$$Q(s,a) \equiv r(s,a) + \gamma V^*(\delta(s,a)) \tag{1}$$

Then $\pi^*(s)$ and $V^*(s)$ in terms of *Q* (*s*, *a*) can be revised as:

$$\pi^*(s) = \arg\max_{a} Q(s,a)$$
$$V^*(s) = \max_{a'} Q(s,a')$$

Taking into account equation (1), this gives

$$Q(s,a) \equiv r(s,a) + \gamma \max_{a'} Q(\delta(s,a),a') \tag{2}$$

The recursive definition of *Q*(*s*, *a*) enables Q-learning algorithm to iteratively approximate Q- values. $\hat{Q}$ is referred as the agent's estimate of the actual function Q. The Q-learning algorithm maintains a large table with entries to each state-action pair. For each entry, the value of $\hat{Q}$ (*s*,*a*) is stored and initially fulfilled with a random number. The agent repeatedly observes its current state s, chooses a possible action a to perform, and determines its immediate reward r(s, a) and resulting new state δ (s, a). The $\hat{Q}$ (s,a) value is then updated according to the following rule:

$$\hat{Q}(s,a) \leftarrow r + \gamma \max_{a'} \hat{Q}(s',a') \tag{3}$$

That is to say, the $\hat{Q}$ -value of current state-action pair is refined based on its immediate reward and the $\hat{Q}$ -value of its next state. After the Q-values of state-action pairs are well estimated by Q-learning algorithm, the agent can reach a globally optimal solution by repeatedly selecting the action that maximize the local values of Q for current state. The actual learning process can be described as follows (Charypar et al., 2004):

1. 1. Initialize the Q-values.
2. 2. Select a random starting state s which has at least one possible action to select from.
3. 3. Select one of the possible actions. This action leads to the next state s′.
4. 4. Update the Q-value of the state action pair (s, a) according to the update rule above.
5. 5. Let s = s′ and continue with step 3 if the new state has at least one possible action. If it has none go to step 2.

2.2 Explore vs exploit

The 2nd step in the learning process does not specify how actions are chosen by the learning agent. In each state the agent basically can choose from two kinds of behavior: either it can explore the state space or it can exploit the information already present in the Q-values. By choosing to exploit, the agent usually gets to states that are close to the best solution so far. Because of this, it can refine its knowledge about that solution and collect relatively high rewards. On the other hand, by choosing to explore states that are further apart from the current best solution, it is possible that it discovers a solution that yields higher rewards than the one already known. The strategy above is similar to the local and global search in most known optimization algorithms.

It is common in Q-learning to use a probabilistic approach to selecting actions. One straightforward strategy is ε-greedy method, where the probability of making a random choice is handled by the parameter ε. In every step, with a probability of 1-ε, the agent exploits the information stored in the Q-values, and with probability ε the agent chooses a random action in order to explore the state space.

In the exploration mode, the ε-greedy method assumes equal selection probabilities across possible actions, whereas the chance of selecting a better action may be increased by taking the current value distribution across alternatives into account. A commonly used method assumes a Boltzmann distribution and selects action a with probability:

$$\Pr(a_i \mid s) = \frac{e^{\hat{Q}(s,a_i)/\tau}}{\sum_j e^{\hat{Q}(s,a_j)/\tau}}$$

where ε is a parameter usually called the temperature. The higher the temperature, the more evenly probabilities are distributed across alternatives and, hence, the higher the system's tendency to explore (Arentze & Timmermans, 2003). As the temperature decreases, the system assigns increasingly higher probability to the highest valued action, and, hence, the lower the tendency to exploit. The value of the temperature parameter (as well as ε) might be a function of time rather than a constant. Then, the system can simulate a tendency to increase exploration in new environments and decrease this tendency as experience is accumulating.

There are two other possible ways of influencing the system's tendency to explore. First, the choice of the initial value for the value function is relevant. When initial values are set to a high level relative to what can be expected, the system will, even for $\varepsilon = 0$ (in the greedy method) or low temperature (in the Boltzmann method), display a high rate of exploration in an early stage. Second, the system may incrementally update an aspiration level (under each state) and switch to an exploration mode each time the currently best alternative (under the concerned state) drops below the aspiration level.

The reinforcement learning is a Markov decision process (MDP), where the functions δ (s, a) and $r(s, a)$ depend only on current state and action-pairs. In our application, we will restrict ourselves to a discrete MDP, for a discussion of a continuous MDP and for more examples, we refer to (Mitchell, 1997). The *Q*-learning algorithm will converge under two conditions (Watkins & Dayan, 1992). First, the immediate reward is bounded, i.e. there exist some positive constant c such that for all state action pairs, $|r(s, a)| < c$. The second condition is that the agent selects actions in such a fashion that it visits all possible state-action pairs infinitely often. Both conditions were met in the experimental results shown in the remainder of the paper.

3. Time and location allocation for activity and travel combinations

In this section, a hypothetical example has been presented to improve the understanding of Q-learning. A similar example has been presented and explained in Charypar et al. (2004), which is repeated here for the sake of clarity. The behavior of the Q-learning algorithm is first explained with respect to the time allocation problem; location allocation is dealt with subsequently. The integration of time and location allocation in a more realistic environment is treated in the next section.

3.1 Time allocation by means of Q-learning

3.1.1 Assumptions

For this first application and for the sake of clarity, the presence of travel modes has been ignored in the fixed sequence of activities. There are a number of other simplifying assumptions which are made to better understand the behaviour of the agent:

- Fixed order of only 4 activities (1 sequence), i.e.: Home – Work – Shop – Leisure
- Time of the day is discretized with a course time slot of 6 hours. The time structure is assumed to be periodic, i.e. 24:00 P.M. is connected to 0:00 A.M.. The duration of each activity is restricted to 12 hours in order to keep the number of state finite.
- A state s is characterized by the activity, starting time of activity and duration (time already spent at activity), and denoted as a triple (a, s, d).
- For a state s, an action may be to Stay ('S') at the current activity for another time slot or to Move ('M') on to perform the next activity.
- No travel time between two activities (ignorance of travel modes)

- Parameter setting: Learning rate $\alpha = 1$; Discounting factor $\gamma = 0.8$; $\varepsilon = 1$ (ε -greedy method applied). For purely discrete worlds, α can be safely set equal to 1. The reason is that since the system is discrete and finite, the trajectory eventually needs to come back to a state where it was before. Once this point has been reached, the system will do exactly the same as in the previous "round". A learning rate of 1 will then lead to the most optimal and fastest learning. The agent should not only be interested in immediate rewards, but in the total discounted reward. As mentioned before, the *discounting factorγ* defines how much the expected future rewards, affect decisions now. High γ means that potential future rewards have a major influence on decisions now - and that one is willing to trade short-term loss for long-term gain. While this value can be chosen arbitrarily, it should be close to 1 since we are interested in finding the *daily* time plan that maximizes the reward. The chosen value has an impact on the learning speed of the algorithm, which is of less importance for the application framework that is presented in this paper. More information can be found in Watkins & Dayan (1992).

In addition to these assumptions, reward tables are artificial and extremely simple, as shown in Table 1.

	Home			Work			Shopping			Leisure		
Start time/Duration	0h	6h	12h	0h	6h	12h	0h	6h	12h	0h	6h	12h
0:00 A.M.	0	6	0	0	0	0	0	0	0	0	3	0
6:00 A.M.	0	4	0	0	3	5	0	0	0	0	3	1
12:00 A.M.	0	2	0	0	0	0	0	5	1	0	3	4
6:00 P.M.	0	1	0	0	0	0	0	0	0	0	3	0

Table 1. An example of a simple reward table for activities

It can be seen from Table 1, that the reward of working 0 hours is 0 and is independent of the starting-time of the work-activity. Arriving at work at 6:00 A.M. gives somebody a reward of 3 (units) at the moment he/she is working for 6 hours (i.e. from 6:00 A.M. - 12:00A.M.) or a reward of 5 (units) at the moment the person is working for 12 hours (i.e. from 6:00 A.M. - 6 P.M.). Arriving at work later than 6 A.M. gives no reward at all. The reward tables for home, shop and leisure are similar.

3.1.2 Evolution of Q-values and state-action pairs

Let us now reconsider the Q-learning algorithm. Since $\alpha = 1$ and $\gamma = 0.8$, the update rule for our simple example is equal to $\hat{Q}(s,a) \leftarrow r(s,a) + 0.8 \max_{a'} \hat{Q}(s',a')$. In the first step of the learning process, all the Q-values of every state-action pair are set equal to zero. Next, a random starting state s will be chosen, which has at least one possible action to select from. In our example, the starting state may be equal to (Work, 0:00 A.M., 6 hours). The third step selects one of the possible actions, which will bring us to the next state s'. Because the exploration probability was set maximal, i.e. $\varepsilon = 1$, the agent will always randomly choose an action in order to explore the state space in an attempt to find a new, better solution than the one already known. (On the contrary, when $\varepsilon = 0$, the agent will choose the action that has the largest Q-value so far.) Suppose the agent randomly chooses to Move on the next activity. The next state turns to be (Shopping, 6:00 A.M., 0 hour). According to the update rule in step 4, the updated Q (s, a) = Q (Work, 0:00 A.M., 6 hours; Move) is still equal to 0 since both the immediate reward and the maximal Q-value of its next state-action pairs are zeros.

Table 2 shows the states that have been visited by the agent in every loop, while Table 3 illustrates the progress of the Q-values for every state-action pair during the execution of the algorithm.

	Home			Work			Shopping			Leisure		
Start time/ Duration	0 h	6 h	12 h	0 h	6 h	12 h	0 h	6 h	12 h	0 h	6 h	12 h
0:00 A.M.	7	8			1							
6:00 A.M.				9 25	10 26		2	3	4			
12:00 A.M.	13 17			14 18			11 15 19 27			12 16 20 28	21 29	
6:00 P.M.	22 30 34	23	24	31 35			32 (36)			5 33	6	

Table 2. Visited states per loop (Numbers denote the loop number)

In the final loop, the state s will be set equal to the state (Shopping, 6:00 A.M., 0 hours). In this artificial example, no travel time has been taken into account. It should be noted that in a realistic scenario, the start time of state s′ should thus be augmented with the travel time which is needed to get from state s to state s′. For now, the algorithm continues with loop 2, which starts again at step 3 of the algorithm procedure. The Q-values stay equal to zero until the 5th loop. In this loop, the action is Stay, which will bring the agent to the state (Leisure, 6:00 P.M., 6 hours) and a 3-unit immediate reward. It is worth mentioning that the immediate rewards are given as "utility per time slice", which corresponds to a coarse version of marginal utility. Also interesting to observe is for instance the 23rd loop, where the agent chooses to stay for another 6 hours when it has already been home for 6 hours (start from 6:00 P.M.). The immediate reward is calculated as 0 – 1 = -1, which means that the agent feels unworthy if continues to Stay. The 24th loop is the first where the Q-values of its next state-action pairs are non-zeros. The immediate reward is equal to 0, but the second part of the update rule looks at the latest updated Q-value for every state-action pair, takes the largest Q-value over all the actions and multiplies this by the discounting factor. In this case the latest updated Q-value for the state-action pair (Work, 6:00 A.M., 0 hours; Stay) is 3 (see loop number 9) and for (Work, 6:00 A.M., 0 hours; Move) it is 0 (initialization). For this reason, the updated Q-value of the 24th loop is equal to = 0 + 0.8 * Max (3, 0) = 2.4. The computation for the other loops is similar (see Table 3).

Loop	Action	Q-value	Loop	Action	Q-value	Loop	Action	Q-value
1	Move	0	13	Move	0	25	Stay	3
2	Stay	0	14	Move	0	26	Move	0
3	Stay	0	15	Move	0	27	Move	0+0.8 max(3,0)=2.4
4	Move	0	16	Move	0	28	Stay	3
5	Stay	3	17	Move	0	29	Move	0+0.8 max(1,0)=0.8
6	Move	0	18	Move	0	30	Move	0
7	Stay	6	19	Move	0	31	Move	0
8	Move	0	20	Stay	3	32	Move	0+0.8max(3,0)=2.4
9	Stay	3	21	Move	0	33	Move	0+0.8max(1,0)=0.8
10	Move	0	22	Stay	1	34	Move	0
11	Move	0	23	Stay	-1	35	Move	0+0.8max(0,2.4) =1.92
12	Move	0	24	Move	0+0.8 max(3,0)=2.4	...	...	...

Table 3. Q-values and state-action pairs

3.1.3 Optimal time allocation

The learning procedure continues until each state-action pair has been visited for a sufficient large number of times and until the corresponding Q-value converges. Then at each state, the agent chooses the action that achieves a maximal Q-value, which means that an optimal policy chart can be constructed as shown in Table 4. Starting from an arbitrary state, the policy will finally guide the agent to its stable and optimal time planning within a day:

Home	:	0:00 A.M.	--	6:00 A.M.
Work	:	6:00 A.M.	--	12:00 A.M.
Shop	:	12:00 A.M.	--	6:00 P.M.
Leisure	:	6:00 P.M.	--	0:00 A.M.

	Home			Work			Shop			Leisure		
Start time/ Duration	0 h	6 h	12 h	0 h	6 h	12 h	0 h	6 h	12 h	0 h	6 h	12 h
0:00 A.M.	S	M	M	M	S	M	M	S	M	M	M	M
6:00 A.M.	S	M	M	S	M	M	S	M	M	M	M	M
12:00 A.M.	M	M	M	M	M	M	S	M	M	S	S	M
6:00 P.M.	M	S	M	M	M	M	M	M	M	S	M	M

Table 4. Policy Chart for iterations going to infinity

For instance, the algorithm will first choose a random start state. Let's say (Shop, 0:00 A.M., 6 hours). The corresponding action in the policy chart is Stay. As a result, the next state is equal to (Shop, 0:00 A.M., 12 hours). According to the policy chart, the agent chooses to Move (since the maximal duration for each activity is 12 hours), and comes to the next states (Leisure, 12:00 A.M., 0 hours). Carrying out the policy in Table 4, the agent sequentially arrives at (Leisure. 12:00 A.M., 6 hours), (Leisure, 12:00 A.M., 12 hours), (Home, 0:00 A.M., 0 hours), (Home, 0:00 A.M., 6 hours), (Work, 6:00 A.M., 0 hours), (Work, 6:00 A.M., 6 hours), (Shop, 12:00 A.M., 0 hours), (Shop, 12:00 A.M., 6 hours), (Leisure, 6:00 PM, 0 hours) and (Leisure, 6:00 PM, 6 hours). Next the agent will Move again to the state (Home, 0:00 A.M., 0 hours), thus forming a cycle within a day, which is the same as the optimal time planning above. It can be seen from the policy chart that an arbitrary start state, such as (Leisure, 0:00 A.M., 6 hours) or (Home, 6:00 A.M., 12 hours), will ultimately lead to the same optimal solution.

3.1.4 Discussion

Finally, some remarks need to be made with respect to the use of the Q-learning algorithm to solve the time allocation problem. First, cycles can also be multiples of 24 hours. For example, an agent can have one full day where it gets up early and goes to bed late, alternated with a less full day where it gets up later and goes to bed earlier. Second, an interesting side-effect of the structure of Q-learning is that the result of the computation is not only the optimal "cycle" through state space, but also the optimal "paths" if the agent is pushed away from the optimal cycle. For example, if an activity takes considerably longer than expected, the Q-values at the arrival state will still point the way to the best continuation of the plan, as shown in the example above. Third, it is possible that some of the Q-values do not converge when their state-action pairs have not been sufficiently visited. Then the agent will nevertheless find a cycle, albeit possibly not the optimal one. In reality, it may be time consuming to visit each state-action pair infinitely in a huge state space with many possible actions, which pushes the agent to a tradeoff between the learning time and solution quality.

3.2 Location allocation by means of Q-learning

Consistent with the time allocation problem, location allocation can also be solved by means of Q-learning. For this purpose, it is assumed that people try to maximize/minimize the reward/cost of its travel in total.

Travel distance may not be an optimal measure for determining the burden of travel because it is plausible in a realistic situation that the distance between location A and location B is shorter than the distance between location A and C, while the travel time may be longer (for instance because of a better road network). Furthermore, it is possible that there is a difference in the transport mode that is used.

Translated into a context of Q-learning, the agent learns to find a travel policy that achieves maximal reward/minimal cost. It is assumed that the immediate reward of traveling between two locations depends upon the travel mode, and has a negative correlation with travel time.

3.2.1 Assumptions

Again, consider a simple example with the following simplifying assumptions to better understand the behaviour of the decision agent:

- One activity-travel sequence: Home – *public transport* – work – *walk* – leisure – *walk* – shop – public transport – Home.
- A state is characterized by the activity and current location, and is denoted as (*a*, *l*).
- For a state, an action is to choose the location where the agent can perform the next activity in sequence. Activities can be carried out in a limited number of locations:
  Home : Location A
  Work : Location B
  Leisure : Location C or D
  Shop : Location E or F
- Only the rewards that come from travel are learned to be maximized.
- Parameter setting: Learning rate $\alpha = 1$; Discounting factor $\gamma = 0.9$; $\varepsilon = 1$ (ε -greedy method applied).

In addition to these assumptions, reward tables are artificial and extremely simple, as shown in Table 5.

	Public transport						Walk					
	A	B	C	D	E	F	A	B	C	D	E	F
A	/	-12	/	/	-14	-16	/	/	/	/	/	/
B	-12	/	/	/	/	/	/	/	-8	-5	/	/
C	/	/	-	/	/	/	/	-8	/	/	-10	-4
D	/	/	/	-	/	/	/	-5	/	/	-6	-6
E	-14	/	/	/	-	/	/	/	-10	-6	/	/
F	-16	/	/	/	/	-	/	/	-4	-6	/	/

Table 5. An example of a simple reward table for travel

3.2.2 Evolution of Q-values and state-action pairs

Taking these simplifying assumptions into account, Home and Work can only be carried out at location A and B. It is obvious that the agent only has to decide about the location of Leisure and Shop activities, and each of them has two possible choices. The remainder of this section illustrates the learning procedure of the agent.

After all state-action pairs are initialized as zeros, a random state *s* will be chosen. It should be recalled that the state is defined by an activity and an origin location. Assume that the agent first visits state (Work, B). In the third step of the learning procedure, the agent chooses a random action in order to explore the state space in an attempt to find a better solution than the one already know. Let us assume that action (destination) C has been chosen to perform the next activity Leisure. The travel mode lies on the sequence and here is walk. The updated *Q* (Work, B; C) thereby equals -8 + 0.9 * max (*Q* (Leisure, C; E), *Q* (Leisure, C; F) = -8. Assume that the agent selects to walk to E for Shop when it is at the new state (Leisure, C), *Q* (Leisure, C; E) turns to be -10 + 0.9 * max (*Q* (Shop, E; A)) = -10. As shown in Table 6, the agent visited these states sequentially. These actions at each state and their corresponding updated Q-values are demonstrated in Table 7.

Origin/Activity	Home	Work	Leisure	Shop
A	4, 8, 12			
B		1, 5, 9, 13		
C			2, 10	
D			6, 14	
E				3, 15...
F				7, 11

Table 6. Visited states per loop

Loop	Action	Q-value	Loop	Action	Q-value
1	C	Q(Work, B; C) = -8	9	C	Q(Work, B; C) = -8
2	E	Q(Leisure, C; E) = -10	10	F	Q(Leisure, C; F) = -28.12
3	A	Q(Shop, E; A) = -14	11	A	Q(Shop, F; A) = -30.85
4	B	Q(Home, A; B) = -12	12	B	Q(Home, A; B) = -16.5
5	D	Q(Work, B; D) = -5	13	D	Q(Work, B; D) = -5
6	F	Q(Leisure, D; F) = -6	14	E	Q(Leisure, D; E) = -18.6
7	A	Q(Shop, F; A) = -26.8	15	A	Q(Shop, E; A) = -28.85
8	B	Q(Home, A; B) = -16.5	...	...	...

Table 7. Q-values and State-action pairs

3.2.3 Optimal location allocation

The Q-values tend to converge when each state-action pair has been visited for a sufficient large number of times. Then at each state, the agent chooses the optimal action that achieves maximal Q-value, thus constructing a policy (chart), as shown in Table 8.

Origin/activity	Home	Work	Leisure	Shop
A	B			
B		D		
C			F	
D			E	
E				A
F				A

Table 8. Policy chart for iterations going to infinity

The optimal location allocation for this sample sequence is thus equal to:

Home (A) - *public transport* - Work (B) - *walk* - Leisure (D) - *walk* - Shop (E) - *public transport* - Home (A)…

According to these stored *Q*-values of each state-action pair, the agent know how to react properly back to the optimal path when something unforeseeable happens. For instance, when location D for Leisure is not available today, the agent carries out Leisure at location C instead. Making use of its *Q*-values information about its two choices at location C, the agent wisely selects F as the location for Shopping. Next, it moves back Home at location A and is situated on the optimal path again.

4. Empirical results

4.1 Optimizing activity-travel pattern allocations

4.1.1 Preface

The previous two sections have independently considered time and location allocation in an artificial environment. In reality, however, the reward function will be more complex, there may exist a more refined time granular; an abundant number of locations may be available for a certain activity, and the distribution of these locations may be more disarrayed. Because of this, it becomes not so straightforward in the planning of time or locations. Furthermore, people will simultaneously take the time and location arrangements into account in order to get a maximal reward in total. It is recalled that the reward of daily activities depends upon the duration as well as start time, people will not simply endeavor to obtain an optimal route for travel, since such a route design may not be perfectly suitable for the time arrangement of daily activities. On the other hand, when people allocate time for activities, they have to consider the flexible travel times since a number of locations are available for the next activity. The time and location arrangements are therefore interacted.

4.1.2 Assumptions

We will integrate the two problems under the framework of Q-learning in a more realistic environment, which can be described as follows:

- The elements of sequences are limited to four kinds of activities (i.e. Home, Work, Shop and Leisure) and four kinds of travel modes (i.e. walk, bike, car and public transport).
- Time of the day is discretized with a refined time slot of 15 minutes, and the maximal duration of each activity is 12 hours.
- A state s is characterized by activity, starting time of activity, time already spent at activity (duration) and the origin location where the activity is performed.
- For a state s, an action a may be to Stay: keep performing the activity at current location for another time slot, or to Move: move to a possible location where it starts to perform the next activity. The travel mode the agent uses to reach these locations is determined by the sequence.

The reward functions of these four activities are illustrated in Figure 1 by means of example. Probably the best way to derive these reward tables in reality is to conduct elaborated stated preference experiments that are able to quantitatively assess the reward that people experience per start time and per time unit that was spent per activity. As a second-best alternative, one may use the frequency information per time frame which is available in the activity diaries as an approximation for the rewards. While frequency is certainly not a synonym for reward, the idea might work fairly well if we have a look at the purpose of our experiment. In our application, the aim is to come up with a time allocation (per activity), that corresponds best with the information that is present in the data. Obviously, some direct relationship is needed between the model and the data to achieve this. So, even though people may not like it to get to work at 7 A.M. (and may report a low reward in a realistic situation), the learning model will assign a lot of activities starting at that point in time if this happens frequently often in the data. However, the frequency information cannot be used entirely without any modification. A simple example can illustrate this.

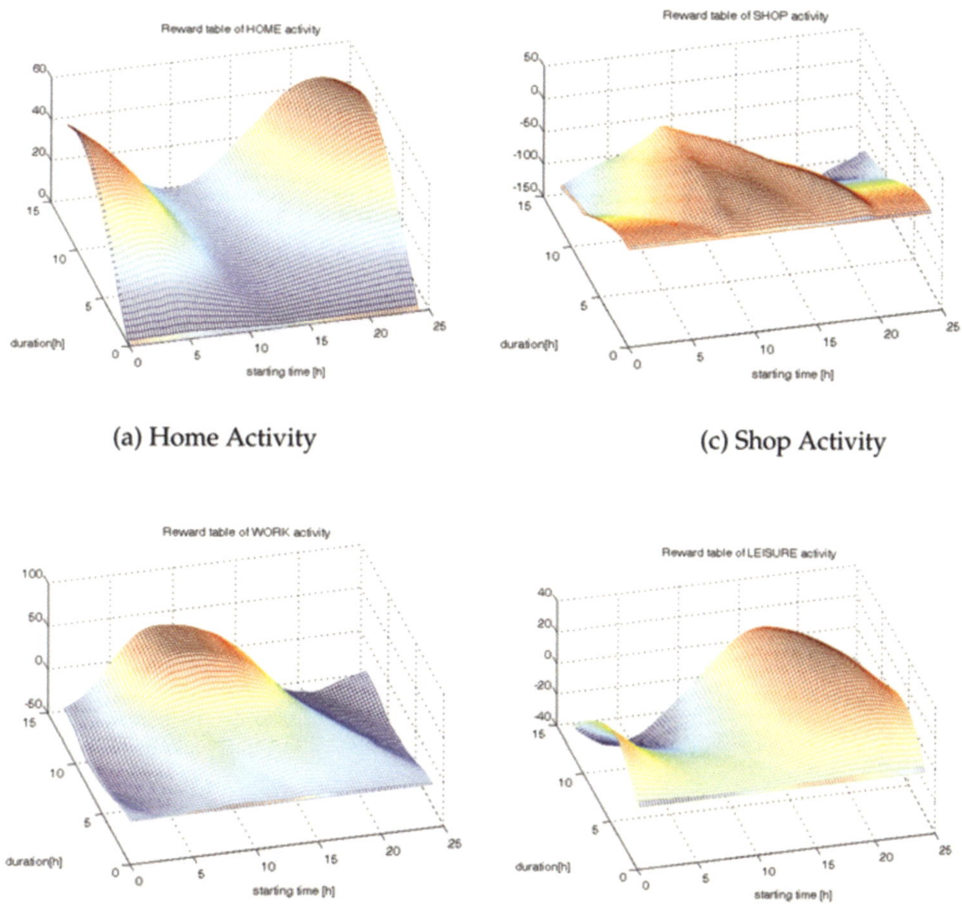

(a) Home Activity

(c) Shop Activity

(b) Work Activity

(d) Leisure Activity

Fig. 1. Reward tables

Suppose that somebody has reported to have end sleeping at 3.15 A.M. and that the time that he/she was already sleeping was 15 minutes. The reward table that is defined by a 3.00 A.M. starting time and a 15 minute duration, needs be incremented by 1 unit. However, assume now that a second person reported to have ended sleeping at 4.00 A.M. and that the time that he/she was already sleeping was 60 minutes. Now, in this case, not only the reward table that is defined by a 3.00 A.M. starting time and a 60 minute duration needs to

be updated, but the 15-, 30- and 45-minute interval needs to be updated as well. A simple program has been established to automate these kind of conversion procedures for the frequency information that is present in the data. This may result in a reward function that looks like Figure 1 where for instance starting to work for 15 minutes at 2:00 A.M. brings a negative reward. However, the agent has a much higher reward if it starts to work at 8:00 A.M. for the same duration. Additionally, assuming that the shop is only available between 8:00 A.M. - 8:00 P.M., the agent will acquire no reward if it starts to shop at 6:00 A.M. or continues to shop at 11:00 P.M.
With respect to location allocation, 100 locations were collected in a city and we recorded the distances among them. These locations are graphically illustrated in Figure 2, by applying the multi-dimensional scaling (MDS) technique (Johnson & Wichern, 1998). Of these 100 locations, 20 locations are available for Shopping, and 15 for Leisure. For each person, there is only one location available, both for Home and for Work.

4.1.3 Reward/cost function

For each travel mode, the travel time among these locations are logged. It is assumed that the reward/cost function in term of travel time is as follows:

$$\text{Reward}\left(t\right) = -c*(b*t)^{a}$$

,where c is identical for all travel modes and is applied to easily control the relative importance of travel compared with daily activities. The parameters b and a are specifically set for each travel mode in order to respectively dominate the range of reward and its evolution trend.

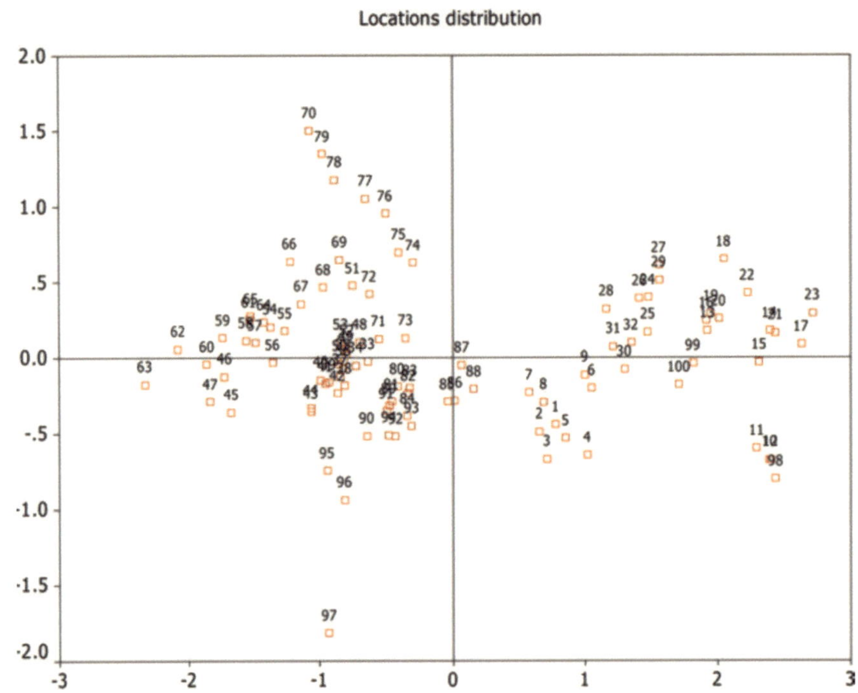

Fig. 2. Location distribution

The setting of these parameters are shown in Table 9 and their corresponding curve is depicted in Figure 3.

	Walk	Bike	Car	Public transport
a	1.6	1.1	0.6	0.8
b	1/12	1/10	1/6	1/8
c	5			

Table 9. Parameter setting for reward functions of each travel mode

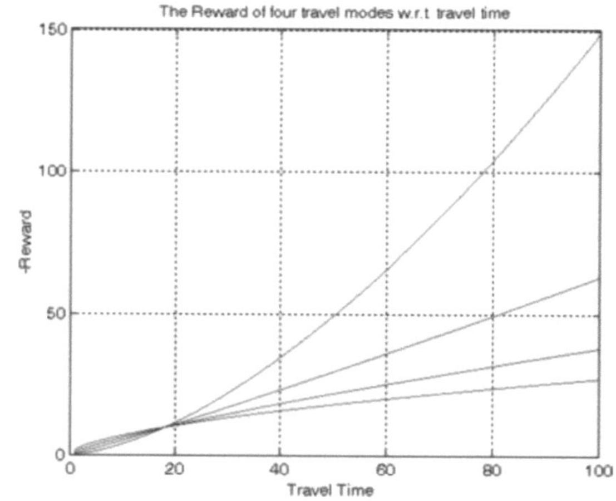

Fig. 3. Reward function curves of each travel mode

In such a complicated environment, it is required for the learning agent to look far into the future in order to find a good daily plan of time and locations. The discounting factor γ is set at 0.99, which is close to one and makes the learning procedure harder to converge. The ε - greedy method that was explained before is adopted and ε is set as 1 in order to explore the state space sufficiently.

Due to the use of discrete time intervals, the starting time of activity is calculated as the ending time of previous activity plus, instead of real travel time, the minimal number of time slots that contains the travel time. It is expected that this adaptation causes trivial influence because of the small time granular.

Furthermore, the discount per time slot should be the same during the learning procedure. As a result, the discount factor is equal to γ^m if it takes the agent m time slots to travel to the next location.

4.1.4 Empirical results

Three sequences were dealt with in this paper by means of example:

1. Home - *car* - Work - *car* - Shop - *car* - Leisure - *car* - Home
2. Home - *public transport* - Work - *public transport* - Home - *bike* - Leisure - *bike* - Shop - *bike* – Home
3. Home - *public transport* - Work - *walk* - Leisure - *walk* - Shop - *public transport* - Home

The optimal behaviour of three persons are presented for each pattern by means of example.

The home and location pair for each person can be listed as follows:
Person A: Home – location 7; Work – location 82
Person B: Home – location 29; Work – location 9
Person C: Home – location 30; Work – location 54
The outputs are displayed in Table 10.

Per.	Seq.	Optimal Behavior
A	1	H(23:15 --07:15, 7), W(07:45 --18:00, 82), S(18:15 --19:45, 87), L(20:00 --23:00, 0)
	2	H(22:30 --06:45, 7), W(07:45 --17:30, 82), H(18:30 --18:30, 7), L(18:45 --20:45, 0), S(21:00 --22:00, 6)
	3	H(23:15 --06:45, 7), W(07:45 --17:30, 82), L(18:45 --20:30, 33), S(21:00 --22:00, 36)
B	1	H(23:30 --07:15, 29), W(07:45 --18:00, 9), S(18:15 --19:45, 11), L(20:00 --23:00, 10)
	2	H(22:30 --06:15, 29), W(07:45 --17:15, 9), H(18:45 --18:45, 29), L(19:15 --20:45, 0), S(21:00 --22:00, 3)
	3	H(23:15 --06:30, 29), W(08:00 --17:45, 9), L(18:30 --20:15, 10), S(21:00 --22:00, 11)
C	1	H(23:30 --07:30, 30), W(08:00 --18:00, 54), S(18:15 --19:45, 55), L(20:00 --23:00, 33)
	2	H(22:30 --06:30, 30), W(07:45 --17:30, 54), H(18:45 --18:45, 30), L(19:00 --20:30, 27), S(21:00 –22:00, 25)
	3	H(23:15 --06:45, 30), W(08:00 --18:00, 54), L(18:45 --20:30, 39), S(21:00 --22:00, 38)

Table 10. Optimal output

*H – Home, W – Work, L – Leisure, S – Shop.

*Each element in the optimal behavior is denoted as Activity (Start time – End time, location).

For example, when person A chooses sequence 2 for everyday life, he/she would like to stay at home from 22:30 P.M. to 6:45 A.M., and then moves by public transport to location 82. At 17:30 PM, he/she stops working and returns home. Person A does not spend in home time (which means that the home activity that was assumed to exist in the given sequence, is skipped) and directly rides bicycle to location 0 for Leisure. After two hours leisure, he heads to location 6 for one hour's shopping. Finally, he starts to move by bike back home at 22:00 P.M.

4.2 Route optimization vs. activity-travel optimization

As mentioned above, the equation Reward $(t) = -c*(b*t)^a$ is applied to calculate the travel reward (cost). We also run our optimization program when c is set as infinite large, which makes the agent arrange his route in a fashion that achieves lowest travel cost. The experiments revealed that for sequences 2 and 3, the route arrangements are the same as those in Table 10, while the situation is probably different for sequence 1. For instance, when c is infinite large and sequence 1 is adopted, person A prefer location 83 than location 87 for Shop, and person C prefer location 39 than location 33 for Leisure. The output is the result of the fact that in sequence 1, traveling by car suffers from low cost and the route arrangement is often subject to the activity arrangement in order to achieve highest reward in total, while

traveling by public transport, bike or walk is costly and the route should also be carefully designed to alleviate the travel cost as much as possible.
Another interesting output, when c is infinitely large, is that the agent will keep performing each activity as long as possible (12 hours in our environment) in order to avoid unnecessary location transfers in everyday life, which is apparently reasonable.

4.3 Back to optimal path gracefully

When unforeseeable events often happen in our life, such as traffic jam or overtime on work, the agent is put off the optimal path. One extraordinary advantage of Q-learning is that the agent, according to the Q-values accumulated in the learning procedure, can wisely choose the appropriate action and move back to optimal path gracefully as it was also mentioned in Charypar & Nagel (2005). We illustrate this characteristic by means of the following two examples.
Example 1: Suppose person A takes sequence 1 as his daily activity-travel pattern. One day, he has to deal with extra tasks and keeps working till P.M. 19:00, which is off his optimal daily arrangement. He then chooses to go shopping at location 87 for 1 hour and 45 minutes. Then he moves to location 0 for leisure and get back home at A.M. 00:00. He will get up at A.M. 07:15 as usual and be on the optimal path again. The adjustment process is as: Work (07:45 --19:00, 82), Shop (19:15 --21:00, 87), Leisure (21:15 --23:45, 0), Home (00:00 --07:15, 7), Work (07:45 --18:00, 82)...
Example 2: Assume person B adopts sequence 2. One morning, he is delayed one hour by traffic jam and starts to work at A.M. 08:45. Based on his experience, he will wisely work for 9 hours. He then arrives at home at P.M. 19:15 and directly moves to location 0 for leisure. After one hour's leisure, he starts to shop at P.M. 21:00, thus returning to optimal path. The process is stated as: Work (08:45 --17:45, 9), Home (19:15 --19:15, 29), Leisure (19:45 --20:45, 0), Shop (21:00 --22:00, 3), Home (22:30 --06:15, 29), Work (07:45 --17:15, 9)...

5. Conclusion and discussion

The methodology presented in this paper was able to allocate time and location information to sequences that consist of activities and transport modes. To the best of our knowledge, activity and location allocations have not yet been integrated and optimized in previous research in order to achieve maximal rewards for a given activity-travel pattern. The methodology was based on the reinforcement learning algorithm which has been used to help the agent search the optimal path in the huge number of states of given environments.
During learning, the Q-learning agent tries some actions (i.e., output values) on its environment. Then, it is reinforced by receiving a scalar evaluation (the reward) of its actions. In a first implementation, it has been assumed that time allocation is dependent on the type of activity, the starting time of the activity and the time already spent at that activity. Also, the sequence of different activities determined the time allocation. Indeed, two sequences that contain a similar activity which has the same starting time and the same time spent at that activity, do not have to (and often will not) receive the same time allocation for that particular activity, as a result of the different sequence order in which other activities occur in both diaries. Technically, the agent will come up with another optimal path, a different policy chart and as a result also a different time allocation for both sequences. The location allocation problem was initially also solved in the assumption that

the allocation is dependent on the travel time between two locations and on the transport mode that has been chosen to reach these locations. Also in this case, it is obvious that the sequence information of activities and transport modes largely determines the allocation.

Then, in a final implementation, the idea to integrate time and location allocation simultaneously, has been conceived. Dealing with both allocations simultaneously, leads to some important advantages. The first advantage is that the reward is not only maximized in either the time or the location facet, but the total reward in a day (i.e. the reward that arises from determining optimal start and end times and the cost that arises from travelling between locations) will be maximized by means of an integrated approach, which is obviously more realistic. The second major advantage is that flexible travel times between two locations can be incorporated. In the first time allocation implementation, it was impossible to achieve this, due to the lack of location information.

The most important drawback of this integrated implementation, is that the magnitude of the importance between the time and location relationship cannot be immediately observed from the data. To this end, a simple conversion function has been proposed and tested in the empirical section. Further research could for instance use other alternative techniques (for instance stated preference) to better specify and understand this relationship. It was also mentioned above that the reward tables used in the experiments can be derived from frequency information that is present in the data. Alternatively, one may also use reward functions or utility functions which include more parameters when determining the utility of an action. As such, apart from the starting time and the duration of the activity, the activity location, the position of the activity within the activity schedule and the activity history are also incorporated in these utility functions. An initial approach has been shown in van Bladel et al. (2006).

As mentioned before, the approach presented in this paper largely relies upon a fixed sequence of activities and transport modes. Alternatively, one may also let the reinforcement algorithm determine this activity-travel sequence autonomously. An initial framework for this has been proposed in Vanhulsel et al. (Vanhulsel et al., 2006) in an application where a key event (obtaining a driver's license) is simulated. However, the approach presented only some initial results and needs further investigation. In addition to this, one may also want to investigate the use of currently unexplored *relational* reinforcement learning approaches (Driessens, 2004a, 2004b; Dzeroski et al., 2001) in this domain, which will employ a relational regression technique in cooperation with a Qlearning algorithm to build a relational, generalized Q-function. As such, it combines techniques from reinforcement learning with generalization techniques from inductive logic programming.

6. Acknowledgement

Davy Janssens acknowledges support as a post-doctoral research fellow from the Research Foundation - Flanders (F.W.O.-Vlaanderen).

7. References

Arentze, T.A. & Timmermans, H.J.P. (2003). Modelling learning and adaptation processes in activity-travel choice: A framework and numerical experiment. *Transportation*, Vol. 30, 37 - 62.

Barto, A.G. & Sutton, R.S. (1981). Associative search network: a reinforcement learning associative memory. *Biological Cybernetics*, Vol. 40, 201 - 211.

Charypar, D.; Graf, P. & Nagel, K. (2004). Q-learning for flexible learning of daily activity plans, *Electronic Proceedings of the Swiss Transport Research Conference (STRC)*, Monte Verita, Czechoslovakia. See http://www.strc.ch

Charypar, D. & Nagel, K. (2005). Q-learning for flexible learning of daily activity plans, *Electronic Proceedings of the 84th Annual Meeting of the Transportation Research Board (CD-ROM)*, Washington, D.C., USA.

Crites, R.H. & Barto, A.G. (1996). Improving elevator performance using reinforcement learning, In: *Advances in Neural Information Processing Systems*, D.S. Touretzky, M.C. Mozer, and M.E. Hasselmo, (Eds.), 1017 – 1023, The MIT Press.

Dijkstra, E. (1959). A note on two problems in connection with graphs. *Numerical Mathematics*, Vol. 1, 269 - 271.

Driessens, K. (2004). *Relational reinforcement learning*, Ph.D. Thesis, Department of Computer Science, K.U.Leuven, Leuven, Belgium.

Driessens, K. & Dzeroski, S. (2004). Integrating guidance into relational reinforcement learning. *Machine Learning*, Vol. 57, 271-304

Dzeroski, S.; De Raedt, L. & Driessens, K. (2001). Relational reinforcement learning. *Machine Learning*, Vol. 43, 7-52

Johnson, R.A. & Wichern, D.W. (1998). *Applied Multivariate Statistical Analysis*, Prentice Hall. Kaelbling, L.P.; Littman M.L. & Moore, A. (1996). Reinforcement learning: a survey. *Journal of Artificial Intelligence Research*, Vol. 4, 237 - 285.

Littman, M.L. (1994). Markov games as a framework for multi-agent reinforcement learning, *Proceedings of the Eleventh International Conference on Machine Learning*, pp.157-163, San Francisco, CA, USA.

Mahadevan, S. & Connell, J. (1992). Automatic programming of behavior-based robots using reinforcement learning. *Artificial Intelligence*, Vol. 55, 311 - 365.

Mitchell, T. *Machine Learning* (1997). McGraw Hill, New York. Moriarty, D.a.L. P. (1998). Learning cooperative lane selection strategies for highways, *Proceedings of the Fifteenth National Conference on Artificial Intelligence*, pp. 684-691, Madison, Wisconsin, USA.

Schaal, S.a.A. C. (1994). Robot juggling: an implementation of memory-based learning. *Control Systems Magazine*, Vol. 14, 57 - 71.

Schneider, J.; Boyan, J. & Moore, A. (1998). Value function based production scheduling, *Proceedings of the Fifteenth International Conference on Machine Learning*, pp.522-530, Madison, Wisconsin, USA.

Sutton, R.S. & Barto, A.G. (1998). *Reinforcement Learning: An Introduction*, MIT Press, Cambridge.

Tesauro, G. (1992). Practical issues in temporal difference learning. *Machine Learning*, Vol. 8, 257 - 277.

Tesauro, G. (1994). TD-Gammon, a self-teaching backgammon program, achieves masterlevel play. *Neural Computation*, Vol. 6, 215 - 219.

Thrun, S. (1995). Learning to play the game of chess, In: *Advances in Neural Information Processing Systems*, G. Tesauro, D. Touretzky, and T. Leen (Eds.), 1069 – 1076, The MIT Press, Cambridge, MA.

Van Bladel, K., Bellemans, T., Wets, G., Arentze, T. & Timmermans, H.J.P. (2006). Fitting S-Shaped Activity Utility Functions Based on Stated Preference Data. *Electronic Proceedings of the 11th International Conference on Travel Behavior Research* (CD-ROM), Kyoto, Japan.

Vanhulsel, M., Janssens, D. & Wets, G. (2006). Calibrating a New Reinforcement Learning Mechanism for Modeling Dynamic Activity-Travel Behavior and Key Events, *Electronic Proceedings of the 85th Annual Meeting of the Transportation Research Board* (CD-ROM), Washington, D.C., USA

Watkins, C. (1989). *Learning from Delayed Rewards*, Ph.D. Thesis, Department of Psychology, University of Cambridge, Cambridge, England.

Watkins, C. & Dayan, P. (1992). Technical note: Q-learning. *Machine Learning*, Vol. 8, 279 - 292.

20

Application on Reinforcement Learning for Diagnosis Based on Medical Image

Stelmo Magalhães Barros Netto, Vanessa Rodrigues Coelho Leite,
Aristófanes Corrêa Silva, Anselmo Cardoso de Paiva,
and Areolino de Almeida Neto
Universidade Federal do Maranhão (UFMA)
Brazil

1. Introduction

The benefit of a medical imaging examination in terms of its ability to yield an accurate diagnosis depends on the quality of both the image acquisition and the image interpretation. During the past century, radiology has grown tremendously due to advances in image detector systems and computer technology.

On the other side, the image interpretation is an error prone task. The number of lawsuits filed against medical imaging professionals that are related to the miss of a diagnosis is close to 70% (Berlin, 1995). The most common errors are perceptual errors that lead to diagnoses misses, representing about 60% of the cases (Renfrew et al., 1992). In cancer diagnoses, some studies show that the risks of false negative diagnoses are up to 75%.

These number of diagnosis errors due to misinterpretation of medical images and the current development in automation methods to help the specialist in this error prone task, lead to the development of novel devices and techniques to assist the specialist in the diagnosis achievement. These systems can provide a second opinion and may be used as a first stage of radiological interpretation (Nab et al, 1992). These systems are commonly named Computer-Aided Diagnosis (CAD) systems and have been developed to assist radiologists and other specialized physicians in the diagnostic setting like early detection of lung cancer in radiographs and CT images.

The system aid may contribute to understand essential features and information hidden in the images which are not readily apparent. Also, the effects between the different image aspects are not distinguishable. The image information and the extracted parameters may be too complex to be solved with conventional techniques. Thus we may use other techniques like Machine Learning methods. Machine Learning methods use these complex sets of data, and can help to model the nonlinear relationships that exist between them, improving medical care.

Machine Learning (ML) aims at providing techniques and methods for accumulating, changing and updating knowledge in computational systems, and in particular mechanisms to help the system to induce knowledge from examples or new data. These

methods are appropriated when we do not have algorithmic solutions, in the absence of formal models, or when we do not know precisely the application domain.
One of the approaches of Machine Learning is reinforcement learning, which emphasizes the individual's learning through interactions with his environment, contrasting with classical machine learning approaches that privilege learning from a knowledgeable teacher, or on reasoning from a complete model of the environment.
In Reinforcement Learning the learner is not told which action to take, but instead must find which actions yield a better reward after trying them. The most distinguishing features of reinforcement learning are trial-and-error search and delayed reward.
In the Machine Learning community, reinforcement learning has been used to solve many complex tasks normally thought of as quite cognitive. For example, a reinforcement learning algorithm has performed the medical diagnosis (Stensmo & Sejnowski, 1996), bioinformatics (Sahba et al, 2006), speech recognition (Rabiner, 1989), spell recognition (Raedt & Bruynooghe, 2004), computational vision and even robots locomotion (Smart, 2002).
The purpose of this chapter is to investigate the adequacy of the reinforcement learning technique to classify lesions based on medical image. We will show the application of this technique with the goal of lung nodules classification between malignant from benign. We will use a set of 3D geometric measures extracted from the lung lesions Computerized Tomography (CT) images.
This work is organized as follows. Section 2 presents a brief overview about the main concepts of Reinforcement Learning theory. Following this, in Section 3 the medical imaging main modalities are described and its use for cancer detection/diagnosis is shown. Specially, we describe the lung cancer problem and some of the methods applied for its diagnose based on medical images and computer supported. Section 4 describes some works proposed in the literature that apply reinforcement learning to medical images, presenting a more detailed description of an application of reinforcement learning for lung cancer lesions classification. Finally, Section 5 presents the final remarks

2. Reinforcement learning

Reinforcement learning (Sutton & Barto, 1998) is a formal mathematical framework in which an agent manipulates its environment through a series of actions, and in response to each action receives a reward value. An agent stores its knowledge on how to choose reward maximizing actions in a mapping from agent internal states to actions. In essence, the agent's "task" is to maximize its reward over time. Good task performance is precisely and mathematically defined by the reward values.
Reinforcement learning is a problem formulation, not a solution technique. The siblings of reinforcement learning are supervised learning and unsupervised learning.
One can assert that Reinforcement Learning (RL) is a training which uses a tip or clue that can be positive or negative. The apprentice is not taught which action he must realize, but some signals are given to him as to allow him to decide/choose a better road.
Is at this point where the RL differentiates from the supervised learning, which necessitates a teacher to teach what is the more appropriated action for each state.

Reinforcement learning is frequently used when there is no good exemplar behavior to be followed, when the environment is unknown or when one wishes to satisfy various goals at the same time. This kind of learning is inspired in children's learning. Children perform random actions and discover cause and effect relationships according to environmental responses (food, water, a teacher's smile, a praising word or a very loud sound, an electric shock, the awful teacher's face or a complaint), they learn which actions are good and which are bad.

Formally in the Reinforcement Learning problem there is an agent and an environment that interact in a sequence of discrete steps, t = 0; 1; 2; 3; ... On each step, the agent perceives that the environment is in a state, st, and selects an action, at. In response, the environment makes a stochastic transition to a new state, st+1, and stochastically emits a numerical reward, rt+1 $\in \Re$. The agent seeks to maximize the reward it receives in the long run. For example, the most common objective is to choose each action as to maximize the expected discounted return.

For each pair state/action, (s,a), there is a reinforcement signal, R(s,a)$\rightarrow\Re$, which is given to the agent when whenever the agent performs the action a in the state s. The agent's relationship with the environment is illustrated in Figure 1.

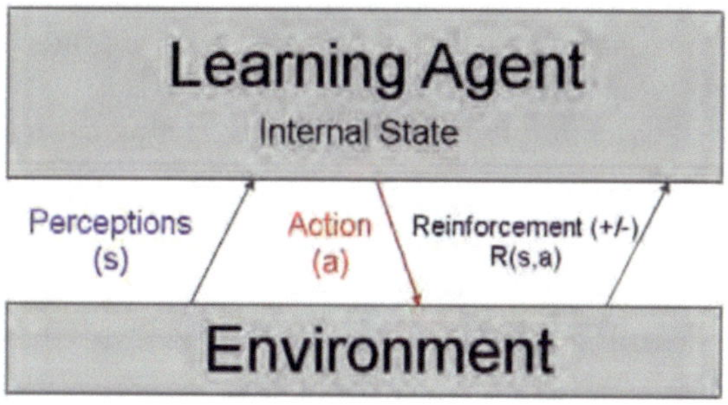

Fig. 1. Reinforcement learning elements

The reinforcement signal is the agent's learning basement. The reinforcement must indicate the goal to be reached. For example, when playing draughts the reinforcement can be given to the agent just at the end of the game, being positive if the agent wins and negative when he loses or be drawn. Doing so, the reinforcement is showing to the agent that his goal is to win the game and not to lose or be drawn. The reinforcement learning problem is to choose actions policy that maximizes the totality of the rewards received by the agent. An actions policy corresponds to a function $\Pi(s) \rightarrow a$, that states which action for each state must be realized by the agent. An agent can follow several action policies, but the learning goal is to calculate the policy that maximizes the sum of the future rewards, i.e., the total of rewards received after adopting that policy. That optimal policy is called Π^*.

2.1 Q-Learning

Q-Learning (Watkins & Dayan, 1992) is one of the methods for solving the reinforcement learning problem. That technique iteratively estimates a function Q(s,a) $\rightarrow\Re$, which determines the sum of expected future rewards when the agent performs the action a in the state s, continuing from there on to act optimally. As that sum can be infinite, whether there is not a final state to be attained, it used a discount factor in the sum parcels. That discount

factor also differentiates the rewards far away from the actual state, giving a higher value to the closest rewards. This way, the function Q defines the sum of the discounted future rewards.
Once it is estimated the function Q, the agent's behavior (actions policy) can be easily determined. As highly valued rewards are linked to a good performance, it is enough for the agent to choose, at each state s, the action a, holding the highest value of Q(s,a). Nevertheless, following this approach, the agent loses a part of his learning capacity. As at each state is always executed the same action (the highest valued action of Q), only that action will have their value updated, being able of perpetuating itself as the best action. This way, during the training phase, when the Q function is being built, it becomes necessary to exchange usufruct and exploitation phases.
To usufruct means that the agent will choose the best action, in the current Q estimative; exploitation means that the agent will choose a random action a', as to have its Q(s,a') value updated and, possibly, may became the best action. However, the decision on which strategy must be adopted at each moment is not trivial, yielding the exploitation /usufruct dilemma.
The inter-change between usufruct and exploitation also occurs in dynamic environments. In these cases, the agent just learns the optimal politics. As the environmental variables are subject to change, it is necessary the agent be constantly updated, updating its optimal policy estimative, which changes with the time.
The value of Q(s,a) is updated along the agent's learning, using the following rule:

$$Q(s,a) \leftarrow Q(s,a) + \alpha[r + \gamma.\max{}_a Q(s',a) - Q(s,a)] \quad (1)$$

Equation 1: Updating rule in the Q-Learning method
where α is the agent's learning rate, r is the reinforcement received by the realization of action a in the state s, and γ is the discount rate. The variable s' indicates the opponent's current state; i.e., the state he is in after having performed the action a in the state s. An important characteristic of that rule is that it does not use any knowledge on the environment dynamics, just the knowledge on the variables defined by the reinforcement learning problem (s, a, s', e r) and about the learning parameters (α and γ). Another particularity is the rule's computational efficiency, which just uses basic operations and comparisons.

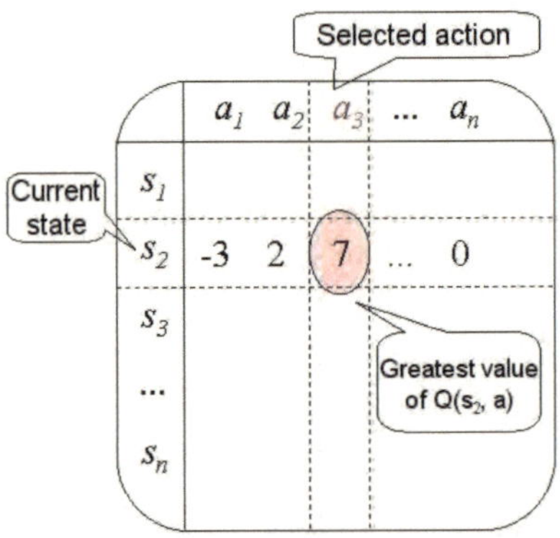

Fig. 2. Learning elements in a Q-Table

One particularity of the Q-Learning method is the way in which the Q function is approximated. The simpler approach, and also the most popular, represents the Q function by a bi-dimensional matrix, called Q-Table, with the states in one dimension and the actions in another. That representation makes possible to easily access to tables' items (for consultation and updating), besides being easier to implement, but has the disadvantage of using a lot of space, turning its use unfeasible in applications with large actions or large states space. In addition, that representation does not generalize the learned knowledge, thus its training needs to simulate all possible situations, becoming very slow. The representation of the reinforcement elements into a Q-Table is illustrated in Figure 2.

3. Medical image

Medical imaging has been undergoing a revolution making possible the execution of medical procedures faster, more accurate, and less invasive. The imaging techniques have the potential to broaden our observation capabilities and understand the biophysical world, leading to a dramatic increase in our ability to apply new algorithms and techniques to model physiological functions and dysfunctions in the patient's body.

From the discovery of X-rays in 1895, images are used as a way of acquiring information on the patients' health state. In 1917 J. Radon elaborated mathematical theories that would allow the tomography reconstruction of images. The use of images spread out from 1967 with the building of the first tomography by G. N. Hounsfield. Nowadays, there are several imaging modalities in the medical area.

In the last two decades there have been significant advances in computerized medical imaging. Such developments led to new imaging modalities in two, three and multi-dimensions, which became important clinical tools in the radiological diagnosis. The various modalities of radiological images are very significant in the medical practice and are also decisive in illnesses treatment. While in the beginning of the last century radiological images were the only way of images acquisition, several new modalities were developed up to now, and are widely used to acquire anatomical, physiological, metabolic and functional information of the human body. Currently, the most common ways of acquisition of medical images are: Computerized Tomography (CT), Magnetic Resonance Imagery (MRI), Single Photon Emission Computerized Tomography (SPECT), Positron Emission Tomography (PET) and Ultrasound.

Today, medical imaging is an essential part of medicine. The pathologies can be observed rather than inferred from symptoms. For example, a specialist can monitor the healing of damaged tissue or the growth of a tumor, and determine an adequate therapy.

Many different imaging techniques are available nowadays and are commonly used in clinical daily practice. Each imaging modality is proper to revealing a particular organ or pathology characteristics (Hendee & Ritenour), but they are complementary as they offer different views of the same tissues or functionalities.

Some imaging modalities are appropriate to image the anatomical morphology. They include radiography, ultrasound (US), computed tomography (CT), magnetic resonance imagery (MRI). On the other side we have the functional modalities that are used to study the metabolism of the tissues. In this class we have scintigraphy, single photon emission computerized tomography (SPECT), positron emission tomography (PET) and the functional magnetic resonance imagery (fMRI). As new techniques are being added every few years the list becomes outdated very quickly (Brooks, 2001). We will briefly describe the principal imaging modalities, for a more detailed description see [http://www.sprawls.org/resources/].

The Ultrasonography is based on high frequency sound waves sent by a transmitter that bounce off the different tissues and organs to produce distinctive patterns of echoes that are captured by a receiver and forwarded to a computer that translates them into an image on a screen. Ultrasound is suitable for abdomen imaging as it distinguish subtle variations among soft, fluid-filled tissues. Additionally, it does not damage tissues with ionizing radiation, but generates very noisy images.

Computerized Tomography (CT) is generated by a number of 2D radiographs transversally acquired around the patient body. The 3D image is then reconstructed by an algorithm using the Radon transform (Helgason, 1980). CT offers high contrast between bone and soft tissue and low contrast among different soft tissues. As CT uses X-Rays we must take into account the effects of ionizing radiation. CT is much proper for imaging the thoracic cage.

The Magnetic Resonance Imaging relies on the relaxation properties of magnetically-excited hydrogen nuclei of water molecules in the body. The patient is briefly exposed to a burst of radio-frequency energy, which, in the presence of a magnetic field, puts the nuclei in an elevated energy state. As the molecules undergo their normal, microscopic tumbling, they shed this energy into their surroundings, in a process referred to as relaxation. Images are created from the difference in relaxation rates in different tissues. MRI uses magnetic fields and non-ionizing radiation in the radio frequency range. Thus, according to actual medical knowledge, is harmless to patients and has much better soft tissue contrast than X-rays, being adequate for brain and spinal cord scans.

It can be noticed that those methods involve sophisticated instrumentation and equipment based on computers for data collecting, image reconstruction and visualization.

Those forms of imaging are valuable because they are not invasive, that is, instruments do not penetrate the patient's body. Besides that, there is no doubt on the quality of the images generated by such equipments, benefiting medical practices such as diagnosis, surgical planning and therapy.

Such images have a high medical content once they store relevant information for the exercise of diverse medical specialties: oncology, gynecology, radiology, pneumology and cardiology, just to cite some. However, as to take the maximum advantage of those images content, specialist of the medical area need to use the computer.

In addition, those images can be processed and handled as to allow the visualization of characteristics initially imperceptible, turning possible better accuracy and important characteristics checking used in diagnosis elaboration. Next, those main features can be quantified and analyzed through programs and computational models to understand their behavior, thus contributing in the diagnosis or just to evaluate the evolution of therapeutic protocol.

Thus, we verify that is necessary to develop computational programs and methods for processing and handling the data obtained through the different medical images acquisition techniques, allowing the enhancement and preservation of the clinical data present in the exam.

The current degree of development reached by the computational modeling techniques together with the fast growing of the computers calculation performance, has allowed the study, development and solution of highly sophisticated models able of aiding, with a rather fair degree of accuracy, in the results of important medical procedures, such as cancer diagnosis, for example.

3.1 Cancer diagnosis

Cancer is the name given to all malignant tumors, and when their size is small, in the form of a nodule. The word derives from the Latin cancer, which means crab. That name is due to the similitude between the crustacean legs and the tentacles of the tumor that infiltrate like roots into the healthy tissue of the body.

There is great difficulty to qualitatively define the benignant or malignant characteristics of the nodule, as well as in the tracking and following of its growth in a reliable way. Commonly, the evaluation of the nodular growth is done by measuring the nodule in the computerized tomography printed film or x-rays using a ruler passed over the image, what results in not so accurate measurements. Even though more accurate measurements could be directly taken with the digital data, many times they are available to physicians, who usually can access only the printed film.

Surgical nodule extraction is a practice applied to the majority of the patients presenting asymptomatic nodule with undetermined etiology, in a patient with etiological data compatible with higher susceptibility to cancer. Nevertheless, many of those interventions could be avoided once most of the times the nodules are benign. Hence, it is fundamental to use more precise techniques to better evaluate the nodular growing and their characteristics, to make possible a more reliably determination of the nodule's benignity or malignancy.

Some factors difficult the nodule's identification and diagnosis, among these are:

- The organ's structures present similar characteristics (shape, densities, etc.) which mixes up one another, turning them confuse;
- In its initial phase, if the nodule is small and has no well defined shape, is hard to diagnostic it;
- Measurements taken by physicians to analyze the nodule's evolution, as for example its diameter, are done handmade, usually using a ruler sweeping over the image;
- Physicians' visual fatigue, emotional factors and experience may influence the diagnostic;
- Finally, in many cases, the image's quality is bad.

One of the most common cancers in the world is lung cancer. It is a leading cause of cancer death in men and women. Cigarette smoking causes most lung cancers.

3.2 Lung cancer

Lung cancer is a serious problem of public health in Europe, United States and many other countries around the world because it is becoming the cancer mortality leader for men and women. The disease is also known as one of the shortest means for survival among other malignancies (Tarantino, 1997). As soon as the diagnosis is made it has been estimated that only 13% of the patients will be alive after 5 years (Lag l, 2002). In Brazil, lung cancer occupies the first place of cancer's death in men and the second in women. It is estimated that it caused 27.170 deaths (17.850 men and 9.320 women) in 2006 (INCA, 2003).

In spite of lung cancer earns the benefit for one of the most efficacious measures of primary prevention, it has been expected that results of recent campaigns against smoking will

become apparent only after two or three decades. While this, lung cancer continues to be present in advanced stages with a global outcome close to 13% in five years (Lag l, 2002).
From the biological point of view, lung cancer is an uncontrolled growth of abnormal cells in one or both lungs, which can reproduce very fast and produce regional and distant metastasis even when the patient is asymptomatic. Lumps of cancer cells (tumors) impair lung's function when obstructs the bronchi but not when they are located in other areas. The pulmonary parenchyma does not have painful nervous terminations and unless the tumor invades precociously the parietal pleura, pain will be a late sign of lung cancer (Silva et al, 2004).
Nowadays, the main chance to discover a lung cancer in its initial stage is an incidental finding of a solitary pulmonary nodule disclosed by Chest X ray or Computed Tomography (CT), indicated to explore some abnormal thoracic clinical manifestation or routine preoperative evaluation. Other possibility, that has become important in recent years, is a CT Screening Lung Cancer Program in high risk patients like heavy smokers that have smoked for more than 30 years (Henschke et al, 2003).
The main problem of the solitary pulmonary nodule is the identification of its nature. Sometimes this is possible only with radiological findings that allow diagnosis of benignity like total, central, lamellar or popcorn calcifications and high fat contents (hamartoma). Alternatively, some data are highly suggestive of malignity like specular margins and pleural tail but unfortunately around 15% of these findings also occur in benign nodules. In many other cases is not possible with simple radiological criteria to know the true nature of the nodule which is classified as undetermined. This situation is particularly frequent in nodules shorter than 1 cm of diameter where benign aetiology can respond for more than 90% of the total (Lillington & Caskey, 1993), (Henschke et al, 2003).
The top row in Figure 1 shows the texture from a slice of two benign (a and b) and two malignant (c and d) nodules. The bottom row in Figure 1 shows their respective 3D shape.

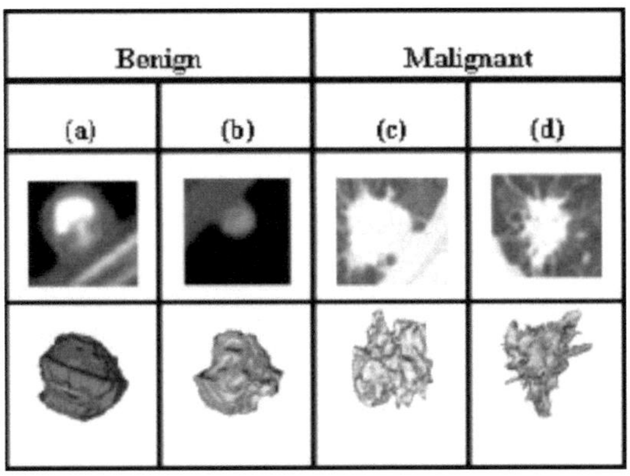

Fig. 3. Benign and malignant lung nodules examples

At radiological examination, solitary pulmonary nodules are approximately round lesions shorter than 3 cm in diameter, completely surrounded by lung parenchyma and can represent a benign or malignant disease. Any larger lesion is named pulmonary mass and should be considered as malignant until counterproof is found. In all of these situations, etiologic definition is paramount to the medical decision. In spite of the gold standard diagnosis be the histological examination - normally obtained by invasive procedures -

image methods and in special CT can aid diagnostic process in analyzing nodule's attributes (Ost et al, 2003).

Radiological characteristics of benignity are well known and based in calcifications or fat texture patterns which change the mean radiological density out of soft tissues range. Malignity does not have similar texture criteria and the diagnosis is normally suggested by an irregular shape associated to some clinical data, like tobacco's load. Venous iodine contrast administration during CT adds some improving in texture resolution in order to discriminate between benign and malignant nodules (Swensen, 1997). Recently, there is a renewed attention to quantify wash-in and washout after contrast injection to obtain a nodule characterization (Jeong et al, 2005). Unfortunately, short diameters and allergic reactions are limiting factors of these techniques. Even the most modern metabolic image method in clinical use, that is the Positron Emission Tomography (PET) superposed to helical CT examination (PET - CT) with images acquisitions before and after 18-fluoro-deoxyglucose intravenous administration, also has important limitations represented by false positive of some inflammatory processes and false negativity of small or indolent cancers (Gould, 2003), (Pepe, 2005), (Giger , 1999).

Some authors have been hypothesizing that quantitative CT data derived from geometric and texture parameters may contribute to differential diagnosis between benign and malignant solitary pulmonary nodules, even without contrast utilization. McNitt-Gray et al. (McNitt-Gray et al, 1999a), (McNitt-Gray et al, 1999b) extracted measurements from nodule's shape, attenuation coefficient, attenuation distribution and texture. They used a discriminant analysis technique with stepwise variable selection procedure to separate benign from malignant nodules. Kawata et al. (Kawata et al, 1997), (Kawata, 1998), (have presented a method to characterize the internal structure of 3-D nodules using computerized tomography images shape index and density to locally represent each voxel. They created a histogram of characteristics based on shape index, called shape spectrum measurements, to store voxels with a given index to define the nodule. Matrices similar to those of the texture-analysis method (Co-occurrence matrix) were also created for shape index and density. The statistical technique discriminant analysis was employed to classify benign and malignant nodules. In Silva et al. (Silva et al, 2004) it was showed that geo-statistical functions as semivariogram, covariogram, correlogram and madogram or some indices of spatial autocorrelation as Moran's Index and Geary's Coefficient, supply good results to discriminate malignant from benign nodules.

4. Application of reinforcement learning on medical image

The diffusion of Reinforcement Learning in various application areas is a subject of considerable ongoing research. It is argued that the successful implementation of such method can help the integration of computer-based systems in the healthcare environment, providing opportunities to facilitate and enhance the work of medical experts and ultimately to improve the efficiency and quality of medical care.

One of the main applications area is the use of Reinforcement Learning to build systems that support and help the specialist in the diagnose task. Based upon patient's information, Fakih & Das (2006) developed a learning based methodology and recommend test(s) that optimize a suitable measurement of diagnostic performance. A comprehensive performance measurement that accounts for the costs of testing, morbidity, and mortality associated with the tests, and time taken to reach diagnosis is developed. The performance measurement also accounts for the diagnostic ability of the tests. The methodology combines tools from the fields of data mining (rough set theory, in particular), utility theory, Markov decision processes (MDP) and reinforcement learning (RL). The rough set theory is used in extracting diagnostic information in the form of rules from the medical databases. Utility theory is used in bringing various non homogenous performance measurements into one cost based measurement. An MDP model together with an RL algorithm facilitates obtaining efficient testing strategies. The methodology is implemented on a sample problem of diagnosing solitary pulmonary nodule (SPN). The obtained results are compared with those from four alternative testing strategies.

(Stensmo & Sejnowski, 1996) used decision and probability theory to construct such systems from a database of typical cases. This simplifies the task of knowledge extraction from physicians who often do not know how they have come to a certain diagnosis. Probability models are constructed using mixture models that are efficiently learned by the Expectation-Maximization algorithm. Problems with missing data are then solved, both for missing data in the case database and during diagnosis (missing data are then not yet conducted observations). Decision theory is used to find the most informative next question to ask, observation to make, or test to do in order to minimize the diagnosis total cost. It is also used to decide when to stop requesting more information. To automatically find good utility values for the decision theoretic model, temporal difference reinforcement learning is used to increase the system accuracy. Results are presented on a case database for heart disease.

On the other hand, we also found in the literature some works using Reinforcement Learning to help the segmentation of medical images. (Shokri & Tizhoosh, 2003) introduced a reinforcement-learning concept to find the optimal threshold for digital images. The proposed approach can integrate human experts knowledge in an objective or subjective way to overcome the shortcomings of the existing methods.

(Peng & Bhanu, 1998) presented a system that achieves robust performance by using reinforcement learning to induce a mapping from input images to corresponding segmentation parameters. This is accomplished by using the confidence level of model matching as a reinforcement signal for a team of learning automata to search for segmentation parameters during training. The use of the recognition algorithm as part of the evaluation function for image segmentation gives rise to significant improvement of the system performance by automatic generation of recognition strategies. The system is verified through experiments on sequences of indoor and outdoor color images with varying external conditions.

(Sahba et al, 2006) introduced a new method for medical image segmentation using a reinforcement learning scheme. They use this novel idea as an effective way to optimally find the appropriate local threshold and structuring element values and segment the prostate in ultrasound images. Reinforcement learning agent uses an ultrasound image and its manually segmented version and takes some actions (i.e., different threshold and structuring element values) to change the environment (the quality of segmented image). The agent is provided with a scalar reinforcement signal determined objectively. The agent uses this objective reward/punishment to explore/exploit the solution space. The values obtained using this procedure can be used as valuable knowledge to fill a Q-matrix. The reinforcement learning agent can use this knowledge for similar ultrasound images as well. The results demonstrated high potential for applying reinforcement learning in the field of medical image segmentation.

4.1 Reinforcement learning for classifying lesions based on medical imaging

4.1.1 Image acquisition

The images herein used were provided by the Fernandes Figueira Institute and the Pedro Ernesto University Hospital - both from Rio de Janeiro city – for a project of CAD tools development. They were obtained from different real patients, providing a total of 39 nodules (29 benign and 10 malignant).

The images were acquired with a Helical GE Pro Speed tomography under the following conditions: tube voltage 120 kVp, tube current 100 mA, image size 512×512 pixels, voxel size 0.67 × 0.67 × 1.0 mm. The images were quantized in 12 bits and stored in the DICOM format (Clunie, 2000).

It is important to stand out that the CT exam was performed with no contrast injection, which may be clinically used in order to increase the diagnosis readiness but also carries some morbidity and occasional mortality by allergic complications.

It is also necessary to highlight that the nodules were previously diagnosed by physicians and that the final diagnosis of benignity or malignancy was further confirmed by histopathological exam of the surgical specimen or by radiological 3-year stability, which explains the reduced size of our sample.

4.1.2 The lung nodules segmentation

In most cases, lung nodules are easy to be visually detected by physicians, since their shape and location are different from other lung structures. However, the nodule's voxel density is similar to that of other structures, such as blood vessels, which makes difficult any kind of automatic computer detection.

Generally speaking, the solitary pulmonary nodule is normally found in Chest X Ray or CT as an unexpected finding. The main reason for this is because the nodule (> 1cm) is easily distinguished from the surrounding structures. If this distinction is difficult the nodule's diagnosis is difficult too. It is common that in an evaluation of an automatic process for segmentation or in a created program to contribute for lung cancer screening, the gold standard is the analysis made by one or more radiologists. For example: it can be difficult for an automatic segmentation program to distinguish between a nodule and the chest wall, but is relatively easy for an experienced observer to separate the two structures. The same occurs with a nodule close to a vascular structure.

Unless the nodule be in a central position close to a hilar vessel, the distinction is not difficult. However, another level of situation is represented for a small nodule (< 1cm). In this setting the radiological diagnosis can be difficult and separation from vascular structures either. References which express the radiologist as a reference point to evaluate computer's analysis are for example (Takashima, 2003).

A semi-automatic segmentation process was performed using a Pulmonary Nodule Analysis System (Silva et al, 2002) called Bebúi. In this, beyond the 3D region growing algorithm with voxel aggregation, two resources help and provide greater control in the segmentation procedure: the barrier and the eraser. The barrier is a cylinder placed around the nodule by the user with the purpose of restricting the region of interest and stopping the segmentation by voxel aggregation from invading other lung structures. The eraser is a resource of the system that allows physicians to erase undesired structures, either before or after segmentation, in order to avoid and correct segmentation errors (Silva et al, 2002).

The Marching Cubes algorithm (Lorensen & Clinie, 1987) is used to build an explicit representation of volume data. The measurements described along the present paper will use this representation. In order to remove irregularities of the reconstructed surface, the Laplacian smoothing technique (Ohtake et al, 2001) is used. Figures 2 (a) and (b) show the result of applying the Marching Cubes algorithm and the Laplacian technique, respectively.

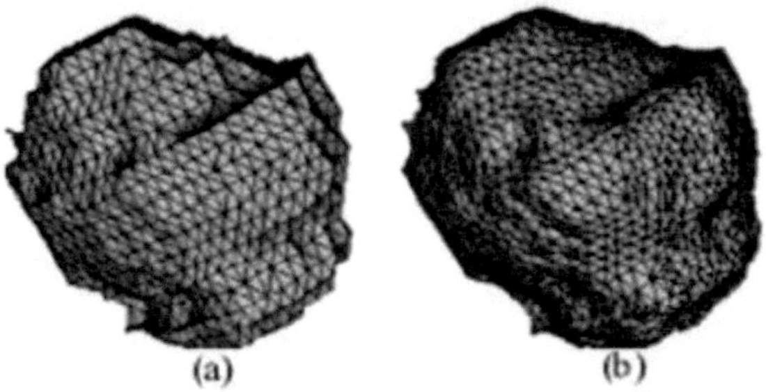

Fig. 4.a) Application of Marching Cubes. b) Application of Laplacian technique.

4.1.3 3D geometric measurements

The measurements to be presented in this section seek to capture information on the nodule's 3D geometry from the CT. The measurements should ideally be invariant to changes in the image's parameters, such as voxel size, orientation, and slice thickness.

1. **Sphericity Index:** The Sphericity Index (SI) measures the nodule's behavior in relation to a spherical object. It is defined as

$$SI = \frac{6\sqrt{\pi}V}{A^{\frac{3}{2}}} \quad (2)$$

   where V is the surface volume and A corresponds to the surface area. Thus, if the nodule's shape is similar to a sphere, the value will be close to 1. In all cases, SI ≤ 1.

2. **Convexity Index:** The Convexity Index (CI) (Smith, 1999) measures the degree of convexity, defined as the area of the surface of object B (A(B)) divided by the area of the surface of its convex hull ($A(H_B)$). That is,

$$CI = \frac{A(B)}{A(H_B)} \quad (3)$$

   The more convex the object is, the closer to 1 will be the value of CI. For all objects, CI ≥ 1.

3. **Curvature Index:** The two measurements presented below are based on the main curvatures kmin and kmax, defined by

$$k_{\min,\max} = H \mp \sqrt{H^2 - K} \quad (4)$$

   where K and H are the Gaussian and mean curvatures, respectively. The values of H and K are estimated using the methods described in (Esse & Drury, 1997).

   - **Intrinsic curvature:** The Intrinsic Curvature Index (ICI) (Smith, 1999), (Esse & Drury, 1997) captures information on the properties of the surface's intrinsic curvatures, and is defined as

$$ICI = \frac{1}{4\pi} \iint \left| k_{min} k_{max} \right| dA \tag{5}$$

Any undulation or salience on the surface with the shape of half a sphere increments the Intrinsic Curvature Index by 0.5, regardless of its size - that is, the ICI counts the number of regions with undulations or saliencies on the surface being analyzed.

- **Extrinsic curvature:** The Extrinsic Curvature Index (ECI) (Smith, 1999), (Esse & Drury, 1997) captures information on the properties of the surface's extrinsic curvatures, and is defined as

$$ECI = \frac{1}{4\pi} \iint \left| k_{max} \right| \left(\left| k_{max} \right| - \left| k_{min} \right| \right) dA \tag{6}$$

Any crack or gap with the shape of half a cylinder increments the *ECI* in proportion to its length, starting at 0.5 if its length is equal to its diameter - that is, the *ECI* counts the number and length (with respect to the diameter) of semi cylindrical cracks or gaps on the surface.

4. **Types of Surfaces:** With the values of extrinsic (H) and intrinsic (K) curvatures, it is possible to specify eight basic types of surfaces [13], [14]: *peak* ($K > 0$ and $H < 0$), *pit* ($K > 0$ and $H > 0$), *ridge* ($K = 0$ and $H < 0$), *flat* ($K = 0$ and $H = 0$), *valley* ($K = 0$ and $H > 0$), *saddle valley* ($K < 0$ and $H > 0$), *minimal* ($K < 0$ and $H = 0$), *saddle ridge* ($K < 0$ and $H < 0$).
The measurements described below were presented in (Koenderink, 1990) for the classification of lung nodules and the results were promising. However, they have computed curvatures H and K directly from the voxel intensity values, while here we compute them with respect to the extracted surface, which is composed by triangles.
In practice, it is difficult to determine values that are exactly equal to zero, due to numerical precision. Therefore we have selected only the types *peak, pit, saddle valley* and *saddle ridge* for our analysis (Koenderink, 1990).
   - **Amount of each Surface Type:**
     This measurement indicates the relative frequency of each type of surface in the nodule, where *APK* (Amount of *peak* surface), *API* (Amount of *pit* surface), *ASR* (Amount of *saddle ridge* surface) and *ASV* (Amount of *saddle valley* surface).
   - **Area Index for each Surface Type:**
     For each surface type, the area occupied in the nodule divided by the total nodule area is computed, where *AIPK* (Area Index for *peak* surface), *AIPI* (Area Index for *pit* surface), *AISR* (Area Index for *saddle ridge* surface) and *AISV* (Area Index for *saddle valley* surface). =>
   - **Mean *Curvedness* for each Surface Type:**
     Curvedness is a positive number that measures the curvature amount or intensity on the surface [13]:

$$c = \sqrt{\frac{k_{min}^2 + k_{max}^2}{2}} \tag{7}$$

The measurements are based on the curvedness and the surface types. For each surface type, the mean curvedness is determined using the curvedness of each surface type, divided by the curvedness number in each surface type. Where, CPK (mean curvedness for peak), CPI (mean curvedness for pit), CSR (mean curvedness for saddle ridge) and CSV (mean curvedness for saddle valley).

4.1.4 Tests and results

The idea of classification is to encounter a path from the pattern presented to a known target, in the present case to a malignant or to a benign pattern. Furthermore the path found should be the shortest in some sense; in such way that the presented pattern seems to be nearer from a known target and therefore it can be considered of the type of the target. Considering the diverse techniques, the Reinforcement Learning (RL) was chosen to find this path, because it can learn without a mathematical model of a path and because it can learn a correct path only using a reward when the target is encountered.

The tests described in this work were carried out using a sample of 36 nodules, 29 benign and 7 malignant. It is important to note that the nodules were diagnosed by physicians and had the diagnosis confirmed by means of surgery or based on their evolution. Such process takes about two years, which explains the reduced size of our sample. The sample included nodules with varied sizes and shapes, with homogeneous and heterogeneous characteristics, and in initial and advanced stages of development.

The stepwise analysis (Lachenbruch, 1975) selected 5 out of the 13 measurements (states), described in Section 4.1.3, to be analyzed by the reinforcement learning classifier. The selected states were ICE, QPK, QSR, QSV and CPI. Each state was discretized in ten different values. The discretization of each state is shown in Table 1.

State	ICE	QPK	QSR	QSV	CPI
1	45 – 492.61	9 – 145.88	5 – 167.55	23 – 369.83	0.24 – 0.27
2	492.61 – 1.39e+3	145.89 – 419.67	167.55 – 492.67	369.83 – 1.06e+3	0.27 – 0.32
3	1.39e+3 – 2.29e+3	419.67 – 693.44	492.67 – 817.78	1.06e+3 – 1.76e+3	0.32 – 0.37
4	2.28e+3 - 3.18e+3	693.44 - 967.22	817.77 - 1.14e+3	1.76e+3 - 2.45e+3	0.37 0.43
5	3.18e+3 - 4.07e+3	967.22 - 1,240	1.14e+3 - 1,467	2.45e+3 - 3.14e+3	0.43 - 0.48
6	4.07e+3 - 4.97e+3	1,241 - 1.51e+3	1,468 - 1.79e+3	3.14e+3 - 3.84e+3	0.48 - 0.53
7	4.97e+3 - 5.86e+3	1.51e+3 - 1.78e+3	1.79e+3 - 2.12e+3	3.84e+3 - 4.53e+3	0.53 0.58
8	5.86e+3 - 6.76e+3	1.79e+3 - 2.06e+3	2.12e+3 - 2.44e+3	4.53e+3 - 5.22e+3	0.58 0.64
9	6.76e+3 - 7.65e+3	2.06e+3 - 2.33e+3	2.44e+3 - 2.77e+3	5.22e+3 - 5.92e+3	0.64 - 0.69
10	7.65e+3 - 8,102	2.33e+3 - 2,473	2.77e+3 - 2,931	5.92e+3 - 6,266	0.69 - 0.719

Table 1. Discretization of each state

With these states and actions, the matrix Q has the following size: $10^5 x 3^5$, because each state has ten different values and each action three possibilities.

The classificator try to reach the state that corresponds to geometric characteristics of the benign or malignant pattern. These are determined by the above defined states, by the increment, constancy and decrement actions over the current value of the corresponding state, at each varaiable state starting from a set of states as initial point. An action is randomly taken with 50% random rate aiming at finding the bests pair state/action for each set of states. The unitary value reinforcement is given to each state change in the case a right pattern is found, conversely, the reinforcement is null.

The learning is done by selecting 19 images of benign and 4 malingnat nodules, and we choose as target the most characteristic bening and malignant nodules. To each image is assigned a learning step for classification and the set of all those images forms an episode.

After training, the knowledge should have been acquired. This is verified with a test of classification with images not used during the training phase. For this purpose nine benign and two malignant images were selected. Figure 3 shows the results obtained, where we used the remaining nine benign and two malignant nodules. In this figure we represent in the x-axis the nodules case, being cases 1 to 9 benign and cases 10 and 11 malignant. On the other hand, the y-axis represents the number of steps from the start point to the target, which means the number of actions taking to reach the case target. When a given case takes a positive number of steps to reach the target, we have a successful classification. Otherwise a negative number represents an incorrect classification and when the classification is not determined we set the number of steps as zero. The obtained data was generated from four experiments, using 20000, 30000, 40000 and 50000 episodes in the training phase.

The number of right classification grows from 45% for 20000 episodes to 81% for 50000 episodes; as shown in Table 2, which indicates a good improvement in the classification success as the number of episodes grows.

Interesting information observed in the results involves the set of 40000 episodes, when the number of successful classification decreased, which should be derived from the random choices used in the training phase, that lead to a poor learning. But, as already proved in RL theorem (Barto et al., 1983), a very high number of episodes drives to a correct learning, generating a very high successful rate in the classification.

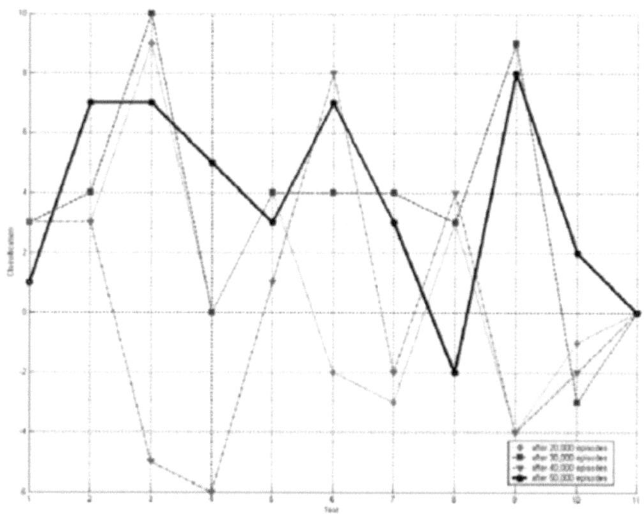

Fig. 5. Application of reinforcement learning.

Due to the relatively small size of the existing CT lung nodule databases and the various CT imaging acquisition protocols, it is difficult to compare the diagnosis performance between the developed algorithms and others proposed in the literature.

Success	Error	Non-Determined	Number of Episodes
45.45%	36.36%	18.18%	20,000
72.72%	9.09%	18.18%	30,000
45.45%	45.45%	9.09%	40,000
81.81%	9.09%	9.09%	50,000

Table 2. Application of Reinforcement Learning.

The number of studied nodules in our dataset is too small to state definitive conclusions, but the preliminary results of this work are very encouraging, demonstrating that a reinforcement learning using nodule shape characteristics, can contribute to discriminate benign from malignant lung nodules on CT images.

Based on these results, we have observed that such shape characteristics provide significant support to a more detailed clinical investigation, and the results were very encouraging when nodules were classified with reinforcement learning.

Nevertheless, there is the need to perform tests with a larger database and more complex cases in order to obtain a more precise behavior pattern.

7. Conclusion

This work presents an overview of current work applying reinforcement learning in medical image applications, presenting a detailed illustration of a particular use for lung nodules classification.

The addressed application of reinforcement learning to solve the problem of lung nodules classification used the 3D geometric nodules characteristics to guide the classification. Even though the results are preliminary we may see that the obtained results are very encouraging, demonstrating that the reinforcement learning classifier using characteristics of the nodules' geometry can effectively classify benign from malignant lung nodules based on CT images.

On the other side, we may observe that this is a machine learning that is not commonly applied to medical images and this is an opportunity for more intensive investment in the research for this area.

But some problems are well known in this application and must be more studied. We should research how to find out a way to shorter the training phase, while maintaining the learning quality. And also must be improved the tests to generate more definitive results and to make possible the comparison with other classifiers.

8. References

Almeida, A.; Heimann, B.; Góes, L. & Nascimento, C.(2003). Avoidance of multiple dynamic obstacles, *Proceedings of International Congress of Mechanical Engineering,* Volume 17, São Paulo

Almeida, A.; Heimann, B.; Góes, L. & Nascimento, C.(2003). Obstacle avoidance in dynamic environment: A hierarchical solution, *Proceedings of Redes Neurais,* pp. 289-294, Volume 6, São Paulo

Barto, A.; Sutton, R. & Anderson, C. (1983) Neuronlike adaptive elements that can solve difficult learning control problems, *IEEE Transactions on Systems, Man and Cybernetics,* 13, 834-846

Berlin, L. & Berlin, J. (1995) Malpractice and radiologists in Cook County, IL: trends in 20 years of litigation. *AJR Am J Roentgenol* 165,781-788

Camponogara, E.; Serra, M. R. G. (2005). *Aprendizagem por Reforço: Uma Primeira Introdução* , CIPEEL, Universidade Federal de Santa Catarina Departamento de Automação e Sistemas, Florianópolis.

Clunie, D.A. (2000) DICOM Structered Reporting, *PixelMed Publishing,* Pennsylvania

D. Brooks (2001) Emerging medical imaging modalities, *IEEE Signal Processing Magazine,* 18, no. 6, 12-13

Doya, K. Reinforcement learning: Computational theory and biological mechanisms, Neural Computation Unit, Okinawa Institute of Science and Technology, Japan, 12-22

Duda, R.O. & Hart, P.E. (1973) *Pattern Classification and Scene Analysis,* Wiley-Interscience Publication, New York

Essen, D.C.V. & Drury, H.A. (1997) Structural and functional analyses of human cerebral cortex using a surface-based atlas, *The Journal of Neuroscience,* 17, 7079-7102

Fakih, S. J. & Das, T. K. (2006) LEAD: A Methodology for Learning Efficient Approaches to Medical Diagnosis, *IEEE Transactions on Information Technology in Biomedicine,* 10, No. 2, April 2006.

Gould, M. K.(2003) *Cost-effectiveness of alternative management strategies for patients with solitary pulmonary nodules,* Ann. Intern. Med. 9, 138, 724-735

Helgason, S. (1980) *The Radon transform,* Birkhäuser, Boston, MA

Hendee, W. & Ritenour, R. (2002) *Medical imaging physics,* 4 ed., Wiley-Liss

Henderson, D.W. (1998) *Differental Geometry: A Geometric Introduction,* Prentice-Hall, Upper Saddle River, New Jersey

Henschke, C.I. et al (2001) Early lung cancer action project: A summary of the findings on baseline screening, *The Oncologist,* 6, 147-152

Hoffman, L. T. & Silva, J. D. S. da. (2004) Um sistema de visão robótica baseada em aprendizagem por reforço, *Instituto Nacional de Pesquisas Espaciais - INPE Programa de Pós-gradução em Computação Aplicada,* São José dos Campos, SP .

INCA (2003), Estimativas da incidência e mortalidade por câncer no Brasil, available in: http://www.inca.gov.br/estimativas/2003/versaofinal.pdf

Jeong, Y. ; Lee, K.; Jeong, S.; Chung, M.; Shim, S.; Kim, H.; Kwon, O. & Kim, S. (2005) Solitary pulmonary nodule: characterization with combine wash-in and washout features of dynamic multidector row CT., Radiology 2, 237, 675-683.

Kawata, Y.; Niki, N.; , Ohmatsu, H.; Kakinuma, R.; Eguchi, K.; Kaneko, M. & Moriyama, N. (1997) Classification of pulmonary nodules in thin-section CT images based on shape characterization, *In: International Conference on Image Processing,* 3, IEEE Computer Society Press, 528-530

Kawata, Y.; Niki, N.; Ohmatsu, , H.; Kakinuma, R.; Eguchi, K.; Kaneko, M. & Moriyama, N. (1997) Classification of pulmonary nodules in thin-section CT images based on shape characterization, in: International Conference on Image Processing, Vol. 3, *IEEE Computer Society Press*, pp. 528–530.

Kawata, Y.; Niki, N.; Ohmatsu, H.; Kakinuma, R.; Eguchi, K.; Kaneko, M. & Moriyama, N. (1988) Quantitative surface characterization of pulmonary nodules based on thin-section CT images, *IEEE Transactions on Nuclear Science,* 45, 4, 2132–2138

Kawata, Y.; Niki, N.; Ohmatsu, H.; Kusumoto, M.; Kakinuma, R.; Mori, K.; Nishiyama, H.; Eguchi, K.; Kaneko, M. & Moriyama, (1999) N.Computer aided differential diagnosis of pulmonary nodules using curvature based analysis, in: *International Conference on Image Analysis and Processing,* Vol. 2, IEEE Computer Society Press, pp. 470–475.

Koenderink, J.J. (1990) *Solid Shape,* MIT Press, Cambridge, MA, USA

Lachenbruch, P. A. (1975), Discriminant Analysis, Hafner Press, New York.

Lag, R. *Seer cancer statistics review,* Tech, National Cancer Institute, Bethesda, MD, available at http://seer.cancer.gov/csr/1975 2002/, accessed on July/2007

Levin, E.; Pieraccini, R. & Eckert, W. *Learning Dialogue Strategies within the Markov Decision Process Framework,* AT&T Labs-Research, Florham Park, USA, 72-79

Lillington, G. A. & Caskey, C. J. (1993) *Evaluation and management of solitary and multiple nodules,* Clin Chest Med, 14, 1, 111–119.

Lorensen, W.E. & Cline, H.E. (1987) Marching cubes: A high resolution 3D surface construction algorithm, *Computer Graphics,* 21, 163–169

McGuiness, G. ; Libby, D. M.; Smith, J. P.; Pasmantier, M. W. & Mietinnen, O. S.(2003) Ct screening for lung cancer: Significance of nodules at baseline according to size, *Radiology,* 30, 1, 11–15.

McNitt-Gray, M. F. ; Hart, E. M. ; Wyckoff, N.; W. Sayre, J. Goldin, J. G. & Aberle, D. R. (1999a) *A pattern classification approach to characterizing solitary pulmonary nodules imaged on high resolution CT: Preliminary results,* Medical Physics 26, 6, 880–888

McNitt-Gray, M. F.; Hart, E. M.; Wyckoff, N.; Sayre, J. W.; Goldin, J. G. & Aberle, D. R.(1999b) *The effects of co-occurrence matrix based texture parameters on the classification of solitary pulmonary nodules imaged on computed tomography,* Computerized Medical Imaging and Graphics, 339–348.

Nab, H.W.; Karssenmeijer, N.; Van Erning L.J.T.H.O. & Hendriks, J.H.C.L. Comparison of digital and conventional mammography: a ROC study of 270 mammograms. *Medical Informatics,* 17, pp. 125–131

Nikolaidis, N. & Pitas, I. (2001) *3-D Image Processing Algorithms***.** John Wiley, New York

Ohtake, Y.; Belyaev, A. & Pasko, A. (2001) Dynamic meshes for accurate polygonization of implicit surfaces with shape features, *In Press, I.C.S., ed.: SMI 2001 International Conference on Shape Modeling and Applications,* 74–81

Ost, D., Fein, A.M., Feinsilver, S.H.(2003) *The solitary pulmonary nodule.* N. Engl. J. Med. 25, 2535–2542

Peng, J. & Bhanu, B. (1998) Closed-Loop Object Recognition Using Reinforcement Learning, *IEEE Transations on Pattern Analysis and Machine Intelligentece*, 20, No. 2, February 1998.

Pepe, G. ; Rosseti, C.; Sironi, S.; Landoni, G.; Gianoli, L.; Pastorino, U.; Zannini, P.; Mezzetti, M.; Grimaldi, A.; Galli, L.; Messa, C. & Fazio, F.(2005) *Patients with known or suspected lung cancer: evaluation of clinical management changes due to 18 F - deoxyglucose positron emission tomography* (18 F - FDG PET) study., Nucl. Med. Commun. 9, 26, 831–837

Rabiner, L. R. (1989) A Tutorial on Hidden Markov Models and Selected Applications in Speech Recognition, *Proceedings of the IEEE*, 77, 2, 257-286

Raedt, L. & Bruynooghe, M (2004) *Relational Reinforcement Learning*, Katholieke Universiteit Leuven - Faculteit Toegepaste Wetenschappen Arenbergkasteel, Belgium

Reeves, A.P. & Kostis, W.J. (2000) Computer-aided diagnosis for lung cancer, *Radiologic Clinics of North America*, 38, 497–509

Renfrew, DL; Franken, E. A.; Jr, Berbaum, KS., et al. (1992) Error in radiology: classification and lessons in 182 cases presented at a problem case conference. *Radiology*, 183,145-150

S. G. A. III, Giger, M. L.; Moran, C. J.; Blackburn, J. T.; Doi, K. & MacMahon, H. (1999) *Computerized detection of pulmonary nodules on CT scans*, Radiographics 19, 5, 1303–1311

Sahba, F.; Tizhoosh, H.R. & Salama, M.M.A. (2006) A Reinforcement Learning Framework for Medical Image Segmentation, *Proceedings of International Joint Conference on Neural Networks*, IJCNN '06. , pp. 511-517

Shokri, M. & Tizhoosh, H. R. (2003) *Using reinforcement learning for image thresholding*, Department of Systems Design Engineering, Faculty of Engineering, University of Waterloo, Canada.

Silva, A. C. & Carvalho, P. C. P. (2002) Sistema de análise de nódulo pulmonar, In: *II Workshop de Informática aplicada a Saùde*, Universidade de Itajai, Itajaí.

Silva, A. C.; Carvalho, P. C. P. & Gattass, M. (2004) *Analysis of spatial variability using geostatistical functions for diagnosis of lung nodule in computerized tomography images*, Pattern Analysis & Applications 7, 3, 227

Silva, A.C.; Carvalho, P.C.P. & Gattass, M. (2004) Diagnosis of solitary lung nodule using semivariogram and skeletonization in computerized tomography images, *Proceedings of 21st Meeting of the Society for Computer Applications in Radiology (SCAR 2004)*

Silva, A.C.; Carvalho, P.C.P. & Gattass, M. (2005) Analysis of spatial variability using geostatistical functions for diagnosis of lung nodule in computerized tomography images, *Pattern Analysis and Applications*, 7, 227–234

Silva, A.C.; Carvalho, P.C.P.; Peixoto, A. & Gattass, M. (2004) Diagnosis of lung nodule using gini coefficient and skeletonization in computerized tomography images, *Proceedings of 19th ACM Symposium on AppliedComputing (SAC 2004)*, pp. 243–248, NY, USA, ACM Press New York (2004)

Smart W. D. (2002) *Making Reinforcement Learning Work on Real Robots*, Ph.D. thesis, Department of Computer Science, Brown University

Smith, A.C. (1999) The Folding of the Human Brain, from Shape to Function, *PhD thesis*, University of London. Available at http://carmen.umds.ac.uk/a.d.smith/phd.html

Stensmo, M & Sejnowski, T. J (1996) Automated Medical Diagnosis based on Decision Theory and Learning from Cases, World Congress on Neural Networks pp. 1227-1 231

Sutton, R. & Barto, A. (1998) *Reinforcement Learning: An Introduction*, MIT Press, Cambridge, MA

Swensen, S. J.(1997) *The probability of malignancy in solitary nodules. application to small radiologically indeterminate nodules*, Arch. Intern. Med. 8, 157, 849–855

Takashima, S.; Sone, S.; Li, F.; Mauyama, Y.; Hasegawa, M. & Kadoya., M. (2003) Indeterminate solitary pulmonary nodules revealed at population-based ct screening of the lung: using first follow-up diagnostic ct to differentiate benign end malignant lesions., *Am J Roentology* 180, 5, 1255–1263.

Tarantino, A.B(1997) 38. In: *Nódulo Solitário Do Pulmão,* 4 edn. Guanabara Koogan, Rio de Janeiro 733–753

Watkins, C. & Dayan, P. (1952) Q-Learning, *Machine Learning*, 8, 3, 279-292

Yin, Peng-Yeng (2002) *Maximum entropy-based optimal threshold selection using deterministic reinforcement learning with controlled randomization,* Department of Information Management, Ming Chuan University Taiwan, 2002.

21

RL Based Decision Support System for u-Healthcare Environment

Devinder Thapa, In-Sung Jung and Gi-Nam Wang
AJOU University
South Korea

1. Introduction

We can imagine a haywire situation with no healthcare centres nearby. In this situation, a high risk patient, away from the medical healthcare center, may get major heart attack or unpredictable sudden stroke, or some other noxious symptoms. Lack of on-time information, proper diagnosis, and decision making system, may sometimes cause the life of the patient. In order to access the timely information and to employ correct diagnosis at anytime and anywhere, use of ubiquitous technologies is becoming ideal test-beds for u-Healthcare environments. However, using ubiquitous device, it would be one of the most crucial requisites to accumulate accurate signals timely and appropriate processing of those signals during such critical circumstances. Furthermore, lack of proper decision support system may delay the treatment, and it may cost a life of the patient. The effort to rectify any of these issues will minimize the time lag between observation and treatment during the emergency circumstances, and helps to reduce the diagnosis time, that can be better utilize for caring the patient.

The objective of this chapter is to combine the agent based decision support system with ubiquitous artefacts and make it more intelligent, so that it can help the doctors to acquire correct and timely diagnosis information and select appropriate treatment choices. Also, designed is a novel interpretation of Markov decision process, providing clear mathematical formulation to connect reinforcement learning agent system. An attempt is given to supervise the dynamic situation by using agent based ubiquitous artefacts and to find out the appropriate solution for emergency circumstances, providing correct diagnosis and proper treatment in time. The well known reinforcement learning can be utilized to model u-healthcare decision support system. The reason for using the RL (Reinforcement Learning) agent based on MDP (Markov Decision Process) model is because it needs less number of parameters compare to other decision trees it also gives approximation method to make trade off between accuracy and speed, in turn, solve the complex number of cases in less time compare to other decision support system (Milos H., Fraser H., 2000).

Organization of this chapter is as follows. Section 2 is a review of the related works, RL agent, and Markov decision model is also explained. Section 3 describes the details scenario of the proposed approach. Similarly, section 4 discusses the formulation of the model and optimal policy finding algorithm of the RL based decision support system. Finally section 5 & 6 concludes the chapter and contains references.

2. Related works

The concept of ubiquitous healthcare system using agent technology is studied in the reference Jakob E. Bardram (2004). Where the author visualized about highly interactive hospital, it will facilitate the doctors to access relevant medical information at anytime and anywhere, using ubiquitous hardware and software. Similar nature of research is explained in the reference work of (Thapa D., et al., 2005). In the reference work of (Wendelken S.M., et al., 2003), the idea of location finder agent using iterative deepening search is described. It can be utilized to design the patient location finder agent in a u-healthcare system. Similarly, the concept of agent based healthcare environment is explained in the reference (Rodriguez M., et al., 2003). Although, the functional architecture of the reference work is different, the conceptual idea is deployable to our work.

In the reference work of (Milos H., & Fraser H., 2000) partially observable Markov decision process [POMDP] can be deployable utilized for the diagnosis and treatment of ischemic heart disease. This work can be theoretically considered as the part of reinforcement learning agent. Although POMDP is more suitable to observe the hidden state of the patient, its exponential growth is prone to state explosion problem. In our work, we deployed MDP assuming the patient state is within the domain of experts' knowledge. In addition, time complexity of the MDP is lesser than POMDP.

All of the existing works are focused on the exploitation of ubiquitous artefacts for the betterment of healthcare system. However, little attention is given to the concept of developing integrated emergency system using reinforcement learning decision support system in a *u*-healthcare environment. The main objective of this research is to design agent based decision support system using reinforcement learning, to reduce the time lag between the onset of the attack and the time that care is administered. Ubiquitous devices combined with agent technology can reduce the time latency, and they can provide suitable on-time treatment information when the patient is away from the hospital premises.

2.1 Reinforcement learning agents

Reinforcement learning (RL) is based on interaction with an environment, from the consequences of action, rather than from explicit teaching. RL methods are intended to address the kind of learning and decision making problems that people face in their everyday lives. Main elements of Reinforcement learning are states $\boldsymbol{s}$, actions $\boldsymbol{a}$, and rewards $\boldsymbol{r}$ as depicted in Fig.1. The reinforcement learning agent (RL-agent) is connected to its environment via sensors. In every step of interaction the agent receives a feedback about the state of the environment s_{t+1} and the reward r_{t+1} of its latest action a_t. The agent chooses an action a_{t+1} representing the output function, which changes the state s_{t+2} of environment. The agent gets a new feedback, through the reinforcement signal r_{t+2}. It involves a decision-making agent interacting with its environment so as to maximize the cumulative reward that it receives over time. The agent perceives aspects of the environment's state and it selects right actions. The agent may estimate a value function and use it to construct better and better decision-making policies over a given time. The main objective of the agent is to maximize the aggregated reinforcement signals. RL could be characterized by a mathematical framework of Markov decision processes (MDPs) (Stuart J. R. and Peter N., 2003).

In medical healthcare system, when we are supposed to take right decision in a right time, reinforcement learning agent, by combining different model and actions, can help a physician to find out the best diagnosis and treatment options in different states of the patient. By using RL algorithms we can choose the best alternative action during the emergency circumstances which can reduce the total cost (time, treatment complexity etc) of the action (diagnosis & treatment) taken by the physician.

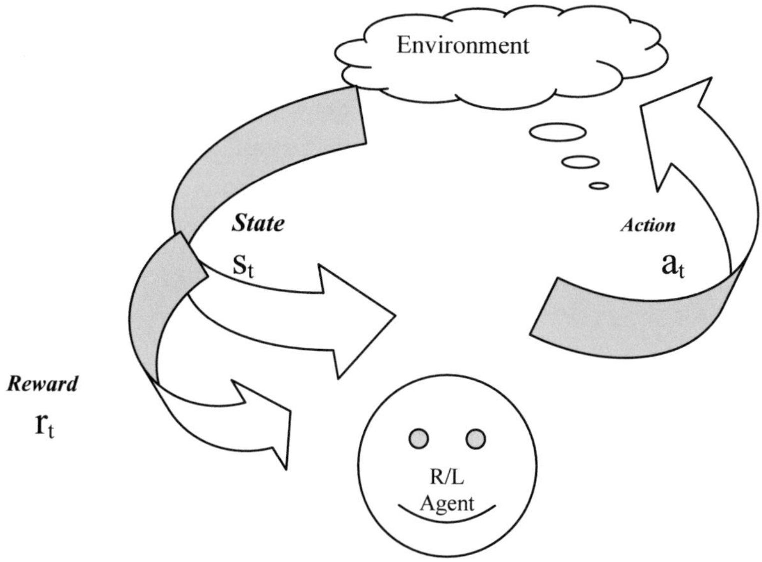

Fig. 1. Reinforcement Learning Agent

2.2 Markov decision process

Reinforcement learning basically uses the MDP concept for implementation. We are using the MDP which is based on shortest route approach to reduce the time latency of the reactive action, as per our approach, time is as much important as efficiency.

An MDP is defined by a set of states ***S***, actions ***A***, Reward ***R***, and transition probabilities ***T*** (Puterman M. L., 1994). A transition function, T: S x A ->P(S), defines the effects of the various actions on the state of the environment. P(S) represents the set of discrete probability distributions over the set ***S***. The reward function, R: S x A→ R, specifies the agent's task to find a policy mapping, choice of action, so as to maximize the expected sum of reward. Two types of decision model can be used to obtain the reward. Infinite horizon uses discount factor $0<\gamma<1$ to control how much effect future rewards have on the optimal decisions, with small values giving significant weight to later rewards. However, finite horizon does not use discount factor and the iteration of certain action is known in advance. This paper deployed the finite horizon decision model.

$$V^*(s) = \max_a (R(s,a) + \sum_{s' \in S} T(s,a,s') V^*(s')), \forall s \in S, \quad (1)$$

$$V^*(s) = \max_\pi E(\sum_{t=0}^{\infty} r_t) \quad (2)$$

$$R(s,a) = \sum_{s' \in S} P(s' \mid s,a) R(s,a,s') \tag{3}$$

Implementation of this model in our approach is to ascertain, current state (patient status at the time of incident), action (medication, no action), transition probabilities (between current state and new state), and reward (cost and complexities) certain payoffs related to this transition. The objective of this model is to find out the optimized action to maximize the reward or cost in a finite discounted horizon as shown in equation 1.

Due to the computation complexities of the pure MDP model we use Bellman's value function recursively; it [eqn. 1] calculates the total reward value by adding all the suboptimal values [eqn. 3] at some finite time horizon

3. Proposed model

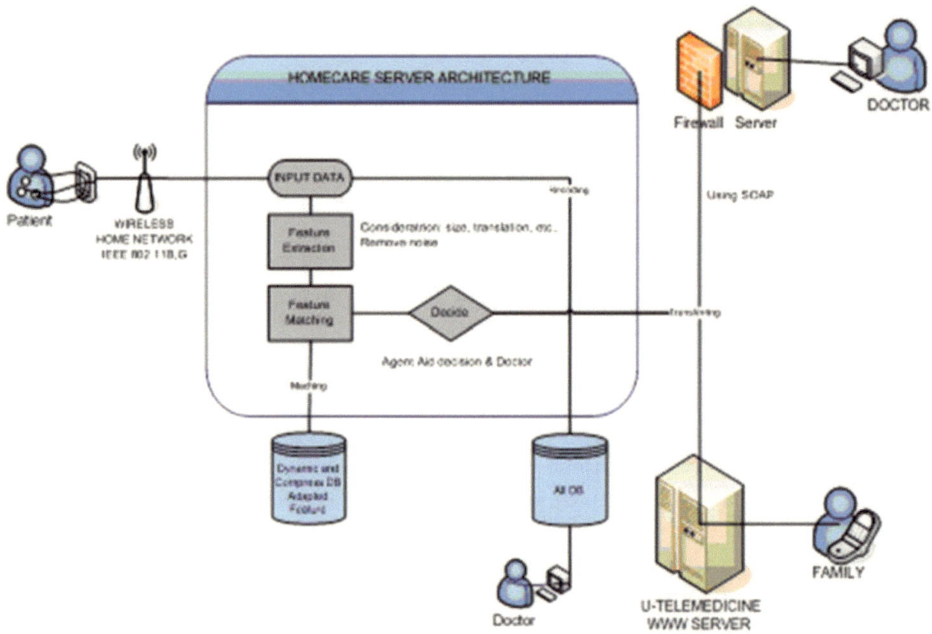

Fig. 2. RL based decision support systems in a u-Healthcare system

Assumption of this research test bed has been made in the ubiquitous environment. As shown in Fig.1, when a high risk patient, far from medical facilities, gets some perilous occurrence in their body, the ubiquitous sensor device attached to their body sends bio signals like (digital sounds of lung, SaO2, EKG) etc. to the home medical server using IEEE 802.11b wireless network.

The home medical server is connected to the hospital knowledgebase server through TCP/IP using internet connection. This signal sends the patient current status to the HIS (Hospital Information Server). On the bases of this crucial input data the decision making agent, based on RL model, make inference of the data and provide entire data history of the patient with best alternate action (diagnosis and treatment) to the related department with minimal time cost. Decision agent also helps to the related physician check his scheduling, and sends the patients profile to the related departments. It helps in timely availability of the crucial information to the right place. The flow of Information processing is depicted in the following figure 2.

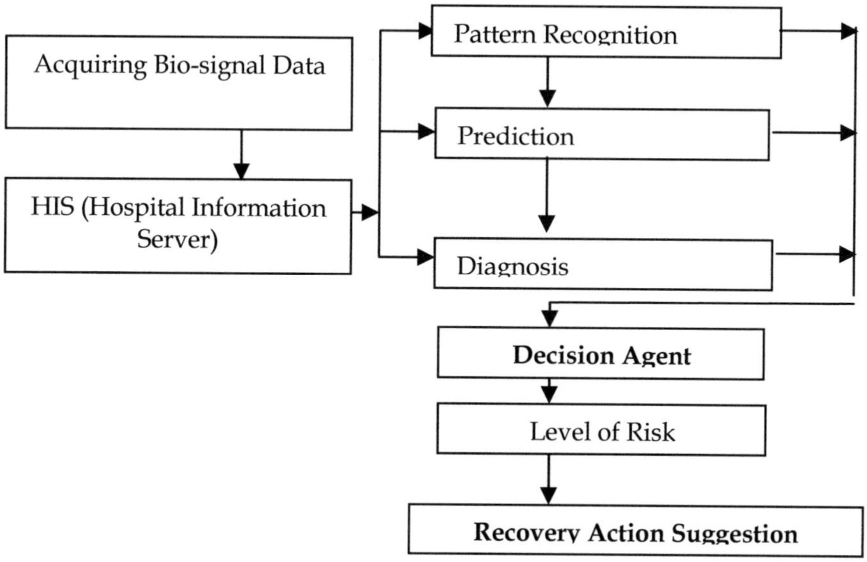

Fig. 3. Flow of information processing in a u-Healthcare system

1. Aquiring bio-signals and pattern recognition can be done by using artificial neural network like back propagation.
2. Prediction & diagnosis can be done by using time series analysis & self organizing feature map (SOM), artificial neural network .
3. RL decision making agent is based on MDP (Markov Decision Process), this chapter particularly describes about this approach.

Final output of the decision making agent will be two fold measurements as shown in fig 4:

- Patient Current State (Level of risk)
  - Normal
  - Serious
  - Emergent

- Emergency Measurement
  -If the (State = Emergent)
  Send SMS Message to Doctor
  Send SMS Message to User Relatives
  Send SMS Message to Ambulance

On the basis of the level of risk it suggests best series of action or optimal policy for the better way of diagnosis and treatment.

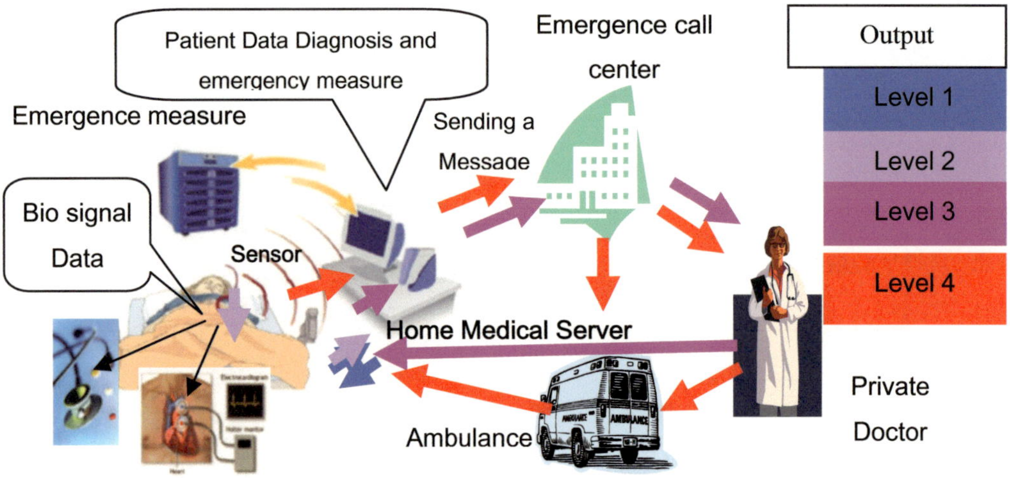

Fig. 4. Complete graphical scenario of RL integrated u-Healthcare System

As soon as the patients reach to the hospital premises information will be ready for the optimal and immediate action by physician. Although this is a conceptual idea, the parallel research on this idea has been going on. Our approach is to make the RL based decision making model more efficient and rational to save the life of the high risk patients in emergency circumstances, with the help of RL integrated ubiquitous artifacts in the u-Healthcare system. The level of risk will be calculated on the basis of the input data described in Table I.

Data	Standard
SaO2	Normal >90% Lack of oxygen: Mild 90~94% Moderate 75-90%
HR (Heart Rate)	Normal 60~100/min Tachycardia >100/min Paroxysmal Tachycardia: 150~250/min
BP (Blood Pressure)	Normal : 120/80mm HG Hypertension: >140/90mmHG Serious Hypertension: >200/140mmHG Hypotonic >100/60mmHG Serious Hypotonic <80/60mmHG
Body Temperature	Normal: 36.5~37Degree Slight fever: Morning >37.2 Evening >37.7 High Fever > 38.3

Table I. Parameters for calculating the level of risk (Source: AJOU university hospital)

4. Formulations to a reinforcement learning problem

In this paper, we assumed that patient current state is fully observable; we have used the MDP model with finite discounted horizon. On the basis of his current available data (like heart beat, pulse rate, respiration, chest pain) as shown in table I, and past history of the patient from Hospital Information Server, it makes different combination of the action (medication or no action or emergency measurement) and reinforce (negative and positive) rewards (cost) with every action to go to next state. Finally, it finds out the best action or minimum cost (time taking) solution.

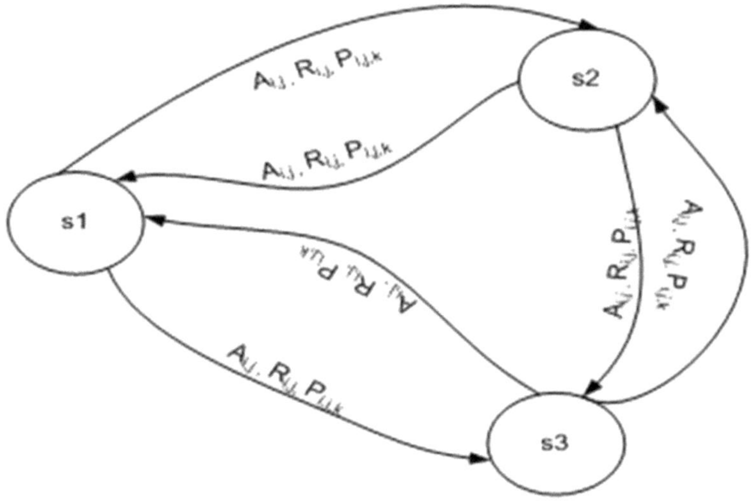

Fig. 5. Symbolic representation of Markov Decision Process

R=Reward, P=Transition probability, A=Action, S=State

Decision Epochs: [Finite time horizon]

$$T=\{1,2,\ldots,N\}, \quad N \leq \infty$$

States(S) = [Normal (s3), Serious (s1), Emergent (s2)]

S= {s1, s2, s3}

Action (A) = [No action(a1), Medication(a2), Medication with emergency measurement(a3)]
$A = \{a_{i,j} \mid i=1,2,3 \text{ and } j=1,2,3\}$, where *i* refers to the state and *j* refers to action

Rewards(R) = {Cost ($r_{i,j}$) | i=1,2,3 and j= integer }

$$R(S1, a_{i,j}) = r_{i,j}$$
$$R(S2, a_{i,j}) = r_{i,j}$$
$$R(S3, a_{i,j}) = r_{i,j}$$
$$\text{If } N \leq \infty$$

Transition Probabilities (pt): [Effect of diagnosis and treatment (p)]

$$pt(s3 \mid s1, a_{1,2}) = p_{1,2,3}$$

For example, if the patient is in the state s1 and the action $a_{1,2}$ will be taken then the probability of patient going to state s3 will be $p_{1,2,3}$. Where p denotes the probability between [0, 1] of transition, and 1, 2, and 3 denotes the action $a_{1,2}$ and state s3 respectively. Calculation of expected Reward or Cost:

Example: $R(S1, a_{1,1}) = R(S1, a_{1,1}, S1)\, pt(S2 \mid S1, a_{1,1}) + R(S1, a_{1,1}, S2)\, pt(S2 \mid S1, a_{1,1})$

4.1 Finding the best policy or the minimum cost function using DP (Dynamic programming) approach

Compared with other methods for solving MDPs, DP methods are actually quite efficient. The (worst case) time DP methods take to find an optimal policy is polynomial in the number of states and actions (Stuart J. R. and Peter N., 2003). If n and m denote the number of states and actions, this means that a DP method takes a number of computational operations that is less than some polynomial function of n and m. A DP method is guaranteed to find an optimal policy in polynomial time even though the total number of (deterministic) policies is m^n. In this sense, DP is exponentially faster than any direct search in policy space could be, because direct search would have to exhaustively examine each policy to provide the same guarantee.

choose an arbitrary policy π'

loop

$\pi := \pi'$

compute the value function of policy π :

solve the linear equations

$$V\pi(s) = R(s, \pi(s)) + \sum_{s' \in S} T(s, \pi(s), s') V_\pi(s') \tag{4}$$

improve the policy at each state:

$$\pi'(s) := \arg\min_a (R(s,a) + \sum_{s' \in S} T(s, a, s') V_\pi(s')) \tag{5}$$

until $\pi = \pi'$

Denote a policy as Л, where Л=action selected in current state. Where $V\pi(s)$ and $\pi'(s)$ are optimal value and control function. We can take Л' as any random policy and $V\pi(s)$ is reward value starting from current state and following the Л policy. Now we can define another greedy policy in terms of Л'(s) and make iteration of the value function $V\pi(s)$ function until $\pi = \pi'$. We consider whether the value could be improved by changing the first action taken. If it can, we change the policy to take the new action whenever it is in that situation. When $\pi = \pi'$ and no improvements are possible, then the policy is considered to be optimal. This model will be helpful to achieve the objective of finding an action or a sequence of actions that optimizes the time cost of diagnosis and treatment in a given finite horizon under emergency circumstances.

5. Conclusion

This paper presents and describes a Reinforcement Learning agent based model used for information acquiring and real time decision support system at emergency circumstances. The well known reinforcement learning is utilized for modeling emergency u-Healthcare system. Markov decision process is also employed to provide clear mathematical formulation in order to connect reinforcement learning as well as to express integrated agent system. This method will be highly effective for the real time diagnosis and treatment of high risk patient during the emergency circumstances, when they are away from the hospital premises. Looking at the growing increase in the research area of ubiquitous devices this approach seems to be very beneficial and life saving for the high risk patient at the time of emergency circumstances. Further pursuing will be to develop some prototype, and simulate the testing data, planning modules, and find out the actual outcome of this approach.

6. Acknowledgement

This work has been partially supported by BK21 (Brain Korea 21st Century) and the Ubiquitous Autonomic Computing and Network Project, the Ministry of Information and Communication (MIC) 21st Century Frontier R&D Program, South Korea.

7. References

Jakob E. Bardram(2004). The Personal Medical Unit -- A Ubiquitous Computing Infrastructure for Personal Pervasive Healthcare. *UbiHealth 2004: The 3rd International Workshop on Ubiquitous Computing for Pervasive Healthcare Applications*

Jung I., Thapa D. and Wang G. N.,(2005). Neural Network Based Algorithm for Diagnosis and Classification of Breast Cancer Tumor, *LNAI 3801, Springer-Verlag Berlin Heidelberg,* (2005), pp. 107–114.

Leong, T. Y. (1998). Multiple perspective dynamic decision making, *Artificial Intelligence,* Vol.105, No. 1-2 (October 1998), pp. 209-261, ISSN: 0004-3702

Lesile P. K., Michael L. L., Andrew W. M. (1996). Reinforcement Learning: A Survey. *Journal of Artificial Intelligence Research, Vol.* 4, (1996), pp. 237-285

Milos H., Fraser H.(2000). Planning Treatment of Ischemic Heart Disease with Partially Observable Markov Decision Process. *Artificial Intelligence in Medicine,* vol. (18), (2000) pp. 221-244

Puterman M. L., (1994). Markov Decision Process: Discrete Stochastic Dynamic Programming. *A Wiley-Interscience publication, John Wiley & Sons, Inc.,* (1994) New York.

Rodriguez M., Favela J., Gonzalez V. and Muñoz M. (2003). Agent Based Mobile Collaboration and Information Access in a Healthcare Environment. *Proceedings of Workshop of E-Health,* Applications of Computing Science in Medicine and Health Care. ISBN: 970-36-0118-9. (December 2003), Cuernavaca, México

Sutton R. S. & Barto A. G. (1998). Reinforcement Learning: An Introduction. *MIT Press* (1998), a Bradford Book, Cambridge, MA

Stuart J. R. and Peter N.(2003). Artificial Intelligence: A Modern Approach IInd edition. *Pearson Education International,* (2003), New Jersey

Thapa D., Jung I., and Wang G.N.(2005). Agent Based Decision Support System using Reinforcement Learning under Emergency Circumstances, *Spriger Lecture Notes in Computer Science (LNCS)*, 3610, (2005), pp. 888-892.

Ulieru, M.; Geras, A: Emergent, (Nov. 2002). Holarchies for e-health applications: a case in glaucoma diagnosis. *IECON 02 (IEEE 2002 28th Annual Conference of the Industrial Electronics Society)*, Volume: 4, 5-8 (Nov. 2002) pp. 2957 - 2961

Watrous, R.L. and Towell, G.(1995). A Patient-adaptive Neural Network ECG Patient Monitoring Algorithm. *In Proceedings Computers in Cardiology*, Vienna, Austria (1995) pp. 229--232.

Wendelken S.M., McGrath S.P. and Blike G.T.(2003). A medical assessment algorithm for automated remote triage. *International conference of the IEEE EMBS*, Mexico, September 17-21,(2003)

22

Reinforcement Learning to Support Meta-Level Control in Air Traffic Management

Daniela P. Alves[1], Li Weigang[2] and Bueno B. Souza[2]
[1] *Brazilian Institute of Information in Science and Technology - IBICT,*
[2] *Department of Computer Science, University of Brasilia - UnB,*
Brazil

1. Introduction

In a complex environment where the messages exchange intensively among the agents, a difficulty task is to decide the best action for new arriving messages during on-line control. A typical form of communication in Air Traffic Flow Management (ATFM) is verbal language to exchange the information and there is almost no digital recording of this communication between pilot and air controller. As the development of distributed computation system [1], the digital message communication is proposed especially for processing the immense amount of messages.

In a real case such as the First Integrated Center of Air Defense and Air Traffic Control - CINDACTA I, in Brasilia, the system monitors 70% of the traffic flow in Brazil. According to the air traffic control procedure in CINDACTA I, Flight Information Region of Brasilia - FIR-BS is divided into 14 sectors and managed by 3 regional supervisors (Sao Paulo, Rio de Janeiro and Brasilia). Every air controller monitors his sector and is responsible to his supervisor. Only supervisor can make a decision to manage the air traffic flow. Any action is realized by air controller according to the decision of supervisor. For example, a decision may be to hold a flight in an airport for more 10 minutes, or assign the priority to another flight in the landing processing.

In CINDACTA I, the monitor system (equipment and operation software) is suitable, but there is no a general system to manage and synchronize the traffic dynamically and to support the decision for adequate traffic management. Supervisor makes the decision just by his experience without quantity analyses of the impact of the action. To resolve this kind of problem, some researches were developed using the solution of Artificial Intelligence and others according to the new conception of ATFM.

A distributed ATM system has been studied in Australia [2]. The advantages of that approach are inherent distribution, autonomy, communication and reliability. Prevôt, from NASA Ames Research Center, has studied a distributed approach for operator interfaces and intelligent flight guidance, management and decision support [3]. An application of multi-agent coordination techniques in ATM, which sets up a methodological framework using multi-agent coordination techniques that supports the collaborative work in ATM has also been presented recently by Eurocontrol [4]. It should be mentioned that the multi-agent

coordination technique is a useful methodological framework, however the research in [4] is limited to a software shell. Due to the huge amount of information traffic in ATFM, its implementation may not be straightforward when brought into practical fields.
A multi-agent system (MAS) for ATFM in grid computing - ATFMGC, was developed recently [5]. The research proposed an approach of cooperation and negotiation among agents using grid computing in a real time traffic synchronization problem. In some aspects such as the agent functions, their knowledge representation and inference processes [6] were developed. Standard of Balancing among Airports (SBA) as a criterion was also used to balance and measure the amount of communication among agents (i.e. airports) and the tolerated delay of the flights [5].
On the other hand, some problems have appeared for the fact of the intense exchange of messages in ATFMGC related with more than 10 airports. For a fixed SBA, it is impossible to efficiently equilibrate the communication. It is necessary to adapt a suitable mechanism to assist the decision process. The System of the Application and Management of the Decision Support Air Traffic Flow Control - SISCONFLUX is still in development [16]. Within this system, the idea is to introduce Meta-Level Control approach [7, 8] in ATFM. During information process, the reinforcement learning [9] is inserted to acquire experience to make Markov decision process more efficiency.
Meta-Level Control approach was developed by Raja and Lesser since 2003 [7, 8] for Multi-Agent System. This research proposed a Module of Evaluation and Decision Support (MAAD) in SISCONFLUX for ATFM with the combination of the Meta-Level Control approach and reinforcement learning algorithms (Q-leanring and SARSA [10]). With the developed system, four strategies of the modifications of the parameters in the Q-learning and SARSA algorithms are studied during reinforcement learning simulation, such as the cases of initial heuristic (IH), epsilon adaptative (EA), performance heuristic (PH) and the combination of above three (IH + EA + PH). The results from simulation and analyses show satisfactory in the traffic management process.
The chapter is organized in five parts: soon after this introduction, section II presents a general view of Meta-Control and algorithms of reinforcement learning. In the third section, the proposed system SISCONFLUX and principal model of this research - MAAD are described including control process and learning algorithms. A case study is illustrated and discussed in section IV. Last section presents the conclusions and future research.

2. Meta-level control and reinforcement learning algorithms

2.1 Meta-level control

Meta-level control is defined as the ability of complex agents operating in open environments to sequence domain and deliberative actions to optimize expected performance [7, 8]. It is an important topic in automatic control and some related fields. Russel and Wefald [11] presented a general approach of meta-reasoning and named as Principles of Meta-Reasoning. Some applications and related works were intensely studied by Raja and Lesser such as [7, 8, 11]. In these researches, an additional layer of meta-control that acts above of the component of control in the system to help the decision process. Reinforcement learning is also introduced to make the agents to learn knowledge from experience for better to make the decision.
The actions of the intelligent agents in the classic architecture are classified in two types: action and action to recover property of control, as the research in [10].

Considering the Meta-Reasoning, Raja and Lesser [7, 8] mentioned another action: the action of Meta-Level Control. It is a process of optimization of the performance of agents for choosing the sequence of actions to recover property and the deliberative of the activities [8].

Reactive controls may be suitable for situations with high restrictions such as: real time, limited resources, among others. There are five types of event triggers that require Meta-Level decision making [8]:

- Arrival of a new task from the environment;
- Presence of a task in the current task set library (current) that it requires negotiation with a non-local agent;
- Failure of a negotiation to reach a commitment;
- Decision to schedule a new set of tasks or to reschedule existing tasks;
- Significant deviation of online schedule performance from expected performance.

According [7, 8], Meta-Level Control is a process of deciding among the following choices: to drop the goal and not do any analysis; to delay goal analysis; reason about the amount of effort to go into goal analysis; and to determine the context of the goal analysis - whether to analyze it a single goal or multiple goals within a single agent perspective; or to analyze single or multiple goals in the context of a facilitating agent's goals.

Meta-Level Control is useful in situations where options for goal analysis are expensive, in other words, the costs or accumulated costs affect agent performance detrimentally. It is useful when the cost of goal analysis is significantly more expensive than cost of meta-level control actions. It is also useful where a choice has to be made about the type of goal analysis and the options for goal analysis have significantly different costs and produce results with significantly different utilities.

2.2 Reinforcement learning

Reinforcement learning is learning what to do and how to map situations to actions - so as to maximize a numerical reward signal [12]. The learner is not told which actions to take, as in most forms of machine learning, but instead must discover which actions yield the most reward by trying them. In the most interesting and challenging cases, actions may affect not only the immediate reward but also the next situation and, through that, all subsequent rewards. These two characteristics - trial-and-error search and delayed reward - are the two most important distinguishing features of reinforcement learning. One of the challenges that arise in reinforcement learning and not in other kinds of learning is the tradeoff between exploration and exploitation.

To obtain a lot of reward, a reinforcement learning agent must prefer actions that it has tried in the past and found to be effective in producing reward. But to discover which actions these are it has to select actions that it has not tried before. The agent has to exploit what it already knows in order to obtain reward, but it also has to explore in order to make better action selections in the future. The dilemma is that neither exploitation nor exploration can be pursued exclusively without failing at the task.

For control problems such as ATFM, reinforcement learning agents can be left to learn in a simulated environment and eventually they will come up with good controlling policies. Some advantages of using reinforcement learning for control problems is that an agent can

be retrained easily to adapt to environment changes, and trained continuously while the system is online, improving performance all the time [12].
The typical mathematical model witch bases Reinforcement Learning is known as Markov Decision Process [10]. This model considers two main conditions:

1. The Markov Property - Situation in which the probability of transition of a state s for a next state s ' depends only on state s and of the action the adopted in s. This means that the current state supplies the enough's information to the learning system decide which action must be taken.
2. Markov Decision Process - is a process in which a set of states S, $s \in S$, $a \in$ set of A(s) action, T set of transitions between states associates with the actions and a set of probabilities P on the joint S that represents a modeling of the transitions between the states.

Two algorithms of reinforcement learning are used in this research, such as: Q-learning and SARSA [12], as mentioned in the following sub-sections.

2.2.1 Q-leanring algorithm

A Q-learning agent learns an action-value function, or Q-function, giving the expected utility of taking a given action in a given state. The essence of the Q-learning algorithm is defined as follows [10 - 15]. At the time *t*, the agent:

1. Visit state s_t and select an action a_t.
2. Receive *r*, reward observed in the following state, from the process of the reinforcement $r(s_t, a_t)$ and observe the next state s_{t+1}.
3. Update the action value :

$$Q_{t+1}(s_t, a_t) \leftarrow Q_t(s_t, a_t)+\alpha[r(s_t, a_t) + \gamma \max_{a'} Q_t((s_{t+1},a_{t+1}) - Q_t(s_t, a_t)] \quad (1)$$

4. Repeat above steps until stopping criterion is satisfied.

Where [12],

s, a are the original state and action, r is the reward observed in the following state.

α : the learning rate, set between 0 and 1. Setting it to 0 means that the Q-values are never updated, hence nothing is learned. Setting a high value such as 0.9 means that learning can occur quickly.

γ: discount factor, also set between 0 and 1. This models the fact that future rewards are worth less than immediate rewards. Mathematically, the discount factor needs to be set less than 0 for the algorithm to converge.

$\max_a$: the maximum reward that is attainable in the state following the current one. i.e. the reward for taking the optimal action thereafter.

2.2.2 SARSA algorithm

The SARSA algorithm is a temporal difference (TD) method that learns action-value functions by a bootstrapping mechanism, that is, by making estimations based on previous estimations. It is an On-Policy algorithm for reinforcement learning and defined as follows [10 - 15]. At the time t, the agent:

1. Visit a state s_t and select an action a_t.
2. Receive *r*, reward observed in the following state, from the process of the

reinforcement $r(s_t, a_t)$ and observe the next state s_{t+1}.
3. Assign $e_t(s_t, a_t) = e_t(s_t, a_t) + 1$
4. Update the action value :

$$Q_{t+1}(s_t, a_t) \leftarrow Q_t(s_t, a_t) + \alpha[r(s_t, a_t) + \gamma\, Q_t((s_{t+1}, a_{t+1}) - Q_t(s_t, a_t)]\, e_t(s_t, a_t) \quad (2)$$

5. For all s, a do $e_t(s_t, a_t) = \gamma\lambda e_t(s_t, a_t) + 1$
6. Repeat above steps until stopping criterion is satisfied.

The major difference between SARSA algorithm and Q-learning, is that the maximum value for some action not taken for the next state is not used for updating the Q-values. Instead, a new action and a reward are selected using the same policy that determined the original action.

3. Proposed model: evaluation and decision support

3.1 Propose of SISCONFLUX

The System of the Application and Management of the Decision Support Air Traffic Flow Control - SISCONFLUX is in development. The system is proposed to make the suitable decisions for the supervisors of controllers of an air traffic control region, the decision restrictive the traffic flow control more effective ahead of determined scenario. Such decision action will represent the solution most adequate for the maintenance of the best condition of flow of traffic in the Flight Information Region of Brasilia - FIR-BS as a whole.

The SISCONFLUX also is proposed to support the decision according to the determined flights, routes or airports condition, to prioritize the traffic flow management. Such prioritized action may be established in agreement the emanated orientation of the responsible agencies for the air traffic flow management in Brazilian airspace.

As a part of this system, the Module of Evaluation and Decision Support (MAAD) is with the function as a module of analysis and learning. Based on the experience of the air traffic controllers and supervisors, MAAD learns the experience and suggest the decision to adjusted traffic flow in the sectors of traffic control do not reach the condition of congestion or saturation. This suggestion is defined by the other subsystem: Module of Balancing of Flow (MBF), which is general manager of the traffic flow to balance the delay (Sky or Grand Holding) in the minimum or accepted condition.

The definition of the control or adjustment of the flow is from series actions which are specified by some parameters in computation system. These actions are defined by air traffic controller and supervisors, for example, to delay a flight in an airport or give priority for a landing flight, etc. In such a way, the subsystem can get the input action from supervisor, according to pre-established parameters. That input will be sent to other integrant modules of the system for the projection of new scenery and restart of the operation cycle.

MAAD is also developed as the interface among the human agents (air controllers and supervisors) and with the other modules of the system. Basically it has the function to catch the experience of the controllers and supervisors, including these variants to the set of results analyzed from the previous modules, besides functioning as origin of data for the system as well.

Once the decisions are accepted by the supervisors, the same ones will be stored and will start to be part of the system as an accepted decision for the data base. Among All the tasks of this module can be mentioned:

- Presentation of the results to the supervisors;
- Collect of data for learning purpose;
- Storage of the set of pairs (state; action);
- Log of events as action of the operators;
- Activities that are considered useful administratively (item in discussion with the command of CINDACTA I).

To support the decision, the technique of Meta-Level Control is modified and applied to the system to improve the performance of the communication between the agents. During the control process, the decision is taken being based on the experience and the knowledge acquired for the agents with reinforcement learning.

MAAD as a learning module inserted in the architecture of the SISCONFLUX (Figure 1) that guarantees the capacity of adaptation in random situations, or either, adaptation to the alterations of the decision environment. The use of reinforcement learning speeds up heuristically the decision procedure, where Q-learning and SARSA algorithms are introduced.

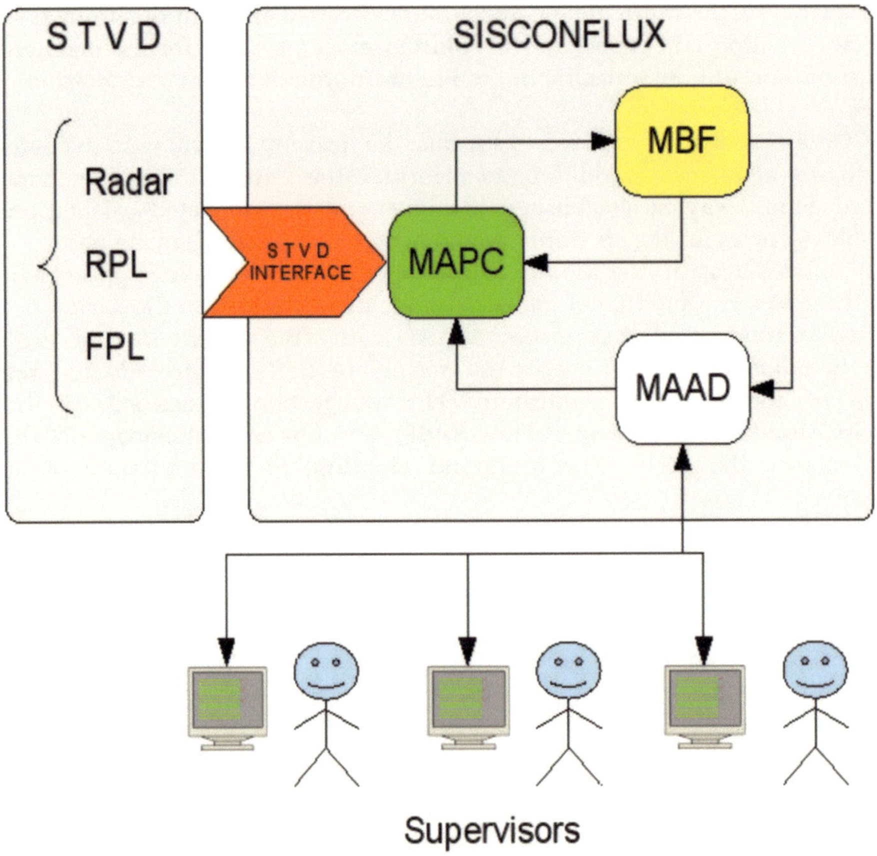

Fig. 1. Architecture of SISCONFLUX

Where:
SISCONFLUX: The System of the Application and Management of the Decision Support Air Traffic Flow Control.
MAPC: Module of Accompaniment and Forecast of Scenery.
MBF: Module of Balancing of Flow.
MAAD: Module of Evaluation and Decision Support.
STVD: System of Treatment and Visualization of Data.
RPL: Plans of Repetitive Flights.
FPL: Plans of Eventual Flights.

Figure 2 shows to a project of functioning of the subsystem and its relationship with the other modules of the SISCONFLUX.

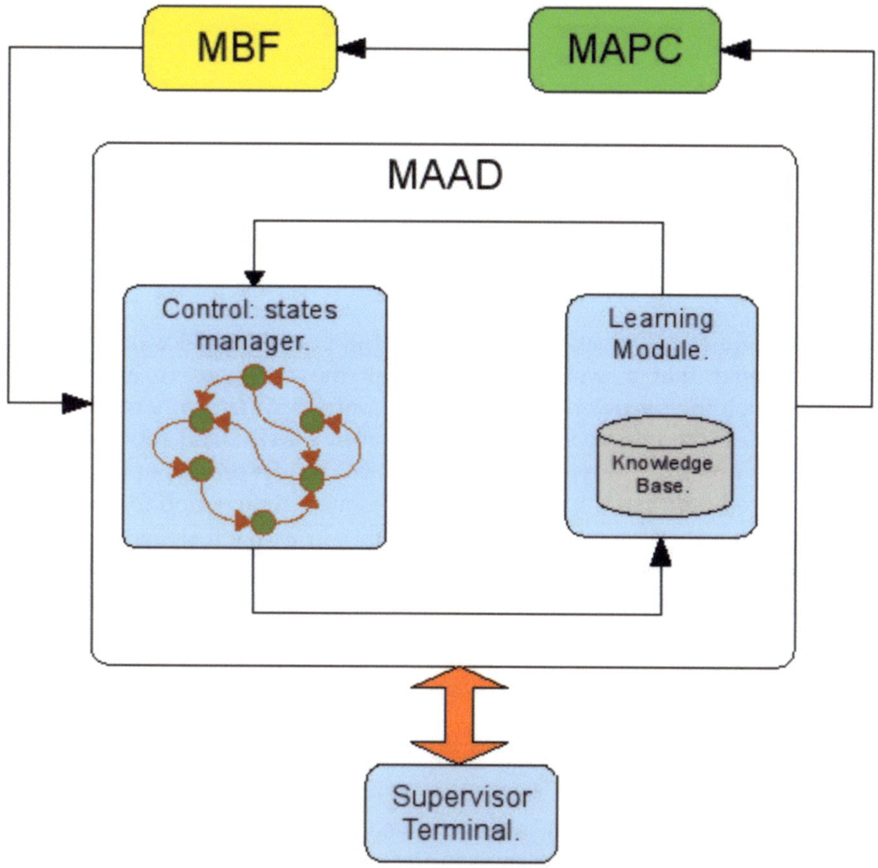

Fig. 2. Relationship among sub-models in SISCONFLUX

3.2 Architecture of module of evaluation and decision support (MAAD)

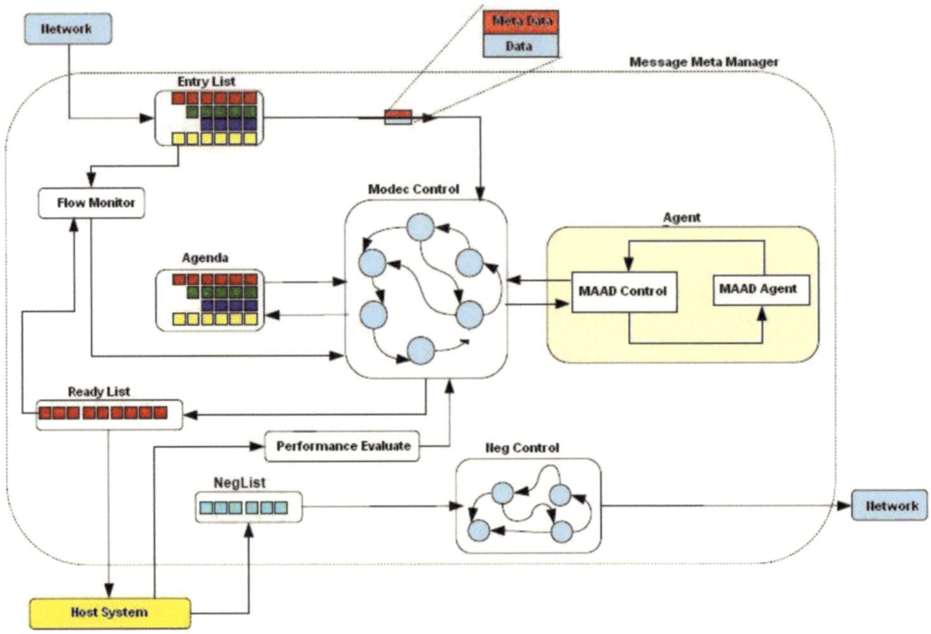

Fig. 3. Architecture of MAAD

The model of Module of Evaluation and Decision Support (MAAD) is developed as a Meta-Level Control layer that a system host receives the messages in a more appropriate sequence, set appointments determined messages and prioritizing others. MAAD consists of two main modules: Module of Decision and Control - MDC and Module Reinforcement Learning - MRL. In such a way, Meta-Level Control uses a set of parameters to associate each message (good utility of the message and maximum state period for the execution) and generate a series of other parameters: the probability of arrive message in the entrance list with high utility, the utility of the messages to set appointments in the agenda list, the period of execution for the message that is in the beginning of the agenda and reason of flow that measures the messages entering to and leaving from MDC. Figure 3 shows the architecture of MAAD.

Exchanging the messages in a distributed system with a manner of communication needs to establish a hierarchy according to aspects of this system. The attributes defined for the system are attached to the message of the Meta-Level Controller that the message encapsulates and sends it. The destination of the message is also processed by a Meta-Controller within the Multi-Agent System, which receives the message and analyzes the enclosed attributes to make the decision in the most appropriate. The manager in Meta-Level Control can decide among three actions: to set appointments of the message for posterior act of receiving; to transfer the message in the system or still to discard it.

The approach of intelligent agent makes use of some aspects of Meta-Level Control as to use the parameters in Meta-Level of the messages for taking efficient decision and without overload the performance of the system in general situation.

3.2 Decision and control approach

The decision process is carried through by MDC which is supported by a Knowledge Base. This base is defined as a part of MRL. The heuristic is used initially in MRL by ad hoc form, where for each state of the environment, it is suggested with an action that in accordance with the previous analysis. However, if dealing with a random environment, it is not always suggested a best action initially. This action may be indicated during a long time. Thus the suggestions are modified in the manner that the agent knows better the environment that it is acting.

The defined heuristic initially is necessary in the situation that the agent does not operate so bad form in the beginning state because it knows very little on the environment.

The state changes are shared by two modules. MDC is developed for controlling the state changes, managing the entrance and the exit of messages and carrying through the communication among the diverse agents. And MRL carries through reinforcement learning for better decision.

Six parameters are used to define a state: p_1, p_2, p_3, p_4, p_5, p_6. They are standardized respectively in the order of the parameters as follows:

- p_1 represents priority of the message that arrives;
- p_2 represents the existing stated period so that the messages can be processed;
- p_3 represents good utility of the set of appointment of the messages;
- p_4 represents the stated period of execution of the messages that are set appointments;
- p_5 represents probability of a arrived message with high priority;
- p_6 represents the reason of flow of the messages in MAAD.

Each parameter will receive a value: high, average or low (see figure 4). When a state has one or more of the six parameters with value not informing, such as 00_2, for project decision, that state will not be studied. In this form, valid states with the six informed parameters will only be dealt by MDC.

For example, the state $(100111011101)_2$, in binary, would present the following values for each parameter: $p_1 = 10$, $p_2 = 01$, $p_3 = 11$, $p_4 = 01$, $p_5 = 11$, $p_6 = 01$, that correspondents the state in decimal form of 2525.

$$\underbrace{11}_{P_1}\quad \underbrace{11}_{P_2}\quad \underbrace{01}_{P_3}\quad \underbrace{01}_{P_4}\quad \underbrace{10}_{P_5}\quad \underbrace{11}_{P_6}$$

Fig. 4. The parameters for state presentation where: $(11)_2$ = High, $(10)_2$ = Medium, $(01)_2$ = Low and $(00)_2$ = Undefined

Given a state of the environment from MDC, it can be transferred to MRL and then an action will be indicated for the environment. The selected action is executed by the environment and then reinforcement behind this action. This action is returned for the agent of learning that influences the impact of the suggested action. This process of interaction enters the learning agent and the environment will continue and allow the accumulation of experience of the Agent for the long time.

If the learning of the agent to consider only reinforcement learning, the general process will be very slow. Thus, a alternative approach to speed up the learning may be interesting. In this form, an adaptation to select randomly between exploitation and exploring may be influenced by the performance of the agent in the environment and the external factors to the environment.

To evaluate the performance of the current state of the system - MAAD, five parameters are considered and to get the final value of AvD:

$$AvD = \frac{(3 \times SDS + 2 \times RF + SEL + SAL + SPL)}{8} \tag{3}$$

where,

SDS (Situation of the Host System): this parameter presents situation of the system which the MAAD serves. It is with weight three in the general evaluation due to the necessity to increase the influence of the system host on the evaluation of performance of the MAAD.

RF (Reason of the Flow): this parameter is used to measure the flow of the messages in MAAD. It is with weight two due to the necessity to show more efficiency of the communication of the messages in MAAD.

SEL (Situation of the Entrance Lists): this parameter is used to measure the queue of entrance messages and can be reduced or increased when the system is more congested or less congested respectively.

SAL (Situation of the Agenda): this parameter is used to measure the Agenda of messages and is reduced or increased when the Agenda in the system is more congested or less congested respectively.

SPL (Situation of the Ready List): this parameter is used to measure the processed messages in the queue and can be reduced or increased when the queue is more congested or less congested respectively.

3.3 Module reinforcement learning – MRL

The agent of reinforcement learning uses two algorithms that are well defined in the literature of reinforcement learning: Q-learning and SARSA [5]. Four strategies of the modifications of the parameters in the Q-learning and SARSA algorithms are studied during reinforcement learning simulation, such as the cases of initial heuristic (IH), epsilon adaptative (EA), performance heuristic (PH) and the combination of above three (IH + EA + PH). In totally, eight modifications have been implemented: four modifications for Q-learning and four modifications for SARSA.

The first modification is the original implementation of Q-learning and SARSA with an initial heuristic (IH). This initial heuristic guides the agent in the start when it still does not have experience of the environment that it is acting. For long time, the rules go being substituted for the successful actions that the agent goes taking.

The second modification is a proposal epsilon adaptative (EA) that it reduces the percentage of exploration while the actions are successful or increases this percentage while the actions negatively influence the evaluation of the performance of the system. There is a version for Q-learning and another one for SARSA.

The third modification uses a definition of heuristic (PH) based on the performance of the MAAD, see Bianchi's work [14]. The policy of this variable considers a heuristic function based on performance. So, the learning algorithm considers these actions which give the best reinforcement associated with the best performance by the heuristic function. An ideal performance is defined as 100% of the evaluation space and a value of performance is measured in the instant of analysis between 0% and 100%. The bigger the performance of the agent, the best is its behavior. The desired situation is to find the politics that allows the agent in the distance to minimize between the current performance and the considered ideal performance.

The fourth and last modification is in the implementation of Q-learning and SARSA when heuristic initial, adapt epsilon and heuristic (IH + EA + PH) is based on the performance.

4. Case study

The case study shows the results from the simulation of the message exchange within the developed system. Each knot in the distributed system presents a layer managed in Meta-Level where the meta-parameters are analyzed for each message. With this consideration, we can see that the classification of the messages is based on the importance of the message without losing: more importance, higher priority.

4.1 Simulation condition

Each message generating source is considered as a knot in the distributed system. The message from this source can be processed by other knots. In a determined moment, if there is less traffic, fewer messages are needed to be processed, in case no congestion arises in the airport system.

In basic simulation, four knots, i.e. four airports, form the study environment. Three of these generating sources send messages to one other knot for analysis. Generally, there is no logical difference among each generating source. The intention of the basic simulation is to identify the adversities of each airport and the important characteristics which need to be treated.

The adversities from each airport are simulated through generation intervals between the messages. To represent a process of intense message exchange, the messages are generated with a short interval. On the other hand, a process of small intensity message exchange is represented with a long interval.

To evaluate the quality of learning, an evaluation module is projected to attribute a note to the agent. Based on a default table of possible good actions for each case, the evaluation module generates the note. This note is generated from the action taken in relation to what it is suggested by the default table and also considering the degree of congestion of the external path. Here, the evaluation of learning quality is done within the mentioned periods. The interval of evaluation between the messages is varied throughout the four simulations. The configuration chosen included 32 periods and intervals between the messages of 1 second for Q-learning and 5 seconds for SARSA.

4.2 Evaluation of the performance of MAAD

Each algorithm is tested with the combination of proposed strategies (as mentioned in last section). In summary, the strategies include the use of heuristics and adapted parameters by

performance that enables the agent to learn flexibly and rapidly.
Figure 5 shows the result of the evaluation of the performance of messages meta-controlling. The curves of performance of Q-learning are worse, in all four evaluations, compared with the curves from SARSA algorithm. The literature justifies this result due to the nature of the two algorithms. While Q-learning makes a search among the possibility actions, SARSA makes a random choice that considers the probability distribution of the actions until the action is selected.

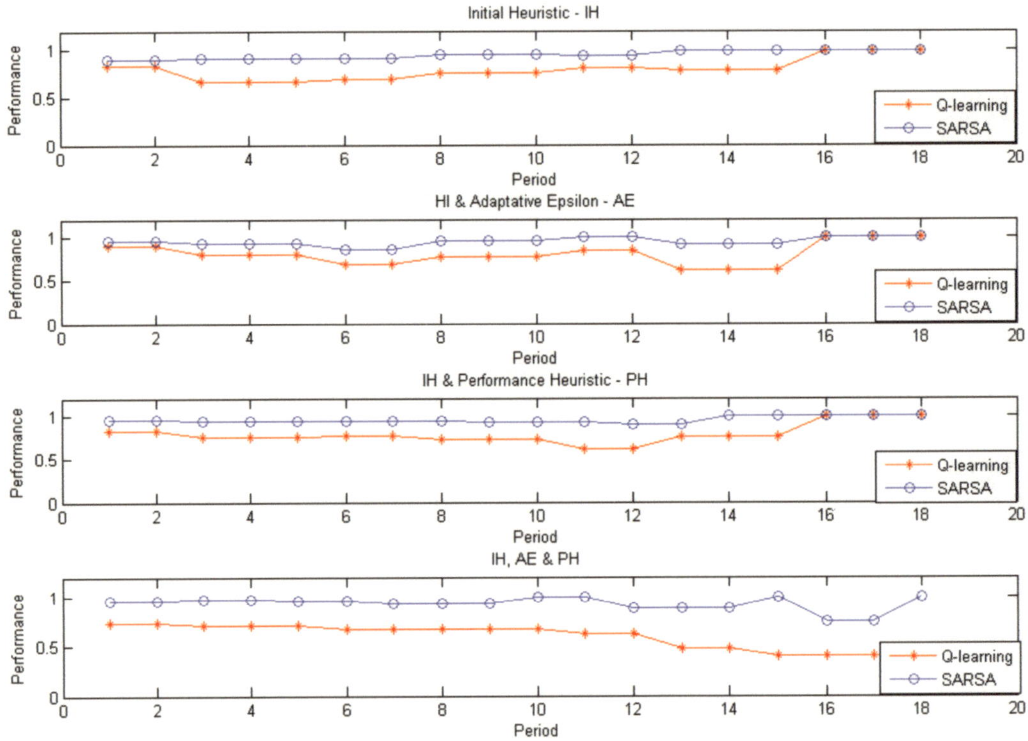

Fig. 5. Evaluation of the Performance of MAAD

As a result, the use of initial heuristic (IH) and epsilon adaptative (EA) present better results with SARSA algorithm. In case of Q-learning, the initial heuristic (IH) and performance heuristic (PH) present better results according to the observed learning performance. However, it is observed that the results of agents learning with Q-learning are worse in comparison with SARSA.

4.3 Evaluation of the quality of the learning and alteration of the *alpha* parameter

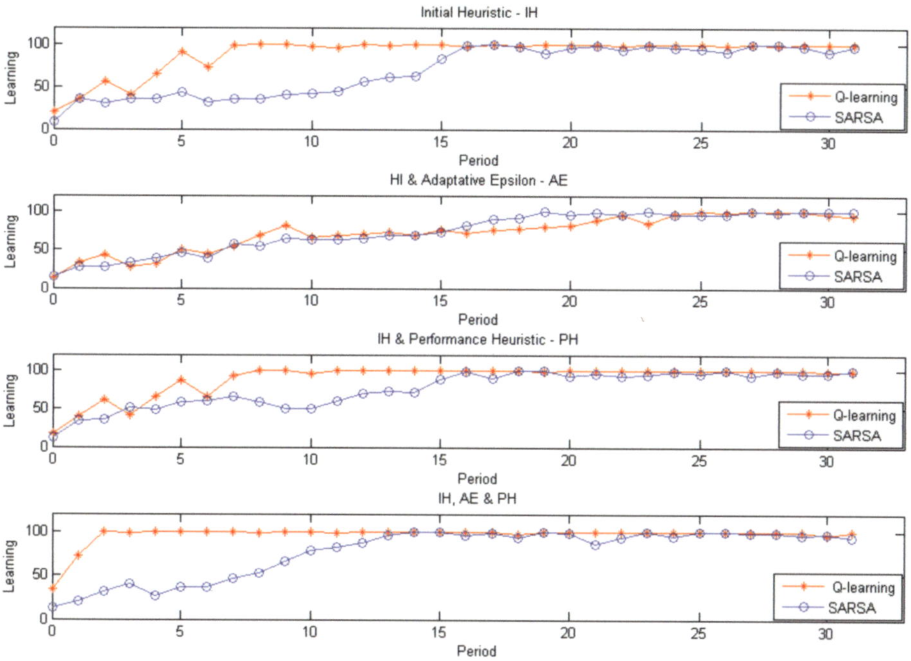

Fig. 6. Evaluation of the Learning Quality for $\alpha = 0.02$

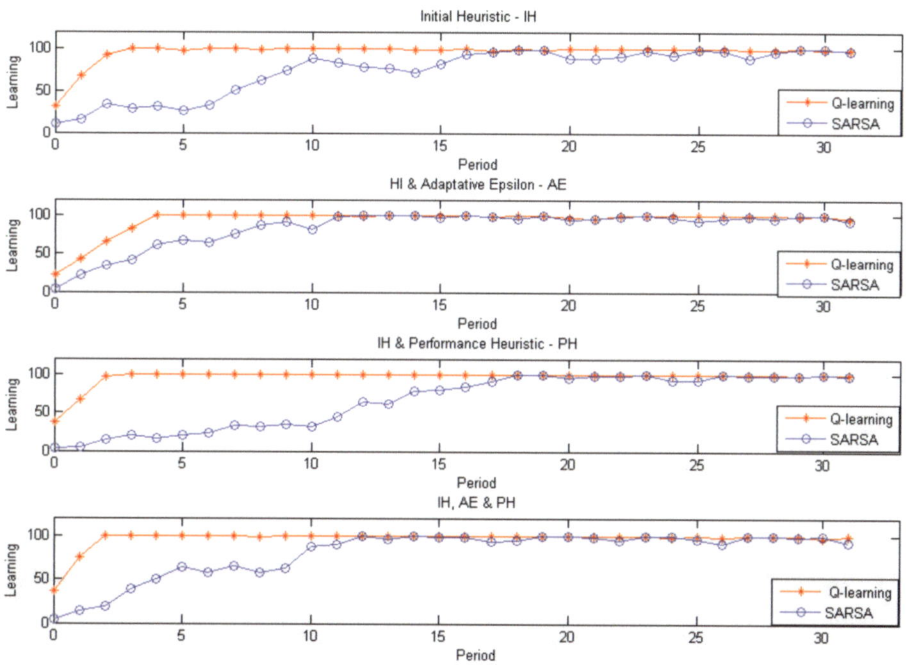

Fig. 7. Evaluation of the Learning Quality for $\alpha = 0.04$

In this case, a vector of uplas (state, action, reward) is defined, considering the acceptable value depending on the environment conditions. When the decision is taken, it is compared with a defined acceptable standard which maximum value is 100%. If a decision is within the acceptable standards, a parameter note is developed and stored in a note vector. After the complete fulfilling of the note vector, with initially one hundred positions, the arithmetic mean of notes is calculated and note value is altered. This guarantees that a good decision will lead to the growth of the note and a bad decision to its decrease.

In figure 6, the system tries to make a decision following the expected standard. In the initial points, some decisions have bad performance. Initially, a note zero is attributed, and to the measure that the module takes good decisions, this note is increased. Some bad decisions should expected. This is one of the characteristics of reinforcement learning. SARSA algorithm has faster execution time than Q-learning (see figures 6 and 7). However, the experiments show that it learns slower to reach maximum note. On the other hand, the Q-learning algorithm takes a lesser amount of periods to reach a maximum note (see figures 6 and 7).

Concerning the results obtained with the change of alpha parameter, it was adjusted for values of 0.02 and 0.04, respectively. With alpha of 0.04, the simulation achieved better results.

5. Conclusions

This research presented a solution for Meta-Level Control application and reinforcement learning in the decision process to improve the efficiency for the exchange of messages within a distributed system in ATFM. As a part of the research of the Evaluation and Decision Support Module (MAAD), the reinforcement learning approach was applied and developed as a sub-module (MRL) with adaptation of two algorithms: Q-learning and SARSA. The Meta-Level Control was developed as another sub-module (MDC) for making decision regarding information process.

One of the advantages of the use of reinforcement learning is that the agents acquire experience during the iteration process with the environment. As a similar form of learning, it utilizes system performance as criteria to verify the performance of the agents in the environment. After analyzing the activities of controllers and supervisors, the hierarquization of these activities in computation module was established, allowing treating more critical situations faster and more effective. At the same time, the controllers and supervisors can get the quantitatively impact from the system for their decisions.

The simulation results from four cases by two reinforcement learning algorithms (Q-learning and SARSA) have shown the correctness and efficiency of the combination of Meta-Level Control and reinforcement learning in a special problem of ATFM. As a stage research report, the simulation is just a part of the internal message process. Other interesting aspect is the evaluation of changes in the value of alpha parameter. The learning quality is influenced by a suitable choice of alpha value.

In further research, it will be pursued the integration of support decision procedures with all modules in SISCONFLUX, to effectively assist the activities of controllers and supervisors. It is intend to consider a heuristic procedure in MAAD to improve the performance, reflecting quantitative criteria of the real life performance of the controllers and supervisors in CINDACTA I. It is also interesting to use other reinforcement learning algorithms such as R-learning or Dyna in the system.

6. Acknowledgements

This research is partially supported by Brazilian National Council for Scientific and Technological Development - CNPq (Proc. 306065/2004-5) and FINATEC - Foundation of Scientific and Technological Enterprises of the University of Brasilia -UnB, Brazil.

7. References

A. S. Tanenbaum and M. V. Steen, Distributed Systems: Principles and Paradigms. Prentice-Hall, 2002.

G. Tidhar, A. Rao, M. Ljunberg, Distributed Air Traffic Management System, Tech. Rep. 25, Australian Artificial Intelligence Institute, 1992.

T. Prevôt, Exploring the Many Perspectives of Distributed Air Traffic Management: The Multi Aircraft Control System MACS, Proc. of the Int. Conference on Human-Computer Interaction in Aeronautics S. Chatty, J. Hansman, and G. Boy (Eds.), pp. 149-154, 2002.

M. Nguyen-Duc, J. P. Briot, A. Drogoul, V. Duong. An application of Multi-Agent Coordination Techniques in Air Traffic Management, Proc. of the IEEE Int. Conference on Intelligent Agent Technology, 2003.

L. Weigang, M. V. P. Dib, A. C. M. A. Melo, C. J. P. Alves, "Multi-Agents System by Grid Computing for Real Time Traffic Synchronization", Journal of the Brazilian Air Transportation Research Society, Vol. 2, pp. 63-82, 2006.

L. Weigang, C. J. P. Alves, N. Omar, "An Expert System for Air Traffic Flow Management". Journal of Advanced Transportation. Vol. 31, N. 3, pp. 343-361, 1997.

A. Raja and V. Lesser, Efficient Meta-Level Control in Bounded-Rational. In Proceedings of Autonomous Agents and Multi-Agent System, pp.1104-1105, Melbourne, Australia, 2003.

A. Raja and V. Lesser, "A Framework for Meta-level Control in Multi-Agent Systems", Autonomous Agents and Multi-Agent Systems, Springer, 2007.

R. S. Sutton and A. G. Barto, Reinforcement Learning: An Introduction. The MIT Press, England, 1998.

S. Russel and P. Norvig, Artificial Intelligence - A modern Approach. Pearson Education, Inc., Second Edition, New Jersey, 2003.

S. Russel, E. Wefald, Principles of Metareasoning, Artificial Intelligence, Vol. 49, pp. 361-395, 1991.

R. S. Sutton, A. G. Barto, Reinforcement Learning: An Introduction. The MIT Press, England, 1998.

P. D. Watkins, Technical note Q-learning. Machine Learning, Vol. 8, pp. 279-292, 1992.

R. A. C. Bianchi and A. H. R. Costa, Uso de Heurísticas para a Aceleração do Aprendizado por Reforço. No XXV Congresso da Sociedade Brasileira de Computação. São Leopoldo, Brasil, 2005.

S. Zhang and F. Makedon, Privacy Preserving Learning in Negotiation. In: Proceedings of the ACM symposium on Applied computing - SAC'05, ACM Press, Santa Fe, pp. 821-825, 2005.

Crespo, A. M. F., Aquino, C. V., Souza, B. B., Weigang, L., Melo, A. C. M. A., Alves, D. P., Sistema Distribuído de Apoio a Decisão Aplicado Ao Gerenciamento Tático do Fluxo de Tráfego: Caso CINDACTA I, em Anais do VI Simpósio de Transporte Aéreo - SITRAER, pp. 317-327, Maringar, 2007.